KU-885-295

EDITOR

David McComb
Colorado State University

Advisory Board

Members of the Advisory Board are instrumental in the final selection of articles for each edition of Annual Editions. Their review of articles for content, level, currentness, and appropriateness provides critical direction to the editor and staff. We think you'll find their careful consideration well reflected in this volume.

STAFF

Ian A. Nielsen, Publisher
Brenda S. Filley, Production Manager
Roberta Monaco, Editor
Addie Raucci, Administrative Editor
Cheryl Greenleaf, Permissions Editor
Deanna Herrschaft, Permissions Assistant
Diane Barker, Proofreader
Lisa Holmes-Doebrick, Administrative Coordinator
Charles Vitelli, Designer
Shawn Callahan, Graphics
Lara M. Johnson, Graphics
Laura Levine, Graphics
Mike Campbell, Graphics
Libra A. Cusack, Typesetting Supervisor
Juliana Arbo, Typesetter
Jane Jaegersen, Typesetter
Marie Lazauskas, Word Processor

To the Reader

In publishing ANNUAL EDITIONS we recognize the enormous role played by the magazines, newspapers, and journals of the *public press* in providing current, first-rate educational information in a broad spectrum of interest areas. Within the articles, the best scientists, practitioners, researchers, and commentators draw issues into new perspective as accepted theories and viewpoints are called into account by new events, recent discoveries change old facts, and fresh debate breaks out over important controversies.

Many of the articles resulting from this enormous editorial effort are appropriate for students, researchers, and professionals seeking accurate, current material to help bridge the gap between principles and theories and the real world. These articles, however, become more useful for study when those of lasting value are carefully *collected, organized, indexed,* and *reproduced* in a *low-cost format*, which provides easy and permanent access when the material is needed.

That is the role played by *Annual Editions*. Under the direction of each volume's *Editor,* who is an expert in the subject area, and with the guidance of an *Advisory Board,* we seek each year to provide in each ANNUAL EDITION a current, well-balanced, carefully selected collection of the best of the public press for your study and enjoyment. We think you'll find this volume useful, and we hope you'll take a moment to let us know what you think.

After 1500 world affairs were increasingly influenced by the power and problems of Western civilization—more so than by any other civilization. Europe and its offspring in North America experienced a transformation during the industrial and scientific revolutions unlike that of other societies. Western guns and ships opened the door to global dominance and the extension of Western culture. Ideas about capitalism, trade, private property, socialism, Christianity, democracy, nationalism, and human rights, for example, traveled on the caravels and the steamboats. It was a European who dispelled the myth of the "sea of pithy darkness" on the western coast of Africa where sea dragons supposedly ate sailors. It was also an intrepid European who discovered the New World and carried trade goods to the distant Far East. It was not a Chinese mariner who sailed up the Hudson River, nor an African who forced open the Japanese ports at gunpoint. It was not an American Indian who transferred potatoes to Ireland or corn to France or manioc to Africa. With all of their faults and virtues, it was the Europeans and later the Americans who ventured around the globe and to the surface of the moon.

The history of the modern world, the period after 1500, therefore, intimately concerns the circumstances of the West and the ambitions of its people. As Westerners reached into the world, they established trading ports, colonies, and carved out overseas empires. Early conquerors in the Americas and the Pacific used swords, horses, dogs, disease, and gunpowder. Later invaders in Africa, China, and India used railroads, telegraphs, quinine, steamboats, and machine guns. This was the time when the English were so widely dispersed that the sun was always shining on the British Empire. Then, after the disasters of two world wars, a depression, and a cold war in the twentieth century, the West retreated. It left behind, however, a residue of ideas, religion, technology, and the English language.

No person, no remote tribe, no plant nor animal was left untouched by this global penetration of the West. Television and motor cars are now everywhere. Wealthy people travel to the Antarctic, the Caribbean, or the Seychelles for vacations. Poorer people wear digital wristwatches and listen to transistor radios. Fax machines utilize telephone lines. Young people worldwide are seen wearing American blue jeans, listening to rock music, and playing soccer or basketball. There is an intermixing of cultures and an interdependence of economies. Indigenous peoples have had to react in one way or another to the Western influence—adopt, adapt, or try to avoid. The human species has become culturally richer for all of the global interconnection, and at the same time increasingly imperiled by diseases, pollution, exploitation, warfare, and overpopulation.

The purpose of this anthology is to give students a sense of the modern world through a selection of timely, fresh, and interesting articles from popular sources. The units are organized into large chronological periods with special segments on the industrial and scientific revolutions and on current global problems. The progress of science and technology is ongoing and still has a pervasive influence upon the history of the world. The subject, moreover, is fundamental in the history of Western civilization. There are other subtopics, however, to be found in the units—war, politics, women's history, for example—that cut through the time periods. The topic guide in this edition can serve as an index for these subjects. Along with the topic guide of that appears *Annual Editions, World History, Volume I,* you can put together a topical reference throughout world history.

The world is not perfect and this is not a perfect anthology. A world history anthology by its nature must be selective and not everything can be covered. Some subjects, moreover, are but imperfectly discussed in recent commentary and so an older article must be used to maintain balance. You may know of some better articles, and so we would like to have your suggestions and comments. Please use the postage-paid rating form at the back of this volume to help us improve the next edition of *Annual Editions: World History, Volume II.*

David McComb

David McComb
Editor

Contents

Unit
1

The Ferment of the West, 1500–1800

Six articles examine the cultural development of the West, including such topics as early religious thinking, women in eighteenth-century society, and the importance of the American Constitution in world events.

The concepts in bold italics are developed in the article. For further expansion please refer to the Topic Guide and the Index.

Unit 2

The Industrial and Scientific Revolutions

Seven selections discuss the revolution in the industrial and scientific world. Topics include the change from cottage industry to factory and the evolution of industry.

The concepts in bold italics are developed in the article. For further expansion please refer to the Topic Guide and the Index.

Unit
3

The West and the World, 1500–1900

Eight articles show how the West extended and dominated much of the world. Topics include the age of discovery, the emergence of Western colonial powers, evolution of Africa, and the European impact on the Far East.

Unit 4

The Twentieth Century to 1950

Eight articles examine the effect of war and depression on modern world history. Topics include the impact of World War I, the formation of the modern Middle East, World War II, and the dynamics of Japan.

Unit 5

The Era of the Cold War, 1950–1990

Six articles discuss the evolution of a new world order. Topics include African independence, the Middle East, the dissolution of the Soviet Union, and China.

Unit 6

Global Problems, Global Interdependence

Six selections examine the effects of interdependence on some world problems, including environmental degradation, the spread of nuclear technology, population growth, the AIDS crisis, and cultural diversity.

The concepts in bold italics are developed in the article. For further expansion please refer to the Topic Guide and the Index.

Topic Guide

This topic guide suggests how the selections in this book relate to topics of traditional concern to world history students and professionals. It is useful for locating articles that relate to each other for reading and research. The guide is arranged alphabetically according to topic. Articles may, of course, treat topics that do not appear in the topic guide. In turn, entries in the topic guide do not necessarily constitute a comprehensive listing of all the contents of each selection.

TOPIC AREA	TREATED IN	TOPIC AREA	TREATED IN
Africa	6. French Revolution, North Africa, and the Middle East 14. Portugal's Impact on Africa 18. Who Was Responsible? 34. Decade of Decline 40. Future of AIDS	Europe	1. Luther 2. Scotland's Greatest Son 3. First Feminist 4. World Transformed 7. Cottage Industry and the Factory System 14. Portugal's Impact on Africa 15. Fateful Moment When Two Civilizations Came Face to Face 16. Discovering Europe, 1493 18. Who Was Responsible? 22. International Economy 25. Sarajevo 26. Social Outcasts in Nazi Germany 31. Berlin 1961 32. Who Broke Down This Wall? 33. Return to History 36. Toxic Wasteland
Americas	15. Fateful Moment When Two Civilizations Came Face to Face 16. Discovering Europe, 1493 17. Potato Connection 18. Who Was Responsible?		
Asia	5. China 19. Macartney Embassy to China 20. Coffee, Tea, or Opium? 21. After Centuries of Japanese Isolation 23. On the Turn—Japan, 1900 24. Japanese Women at Work 27. '... Heavy Fire ... Unable to Land ... Issue in Doubt' 28. Making It Happen 29. Why We Dropped the Bomb	France	3. First Feminist 4. World Transformed 5. China 6. French Revolution, North Africa, and the Middle East 10. Scientific Importance of Napoleon's Egyptian Campaign 25. Sarajevo
China	5. China 19. Macartney Embassy to China 20. Coffee, Tea, or Opium?	Geography	10. Scientific Importance of Napoleon's Egyptian Campaign 13. Scientific Legacy of Apollo 14. Portugal's Impact on Africa 16. Discovering Europe, 1493 17. Potato Connection 18. Who Was Responsible? 21. After Centuries of Japanese Isolation 33. Return to History 36. Toxic Wasteland 39. Can the Growing Human Population Feed Itself?
Cold War	30. Heating Up the Cold War 31. Berlin 1961 32. Who Broke Down This Wall? 36. Toxic Wasteland		
Colonization	10. Scientific Importance of Napoleon's Egyptian Campaign 15. Fateful Moment When Two Civilizations Came Face to Face 18. Who Was Responsible?	Germany	1. Luther 25. Sarajevo 26. Social Outcasts in Nazi Germany 31. Berlin 1961 32. Who Broke Down This Wall?
Economics	2. Scotland's Greatest Son 7. Cottage Industry and the Factory System 18. Who Was Responsible? 19. Macartney Embassy to China 20. Coffee, Tea, or Opium? 21. After Centuries of Japanese Isolation 22. International Economy 24. Japanese Women at Work 34. Decade of Decline	Great Britain	2. Scotland's Greatest Son 3. First Feminist 7. Cottage Industry and the Factory System 8. For a While, the Luddites Had a Smashing Success 19. Macartney Embassy in China 20. Coffee, Tea, or Opium? 22. International Economy 25. Sarajevo
Environment	13. Scientific Legacy of Apollo 17. Potato Connection 34. Decade of Decline 36. Toxic Wasteland 38. Sowing Success, Reaping Guns 39. Can the Growing Human Population Feed Itself? 40. Future of AIDS	India	38. Sowing Success, Reaping Guns

TOPIC AREA	TREATED IN	TOPIC AREA	TREATED IN
Industrial Revolution	2. Scotland's Greatest Son 7. Cottage Industry and the Factory System 8. For a While, the Luddites Had a Smashing Success 24. Japanese Women at Work	**Soviet Union**	30. Heating Up the Cold War 31. Berlin 1961 32. Who Broke Down This Wall? 33. Return to History 36. Toxic Wasteland
Japan	21. After Centuries of Japanese Isolation 23. On the Turn—Japan, 1900 24. Japanese Women at Work 27. '. . . Heavy Fire . . . Unable to Land . . . Issue in Doubt' 29. Why We Dropped the Bomb	**Technology**	2. Scotland's Greatest Son 7. Cottage Industry and the Factory System 8. For a While, the Luddites Had a Smashing Success 9. Looking beyond Aristotle and Alchemy 12. How Von Neumann Showed the Way 17. Potato Connection 28. Making It Happen 36. Toxic Wasteland 37. Nuclear Epidemic 38. Sowing Success, Reaping Guns 39. Can the Growing Human Population Feed Itself?
Middle East	6. French Revolution, North Africa, and the Middle East 35. Islam		
Politics	4. World Transformed 5. China 6. French Revolution, North Africa, and the Middle East 19. Macartney Embassy to China 21. After Centuries of Japanese Isolation 26. Social Outcasts in Nazi Germany 29. Why We Dropped the Bomb 30. Heating Up the Cold War 31. Berlin 1961 32. Who Broke Down This Wall? 33. Return to History 37. Nuclear Epidemic 38. Sowing Success, Reaping Guns 41. Cultural Diversity	**United States**	11. James Watson and the Search for Biology's 'Holy Grail' 12. How Von Neumann Showed the Way 13. Scientific Legacy of Apollo 21. After Centuries of Japanese Isolation 22. International Economy 27. '. . . Heavy Fire . . . Unable to Land . . . Issue in Doubt' 28. Making It Happen 29. Why We Dropped the Bomb 30. Heating Up the Cold War 31. Berlin 1961 32. Who Broke Down This Wall?
Population	15. Fateful Moment When Two Civilizations Came Face to Face 17. Potato Connection 18. Who Was Responsible? 26. Social Outcasts in Nazi Germany 39. Can the Growing Human Population Feed Itself? 40. Future of AIDS 41. Cultural Diversity	**Warfare**	4. World Transformed 15. Fateful Moment When Two Civilizations Came Face to Face 20. Coffee, Tea, or Opium? 25. Sarajevo 26. Social Outcasts in Nazi Germany 27. '. . . Heavy Fire . . . Unable to Land . . . Issue in Doubt' 28. Making It Happen 29. Why We Dropped the Bomb 30. Heating Up the Cold War 31. Berlin 1961 37. Nuclear Epidemic 38. Sowing Success, Reaping Guns
Religion	1. Luther 35. Islam 38. Sowing Success, Reaping Guns		
Science	10. Scientific Importance of Napoleon's Egyptian Campaign 11. James Watson and the Search for Biology's 'Holy Grail' 12. How Von Neumann Showed the Way 13. Scientific Legacy of Apollo 28. Making It Happen 37. Nuclear Epidemic 40. Future of AIDS	**Women**	3. First Feminist 24. Japanese Women at Work

The Ferment of the West, 1500–1800

The voyages of discovery in the fifteenth and sixteenth centuries are symbolic of the spirit of adventure and curiosity that carried Western civilization around the globe. The unique character of the civilization was formed by many events, and the purpose of this first unit is to give some explanation of the important elements. One of the major episodes was the Protestant Reformation. Martin Luther started it with protests against the dominant Roman Catholic Church and triggered an avalanche that not only contributed to theology, but also fed the skepticism of the time. If people could doubt the church fathers and think for themselves, they could challenge leadership in other areas of life as well.

Adam Smith did not issue a challenge, but rather offered a definition about the new economy of the Industrial Revolution. Smith, the first great economist, argued that laissez-faire and the "invisible hand" of the marketplace would work to supply all the goods that people wanted. If left alone without governmental interference, manufacturers would produce what was needed and in the correct amount—a case of supply and demand. His concepts of capitalism have been much modified by subsequent conditions, such as social welfare and large multinational corporations, but capitalism was not destroyed by suppressed workers as Karl Marx later predicted. It turned out to be a flexible economic system that at present has triumphed over the socialism of communism. John Kenneth Galbraith, an outstanding economist himself, describes Adam Smith in his essay "Scotland's Greatest Son."

Sigmund Freud, the man who opened the field of psychology at a later period, once lamented, "What do women want?" Mary Wollstonecraft had an answer long before the days of Freud. She wanted recognition that the female mind was as good as the male's mind, and that women should be treated in a reasonable fashion. She was able to make a career with her writing, and she lived an emancipated life at a time when women were not so free. The rights of women fall under the concept of liberalism, an ideal that was an integral part of both the American and French Revolutions. Mary Wollstonecraft was a participant of that era.

The American Revolution produced both the Declaration of Independence and the Federal Constitution of 1787. The Constitution provided an outline for a practical republican government that has endured for over 200 years. Important are the first ten amendments, the liberal agenda that provide guarantees for personal freedoms. Ideas in the Constitution, many taken from European sources, influenced the participants of the French Revolution.

In contrast to the revolt in the United States, a peripheral frontier nation, the French Revolution turned out to be more startling for Europe and the world. France was the most enlightened country in Europe at the time, and its upheaval was a threat to the neighboring monarchies. The subsequent wars, despite the fact that Napoleon became a dictator, spread the spirit of the French Revolution. In "A World Transformed," Keith Baker examines the ideas of the French revolt, while the remaining two articles track the influence of the revolutions in China, North Africa, and Middle East. It took time for the thoughts to penetrate, and even then the liberal ideals were subject to moderation by the local culture. It is of interest that the students in revolt at Tiananmen Square in China put together a goddess of liberty as a symbol of their cause to show on the television screens of the world.

Looking Ahead: Challenge Questions

Why are the philosophies of Martin Luther, Adam Smith, and Mary Wollstonecraft important?

What effect did Luther, Smith, and Wollstonecraft have on their contemporaries?

Define a "feminist." Does Wollstonecraft fit that definition?

What was the role of women at the time of the French Revolution?

What was the role of violence in the French Revolution? Why was it necessary?

Why did the liberal revolutions occur in the West?

Trace the influence of the French Revolution around the world. How long did it take for the ideas to spread? Through what channels did the ideas spread?

LUTHER SCHLÄGT DIE 90 SÄTZE AN.

Luther: Giant of His Time and Ours

Half a millennium after his birth, the first Protestant is still a towering force

It was a back-room deal, little different from many others struck at the time, but it triggered an upheaval that altered irrevocably the history of the Western world. Albrecht of Brandenburg, a German nobleman who had previously acquired a dispensation from the Vatican to become a priest while underage and to head two dioceses at the same time, wanted yet another favor from the Pope: the powerful archbishop's chair in Mainz. Pope Leo X, a profligate spender who needed money to build St. Peter's Basilica, granted the appointment—for 24,000 gold pieces, roughly equal to the annual imperial revenues in Germany. It was worth it. Besides being a rich source of income, the Mainz post brought Albrecht a vote for the next Holy Roman Emperor, which could be sold to the highest bidder.

In return, Albrecht agreed to initiate the sale of indulgences in Mainz. Granted for good works, indulgences were papally controlled dispensations drawn from an eternal "treasury of merits" built up by Christ and the saints; the church taught that they would help pay the debt of "temporal punishment" due in purgatory for sins committed by either the penitent or any deceased person. The Pope received half the proceeds of the Mainz indulgence sale, while the other half went to repay the bankers who had lent the new archbishop gold.

Enter Martin Luther, a 33-year-old priest and professor at Wittenberg University. Disgusted not only with the traffic in indulgences but with its doctrinal underpinnings, he forcefully protested to Albrecht—never expecting that his action would provoke a sweeping uprising against a corrupt church. Luther's challenge culminated in the Protestant Reformation and the rending of Western Christendom, and made him a towering figure in European history. In this 500th anniversary year of his birth (Nov. 10, 1483), the rebel of Wittenberg remains the subject of persistent study. It is said that more books have been written about him than anyone else in history, save his own master, Jesus Christ. The renaissance in Luther scholarship surrounding this year's anniversary serves as a reminder that his impact on modern life is profound, even for those who know little about the doctrinal feuds that brought him unsought fame. From the distance of half a millennium, the man who, as Historian Hans Hillerbrand of Southern Methodist University in Dallas says, brought Christianity from lofty theological dogma to a clearer and more personal belief is still able to stimulate more heated debate than all but a handful of historical figures.

Indeed, as the reformer who fractured Christianity, Luther has latterly become a key to reuniting it. With the approval of the Vatican, and with Americans taking the lead, Roman Catholic theologians are working with Lutherans and other Protestants to sift through the 16th century disputes and see whether the Protestant-Catholic split can some day be overcome. In a remarkable turnabout, Catholic scholars today express growing appreciation of Luther as a "father in the faith" and are willing to play down his excesses. According to a growing consensus, the great division need never have happened at all.

Beyond his importance as a religious leader, Luther had a profound effect on Western culture. He is, paradoxically, the last medieval man and the first modern one, a political conservative and a spiritual revolutionary. His impact is most marked, of course, in Germany, where he laid the cultural foundations for what later became a united German nation.

When Luther attacked the indulgence business in 1517, he was not only the most popular teacher at Wittenberg but also vicar provincial in charge of eleven houses of the Hermits of St. Augustine. He was brilliant, tireless and a judicious administrator, though given to bouts of spiritual depression. To make his point on indulgences, Luther dashed off 95 theses condemning the system ("They preach human folly who pretend that as soon as money in the coffer rings, a soul from purgatory springs") and sent them to Archbishop Albrecht and a number of theologians.*

The response was harsh: the Pope eventually rejected Luther's protest and demanded capitulation. It was then that Luther began asking questions about other aspects of the church, including the papacy itself. In 1520 he charged in an open letter to the Pope, "The Roman Church, once the holiest of all, has become the most licentious den of thieves, the most shameless of brothels, the kingdom of sin, death and hell." Leo called Luther "the wild boar which has invaded the Lord's vineyard."

The following year Luther was summoned to recant his writings before the Diet of Worms, a council of princes

---

*Despite colorful legend, it is not certain he ever nailed them to the door of the Castle Church.

convened by the young Holy Roman Emperor Charles V. In his closing defense, Luther proclaimed defiantly: "Unless I am convinced by testimony from Holy Scriptures and clear proofs based on reason—because, since it is notorious that they have erred and contradicted themselves, I cannot believe either the Pope or the council alone—I am bound by conscience and the Word of God. Therefore I can and will recant nothing, because to act against one's conscience is neither safe nor salutary. So help me God." (Experts today think that he did not actually speak the famous words, "Here I stand. I can do no other.")

This was hardly the cry of a skeptic, but it was ample grounds for the Emperor to put Luther under sentence of death as a heretic. Instead of being executed, Luther lived for another 25 years, became a major author and composer of hymns, father of a bustling household and a secular figure who opposed rebellion—in all, a commanding force in European affairs. In the years beyond, the abiding split in Western Christendom developed, including a large component of specifically "Lutheran" churches that today have 69 million adherents in 85 nations.

The enormous presence of the Wittenberg rebel, the sheer force of his personality, still broods over all Christendom, not just Lutheranism. Although Luther declared that the Roman Pontiffs were the "Antichrist," today's Pope, in an anniversary tip of the zucchetto, mildly speaks of Luther as "the reformer." Ecumenical-minded Catholic theologians have come to rank Luther in importance with Augustine and Aquinas. "No one who came after Luther could match him," says Father Peter Manns, a Catholic theologian in Mainz. "On the question of truth, Luther is a lifesaver for Christians." While Western Protestants still express embarrassment over Luther's anti-Jewish rantings or his skepticism about political clergy, Communist East Germany has turned him into a secular saint because of his influence on German culture. Party Boss Erich Honecker, head of the regime's *Lutherjahr* committee, is willing to downplay Luther's antirevolutionary ideas, using the giant figure to bolster national pride.

Said West German President Karl Carstens, as he opened one of the hundreds of events commemorating Luther this year: "Luther has become a symbol of the unity of all Germany. We are all Luther's heirs."

After five centuries, scholars still have difficulty coming to terms with the contradictions of a tempestuous man. He was often inexcusably vicious in his writings (he wrote, for instance, that one princely foe was a "faint-hearted wretch and fearful sissy" who should "do nothing but stand like a eunuch, that is, a harem guard, in a fool's cap with a fly swatter"). Yet he was kindly in person and so generous to the needy that his wife despaired of balancing the household budget. When the plague struck Wittenberg and others fled, he stayed behind to minister to the dying. He was a powerful spiritual author, yet his words on other occasions were so scatological that no Lutheran periodical would print them today. His writing was hardly systematic, and his output runs to more than 100 volumes. On the average, Luther wrote a major tract or treatise every two weeks throughout his life.

The scope of Luther's work has made him the subject of endless reinterpretation. The Enlightenment treated him as the father of free thought, conveniently omitting his belief in a sovereign God who inspired an authoritative Bible. During the era of Otto von Bismarck a century ago, Luther was fashioned into a nationalistic symbol; 70 years later, Nazi propagandists claimed him as one of their own by citing his anti-Jewish polemics.

All scholars agree on Luther's importance for German culture, surpassing even that of Shakespeare on the English-speaking world. Luther's masterpiece was his translation of the New Testament from Greek into German, largely completed in ten weeks while he was in hiding after the Worms confrontation, and of the Old Testament, published in 1534 with the assistance of Hebrew experts. The Luther Bible sold massively in his lifetime and remains today the authorized German Protestant version. Before Luther's Bible was published, there was no standard German, just a profusion of dialects. "It was Luther," said Johann Gottfried von Herder, one of Goethe's mentors, "who has awakened and let loose the giant: the German language."

Only a generation ago, Catholics were trained to consider Luther the arch-heretic. Now no less than the Vatican's specialist on Lutheranism, Monsignor Aloys Klein, says that "Martin Luther's action was beneficial to the Catholic Church."

Like many other Catholics, Klein thinks that if Luther were living today there would be no split. Klein's colleague in the Vatican's Secretariat for Promoting Christian Unity, Father Pierre Duprey, suggests that with the Second Vatican Council (1962–65) Luther "got the council he asked for, but 450 years too late." Vatican II accepted his contention, that in a sense, all believers are priests; while the council left the Roman church's hierarchy intact, it enhanced the role of the laity. More important, the council moved the Bible to the center of Catholic life, urged continual reform and instituted worship in local languages rather than Latin.

One of the key elements in the Reformation was the question of "justification," the role of faith in relation to good works in justifying a sinner in the eyes of God. Actually, Catholicism had never officially taught that salvation could be attained only through pious works, but the popular perception held otherwise. Luther recognized, as University of Chicago Historian Martin Marty explains, that everything "in the system of Catholic teaching seemed aimed toward appeasing God. Luther was led to the idea of God not as an angry judge but as a forgiving father. It is a position that gives the individual a great sense of freedom and security." In effect, says U.S. Historian Roland Bainton, Luther destroyed the implication that men could "bargain with God."

Father George Tavard, a French Catholic expert on Protestantism who teaches in Ohio and has this month published *Justification: An Ecumenical Study* (Paulist; $7.95), notes that "today many Catholic scholars think Luther was right and the 16th century Catholic polemicists did not understand what he meant. Both Lutherans and Catholics agree that good works by Christian believers are the result of their faith and the working of divine grace in them, not their personal contributions to their own salvation. Christ is the only Savior. One does not save oneself." An international Lutheran-Catholic commission, exploring the basis for possible reunion, made a joint statement along these lines in 1980. Last month a parallel panel in the U.S. issued a significant 21,000-word paper on justification that affirms much of Luther's thinking, though with some careful hedging from the Catholic theologians.

There is doubt, of course, about the degree to which Protestants and Catholics can, in the end, overcome their differences. Catholics may now be permitted to sing Luther's *A Mighty Fortress Is Our God* or worship in their native languages, but a wide gulf clearly remains on issues like the status of Protestant ministers and, most crucially, papal authority.

During the futile Protestant-Catholic reunion negotiations in 1530 at the Diet of Augsburg, the issue of priestly celibacy was as big an obstacle as the faith *vs.* good works controversy. Luther had married a nun, to the disgust of his Catholic contemporaries. From the start, the marriage of clergy was a sharply defined difference between Protestantism and Catholicism, and it remains a key barrier today. By discarding the concept of the moral superiority of celibacy, Luther established sexuality as a gift from God. In general, he was a lover of the simple pleasures, and would have had little patience with the later Puritans. He spoke offhandedly about sex, enjoyed good-natured joshing, beer drinking and food ("If our Lord is permitted to create nice large pike and good Rhine wine, presumably I may be allowed to eat and drink"). For his time, he also had an elevated opinion of women. He cherished his wife and enjoyed fatherhood, siring six children and rearing eleven orphaned nieces and nephews as well.

But if Luther's views on the Catholic Church have come to be accepted even by many Catholics, his anti-Semitic views remain a problem for even his most devoted supporters. Says New York City Rabbi Marc Tanenbaum: "The anniversary will be marred by the haunting specter of Luther's devil theory of the Jews."

Luther assailed the Jews on doctrinal grounds, just as he excoriated "papists" and Turkish "infidels." But his work titled *On the Jews and Their Lies* (1543) went so far as to advocate that their synagogues, schools and homes should be destroyed and their prayer books and Talmudic volumes taken away. Jews were to be relieved of their savings and put to work as agricultural laborers or expelled outright.

Fortunately, the Protestant princes ignored such savage recommendations, and the Lutheran Church quickly forgot about them. But the words were there to be gleefully picked up by the Nazis, who removed them from the fold of religious polemics and used them to buttress their 20th century racism. For a good Lu-

theran, of course, the Bible is the sole authority, not Luther's writings, and the thoroughly Lutheran Scandinavia vigorously opposed Hitler's racist madness. In the anniversary year, all sectors of Lutheranism have apologized for their founder's views.

Whatever the impact of Luther's anti-Jewish tracts, there is no doubt that his political philosophy, which tended to make church people submit to state authority, was crucial in weakening opposition by German Lutherans to the Nazis. Probably no aspect of Luther's teaching is the subject of more agonizing Protestant scrutiny in West Germany today.

Luther sought to declericalize society and to free people from economic burdens imposed by the church. But he was soon forced, if reluctantly, to deliver considerable control of the new Protestant church into the hands of secular rulers who alone could ensure the survival of the Reformation. Luther spoke of "two kingdoms," the spiritual and the secular, and his writings provided strong theological support for authoritarian government and Christian docility.

The Lutheran wing of the Reformation was democratic, but only in terms of the church itself, teaching that a plowman did God's work as much as a priest, encouraging lay leadership and seeking to educate one and all. But it was Calvin, not Luther, who created a theology for the democratic state. A related aspect of Luther's politics, controversial then and now, was his opposition to the bloody Peasants' War of 1525. The insurgents thought they were applying Luther's ideas, but he urged rulers to crush the revolt: "Let whoever can, stab, strike, kill." Support of the rulers was vital for the Reformation, but Luther loathed violent rebellion and anarchy in any case.

Today Luther's law-and-order approach is at odds with the revolutionary romanticism and liberation theology that are popular in some theology schools. In contrast with modern European Protestantism's social gospel, Munich Historian Thomas Nipperdey says, Luther "would not accept modern attempts to build a utopia and would argue, on the contrary, that we as mortal sinners are incapable of developing a paradise on earth."

Meanwhile, the internal state of the Lutheran Church raises other questions about the lasting power of Luther's vision. Lutheranism in the U.S., with 8.5 million adherents, is stable and healthy. The church is also growing in Third

World strongholds like racially torn Namibia, where black Lutherans predominate. But in Lutheranism's historic heartland, the two Germanys and Scandinavia, there are deep problems. In East Germany, Lutherans are under pressure from the Communist regime. In West Germany, the Evangelical Church in Germany (E.K.D.), a church federation that includes some non-Lutherans, is wealthy (annual income: $3 billion), but membership is shrinking and attendance at Sunday services is feeble indeed. Only 6% of West Germans—or, for that matter, Scandinavians—worship regularly.

What seems to be lacking in the old European churches is the passion for God and his truth that so characterizes Luther. He retains the potential to shake people out of religious complacency. Given Christianity's need, on all sides, for a good jolt, eminent Historian Heiko Oberman muses, "I wonder if the time of Luther isn't ahead of us."

The boldest assertion about Luther for modern believers is made by Protestants who claim that the reformer did nothing less than enable Christianity to survive. In the Middle Ages, too many Popes and bishops were little more than corrupt, luxury-loving politicians, neglecting the teaching of the love of God and using the fear of God to enhance their power and wealth. George Lindbeck, the Lutheran co-chairman of the international Lutheran-Catholic commission, believes that without Luther "religion would have been much less important during the next 400 to 500 years. And since medieval religion was falling apart, secularization would have marched on, unimpeded."

A provocative thesis, and a debatable one. But with secularization still marching on, almost unimpeded, Protestants and Catholics have much to reflect upon as they scan the five centuries after Luther and the shared future of their still divided churches.

—By Richard N. Ostling. Reported by Roland Flamini and Wanda Menke-Glückert/Bonn, with other bureaus.

Scotland's Greatest Son

In *The Wealth of Nations* Adam Smith gave the world a new
and witty and literate perception of
the dismal science. But what would he have said about ITT?

JOHN KENNETH GALBRAITH

In June of 1973 economists gathered from all over the world in the Royal Burgh of Kirkcaldy, immediately across the Firth of Forth from Edinburgh, to celebrate the two hundred and fiftieth anniversary of the birth of the town's — most would say Scotland's—greatest son. That was Adam Smith, who was born there in 1723, the son of the local collector of customs, and who, after study at the evidently excellent local school, went on to the University of Glasgow and then to Balliol for six years. Returning to Scotland, he became, first, professor of logic and then, in 1752, professor of moral philosophy at Glasgow. This chair he resigned in 1764 to travel on the Continent as the well-paid tutor of the young Duke of Buccleuch, a family possessed to this day of a vast acreage of dubious land on the border. In Europe Smith made the acquaintance of the physiocratic philosophers and economists Quesnay and Turgot, as well as Voltaire and other notable contemporaries, and used his time and mind well. He then returned to Kirkcaldy where, for the next twelve years, subject to lengthy sojourns in London and to the despair of some of his friends who feared he would never finish, he engaged himself in the writing of *The Wealth of Nations*.

This great book was published in 1776, a few weeks before the Declaration of Independence, and if there is coincidence in the dates, there was also association in the events. Unlike his friend David Hume (who died that August), Smith deplored the separation. He had wanted instead full union, full and equal representation of the erstwhile colonies in Parliament, free trade within the Union, equal taxation along with equal representation, and the prospect that, as the American part developed in wealth and population, the capital would be removed from London to some new Constantinople in the West. Practical men must have shuddered.

However, *The Wealth of Nations*, at least among the knowledgeable, was an immediate success. Gibbon wrote, "What an excellent work is that with which our common friend Mr. Adam Smith has enriched the public . . . most profound ideas expressed in the most perspicacious language." Hume, in a much quoted letter, was exuberant:

Euge! Belle! Dear Mr. Smith. I am much pleased with your performance, and the perusal of it has taken from me a state of great anxiety. It was a work of so much expectation, by yourself, by your friends, and by the public, that I trembled for its appearance, but am now much relieved . . . it has depth and solidity and acuteness, and is so much illustrated by curious facts that it must at last attract the public attention.

The public response—to two volumes costing £1 16s., the equivalent of perhaps thirty dollars today—was also good. The first edition was soon sold out, although this intelligence would be more valuable were the size of the edition known. Smith spent the next couple of years in London being, one gathers, much fêted by his contemporaries for his accomplishment, and then, having been appointed Commissioner of Customs in Edinburgh, an admirable sinecure, he returned to Scotland. He died in Edinburgh in 1790.

By this time, *The Wealth of Nations*, though at first ignored by politicians, was having an influence on men of affairs. A year and a half after Smith's death, Pitt, introducing his budget, said of Smith that his "extensive knowledge of detail and depth of philosophical research will, I believe, furnish the best solution of every question connected with the history of commerce and with the system of political economy." Not since, in the nonsocialist world at least, has a politician committed himself so courageously to an economist.

Smith has not been a popular subject for biographers. He was a bachelor. His best-remembered personal trait was his absent-mindedness. Once, according to legend, he fell into deep thought and walked fifteen miles in his dressing gown before regaining consciousness. His manuscripts, by his instruction, were destroyed at his death. He disliked writing letters, and few of these have survived. The papers of those with whom he did correspond, or which reflected his influence, were destroyed, mostly because of lack of interest, and some, it appears, as late as 1941 or 1942. Adam Smith's only other major published work, *The Theory of Moral Sentiments*, reflects interests antecedent to those in political economy. It is often cited by scholars but little read. No biography of Adam Smith has superseded that by John Rae, published nearly eighty years ago.

If Smith's life has attracted little attention, perhaps it is because so much attention has centered on *Inquiry into the Nature and Causes of the Wealth of Nations,* to give the title of his masterpiece its full resonance. With *Das Kapital* and the Bible, *Wealth of Nations* enjoys the distinction of being one of the three books that people may refer to at will without feeling they should have read it. Scholarly dispute over what is Smith's principal contribution has gone on endlessly. This is partly because there is so much in the book that every reader has full opportunity to exercise his own preference.

Exercising that preference, I have always thought that two of Smith's achievements have been neglected. One, mentioned by Gibbon, is his gift for language. Few writers ever, and certainly no economist since, have been as amusing, lucid, or resourceful—or on occasion as devastating. Most rightly remember his conclusion that "People of the same trade seldom meet together, even for merriment and diversion, but the conversation ends in a conspiracy against the public, or in some contrivance to raise prices." There are many more such gems. He noted that "The late resolution of the Quakers in Pennsylvania to set at liberty all their negro slaves may satisfy us that their number cannot be very great." And, anticipating Thorstein Veblen, that "With the greater part of rich people, the chief enjoyment of riches consists in the parade of riches." On the function or nonfunction of stockholders, no one in the next two centuries was more penetrating in however many words: "[Stockholders]

seldom pretend to understand anything of the business of the company, and when the spirit of faction happens not to prevail among them, give themselves no trouble about it, but receive contentedly such half-yearly or yearly dividend, as the directors think proper to make to them." One of Smith's most famous observations, it may be noted, is not in *Wealth of Nations.* On hearing from Sir John Sinclair in October, 1777, that

MARY EVANS PICTURE LIBRARY, LONDON

Gussied up and properly shod (he usually wore his bedroom slippers), Smith appears in an engraving of 1790, the year of his death.

Burgoyne had surrendered at Saratoga and of his friend's fear that the nation was ruined, Smith said, "There is a great deal of ruin in a nation."

Also neglected now are the "curious facts" that enchanted Hume and of which *Wealth of Nations* is a treasure house. Their intrusion has, in fact, been deplored. As a writer Smith was a superb carpenter but a poor architect. The facts appear in lengthy digressions

that have been criticized as such. But for any discriminating reader it is worth the interruption to learn that the expenses of the civil government of the Massachusetts Bay Colony "before the commencement of the present disturbances," meaning the Revolution, were only £18,000 a year and that this was a rather sizable sum compared with New York and Pennsylvania at £4,500 each and New Jersey at £1,200. (These and numerous other details on the Colonies reflect an interest John Rae believes was stimulated by Benjamin Franklin, with whom Smith was closely acquainted.)

Also, were it not for Smith we might not know that after a bad storm, or "inundation," the citizens of the Swiss canton of Underwald (Unterwalden) came together in an assembly where each publicly confessed his wealth to the multitude and was then assessed *pro rata* for the repair of the damage. Or that, at least by Smith's exceptionally precise calculation, Isocrates earned £3,333 6s. 8d. (upward of 50,000 dollars) for what "we would call one course of lectures, a number which will not appear extraordinary from so great a city to so famous a teacher, who taught, too, what was at that time the most fashionable of all sciences, rhetoric." Or that Plutarch was paid the same. Or, continuing with professors, that those who are subject to reward unrelated to their capacity to attract students will perform their duty in "as careless and slovenly a manner" as authority will permit and that in "the university of Oxford, the greater part of the public professors [those with endowed chairs] have, for these many years, given up altogether even the pretence of teaching."

So no one should neglect Smith's contribution to expository prose and "curious facts." Now as to economic thought and policy. Here a sharp and

ADAM SMITH ON SELF-INTEREST:

"It is not from the benevolence of the butcher, the brewer, or the baker that we expect our dinner but from their regard to their self-interest. We address ourselves not to their humanity, but to their self-love, and never talk to them of our necessities, but of their advantages."

obvious distinction must be made between what was important in 1776 and what is important now. The first is very great; the second, save in the imagination of those who misuse Smith as a prophet of reaction, is much less so. The business corporation, which Smith deplored, and the wealth that accumulated in consequence of his advice combined against him. But first we must consider his meaning in 1776.

Smith's economic contribution to his own time can be thought of as falling into three categories—method, system, and advice. The second, overflowing onto the third, is by far the most important.

As to method, Smith gave to political economy, later to become economics, the basic structure which was to survive almost intact at least for the next hundred and fifty years. This structure begins with the problem of value—how prices are set. Then comes the question of how the proceeds are shared—how the participants in production are rewarded. This latter involves the great trinity of labor, capital, and land. Along the way is the role of money. Thereafter come banking, international trade, taxation, public works, defense, and the other functions of the state. Other writers, notably the physiocrats, had previously given political economy a fairly systematic frame, although, as Alexander Gray observed, they had "embellished it with strange frills." But it was Smith who, for the English-speaking world, provided the enduring structure.

The structure, in turn, was more important than what it enclosed. Although Smith's treatment of value, wages, profits, and rents was suggestive and often incisive, it was, in all respects, a begin-

ning and not an end. So it was regarded by Ricardo, Malthus, and the two Mills. Thus, as one example, Smith held that the supply of workers would increase *pari passu* with an increase in the sustenance available for their support. Ricardo translated this thought into the iron law of wages—the rule that wages would tend always to fall to the bare minimum necessary to sustain life. And Malthus, going a step further, adduced his immortal conclusion that people everywhere would proliferate to the point of starvation. Subsequent scholars —the marginal-utility theorists, Alfred Marshall, others—added further modifications to the theory of prices, wages, interest, profits, and rent, and yet further transmutations were of course to follow. Smith was left far behind.

For Smith, the structure he gave to economics and the explanation of economic behavior that it contained were only steps in the creation of his larger system—his complete view of how economic life should be arranged and governed. This was his central achievement. It provides a set of guiding rules for economic policy that are comprehensive and consistent without being arbitrary or dogmatic.

The Smithian system requires that the individual, suitably educated, be left free to pursue his own interest. In doing so, he serves not perfectly, but better than by any alternative arrangement, the common public purpose. Self-interest or selfishness guides men, as though by the influence of an unseen hand, to the exercise of the diligence and intelligence that maximize productive

effort and thus the public good. Private vice becomes a public virtue.

In pursuit of private interest, producers exploit the opportunities inherent in the division of labor—in, broadly speaking, the specialized development of skill for the performance of each small part of a total task of production. Combined with the division of labor is the natural propensity of man "to truck, barter or exchange." The freedom of the individual to do his best both in production and in exchange is inhibited by regulation and taxation. Thus the hand of the state should weigh on him as lightly as possible. The limiting factor on the division of labor—roughly, the scale of specialized productive activity —is the size of the market. Obviously, this should be as wide as possible.

There follows Smith's special case against internal, monopolistic, or international restrictions on trade. The case against international barriers gains force from the fact that both well-being and national strength derive not from the accumulation of precious metal, as Smith's mercantilist precursors had held, but as one would now say and as Smith in effect did say—from the productivity of the labor force. Given an industrious and productive labor force, in the most majestic of Smith's arguments, the supply of gold will take care of itself.

Such, in greatest compression, is the Smithian system—the one that Pitt proclaimed as "the best solution of every question connected . . . with the system of political economy."

Smith's third contribution was in the field of practical policy. His advice—on banking, education, colonies, taxation (including the famous canons and extending even to recommendations for the reform of taxation in France), public works, joint-stock companies, agriculture—was infinitely abundant. It could be that no economist since has offered so much. With many exceptions and frequent modifications to fit the circumstance, it is in keeping with Smith's system. The bias in favor of freeing or unburdening the individual to pursue his

"Poverty, though it no doubt discourages, does not always prevent marriage. It seems even to be favourable to generation. A half-starved Highland woman frequently bears more than twenty children, while a pampered fine lady is often incapable of bearing any, and is generally exhausted by two or three. . . . But poverty is extremely unfavourable to the rearing of children. The tender plant is produced, but in so cold a soil and so severe a climate, soon withers and dies."

interest is omnipresent, and so is his belief that men will toil effectively only in the pursuit of pecuniary self-interest. There will be occasion for a further word on this advice; now we must see what of Smith survives.

Needless to say, the mordant language and the curious facts survive; it is too bad they are not more read and enjoyed. Also, Smith's concept of the economic problem—and the division of the subject between value and distribution—are still to be found in that part of the textbooks that economists call microeconomics (and those given to tasteless insider abbreviation call "micro"). His particular conclusions as to how prices, wages, rents, and return to capital are determined, and his views on gold, paper currency, banks, and the like, are now only of antiquarian interest.

Nor does much of the abundant advice just mentioned have modern meaning. It better illuminates life in the eighteenth century than any current problems. Until recently the textbooks on taxation included reverent mention of Smith's four great canons. But no one now coming to them without knowledge of their author would think them very remarkable. That taxes should be certain or predictable and arbitrary in their bite; that they should be so levied and collected as to fit the reasonable convenience of the taxpayer; and that the cost of collection should be a modest part of the total take was important in 1776. But these three things are pretty well accepted now.

Smith's fourth canon, that the "subjects of every state ought to contribute towards the support of the government, as nearly as possible, in proportion to their respective abilities; that is, in proportion to the revenue which they respectively enjoy under the protection of the state," could be taken as an enduring prescription for a proportional (i.e., fixed percentage) as distinct from a progressive income tax. Some beleaguered rich have so argued. In fact, Smith was speaking only of what seemed possible and sensible in his own time. He would have moved with the times. It might be added that his modest prescription gives no comfort to tax shelters, special treatment of state and municipal bonds, the oil-depletion allowance, or those who believe that they were intended by nature to be untroubled by the IRS. Numerous of the big rich in the United States would find even Adam Smith's proportional prescription rather costly as compared with what they now pay.

The next and more interesting question concerns Smith's system—his rules for guiding economic life. What of that survives? Is economic life still guided in appreciable measure by the unseen hand of self-interest—in modern language, by the market? What has happened to the notion of the minimal state, and is it forever dead? And what of Smith's plea for the widest possible market both within and between nations?

In truth, time has dealt harshly with Smith's system. On one important mat-

ter he was simply wrong. Further damage was done by an institution, the business corporation, for which he saw little future and which, on the whole, he deplored. And his system was gravely impaired by the very success of the prescription that he offered.

Smith's error was his underestimate of man's capacity, perhaps with some social conditioning, for co-operation. He thought it negligible. Men would work assiduously for their own pecuniary advantage; on shared tasks, even for shared reward, they would continue to do as little as authority allowed. Only in defeating or circumventing that authority—in minimizing physical and intellectual toil, maximizing indolence and sloth—would they bring real effort and ingenuity to bear. But not otherwise. People work only if working for themselves. There is no more persistent theme in *Wealth of Nations*. It is why government tasks are poorly performed. It is why civil servants are an uncivil and feckless crew. It is his case against the British bureaucracy in India. It is why the Oxford professors lapse into idleness. And it is why, in Smith's view, joint-stock companies, except for routine tasks, have little to commend them. Their best chance for survival, one to which the minds of the directors almost invariably turn, is to obtain a monopoly of their industry or trade, a tendency to which Smith devotes some of his finest scorn. Otherwise, their employees or servants devote themselves not to enriching the company but to enriching themselves or not enriching anyone.

In fact, experience since Smith has shown that man's capacity for co-operative effort is very great. Perhaps this was the product of education and social conditioning, something that no one writing in the eighteenth century could have foreseen. Perhaps Smith, handicapped by his environment, judged all races by the Scotch (as we are correctly called). Most likely he failed to see the pride people could have in their organization, their desire for the good opinion or esteem of their co-workers, maybe what Veblen called their instinct to workmanship.

In any case, governments in the performance of public tasks, some of great technical and military complexity, corporations in pursuit of growth, profit, and power, and socialist states in pursuit of national development and power have been able to enlist a great intensity of co-operative effort. And both corporate and socialist economic activities have been able to unite an instinct to co-operation with a promise of individual economic reward and gain from both. At least in the industrialized world, highly organized forms of economic activity enlist a great intensity of co-operative effort.

The most spectacular example of co-operative effort—or perhaps, to speak more precisely, of a successful marriage of co-operative and self-serving endeavor—has, of course, been the corporation. This, for the reasons just noted, Smith did not think possible. And the development of the corporation, in turn, was destructive of the minimal state that Smith prescribed.

For this there were several reasons. The corporation had needs—franchises, rights-of-way, capital, qualified manpower, technical support, highways for its motor cars, airways for its airplanes—which only the state could supply. A state that served its corporations satisfactorily quickly ceased, except in the hopes of truly romantic conservatives, to be minimal.

Also, a less evident point, the economy of the great corporation, when combined with that of the unions (which were in some measure the response to it), was no longer stable. The corporation retained earnings for investment; there was no certainty that all of such savings would be invested. The resulting shortage of demand could be cumulative, for wages and prices would no longer adjust to arrest the downward spiral. And in other circumstances wages and prices might force each other up to produce an enduring and cumulative inflation. The state was called upon to offset the tendency to recession by stabilizing the demand for goods. This was the message of Keynes. And the state had to intervene to stabilize prices and wages if inflation were to be kept within tolerable limits. Both actions were heavy blows at the Smithian state.

The corporation, as it became very large, also ceased to be subordinate to the market. It fixed prices, sought out supplies, influenced consumers, and otherwise exercised power not different in kind from the power of the the state itself. As Smith would have foreseen, this power was exercised in the interest of its possessors, and on numerous matters—the use of air, water, and land—the corporate interest diverged from the public interest. It also diverged where, as in the case of the weapons firms, the corporation was able to persuade the state to be its customer. Corporate interest did not coincide with the public interest as the Smithian system assumed. And there were yet further appeals to the government for redress and further enhancement of the state. This development, on which I will have a later word, has proceeded with explosive speed, especially since World War II.

Finally, Smith's system was destroyed by its own success. In the nineteenth century and with a rather deliberate recognition of their source, Britain was governed by Smith's ideas. So, though more by instinct than by deliberate philosophical commitment, was the United States. And directly, or through such great disciples as the French economist J. B. Say, Smith's influence extended to Western Europe. In the context of time and place, the Smithian system worked; there was a vast release of productive energy, a great increase in wealth, a large though highly uneven increase in living standards. Then came the corporation with its superior access to capital (including that reserved from its own earnings), its great ability to adapt science and technology to its purposes, and its strong commitment to its own growth through expanding sales and output. This, and by a new order of magnitude, added to the increase in output, income, and consumption.

This was the next nail. It is not possible to combine a highly productive economy with a minimal state. Public regulation had to develop in step with private consumption; public services must bear some reasonable relationship to the supply of private services and goods. Both points are accepted in practice if not in principle. A country cannot have a high consumption of automobiles, alcohol, medication, transportation, communications, or even cosmetics, without rules governing their use. The greater the wealth, the more men needed to protect it, and the more required to pick up the discarded containers in which so much of it comes. And in rough accord with increased private consumption goes an increased demand for public services—for education, health care, parks and public recreation, postal services, and the infinity of other things that must be provided, or are best provided, by the state.

Among numerous conservatives there is still a conviction that the society of the minimal state was deliberately destroyed by socialists, planners, *étatists*, and other wicked men who did not know what they were about, or knew all too well. Far more of the responsibility lies with Smith himself. Along with the corporation, his system created the wealth that made his state impossible.

In one last area, it will be insisted, Adam Smith does survive. Men still respect his inspired and inspiring call for the widest possible market, one that will facilitate in the greatest degree the division of labor. And after two centuries the dominant body of opinion in industrial nations resists tariffs and quotas. And in Europe the nation-states have created the ultimate monument to Adam Smith, the European Economic Community. In even more specific tribute to Smith, it is usually called the Common Market.

13

Even here, however, there is less of Smith than meets the eye. Since the eighteenth century, or, for that matter, in the last fifty years, domestic markets have grown enormously. That of insular Britain today is far greater than that of imperial Britain at the height of empire. The technical opportunities in large-scale production have developed enormously since 1776. But national markets have developed much, much more. Proof lies in the fact that General Motors, IBM, Shell, Nestlé, do not produce in ever larger plants as would be the case if they needed to realize the full opportunities inherent in the division of labor. Rather, they produce the same items in numerous small plants. Except perhaps in the very small industrial countries— Holland, Belgium, Luxembourg— domestic markets have long been large enough so that even were they confined to the home market, producers would realize the full economies of scale, the full technical advantages of the division of labor.

The Common Market, and the modern enlightenment on international trade, owe much more to the nontechnical needs of the modern multinational corporation than they do to Adam Smith. The multinational corporation stands astride national boundaries. Instead of seeking tariff support of the state against countries that have a comparative advantage, it can go to the advantaged countries to produce what it needs. At the same time, modern marketing techniques require that it be able to follow its products into other countries to persuade consumers and governments and, in concert with other producers, to avoid the price competition that would be disastrous for all. So, for the multinational corporation, tariffs, to speak loosely and generally, are both unnecessary and a nuisance. It would not have escaped the attention of Adam Smith, although it has escaped the attention of many in these last few years, that where there are no corporations, the Common Market is less than common and very

much less than popular. The tariff enlightenment following World War II has resulted not from a belated reading of *Wealth of Nations* but from the much more powerful tendency for what serves the needs of large enterprises to become sound public policy.

But if time and the revolution that he helped set in motion have overtaken Smith's system and Smith's advice, there is one further respect in which he remains wonderfully relevant. That is in the example he sets for professional economists—for what, at the moment, is a troubled, rather saddened discipline. Smith is not a prophet for our time, but, as we have seen, he was magnificently in touch with his own time. He broke with the mercantilist orthodoxy to bring economic ideas abreast of the industrial and agricultural changes that were only then just visible on the horizon. His writing in relation to the Industrial Revolution involved both prophecy and self-fulfilling prophecy. He sensed, even if he did not fully see, what was about to come, and he greatly helped to make it come.

The instinct of the economist, now as never before, is to remain with the past. On that, there is a doctrine, a theory— one that is now wonderfully refined. And there are practical advantages. An economist's capital lies in what he knows—sometimes what he learned in graduate school. Or he has investment in a textbook. To adhere to and articulate the accepted view protects this investment. It also keeps a scholar clear of controversy, something that is usually regarded as a trifle uncouth or indecent. To stay with what is accepted is also consistent with the good life—with the fur-lined comfort of the daily routine between suburb, classroom, and office. To this blandishment, economists are no more immune than other people. The tragedy lies in their resulting obsolescence. As the economic world changes, that proceeds relentlessly, and it is a painful thing.

Remarkably, the same institution, the corporation, which helped to take the

economic world away from Adam Smith, has, in its explosive development in modern times, taken it away from the mature generation of present-day economists. As even economists in their nonprofessional life concede, the modern corporation controls prices and costs, organizes suppliers, persuades consumers, guides the Pentagon, shapes public opinion, buys presidents, and is otherwise a dominant influence in the state. It also, alas, in its modern and comprehensively powerful form, figures not at all in the accepted economic theory. That theory still holds the business firm to be solely subordinate to the market, solely subject to the authority of the state, and ultimately the passive servant of the sovereign citizen. There is no ITT in the system. So there is no control of prices, no weapons culture, no dangerously laggard industries, no deeply endemic inequality—there is only incidental damage to the environment arising from minor and hitherto uncelebrated defects (what are called external diseconomies) in the price system. To have to lose touch with reality is the tragedy. And matters are made worse by a younger generation of scholars that accepts and explores the problem of economic power and struggles, sometimes rather crudely, to come to terms with it. Older scholars are left with the barren hope that they can somehow consolidate their forces and thus exclude the threat. It is a fate that calls less for criticism than for compassion.

It is not a fate that Adam Smith would have suffered. Given his avid empiricism, his deep commitment to reality, his profound concern for practical reform, he would have made the modern corporation and its power, and the related power of the unions and the state, an integral part of his theoretical system. His problem would have been different. With his contempt for theoretical pretense, his intense interest in practical questions, he might have had trouble getting tenure in a first-rate modern university.

The First Feminist

In 1792 Mary Wollstonecraft wrote a book to prove that her sex was as intelligent as the other: thus did feminism come into the world. Right on, Ms. Mary!

Shirley Tomkievicz

The first person—male or female—to speak at any length and to any effect about woman's rights was Mary Wollstonecraft. In 1792, when her *Vindication of the Rights of Woman* appeared, Mary was a beautiful spinster of thirty-three who had made a successful career for herself in the publishing world of London. This accomplishment was rare enough for a woman in that day. Her manifesto, at once impassioned and learned, was an achievement of real originality. The book electrified the reading public and made Mary famous. The core of its argument is simple: "I wish to see women neither heroines nor brutes; but reasonable creatures," Mary wrote. This ancestress of the Women's Liberation Movement did not demand day-care centers or an end to women's traditional role as wife and mother, nor did she call anyone a chauvinist pig. The happiest period of Mary's own life was when she was married and awaiting the birth of her second child. And the greatest delight she ever knew was in her first child, an illegitimate daughter. Mary's feminism may not appear today to be the hard-core revolutionary variety, but she did live, for a time, a scandalous and unconventional life—"emancipated," it is called by those who have never tried it. The essence of her thought, however, is simply that a woman's mind is as good as a man's.

Not many intelligent men could be found to dispute this proposition today, at least not in mixed company. In Mary's time, to speak of *anybody's* rights, let alone woman's rights, was a radical act. In England, as in other nations, "rights" were an entity belonging to the govern-ment. The common run of mankind had little access to what we now call "human rights." As an example of British justice in the late eighteenth century, the law cited two hundred different capital crimes, among them shoplifting. An accused man was not entitled to counsel. A child could be tried and hanged as soon as an adult. The right to vote existed, certainly, but because of unjust apportionment, it had come to mean little. In the United States some of these abuses had been corrected—but the rights of man did not extend past the color bar and the mas-culine gender was intentional. In the land of Washington and Jefferson, as in the land of George III, human rights were a new idea and woman's rights were not even an issue.

In France, in 1792, a Revolution in the name of equality was in full course, and woman's rights had at least been alluded to. The Revolutionary government drew up plans for female education—to the age of eight. "The education of the women should always be relative to the men," Rousseau had written in *Emile*. "To please, to be useful to us, to make us love and esteem them, to educate us when young, and take care of us when grown up, to advise, to console us, to render our lives easy and agreeable; these are the duties of women at all times, and what they should be taught in their infancy." And, less prettily, "Women have, or ought to have, but little liberty."

Rousseau would have found little cause for complaint in eighteenth-century En-gland. An Englishwoman had almost the same civil status as an American slave. Thomas Hardy, a hundred years hence, was to base a novel on the idea of a man casually selling his wife and daughter at public auction. Obviously this was not a common occurrence, but neither is it wholly implausible. In 1792, and later, a woman could not own property, nor keep any earned wages. All that she possessed belonged to her husband. She could not divorce him, but he could divorce her and take her children. There was no law to say she could not grow up illiterate or be beaten every day.

Such was the legal and moral cli-mate in which Mary Wollstone-craft lived. She was born in London in the spring of 1759, the second child and first daughter of Edward Wollstonecraft, a prosperous weaver. Two more daughters and two more sons were eventually born into the family, making six children in all. Before they had all arrived, Mr. Wollstonecraft came into an inheritance and decided to move his family to the country and become a gentleman farmer. But this plan failed. His money dwindled, and he began drinking heavily. His wife turned into a terrified wraith whose only interest was her eldest son, Edward. Only he escaped the beatings and abuse that his father dealt out regularly to every other house-hold member, from Mrs. Wollstonecraft to the family dog. As often happens in large and disordered families, the eldest sister had to assume the role of mother and scullery maid. Mary was a bright, strong child, determined not to be bro-ken, and she undertook her task energet-ically, defying her father when he was violent and keeping her younger brothers and sisters in hand. Clearly, Mary held the household together, and in so doing forfeited her own childhood. This ex-perience left her with an everlasting gloomy streak, and was a strong factor in making her a reformer.

At some point in Mary's childhood, another injustice was visited upon her, though so commonplace for the time that she can hardly have felt the sting. Her elder brother was sent away to be educated, and the younger children were left to learn their letters as best they could. The family now frequently changed lodgings, but from her ninth to her fifteenth year Mary went to a day school, where she had the only formal training of her life. Fortunately, this included French and composition, and somewhere Mary learned to read critically and widely. These skills, together with her curiosity and determination, were really all she needed. The *Vindication* is in some parts long-winded, ill-punctuated, and simply full of hot air, but it is the work of a well-informed mind.

Feminists—and Mary would gladly have claimed the title—inevitably, even deservedly, get bad notices. The term calls up an image of relentless battle-axes: "thin college ladies with eye-glasses, no-nonsense features, mouths thin as bologna slicers, a babe in one arm, a hatchet in the other, grey eyes bright with balefire," as Norman Mailer feelingly envisions his antagonists in the Women's Liberation Movement. He has conjured up all the horrid elements: the lips with a cutting edge, the baby immaculately conceived (one is forced to conclude), the lethal weapon tightly clutched, the desiccating college degree, the joylessness. Hanging miasmally over the tableau is the suspicion of a deformed sexuality. Are these girls man-haters, or worse? Mary Wollstonecraft, as the first of her line, has had each of these scarlet letters (except the B.A.) stitched upon her bosom. Yet she conformed very little to the hateful stereotype. In at least one respect, however, she would have chilled Mailer's bones. Having spent her childhood as an adult, Mary reached the age of nineteen in a state of complete joylessness. She was later to quit the role, but for now she wore the garb of a martyr.

Her early twenties were spent in this elderly frame of mind. First she went out as companion to an old lady living at Bath, and was released from this servitude only by a call to nurse the dying Mrs. Wollstonecraft. Then the family broke up entirely, though the younger sisters continued off and on to be dependent on Mary. The family of Mary's dearest friend, Fanny Blood, invited her to come and stay with them; the two girls made a small living doing sewing and handicrafts, and Mary dreamed of starting a primary school. Eventually, in a pleasant village called Newington Green, this plan materialized and prospered. But Fanny Blood in the meantime had married and moved to Lisbon. She wanted Mary to come and nurse her through the birth of her first child. Mary reached Lisbon just in time to see her friend die of childbed fever, and returned home just in time to find that her sisters, in whose care the flourishing little school had been left, had lost all but two pupils.

Mary made up her mind to die. "My constitution is impaired, I hope I shan't live long," she wrote to a friend in February, 1786. Under this almost habitual grief, however, Mary was gaining some new sense of herself. Newington Green, apart from offering her a brief success as a schoolmistress, had brought her some acquaintance in the world of letters, most important among them, Joseph Johnson, an intelligent and successful London publisher in search of new writers. Debt-ridden and penniless, Mary set aside her impaired constitution and wrote her first book, probably in the space of a week. Johnson bought it for ten guineas and published it. Called *Thoughts on the Education of Daughters,* it went unnoticed, and the ten guineas was soon spent. Mary had to find work. She accepted a position as governess in the house of Lord and Lady Kingsborough in the north of Ireland.

Mary's letters from Ireland to her sisters and to Joseph Johnson are so filled with Gothic gloom, so stained with tears, that one cannot keep from laughing at them. "I entered the great gates with the same kind of feeling I should have if I was going to the Bastille," she wrote upon entering Kingsborough Castle in the fall of 1786. Mary was now twenty-seven. Her most recent biographer, Margaret George, believes that Mary was not really suffering so much as she was having literary fantasies. In private she was furiously at work on a novel entitled, not very artfully, *Mary, A Fiction.* This is the story of a young lady of immense sensibilities who closely resembles Mary except that she has wealthy parents, a neglectful bridegroom, and an attractive lover. The title and fantasizing contents are precisely what a scribbler of thirteen might secretly concoct. Somehow Mary was embarking on her adolescence—with all its daydreams—fifteen years after the usual date. Mary's experience in Kingsborough Castle was a fruitful one, for all her complaints. In the summer of 1787 she lost her post as governess and set off for London with her novel. Not only did Johnson accept it for publication, he offered her a regular job as editor and translator and helped her find a place to live.

Thus, aged twenty-eight, Mary put aside her doleful persona as the martyred, set-upon elder sister. How different she is now, jauntily writing from London to her sisters: "Mr. Johnson . . . assures me that if I exert my talents in writing I may support myself in a comfortable way. I am then going to be the first of a new genus . . ." Now Mary discovered the sweetness of financial independence earned by interesting work. She had her own apartment. She was often invited to Mr. Johnson's dinner parties, usually as the only female guest among all the most interesting men in London: Joseph Priestley, Thomas Paine, Henry Fuseli, William Blake, Thomas Christie, William Godwin—all of them up-and-coming scientists or poets or painters or philosophers, bound together by left-wing political views. Moreover, Mary was successful in her own writing as well as in editorial work. Her *Original Stories for Children* went into three editions and was illustrated by Blake. Johnson and his friend Thomas Christie had started a magazine called the *Analytical Review,* to which Mary became a regular contributor.

But—lest anyone imagine an elegantly dressed Mary presiding flirtatiously at Johnson's dinner table—her social accomplishments were rather behind her professional ones. Johnson's circle looked upon her as one of the boys. "Wollstonecraft" is what William Godwin calls her in his diary. One of her later detractors reported that she was at this time a "philosophic sloven," in a dreadful old dress and beaver hat, "with her hair hanging lank about her shoulders." Mary had yet to arrive at her final incarnation, but the new identity was imminent, if achieved by an odd route. Edmund Burke had recently published his *Reflections on the Revolution in France,* and the book had enraged Mary. The statesman who so readily supported the quest for liberty in the American colonies had his doubts about events in France.

Mary's reply to Burke, *A Vindication of the Rights of Men*, astounded London, partly because she was hitherto unknown, partly because it was good. Mary proved to be an excellent polemicist, and she had written in anger. She accused Burke, the erstwhile champion of liberty, of being "the champion of property." "Man preys on man," said she, "and you mourn for the idle tapestry that decorated a gothic pile and the dronish bell that summoned the fat priest to prayer." The book sold well. Mary moved into a better apartment and bought some pretty dresses—no farthingales, of course, but some of the revolutionary new "classical" gowns. She put her auburn hair up in a loose knot. Her days as a philosophic sloven were over.

Vindication of the Rights of Woman was her next work. In its current edition it runs to 250-odd pages; Mary wrote it in six weeks. *Vindication* is no prose masterpiece, but it has never failed to arouse its audience, in one way or another. Horace Walpole unintentionally set the style for the book's foes. Writing to his friend Hannah More in August, 1792, he referred to Thomas Paine and to Mary as "philosophizing serpents" and was "glad to hear you have not read the tract of the last mentioned writer. I would not look at it." Neither would many another of Mary's assailants, the most virulent of whom, Ferdinand Lundberg, surfaced at the late date of 1947 with a tract of his own, *Modern Woman, the Lost Sex*. Savagely misogynistic as it is, this book was hailed in its time as "the best book yet to be written about women." Lundberg calls Mary the Karl Marx of the feminist movement, and the *Vindication* a "fateful book," to which "the tenets of feminism, which have undergone no change to our day, may be traced." Very well, but then, recounting Mary's life with the maximum possible number of errors per line, he warns us that she was "an extreme neurotic of a compulsive type" who "wanted to turn on men and injure them." In one respect, at least, Mr. Lundberg hits the mark: he blames Mary for starting women in the pernicious habit of wanting an education. In the nineteenth century, he relates, English and American feminists were hard at work. "Following Mary Wollstonecraft's prescription, they made a considerable point about acquiring a higher education." This is precisely Mary's prescription, and the most dangerous idea in her fateful book.

"Men complain and with reason, of the follies and caprices of our Sex," she writes in Chapter 1. "Behold, I should answer, the natural effect of ignorance." Women, she thinks, are usually so mindless as to be scarcely fit for their roles as wives and mothers. Nevertheless, she believes this state not to be part of the feminine nature, but the result of an equally mindless oppression, as demoralizing for men as for women. If a woman's basic mission is as a wife and mother, need she be an illiterate slave for this?

The heart of the work is Mary's attack on Rousseau. In *Emile* Rousseau had set forth some refreshing new ideas for the education of little boys. But women, he decreed, are tools for pleasure, creatures too base for moral or political or educational privilege. Mary recognized that this view was destined to shut half the human race out of all hope for political freedom. *Vindication* is a plea that the "rights of men" ought to mean the "rights of humanity." The human right that she held highest was the right to have a mind and think with it. Virginia Woolf, who lived through a time of feminist activity, thought that the *Vindication* was a work so true "as to seem to contain nothing new." Its originality, she wrote, rather too optimistically, had become a commonplace.

Vindication went quickly into a second edition. Mary's name was soon known all over Europe. But as she savored her fame—and she did savor it—she found that the edge was wearing off and that she was rather lonely. So far as anyone knows, Mary had reached this point in her life without ever having had a love affair. Johnson was the only man she was close to, and he was, as she wrote him, "A father, or a brother—you have been both to me." Mary was often now in the company of the Swiss painter Henry Fuseli, and suddenly she developed what she thought was a Platonic passion in his direction. He rebuffed her, and in the winter of 1792 she went to Paris, partly to escape her embarrassment but also because she wanted to observe the workings of the Revolution firsthand.

Soon after her arrival, as she collected notes for the history of the Revolution she hoped to write, Mary saw Louis XVI, "sitting in a hackney coach . . . going to meet death." Back in her room that evening, she wrote

to Mr. Johnson of seeing "eyes glare through a glass door opposite my chair and bloody hands shook at me . . . I am going to bed and for the first time in my life, I cannot put out the candle." As the weeks went on, Edmund Burke's implacable critic began to lose her faith in the brave new world. "The aristocracy of birth is levelled to the ground, only to make room for that of riches," she wrote. By February France and England were at war, and British subjects classified as enemy aliens.

Though many Englishmen were arrested, Mary and a large English colony stayed on. One day in spring, some friends presented her to an attractive American, newly arrived in Paris, Gilbert Imlay. Probably about four years Mary's senior, Imlay, a former officer in the Continental Army, was an explorer and adventurer. He came to France seeking to finance a scheme for seizing Spanish lands in the Mississippi valley. This "natural and unaffected creature," as Mary was later to describe him, was probably the social lion of the moment, for he was also the author of a bestselling novel called *The Emigrants*, a farfetched account of life and love in the American wilderness. He and Mary soon became lovers. They were a seemingly perfect pair. Imlay must have been pleased with his famous catch, and dear, liberated girl that she was—Mary did not insist upon marriage. Rather the contrary. But fearing that she was in danger as an Englishwoman, he registered her at the American embassy as his wife.

Blood was literally running in the Paris streets now, so Mary settled down by herself in a cottage at Neuilly. Imlay spent his days in town, working out various plans. The Mississippi expedition came to nothing, and he decided to stay in France and go into the import-export business, part of his imports being gunpowder and other war goods run from Scandinavia through the English blockade. In the evenings he would ride out to the cottage. By now it was summer, and Mary, who spent the days writing, would often stroll up the road to meet him, carrying a basket of freshly-gathered grapes.

A note she wrote Imlay that summer shows exactly what her feelings for him were: "You can scarcely imagine with what pleasure I anticipate the day when we are to begin almost to live together; and you would smile to hear how many plans of employment I have in my head, now that I am confident that my heart has found peace . . ." Soon she was pregnant. She and Imlay moved into Paris. He promised to take her to America, where they would settle down on a farm and raise six children. But business called Imlay to Le Havre, and his stay lengthened ominously into weeks.

Imlay's letters to Mary have not survived, and without them it is hard to gauge what sort of man he was and what he really thought of his adoring mistress. Her biographers like to make him out a cad, a philistine, not half good enough for Mary. Perhaps; yet the two must have had something in common. His novel, unreadable though it is now, shows that he shared her political views, including her feminist ones. He may never have been serious about the farm in America, but he was a miserably long time deciding to leave Mary alone. Though they were separated during the early months of her pregnancy, he finally did bring her to Le Havre, and continued to live with her there until the child was born and for some six months afterward. The baby arrived in May, 1794, a healthy little girl, whom Mary named Fanny after her old friend. Mary was proud that her delivery had been easy, and as for Fanny, Mary loved her instantly. "My little Girl," she wrote to a friend, "begins to suck so manfully that her father reckons saucily on her writing the second part of the Rights of Woman." Mary's joy in this child illuminates almost every letter she wrote henceforth.

Fanny's father was the chief recipient of these letters with all the details of the baby's life. To Mary's despair, she and Imlay hardly ever lived together again. A year went by; Imlay was now in London and Mary in France. She offered to break it off, but mysteriously, he could not let go. In the last bitter phase of their involvement, after she had joined him in London at his behest, he even sent her—as "Mrs. Imlay"—on a complicated business errand to the Scandinavian countries. Returning to London, Mary discovered that he was living with another woman. By now half crazy with humiliation, Mary chose a dark night and threw herself in the Thames. She was nearly dead when two rivermen pulled her from the water.

Though this desperate incident was almost the end of Mary, at least it was the end of the Imlay episode. He sent a doctor to care for her, but they rarely met again. Since Mary had no money, she set about providing for herself and Fanny in the way she knew. The faithful Johnson had already brought out Volume I of her history of the French Revolution. Now she set to work editing and revising her *Letters Written during a Short Residence in Sweden, Norway, and Denmark,* a kind of thoughtful travelogue. The book was well received and widely translated.

And it also revived the memory of Mary Wollstonecraft in the mind of an old acquaintance, William Godwin. As the author of the treatise *Political Justice,* he was now as famous a philosophizing serpent as Mary and was widely admired and hated as a "freethinker." He came to call on Mary. They became friends and then lovers. Early in 1797 Mary was again pregnant. William Godwin was an avowed atheist who had publicly denounced the very institution of marriage. On March 29, 1797, he nevertheless went peaceably to church with Mary and made her his wife.

The Godwins were happy together, however William's theories may have been outraged. He adored his small step-daughter and took pride in his brilliant wife. Awaiting the birth of her child throughout the summer, Mary worked on a new novel and made plans for a book on "the management of infants"—it would have been the first "Dr. Spock." She expected to have another easy delivery and promised to come downstairs to dinner the day following. But when labor began, on August 30, it proved to be long and agonizing. A daughter, named Mary Wollstonecraft, was born; ten days later, the mother died.

Occasionally, when a gifted writer dies young, one can feel, as in the example of Shelley, that perhaps he had at any rate accomplished his best work. But so recently had Mary come into her full intellectual and emotional growth that her death at the age of thirty-eight is bleak indeed. There is no knowing what Mary might have accomplished now that she enjoyed domestic stability. Perhaps she might have achieved little or nothing further as a writer. But she might have been able to protect her daughters from some part of the sadness that overtook them; for as things turned out, both Fanny and Mary were to sacrifice themselves.

Fanny grew up to be a shy young girl, required to feel grateful for the roof over her head, overshadowed by her prettier half sister, Mary. Godwin in due course married a formidable widow named Mrs. Clairmont, who brought her own daughter into the house—the Claire Clairmont who grew up to become Byron's mistress and the mother of his daughter Allegra. Over the years Godwin turned into a hypocrite and a miser who nevertheless continued to pose as the great liberal of the day. Percy Bysshe Shelley, born the same year that the *Vindication of the Rights of Woman* was published, came to be a devoted admirer of Mary Wollstonecraft's writing. As a young man he therefore came with his wife to call upon Godwin. What he really sought, however, were Mary's daughters—because they were her daughters. First he approached Fanny, but later changed his mind. Mary Godwin was then sixteen, the perfect potential soul mate for a man whose needs for soul mates knew no bounds. They conducted their courtship in the most up-to-the-minute romantic style: beneath a tree near her mother's grave they read aloud to each other from the *Vindication.* Soon they eloped, having pledged their "troth" in the cemetery. Godwin, the celebrated freethinker, was enraged. To make matters worse, Claire Clairmont had run off to Switzerland with them.

Not long afterward Fanny, too, ran away. She went to an inn in a distant town and drank a fatal dose of laudanum. It has traditionally been said that unrequited love for Shelley drove her to this pass, but there is no evidence one way or the other. One suicide that can more justly be laid at Shelley's door is that of his first wife, which occurred a month after Fanny's and which at any rate left him free to wed his mistress, Mary Godwin. Wife or mistress, she had to endure poverty, ostracism, and Percy's constant infidelities. But now at last her father could, and did, boast to his relations that he was father-in-law to a baronet's son. "Oh, philosophy!" as Mary Godwin Shelley remarked.

If in practice Shelley was merely a womanizer, on paper he was a convinced feminist. He had learned this creed from Mary Wollstonecraft. Through his verse Mary's ideas began to be disseminated. They were one part of that vast tidal wave of political, social, and artistic revolution that arose in the late eighteenth century, the romantic movement. But because of Mary's unconventional way of life, her name fell into disrepute during the nineteenth century, and her book failed to exert its rightful influence on the development of feminism. Emma Willard and other pioneers of the early Victorian period indignantly refused to claim Mary as their forebear. Elizabeth Cady Stanton and Lucretia Mott were mercifully less strait-laced on the subject. In 1889, when Mrs. Stanton and Susan B. Anthony published their *History of Woman Suffrage,* they dedicated the book to Mary. Though Mary Wollstonecraft can in no sense be said to have founded the woman's rights movement, she was, by the late nineteenth century, recognized as its inspiration, and the *Vindication* was vindicated for the highly original work it was, a landmark in the history of society.

A WORLD TRANSFORMED

Keith Michael Baker

Keith Michael Baker is professor of history at Stanford University. Born in Swindon, England, he received a B.A. (1960) and an M.A. (1963) from Cambridge University, and a Ph.D. from the University College at the University of London (1964). He is the author of Condorcet: From Natural Philosophy to Social Mathematics *(1975), and editor of* The Political Culture of the Old Regime *(1987) and* The Old Regime and the French Revolution *(1987). This essay is adapted from an article that appeared in* France *magazine, and is reprinted by permission.*

My dear philosopher, doesn't this appear to you to be the century of revolutions...?" So wrote Voltaire to his fellow apostle of enlightenment and reform, the mathematician d'Alembert, in 1772. The remark was more prescient than its writer knew. Within a few years, the elegant, aristocratic, and oppressive France to which Voltaire belonged was to explode.

The traditional social order whose injustices Voltaire had done much to publicize was to be swept away. His countrymen were to be seized with a passion to create a new society whose ramifications went far beyond anything the philosopher had expected or desired. Novel ideas, radically different modes of political practice, unprecedented forms of civic and military mobilization, were to fan out from Paris across Europe, as the French set out in 1789 to do nothing less than make the world anew.

The events that began to unfold in France in 1789 gave a profoundly new meaning to the notion of "revolution," a meaning that has transformed world history and touched the lives of all nations.

When Voltaire's contemporaries heard the term, they generally thought of abrupt and unexpected changes occurring in human affairs, without the conscious choice of human actors. A new sense of the meaning of the word revolution was beginning to meld in the minds of Frenchmen when they heralded the outcome of the American War of Independence as "the American Revolution." But it was not until 1789 that these various elements fused so dramatically into a powerful new conception.

In presenting their actions to the world, the spokesmen of 1789 conceived of "the French Revolution" as a radical break with the past achieved by the conscious will of human actors, not simply a historical mutation suffered passively by them. No longer a simple moment of change, a revolution became an act of universal significance, pregnant with meaning for humankind and its future. Although carried out by a single people, the revolution was seen by its actors as the conjuncture of eternity and the present, with the fate of all humanity hanging in the balance. The modern conception of revolution was born.

If our own century, too, has been a century of revolutions, this is because men and women throughout the world have continued to play out, in one way or another, that script for modern politics invented by the French in 1789. Not only the modern notion of revolution itself but our contemporary political vocabulary—the distinction between "Right" and "Left"; the notions of nationalism, liberalism, conservatism, socialism; even our modern understanding of democracy and human rights—derive, directly or indirectly, from the French Revolution. Two centuries later, in the bicentennial year of the French Revolution, we find ourselves still confronted by the challenge

From *The Wilson Quarterly*, Summer 1989, pp. 37-45. © 1989 by the Woodrow Wilson International Center for Scholars. Reprinted by permission.

of understanding the meaning and implications of its extraordinary events.

This challenge is a particularly fascinating one for Americans. For the French Revolution was at once closely linked to the American Revolution, inspired by many of the same ideals, and yet radically different in its course, its implications, and its outcomes. The most immediate link between the two revolutions was financial and political. The French monarchy that undertook to support the Americans in their War of Independence against the British was already crippled by accumulated debts from previous wars. It could not long continue to support these debts, nor to incur new ones, while enjoying an inefficient and inequitable tax system. Yet Louis XVI (1774–92) could not reform this system without admitting some version of the principle of consent to taxation, which the absolute monarchy had resisted for almost 200 years. Paradoxically, the monarchy also found itself in the position of supporting and popularizing American arguments for liberty and government by consent as part of its war against the British.

When French participation in the American war eventually pushed the monarchy into virtual bankruptcy (as Turgot, the finance minister from 1774 to 1776, predicted it would), the government was forced to press for extensive reform of the administrative and fiscal system, including the elimination of traditional tax privileges enjoyed by the nobility and the clergy. The nobility and clergy seized upon the American example and refused taxation without representation: They countered the government's reform initiatives with demands for government by consent, fiscal responsibility, and an end to arbitrary power. To resolve the resulting conflict, Louis XVI, on August 8, 1788, was forced to call the meeting of the Estates General for May of the following year. It was a thrilling moment. Every French king since 1614 had refused to consider convening the ancient consultative assembly of deputies from the three social orders (Estates).

Imagine the excitement, the expectations of reform, and the hopes for relief of grievances occasioned at every level of society by this momentous decision of an absolute monarch to call representatives of his people together in a general assembly for the first time in almost two centuries.

Imagine, too, the political problems involved in this resurrection of an institution long thought dead. How was the Estates General to meet, and how were its deputies to be chosen? We can get some sense of the difficulty of resolving these questions if we reflect upon what it would be like if no national assembly had met in America since the Constitutional Convention and it suddenly became necessary to call one today. Should Vermont be given the same proportion of delegates it sent in 1787; and what about the (then-nonexistent) state of California? Would the electoral procedures be the same as they were in 1787? And what about the requirements for eligibility to vote or to be elected? Questions such as these would amount to deciding the nature of national political identity and the meaning of citizenship all over again.

In fact, on crucial points of detail, the French government had no reliable records of how the elections of deputies to the Estates General had been conducted almost 200 years earlier. Abandoning its traditional propensity for secrecy and absolute authority in deciding important matters, it even turned to the public at large for information and advice regarding the appropriate forms of election (though this may also have been a political tactic to divide and defuse opposition to royal policies). Profound disputes arose over whether the procedures used by the deputies in 1614 to vote on measures should again be followed in a society changed by the passage of two centuries. In the waning months of 1788, as the date for the meeting of the Estates General approached and the government hesitated to announce the procedures to be followed, France was consumed by a bitter pamphlet war.

In 1614, the three Estates of the realm—the clergy, the nobility, and the unprivileged remainder of the people, the so-called Third Estate—had sent three separate delegations, each deliberating and voting separately, with essential issues decided by a majority of two out of the three Estates. Hoping to defend traditional privileges, many pamphleteers who wrote on behalf of the clergy and the nobility at the end of 1788 argued for the continuation of these procedures as part of the "ancient constitution" of the realm. The pamphlets emanating from the Third Estate argued for a modification of the traditional procedures that would favor its interests: They demanded that the Third Estate elect a number of deputies equal to those of the combined privileged orders and that the decisions of the Estates General be made by a majority of all the deputies voting as a single body. Their authors calculated that deputies of the Third Estate would then form a majority together with liberal deputies from the clergy and nobility.

But the most celebrated pamphlet of this period—indeed, of the entire French Revolution—went far beyond these claims on behalf of the Third Estate. In fact, it was written by a member of the minor clergy, Emmanuel-Joseph Sieyès, one of those sons of the unprivileged who used a clerical career as an avenue for social advancement, only to find their ambitions blocked by the hold of the aristocracy on important positions within the church. Sieyès turned his personal frustrations into an indictment of the entire regime. Published at the very beginning of 1789, his celebrated pamphlet, *What Is The Third Estate?*, did for the French what Tom Paine's *Common Sense* had done for the Americans little more than a decade earlier. It recast the terms of public debate, and, by doing so, transformed the political situation into a moment ripe for revolution.

Sieyès's argument was radical in its simplicity. Where more moderate spokesmen for the Third Estate objected that the privileged were a minority whose power and pretensions within the nation should be reduced, Sieyès asserted that they could form no part of the nation at all. If a nation, Sieyès argued, were a civil society satisfying the needs of its members through productive economic activities, then the idle and unproductive privileged classes were no more than parasites upon it. Or if a nation were a political association of citizens living equally under a common law, then the claims of the privileged to unequal status and a separate legal identity automatically set them outside it. In either case, Sieyès proclaimed, the Third Estate constituted the entire nation in and of itself.

So even before the Estates General had met, Sieyès had announced the fundamental principle of the French Revolution: A nation is and must be one and indivisible. This claim implied a complete rejection of the traditional social and political order in France, which assumed a multiplicity of heterogeneous entities made one only by their common subjection to the sovereign will of the king. Sieyès's argument was a radical refutation of the assumption that the division of the Estates General into three separate assemblies was or could be legitimate. Three assemblies meeting separately could never represent the common will of an indivisible nation.

Indeed, in an argument with profound consequences for subsequent French history, Sieyès went so far as to argue that the national will could never be bound by any existing constitutional form. The nation was a pure political being, prior to any constitution; it had only to express its will, in any manner, for existing political and legal arrangements to be suspended. "The nation," he argued, "is all that it can be by the very fact of its existence. Not only is the nation not subject to a constitution, but it *cannot*, it *must not* be."

This is an amazing conclusion, well worth reflecting upon, because its implications transformed an entire world. By arguing that the nation is the natural and essential human collectivity in which individuals must secure their liberty, citizenship, and rights, Sieyès called upon the French to break with the past. The French not only took up this call but fashioned it into the modern principles of national sovereignty and national self-determination, which they announced in the name of all peoples. The entire history of the 19th and 20th centuries has been shaped (for better or worse) by the efforts of one people after another to recover their national identity and to exercise their sovereignty in a state of their own. Nationalism as a political ideology dates from the French Revolution.

Sieyès's arguments also made the French Revolution, from the very beginning, far more radical than the American Revolution. The Americans could resist the tyranny of George III and his Parliament by invoking the rights of Englishmen and the tradition of the Common Law. In repudiating British rule, they were not renouncing their entire history. The logic of Sieyès's argument, by contrast, necessarily implied a radical break with the past. The authority of history was shattered forever by his call to the principles of natural right and sovereign will.

Natural rights, the new idea of nationality, the necessity of a radical break with the past—these were the revolutionary principles Sieyès offered his compatriots in 1789. They were not slow to accept these principles—for themselves and in the name of humanity at large. The message of *What Is The Third Estate?* was clear: Because the Third Estate constituted the entire nation, the deputies it sent to the Estates General were really the sole national representatives and should act accordingly.

And this indeed is what they decided to do. When the Estates General met on May 5, the Third Estate deputies refused to form a separate chamber. Six weeks later, they broke the resulting political deadlock by proclaiming themselves a National Assembly which alone could express the national will. This was their first revolutionary act. It was reaffirmed three days later, on June 20, 1789, when they swore in the famous Tennis Court Oath not to disperse until the nation had been given a new constitution. And it was doubly confirmed: first, when Louis XVI capitulated by ordering the deputies of the nobility and the clergy to join the new National Assembly; second, when the people of Paris stormed that great citadel of despotism, the Bastille, in order to save the Assembly from the threat of being forcibly dispersed by the royal armies. A "nation" had spoken, not only through its representatives but also through popular action.

Popular action was to drive the Assembly even further in realizing the logic of a revolutionary break with the past. The fall of the Bastille on July 12–14, 1789, was the signal for disorders throughout France, as townspeople overthrew municipal oligarchies, and peasants impatient for reforms attacked the castles of the aristocracy and destroyed the records of hated feudal exactions. These actions left the new representatives of the nation no choice but to exercise the sovereignty they had claimed on its behalf.

In an emotion-laden session lasting far into the night of August 4, 1789, the deputies extended revolutionary principles far beyond anything they had originally intended. They declared the "feudal regime" abolished: Not only feudal dues but the privileges of the nobility and the clergy, as well as of provinces and towns—in a word, the entire administrative, financial, and judicial order of what was soon to be called the Old Regime—were in principle swept away. This celebrated "holocaust of privileges," perhaps the most momentous act of the entire French Revolution, in effect created the modern individual, a person free from traditional status bonds, in a new society that was to be based on property, contract, and individual rights. It also inaugurated a philosophical and psychological dynamic which set the French to exploring the hazardous modern conviction that society can be made anew through the exercise of political will.

Even before the dramatic "Night of the Fourth of August," the assembly had been debating the necessity of a Declaration of Rights. Some members, inspired by the American Declaration of Independence, called for a declaration to proclaim to the nation and to humankind at large the abstract principles upon which the new constitution should be based. Others, fearing social disorder as a consequence of an abstract declaration of rights, preferred the enactment of specific positive laws to prevent abuses of power. After August 4, 1789, however, the outcome was clear. Within three weeks, the assembly had drafted its statement of the philosophical principles upon which a new constitution would rest and a new society be inaugurated. Coincidentally, the Declaration of the Rights of Man and of the Citizen was adopted within a few days of the vote on the Bill of Rights in the U.S. Congress.

Drawing as they did upon a common philosophical heritage, sharing a common concern to protect individual citizens from any exercise of arbitrary power, these two great enactments of the principles of human rights nevertheless differ in fundamental ways. The American Bill of Rights took the form of amendments to the Constitution. Individuals in America were protected from arbitrary

THE UNFOLDING OF A REVOLUTION

We know the exact moment when the idea of— even the word for—revolution was first used in its modern political sense. On the night of July 14, 1789, the Duc de La Rochefoucauld-Liancourt informed Louis XVI that the Bastille prison had been stormed and royal troops had defected before a popular attack. The King's response was almost nonchalant: "C'est une révolte." Liancourt corrected him, "Non, Sire, c'est une révolution."

The King was familiar with revolts; they were popular defiances which could be put down with the means at his disposal. In using the old astronomical term, revolution, Liancourt was not suggesting, however, that there would be a revolving or return. It was, rather, the "irresistibility," such as propels heavenly bodies in their courses, which Liancourt saw entering human events. Control was now out of the hands of the king and his ministers.

The irresistibility Liancourt noted would sweep away much of the world as it was known. Below is a calendar of a world transformed.

1789

May 5: Pressed by a desperate need for revenues, Louis XVI convenes the Estates General, the first national parliament to meet in nearly 200 years. Without any living precedent to guide it, the Third Estate (the new middle class) pits itself against the aristocracy. In June, the Third Estate declares itself The National Assembly, determined to write a new constitution.

July 14: A Parisian mob liberates the Bastille, a nearly empty prison but a symbol of the oppressions of the *ancien régime.* Its "liberation" incites revolutionary actions throughout France.

July 20–August 6: Peasants arm themselves against looting brigands in the countryside but instead turn upon the castles and burn the records of their manorial debts and feudal obligations. Feudalism is, in effect, ended.

October 5-6: A Parisian crowd made up largely of women, the so-called Women's March, proceeds to Versailles and forces the King to return to Paris, where he is now forced to reside.

November 2: The property of the clergy is confiscated and put on sale. Although the sales initially benefit only those who already have property, the Revolution is propelled toward a new redistribution of landed wealth.

1790–1791

February: Religious orders are abolished in France. The church of France becomes a national church, with priests ordered to swear loyalty to the *Civil Constitution of the Clergy.* The resulting schism will later spark the counter-Revolution.

February 1790–June 1791: The constitutional monarchy, based on the English model from the Revolution of 1688, proves ineffective. The Marquis de Lafayette's compromises fail to reconcile an aristocracy living on feudal dues and a peasantry determined to do away with them. Civil war rages in many regions of the country.

June 21, 1791: Louis XVI, disguised as a valet, attempts to flee the country, only to be captured at Varennes. Thus ends the experiment with constitutional monarchy. Sympathetic to Louis's plight, Prussia and Austria threaten intervention, while inside France almost every interest sees its salvation in a foreign war.

1792

April 20: The Legislative Assembly—led by the progressive bourgeoisie, the Girondins—declares war on Austria. Ensuing military defeats, combined with economic crisis, revive popular discontent and raise revolutionary sentiment to a fever pitch.

August 10–11: Spurred by popular insurrection, the Assembly abolishes the monarchy and forms a convention to write a new constitution. Active participation of the *sans-culottes* (literally, without trousers, or those who wear britches; in other words, lower-class artisans who have little or no property) leads to universal suffrage and the arming of lower-class citizens. During this so-called Second Revolution the more moderate Girondins lose control.

September 20: A new National Convention is elected. The Revolutionary Army finally halts the invasion of Prussian troops just north of Paris at Valmy. Witnessing the battle, the poet

Goethe declares, "From this day and this place dates a new era in the history of the world."

September 22: Under the new calendar, this day is designated the first day of the new era—Vendémiaire I, Year I. The new calendar (which remains in effect till January 1, 1806) reveals the revolutionary inclination to remake everything, including time.

December 11: The trial of Louis XVI begins. On January 14, 1793, he is declared guilty and on January 21, executed.

1793

February 1: The Convention declares war on Great Britain and the Netherlands and, a month later, on Spain. The government passes into the hands of the far more radical Montagnards under Robespierre's leadership.

March: A series of defeats is suffered by the Revolutionary Army, as counter-Revolution breaks out.

September 25: The Convention silences all opposition. The Committee of Public Safety, led by Robespierre, commences a series of public trials and executions, which becomes the infamous "Terror." By December 1, there are 4,595 prisoners in the jails of Paris.

October 16: Marie-Antoinette is executed.

November 10: The Cathedral of Notre Dame is converted into the Temple of Reason. A tide of de Christianization leads to the closing of Parisian churches; elsewhere, cemeteries bear the slogan, "Death is an eternal sleep."

December 6: The Convention, pressed by Robespierre who fears alienating neutral foreign powers, reaffirms the principle of worship. In effect, the 12-member Committee of Public Safety under Robespierre takes the revolutionary momentum away from the popular insurrections.

1794

December (1793) to July: The revolutionary government stabilizes itself—chiefly by executing its enemies and stifling internal dissent. Production, distribution, and profits are all strictly controlled in order to generate revenues for conducting the war. By spring, the government has amassed an army of a million men, an unprecedented instrument for waging war.

July 27–28: The irony of the Revolution is that its success leads to its demise. With its enemies on the right and left liquidated, with popular insurrections subdued and victory in its foreign wars likely, the revolutionary government can no longer intimidate the Convention. In July, the government falls into internal dissension, and during two dramatic days—8 and 9 Thermidor—Robespierre is outmaneuvered by a ramshackle coalition of his enemies. The execution of Robespierre, Saint-Just, and their partisans on 10 Thermidor is the date cited by many historians to mark the end of the Revolution.

Aftermath

During the next two years, known as the Thermidorian reaction, the Notables, or "men of substance," attempted to force the *sans-culottes* out of political life and also to abandon the controlled economy. But the government they formed under the Directory floundered, equally afraid of royalism and democracy. Moreover, it proved impotent in the face of persistent financial and social crises. The more discredited the Directory became, however, the greater rose the prestige of its conquering generals, especially of the victorious general of the Italian Campaign of 1796–97—Napoleon Bonaparte. In 1799, the Coup d'État of 18 Brumaire brought Napoleon to power, initially as First Consul, then as Consul for Life, and finally as Emperor. Yet even as he became Emperor, Napoleon consolidated and exported many revolutionary reforms—from judicial equality to the metric system—and indeed, in the eyes of aristocratic Europe, Napoleon remained the "soldier of the Revolution."

government by the judiciary functioning under specific rules already stated in the Constitution. The Declaration of the Rights of Man, by contrast, was adopted before the National Assembly had even begun to enact a new constitution. It enunciated the universal, founding principles which a constitution had to implement, and became the philosophical measure against which any constitution might be found wanting.

The Declaration thus preceded the French Constitution eventually adopted in 1791. And within months of its implementation, that Constitution was repudiated in the name of the very principles enshrined in the Declaration. It was to be the first of many so repudiated, as the French sought not only during the revolutionary period but throughout the 19th century to match successive constitutions to the universal principles set forth in the Declaration.

None of these principles was more important, none made the achievement of a stable constitution more difficult in France, than that enunciated in Article III: "The source of all sovereignty resides essentially in the nation." The statement clearly echoed clauses in the American Constitution insisting that the source of all power inhered in the people. But the French were to give the proposition a more radical meaning, which led them almost immediately to reject the Anglo-American example of a separation and balance of powers.

The American Constitution was, in fact, one of the models considered when the Assembly turned from drafting the Declaration of the Rights of Man to a debate over constitutional principles. Within two weeks, however, the Anglo-American model had been definitely rejected in accordance with principles already announced by Sieyès in *What Is The Third Estate?* For a majority of the deputies, national sovereignty was by definition one and indivisible. The idea of the balance of powers—far from being a safeguard of liberty—appeared to be a recipe for constitutional confusion and an impediment to the univocal expression of a supreme national will. Preferring arguments drawn from

Rousseau's *Social Contract* to those in Montesquieu's *Spirit Of the Laws*, they looked for liberty not in a constitutional balancing of interests but in the undivided authority of a single legislative assembly made directly responsible for its deliberations and actions to the will of people.

This decision goes a long way to explain the very different constitutional and political histories of the two countries during the past two centuries. The American Founders sought to secure individual rights by dispersing power through a system of checks and balances. The French Founders sought to secure human rights by constructing a unitary form of government, based on the general will emanating from the citizens as a single body. They opted, in other words, to limit particular powers and functions by generalizing power and extending it to all.

From a constitutional perspective, this choice made the representation and delegation of power profoundly difficult. For as soon as a representative body was elected to legislate for the nation, or its deliberations issued in laws or decrees, there was the risk of these actions being perceived as emanating from a particular will which no longer corresponded to the general will of the nation. The dramatic assertions of popular will during the subsequent years of the French Revolution and the Napoleonic experiment with referendums would be replayed through the course of the following century, in efforts to resolve this problematic relationship between sovereignty and representation created by the National Assembly in 1789. The problem has remained at the heart of the fertile history of French experimentation with constitutional forms down to our day.

The American and French revolutions were closely linked in time and, initially, in spirit. But while the Americans attempted in their Revolution to perfect the work of history, the French opted for the far more radical experiment of a philosophical break with the past that would create the world anew. In this bicentennial year of 1989, we are still living amid the consequences of decisions and actions taken 200 years ago on the other side of the Atlantic.

1789
AN IDEA
THAT CHANGED
THE WORLD

China: rethinking the Revolution

ZHILIAN ZHANG

Zhilian Zhang, of China, is a professor of history at Beijing University. President of the Association for the Study of French History, a member of the International Commission on the History of the French Revolution, and editor-in-chief of a general history of France, his published works include an essay entitled From the Gauls to De Gaulle.

Reform or revolution? This was the dilemma faced by Chinese élites in the nineteenth century. The example of the French Revolution was at the core of their debates.

IN China, the influence of the French Revolution was not immediately felt, and it was only a century later that the ideals of 1789 were explicitly voiced.

There were geographical as well as sociological reasons for this time-lag. In the days of sailing ships, a despatch took at least eight months to reach Peking from London. Lord Macartney, head of the first official British mission to China, left Portsmouth in September 1792, and did not reach Peking until August 1793.

The imperial court where he was received had already heard of the events in France, and rumours of the upheaval caused by the Revolution made anything new subject to suspicion. At the height of its power and prosperity, China had no need to think of change. The country had a stable social structure, with no bourgeoisie, no ideological contention, no political opposition. If the peasants were unhappy, they were not yet organized. In China, the time was not ripe for reform, still less for revolution.

During the nineteenth century pressure for social and political change began to mount.

Reprinted with permission from *The UNESCO Courier*, June 1989, pp. 44-47.

Peasant unrest (from the White Lotus uprisings in the 1790s, to the Taiping insurrection of 1850-1864), foreign aggression (from the First Opium War with Britain of 1839-1842 to the French expeditions of the 1880s), economic decline and widespread corruption, continuous population growth—all these factors sapped the foundations of the Middle Empire. The crisis became acute on the eve of the twentieth century following defeat at the hands of Japan.

Such were the conditions in which Chinese élites began to study the French Revolution in the hope of finding solutions to their own problems.

Monarchs who lose the people's confidence

The first significant commentary inspired by the French Revolution was written by the reformer Wang Tao (1828-1897). In his *Compendium on France* he wrote: "Does the calamitous violence of republican government always lead to such excesses? When the rebel parties, in their cruel fury, do not shrink from committing regicide, where are a country's laws? What has happened to the rulers of nature? It is as if Heaven and Earth had been reversed and the world was upside down... In all of history surely there has been no rebellion worse than this. And yet, at the origin of these calamities, we find the inability [of the monarch] to conciliate the masses and win the confidence of his subjects. Presuming upon their high position, these monarchs fail to identify with popular fortunes. And mounting resentment is enough to bring about the demise of royalty... Such being the case, can rulers do as they please and behave irresponsibly?"

Wang Tao condemned the rebels but held the king responsible for the calamity because he had alienated himself from the people. This was a lesson that rulers should draw from the Revolution.

The stirrings of reform

The tide for radical change rose higher in the 1890s and a generation of reformers emerged, with Kang Youwei (1858-1927) and Liang Qichao (1873-1929) in the forefront. Kang won the confidence of the Emperor Guangxu (but not that of the Empress Dowager), and dreamt of reforming the Empire "from the top". True to the classical Chinese tradition of using the past to serve current policies, he was nevertheless an innovator in that he used the history of a foreign country to convince the emperor and the court.

In the preface to his *Account of the French Revolution*, dedicated to Guangxu, Kang uncon-

ditionally condemned the excesses of this "bloody revolt": "There has never been anything more disastrous than the atrocities of modern revolution." His censure of Louis XVI was no less severe: "Divine right is not granted permanently. Only by virtuous means can you keep it; otherwise, it will be taken from you. Louis XVI's promise to grant a constitution did not come from his own initiative but was given under pressure. His hesitation and oscillation, his initial recourse to arms and later disbandment of his guards, and finally his appeal to foreign intervention and flight to Varennes, stirred up the indignation of the people to such an extent that he was sent to the guillotine and scorned by the world."

Kang felt that popular feelings should be calmed rather than excited, because the populace, once aroused to action, is like a rock rolling down a steep hill; nothing can halt its course. "It may have been possible for a single person to tyrannize an ignorant mass. But once the people realize that the world is made for all and not just for a few, they envy the rich and strive for power and prestige."

Kang conceded that all modern constitutional governments originated in the French Revolution: "In spite of its aberrations and tyrannical violence, it was aided by the trend of the times and the spirit of the people. Like a huge storm sweeping over and transforming the great earth, it was indeed something frightening. As there has not been anything as grandiose in the annals of political change, it may also serve as an example."

According to Kang Youwei, the obvious lesson was that a reform programme should be launched from above and a constitutional monarchy be established before the rebellious people took matters into their own hands and imposed radical changes from below.

Kang's contemporary Liang Qichao was one of the first writers to introduce the ideas of the Enlightenment to the Chinese. In his *Life of Madame Roland*, he called the Revolution "the Mother of European Civilization"; but he repeatedly cited the alleged final words of his heroine on the scaffold: "Oh, Liberty, what crimes are committed in thy name!" He rejected oppression and revolution in the same breath. He was an advocate of "destruction without bloodshed". He warned the conservatives in high places that to ignore the aspirations of the people would lead to a new outbreak of the Terror. At the same time, he made clear to the "pushers in low places" that if they unleashed the passions of the masses, the result would be a blood bath and anarchy, as in France.

The reforms proposed by Kang and his followers, although mild, were not accepted by those in power. Six reformers were decapitated. Kang was obliged to flee to Hong Kong, while Liang sought refuge in Japan. The attempt at change was nipped in the bud.

Bloodshed, the price of liberty

A reaction was bound to assert itself from the revolutionary camp. Not only in China, but also in Japan where many radicals took shelter following the failure of the reforms. A torrent of pamphlets and political papers imbued with the ideas of 1789 appeared. In the first decade of the twentieth century, the French Revolution became the model for the struggle against feudal oppression.

A radical interpretation of the French Revolution emerged from the writings of the revolutionists. Rebutting the counter-revolutionary ideas of Kang Youwei, they stressed the necessity of propagating in China ideas of Enlightenment and revolution. They exalted the spirit of sacrifice and recourse to violence. They appealed to men and parties to unite. For the first time, the names of Montesquieu, Voltaire, Rousseau, Turgot, Helvétius, Sieyès and Fourier were on the lips of Confucian scholars. Journals published commentaries on the Declaration of the Rights of Man and of the Citizen. Several versions of the *Marseillaise* were circulated.

Criticizing as ridiculous the notion of "destruction without bloodshed", the revolutionists upheld, on the contrary, that the success of the revolution depended on violence and sacrifice. Ready to give their lives, they vowed "to sacrifice themselves for the rights of the people and to buy liberty with bloodshed". Was that not how despotism had been abolished and natural rights restored in France? A staunch revolutionist from Hunan exclaimed: "Have you not known the affairs in France, the homeland of the *Social Contract*, the battlefield of freedom? All was accomplished through violence. The Revolution of 1789 was indeed tragic and violent; those of 1830 and 1848 were no less so. The guillotined head of the King was paraded through the streets of Paris, while the throngs of people cried out *Vive la liberté!* Thrice have they driven away their king, fourteen times have they changed their constitution—always with much bloodshed. Yet France has become a strong nation."

But how was the unity of the revolutionary movement and its leaders to be preserved? The Chinese revolutionists expressed great admiration for the Jacobin Club which appeared to them as a "driving force of the Revolution". But they noticed with regret that political and personal rivalries between Girondins and Montagnards, then between Dantonists and Robespierrists, finally led to the downfall of democracy. A revolutionary patriot, Liu Yazi, drew an analogy between the disputes of leaders in the French Revolution and the quarrels of leaders in the Taiping Heavenly Kingdom, as a warning to his comrades.

Thus the long debate on the virtues and crimes of the French Revolution gradually reinforced the conviction of those who believed that China needed revolution, not piecemeal change.

A great 'social laboratory'

A new generation of revolutionary leaders came to the forefront. Many of them discovered their calling while listening to accounts of the storming of the Bastille. In June 1920, a twenty-two-year-old Chinese youth wrote these lines for a classmate who was leaving to study in France:

> *On your return, you will*
> *Hoist the Flag of Liberty*
> *Sing the Song of Independence*
> *Fight for the Rights of Women*
> *And seek for Equality*
> *In the great social laboratory.*

The author's name was Zhou Enlai.

The French Revolution, North Africa, and the Middle East

Antony T. Sullivan

Antony T. Sullivan is an associate of the Center for Near East and North African Studies at the University of Michigan. He is the author of Thomas-Robert Bugeaud, France and Algeria, 1784–1849: Politics, Power and the Good Society (*Archon Books, 1983) and* Palestinian Universities under Occupation (*American University in Cairo Press, 1988).*

When French infantry shattered Egypt's Mamluk cavalry near the Pyramids on July 21, 1798, the French Revolution erupted into the world of Islam. Little would be the same thereafter. France, more than any other Western power, became the engine of modernization across a vast territory bordering the eastern and southern Mediterranean. Probably nowhere else in the Third World has the French Revolution had more impact than in the Middle East and North Africa. Certainly, nowhere else has the struggle between Western models and indigenous traditions become more acute. Today, the intense cultural debate opened by the French Revolution continues to agitate Arabs and Muslims, and its ultimate consequences remain uncertain.

Earlier major events in the West had no great influence on the Muslim world. For example, the cultural and other changes wrought by Christianity did not strongly impress Muslims. They believed that God's revelation to Christians had long since been superseded by His definitive revelation to Muhammad. Christian "truth" at best reflected imperfectly a truth that Muslims alone possessed in entirety. Almost two centuries of occupation of a portion of the Muslim heartland by Christian Crusaders failed to stimulate significant Muslim curiosity about the worldview of their opponents. Revolutionary France, with its aggressive secularism and anti-Christian ideology, combined with its success in mobilizing society through a new and fervent nationalism, persuaded Muslims that by following its example they might discover the key to Western power without compromising their own cultural authenticity. Today, the hopes of many have been disappointed. On the one hand Muslims perceive their societies as both powerless and dependent, and on the other as contaminated by an alien cultural incrustation.

In Egypt, revolutionary France arrived directly and in force. France's ruling Directory, determined to rid itself of the young Bonaparte, who had brought it to power and whom it had come to suspect of plotting a *coup*, dispatched Napoleon overseas with orders to occupy Egypt and threaten British links with its colony of India. Evading the British fleet commanded by Admiral Horatio Nelson, Napoleon landed with some thirty thousand troops at Alexandria on July 1, 1798.

During the next three years France ruled Egypt, and in 1799 even struck northeastward through the Levant as far as Acre, where some of the defeated Mamluk governors of Egypt had taken refuge. There, Napoleon suffered his first military defeat and was forced to withdraw without subduing the city. In late August 1799, he secretly departed Egypt and returned to France, leaving behind an army that ruled the country for another year and a half. Less than three months after his return, the Directory's worst fears were realized. Napoleon sent troops to expel its members and occupy its chambers, thereby making himself master of France. In 1804 he crowned himself emperor, achieving a symbolic acme of power which dazzled the Islamic world quite as much as it did Europe.

The French occupation of Egypt greatly accelerated a process of modernization whose first stirrings can be traced to the rule of Mamluks Ali Bey and Muhammad Bey Abu al-Dhahab (1760–1775). French authorities did so primarily by discrediting Mamluk authority and replacing it with the authority of a militarily powerful, enlightened, and putatively tolerant France. Napoleon at first

This article originally appeared in *The World & I*, July 1989, pp. 563-570. Reprinted with permission from *The World & I*, a publication of The Washington Times Corporation. © 1989.

posed as a friend of Islam and proclaimed his intention to liberate Egypt from tyranny by providing it with institutions for responsible self-government. Such institutions, of course, were to be under close French supervision. In fact, Napoleon established an Egyptian Administrative Council in Cairo responsible for civil government. This council was given the right to elect its own president and appoint a range of lesser officials. Provincial councils were established in much of the rest of the country. For the first time, an indigenous Egyptian elite consisting largely of the religious leadership (the 'ulema) tasted a limited form of self-government. Despite the brief duration of Napoleon's experiment, Egypt's first experience with restricted popular sovereignty was not forgotten.

In addition, Napoleon founded a think tank as a base for the 167 French scholars who accompanied his expedition. That organization, the Institute of Egypt, undertook research and development in a broad range of areas related to Egypt's political economy, infrastructure, and history. Studies were conducted on Egyptian agricultural and water resources, and French engineers were commissioned to improve roads and canals. Factories were designed, many for the purpose of manufacturing gunpowder. Research was undertaken on Egypt's educational and legal systems. Archaeological and topographical surveys were launched, and Egyptian fauna studied. From the Institute came a remarkable twenty-three-volume work, *Description de l'Egypte*, which was published between 1809 and 1829 and introduced Egypt and Islam to nineteenth-century Europe. Most important, however, was the intellectual impact the Institute had on Egypt's small but influential religious elite.

In particular, many of the 'ulema were impressed by the systematic ordering of knowledge and the scientific methodology that characterized French scholarship at the Institute. The spirit of rationalism, so characteristic of the contemporary West, entered Egypt and the modern Islamic world largely through Napoleon's Institute of Egypt. The fact that the Institute established Egypt's first Arabic printing press and began to

publish two journals in Arabic only enhanced France's reputation as both enlightened and progressive. Thanks largely to the Institute's work, the French Revolution succeeded in striking root in Egypt only a decade after its outbreak. During the reign of Muhammad Ali (1805–1849) and his immediate successors, Egyptian modernization proceeded under increasing French tutelage.

Muhammad Ali, an Ottoman army officer of Albanian extraction, arrived in Egypt in 1801 and seized power four years later. Determined not to be overthrown and to increase

> The French occupation of Egypt greatly accelerated a process of modernization.

Egypt's military power, he aped France's *levée-en-masse* by conscripting Egyptian peasants into a new-model army. No military obligation had been imposed on the Egyptian peasantry during the previous five thousand years, and Muhammad Ali's conscription proved highly unpopular. Nevertheless, he pressed ahead. By the early 1830s an Egyptian army of some one hundred thousand men had become the most powerful military force in the Eastern Mediterranean. Indeed, French support in 1832 enabled Muhammad Ali to come close to occupying Constantinople and destroying the Ottoman Empire, of which Egypt remained nominally a part. Throughout his various military campaigns in Arabia, the Sudan, Greece, and Lebanon, French military advisers accompanied Muhammad Ali's troops, cementing the alliance between a modernizing Egypt and the Parisian heirs of the French Revolution.

At home, Muhammad Ali founded

Egypt's first indigenous institutions for advanced professional training in such subjects as engineering, medicine, and public administration. Many of the instructors were French and taught in that language. Moreover, Ali imported French technicians to provide advice on the establishment of new industries, the creation of a new system of irrigation, and the construction of a canal to link Cairo with Alexandria. Egypt under Muhammad Ali became the first Third World state to attempt an industrial revolution: Factories for the manufacture of cotton textiles, paper, and soap were all established by state initiative. Students were frequently sent to France for higher education, and many returned to direct the new manufacturing enterprises.

In 1854 Ferdinand de Lesseps, French consul-general during the 1830s in Alexandria, who had befriended Muhammad Ali's eldest son Sa'id, used his relationship with Egypt's new ruler to obtain a concession for construction of the Suez Canal. During the subsequent fifteen years, de Lesseps' *Compagnie Universelle du Canal Maritime de Suez* built one of the great monuments of the nineteenth century. When the canal opened in 1869 under the patronage of Muhammad Ali's French-educated grandson, the Khedive Isma'il, and representatives of the principal European powers, French influence in Egypt was ubiquitous. Even after France's displacement by England after 1882 as the main foreign influence in the country, Egypt's exigent thrust into modernity which the French Revolution had spawned continued.

THE FRENCH REVOLUTION AND THE OTTOMAN EMPIRE

While Napoleon was in Egypt, French revolutionary ideas were also entering the Ottoman Empire through Constantinople. There, Sultan Selim III (1789–1807) was as concerned with military reform as was Muhammad Ali, and sought from revolutionary France the latest in military training, tactics, and technology. With French counsel, Selim created a six hundred-man infantry battalion organized and equipped on European lines, which he hoped might be the first step toward dissolution of the decadent Janissary corps. With the same goal in mind, he established military and naval academies to train a new breed of officer. In so doing, Selim began to develop a professional elite that spoke French and looked to France for advice and support. Selim established Ottoman embassies in the major European capitals, proposed the abolition of tax farming, encouraged the translation of foreign books, and even toyed with the idea of creating a consultative assembly. Although he was brutally overthrown in 1807 and many of his supporters were massacred, the process of modernization Selim began did survive. Three decades later, it assumed new life.

Indeed, political modernization inspired the entire *Tanzimat* ("reorganization"), the Ottoman Empire's great period of nineteenth-century reform. Between 1839 and 1878 an attempt was made to incorporate the secularism and egalitarianism of the French Revolution into the empire's legal and bureaucratic codes. For example, a system of impartial and predictable justice was proclaimed for non-Muslims as well as Muslims, and ethnicity or religion was decreed irrelevant to public office, state employment, or military service. During the 1860s the Young Ottomans, a coterie of technocrats fluent in French and deeply influenced by Rousseau, urged Sultan Abdul Aziz to prepare a constitution and establish a parliament. They advocated a common patriotism for Turks, Armenians, Arabs, and all other communities in the empire. Although forced into exile in Paris by the early 1870s, Namek Kemal, Ibrahim Shinasi, and other reformers did assist the Ottoman Empire to accelerate a process of political rationalization that helped to delay its collapse until after World War I. Their efforts, and the larger Tanzimat of which they were a part, constituted one important bridge whereby the ideas of the French Revolution ultimately reached the eastern Arab world early in the twentieth century. None of those ideas was more important than the idea of nationalism, which was fundamental to all Middle Eastern political discussion until only fifteen years ago.

However, France had long since returned to North Africa. Only some three decades after Napoleon's Egyptian campaign, France occupied the Ottoman Empire's western province of Algeria. After 1830, France moved inexorably to round out its conquest in the Maghreb by adding Tunisia in 1881 and finally taking the independent kingdom of Morocco in 1911–12.

THE REVOLUTION IN ALGERIA

In Northwest Africa, the new age of liberty proclaimed by the French Revolution ran athwart the harshness of French colonial power. Disil-

> While Napoleon was in Egypt, French revolutionary ideas were also entering the Ottoman Empire through Constantinople.

lusionment was especially deep in Algeria, despite (or rather because of) its formal incorporation as a part of the *métropole*. The bitterness that ultimately led to Algeria's savage war of independence (1954–1962) was fostered by France's reluctance to apply its own Declaration of the Rights of Man to those who were neither French nor European. The disparity between what Muslims and Arabs understood the French Revolution to have promised, and how they observed France to act as imperial master, had a resonance that echoes still.

In Algeria, French rule began badly. In 1830, French troops in Algiers' Casbah contributed to what soon became the almost total destruction of indigenous institutions by lighting their pipes with official Algerian state papers. Sections of Algerian cities were demolished, roads were built through cemeteries, and, during the 1840s, at least two Algerian tribes were incinerated by French

soldiers after they took refuge in caves. During its first four decades in Algeria, France frequently employed a scorched-earth policy to subdue Algerian resistance. After 1870, and especially as the European settler population increased, France developed a two-tiered and unequal system of justice for *colons* on the one hand and *indigènes* on the other. During the 1930s and 1940s, such moderate Algerians as Ferhat Abbas called on France to be faithful to its own revolutionary heritage and grant Algerian petitions for reform. In the end all failed; France finally relinquished Algeria in 1962 after employing even more violence than it had once used to conquer that territory.

In Algeria and elsewhere in French North Africa, an important aspect of the new imperialism that Napoleon had inaugurated was France's self-proclaimed *mission civilisatrice*. Nationalism, imperialism, and a sure sense of cultural superiority subsisted together easily and led France to attempt to uplift and educate some of those it ruled, even while depriving them of their ancestral lands and shattering the integrity of tribal society. Even for that small elite of Algerian Muslims that received the best education metropolitan France could offer, few could hope to acquire French citizenship with full civil and political rights. To do so, Muslims were required to repudiate Islamic law, particularly as it related to marriage and the inheritance of property. Only a handful of Algerians ever rejected those traditions they had inherited as Muslims. One might indeed become an *évolué*, as the French described those it had educated most highly, but as a practicing Muslim one could still not be accepted as truly French in the new France that the Revolution had created.

One salient example of France's "civilizing" mission was the campaign of Monseigneur Lavigerie, named archbishop of Algiers in 1867, to uplift and re-Christianize North Africa. For Lavigerie, North Africa's Christian past constituted the prologue to a Christian future. The non-Arab, Berber third of Algeria's Muslim population should be reminded of its Christian roots, Lavigerie maintained, and this people might be used as a wedge to initiate a Christian reconquest of the Maghreb. To begin that reconquest he collected 1,753 Muslim orphans and began to educate them in a Christian ethos, hoping that they might ultimately be converted and constitute the nucleus of a native clergy. The archbishop rejected all appeals from the orphans' relatives to halt such proselytism. In Lavigerie's view, Christianity was indistinguishable from Western civilization, and it was the duty of France's army and bureaucracy, as well as the church, to propagate both. A royalist in religion as well as in politics, Lavigerie worked especially against the secular universalism that had made the French Revolution accessible to the world of Islam. The intense cultural chauvinism demonstrated by Lavigerie was understood by Muslims to be an integral part of French imperialism. Gradually, the stage was set, both in the Maghreb and elsewhere, for a counterattack in the name of Islamic authenticity.

Nevertheless, France today retains an important role throughout northwest Africa. France is one of Algeria's most important trading partners, Algerian government ministries continue to conduct much of their business in French, and French remains the language of instruction at Algerian universities in most technical and some social science and humanistic fields. On occasion, Algerians even express regret that almost all Europeans left shortly before independence. Some Algerian Muslims now believe that were they still present, the Europeans might help to reinvigorate Algeria's failing economy. Currently, eight hundred thousand Algerian Arabs and Berbers live in France, constituting one additional link between France and its former colony. Tunisia and Morocco, too, retain close ties with France, ties made stronger by the absence of any legacy of a bitter war for independence.

In Lebanon, France has a special interest, and has long played an important role in education and professional training. Saint-Joseph University, founded in 1875 and closely linked with the University of Lyons, has for generations molded an important section of the Lebanese (and

> The secular modernity that the French Revolution promised the Middle East is under siege by Islamic fundamentalism.

especially Maronite) governmental elite. French remains its primary language of instruction. Holy Spirit University in Kaslik, north of Beirut, boasts of its French and ultramontane Christian orientation. It has been associated with some of the more extreme elements of political Maronitism, and wages a *Kulturkampf* reminiscent of the one waged long since by Archbishop Lavigerie in North Africa. Like Saint-Joseph, Holy Spirit University teaches primarily in French and uses a French grading system. The Sagesse Law Institute also contributes to French influence in Lebanon, as do the high-school programs modeled on the French baccalaureate at such private secondary schools as the Collège Protestant and International College.

Presently, the secular modernity that the French Revolution once seemed to promise the Middle East and North Africa is under siege by Islamic fundamentalism. Indeed, the campaign currently being waged by Muslim fundamentalists in the name of Islamic authenticity should be understood as a repudiation of the French Revolution and all its works. This campaign is especially bitter in Lebanon, where the political separatism and cultural triumphalism of French-speaking Maronites has gravely weakened the transsectarian inclusiveness of traditional Arab nationalism. Today, Muslim fundamentalists regard the defection of Maronites from the Levantine body politic as an open wound inflicted by French culture on Arab society. Arabization and Islamization, long under way in North Africa and accelerating in Lebanon, are the Muslim world's response to what are perceived as the alienating blandishments of revolutionary France. Secular, leftist, and nationalistic military regimes are a principal target of Muslim wrath. Although Islam's counterattack will certainly not succeed in extirpating all of the French Revolution's legacy, Muslim disillusionment with the cultural syncretism of the past two hundred years will doubtless continue to refashion that legacy during the rest of this century and beyond.

The Industrial and Scientific Revolutions

The events that brought global supremacy to the West were the industrial and scientific revolutions. It can be argued that China was at the same technological level as Europe in 1500, but China did not remain competitive because of changes in the West. It is the development of industry and science in the eighteenth century, along with the early agricultural revolution of 10,000 years ago, that mark the two greatest transformations in human history. This unit explores the industrial and scientific change that gave Western civilization its unique advantage.

Industrialization started in England, where favorable economic, religious, and government policies prevailed, and because England possessed the resources, need, and opportunity for industrialization. The nation had used up its forests and turned to coal for fuel. As the miners dug deeper, drainage became necessary and the Newcomen engine, a device designed by Thomas Newcomen to pump water from mines, resulted. The engine gave the world portable energy, and people escaped the vagaries of wind power and streams.

Mechanization spread in the English textile industry through a series of complementary inventions that increased the output of weavers and spinners. Factories gradually replaced the small-scale, at-home, cottage weavers, which had a long-run benefit of an increased standard of living. In the short run, however, workers suffered, and in the early nineteenth century, destructive bands called Luddites roamed the English countryside destroying the hated machines. This lawlessness was suppressed by governmental force, but since that time whenever skilled workers have been replaced by machines, the whispered voice of "Ned Ludd" can be heard. From England the innovations in manufacturing spread to the mainland and later to the United States and Japan. In unit 4 the effects of this revolution upon Japanese women can be seen as an echo of what had happened earlier with workers elsewhere.

The Industrial Revolution was not a revolt in the sense of a quick, dramatic uprising like the French Revolution. It was slower than that with roots that go back into the Middle Ages. In a sense, the Industrial Revolution has never stopped and some historians argue that it continues with the use of robotics in manufacturing and computers to make decisions.

Parallel to the Industrial Revolution was the scientific revolution that provided a means of discovering the truth about natural phenomena. Science emerged from a shift of interest from religious to earthly affairs during the Renaissance and a loosening of the grip of the Roman Catholic Church during the Reformation.

Copernicus started the scientific revolution in astronomy by placing the sun at the center of the solar system and Earth as a planet in orbit. Galileo, who combined his technical skills at telescope construction with his scientific curiosity, discovered four new planets, the stars of the Milky Way, the mountains of the moon, and the moons of Jupiter. This gave credence to Copernican thought. Galileo was a transitional man with one foot in the medieval world and the other in the modern world. Georgius Agricola was another such individual whose curiosity about the world drove him in many directions. Although he remained a Roman Catholic in a Protestant land, he was respected as a community leader and an expert on mining and minerals.

Along with the political ideas of the French Revolution, science also traveled with the military exploits of Europeans, as Charles Gillispie demonstrates with his article about the scientific exploration of Egypt by part of Napoleon's army. Although they did not understand everything at the time, Napoleon's scientists and engineers carefully collected and recorded information that later proved useful in explaining the ancient civilization of Egypt. In this manner European scholarship, particularly archaeology and history, helped Egypt recapture its lost past.

The scientific revolution, like the Industrial Revolution, continues today. Perhaps the greatest story of modern science is the explanation of life itself, as noted by Stephen Hall in his commentary about James Watson, one of the discoverers of DNA. Computers represent a combination of science and technology, and John Von Neumann, a mathematical genius, indicated a correct pathway for the development of this practical tool that is part of continuing industrialization.

Space exploration would not be possible without the computers that help calculate trajectories and the responses necessary to escape the gravity of Earth. With such technology, scientific information has been gathered, part of the legacy of the Apollo missions that help explain our place in the solar system and the universe. Such knowledge can raise religious questions, as can the DNA experiments of James Watson. Still, the flights

HE THAT HATH A TRADE HATH AN ESTATE. AT THE WORKING MANS HOUSE HUNGER LOOKS IN, BUT DARES NOT ENTER.

INDUSTRY PAYS DEBTS, WHILE DESPAIR INCREASETH THEM.

of the Apollo missions represent a triumph for science and technology. Space flights demonstrate the power and unique abilities of Western civilization.

Looking Ahead: Challenge Questions

Compare the characteristics of cottage industry and the factory system. Why did the factory system of production win out over the cottage system?

What was the complaint of the Luddites? Why did they lose?

Why is science and industry seen as a unique characteristic of Western civilization? Is it really unique?

Discuss Georgius Agricola as a "Renaissance Man," a person who can do many things.

Compare Georgius Agricola, Martin Luther, and Adam Smith.

What are the characteristics of a "scientific" mind?

Debate the statement that the only good science is applied science (science that has a practical result).

Describe the Apollo missions and their accomplishments. Then, answer the question, "So what?"

Cottage Industry and the Factory System

Duncan Bythell

AT THE CENTRE OF MOST PEOPLE'S picture of Britain's industrial revolution in the nineteenth century stands the dark, satanic mill, where an exploited and dispirited army of men, women and children is engaged for starvation wages in a seemingly endless round of drudgery: the pace of their labour is determined by the persistent pulse of the steam engine and accompanied by the ceaseless clanking of machines; and the sole beneficiary of their efforts is the grasping, tyrannical, licentious factory master, pilloried by Charles Dickens in that loud-mouthed hypocrite and philistine, Mr. Bounderby. Crude and exaggerated though this image is, it depicts very clearly the main features of the pattern of production which became widespread in the manufacturing industries, not only of Britain, but also of the other advanced countries, by the end of the nineteenth century. For it highlights the emergence of the factory, where hundreds labour together under one roof and one direction, as the normal type of work-unit; it stresses the new importance of complex machine-technology in the process of production; and it emphasises that, because ownership of these machines, of the building which houses them and the engine which drives them, rests with the private capitalist, there exists an unbridgeable gulf between him and his property-less wage-earning employees.

This system of production, which is usually assumed to have been pioneered and rapidly adopted in Britain's textile industries around the end of the eighteenth century, did not, of course, emerge in a wholly non-industrial world. The popular picture suggests that it replaced – or rather, brutally displaced – an earlier type of organisation, variously referred to as 'the domestic system', the 'outwork system', or simply as 'cottage industry', which differed totally from the factory system. Whereas the latter concentrates workers under one roof in an increasingly urban enviroment, the former disperses employment into the homes of the workers, most of whom live in the countryside. Although the modern mill is filled with the factory master's costly machinery, the domestic workshop houses simple and traditional hand-tools – the spinner's wheel, the weaver's loom, the cordwainer's bench, the nail-maker's forge, and the seamstress' humble pins and needles – which actually belong to the worker. And whilst the factory system implies clear class division, with the wage-earner firmly subordinated to, and perpetually at odds with, his employer, the domestic system gives the head of the household an independent, quasi-managerial status, which enables him to control his own time and to direct, in a 'natural' fatherly way, the efforts of his family team.

The unspoken assumption is that, in the undisciplined, fulfilling, and relatively classless world of cottage industry, the common man was certainly happier, even if he was materially worse off, than his grandson. Only in the last desperate phase, when the dwindling band of domestic handworkers found themselves competing hopelessly against the new generation of factory machine-minders, is the idyllic image tarnished; and the haunting picture of the doomed handloom weaver, striving in his cellar to match the output of his wife and children who have been forced into the factory, reinforces the notion that, between old and new systems, there is nothing but contrast, conflict, and competition.

Any concept of historical change based on snapshots taken on separate occasions tends to emphasise differences and discontinuities. In the caricature of the domestic and factory systems just presented, they appear to be completely antithetical. Yet on closer examination, the story of most industries which 'modernised' in the course of the nineteenth century is full of important elements of *continuity* and *complementarity* between the factory and the pre-factory stages of their development; and it is on these two dimensions, rather than on the stark contrasts suggested by the traditional stereotype, that I want to focus attention.

Let us consider continuity first. A number of historians have recently suggested that the existence of the domestic system of production in such industries as textiles was one of the main features

Factory spinning

 From *History Today*, April 1983, pp. 17-23. © 1983 by History Today, Ltd., 20 Old Compton Street, London W1V 5PE. Reprinted by permission.

distinguishing the pre-industrial economies of Europe from the Third World countries of today; and although they prefer the abstract concept of 'proto industrialisation' to the well-established and perfectly adequate term 'domestic system', they are essentially claiming that the industrial revolutions of the nineteenth century could not have taken place without the prior development of a form of production which, in their view, was to provide both the capital and the labour needed for modern industrial development.

In making this claim, proponents of the theory of 'proto industry' are drawing attention to one of the most important, but often misunderstood, features of the classic domestic system – the fact that it already showed a clear distinction between the capitalists who controlled it and the wage-earners who depended upon it for their livelihood. For the domestic system, no less than the factory system which replaced it, was a method of mass-production which enabled wealthy merchant-manufacturers to supply not only textile fabrics, but also items as diverse as ready-made clothes, hosiery, boots and shoes, and hardware, to distant markets at home and abroad. In order to do so, they, like the factory masters who followed them, bought the appropriate raw materials and hired wage-labour to convert them into finished products. The pay roll of some of these merchant-manufacturers could run into many hundreds: in the late 1830s, for example, Dixons of Carlisle, cotton manufacturers, employed 3,500 handloom weavers scattered over the border counties of England and Scotland and in Ulster; a decade or so later, Wards of Belper, hosiers, provided work for some 4,000 knitting frames in the counties of Derbyshire, Nottinghamshire, and Leicestershire; and as late as the 1870s, Eliza Tinsley and Co. put out work to 2,000 domestic nail- and chain-makers in the west Midlands.

To service and co-ordinate such large and scattered forces required an elaborate system of communication and control in which the key figures were the agents – variously known as 'putters-out', 'bagmen', and 'foggers' – who were the equivalents of the modern supervisor or shop-floor manager. Certainly, the workers whom these great men employed generally owned their own tools, although in the case of an elaborate piece of machinery like the knitting frame they often had to hire it; and most of them worked on their own premises – although, again, it was by no means rare for the individual weaver, knitter, or nail-maker to rent space and tools in another man's shop. But except in a few minor rural trades like straw-plaiting and lace-making in the south and east Midlands, they neither provided their own raw materials, nor had they any interest in marketing the goods they helped to make. They were, in short, wage-earners who happened to own some of the tools of their trade. But the trade in which they worked was organised by capitalists; and far from making goods to sell to local customers, they were often, all unknowing, supplying the wants of West Indian slaves and North American frontiersmen.

The crux of the argument about continuity between domestic and factory systems of mass-production turns on whether it was actually the case that the firms which set up the first modern factories in a particular industry were already active in it on a putting-out basis, and whether the last generation of domestic workers transformed themselves into the new race of factory hands. Of course, no one is maintaining that continuity was direct and complete in every single industry or region where such a transition occurred: indeed, there were areas such as East Anglia or the Cotswolds where the change-over simply did not take place, and where a once important industry gradually vanished as the old domestic system dwindled and died. But where 'modernisation' did happen in traditional outwork industries in the course of the nineteenth century, as it did in the textile industries of Lancashire and Yorkshire and in the hosiery trade of the east Midlands, historians seem to be agreed that it was existing firms which played a leading role, albeit cautiously and belatedly in some instances, in setting-up the factory system and in embodying some of their capital in buildings and machines; in other words the fortunes made, and the expertise in marketing and managing acquired, in the old system of production were important in enabling the new system to develop.

There is less agreement, however, as to how far the existing hand-workers in any particular industry really did shift over to the factory. The theory of 'proto industry' suggests that the domestic system had created a country-dwelling but landless proletariat in many ways at odds with the traditional rural society around them: they had only a minimal involvement in the agrarian economy, and were therefore rootless and prone to migration; they possessed manual skills irrelevant to farming activities; and as wage-earners, they were obliged to respond to the pressures and the opportunities of a market economy in which the price of survival was adaptability. In terms of both work-skills and mental outlook, that is to say, they were already well-equipped to form the first generation of the modern industrial labour force.

But did this actually happen? The traditional picture suggests not, because it depicts a stubborn refusal to come to terms with changed circumstances and, indeed, a downright hostility to 'machinery' which, in the Luddite movement of 1811-16 in the Midlands and the various outbreaks of loom-smashing in Lancashire and elsewhere, sometimes erupted in violence. Clearly, the worker's readiness to change with the times depended partly on age, and partly on opportunity. Case studies based on census returns for Lancashire weaving villages during the crucial phase of transition in the middle of the nineteenth century suggest that, once a powerloom shed had been started locally, the younger married men were ready enough to take work in it, but that the elderly were either reluctant to do so, or were debarred by the employer, and therefore stuck to the handloom. But until there was a mill virtually on the spot, most of these villagers believed they had little option but to stick to the handloom, and for want of other opportunity they continued to bring their children up to it. Probably the most important strand of continuity in the labour force was in fact provided by the children of the last generation of hand-workers: by and large, a trade dies out because it stopped recruiting sometime before; and the demise of occupations like handloom weaving was finally assured when families were willing and able to put their offspring into something different, instead of forcing them to follow automatically in father's footsteps.

By highlighting the division between capital and labour which characterised the domestic no less than the factory system of production, and by considering the continuity which this engendered, the new theory of 'proto industry' has pinpointed certain popular misconceptions about the nature of cottage industry. First of all, it must be clear that when economic historians refer to 'outwork' or 'cottage industry' they are *not* talking about a world where each family simply makes manufactured goods for its own use – although in even the most advanced societies elements of the home-made and the do-it-yourself survive. Nor are they discussing the self-employed craftsman or genuine artisan – the village shoe-maker and tailor, or the more sophisticated urban wig-maker or cabinet-maker – who produced and sold 'one-off' goods directly to the order of their local customers, and whose successors are still to be found in some parts of the modern economy. Indeed – and this is a second error which needs to be corrected – in the strict sense they are not dealing with 'skill' or 'craft' at all. As a method of mass-production, the greater part of cottage industry involved the

The weaver at his domestic hand loom (above) contrasts sharply with work on a factory power loom (below).

making of plain, simple, inexpensive goods by hands which, although they became more nimble and adept with experience, had neither needed nor received much initial training. Weaving heavy woollens and hammering nails and chains required a certain strength; but weaving plain calico, knitting coarse stockings, sewing buttons on shirts, plaiting straw, and sticking matchboxes together with glue called for neither brain nor brawn. A seven-year apprenticeship to learn the 'mysteries' of most domestic industries was unnecessary, when the work merely involved the monotonous repetition of a few simple

movements of the fingers; and because the work was unskilled and undemanding it was considered particularly suitable for women and children. Domestic industry, like factory industry, involved the worker in much mindless drudgery; the chief difference was that, in working at home with hand-tools, the wage-earner could go at his or her own pace, instead of having to keep up with the steam engine.

Thirdly, just as we need to abandon the notion that the domestic system was all about skilled craftsmen, so we must reject the idea that it was predominantly about 'men' at all. One of the advantages

which the old terms 'domestic system' and 'cottage industry' have over 'proto industry' is that they suggest an important feature which old-style mass-production shared with the early textile mills: a domestic or cottage workshop called on the efforts of housewife, grandparents, and children of both sexes, as well as those of the household's head. Thus the average weaving or knitting family would run two or three looms or frames, and in addition would operate any ancillary machinery needed to prepare or finish the work. Because it worked as a team, the domestic work unit could also practice division of labour, so that each member could specialise on just one stage in the sequence of production. Like any other family business, a workshop involved in the domestic system was a collective enterprise to which all contributed who could: and only when the household included no children old enough to do even the simplest tasks did it depend for its income on what a man could earn by his own unaided efforts. Because the capitalist-controlled outwork industries made particular use of women's and children's labour in this way, female workers were generally in a clear majority in the work force; and in the mass-production section of the needlework trades, where outwork remained particularly important until late in the nineteenth century, and which included men's tailoring and shirt-making as well as dress-making and lace stitching, the preponderance of women was especially striking.

Fourthly, we must not imagine that, in a capitalist controlled industrial system such as outwork was, relations between masters and operatives were marked by much sweetness and light. Since the main tie between them was the cash nexus, disputes about wages could be frequent and bitter. Most employers in the industries which used the domestic system operated in a tough competitive environment, and their likely reaction to a spell of bad trading conditions would be to cut the piece-rates they paid their workers. Most of the scattered rural outworkers were disorganised and docile, and could offer little, if any, resistance; and in any case, for women and children a pittance was deemed better than no work at all. But the adult men – especially those who lived in the towns, and did the better-class work which needed more strength or skill – were another matter. They had a clear conception of the work and wages proper for a man, and they were better able to take collective action against underpaying masters and weak-willed blacklegs who broke the conventional rules.

As a result, at different times in the late eighteenth and early nineteenth centuries, fierce strikes broke out in such towns as Manchester, Coventry, Barnsley and Norwich, major centres of handloom weaving; among the urban framework knitters of Nottingham and Leicester; and among the nail-makers of the Black Country. At a time when formal trade unionism was a shadowy affair, and in difficult political and economic circumstances, some at least of Britain's industrial outworkers played their part in sustaining patterns of collective bargaining which, *faute de mieux*, sometimes involved great violence; whilst the support these disgruntled men gave to the various campaigns for parliamentary reform between the 1790s and the 1850s has been frequently noted by historians.

Once we have abandoned such misconceptions about the nature of the domestic system as it had come to exist by the end of the eighteenth century, it is easier to see the similarities and the points of continuity between it and the factory system which was eventually and gradually to supersede it. And when we realise that the domestic system, far from being some prehistoric monster which expired when the first cotton factory was built, actually expanded and persisted in many industries and regions until well into the second half of the nineteenth century, we become aware, not only that the two types of mass-production overlapped in time, but also that they complemented each other,

(Above left) The Domestic Rope Maker; from *The Book of Trades*, 1804. (Above right) Making ropes by Huddart's Machinery.
(Below left) An outworker making pins at home: (below right) a needle pointer at work in a factory in Redditch, Worcester.

rather than competed. The textile industries usually occupy the forefront of any discussion of the domestic and factory systems; and in view of their wide geographic dispersal, their rapid expansion, and the hundreds of thousands they had come to employ by the late eighteenth century, this is entirely appropriate. But because, starting with the spinning branch of the British cotton industry in the 1770s, it was in these industries that the complete triumph of the factory system was achieved earliest, attention has been deflected from the many other trades – particularly shoe-making, clothing, and some branches of hardware – where the domestic system actually became more, rather than less, important. For although the first half of the nineteenth century saw the disappearance into the factory first of spinning and then of weaving in Lancashire and Yorkshire, it also witnessed the expansion of mass-production by outwork methods in the ready-made clothing trades and in the boot and shoe industries. And apart from the fact that these growing industries increased output by traditional rather than modern methods, there were other, less expansionary trades – such as Midlands hosiery and Black Country nail-making – which remained fossilised at the 'domestic' stage of development until well after 1850. In addition, the latter part of the nineteenth century actually saw a number of new, small-scale manufactures, such as paperbag and cardboard-box making, establish themselves as cottage industries. Thus, if outwork had more or less disappeared from the staple textile industries by the 1850s, it was more firmly entrenched than ever in and around many of the industrial towns of the Midlands and the south of England, and, above all, in what were to become known as the 'sweated trades' of London. Why was this?

The pioneering experience of the textile industries suggests some of the answers. Contrary to popular belief, even in the cotton industry, the transition from the domestic to the factory system was a slow, piecemeal affair, which took three generations; and in wool, linen and silk, the process was even more protracted. The reason was simple: the first power-driven machines of the 1770s revolutionised *spinning* only; and by making it possible to produce thread on a scale and at a price which would have been inconceivable in the days of the spinning wheel, they simply created a good deal more work for a great many more workers – in this case, the weavers – at the next stage in the production process. And so long as enough extra weavers could be found at wages the employers were prepared to pay, there was no need to think of replacing the handloom with some labour-saving device, as yet uninvented. Thus between 1780 and 1820, the growth of spinning factories marched *pari passu* with a vast increase in the number of handloom weavers' shops; and technical progress in one section of the industry merely led to the multiplication of traditional handwork in associated sections.

The Croppers of the West Riding of Yorkshire were much involved in the machine-wrecking Luddite movement of 1812.

The same thing was to happen in other industries later: when lace-making was mechanised in Nottingham from the 1820s, there was a consequent increase in the amount of stitching, finishing and mending for hand-sewers in their homes; when machines were first used to cut out the components of a stock-sized shoe or coat, they made more unskilled assembly work for domestic workers; and even when the sewing machine had transformed the traditional needlework trades, it did not necessarily drive them out of the home into the factory, because, as a compact, hand-powered, and relatively inexpensive tool, it could be used in a domestic workshop as effectively as in a large factory. In all these ways, factory and domestic systems often co-existed and complemented each other in a given industry. Since it was rarely either possible or necessary for new techniques to be introduced simultaneously at every stage in the process of manufacture, flexible combinations of centralised factory work at one stage, and cottage industry at the next, were perfectly practicable.

There was often a regional dimension to the co-existence of these two types of mass-production, and it was here that elements of competition emerged between them. In the classic case of cotton weaving, for example, the handloom survived as the dominant machine in some parts of Lancashire for almost a generation after it had largely given way to the powerloom in others: in large towns such as Stockport, Oldham and Blackburn, factory production was taken up in the 1820s by manufacturers who already operated spinning mills; but it made little progress in the small towns and villages of north-east Lancashire, such as Padiham, Colne and Haggate before the 1840s. In part, this reflected local differences in the availability of labour and capital, for the more remote rural areas were richer in the former than in the latter. But independent of such regional differences, there was also a qualitative side to this 'staggered' adoption of the powerloom, because the early, clumsy factory looms could cope better with the plain types of cloth than with fancy or patterned goods. Other industries were later to show similar disparities in the rate at which different districts and sections adopted new techniques: for example, the boot and shoe industry of Leicester

Merchants in the Cloth Hall, Leeds in 1814. Merchants used cottage industries as a method of mass-production to supply their buyers.

seems to have relied more on factory production and less on outwork than did that of Northampton in the second half of the nineteenth century; whilst in the 1890s, cottage industry was more apparent in the ready-made clothing trade of London than in that of Leeds.

In short, the domestic system of mass-production in British industry took a long time a-dying during the nineteenth century. It might expand in one trade at the very time that it was contracting in another; in some industries, it could enjoy a harmonious co-existence with factory production for many years, whilst elsewhere it might struggle on in arduous competition for a generation or more. Why was this? How could this technically primitive form of large-scale production remain viable for so long in important parts of the world's first industrial economy?

To find the answer, we must try to fathom the minds of the entrepreneurs in the different industries, as they calculated how best, in a complex and competitive world, to get their goods to market with least cost and least trouble to themselves. A manufacturer who had grown up with the domestic system as the dominant mode of production in his trade would need strong inducements to abandon it, because under normal circumstances it offered him many advantages. If his employees provided their own tools and workrooms, he himself was spared the need to tie up his own capital in bricks and mortar and in machinery; and in times of periodic trade depression or slack seasonal demand – and most of these industries were subject to one or other of these risks, if not, indeed, to both of them – it was the worker, not his employer, who suffered when plant and equipment were standing idle. It was not that these great merchant-manufacturers lacked capital – indeed it required remarkably little fixed capital in most of these industries to build or rent a small factory and fill it with new or second-hand machinery; nor was it generally the case that appropriate new techniques were not available – the time-lag between invention and adoption of a new machine is a recurrent feature in many of these trades; it was rather the case that their capital under the domestic system was embodied in unused raw materials, goods 'in the make', and stocks in the warehouse.

Nevertheless, because it involved more sophisticated machinery, the application of power, and the construction of large, purpose-built work premises, the factory system of production was capital-intensive, rather than labour-intensive. By contrast, what an employer had to rely on to keep cottage industry viable was an abundance of cheap, unskilled, and unorganised labour. So long as he could find enough workers who had no choice but to take his work at the wages he was prepared to offer – no matter how low these might be – he could meet his production targets and reap his expected profits. From the late eighteenth to the late nineteenth centuries, there were many regions of Britain which could provide just such supplies of labour: a high and sustained rate of population increase, together with the greater commercialisation of agriculture, tended to create pools of unemployed or under-employed workers in many rural areas; and in so far as these impoverished country people moved off to the towns in search of more work and better wages, they often merely added to the chaos and confusion in the unskilled urban labour markets.

But what kept the domestic system alive after the mid-nineteenth century more than anything else was the continued availability – long after most adult men had deserted these low paid, dead-end jobs – of female and child labour: incapable of collective self-defence, and often deliberately ignored by their better organised menfolk; accustomed to regarding any earnings, however minute, as a worthwhile contribution to family income; and often only able to work on a part-time or casual basis – they were ideal for many employers' purposes. And in a perverse way, because it thrived on family labour, the domestic system actually helped to perpetuate its own labour force: because cottage industry, by enabling the whole household to earn, acted as a great inducement to early marriages and large families, and thus contributed to the 'population explosion' which was so important a feature of Britain's industrial revolution.

Because labour could be much cheaper in one part of the country than in another, an old-fashioned employer who stuck to outwork could still hope to compete with his more ambitious and enterprising fellows elsewhere who had switched over to factory production. Only in the last quarter of the nineteenth century did a combination of new circumstances – including rural depopulation, compulsory schooling (which both kept young children out of the labour market and widened their horizons), rising real incomes (which made small supplementary earnings less essential to a family), and more 'chivalrous' male

Gathering Teasels in the West Riding of Yorkshire, an aquatint after George Walker. Teasels are still used to raise the nap on woollen cloth.

(Below) *The Preemer Boy,* 1814; aquatint after George Walker. 'Preeming' is detaching, with an iron comb, the bits of wool on the teasel.

only stay in business if they themselves adopted American methods of production. Both the cotton manufacturers of the 1820s and the boot and shoe manufacturers of the 1890s had to overcome strong opposition from workers still suspicious of machinery and still attached (in spite of the precarious economic position in which it left them) to the domestic system: but once the entrepreneurs in any industry had concluded, for whatever reasons, that the disadvantages of cottage industry outweighed the benefits, its days were numbered.

From the worker's point of view, even if we forget the caricature, the dark satanic mill offered an uninviting prospect; but it is hard to escape the conclusion that the domestic system was in many ways even less agreeable. Even where cottage workers were not directly competing with factory workers – and I have suggested that it would be wrong to put too much emphasis on this side of the story - most of them were poorly paid, and likely to be alternately overworked and under-employed. Worst of all, they were subject to all kinds of abuses, not only from employers and their agents, but often from heads of households and fathers of families who connived, however reluctantly, in the exploitation of their own wives and children. Men may have been unwilling to accept the separation of home and workplace which the gradual replacement of the domestic system by the factory system involved: but in its long-term implications for family life, it was probably one of the most beneficial, as well as one of the most fundamental, of all the changes brought about by the industrial revolution.

attitudes towards women as workers – help gradually to eliminate some of the sources of cheap labour and thus undermine one of the domestic system's chief props.

Changes in market conditions, as well as the increasing difficulty of finding suitable labour, could also be instrumental in persuading entrepreneurs to abandon old-style mass-production in favour of the factory. When, for example, attractive new export markets opened up for the English cotton industry in Latin America in the early 1820s, Lancashire manufacturers knew that they would be better able to increase output by introducing powerlooms than by seeking out more handloom weavers at higher wages; and when, more than two generations later, British boot and shoe manufacturers were faced with an 'invasion' of their own home market by cheap mass-produced, factory-made American imports, they recognised that they could

FOR FURTHER READING:
D. Bythell, *The Sweated Trades* (Batsford, 1978); J. L. and B. Hammond, *The Skilled Labourer* (London, 1919); G. Stedman Jones, *Outcast London* (Oxford University Press, 1971); P. Kriedte, H. Medick and J. Schlumbohm, *Industrialization before Industrialization* (Cambridge University Press, 1981); D. Levine, *Family Formation in an Age of Nascent Capitalism* (Academic Press, 1977); J. M. Prest, *The Industrial Revolution in Coventry* (Oxford University Press, 1960); E. P. Thompson, *The Making of the English Working Class* (Gollancz, 1963; Penguin Books).

For a while, the Luddites had a smashing success

In 1811, desperate English weavers made a name for themselves by trying to destroy machines that destroyed their livelihood

Bruce Watson

Neo-Luddite Bruce Watson regards technology with awe and suspicion.

On a cold April night in England's Midlands, a band of defiant and determined men took up arms against the most relentless foe in history. Their enemy held no territory. It had no weapons or soldiers. It had no battle plans. But if these troops gave the slightest ground, the invader would sweep over them, stealing their food, their children, their livelihood.

All day, word spread throughout the rolling, green valleys between Leeds and Manchester. Whispers passed through mills and pubs, among anxious folks on muddy streets, down quaint country lanes that gave no hint of the desperation behind closed doors. With a wink of an eye, strangers recognized another secret soldier. With a hush, they gave the word: the General requires our services. Meet at the Dumb Steeple near on midnight. Bring a weapon. Here's a musket ball, a pint of gunpowder. If you know a lad you can trust, bring him to the St. Crispin Inn and old John Baines'll see he's "twisted-in." Cartwright's mill is armed to the teeth, rumor has it. There'll be trouble, all right. But by the soul of Ned Ludd, this enemy must be stopped.

Approaching midnight, more than 200 men gather in an open field. Some wear masks. Others blacken their faces. Disguised in coats turned inside out, checkered shirts and smocks, they pass a bottle of rum around to bolster their spirits. On command they line up. The musketmen, ten abreast, go first. Then the pistoleers. Hammer and hatchet men fill the third ranks, while a gang armed with pikes, hedge stakes, bludgeons and bare arms brings up the rear. Silently moving down into the sleeping valley, they march toward a battle that, in some sense, has never ended from that day to this. The year is 1812. Their target: technology.

In the late 20th century, an uneasy truce prevails between man and machine. Modern workers riffling through arcane instruction manuals and cursing at last-minute breakdowns, may well dream of smashing a computer to bits—or bytes. Yet somehow, coaxing hardware and software, we get the job done. But the men who marched through the Spen Valley that night in 1812 stood eyeball-to-eyeball with technology, and they did not blink. Machines offered them no Faustian bargain, only repetitive labor at best, at worst unemployment, hunger and ruin for their families. These first soldiers in the struggle against machines have been nearly forgotten in our headlong rush toward a high-tech future. They are remembered in name only—the Luddites. According to *Webster's*: "**Luddite** *n* 1: A member of any various bands of workers in England (1811–16) who destroyed industrial machinery in the belief that its use diminished employment 2: Any opponent of new technologies or technological change."

The word, now bandied about the office among enemies of the microprocessor and its offspring, was once a call to arms. Between 1811 and 1816, to be a Luddite in England's textile district was to stand for humanity, craftsmanship, and a way of life as endangered by the Industrial Revolution as any dinosaur by ice age or meteor. A Luddite was a brother, a father, a son and a secret. A Luddite was a cropper, a weaver, a hero and a soldier loyal to General Ludd. Eventually, up against the largest force of British troops ever before assembled to put down local rebellion, the Luddites steadily waged an uncompromising guerrilla war.

"We will never lay down Arms [till] The House of Commons passes an Act to put down all Machinery hurtful to Commonality,

and repeal that to hang Frame Breakers. . . . We petition no more—that won't do—fighting must." To the mill owner who received this threat signed "General of the Army of Redressers, Ned Ludd, Clerk," the army needed no introduction. By the end of 1811, Luddite bands were smashing machines throughout England's Midlands. But who was this Ned Ludd? According to legend, the lad who gave his name to a movement was never a Luddite himself. Ned Ludd (or Lud or Ludlam) was a mere apprentice knitter in England's wool district during the 1770s. Ordered by his father to get on with his work, Ludd rose up in a fury, took a hammer and smashed his knitting frame into a heap of broken parts. Adolescent temper had fired a shot heard round the textile district, a shot that would be remembered when the machines came to the Midlands.

In the early 19th century the world's most advanced technology was the steam engine, which had already propelled Fulton's steamboat in America and set power looms to weaving in England's new cotton mills. It was a time when, with no help from the machine, human genius and megalomania had put their stamp on the world. Beethoven, Goethe, Wordsworth, Austen, Goya and Napoleon were at work.

England's moors seemed quiet, but in 1811 word came to London that workers in the Midlands were up to some mischief. The first decade of the 19th century was hard on the land. Bad harvests cut grain supplies and tripled prices. The British were on the verge of war with Napoleon and America. Parliament cut off trade with both, leaving nearly half the wool industry unemployed. But the handwriting that spelled doom for skilled textile workers was written on the largest wall anyone had seen in the Midlands, the factory wall.

Angry workers had invaded shops, taken the jack-wires from knitting machines, broken a few others. In March a crowd of men trooped from Nottingham to nearby villages. They were armed with swords, pistols, hatchets and blacksmith's hammers. Though they looked like a mob, their actions were anything but chaotic. Entering small shops, a few smashed stocking frames to bits while others stood guard at the door. They harmed no one, just the frames that made cheaper stockings with less-skilled labor.

Similar attacks followed. Rumor said the men called themselves "Ludds," "Ludders" or "Luddites," and legends spread about the heroes who dared to say no to the machines that stole their jobs. In pubs and homes, magistrates' questions met silence. Ned Ludd? Never heard of such a lad. *General* Ludd? You must be daft, guv'ner. By April 1811, more than 200 frames lay broken across Nottinghamshire. When a local militia and yeoman cavalry assembled in the region, the secret army lay low for the summer.

These days there are neo-Luddites among us. They complain that words should not be "processed," want phones answered by warm-blooded receptionists and insist that no matter how small a computer becomes, there's nothing "personal" about it. Neo-Luddites like to think the original machine-haters shared their techno-nightmares. But England's Luddites expressed their philosophy in threats alone, and their motives were simple. They were hungry. They were unemployed. Although a comet hung over the green hills of England's woolen district in September 1811, they did not have to look into the sky for omens. Their craft was unraveling like a poorly woven cloth.

"I have five children and a wife, the children all under 8 years of age," one poor weaver told a local magistrate. "I get 9d. clear (per week). . . . I work sixteen hours a day to get that. . . . It will take 2d. per week coals, 1d. per week candles. My family live on potatoes chiefly and we have one pint of milk per day."

Before 1750, England's textile district had been a craftsman's paradise where wool was king, weavers princes and machines unwelcome. There were pre-Luddites, among them true royalty. As early as 1552 Edward VI banned a simple gig mill, which sheared wool; later, his sister, Elizabeth I, all but outlawed production of a stocking loom. "I have too much love for my poor people who obtain their bread by the employment of knitting," the queen said, "to give my money to forward an invention that will tend to their ruin." In 1675, weavers destroyed looms that could weave as much as 20 men. In 1768 sawyers tried to demolish a mechanical sawmill.

It was a question of craftsmanship. Wool shorn from sheep in yonder fields and flax grown locally were spun at home by women, the wool woven on hand looms in small mills or workshops, stretched on frames, "teasled" with wire brushes to ruffle the texture, and finally sheared by hefty men called croppers. In the West Riding district of Yorkshire alone, there were more than 3,000 croppers proudly bearing the marks of their trade, huge forearms from wielding the 50-pound shears, and crescent-shaped calluses on their right wrists where the shear handles repeatedly scraped the skin.

But while America and France fought bloody political revolutions, England was in the progressive throes of the Industrial Revolution. In only 40 years, beginning around 1740, English inventors created the spinning jenny, the boring mill and a screw-cutting lathe. Crucible steel became commercially viable, the first iron rails were cast, and James Watt's steam engine was fired up for the first time. When those cunning catalysts Progress and Profit teamed up, no king, queen or law could stop them.

By the 1790s, factory bells rang through the textile district, tolling for cottage industries. Never mind that construction of the first cotton mills drew menacing, angry crowds. It was a question of simple arithmetic and sheer efficiency. By hand, it took one man 88 hours to finish the same amount of cloth that a machine could shear in 18. Other machines—wider looms, broader frames to make stockings out of pieces instead of whole cloth—used steam power and unskilled labor to spin wool into money.

By the early 1800s manufacturers were ignoring the law and mechanizing the wool trade. Outraged by the shoddy machine work that threatened their centuries-old craft, between 1803 and 1806 workers raised the astonishing amount of £10,000 to lobby for enforcement of antimachine laws. To no avail. In 1809 Parliament repealed all laws regulating the wool industry—including those prohibiting the use of machines. Defenseless against steam-driven progress, men remembered Ned Ludd and prepared to fight. No one could say the mill owners were not warned: "Wee Hear in Formed that you got Shear in me sheens and if you Dont Pull them Down in a Forght Nights Time Wee will pull them Down for you Wee will you Damd infernold Dog."

After that the Luddites rose in full force. In early November 1811, a workers' army led by a man calling himself "Ned Lud" marched to a workshop in Bulwell. Axes and hammers smashed the door. Shots came from the windows. Luddites fired back. A wave of attackers retreated into the darkness, regrouped, charged and entered. A few jumped the owner and stood over him while others moved through the workshop smashing frames. The job done, they gathered outside and took roll. One man was missing. The war against technology had its first casualty, John Westley, a Luddite killed by gunfire.

Vowing vengeance, the army scattered into the night. New Luddites were recruited, swearing themselves to silence and learning a tangled set of signals for spotting other followers of General (or sometimes King) Ludd. In a crowd, a Luddite raised his right hand over his right eye. If another Luddite was present, he raised his left hand over his left eye. Following other hand gestures, coded questions were exchanged. Soon, Luddite regiments carrying sticks and guns were marching in fields while a rich lore of songs and poems spread throughout the Midlands, traveling by word of mouth. People sang of "the Atchievements of General Ludd" and compared him to Robin Hood.

All that winter Luddites were a secret by day and a scourge by night. Each morning, mill owners tallied the damage: "Seven frames broken at Holbrook, eighteen at Pentrich." Requests for protection brought only a few dozen troops. The British Government, preoccupied with arming Wellington against Napoleon's forces in Spain and Portugal, dismissed the machine breakers as idle mobs, and the Luddites hammered technology with an ease that today's machine haters can only envy: "Nine frames broken at Basford, two at Bulwell." Then in January 1812, with attacks occurring every night, 3,000 troops marched north into the Midlands. With soldiers advancing, the poor rioting in the streets for bread, and armies of the night bludgeoning machines, the whole region had the "appearance of a state of war," as the London *Times* declared.

In February, Parliament debated making frame breaking punishable by death. A vast majority approved, but rising to the defense of the Luddites was a rather good-looking young chap making his first speech in the House of Lords. Having visited the Midlands, Lord Byron had seen the hunger. "However we may rejoice in any improvement in the arts which may be beneficial to mankind," he wrote a fellow peer, "we must not allow mankind to be sacrificed to improvements in Mechanism." Some have said that Byron was just a rebel in search of a cause, but in defense of the Luddites he was both eloquent and romantic.

"All the cities you have taken," he declared, "all the armies that have retreated before your leaders, are but paltry subjects of self-congratulation if your land divides against itself, and your dragoons and executioners must be let loose against your fellow citizens." Byron proposed that frame breaking be punished by mere imprisonment, but his amendment was summarily rejected by the House of Commons. Only a week later, he published *Childe Harold's Pilgrimage*, a narrative full of wit and adventure that became one of the best-sellers of the age. The poet was soon lost in his celebrity, and frame breaking became a capital offense. Actually catching a frame breaker was another matter. Soldiers learned what local constables knew—that any Luddite was a prophet with great honor in his own county. No matter how many people had seen Luddites marching, heard whispers or had one in the family, their whereabouts and strategy were kept close to the heart. Meanwhile the threats and violence escalated.

By April 1812 every small town had its own band of Luddites, and the machine breakers were ready to attack their most hated foes. In the Colne Valley, mill owner William Horsfall had boasted that he would ride "up to his saddle girths in Luddite blood." At nearby Rawfolds Mill, William Cartwright, defying all threats, had relentlessly mechanized and fortified the place. Its iron-studded front door hid stairs laced with 16-inch metal spikes, a large vat of sulfuric acid to pour onto attackers, and armed guards sleeping inside. A bell on the roof was ready to call troopers from nearby barracks. More fortress than mill, Rawfolds was ready.

In a room above a pub, according to local lore, croppers and weavers, some as young as 16, met to decide on their target. Ultimately, they spun a shilling. Heads, Cartwright; tails, Horsfall. It came up heads.

The night of April 11 was especially cold. In a field near the Dumb Steeple, less than a mile from Robin Hood's grave, more than 300 Luddites gathered. Marching north along the packhorse tracks on Hartshead Moor, then past the home of Patrick Brontë,

whose daughter Charlotte would later describe the Rawfolds attack in her novel *Shirley*, they went quietly so as not to arouse the sleeping regiments quartered nearby. Other Luddites from nearby Leeds failed to show at their appointed meeting place, but the army, too eager to turn back, pressed on until it came to the mill on the Spen River. Two men jumped the guards outside and gagged them. "Hatchet men, advance!" came the order. In regimental formation, men approached the mill. Inside, a barking dog awoke Cartwright. When he opened the door of his makeshift bedroom, musket fire shattered the ground-floor windows, and sledgehammers hit the door.

Cartwright frantically passed out muskets. In their nightshirts, his men began firing down on the attackers, all except one who refused to shoot lest he hit his brother. On the roof, the bell pealed. Within minutes, the attackers broke all but 9 of the mill's 300 windows. But the front door wouldn't budge and the repeated clanging of the bell promised that regiments of the king's soldiers would be arriving any second. Luddite leaders struggled to keep their company together. Sledgehammers pounded the door and smashed holes in it but couldn't get it open. After 20 minutes General Ludd's troops fell back. Some helped the wounded back to safety. Others just bolted. Rawfolds had held.

When the toll was taken inside, only Cartwright had been wounded. But outside, two Luddites lay dying, and no one knew how many others were hit. Following the battle, food riots and machine breaking spread across the whole region. "Vengeance for the blood of the innocent" was scrawled on cottage doors. In marketplaces and town squares, outnumbered magistrates read the Riot Act and filled the jails. British officials hired spies to infiltrate Luddite meetings. Paid for their stories, informers fed the government's worst fears with wild exaggeration: 10,000 Luddite supporters and 30,000 guns ready for shipment from Ireland; huge caches of weapons.

Anonymous letters to the Home Secretary predicted a nationwide Luddite uprising. Behind this specter of mass revolt was a single general. Or was he?

His name crossed valleys and hills. It was posted on public notices, whispered in back rooms. A few threats were signed by Lady Ludd, Eliza Ludd or King Ludd, but most bore the imprimatur of the general himself. Street urchins taunted passing soldiers, shouting "I'm General Ludd!" Magistrates questioned informers, but no matter where they looked, they could not find the leader of the Luddites.

Throughout the insurgency, General Ludd's poems and songs made it clear that machines, not men, were his target: "The guilty may fear but no vengeance he aims / At the honest man's life or Estate, / His wrath is entirely confined to wide frames / And to those that old prices abate." But with the machines so well defended, Luddites began to wage their war by other means. Night raiders stole weapons for future battles. A factory and the owner's house were torched. Just after Rawfolds, William Horsfall rode up to his saddle girths not in Luddite blood but in his own, shot to death by Luddites.

On May 9, 1812, a paper was posted in Nottingham, calling for the death of Spencer Perceval, the British Prime Minister. Two days later, Perceval was assassinated by a lone gunman while entering the lobby of the House of Commons. Cheers, bonfires and celebrations swept the Midlands. Though the assassin turned out to be a deranged avenger with no ties to the Luddites, the lack of a conspiracy did not calm British officials, who had seen enough of insurrection in France and their former colonies in North America. Was a revolution brewing in the Midlands?

An unwritten law of human nature says that change, to be accepted, must come incrementally. Creeping mechanization—a better mousetrap here, a more efficient whirligig there—disturbs only the true technophobes. The rest of us just buy the machines we think we'll need, learn the basics

and try not to lose the warranties. But whenever a barrage of machines swiftly shoves a society from agriculture toward industry or from industry toward information, the forces of opposition rally.

In the late 20th century a sea of troubling technology sweeps through the workplaces and marketplaces. All at once, it seems, everything that used to have a dial becomes digital, and everything once done face-to-face is "interfaced." Fax machines, computers, laser printers, voice mail, E-mail, cordless phones, cellular phones, camcorders, CD players, and extended families of compact, portable and personal devices raise questions about the uses of technology and make doubters out of dutiful workers.

Political theorist Langdon Winner writes: "Rapidly evolving technologies would seem to provide us an occasion to pause and take stock, to ask . . . which factors ought to guide our choices about technology?" Writer Wendell Berry raises a dilemma implicit in the Luddite uprising: "Is the obsolescence of human beings now our social goal? One would conclude so from our attitude toward work, especially the manual work necessary to the long-term preservation of the land, and from our rush toward mechanization, automation, and computerization."

Reviving the old tradition, neo-Luddites arise. Only a few, however, seek open confrontation, most notably members of the environmental group Earth First!, who disable bulldozers and logging equipment (SMITHSONIAN, April 1990). It is perhaps just as well. Before taking up arms, any aspiring neo-Luddite should consider the fate of his or her eponymous ancestors.

For in the summer of 1812, General Ludd met his match, another British general, one Thomas Maitland. Before taking command of British troops in the Midlands, Maitland had put down uprisings in India and the West Indies. Having also helped French royalists battle a bunch of rowdy Parisian citizens in 1789, the stern Scot knew revolution when he saw it.

This was no revolution, he concluded. This was starvation.

Moving into the embattled region, Maitland's army entered a world as distant from London as a common weaver's life was from an aristocrat's. In the Manchester markets, a penny that bought three pounds of potatoes the year before now bought only one. Among those sentenced to hang was an old woman who had stolen potatoes, then jumped on a butter cart and sold its contents to a hungry crowd. Into this situation marched 7,000 men, 1,400 of them mounted, joining the 5,800 already there. Local militia brought the total to 35,000, more than Wellington had taken with him in 1808 to fight in Portugal.

Maitland's tactics were as simple as "divide and conquer." In widely circulated fliers, he guaranteed pardons to those who renounced their oaths to General Ludd, offered cash money to informers and waged a campaign of intimidation. "Fear, and fear alone" would conquer the Luddites, Maitland decided. All summer, it was the weapon of choice.

Troops began chasing Luddites at night, breaking up meetings, taking prisoners and extracting confessions in closed rooms, which one captain wryly described as "dancing school." Hundreds of Luddites turned themselves in. Others gave evidence against their leaders. As Maitland had suspected, there was no General Ludd. Angry Ned Ludd's name had been taken up by the leader of each regional army. Hunger and desperation alone had united the Luddites.

In September, following weeks of sporadic midnight raids, an anonymous letter gave Maitland whole lists of pubs where Luddites met. Arrests brought more information, and soon all the Luddite leaders were in custody. "I think General Ludd has left this neighbourhood," a constable wrote his commanding officer in October. "We are very quiet only I often get a delightful letter threatening to blow out my brains."

The cry now was "Blood for Blood Says General Ludd," but despite such threats against judge and jury, justice was swift. In York 17 Luddites were hanged, 7 acquitted, the rest imprisoned or exiled. And so it went.

While today's Luddites proudly recall their predecessors, the name has a pejorative meaning. Novelist Tom Clancy, whose technothrillers make a high priest out of high tech, pinned the name on opponents of President Ronald Reagan's Strategic Defense Initiative. Any teacher who was suspicious of computers in the classroom quickly earned the label. Central to the anti-Luddite argument is the notion that machines create jobs and make life better.

Perhaps. But for the crushed Luddites themselves, machines brought no golden future. Having lost a war against technology, they lost the peace as well. By 1817, nearly 1,500 shearing machines were doing a cropper's job in Yorkshire alone, and by the time thousands of croppers petitioned Parliament for help, more than three-quarters of them were unemployed. Their craft had simply disappeared. The Luddites had always feared the worst, but the eventual squalor of the factories and mills could only be described by a writer of consummate skill, Charles Dickens, who was born during the Luddite uprising.

Periodic machine breaking continued. In 1830, threshing machines were smashed by followers of a mythical "Captain Swing," and whenever recession laid off workers, a few gig mills were hammered. In Midlands villages, the midnight meetings, drills and incendiary rhetoric continued off and on for 40 years. Old machine breakers kept their oaths of secrecy and sang Luddite songs to their grandchildren. But the men who wielded the first blows against technology passed on, leaving only their name and spirit to inspire those who wonder if humanity is the master of its machines—or vice versa.

Additional reading

Land of Lost Content: The Luddite Revolt by Robert Reid, Heinemann (London), 1986
The Luddites: Machine-Breaking in Regency England by Malcolm I. Thomis, Schocken Books (New York), 1972
The Risings of the Luddites, Chartists and Plug-Drawers by Frank Peel, Augustus M. Kelley Publishers, 1968
The Making of the English Working Class by E. P. Thompson, Pantheon Books, 1964

Looking beyond Aristotle and Alchemy

March 1994 marks the 500th anniversary of the birth of Georgius Agricola, a pioneering geoscientist whose studies give him claim as the father of mineralogy and physical geology.

William J. McPeak

William J. McPeak is a member of the American Geophysical Union, an affiliate of the Institute for Historical Study of San Francisco, and an independent scholar who has contributed several articles to History of the Geosciences: An Encyclopedia *(Garland Press).*

"We lost, on November 21th [1555], that distinguished ornament of our Fatherland, Georgius Agricola, a man of eminent intellect, of culture and of judgment . . . to a four-days fever." So in part read the letter of Georg Fabricius to the great intellectual and educator Philipp Melanchthon. Both men were Protestants; one was a lifelong friend of Agricola's, the other an admiring correspondent. Fabricius also noted that Agricola, a Catholic dying in the small, predominantly Protestant mining town of Chemnitz in Saxon Germany, had been refused burial in Chemnitz's Cathedral of St. Jacob, formerly Catholic and now Protestant. The tragedy was that Agricola, one of the great intellectuals of Saxon Germany, had been the faithful, ever-selfless mayor of Chemnitz for almost 11 years. With religious feelings running high in that year of the Peace of Augsburg, which would temporarily halt the religious conflict of the Reformation, Agricola was borne nearly 40 miles to the Catholic town of Zeitz and interred in the cathedral there. This incident is the only known case of ill feeling against a man whose life was a celebration of dedication to integrity and the scientific spirit.

Agricola's world

The sixteenth century was a period of global exploration and discovery, of intellectual, political, and religious ferment. It was an era of transition, not just of a rebirth of ancient Greek and Roman culture, as the name Renaissance might suggest. Most important, the century strove to provide a clearinghouse of human thought and endeavor, in part through the printing process inaugurated by Johannes Gutenburg circa 1450.

The natural world was still generally viewed in accordance with the ideas of the ancient Greeks. Though sometimes scrutinized critically in the Middle Ages, the thought of Aristotle (384–322 B.C.) continued to provide the foundation of the natural sciences. Aristotelianism systemized the physical world, but the system it imposed was challenged by discrepancies observed and recorded. The best scientific minds of the Renaissance collected everything from plants and rocks to sightings of rainbows and comets. They dabbled in the processes of incipient inductive and experimental thinking. Yet Aristotle was spared displacement because no other system rivaled his. Limited attempts at just such a new ordering of nature did appear in Renaissance science. One of these, meant to explain the solid matter of the terrestrial world, was the work of Agricola. It would remain influential for 200 years and be an important step toward the modern chemical interpretation of matter.

Georg Bauer, commonly known as Georgius Agricola, was born in Glauchau, Saxony, in eastern Germany on March 24, 1494. His parents are unknown, but their simple origin is apparent in the name Bauer, meaning "farmer" or, more familiarly, "peasant." The only recorded reference to siblings is a mention in the Zwickau town-council records of a single brother to "Agricola." When Georg was young, his teachers Latinized his name, as was the fad among Renaissance intellectuals, to "Georgius Agricola."

At 20 Agricola entered the University of Leipzig, about 50 miles northwest of Zwickau. In 1518, after earning a bachelor of arts degree, he became the vice principal of the municipal school of Zwickau, where he taught Greek and Latin. In 1520 he became principal. That same year, fellow Saxon Martin Luther—the son of a peasant miner—having turned Roman Catholic Europe upside down with his call for Germans to break with the Roman doctrine and the pope, was excommunicated. One of Agricola's assistants was Johann Förster, who would collaborate with Luther in the translation of the Bible into German in 1521.

The view that Rome was feeding off the German people had been building and was prevalent among German nobles and intellectuals. Agricola, in a lather of youthful indignation, even coined some antipapal epigrams of his own during the early stages of dissent. But by 1522, as the break with the church became more violent, many thoughtful Europeans had rejected Luther as a demagogue. The desire to reform the church from within was best summed up in the thought of the greatest humanist of the north, the Dutch scholar Desiderius Erasmus. Agricola remained loyal to the church, in the Erasmian spirit. Upon returning for medical studies (1522) and a lecture stint at the University of Leipzig, he found himself in a hotbed of Lutheranism. About 1524 he opted for the universities of Italy, where the atmosphere of strife and dissension was replaced by one of warm scholarship.

A life's work in the making

For a young northern humanist scholar, the passage southward to the birthplace of the Renaissance was no less than a pilgrimage. Agricola drank deeply from the wellsprings of ancient knowledge, completing the courses for the doctor's degrees in medicine, philosophy, and natural science at Bologna and Padua and capping off his clinical studies as a physician in Venice in 1526. In the meantime he had been investigating the most exciting application of the humanist spirit: the printing press. In Venice he had inspected the premier printing houses of Italy, the first among them being the Aldine Press founded by Aldus Manutius.

While finishing his studies, Agricola worked at the Aldine Press, collaborating in editing the treatises of the Roman physician Galen. It was in Italy that Agricola met Erasmus, the most celebrated mind of Europe, who had been general editor and adviser to the printer Johann Froben in Basel, Switzerland, since 1521. Erasmus encouraged Agricola to write and write Agricola would.

Agricola was back in Saxony later in 1526, making the fateful decision to become town physician in Joachimsthal, a burgeoning mining community about 20 miles south of Zwickau. Barely a decade old, Joachimsthal was located on the eastern slopes of the Erzgebirge Mountains near some of the richest precious-mineral lodes in central Europe. Agricola's interest in the natural sciences bloomed in this stark, mountainous locale, which would be home, laboratory, and inspiration from 1527 to 1533. As he visited mines and learned about mineral analysis and the mining arts, he took notes and talked shop with the mining personnel. In this way he met Lorenz Berman, an unusually well-educated member of the mining fraternity. The association spurred Agricola to learn all he could and to consult the histories of mining available in Greek and Latin. Agricola had the penchant of Renaissance professional men for avocational diversion, but this was to become a consuming scientific interest. His aim was to describe all aspects of solid earth, ranging from the constituents of minerals and rocks to the practical arts required to assay, mine, and process them.

Agricola compiled the assimilated knowledge and insights from his studies into a book, *Bermannus* (1530), which summarized mining topics and briefly covered mineralogical and geological topics as well. Framed in the popular humanist-dialogue convention of the day, *Bermannus* is composed of discussions between an experienced miner, modeled on Berman, and two scholarly physicians as they wandered through central European mining areas. It presented an outline of subject matter that would occupy Agricola for the rest of his life.

In 1529 Agricola sent his manuscript to Erasmus at the Froben Press in Basel. Erasmus was impressed and saw to its editing, then added his own enthusiastic letter of approval as an introduction before personally supervising the printing. The honor of having a letter from Erasmus as recommendation for publication was shared only by Agricola, Thomas More, and three of their contemporaries. *Bermannus* is important because it provides the overture to Agricola's revamping of mineral classification, in which the then-conventional, confusing use of colors and simple properties was replaced with a much-expanded descriptive terminology.

Earthly matters

Agricola was a competent physician. He treated and explained the dangers of mining, ranging from falls, cave-ins, and fires to poisonous gases and occupational diseases. He also applied observation to his diagnoses and evidently introduced the practice of quarantine to Germany. However, Agricola was becoming increasingly involved in his scholarly studies of metals and related topics. Later in 1530 Agricola resigned his post at Joachimsthal and began a fact-finding tour to many mining areas. After completing his research in 1533, he accepted the physician's post at the mining center of Chemnitz (until recently, Karl Marx Stadt) in eastern Saxony. That year saw publication of *De mensuris et ponderibus*, a small work that discussed Greek and Roman weights and measures and their correlation with those of Saxony. It contained the promise of a future book on metals. Not much is available on his life for the first decade at Chemnitz, but Agricola probably was preparing this work, *De re metallica*, his most important and comprehensive legacy to geoscience and technology. The one personal record from this period is of his marriage, evidently his second, to the widow Anna Meyner in 1543. There were at least five subsequent children in addition to previous offspring.

Except for ancient sources and portions of medieval alchemical texts, little geological and mining lore was available. The most up-to-date information on extracting ores and smelting came from manuscript "recipe booklets" with origins in early fifteenth-century Germany. Passed-down oral instructions were more prevalent. Nonetheless, books based on this information appeared, beginning in about 1500, under the generic title *Nützlich Bergbüchlein* (Useful little mining book). About 1510, assaying and refining recipe booklets appeared. Called *Probierbüchlein* (Little assay book), they were anonymous until the middle of the sixteenth century. A first, limited attempt at a comprehensive treatment was *De la pirotechnia* (1540), a modestly illustrated work by the Sienese technologist Vannoccio Biringuccio.

In 1544 Agricola's important series of mineralogical and geological treatises went to the Froben Press. Printed in 1546, this collection of collateral treatises included a newly amended version of *Bermannus*. Of greatest importance was *De natura fossilium*, literally meaning "concerning things dug up." This work of mineralogy was the first systematic attempt at classification of minerals. Earlier books employed a confusing assortment of Greek, Roman, German, and alchemical terms relating to color and physical appearance. Agricola's nomenclature employed the universal Latin of the Renaissance scholar and was based on solubility, fusibility, odor, taste, homogeneity, and such external properties as color, hardness, and luster.

This classification method yielded five basic orders and six suborders. Agricola was the first thinker to classify bismuth (which, like mercury, is a liquid) and antimony as primary metals, and he classified 20 more mineral species than the 60 or so

Probier büch=
lein/auff Gold/Silber/Kupffer/
vnd Bley/Auch allerlay Metall
wie man die zů nuß arbayten vñ
Probieren soll.

Alle Münßmayßtern/Wardeyn/Golc
werckern/Berckleüten/vñ kaufleütē
der Metall zů nuß mit grossem fleyß zů
samen gebracht.

COURTESY DOVER PUBLISHING

■ Before the publication of Agricola's major treatise on metallurgy, only small compilations of folk wisdom, such as this *Probierbüchlein* (Little assay book), were available.

known since antiquity. His was a qualitative chemistry based on the content of matter as dictated by the Aristotelian theory of four elements. Until chemical composition based in atomic theory began to see light 200 years later, Agricola's mineralogy would endure, and a portion of his classification endures even today.

The other treatises in this collection contain historical and geographical information about subjects including metals, mines, and liquid and gas flow from the earth. *Rerum metallicarum interpretatio* (Concerning the identification of metals) was a clear and comprehensive listing of 500 Latin and equivalent German mineralogical and metallurgical terms that had initially appeared appended to *Bermannus*. Ranking close to the mineralogical treatise in importance was *De orta et causis subterraneorum* (The origin and causes of the subterranean earth), a seminal work of physical geology that discusses the chemical products and phenomena of the earth and the reasoning behind Agricola's system for classifying minerals. Although his chemistry is still Aristotelian in that it is based on the four elements of air, earth, fire, and water, Agricola made an important departure by avoiding wholesale use of the term *exhalations*. According to Aristotelian thought, these elementally derived, terrestrial compounds and by-products were the source of everything from wind to comets.

Agricola analyzed solid earth by observation and inductive reasoning. Among his main contributions were the first comprehensive explanations of terrain building, erosion and destruction, and ore deposition. He noted that wind and water built up mountains and subsequently dug out plains and valleys; these factors and "fire in the interior of the earth" caused destruction through water erosion, wind sculpting, and earthquakes. Ore channels were created when percolation and circulation of surface water, groundwater, and condensed steam mixed with mineral compounds. Though Agricola considered the limited case of erosion rather than the more common fissuring of mineral and rock strata, his description of ore deposition antedated modern concepts of circulation, suspension, and solution by 300 years. Always concerned with accuracy of information, Agricola managed through the remainder of his busy life to significantly revise the collateral collection, which was republished posthumously in 1558.

Unexpected public life

In 1546 Agricola was named mayor of Chemnitz. Already, his fame was attracting patronage: the dream of every Renaissance scholar. By 1543 he enjoyed the favor of Maurice, duke of Saxony,

and was given a house in Chemnitz for life and privileges customarily reserved for nobility. Because Agricola remained a staunch Catholic and Saxony was the cradle of the Reformation, his appointment was unusual. For his patron Maurice, to whom he dedicated the collected works, Agricola served as an envoy to the Catholics and an adviser of unusual candor and integrity.

The Reformation had divided Germany, with most northern nobles turning Protestant both as a political expedient against the Holy Roman Emperor Charles V, an Austrian Catholic, and to bring economic relief from the monetary demands of the church of Rome. Agricola's public appointment coincided with the outbreak of what became known as the Schmalkaldic War, Charles' chance to deal with the league of rebellious Protestant leaders after the unwelcome diversion of a generation of territorial war with Francis I of France. That Agricola should serve as envoy to the emperor and other Catholic nobles was logical, for Maurice understood the futility of war with Charles. He therefore made a secret pact with the emperor. As the war was played out, Chemnitz endured periodic occupations by both sides, despite Agricola's efforts to

fortify the town against invasion. When the smoke cleared a year later, Maurice's reward for loyalty to the emperor was sole control of Saxony; Agricola won new terms as mayor and yet more trips to regional councils representing the duke and Chemnitz.

Mining made easy

All the while Agricola had been working on his mining and metals opus, even planning for an early publication in 1546. Not until 1550, however, was the text

GEORGII AGRICOLAE
DE RE METALLICA LIBRI XII. QVI-
bus Officia, Inftrumenta, Machinæ, ac omnia deniqʒ ad Metalli-
cam fpectantia, non modo luculentiffimè defcribuntur, fed & per
effigies, fuis locis infertas, adiunctis Latinis, Germanicísqʒ appel-
lationibus ita ob oculos ponuntur, ut clarius tradi non poffint.

EIVSDEM
DE ANIMANTIBVS SVBTERRANEIS Liber, ab Autore re-
cognitus:cum Indicibus diuerfis, quicquid in opere tractatum eft,
pulchrè demonftrantibus.

BASILEAE M. D. LVI.
Cum Priuilegio Imperatoris in annos v.
& Galliarum Regis ad Sexennium.

■ *Left:* As with his earlier works on the classification of metals and geological processes, Agricola's last book, *De re metallica* (1556), established new standards of scholarship for its subject matter, in this case, mining processes. The text was illustrated with hundreds of woodcuts. *Above:* In Agricola's day, pumps and pipes for draining water from mines were made of wood.

COURTESY DOVER PUBLISHING

Left: **Smelting ore in a furnace designed so metal residues could be scraped from its roof and resmelted.**

completed, proved by the December 1550 date of its dedication to Duke Maurice and his younger brother Augustus. Beyond completing the text lay another major barrier to publication: Agricola had decided that it should be illustrated with an accuracy not yet attempted. He had wanted to copiously illustrate *De re metallica*—with all its descriptions of mining exploration, surveying, ore assaying, tools, smelting, and other metallurgical instructions and apparatuses—so that anyone, including posterity, could understand the techniques and processes involved. An artist named Basilius Wefring sketched out many depictions, and Agricola noted hiring illustrators to do the work in the best possible manner. In the sixteenth century most people were illiterate and depended on woodcut depictions for news and religion, so he may have had nonreaders in mind as well. Handling the significant out-of-pocket expenses, Agricola finally had a set of satisfactory woodblocks in hand.

It was not until 1553 that the manuscript was shipped off to the Froben Press and another three years before its actual publication, a year after Agricola's death. The work was divided into 12 books and represented not just a vast array of techniques and processes but the first comprehensive and clear exposition of that information, graced by unique technical illustrations. Although blocks and pulleys, windlasses, waterwheels, geared wheels, and chain-and-piston pumps were of ancient origin, Agricola's illustrations indicated the advance in size and applications of these mechanisms by the sixteenth century. Through the course of his treatise he described windlass mechanisms for hauling earth and water from mines; bucket, piston, and rag-and-chain pumps for siphoning off the constant groundwater seepage; and a variety of ventilators—from large fans, bellows, and transverse paddles to windmills and rotating-drum circulators. Agricola noted all the separating processes for basic metals and was the first author

to describe gold amalgamation with mercury, the various gold-smelting processes, cementation (the process of separating precious metals) with niter, and the latest lead-smelting techniques.

De re metallica would endure as a basic textbook for nearly 200 years after Agricola's death. As a record to posterity, it remains one of the landmarks of applied science, as do *De natura fossilium* and *De orta et causis subterraneorum* for geoscience. During the early years of this century enthusiastic professionals exploring the history of science turned to Agricola's work, the most famous of them being President Herbert Hoover, a former mining engineer. The perspective on Agricola today is multifaceted, with the most extreme revisionist view casting him as a self-serving mining capitalist, a view that is challenged by those who attempt to see him in historical context.

The Chemnitz known as Karl Marx Stadt in East Germany is once again Chemnitz in an undivided Germany. This year, a conference at Chemnitz's Mining Museum will commemorate Georgius Agricola and his place in the history of science. Today, one encounters a perplexing dichotomy: The ideal of science as the source of knowledge and technology for the betterment of society contrasts with the realities of fragmented scientific knowledge and of technology that disrupts ecological and social systems. Yet as food for thought, scientific history serves up the past's legacy, and the Renaissance may well be made to order for the present. Sharing in transitional uncertainty and the compromise that must accompany it, we can gain perspective from the idealistic humanist thinkers of the sixteenth century, in particular, from Georgius Agricola, whose life is a reassurance that knowledge and human integrity can transcend all boundaries.

The Scientific Importance of Napoleon's Egyptian Campaign

Bonaparte's invasion of Egypt brought French scientists and engineers to the Nile. Their work, in turn, brought the splendors of the Nile to Europe

Charles C. Gillispie

CHARLES C. GILLISPIE is a historian of science who is known as editor of the *Dictionary of Scientific Biography*. After completing undergraduate work in chemistry at Wesleyan University, he received his doctoral degree in history from Harvard University. Since 1947 Gillispie has taught at Princeton University, where he is now professor emeritus and where he established the program in history of science in the 1960s.

On the first of July 1798, an armada of 400 ships appeared off the coast at Alexandria. By the end of the day, longboats had put ashore an army of 36,000 men under the command of Napoleon Bonaparte. Meeting with no resistance, he immediately marched his troops, sweltering in their woolen Alpine uniforms, through the oven of the desert to rout the Mameluke rulers of Egypt in the Battle of the Pyramids on July 21. Ten days later Admiral Horatio Nelson destroyed the French fleet, marooning the expeditionary force in the land it was to control and explore for the next three years.

Bonaparte abandoned his soldiers a year later, slipping through the British blockade and returning to France to seize power in the coup d'état of November 9, 1799. Among the handful of retainers he took with him were Gaspard Monge and Claude-Louis Berthollet, the leading members of the first scientific task force to accompany a military expedition. Their colleagues from the Commission of Science and Arts—a group of 151 scientists, engineers, medical men and a few scholars—were left behind with the army. The elite among them were elected to the Institute of Egypt, founded on Bonaparte's initiative as a colonial adaptation of the Institute of France. Serving as permanent secretary throughout the occupation was

Jean-Baptiste Fourier, who had yet to invent the analysis that bears his name.

The most famous discovery of the expedition remains the Rosetta stone, now in the British Museum. The French surrendered it with immense reluctance to the British forces that expelled them from Egypt late in 1801. The commission of technical experts accomplished a great deal else of scientific interest in the land of the pharaohs. A compilation of monumental dimensions contains the record of their archaeological surveys; of their research into the physical and chemical phenomena as well as the natural history peculiar to the region;

SOUTH GATE OF KARNAK was drawn by members of Napoleon's Commission of Science and Arts as they imagined it to have been originally. The scene might have served as a stage set for the grand march in Verdi's *Aida:* while the populace looks on, a Theban king passes through the triumphal arch, preceded by retainers and followed by his prisoners.

and of their inquiries into the sociology of an exotic country.

La Description de l'Égypte, printed between 1809 and 1828, required a specially designed piece of mahogany furniture to house it. Ten folio volumes of plates measuring 20 by 26 inches and two atlases, 26 by 40 inches each, contain 837 copper engravings (50 in color and many with multiple illustrations). A third atlas consists of a topographical chart of Egypt and the Holy Land in 47 sheets. Nine accompanying volumes of text dwarf any modern encyclopedia. They comprise approximately 7,000 pages of memoirs, description and commentary. The whole is divided into three parts: ancient Egypt, modern Egypt and natural history.

The archaeological plates of part one, which make up just over half the total wealth of illustrations, created the first modern vision of Egyptian antiquity. It was in contemplating the sweep and detail of those enormous and powerful engravings that Europeans took the measure of the valley of the Nile. Earlier Western awareness of the land of the

pharaohs had consisted mainly of hearsay about the scale and orientation of the Pyramids and the mystery of the Sphinx. Of Upper Egypt nothing was known beyond the odd traveler's tale of some giant arm, say of Shelley's *Ozymandias,* thrusting out of the sand. An account by the artist Vivant Denon, who accompanied the soldiers in their campaign up the Nile, conveys the impact of rounding a bend in the river and coming on the temples of Karnak and Luxor amid the ruins of Thebes: "The whole army, suddenly and with one accord, stood in amazement…and clapped their hands with delight."

The contributors to *La Description de l'Égypte* captured on paper all the monuments, starting in the south at the Isle of Philae. Drawing, measuring and excavating along the way, they moved downstream through Kom Ombo and Edfu—close by the Nile on the right and left banks, respectively—and past Esna, slightly set back from the river to the west. Their party paused longest amid the vast array of

Thebes, awed by Medinet Habu, the Ramasseum and the colossal statues of Memnon, behind which lie the tombs in the Valley of the Kings and facing which loom the enormous piles of Luxor and Karnak across the Nile. Downstream they came upon the architectural and artistic climax of Dendara. After recording these masterpieces, the group continued north to Memphis and the Pyramids at Giza.

Each site is depicted in a sequence of eight to 10 plates, beginning with topography. Next comes a panorama of the structure in its condition at the time, choked with sand, columns cracked and tumbled, ramparts crumbling, the overall majesty somehow enhanced. Architectural drawings follow, providing ground plans, sections and elevations. Several sheets then depict architectural detail, bas-reliefs and other sculptures as well as surfaces covered with inscriptions. Finally, having scrupulously exhibited what they saw, the designers let themselves go and in the last plate of each series restored the entire structure in the mind's eye.

These creations were the works not of artists or archaeologists but of engineers and a few architects. They were very young engineers, recent graduates and some undergraduates of the École Polytechnique, founded in 1794, where drafting and surveying were major subjects. Equipped with drawing board, graph paper, pencil, ruler and compass, trained engineers were able to produce a sketch of any structure. The drawing could be developed into a finished picture after they had measured all dimensions. The completed engravings re-create the experience of standing before the facade of Karnak or gazing across the sands at the Pyramids with an immediacy not felt in perusing the most modern, the most elaborate of photographic albums.

It was not, of course, for artistic purposes that Bonaparte included these well-educated youngsters in the expedition. Their main responsibility was to build or mend fortifications, roads, bridges, canals and public works. Indeed, the men did discharge their mundane tasks, as they would have done in France. Nevertheless, Egypt was the great adventure of their lives. One team even succeeded in the archaeological feat of excavating the route of the canal that had linked the Red Sea to the Mediterranean in ancient times. (They had the misfortune, however, to calculate that sea level at the former end was 33 feet higher than at the latter—a conclusion that was dead wrong because sea level is sea level the world over.)

The men of the expedition had known nothing of the country when they embarked from France, not even that Egypt was their destination. That information had been kept secret from all but the high command. The members of the Commission of Science and Arts had no guides to the symbolism and significance of what they saw other than the historians and geographers of antiquity: Herodotus, Strabo and Diodorus of Sicily. The elementary facts provided to tourists in the most superficial of modern guidebooks were unknown to them. They supposed small structures to be shrines, middling ones to be temples and the greatest to be palaces. They took the crowns of Upper and Lower Egypt for elaborate coiffures.

Even so, confronted with hundreds of bas-reliefs and thousands of hieroglyphs, the young engineers copied the lot so faithfully that in many instances they preserved the evidence of inscriptions and structures that have since disappeared. For example, the temple of Isis across the Nile from Esna was destroyed in 1828 during the regime of

RUINS OF THE SOUTH GATE of Karnak were depicted as they stood when the engineers came upon them. The remains of the small temples of Apet and Khons can be seen in the foreground, and part of the great temple lies in the center background. The first plate of each architectural series in *La Description de l'Égypte* was devoted to an accurate illustration of a monument as it appeared in 1799.

2. THE INDUSTRIAL AND SCIENTIFIC REVOLUTIONS

TEMPLE OF ISIS, across the Nile River from the ruins of Esna, was destroyed in 1828 during the regime of Mehemet Ali, the modernizer of Egypt. *La Description de l'Égypte* is an important resource for archaeology because it contains several plates preserving the record of structures and inscriptions that no longer exist.

Mehemet Ali. It could be said that Egyptology began with *La Description de l'Égypte*—except that the authors had no clue to the meaning of what they were recording. The opportunity afforded the admirer of their work is, therefore, unique in the history of science. These plates display the subject matter of a science in the absence of the science. It was only in 1822 that Jean-François Champollion succeeded in matching the name Ptolemy in the three scripts—hieroglyphic, demotic and Greek—inscribed on the Rosetta stone. Not until the 1850s were scholars able to construe whole texts.

As for science in the ordinary sense, the Egyptian environment created exceptional opportunities. Monge's explanation of mirages is the most famous memoir contributed to the institute. The sight of island villages shimmering in the waters of an ever receding lake had tormented the army during the grueling march from Alexandria. In a paper read before his colleagues on August 28, 1798, four weeks after Cairo was taken, Monge interpreted the illusion as the effect of light rays from beyond the horizon reflected from the surface of a layer of air superheated at ground level by the sun-soaked sand. Although modern optics attributes the effect to a dual refraction within the surface layer, Monge had the underlying physics right.

A memoir by his fellow senior scientist, Berthollet, had greater consequence, both for the author's career and for his science. Berthollet's *Observations sur le natron* may be considered the point of departure for physical chemistry. Highly saline lakes in a dried-up river basin some 60 miles west of Cairo were known

then by the name "natron," Greek for "soda." Surrounding them are limestone formations on which deposits of that commodity occurred naturally. Interspersed among those patches were stretches where clay predominated—in those areas the soil was full of salt and free of soda. Berthollet deduced that in the limestone sectors, the lime (calcium carbonate) decomposed salt (sodium chloride) in the presence of heat and humidity. The resulting encrustation of natron (sodium carbonate) dried out and solidified on the surface. The accompanying product, calcium chloride, being extremely deliquescent, took up water and seeped away into the ground.

The significant feature of Berthollet's finding was that the reaction known in the laboratory was the exact reverse. Chemists concerned with affinities between substances normally supposed that the chemical nature of reagents was what controlled the direction of a reaction. Here, though, was an instance in which physical factors predominated. Berthollet began the paper reporting these observations in Egypt and completed it in Paris. There he developed the argument into the central theme of his major work published in 1803, *Essai de statique chimique,* which treats the effects of pressure, heat, light and the relative concentration of reagents in determining the course of reactions.

It was, however, the young naturalists, rather than the two senior scientists, whose presence in Egypt might have been expected to make a significant difference to their discipline. Twelve in number, they made up the second largest contingent of the expedition, after the engineers, and were investigating a flora and fauna unknown in Europe. Indeed, two of the authors did make

names for themselves. When they embarked for Egypt, Étienne Geoffroy Saint-Hilaire was in the early stage of his career, and Jules-César Lelorgne de Savigny was at the very beginning of his. Savigny took responsibility for invertebrate zoology and for ornithology as well as for a few reptiles; Geoffroy covered all the other vertebrates.

Geoffroy and Savigny were naturalists of similar interests and very dissimilar scientific personalities. In contrast to Georges Cuvier, not much their elder but already dominant in the Paris Museum of Natural History, both were zoologists whose research moved beyond taxonomy, the work of classification, to morphology, the study of form and structure. The former had been the main preoccupation of the natural history of the 18th century; the latter became an important subdiscipline of the emerging science of biology in the 19th century. Geoffroy made the transition in the spirit of romanticism and Savigny in service to precision.

Geoffroy was of a generous, even effusive disposition. His letters to his colleagues of the museum, and especially to Cuvier (who had refused to join the expedition), are almost embarrassing in their protestations of friendship—the more so because his pleas for assurance that he had not been forgotten went unanswered. Geoffroy also had an eye for novelty. The more spectacular the creature, the more eagerly he described and dissected it. The crocodile, the great Nile tortoise, the *polyptère bichir* (a lungfish with 16 dorsal fins), the torpedo ray and the thunder-fish were among the dramatic forms he opened with his scalpel. In one respect, Geoffroy's style is reminiscent of the great Georges-Louis Leclerc de Buffon's in the preceding century. Geoffroy's accounts include character sketches of the animals—their habits, their conduct, almost their morality. His anatomies were, however, highly skilled. The detail is exact. The drawings and descriptions are clear. He knew the literature.

The morphological direction that Geoffroy's interests were taking became evident in three memoirs on the anatomy of fish published in 1807. He had just had a revelation, Geoffroy wrote, while working on his ichthyology for *La Description de l'Égypte*. Until then, he had concurred with the accepted opinion among naturalists that in important respects the internal organization of fish was categorically different from that of vertebrates generally. Now, on closely examining his Egyptian specimens and Cuvier's collection, he reports that he is thrilled to find that the very organs that had most stubbornly resisted comparison actually exhibit profound analo-

gies with the parts of other vertebrates.

The shift toward morphology led Geoffroy to compose his principal work, *Philosophie anatomique*, between 1818 and 1822. His argument is that differences in the organization of all classes of vertebrates represent variations on a fundamental unity of plan, a notion he later extended to invertebrates. The extravagance of these ideas was in conflict with Cuvier's commitment to the fixity of species and involved the two

CIRCULAR ZODIAC OF DENDARA had been set into the ceiling of a shrine off the Osiris Chapel of the temple. The two engineers who produced the drawing had to work by candlelight lying flat on their backs in the gloom of a closed chamber. In 1821 this masterpiece was moved to Paris, where it is now on display in the Louvre.

former friends in a notorious confrontation in 1830.

Unlike Geoffroy, Savigny first made his name through a small work of broad interest, and only much later did he move from generalization toward specialization. His *Histoire naturelle et mythologique de l'ibis,* published in 1805, is a charming combination of classical erudition and zoological precision. The veneration of the white ibis in ancient Egypt reflected its supposed appetite for flying snakes, which, according to legend, would have otherwise invaded the land. In fact, Egypt was in no danger from snakes, winged or earthbound, except as symbols of evil. Moreover, the ibis is a wading bird and eats no snakes. The real source of its sacred character was its arrival on the summer winds. It reappeared annually as the harbinger of life-giving waters, hence its identification with Toth, the ibis-headed equivalent of Mercury. Savigny notes that if the stomach cavities of ibis mummies held the remains of snakes, and typically they did, it was because the embalmers had served truths deeper than mere facts of natural history.

His book a fine success, Savigny settled down to put his Egyptian specimens in order. Still, he found himself at a loss to ascribe distinguishing characters to the manifold types of insects and crustaceans he had collected. No entomologist had yet identified systems of organs generally disposed in a regular manner—as Linnaeus had done with the sex organs of plants—so that variations might be compared from species to species and genus to genus. Working with some 1,500 specimens, Savigny began the search by detaching the external features and making separate drawings of each. Few of the creatures were as much as a centimeter long, and most of them were much smaller. A survey of his thousands of drawings yielded the key to classification. Because the same elements of mouthparts occurred in all forms, the modifications of these structures afforded the most reliable comparisons between species.

Savigny devoted his first paper to moths and butterflies, the most controversial case. In this report he took issue with his seniors, Cuvier and the foremost entomologist in France, Pierre André Latreille, both of whom considered that the jaws of the caterpillar disappear on its metamorphosis into a butterfly. Not so, Savigny found. He was able to discern forms of miniature lips, mandibles and jaws so modified as to be virtually unrecognizable—a finding for which Cuvier and

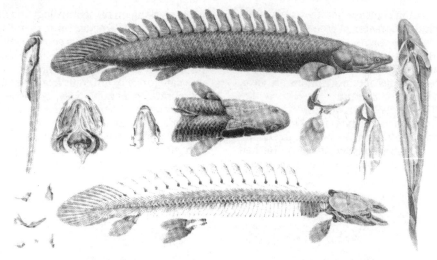

NATURAL HISTORY PLATES and monographs depict the flora, fauna and mineral species of the Nile valley. Étienne Geoffroy Saint-Hilaire, who drew this lungfish (*top*), had a penchant for creatures of unusual or extravagant form. Drawings by the mining engineer François-Michel de Rozière, such as this sample of breccia (*right*), set a new standard for precise geological illustration.

Latreille gave him full credit. These criteria enabled Savigny to establish the morphological definition of the class of insects proper: the hexapods, which have six legs and two antennae.

In his next memoir, Savigny turned to the second great division of articulated invertebrates—the myriapods (including centipedes), arachnids and crustaceans—which Linnaeus had lumped together under the designation "insect." Mouthparts are again the key to classification. So extraordinary were the variations that Savigny adduced homologies with a daring and virtuosity quite uncharacteristic of the staid world of taxonomy. In certain groups, such as crabs, organs that serve for mastication are comparable to those that other orders use for locomotion: what are feet in hexapods appear to be transformed into jaws in crabs. Later work on the ascidians, or tunicate worms, was no less startling. Savigny showed that creatures vaguely called zoophytes, far from being instances of extreme simplicity, exhibit complex colonial arrangements. A final study on annelids advanced the systematization of Cuvier's class of red-blooded worms.

Savigny's work, in short, marks the beginning of zoological studies of homology in general. At the same time, his accuracy in detail was such that his plates on mollusks were reprinted as late as 1926, not for antiquarian but for scientific reasons. He never com-

pleted a comprehensive treatise, however; Savigny was unable even to prepare the annotations to accompany his plates in *La Description de l'Égypte.* As he worked on their infinitely fine detail, he suffered recurrent attacks of a neurological disorder that robbed him of effective eyesight when it set in permanently in 1824. He attributed the problem to the late onset of the ophthalmia that had afflicted many members of the Egyptian expedition. In fact, in the diagnosis of modern specialists, a temporal mode epilepsy may probably have been responsible. Unable to support the light of day, Savigny passed the last 30 years of his life enveloped in a black veil whenever the shutters were opened. His only remaining publication was a taxonomy of the highly systematic hallucinations produced by the turbulence in his optic nerve, an aurora borealis inside his head.

The botany in *La Description de l'Égypte* is a little disappointing when compared with the zoology, but the mineralogy is intriguing indeed. There are 15 magnificent plates, comprising more than 100 illustrations of the petrology of Egypt, together with an extensive monograph on the physical geography of the country. The author, François-Michel de Rozière, was a mining engineer who made no other contribution to formal science and scholarship. Like Savigny, he treated highly specialized subject matter in a manner that held general interest.

Mineralogy was even then differentiating itself from natural history and entering into the emerging discipline of geology. Rozière designed his plates expressly to exemplify the importance of the graphic arts for the new science. Geologists had yet to develop a language like that of chemistry or botany that permitted identifying minerals by specific names. The descriptions of rocks in geologic writings were meaningless in the absence of the specimen in question. A properly executed illustration could supply the lack, and Rozière took pains to ensure that his drawings were not merely pictures of the particular rocks on his table at the moment but schematic renderings of all the distinguishing features of the type each one represented. The elements were to be written down in a description, but the form, the color, the mixture and, above all, the texture—in short, the properties required for recognition—needed to be shown graphically.

Rozière's monograph is entitled *On the Physical Constitution of Egypt and on Its Relation with the Ancient Institutions of the Country*. Had the author been a philosopher or an ideologist of some sort, the argument would have been thought daring because his purpose was to show how culture derives from material circumstances and not from divine dispensation or other transcendental factors. Composed by this mining engineer, the treatment is merely matter of fact. In no other country, Rozière observes, has a highly developed society such as that of ancient Egypt ever exhibited such dependence on a single set of physical factors. Everything in the laws of the land and the customs of the people derives from the behavior of the Nile. The rise and fall of the river not only shaped the civilization of Egypt but also accounted for the influence of its culture on the theogonies, the sciences, and the arts and crafts of all antiquity. The phenomenon, moreover, is one that can be studied in an isolation comparable to that of a laboratory, which for these purposes Egypt was.

It is in part two of *La Description de l'Égypte*, concerned with the country as it was at the end of the 18th century, that the work most largely fulfills the promise of its title. Memoirs and stud-

DIVINE HARPIST from the wall of the tomb of Ramses the Third is among the 50 color illustrations in the document.

59

ies on topography occupy much of the text. The engineering parties that ran the traverses from which maps were constructed had a mission beyond mere cartography. Surveyors fanning out through all the villages across the delta and up the Nile were instructed to take what amounted to a census, reporting the number of inhabitants and families, their status and occupations, the mode of agriculture, the population of horses and camels, the practice of animal husbandry, the types of commerce and industry, the location of quarries, of oases, of canals, of towpaths, the means of transport and communication as well as the ethnic and religious character of the people, both settled and nomadic.

Topography was a subject of medical and physical concern because the goal of 18th-century medicine was to balance the environment and the physiological constitution of men, women and children. The head physician of the expedition was Nicolas Desgenettes, and the head surgeon was Dominique Jean Larrey. The Egyptian setting being dramatic, Desgenettes composed a *Topographie physique et médicale de l'Égypte,* which included collaboration from the astronomer Nicolas-Antoine Nouet. Throughout the occupation, Desgenettes assembled data on the population dynamics of Egypt, compiled a necrology of Cairo for the three years the French were in control and composed a classic of military medicine that set out policies for sanitation, public health and the organization of hospitals.

Larrey, for his part, wrote mainly about disease. He gave clinical descriptions of ophthalmia (usually trachoma), bubonic plague, tetanus, yellow fever, leprosy, elephantiasis, and testicular atrophy and gigantism. In his view, the etiology of plague, fever and tetanus clearly involved a specific external agent, for which he sometimes used the word "virus" and sometimes "germ." His concept of disease was as specific and objective as anything that entered into 19th-century medicine from the new clinical practice in Paris, an approach that he appears to have anticipated and developed on his own.

Among the memoirs and monographs in part two of *La Description de l'Égypte* are many covering topics that nowadays would be classified as social science or humanities. These include anthropolo-

BLACK AND WHITE IBISES were illustrated by Jules-César Lelorgne de Savigny, a founder of morphology. His book on the natural history of the ibis notes that the white ibis, venerated by the Egyptians for protecting their land from serpents, never eats snakes. Ancient embalmers respected and conserved the myth, however, by placing snakes in the stomach cavities of the birds they mummified.

gy (both cultural and physical), demography, meteorology, political science, sociology, geopolitics, agronomy, microeconomics, medieval history, administrative history, linguistics and musicology—disciplines that did not yet exist for the most part. The authors of these pieces also were engineers, scientists and military men, people trained to be systematic, who knew how to look around them and take the measure of what they saw.

Their attitude is that of observers of phenomena. They often said to one another that no other country in the world, and certainly not France, had ever been the subject of such thorough study as theirs on Egypt. That fact began to change when they returned to France. Most of them continued in the service of the state. The voracious fact-gathering they had practiced in Egypt became characteristic both of the Napoleonic regime and the monarchy restored in 1815. One engineer, Chabrol de Volvic, is a fair example. As a youngster, he designed many of the plates on antiquity and composed an essay on the customs of the modern inhabitants of Egypt. Chabrol finished his career as prefect of the Seine in the 1820s. He then ordered the compilation of an urban topography, *Statistique de la Ville de Paris,* in effect an application to the capital of France of the techniques of deep description he and his colleagues had employed in Egypt.

Above and beyond the enormous compilation of information on Egypt, the significance of the participation of science in the expedition lies in the relation it portended between formal knowledge and politics. Unlike the mercantile colonialism that preceded it, the occupation of Egypt had a cultural component. Technical competence was at the forefront of culture. Bonaparte understood that point, not abstractly but intuitively, as he understood whatever related to the exercise of power. His was the impulse that implanted a clone of French science on the banks of the Nile. The British in India, the Dutch in Indonesia, the Spaniards and Portuguese in America—earlier imperialism had not attempted anything of the kind. The spread of European science and its appurtenances to African and Asian societies under the aegis of military conquest and political power began with the French conquest of Egypt.

The motivation that Fourier ascribes to Bonaparte in the preface may be read as a prophetic rationale: "He was aware of the influence that this event [the conquest of Egypt] would have on the relations of Europe with the East and with the interior of Africa as well as on maritime affairs in the Mediterranean and the future of Asia. He set himself the goals of abolishing the tyranny of the Mamelukes, of extending irrigation and agriculture, of instituting regular commerce between the Mediterranean and the Arabian Sea, of fostering commercial enterprises, of offering useful examples of European industry to the Orient, and finally of improving the standard of living of the inhabitants and procuring them all the advantages of an improved civilization. These objectives would be unattainable without the continual application of science and the technical arts."

FURTHER READING

SCIENCE AND POLITY IN FRANCE AT THE END OF THE OLD REGIME. Charles C. Gillispie. Princeton University Press, 1980.
SCIENTIFIC ASPECTS OF THE FRENCH EGYPTIAN EXPEDITION: 1798–1801. Charles C. Gillispie in *Proceedings of the American Philosophical Society,* Vol. 133, No. 4, pages 447–474; December 1989.
MONUMENTS OF EGYPT: THE COMPLETE ARCHAEOLOGICAL PLATES FROM THE *DESCRIPTION DE L'EGYPTE.* Fourth printing. Edited by Charles C. Gillispie and Michel Dewachter. Princeton Architectural Press, 1994.

James Watson and the search for biology's 'Holy Grail'

A 15-year effort to map all the genes on every human chromosome begins . . . raising new hopes and ethical quandaries

Stephen S. Hall

Stephen Hall is a freelance writer living in New York City. He last wrote for Smithsonian *on the links between molecules, emotions and health, in June 1989.*

When he first came to Cold Spring Harbor Laboratory in the summer of 1948, Jim Watson was a young biological Cassius, hungry to find an important scientific problem, preparing to hoist himself onto the shoulders of giants named Salvador Luria, Max Delbrück and Renato Dulbecco. Born in Chicago and raised in the shadow of its steel mills, the 20-year-old Watson was struck by the natural beauty and monied estates of Long Island's North Shore, but he was struck even more by the company it attracted. "There were only bright people here," he recalls, relief still evident in his voice. "The summer was dominated by—well, Dulbecco came with Luria and we did experiments, and

it was exciting. You know, What was the gene?" In five years, Watson and Francis Crick would answer that question by discovering the structure of DNA. Biology has never been the same.

Now, nearly four decades after that seminal discovery, James Dewey Watson—an architect of his own career if ever there was one—has set off to fashion one final piece in the grand symmetry that marks his extraordinary life in science. Once a biological tourist at Cold Spring Harbor, Watson is now in his 22d season as director of the venerable laboratory, which this year celebrates its centennial. And at age 61, when he could have maintained respectability merely by collecting his honorary degrees, Watson has taken on a project sometimes called "biology's moon shot." Known as the Human Genome Initiative, it aspires to identify and map every gene in our chromosomes, parsing DNA's "grammar of life" down to its biochemical sentences, words and letters. "Never will a more important set of instruction books be made available to human beings," Watson vows. And never will a more appropriate set of bookends frame a scientist's career.

Arguably the best-known biologist in America, winner of the Nobel Prize in 1962, famous for his best-selling science memoir, *The Double Helix*—infamous for its breezy, abrasive style—Watson has played a major role in shaping the direction of biological research since the 1950s. He had absolutely nothing to prove when, in 1988, National Institutes of Health director James Wyngaarden asked him to coordinate NIH's effort in its massive and controversial project. So why did he agree to do it?

Watson considers the question only briefly. He is no longer the skinny, leering lad of the archival photographs, with the exaggerated grin and flip of hair straight out of the Social Realists, cousin to one of Edward Hopper's loners or Thomas Hart Benton's earnest Midwestern string beans. The hair is gray and thinner after all these years, but still wild, tufted like pulled cotton; the voice soft, yet hectic. "No one else wanted to do it," he replies, arching his eyebrows. "And someone had to."

That's not the real reason, of course. Since that first summer at Cold Spring Harbor, Watson has instinctively drifted toward the key questions of biology, and for the past 35 years those questions have danced around the maypole of the double helix. The genome project promises a kind of culmination: complete explication of the molecule. So he commutes to NIH headquarters in Bethesda, Maryland, two days a week and wows Congressional committees with his outspoken, oddly patriotic view of the initiative, and has assumed highly visible leadership of a project that will cost about $3 billion, take 15 years and, it is argued, revolutionize biomedicine in the 21st century.

For Watson and the generation of biologists who initiated this grand intellectual crusade, the genome—the genetic blueprint of the organism—is the final prize. Walter Gilbert, a Nobel laureate who worked with Watson in the early '60s at Harvard, calls the genome the "Holy Grail" of genetics. Norton Zinder of Rockefeller University prefers the "Rosetta stone."

What makes this chapter of Watson's story particularly intriguing is that he has placed himself at the crossroads of great social and scientific controversy. Many fear the genome project will destroy the "small science" feel of biology and divert funds from worthy research. Even Watson's old mentor, Salvador Luria, has blasted the venture as a pet project of a "small coterie of power-seeking enthusiasts" who may be leading us into a "kinder, gentler program to 'perfect' human individuals by 'correcting' their genomes. . . ."

The genome project promises great strides in the diagnosis and treatment of disease, but that sunny picture trails clouds of heavy social weather: the possibility of eugenics, of abuses of genetic privacy, of human tragedy inherent in diagnosing fatal diseases without being able to treat them. Without question, the project will take abstract medical, legal and ethical dilemmas and dump them upon nearly every hearth and home. Ironically, the only scientist with enough power and visibility to influence the ethical climate in which this

new genetic future is forged may be James Watson. So when he says, "I may have to visibly take the heat," he might be alluding not only to the current controversies, but ultimately to how history views his overall stewardship of the project.

"You really want to get the problem solved"

"His dominant moral value," says one associate, "is good science." As a good scientist, Watson believes, "You really are curious about the laws of nature, and you want people to understand them. If you can help in that, that's great. But you really want to get the problem solved and not your own reputation furthered." He pauses to give a short laugh. "I enjoy myself most," he says, "in the company of people whom I find brighter than myself, rather than the other way around." Even more than place, home for Watson has always been the company of such people.

He was born on April 6, 1928, into what he describes as a "poor family" on the South Side of Chicago. His Episcopalian father was a bill collector ("It was an awful job," Watson says; "he would have been better as a schoolteacher, but he never ended up that way"). His Scotch-Irish mother, a Catholic, worked as a secretary at the University of Chicago and served as a Democratic precinct boss. Watson's childhood was shaped by the Great Depression, not just its poverty but its embrace of public service, its New Deal populism, and its model of forceful and charismatic leadership in the person of Franklin Roosevelt, whose name often pops up in Watson's conversation. But one of his earliest conflicts, no doubt, was reconciling that populist sentiment with the estranging brilliance of his own intellect. As a child, he was small, unathletic, bookish and, one gathers, as prickly and undiplomatic as he is known to be today. "I wasn't a popular kid," he recalls, "and I suspect it was because I would generally say something which I thought was true. In those days, I used to think manners were terrible, you know. The truth was important and manners often hid the truth." He expectorates one of his laughs, as if what he has said is so obvious there was hardly any reason to say it at all.

He sought the company of adults and the comfort of adult activities, especially reading. His father, a voracious reader, also introduced his son to bird-watching. With his mother, Watson argued the relative importance of nature versus nurture (young Watson, a self-described "leftist," recalls that he argued the side of environment, while his mother championed heredity).

As a youngster, Watson competed on the *Quiz Kids* radio show; he lasted three sessions before tripping up, he claims, on questions about Shakespeare and the Old Testament ("If I'd known the religious questions," he has said, "my father would have been angry at me"). He attended the University of Chicago high school, graduated at age 15 and earned a degree in zoology at the University of Chicago in 1947, before pursuing graduate studies at Indiana University.

Bird-watching acquainted Watson with the beauty of nature; Erwin Schrödinger's book *What Is Life?* introduced him to life's central mystery. Schrödinger described the gene as the crucial entity in the study of biology; unfortunately, in the 1940s no one knew exactly what a gene was, what it looked like or how it worked. As he has done throughout his career, Watson smelled its importance and attached himself to a fraternity of brilliant men—it was always men—hot on the trail of the central question.

The story of the discovery of the structure of DNA is told in unforgettable fashion in Watson's racy and candid memoir, *The Double Helix*. Armed with his PhD, at age 21 he headed off to Europe to find the gene. He worked first in Copenhagen on a Merck fellowship, then grew bored with biochemistry and decided the answer was best pursued at the Cavendish Laboratory in Cambridge, England. His training in genetics complemented the strength of Cambridge, where the British enjoyed a reputation for using x-ray pictures to determine the three-dimensional structure of important molecules, and so he was uniquely positioned to solve the problem. "I was as trained to find the structure of DNA," Watson has since observed, "as Prince Charles is trained to be king."

In Cambridge, Watson teamed up with the 35-year-old Francis H. C. Crick, a scintillating intellect with hardly a credit to his threadbare academic resumé. "Jim and I hit it off immediately," Crick wrote in his recent autobiography, *What Mad Pursuit*, "partly because our interests were astonishingly similar and partly, I suspect, because a certain youthful arrogance, a ruthlessness, and an impatience with sloppy thinking came naturally to both of us." Crick noted that "Watson was regarded, in most circles, as too bright to be really sound." These two bad boys of biology—arrogant, opportunistic, behaving "insufferably" in Crick's estimation—puzzled their way to success without performing a single experiment. With the American chemist Linus Pauling as a rival, Watson and Crick used x-ray pictures of DNA, produced by Rosalind Franklin and Maurice Wilkins of King's College in London, to divine the shape of this most central molecule. By the spring of 1953, they had determined that it was a double helix; by 1962, Watson and Crick—with Wilkins—had their Nobel Prize.

The self-confidence to think big

It is tempting to view everything that followed as anticlimax, yet Watson reinvented his role in science in the '60s. He stopped being an experimentalist and started being an impresario, a "mover of people." He grabbed the compass and charted the course of research. He attracted grant money. He recruited young

talent, mindful of the soil in which he himself flourished. "I think it's important that you establish conditions where people will really become important early in life," he says, "because it gives them the self-confidence to think big."

That process began in earnest at Harvard University, where Watson took an assistant professorship in 1955, and continued at Cold Spring Harbor, where he assumed the directorship in 1968. That same year, at age 39, he married Elizabeth Lewis, his 19-year-old laboratory assistant. Watson and his wife moved into the 19th-century Airslie House, a hilltop mansion once owned by Louis Comfort Tiffany, where they have raised their two sons, Rufus and Duncan.

When he sat down to write his account of the discovery of the structure of DNA, Watson began with an enigmatic anecdote about a fellow scientist who apparently snubbed him one day simply by asking, "How's Honest Jim?" It adverts, Watson says, to the belief that Watson and Crick pirated Rosalind Franklin's x-ray data en route to their discovery. "You know, 'Honest Jim' was the name you'd give to a used-car salesman," Watson admits now. Yet he adopted it as the title of the manuscript he began to circulate privately; published in 1968 as *The Double Helix*, its disparaging and sometimes damaging tone caused a firestorm of controversy even as it climbed the best-seller charts.

Still known for speaking his mind, Watson has not disappointed his critics in his first year as genome czar at NIH. He has talked about divvying up the 23 pairs of human chromosomes and assigning them to different countries (that trial balloon was roundly booed down). He has criticized Japan's reluctance to commit money to genome research and has threatened to withhold data (he told a recent gathering of scientists, "I am for peace, but if there will be war, I will fight it!"). He attacks European scientists as "a bunch of idiots" for declining to publicly discuss the ethical implications of genome research.

Watson has been "something of a wild man"

The journal *Science* recently observed, "To many in the biological community, [Watson] has long been something of a wild man, and his colleagues tend to hold their collective breath whenever he veers from the script"; one former Cold Spring Harbor board member remarks that Watson has perfected the use of "petulance as a management tool." But colleagues argue that there is always strategy behind his antagonistic style. Watson himself says, "I would not dare take this on unless I thought I had the support of the major people doing it. I don't make unilateral decisions."

It is precisely Watson's candor and integrity, and his willingness to take the heat, that have earned that support. "If it were not Jim—if it were headed by an ordinary person—then I believe the project would not have acquired the degree of acceptance that it has in the scientific community," says David Botstein, a vice president of Genentech and probably the project's most articulate and longstanding critic. "I'm convinced he's the right person in the sense that he is the person who scientifically carries the most credibility for this project," agrees Sydney Brenner of the Medical Research Council in England. "Jim is actually *the* heroic figure of science, in terms of the whole development of this area."

To contemplate the enormousness of the task, consider a freckle on the back of your hand. The average freckle contains several thousand cells. Each one of those cells contains 23 pairs of chromosomes. The amount of DNA in each bundle of chromosomes, if unfurled, would form an invisible thread reaching about six feet in length. Interspersed randomly along that six feet of information are somewhere between 50,000 and 100,000 genes. What biologists now propose to do is to locate each one of those genes, pinpoint its specific location on a specific chromosome (a process called mapping) and ultimately decode the biochemical information down to the so-called "letters" of inheritance, the four basic constituents (referred to by their first letters—A, C, G and T) of all genes. In the double helix these letters are linked in pairs, whose sequence on a gene makes it different from any other. These sequences involve 3 billion pairs in all; to date, biologists have deciphered about 35 million.

Yet the genome project commences at a time when there is not enough money to fund much deserving basic research, and Watson seems to view the initiative as an opportunity for biologists to reposition the field. "I think the genome is a way of actually focusing medical research," he says. "I think American biomedical research is in a crisis generated by its own success. There are too many good things to do, and it's been enormously successful from the viewpoint of basic science. But except for the help that it's given to AIDS— finding the virus, getting the test for the blood—it hasn't had any major obvious impacts on too many people's lives. And it isn't curing AIDS. I think that many major diseases will be understood when we can get their genetic basis. And I think we may have to produce another Salk vaccine or something like that, so people can see that the implications are worth it."

Watson has two priorities: to bring the project home under cost and to identify key genes related to human disease. An estimated 4,000 human diseases have a genetic component. Some diseases, like sickle-cell anemia, stem from a single misplaced letter in a single gene; in other illnesses, like hypertension, diabetes, some cancers and heart disease, there is an ensemble of genes playing a dissonant chord together.

Since 1911, when color blindness was linked to the male X chromosomes, biologists have plodded through the genome in search of genes linked to human disease,

but the work has exploded in the past decade. In August 1989, for example, teams from the University of Michigan and Toronto's Hospital for Sick Children announced the isolation of a gene whose malfunction causes cystic fibrosis, which afflicts 1 in 2,000 newborn children. The discovery exemplifies the power of modern genetics, but also the limitations. Finding the gene does not guarantee finding a cure (the genetic glitch of sickle-cell anemia has been known for 15 years, but no cure is in sight). During the past five years the Cystic Fibrosis Foundation has spent $120 million trying to locate the gene. It is being argued that spending about $200 million a year over a 15-year period for the whole genome will be more cost-effective, and more egalitarian, in locating *all* human genes.

Watson believes that maladies like schizophrenia, alchoholism and Alzheimer's disease might yield the first fruits of the genome project. "We have to get some real results in the next five years," he says. "I mean, better maps to human disease genes. I think you should have goals like that. Find the gene for something which you might not have found if you didn't have the human genome mapped. If you want to understand Alzheimer's disease, then I'd say you better sequence chromosome 21 as fast as possible. And it's unethical and irresponsible *not* to do it as fast as possible."

Over the past decade, scientists like Charles Cantor (who leads one of the Department of Energy's three complementary genome centers) at the Lawrence Berkeley Laboratory in California have developed sophisticated techniques of genetic cartography, organizing chromosomes into manageable districts just as states are divided into counties. Leroy Hood's lab at Caltech, meanwhile, has developed an automated sequencing machine that can read out 7,000 letters of DNA in a day. Hood's lab is also working on a computer scanning system that can search and read 30 million genetic letters in three seconds. Watson plans to designate three genome centers in 1990 to centralize this type of technology development. In the meantime, researchers will hone their mapping and sequencing techniques on other organisms—bacteria, yeast, a tiny worm, the good old fruit fly, mice and perhaps even a plant—to study similarities between species.

Still, the technical obstacles are complex, as are the analogies invoked to describe them. Eric Lander, a geneticist, describes it this way: "It's as if I took six sets of the *Encyclopaedia Britannica* and shredded them, and spread the pieces all over the floor, and asked you to reconstruct the books. How do you do that? You look for pages that overlap, so you need multiple copies of the books. You would spend a year or two or three just gluing these copies together in the correct order. And then you have to read the thing. *That's* the genome project." Once the encyclopedia is in hand, Watson adds, "we will be interpreting it a thousand years from now."

Just how rapidly progress is being made was apparent in October of last year, when some 800 biologists jammed a hotel ballroom in San Diego for a meeting called—with the promise of many sequels—"Human Genome I." To the degree that technology drives science, one could hear the genome project's motor racing. Indeed, Watson declared that the 15-year project would officially begin October 1, 1990. But the San Diego gathering typified scientific meetings in another respect: in two and a half days of talks and presentations, exactly 30 minutes was set aside for the discussion of the project's social implications.

Of all the hats Watson will wear as genome project leader, none would appear more ill-fitting at first, or more important, than that of moral ombudsman. Watson is not visibly comfortable with "the ethics thing," as he once termed it; and when it is suggested that, by virtue of his fame and influence, his opinions on ethical issues will likely carry disproportionate weight with Congress and the public, he recoils from the notion like a child ordered to eat peas. "I can't do that," he demurs, "because I'm not, you know, a real player."

His visibility and credibility, however, make him the major player. Protestations notwithstanding, Watson has already taken a surprisingly aggressive fiscal stance to insure that ethical issues get a full public airing. He has declared that 3 percent of the NIH project's budget—over 15 years this portion could approach a substantial $90 million—must be devoted to study and research on the ethical implications of mapping the human genome. That outlay may represent the largest targeted funding of biomedical ethics in the modern era.

"The fact that Watson opens his mouth and utters the word 'ethics' changes the whole valence," says Nancy S. Wexler of Columbia University, who heads NIH's working group on ethics for the genome project. "Other people start to think, 'Gee, this must be important. This is something we should pay attention to.'" Biologist Maynard Olson of Washington University, a member of NIH's Genome Advisory Board, calls Watson's commitment of money for studying ethics "a courageous and precedent-setting position to take." And it is not universally applauded among his colleagues. One of Watson's closest associates observes, "There is a vigorous debate within the genome scientific constituency about the wisdom of supporting ethical, legal and social analysis, and if you took a vote, my guess is that it would be 60-40 or more against Watson. So it is all the more remarkable that he would stick his neck so far out."

Watson has stacked his ethics committee with, if anything, thinkers who have been historically attuned to misuses of scientific knowledge. Its members include Jonathan Beckwith of the Harvard Medical School, a thoughtful critic of genetic technologies; Patricia King, a bioethicist at Georgetown University; Robert F. Murray jr. of Howard University, an expert on the early abuses of genetic screening for sickle-cell anemia and the potential of such programs to feed racial prejudice; and Nancy Wexler, a neuropsychologist who faces the consequences of genetic screening because Huntington's disease, which is invariably fatal, runs in her family. The group's mission, Wexler says, is to "anticipate now the abuses that *can* occur and then prevent them *before* they occur."

Genetic screening is nothing new, as scientists are quick to point out, but the genome project will generate hundreds of disease-related tests, and the sheer volume means that prenatal testing and genetic diagnosis will probably touch every life. Scientists promise a new age of medicine, when doctors will use the genetic profile of newborns to detect genetic susceptibilities to disease and will prescribe preventive steps necessary to forestall illness later in life. But such advance knowledge also invites misuse.

Will employers demand human genetic screening before hiring? Will insurance companies demand genetic profiles of its clients and centralize the information? Will insurers decline to pay medical expenses if a fetus with a lifelong genetic disability is brought to term? Will law enforcement agencies seek access to genetic information? (The FBI already maintains a DNA databank on criminals.) How will doctors counsel a family in which medical science can diagnose a fatal illness, like Huntington's disease, but to whom it can offer no cure? And with a complete catalog of genes at our disposal, will we be able to resist the temptation to tinker with genes, not only to cure disease in individuals (somatic-cell gene therapy) but also to rewire family genomes by retooling germ-line, or reproductive, cells? The groundwork for this type of genetic reengineering is already being laid. "We must not shy away from the germ line," declared *Science* editor Daniel Koshland at Human Genome I.

What Watson tells his colleagues about all this may be more important than what he tells an interviewer. Here is what he said in San Diego: "It would be naive to say any of these answers are going to be simple. About all we can do is stimulate the discussion, and essentially lead the discussion instead of having it forced on us by people who say, 'You don't know what you're doing.' We have to be aware of the really terrible past of eugenics, where incomplete knowledge was used in a very cavalier and rather awful way, both here in the United States and in Germany. We have to reassure people that their own DNA is private and that no one else can get at it. We're going to have to pass laws to reassure them. [But] we don't want people rushing and passing laws without a lot of serious discussion first."

Can Watson foresee the misuse of genetic material in our society, perhaps 50 or 100 years down the road? "Sure," he replies. "That's why I'm talking about laws.

But I think you see a misuse of everything. You see a misuse of pesticides. You see a misuse of high school athletics. You see a misuse of aspirin, of automobiles. So I don't think it should make us upset to say that there will be a misuse."

And when he is asked about what area in the future may be the ripest for misuse of genome information, Watson pauses a long time, hands clasped over his head, and uncharacteristically sidesteps the question. "I don't have a good feeling for where it could be misused the most," he says. And later; "I think people can't really think about things before they are *real.*"

Here, the scientist vies with the New Deal populist. "We're a democracy and the people finally make their decisions," says the populist. "If some process is regarded as repulsive to a majority of the people, we better know." Pause. "Now," adds the scientist, "one hates to have something discovered that's considered repulsive, unless it's been talked about enough to know whether it really *is* repulsive."

Watson has a better record at looking forward than he allows. In 1971, in an essay for the *Atlantic* called "Moving Toward the Clonal Man," he warned of the coming dilemmas of reproductive technologies and argued against what he termed the "laissez-faire nonsense" that science inevitably makes the world better. Test-tube babies, *in vitro* fertilization and surrogate parenting sounded futuristic back then, as some of the genome's potential dilemmas sound in 1990. But as "Honest Jim" wrote in 1971, ". . . if we do not think about it now, the possibility of our having a free choice will one day suddenly be gone."

HOW VON NEUMANN SHOWED THE WAY

T. A. Heppenheimer

T. A. Heppenheimer writes frequently on science. His most recent book is *The Coming Quake: Science and Trembling on the California Earthquake Frontier* (Times Books, 1988).

Before there could be hardware or software, there had to be a vision of exactly how computers would work. A handful of brilliant mathematicians, chief among them John Von Neumann, saw the future.

There were ten people in the party, and they were about to descend into the Grand Canyon. The guide wore a cowboy hat and leather chaps; a coil of rope hung from his saddle. Most of the others were dressed for a day outdoors, wearing hats, loose-fitting shirts, and the like. At the rear of the group was John Von Neumann—hatless and in the formal suit and tie of a banker. Moreover, while everyone else sat on a mule facing right, his faced left.

Von Neumann had been following his own rules for years. He owned a photographic memory that held the complete texts of works of literature and one of the world's largest collections of off-color limericks. Yet he would phone home to ask his wife to help him remember an appointment. He loved to throw parties—and sometimes would steal away to work in his office while his guests remained downstairs. Among his friends he was nearly as well known for his traffic accidents as for his accomplishments in mathematics. A strong supporter of the military, he was fond of attending nuclear-weapons tests. He died of cancer at the age of fifty-three.

Through it all, he was one of the century's most creative and productive mathematicians, lifting his intellectual scepter across a host of technical fields. Mostly he worked with pencil and paper, but in the years after 1945, for the first time in his life, he set himself the task of managing the design and construction of a piece of equipment. This was the Institute for Advanced Study computer, and it set the pattern for subsequent computers as we know them today.

What distinguished this IAS machine was programmability. It embodied Von Neumann's insistence that computers must not be built as glorified adding machines, with all their operations specified in advance. Rather, he declared, they should be built as general-purpose logic machines, built to execute programs of wide variety. Such machines would be highly flexible, readily shifted from one task to another. They could react intelligently to the results of their calculations, could choose among alternatives, and could even play checkers or chess.

This represented something unheard of: a machine with built-in intelligence, able to operate on internal instructions. Before, even the most complex mechanisms had always been controlled from the outside, as by setting dials or knobs. Von Neumann did not invent the computer, but what he introduced was equally significant: computing by use of computer programs, the way we do it today.

The roots of this invention lay not in electronics but in the higher reaches of mathematics, in a problem that tantalized specialists in mathematical logic during this century's early decades: the challenge of establishing basic foundations for math. These would take the form of an explicit set of definitions and axioms, or fundamental statements, from which all known results might be derived.

Everyone expected that such foundations could be constructed if people were only clever enough. David Hilbert of Göttingen University, widely regarded as the world's leading mathematician, summarized this viewpoint in a 1900 address: "Every mathematical problem can be solved. We are all convinced of that. After all, one of the things that attracts us most when we apply ourselves to a mathematical problem is precisely that within us we always hear the call: here is the problem, search for the solution; you can find it by pure thought, for in mathematics there is no *ignorabimus* [we will not know]."

In fact, however, a powerful *ignorabimus* lay at the center of the problem of mathematical foundations. The man who demonstrated this was Kurt Goedel, a logician at the University of Vienna. He was a smallish man with an earnest expression and a thick pair of glasses; he appeared even smaller than he was because of his reluctance to eat. Psychological depressions and other illnesses dogged him throughout much of his life, made more serious at times by his distrust of doctors. In contrast with the gregarious and hearty Von Neumann, Goedel was solitary in his habits, but he did form a few close relationships. One was his lifelong marriage to Adele Nimbursky, a former cab-

He insisted that the computers must be highly flexible general-purpose logic machines — not rigid glorified adding machines.

aret dancer. Another was a warm friendship with Albert Einstein.

In two epochal papers, published in 1931, when he was twenty-five, Goedel showed that no foundations could be constructed. More particularly, he showed that if anyone tried to set forth such foundations, it would be possible to devise mathematical statements that were "formally undecidable"—incapable of being proved or disproved using the proposed foundations. Anil Nerode of Cornell University describes this conclusion as "the paper that everyone read, because it was the most signal paper in logic in two thousand years."

In particular, this work offered two major results for the eventual development of computer science. To prove his theorems, Goedel introduced a notation whereby statements in mathematical logic were encoded as numbers. Every such statement could be expressed as an integer, usually a very large one, and every integer corresponded to a statement in logic. This introduced a concept that would be key to the later advent of computer programming: that not only numerical data but also logic statements—and by extension, programming instructions—could be expressed in a common notation. Further, Goedel's work showed that this notational commonality could give results of the deepest significance in mathematics.

Among the mathematicians who soon took up the study of these matters was Alan Turing, of Cambridge University. Turing was a vigorous man, fond of running and cycling, and sometimes eccentric. Issued a gas mask, he wore it to prevent hay fever. Fearing that British currency would be worthless in World War II, he withdrew his savings and purchased two ingots of silver, buried them in his yard—and then failed to draw a suitable treasure map that would permit him to find them. And when his bicycle developed the habit of having its chain come

loose, he refused to take it in for repairs. Instead he trained himself to estimate when this was about to happen so he could make timely preventive fixes by himself.

Turing was a twenty-five-year-old undergraduate when he made his major contribution to computer science. It came in a 1937 paper, "On Computable Numbers," in which he specifically dealt with an imaginary version of the computer. This idealized machine was to follow coded instructions, equivalent to computer programs. It was to deal with a long paper tape that would be marked off in squares, each square either black or white and thus representing one bit of information. On this tape, in response to the coded commands, the machine would execute a highly limited set of operations: reading, erasing, or marking a particular square and moving the tape.

Analyzing this idealized computer, Turing proved that it offered properties closely related to Goedel's concept of formal undecidability. What was important for computer science, however, was another realization: that with sufficiently lengthy coded instructions this simple machine would be able to carry out any computation that could be executed in a finite number of steps. Here, in its essential form, was the concept of a general-purpose programmable computer.

The basic idea of a calculating machine was not new. The first crude adding machines dated to the seventeenth century. In the nineteenth century Britain's Charles Babbage, assisted by Lady Ada Lovelace, had struggled to invent an "Analytical Engine" that was really a crude mechanical computer. What was new and pathbreaking in Turing's work was that for the first time he gave a clear concept of what a computer should be: a machine that carries out a few simple operations under

the direction of a program that can be as intricate as one may wish.

These developments were very interesting to John Von Neumann. As a student in Germany (he was born in Hungary in 1903), he had worked closely with Hilbert himself, plunging deeply into the search for mathematical foundations. He had shared Hilbert's belief that such foundations could in fact be constructed, had written a paper that contributed some mathematical bricks to the intellectual masonry—and was surprised and chagrined by Goedel's proofs. He had not thought that formal undecidability might exist, and he came away with the feeling that Goedel had scooped him.

He had plenty of reasons to feel confident, however. The son of a Budapest banker who had received a minor title of nobility, the source of his "Von," he had shown himself very early to be a *Wunderkind*, dividing eight-digit numbers in his head at age six and talking with his father in ancient Greek. By age eight he was doing calculus and demonstrating a photographic memory: he would read a page of the Budapest phone directory and recite it back with his eyes closed. His father's wealth made it easy for him to attend the University of Budapest, from which he traveled widely: to the University of Berlin, to Zurich and its equally famous university, and to Göttingen, the world's center of mathematics. At age twenty-two he received his Ph.D. Nor did he keep his genius to himself; his daughter Marina, born in 1935, would rise to become a leading economist in the United States.

Von Neumann had made his reputation during the 1920s, establishing himself as clearly one of the world's outstanding mathematicians. Particularly significant was his work in developing a rigorous mathematical basis for quantum mechanics. That brought him an invitation to Princeton University, which he joined in 1930, when he was twenty-six. "He was so young," says a colleague

You didn't program ENIAC; you laboriously set it up, using patch cords.
Von Neumann joined the group to figure out a better way.

from around that time, "that most people who saw him in the halls mistook him for a graduate student." Then in 1936 Turing came to Princeton to do his graduate work; he was twenty-four. Von Neumann, who had moved to the Institute for Advanced Study in 1933, was quite interested in Turing's work and offered him a position as his assistant after he received his doctorate, but Turing chose to return to Cambridge.

Meanwhile, Von Neumann was doing much more than reading his colleagues' papers. During the early 1940s he began to work extensively on problems of fluid flow. These problems were widely regarded as nightmares, marked by tangles of impenetrable equations. To Von Neumann that meant they were interesting; understanding them could lead to such consequences as accurate weather prediction, and because such problems posed intractable difficulties, they were worthy of his attention.

Then came the war and the Manhattan Project. Von Neumann's expertise in fluid flow now took on the highest national importance. As the work at Los Alamos advanced, he became responsible for solving a problem that was essential to building the plutonium bomb. This was to understand the intricate physical processes by which a thick layer of high-explosive charges, surrounding a spherical core of plutonium, could detonate to produce an imploding shock wave that would compress the core and initiate the nuclear explosion.

As his colleague George Kistiakowsky later wrote, high explosives had been "looked upon as blind destructive agents rather than precision instruments." In the plutonium bomb, however, it would be essential to predict with some accuracy the behavior of the shock waves that would converge on the core. Even Von Neumann's brilliance was inadequate for this. He had hoped that ingenuity and insight would enable him to simplify the pertinent equations to a form both solvable and sufficiently accurate. His collaborator Stanislaw Ulam insisted that it would be necessary to face their full complexity and calculate them, in an age when there were no computers, using methods that would later be programmed to run on computers. Fortunately, the Los Alamos lab was due to receive a shipment of IBM calculating machines. Stanley Frankel, another Los Alamos man, set up a lengthy sequence of steps that these machines could carry out, with Army enlistees running them. It amounted to a very slow computer with human beings rather than electronic devices as the active elements, but it worked. Von Neumann got the solutions he needed, and he proceeded to design the high-explosive charges for Fat Man, the bomb dropped on Nagasaki.

Meanwhile, at the University of Pennsylvania, another effort as secret as the Manhattan Project was under way: the construction of the first electronic computer. This was ENIAC (Electronic Numerical Integrator and Computer), an Army-sponsored project intended for use in calculating the trajectories of artillery shells. Its employment of vacuum tubes rather than people as active elements represented a decided advance, but while the potential value of such tubes for high-speed computing was widely appreciated, the tubes of the day were not particularly reliable. That did not matter when only a few were needed, as in radar or radio, but it would matter greatly in a computer, where a single failed tube could vitiate a lengthy calculation. (Because of this, Harvard's Howard Aiken had gone to work on a computer that would use the electromechanical switches of telephone circuitry. They were far slower than vacuum tubes, but still much faster than human beings, and they were reliable.)

The ENIAC project leaders, John W. Mauchly and J. Presper Eckert, Jr., solved the reliability problem in a simple way. They were working with tubes whose manufacturers had guaranteed a service life of twenty-five hundred hours. With 17,468 tubes in ENIAC, that meant one could be expected to fail, on the average, every eight minutes—and with major computations requiring weeks of operation, this was quite unacceptable. Eckert, however, simply "unloaded" the tubes, arranging it so that they would handle no more than one-half of their rated voltage and one-fourth of their rated current. This reduced the failure rate from one every eight minutes to about one every two days, which was sufficient for practical operation.

The Army's representative on the project was Lt. Herman H. Goldstine, who had taught mathematics at the University of Michigan. He was working out of the Aberdeen Proving Grounds in Maryland, where Von Neumann was a consultant. One day in August 1944 he saw Von Neumann waiting for a train. "I had never met this great mathematician," Goldstine recalled. "It was therefore with considerable temerity that I approached this world-famous figure, introduced myself, and started talking. Fortunately for me Von Neumann was a warm, friendly person who did his best to make people feel relaxed in his presence. The conversation soon turned to my work. When it became clear to Von Neumann that I was concerned with the development of an electronic computer capable of 333 multiplications per second, the whole atmosphere changed from one of relaxed good humor to one more like the oral examination for a doctor's degree in mathematics."

Von Neumann's "Report on the EDVAC" envisioned a computer using programs as the brain uses memory. Soon he was building one.

ENIAC was a large air-conditioned room whose walls were covered with cabinets containing electronic circuitry—three thousand cubic feet of it. It weighed thirty tons and drew 174 kilowatts of power. Its computational speed and capability would fail to match the hand-held programmable calculators of the mid-1970s, but even so, it was such an advance over all previous attempts at automatic computation as to stand in a class by itself. Still, it was not without its faults, as its builders were well aware. Its main memory (random-access memory) could hold only a thousand bits of information—the equivalent of about three lines of text. And it was completely lacking in any arrangements for computer programming.

You did not program ENIAC; rather, you set it up, like many other complex systems. Although it was a general-purpose computer, able to solve any problem, it relied on physical interconnections. You prepared for a particular problem by running patch cords between jacks and other plugs, with cabling up to eighty feet long. The task could take two days or longer. In a 1943 report the builders admitted that "no attempt has been made to make provision for setting up a problem automatically," adding that "it is anticipated that the ENIAC will be used primarily for problems of a type in which one setup will be used many times before another problem is placed on the machine."

By the summer of 1944, however, Eckert, Mauchly, and their colleagues were already beginning to think seriously about ENIAC's successor. This would have the name EDVAC (Electronic Discrete Variable Automatic Computer). As early as January of that year Eckert had described a computer in which an "important feature" was that "operating instructions and function tables would be stored in exactly the same sort of memory device as that used for numbers." Eckert was also inventing an appropriate memory device: a "delay line," or long tube filled with mercury in which bits of data would take the form of pressure pulses traversing the tube at high speed. And in October 1944, at Goldstine's urging, the Army awarded a $105,600 contract for work on the EDVAC concept.

Into this stimulating environment stepped Von Neumann. He joined the ENIAC group as a consultant, with special interest in ideas for EDVAC. He helped secure the EDVAC contract and spent long hours in discussions with Mauchly and Eckert. "He was really racing far ahead and speculating as to how you build better computers, because that's what we were talking to him about," Mauchly later said. "We said we don't want to build another of these things [ENIACs]. We've got much better solutions in many ways."

Von Neumann's particular strength was the logical structure of a computer, the details of its logic operations. His leadership made the EDVAC discussions more systematic. Before his arrival Eckert and Mauchly had relied mostly on informal conversations; with Von Neumann there were regular staff meetings with recorded minutes. As Goldstine reported to his boss, Von Neumann was "devoting enormous amounts of his prodigious energy to working out the logical controls of the machine. He also has been very much interested in helping design circuits for the machine."

In late June 1945, working at Los Alamos, Von Neumann completed a 101-page document titled "First Draft of a Report on the EDVAC." In his clear and penetrating way, he set forth an overview of the design of a digital computer that would feature stored-program operation. It had much more than circuitry and logic; it reflected Von Neumann's broad interests by drawing on the work of Warren McCul-loch, a neurophysiologist who in 1943 had published a description of the functioning of the human brain. Von Neumann boldly drew comparisons between his electronic circuits and the brain's neurons, emphasizing that just as the brain relies on its memory, so the computer would depend on its programs. Goldstine soon was distributing copies to interested scientists. In time the "First Draft" would become one of the most influential papers in computer science.

Goldstine circulated the draft with only Von Neumann's name on the title page. In a later patent dispute, Von Neumann declined to share credit for his ideas with Mauchly, Eckert, or anyone else. So the "First Draft" spawned the legend that Von Neumann invented the stored-program computer. He did not, though he made contributions of great importance. But by writing the "First Draft," and subsequent reports, he gave a clear direction to the field. The prestige of his name ensured that he would be followed. "The new ideas were too revolutionary for some. . . ," said the British computer expert Maurice Wilkes. "Powerful voices were being raised to say that . . . to mix instructions and numbers in the same memory was to go against nature." Von Neumann stilled such doubts.

As 1945 proceeded, he became convinced that he should not merely write about stored-program computers but should take the lead in another way: by building one. Raising money for such a project would be no problem; he knew his way around Washington. The problem was that his home base was, and had been since 1933, the Institute for Advanced Study, in Princeton, New Jersey. Founded by the department-store magnate Louis Bamberger and his sister, Carrie Fuld, it was a center for pure contemplation and thought, a place where Einstein and Goedel would feel at home and spend much of their careers. To propose build-

All the later technical advances would merely offer better ways to implement the basic concept that Von Neumann had described.

ing a computer at IAS was like offering to install a radar facility in St. Peter's Basilica.

Von Neumann overcame his colleagues' objections by playing the IAS against two other institutions that wanted him, the University of Chicago and the Massachusetts Institute of Technology. At MIT Norbert Wiener, a colleague from Von Neumann's Göttingen days and himself a pioneer in computing, offered Von Neumann the chairmanship of the mathematics department, emphasizing that he would be free to work on his "favorite projects." Chicago offered to set up an Institute of Applied Mathematics with Von Neumann as its head. Faced with such offers and wanting to keep Von Neumann as one of their own, his IAS colleagues gave in and granted permission, consoling themselves with the thought that the new computer might after all be useful in research.

Then the ENIAC group broke up. The source of this was a new director of research at the University of Pennsylvania, where the computer had been built, Irven Travis. Travis had spent his war in the Navy and proposed to run a tight ship now that he was back in the civilian world. He soon was quarreling with Eckert and Mauchly over the issue of patents. The two ENIAC inventors saw great commercial prospects in computers and had a letter from the university president that agreed they could hold patents on ENIAC. Travis, however, insisted that they must sign patent releases. He made no bones about it; in one meeting with Mauchly he stated, "If you want to continue to work here at the university, you must sign these agreements." Mauchly and Eckert refused and were soon out on their own as independent entrepreneurs.

By the summer of 1946, then, three groups were seeking to build a stored-program computer along the lines of the "First Draft." Eckert and Mauchly had by far the most experience in this area, but were out in the cold with little money, few contacts, and slight business experience. The remnants of the ENIAC group, at the University of Pennsylvania, had few good people but were committed by contract to build an EDVAC, and build it they would, however slowly. Von Neumann had the overall vision, the charismatic reputation, the genius, and the acquiescence of the IAS. What he lacked was experience in project management.

Of these deficiencies, Von Neumann's was the most easily remedied. He had technical support from RCA, which had built a lab in Princeton. He had Herman Goldstine, who left the Army to join him. And at Norbert Wiener's recommendation he hired Wiener's wartime assistant, Julian Bigelow, who had worked on radar-guided fire control of antiaircraft guns and who knew how to build electronic systems of a very demanding character.

The computer was to be built in the boiler room of Fuld Hall, the main building at the IAS. As Bigelow describes the work, "Von Neumann would put half-finished ideas on the blackboard and Goldstine would take them back down and digest them and make them into something for the machine. On the other hand, Von Neumann often had only the foggiest ideas about how we should achieve something technically. He would discuss things with me and leave them completely wide open, and I would think them over and come back with an experimental circuit, and then my group would test it out."

When completed—in a building of its own, well across the IAS campus— the computer had only twenty-three hundred vacuum tubes, considerably fewer than ENIAC's almost eighteen thousand. It was fully automatic, digital, and general-purpose, but like other programmable computers of its generation, it was built years in advance of programming languages such as For-

tran or Pascal. Its commands instead were written directly in machine language, long strings of ones and zeros. An expression such as "A + B," for instance, might be rendered as something like 01101101 10110110 01110011; a significant program would feature many pages written in such notation. In Bigelow's words, there were "none of the tricks that we now have. This was a case where Von Neumann was so clever technically that he had no problem with it. And he couldn't imagine anyone else working with a computer who couldn't program in machine code."

How significant was this IAS computer? The science historian Joel Shurkin, who has sought to assess fairly the claims of various inventors as to priority, writes that "Von Neumann's technical contributions are manifest and beyond controversy. The machine he designed would be faster than anything else. . . . While all the other computer makers were generally heading in the same direction, Von Neumann's genius clarified and described the paths better than anyone else in the world could. Moreover, many of the developments in programming and in machine architecture at the institute profoundly influenced future computer development. . . . While others were using crude digital instructions for their machines, Von Neumann and his team were developing instructions (what scientists call codes) that would last, with modification, through most of the computer age."

The machine received its baptism with the nation again at war, in Korea, and with the hydrogen bomb now a matter of highest priority. Von Neumann, who had maintained his leadership in nuclear-weapons work, arranged to run a problem dealing with H-bomb physics. It would be the most extensive computation ever carried out. "It was computed in the summer of 1950," says Bigelow, ". . . while the machine had clip leads on it. We had engineers there to keep it running and it ran for sixty days, day and night, with very few errors. It did a nice job."

The way was open, then, for the computer to sweep all before it. There would be substantial technical advances: programming languages beginning in the mid-1950s, then transistors, integrated circuits, and microprocessors. But these would merely offer better ways to implement the basic concept—the stored-program computer—that Von Neumann had described in his 1945 "First Draft."

As if computation carried with it some dreadful incubus, a number of its pioneers would die amid tragedy. Alan Turing was the first, in 1954, at age forty-one. Convicted in England of soliciting sexual favors from a teen-age boy, he was given a choice of prison or hormone treatments. He chose the hormones and soon found his breasts growing. Driven to despair, he made up a batch of cyanide in a home laboratory and died an apparent suicide.

For Von Neumann it was even worse. In the summer of 1955 he was diagnosed with bone cancer, which soon brought on excruciating pain. In the words of his friend Edward Teller, "I think that Von Neumann suffered more when his mind would no longer function than I have ever seen any human being suffer." Toward the end there was panic and uncontrolled terror. Early in 1957 he too was gone.

For Kurt Goedel it was his own personal demons that would drive him to death. In an epic escape from Nazi-occupied Austria, he and his wife had crossed the Soviet Union and then the Pacific to reach the United States. From 1940 to 1976 he was himself a member of the IAS. The author Edward Regis describes him, in his last years, as "a cadaverous old man shuffling past alone, dressed in his black coat and winter hat." After his wife underwent surgery and was placed in a nursing home, in 1977, Goedel refused to take any food. He starved himself to death. When he died early the next year, the death certificate of this great logician stated that the cause was "malnutrition and inanition caused by personality disturbance."

John Mauchly's later years were racked by deep bitterness. He was bitter at Von Neumann for not giving him credit as a co-inventor of the stored-program computer and at Goldstine for being one of Von Neumann's most effective supporters. Mauchly, along with Eckert, had struggled through lean years but then won success by building UNIVAC, the first commercially successful computer. The firm of Remington Rand brought them in—and eventually the roof fell in. In a major lawsuit their ENIAC patent was invalidated, with the judge ruling that they were not even the true inventors of the electronic computer. "Lawyers keep making money," said Mauchly toward the end. "We've got down to the point where maybe we can buy some hot dogs with our Social Security." In 1980 he died from a disfiguring genetic disease.

Nor were the pioneering institutions spared, though for them the incubus brought ill-considered abandonment of the computer field rather than unpleasant death. The University of Pennsylvania never recovered from the effects of Irven Travis's decisions, which cost that school its best computer people. The computer group did manage to build EDVAC, or at least enough of it to satisfy the Army, but it amounted to a last try by this group and led to no new projects. And after Von Neumann died, the IAS abandoned computer science altogether, shipping his computer to the Smithsonian.

The room where it was built, writes Regis, "is not treated as a historical site. No plaque or bust commemorates the birth of the stored program computer within. The room, at the end of a dark and lonely hallway, today houses the Institute's stationery supplies, and boxes of file folders, pads of paper, and inter-departmental mail envelopes reach almost to the ceiling."

Yet elsewhere at the IAS, and around the world, are today's computers, which still follow the directions Von Neumann set forth in his "First Draft" and subsequent writings and that he demonstrated in his project at the IAS. These computers, rather than plaques or busts cast in bronze, are among the true monuments to the cheerful and highly creative man who was John Von Neumann.

The Scientific Legacy of Apollo

*The retrieved lunar rocks have helped settle questions
about the moon's origin, its composition and even the
early conditions that affected life on the earth*

G. Jeffrey Taylor

G. JEFFREY TAYLOR, who received his Ph.D. in geology from Rice University in 1970, is a professor at the Hawaii Institute of Geophysics and Planetology, School of Ocean and Earth Sciences and Technology, University of Hawaii at Manoa in Honolulu. He chairs the lunar exploration science working group, a committee that advises the National Aeronautics and Space Administration on future lunar missions. He has recently become active in studies of the dynamics of lava flows on the earth, the moon, Mars and Venus. His belief that education is a prime justification for a vigorous space program has led him to develop instructional materials for use in grades 4 through 12.

When Neil A. Armstrong and Edwin "Buzz" Aldrin, Jr., dug into the moon's surface 25 years ago, they were doing more than collecting dry, dark dirt. They were time traveling. Their journey in *Apollo 11* across 380,000 kilometers of space sent them back billions of years. Armstrong, Aldrin and the 10 astronauts who followed returned with samples that contain a fascinating history of the moon and the earth. The rocks have indicated the moon's violent and surprising origin, its composition and its age. Instruments placed on the surface enabled geophysicists to reconstruct the satellite's internal structure and activity. Without the Apollo program, none of these discoveries could have been made.

By traveling to the moon, we also learned about the earth. Volcanism, folding, faulting, mountain building, weathering and glaciation have erased or modified most of the earth's ancient history. Fortunately, the moon was not so energetic a geologic engine. It was active enough in its first billion years to produce an intriguing and complex array of products, but not so vigorous that it completely eradicated the chronicle of what had happened. By comparing the moon's craters, lava flows and volcanic debris with corresponding formations on the earth, workers can test theoretical models of the mechanisms that created such features here.

The Apollo missions, of course, did not instantly modify the thinking about our nearest celestial neighbor. It took several years to analyze the samples

and to form reasonable theories based on those empirical findings. The landings recovered 382 kilograms of moon material from six sites. The rocks quickly oxidize when exposed to air, so they are preserved in a dry, nitrogen-filled chamber at the National Aeronautics and Space Administration Lyndon B. Johnson Space Center in Houston.

Among the first questions the samples resolved was the moon's age. Isotopic dating showed that the moon formed at the same time as did the earth, 4.5 billion years ago. The rocks also indicated that the moon was geologically active until about two billion years ago. Other major questions took longer to answer.

In fact, investigators did not achieve a consensus on a theory of the moon's origin until 1984, 12 years after the last Apollo mission flew. The agreement emerged from a conference I organized with William K. Hartmann of the Planetary Sciences Institute in Tucson and Roger J. Phillips, now at Washington University. The meeting was held in Kona, on the big island of Hawaii. Given the tenacity with which scientists cling to their views, none of us suspected that one of the hypotheses of lunar origin would spring forth as a leading candidate above the others. Certainly none of us thought the postconference favorite would not be one of the three classic hypotheses. Each of these hypotheses had what some considered to be fatal flaws. Each also had ardent supporters. It is a testament to human persistence and imagination that so

many scientists tried so hard to adapt their preferred idea to a growing list of facts. Many houses of cards came tumbling down in Kona.

The least favorite classic idea going into the conference was the capture hypothesis. In its original form the capture hypothesis held that the earth seized a fully formed moon that came whizzing in from elsewhere in the solar system. In principle, such capture is possible but unlikely. A body passing near the earth would probably collide with it or get a gravitational boost that would alter its orbit so much that it could never meet up with the earth again. The chances of the orbits of the moon and the earth being exquisitely right for a capture is so minuscule that all but a few scientists had rejected the idea.

The Apollo mission helped to put that theory to rest. Lunar samples showed that the moon and the earth have similar quantities of oxygen isotopes, suggesting a close kinship. If the moon had formed elsewhere in the solar system, it would probably have had a different isotopic oxygen composition from that of the earth.

The second classic lunar genesis idea presented was the fission hypothesis. This theory has a long and honorable history. George Darwin, the second son of Charles's 10 children, first proposed it. He postulated that the earth, during a period after it formed a core, was at one time spinning extremely fast. It bulged so much at the equator that eventually a small blob spun off, becoming the moon. The scenario would account nicely for a crucial feature of the moon deduced by astronomers more than 100 years ago. Based on the satellite's orbital characteristics and size, the investigators calculated that the moon must be less dense than the earth. The low density implies that the moon must have only a small metallic core, if it harbors one at all. The fission idea would explain this fact: a fissioned moon is composed mostly of the earth's mantle (the layers between the crust and the core).

Subsequent calculations showed that the earth would have to have been rotating once every 2.5 hours in order to have spun off the material that became the moon. This short day is among the chief problems with the hypothesis: no one can figure out how the earth would have been spinning so fast in the first place. The models that described planetary formation as an accumulation of dust grains indicated that the earth would end up spinning rather slowly, if at all. Incorporating events that add angular momentum—most notably, impacts of planetesimals up to a few hundred kilometers across—did not help. Computer simulations showed that for every object that struck the earth to add clockwise spin, another impact would cause the planet to spin counterclockwise. Even if there were a mechanism for imparting enough angular momentum into the earth, advocates of the fission hypothesis had to find a way to eliminate much of the rotational energy. The earth-moon system of today does not have nearly the amount of

momentum needed to initiate separation of the two bodies from one another. Nevertheless, the calculations left enough room for intellectual maneuvering to keep the fission hypothesis from being discounted on dynamical grounds alone.

The Apollo program provided a new test. If the moon split from the earth in this manner, it ought to have exactly the same composition as the earth's rocky material near the surface (specifically, the crust and mantle). The moon and the earth do have identical amounts of oxygen isotopes, which indicates that the two bodies are related in some way. But the compositional similarity ends there. Crucial data came from lunar samples, a network of seismometers left behind and spectroscopic studies by the Apollo 15 and 16 missions. They enabled researchers to conclude that the moon and the earth have different chemical compositions.

For example, the moon has much less volatile material—substances that boil away easily—than does the earth's mantle. The satellite completely lacks any water-bearing minerals: it is bone-dry. It also lacks other kinds of volatile elements, from common ones such as potassium and sodium to more exotic chemicals such as bismuth and thallium. Scientists also discovered that the moon is enriched in nonvolatile substances relative to the earth. Called refractories, these elements are the opposite of volatiles: they boil at high temperatures. It appears that refractories such as aluminum, calcium, thorium and the rare-earth elements are present

in the moon at concentrations that are about 50 percent higher than those in the earth. Another bit of damaging evidence against the case for fission comes from the ratio of iron oxide to magnesium oxide. The ratio of these common compounds seems to be about 10 percent higher in the moon than it is in the crust and mantle of the earth.

Despite the evidence, fission proponents did not yield. They developed schemes to drive off volatiles and enrich refractories; they widened the error bars in the iron oxide to magnesium oxide ratios sufficiently to claim that the two bodies are indistinguishable. But in the long run the Apollo program findings have convinced most investigators that the fission model fails the compositional test.

The third classic idea is the double planet hypothesis, by which the moon and the earth formed concurrently from a cloud of gas and dust. Thus, the raw materials for the moon came from a ring of material in orbit around the earth. As the earth grew, so did the ring and the embryonic moon within. This hypothesis always had trouble explaining why the moon has such a small metallic core compared with that of the earth. Richard J. Greenberg and Stuart J. Weidenschilling and some of their colleagues at the Planetary Sciences Institute and at the University of Arizona tackled the question during the year before the Kona conference. They suggested that the orbiting ring of material acts as a compositional filter. The rocky parts of incoming bodies break up easily and are incorporated into the ring;

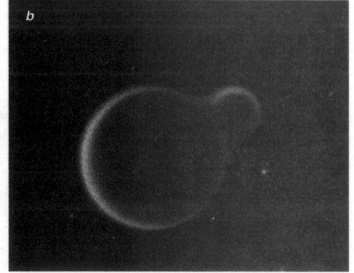

SCENARIOS OF LUNAR FORMATION varied widely before the Apollo missions. The capture hypothesis (*a*) depicts the moon as a body caught by the earth's gravity. In the fission idea (*b*), rapid rotation caused a piece of the early earth to

metallic parts pass through to become part of the earth.

Much debate centered on the efficacy of the process, and many researchers raised doubts about whether the incoming bodies would have been separated into cores and mantles. Although the binary planet hypothesis explains the similarity of the composition of the earth and the moon with respect to oxygen isotopes, it does not account for the differences in volatiles and refractories. Most important, it runs into the angular momentum problem. That is, it does not explain how the earth's rotation came to be 24 hours, which is faster than predicted by simple accretion models, and how the ring could have acquired enough circular motion to stay in orbit.

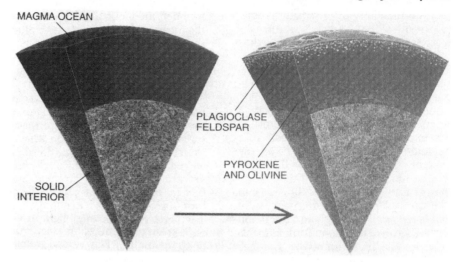

As we were organizing the Kona meeting, I wondered what new twists the proponents for these fatally flawed ideas would devise. Although modifications were indeed presented, we were all surprised by the enthusiastic reception given to a long-ignored idea: the giant impact theory. Among the most surprised was conference co-organizer Hartmann, and he was one of the inventors of the notion. By the end of the deliberations, a clear consensus formed in support of the idea that the impact of a large projectile with the growing earth dislodged the material that would form the moon. Of course, skeptical diehards and others desperately clinging to one of the old ideas remained, but the giant impact theory of lunar origin enchanted most participants.

The idea was not really brand-new. Like an actor who achieves "overnight success" after years of small roles, the giant impact theory was a bit player for a long time. Hartmann and his colleague Donald R. Davis proposed the impact theory in 1975. They had been investigating the accumulation of planets from smaller objects and noticed that numerous large bodies would have wandered near the earth. A few could have been as large as Mars. Hartmann and Davis hypothesized that the earth collided with such an object. As a result, some of the debris was launched into orbit, providing raw material for the moon. Alastair G. W. Cameron of the Harvard-Smithsonian Center for Astrophysics and William R. Ward of the Jet Propulsion Laboratory in Pasadena, Calif., independently suggested the same idea one year later as they tried to resolve the angular momentum problem.

They also addressed the details of the mechanism by which the material could achieve orbit and not fall back to the earth.

The work of Hartmann and Davis had been anticipated almost 30 years before by the late geologist Reginald A. Daly of Harvard University. Two distinguished pioneers of lunar science, Ralph B. Baldwin of the Oliver Machinery Company in Grand Rapids, Mich., and Don E. Wilhelms of the U.S. Geological Survey in Menlo Park, Calif., found that Daly had suggested in 1946 that the moon formed from the earth by the glancing impact of a planet-size object. Although Daly's analysis contains errors, the giant impact idea is clearly stated in this insightful but completely ignored paper. Even if Daly's work had been widely read, it might have been discounted: the paper was published before scientists realized that impacts were an im-

break off and become the moon. In the double planet hypothesis (c), dust grains accumulated to form the earth and moon.

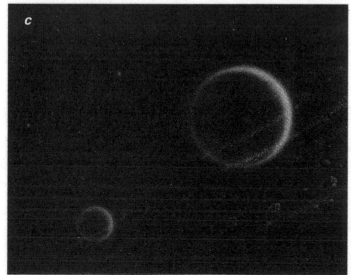

The now dominant giant impact theory (d) states that a huge collision flung into orbit debris that became the moon.

portant planetary process [see "Prematurity and Uniqueness in Scientific Discovery," by Gunther S. Stent; SCIENTIFIC AMERICAN, December 1972].

Although the giant impact hypothesis lay in obscurity until the announcement at Kona, nothing since that 1984 conference has shaken its firm position as the leading theory. It simply explains too many observations. The moon lacks metallic iron at its center because the core of the impactor stuck to the earth, so the moon formed from the silicate parts of both objects. The difference in the ratio of iron oxide to magnesium oxide between the earth and the moon exists because the moon formed mostly from the impactor. (One assumes that the projectile harbored less iron oxide than does the earth.)

The moon is dry because of the incalculable amount of heating that took place during the collision: the high temperatures evaporated all water and other volatiles. The refractories enriched the moon's composition because they recondensed quickly after heating and so were incorporated. The identical oxygen isotopic composition of the earth and the moon arises because the impactor and the earth formed in the same region of the evolving solar system. Finally, the hypothesis explains the most difficult problem: the angular momentum of the earth-moon system. The projectile must have struck the earth off-center, away from the central axis. This type of blow would have sped up the earth's rotation to its current value.

The most enticing aspect of the giant impact theory is that such a collision is a natural consequence of planet formation. No unusual or ad hoc circumstances need to be invoked. Such catastrophes, while enormous, are not unlikely. Indeed, planetary scientists now appeal to giant impacts to explain the composition of Mercury and the large tilt of Uranus. Without this colossal event early in the history of the solar system, there would be no moon in the sky. The earth would not be rotating as fast as it does, nor would it have such strong tides. Days might even last a year, as they do on Venus. But then, we probably would not be here to notice.

In addition to settling the question of the moon's origin, the Apollo samples enabled researchers to deduce the satellite's structure and evolution. The moon's features appear to have been reworked quite a bit by internal processes, though to a much lesser extent than those of the earth. A gigantic body of magma hundreds of kilometers deep, which apparently surrounded the moon and helped to form the lunar crust and mantle, precipitated the events. Indeed, this magma ocean theory has reigned as a central tenet of lunar science since Apollo 11 returned the first samples.

The Eagle landed on the surface of a mare in the Sea of Tranquillity, one of the dark gray areas that paint the features of the man-in-the-moon. They are the remnants of vast lava flows that leaked out onto the surface billions of years ago. Armstrong and Aldrin returned mostly samples from underfoot—basaltic bedrock rich in titanium. They also returned samples of the lunar regolith. The regolith is the loose debris that falls back to the moon after meteoroid impacts have kicked them up. It is the moon's version of soil, covering most of the surface to depths as great as 20 meters.

The samples of regolith contain a small percentage of white stones and pebbles composed chiefly of calcium and aluminum silicates known as plagioclase feldspar. Some rocks, called anorthosites, were composed of nothing but such feldspar. John A. Wood of the Harvard-Smithsonian Center for Astrophysics and Joseph V. Smith of the University of Chicago independently suggested that these anomalous particles decorating the Apollo 11 regolith were tossed there by impacts on distant highland terrain (the light-colored areas of the moon). Thus, they argued, the highlands must be dominated by feldspar-rich rocks. This bold extrapolation was confirmed by Apollo 16 and other craft that had touched down on the highlands. Remote chemical measurements conducted by the orbiting Apollo 15 and Apollo 16 command modules, along with telescopic observations of the highlands by my colleague B. Raymond Hawke of the University of Hawaii and his co-workers, also provided critical evidence.

But that extrapolation was not enough for Wood and Smith. They wondered why the highlands were so rich in plagioclase feldspar. The material might have accumulated on top of magma, like ice cubes floating in a glass of water. Such events happen on the earth in large magma bodies called layered intrusions. The structures form when dense minerals sink and lighter ones rise. Wood and Smith proposed that feldspar floated in a magma "sea," eventually creating the lunar crust. The heavy minerals composed of iron and magnesium silicates—olivine and pyroxene—sank to create the mantle. Moreover, the workers argued, if all the highlands are rich in feldspar, then the magma must have been everywhere, encircling the moon. Thus was born the magma ocean, an idea not even conceived of before the Apollo missions.

Further support for the magma ocean concept comes from a seemingly unconnected group of rocks, the mare basalts. These rocks are rich in olivine and pyroxene—the heavy material that sank in the magma ocean. They erupted onto the surface in the form of lava three billion years ago. Most important, these basalts lack a trace element called europium. The plagioclase feldspar from the highlands, however, is enriched in this element. In fact, the enrichment in the highlands is about equal to the depletion in the mare basalts. The findings bolster the presumption that both the maria and the highlands emerged from the magma ocean. During their formation, the feldspar-rich highlands simply grabbed more of the europium than did the mare basalts.

The presence of a magma ocean prompts a question. How was it created in the first place? Specifically, from where did the energy necessary to liquefy planetary material come? The process of core formation may have supplied some energy: the sinking of metallic iron releases heat. The immense impact that led to the formation of the moon contributed a further boost of energy. Geophysicists have examined the problem in detail and concluded that the giant impact led to the formation of a large amount of molten material. So great was the melting that up to 65 percent of the projectile and the earth became magma.

The concept of the magma ocean is now being applied to other planets as well. It is changing the way scientists look at the evolution and early history of the solar system. In the laboratory, experimenters try to determine how minerals form in magma and how trace elements are partitioned between the magma and crystallized materials. Another community of researchers investigates processes that could have operated in a magma ocean on the earth 4.5 billion years ago (the active geology of the planet since then has removed all evidence of a magma ocean). I have been marshaling evidence that some asteroids, especially those that formed iron cores, also bore magma oceans early in their histories. All this research was spawned because creative and bold scientists attached special importance to a few dozen little chunks of white rock in a charcoal-gray pile of dirt from the moon.

Although the evidence is compelling, some investigators are still skeptical about the magma ocean theory: they cite the existence of lunar highlands that lack feldspar. The final proof requires a global survey from a lunar orbit of the highlands' crust. The *Clementine* probe, a Department of Defense mission to test advanced sensors, has recently completed its mission to map the moon spectroscopically. (NASA has no planned missions to explore the moon.) Information from *Clementine's* sensors may provide the crucial data to establish the amount of plagioclase feldspar in the crust.

After the giant impact and the structural formation induced by the magma ocean, the moon experienced another step in its evolution: impact cratering. This major geologic process in fact still affects the planets. Its importance was not always appreciated. Before the space age, many scientists claimed that volcanism formed lunar craters and cavities. But as the Apollo missions approached, understanding of impact processes and products increased tremendously. Geologists proved that many circular structures on the earth were formed by collision with an extraterrestrial object. They studied them in order to establish the key characteristics of such features. Others made craters in laboratories, using high-speed guns that propelled projectiles at velocities of several kilometers a second, which smashed into targets.

The first person to assemble strong evidence for an impact origin for lunar craters was the renowned geologist Grove K. Gilbert, whose contributions ranged from basic mapping to hydrogeology. In 1893 he published a classic paper called *The Face of the Moon*, the first geologic study of the earth's satellite. Gilbert correctly identifies the maria as vast lava plains. He also describes the craters and explains why they could not be volcanic. Like Daly's paper about the origin of the moon, this one was also forgotten for decades. In fact, the impact-cratering idea did not return until the early 1940s, when Baldwin began studying the moon. Ironically, Baldwin became aware of Gilbert's important work in a letter from Daly in 1948.

The highlands are especially battered, and the rocks show it. Most samples have been melted, mixed, crushed and compressed by shock waves. These rocks, called breccias, are as complicated as an M. C. Escher print. The ages of highland breccias are surprising. In 1974 Fouad Tera, Dimitri A. Papanastassiou and Gerald J. Wasserburg of the California Institute of Technology pointed out that there are two sharp delineations

of ages of highland rocks. The first is at around 4.4 billion years, which Tera and his colleagues took to be the end of primary lunar differentiation (basically, when the magma ocean stopped crystallizing). The other takes place at about 3.9 billion years. This second age, they reasoned, represents a time of intense bombardment that completely wiped out any evidence of previous bombardments; the impacts "reset" the ages of the surface rocks. They dubbed this period of fierce impact bombardment the "lunar cataclysm." The idea states that most of the basins and large craters on the moon formed in a narrow time interval, roughly 3.85 to four billion years ago. Indeed, of the samples dated, the ages of virtually all the rocks from the Apollo program flights and the Russian automated Luna 20 mission are in the 3.85- to 3.95-billion-year range.

Some people did not like the cataclysm idea. Baldwin argued that the apparent clustering of ages was an illusion. The data in effect were contaminated by the widespread distribution of ejected debris. Specifically, the debris originated from the immense event responsible for the formation of the Imbrium basin, a 1,300-kilometer-wide dent that corresponds to the man-in-the-moon's right eye. Baldwin also argued that the elevated parts of large basins have gradually sunk down, indicating they formed before 3.95 billion years ago, perhaps as much as 4.3 billion years ago. Hartmann believes the cluster of ages around 3.9 billion years represented the last of a declining flux of projectiles left over from planetary accretion. The paucity of samples from before that period was the result of what he called a "stone wall." As older rocks were reheated by impacts, their ages were continuously reset to 3.9 billion years. Therefore, only the last impact events are recorded. Hartmann's and Baldwin's arguments persuaded most investigators. So the possibility that a cataclysm—the dramatic pickup in the impact rate between 3.85 and four billion years ago—was cast aside or at least ignored.

The cataclysm's exile lasted more than a decade, until Graham Ryder of the Lunar and Planetary Institute in Houston vigorously revived the idea in 1990. Ryder makes three points. One is that ages of rocks are not so easily reset. Recent work on the effects of impacts on ages demonstrates that the only materials whose ages are affected are those that melt during the impact and, perhaps, a small percentage of other rocks in the target. Most rocks are

crushed up and tossed around but not heated substantially.

Ryder also argues against Hartmann's stone-wall idea. He draws attention to samples of lava flows found among the *Apollo 14* specimens. These rocks range in age from 3.9 to 4.3 billion years. They indicate that the ages of samples can be preserved even though they would have been the most prone to demolition because of their position on the lunar surface.

Ryder's third main contention challenges the notion that all the samples reflect the age of the huge Imbrium basin. Indeed, most workers now feel the idea is probably too simplistic. The highlands harbor many chemically distinct groups of rocks melted by impact, a fact that suggests several collisions. The ages of the rocks cluster between 3.85 and 3.95 billion years.

Still, the question of the exact number of properly dated events remains. So does the issue of what number of impacts constitutes a cataclysm. The differing viewpoints expressed in the cataclysm hypothesis and the stone-wall idea stem in part from two ways of looking at the moon. Ryder advocates cataclysm because he has some confidence in what lunar samples are telling us. Hartmann is more concerned with how planets accrete and thus prefers the stone-wall theory. Reconciling the two perspectives requires more samples from the moon. Especially useful would be specimens from deposits of impact melt inside large basins. Dating them would yield direct, unambiguous ages of each basin from which the samples were collected.

In all likelihood, the bombardment that cratered the moon was not unique. It appears to have occurred throughout the inner solar system. Ancient cratered terrains exist on Mars and Mercury—indeed, Mercury looks much like the moon. (Venus is so active that its earliest features could not have survived.) Numerous projectiles probably hit the early earth as well. The lunar craters can provide some estimate of the size of some of the objects that crashed into the earth. The moon has 35 basins larger than 300 kilometers wide. Even if only half of these basins formed between 3.85 and four billion years ago, the conclusion is inescapable that during the same period the earth would have experienced more than 300 comparable impacts. (The earth is a bigger target, both in terms of cross-sectional area and mass, so it tends to be hit by about 20 times as many projectiles.) Of these, between

15 and 20 would have been monumental, forming basins larger than 2,500 kilometers in diameter. This size, equal to that of the largest lunar basin, is about half the distance across the continental U.S.

Such impacts would have had dramatic consequences. One affected characteristic would have been the earth's geology. Large impacts would have altered any convection patterns in the mantle that may have driven early plate tectonics. They would also have rapidly excavated hot material from the mantle. Brought to the surface, the hot rocks would have melted instantly, producing vast amounts of magma. The residual craters may have collected sediments. Such material may have eroded from the higher areas on the rims of the craters or from the central peaks. The sedimentation could have led to the formation of the first continents.

Life would have had a difficult time thriving during this time. The most dramatic events would have been capable of vaporizing all liquid water on the planet. It seems unlikely that life would have survived anywhere. It would thus have been forced to start over. In fact, Christopher F. Chyba of the NASA Ames Research Center at Moffett Field, Calif., suggests that several sterilization events occurred before the impact rate settled down about 3.8 billion years ago. Only since then would life have been able to take a permanent hold on the earth. Indeed, strong evidence exists that organisms arose by 3.6 billion years ago, only about 200 million years after the bombardment subsided. Recent work indicates that self-replicating molecules can develop quickly, so the 200-million-year period is a reasonable time frame for organisms to emerge.

Large impacts have also been invoked to explain major extinctions on the earth. The impact hypothesis is especially well documented at the Cretaceous-Tertiary boundary, which resulted in the end of half of the living species, including the dinosaurs, 65 million years ago. The main lines of evidence stem from a global enrichment of iridium at the boundary and the presence of shocked forms of quartz and feldspar. Teams spearheaded by Alan R. Hildebrand of the University of Arizona and Virgil L. "Buck" Sharpton of the Lunar and Planetary Institute have identified the site of the probable impact. The crater, called Chicxulub, is completely hidden by sediments forming the Yucatán Peninsula. It was originally discovered in 1981 through gravity surveys and through drilling activities by Pemex, Mexico's national oil company.

Apollo's Influence on Lunar Science

TOPIC	PRE-APOLLO VIEW	CURRENT VIEW
Origin	Captured, derived from the earth or formed with the earth as a dual planet	Giant impact on the earth, followed by formation of the moon from debris
Craters	Most impact, some volcanic	Almost all impact; dynamics of ejected debris determined
Presence of volatiles (such as water)	Unknown, although some scientists thought water had flowed on the moon's surface	Mostly dry, but water brought in by impacting comets may be trapped in very cold places at the poles
Rock ages	Uncertain, but probably ancient (more than a few billion years)	Highlands: most rocks older than 4.1 billion years, with anorthosites 4.4 billion years. Maria: some as young as about two billion years, others as old as 4.3 billion years
Magma ocean	Not conceived of	Anorthosites formed from magma ocean; other highland rocks formed after that
Composition of maria	Unknown	Wide variety of basalt types
Composition of highlands	Unknown	Wide variety of rock types, but all containing more aluminum than do mare basalts
Composition of mantle	Unknown	Varying amounts of mostly olivine and pyroxene

The structure is 300 kilometers in diameter and 65 million years old.

Some scientists have proposed that such mass extinctions are not happenstance events but in fact recur periodically. Proving this hypothesis by looking at features on the earth is not possible. Besides uncertainties in the fossil record, too few terrestrial craters have been dated accurately. Without a correct historical record, a search for periodicity is futile.

The moon's surface may hold the evidence: it is teeming with craters formed during the past 600 million years. Friedrich Hörz of the NASA John-

son Space Center estimates that 5,000 of them are larger than five kilometers in diameter. Even in a local region, say, within a 100-kilometer radius, there are 500 craters wider than one kilometer. But an accurate determination of age requires samples.

Indeed, to fill in missing data about the earth's origin and early history, we must return to the moon. The origin problem seems to be solved, but the details remain sketchy. The existence of the magma ocean is not proved to everyone's satisfaction. We need to determine the overall composition of the moon, which can be done with spectroscopic surveys from orbit and seismographic studies on the surface. More samples from key localities in the lunar highlands would allow us to unravel the processes that operated inside a complicated magma ocean body. The bombardment history of the moon will never be worked out without samples from identifiable impact deposits inside craters. Moreover, new missions do not have to be as expensive or complex as was Apollo. Automated probes can do the job for us.

Of course, the nation and the world may decide they cannot afford to send a fleet of orbital and surface missions to the moon. In that case, we will never know the details of the formation, early melting and bombardment history of the moon and the earth. Only by continuing the legacy of Apollo can we hope to complete our understanding of our place in the solar system.

FURTHER READING

LUNAR SOURCE BOOK: A USER'S GUIDE TO THE MOON. Edited by Grant Heiken, David Vaniman and Bevan M. French. Cambridge University Press, 1991.

TO A ROCKY MOON: A GEOLOGIST'S HISTORY OF LUNAR EXPLORATION. Don E. Wilhelms. University of Arizona Press, 1993.

The West and the World, 1500–1900

The small nation of Portugal, looking for trade opportunities, began the first great European explorations in the fifteenth century. Probing farther and farther down the unknown western African coastline, the Portuguese captain, Bartholomew Dias, reached the Cape of Good Hope before the end of the century. In the years that followed, the possession of the land changed several times, but in the twentieth century it attracted more immigrants from Portugal than ever before. David Birmingham writes about the impact of this small colonizing nation in his article "Portugal's Impact on Africa."

Africa was not an easy land to invade. There were waterfalls near the coastline and deadly diseases. Penetration into unknown Africa had to await the invention of steamboats and the discovery of quinine as a prophylactic for malaria. Superior firearms also aided the Europeans when the conquest finally occurred in the nineteenth century. Meanwhile, a flourishing trade developed on the west coast of Africa to match that of Islamic merchants trading across the Sahara Desert with camel caravans. Native chiefs sold their captives to Christian and Islamic slavers who carried their human cargo to the Middle East, Europe, and the Americas. There has been a long argument about the responsibility for slavery, as Elikia M'Bokolo notes in his essay "Who Was Responsible?" but in general the power lay on the side of the outsiders. It was the Africans who suffered.

In the Americas the slash of the Spanish sword quickly brought the civilizations of the Inca and Aztec to a close. Charles Mee Jr. writes about the meeting of Cortés and the Aztecs that resulted in the unthinking destruction of art and knowledge of the New World. The vast majority of people migrated westward and very few Native Americans traveled to Europe, as Harald Prins and Bunny McBride note. But there was a highly significant migration of food stuffs around the world. This "Columbian Exchange" as it is sometimes called, involved horses, wheat, and smallpox, for example, going from Europe to America. In return, Europe received potatoes, corn, and cocoa. Alfred Crosby, a professor at the University of Texas, explains that this exchange had a worldwide impact and is more significant than all the treasure extracted by the conquistadors.

During the first phase of imperialism from 1500 to 1800, Europeans often dealt with foreign peoples on a level of equality. When Lord Macartney of Lissamore tried to open trade with China, however, his effort met with failure, as Paul Gillingham explains in the article "The Macartney Embassy to China, 1792–94." There was nothing of Western culture that interested the Chinese government at the time. This was a fatal arrogance, and a half century later British warships forced the Chinese to accept opium as an item to balance the tea trade. The Chinese government could not stand against the military supremacy of the British. In similar manner, the Japanese who had embraced isolation for 200 years found themselves humiliated by the naval guns of an American fleet that forced them to open their country to trade. The nineteenth century was marked by territorial acquisition in India, Southeast Asia, China, and Africa as the West completed its conquest of the world.

Looking Ahead: Challenge Questions

What is the importance of technology in the expansion of the West?

What was the motivation of Westerners in their global explorations?

What was the "Columbian Exchange"? What items were involved? What were the long-run consequences of the exchange?

Would you consider African slavery as part of the "Columbian Exchange"?

Who was responsible for the slave trade?

What was the motivation of the British during the Macartney mission? Was it the same during the Opium War?

Does "might make right" in regard to the Opium War, and in regard to the relationships between the United States and Japan in the 1850s?

PORTUGAL'S IMPACT ON AFRICA

Poverty the spur – Bartholomew Dias' voyage to the Cape of Good Hope five hundred years ago marked the apex of an extraordinary Portuguese expansion overseas and the start of a fateful European impact on South Africa.

15th-century tin-glazed bowl showing a Portuguese sailing ship.

David Birmingham

FIVE HUNDRED YEARS AGO, IN 1488, Bartholomew Dias, a Portuguese seaman, reached the Cape of Good Hope on the furthest tip of South Africa. This was the last stage of the Portuguese exploration of the Atlantic coast and its islands. It was also the beginning of five centuries of often strained relations between Europe and South Africa. Two questions arise out of this turning point in the world's fortunes. The first is how did Portugal, a relatively remote and impoverished land at the far ends of medieval Europe, become the pioneer of Atlantic colonisation? And secondly, what were the long-term consequences of the opening of South Africa to alien influences?

The Portuguese domination of the eastern Atlantic took place in six stages, each of which pioneered a new set of colonial experiments. Bartholomew Dias was the heir to two centuries of trial and error as Portugal sought escape from its chronic poverty. The fact that Portugal was able to succeed in becoming an international power was due primarily to the superb shelter which the harbour of Lisbon provided to mariners on the otherwise inhospitable coast of south-eastern Europe.

Lisbon had been a harbour in Phoenician times when Levantine traders needed a haven on the long haul to Britain. It was also used by the Roman and Arab empires, although their primary interest lay in land-based domination. In the thirteenth century sea-power revived and Genoa succeeded in breaking out of the Mediterranean into the Atlantic. The great economic centres of northern Italy and of lower Germany, (hitherto linked by land-routes through the great markets of Lyons and Nuremburg) were now joined by Genoese on the safer maritime route. Lisbon again became a thriving port. The Portuguese learnt about ship-building from the Low Countries and about sea-faring from Italy and Catalonia. At one time the Portuguese monarchy hired no less than six Genoese admirals, although the most famous of them, Christopher Columbus, sought fame by transferring his allegiance to the rival port of Seville in Castile.

The rise of Lisbon as the maritime gateway between northern and southern Europe led to the growth of an urban middle class with merchant and banking skills learnt from Italy. It was this middle class which became the driving force behind the Portuguese search for new wealth overseas. It found its patron in the royal prince, Pedro, brother of the vaunted Henry the Navigator. Portugal was unusual in that the nobility, lacking any other source of wealth in a country of agrarian poverty, showed a willingness to engage in merchant adventures. They were greatly helped by the thriving Jewish community of Lisbon, a community spasmodically enhanced by refugees fleeing persecution in other parts of Christendom. Jewish scholars were not hampered by Christian concepts of the world as portrayed in the scriptures and were able to take a much more scientific look at the evidence needed to draw maps and collate intelligence on economic prospects overseas.

The crises which drove Portugal to expansion were always crises over the price of bread. Throughout the Middle Ages Lisbon had been a hungry city. Access to the farm lands of the interior was inhibited by poor river navigation and expensive long-distance cartage. Grain was therefore not sought from domestic sources but from overseas shippers. Both Spain and Britain became key sup-

From *History Today*, June 1988, pp. 44-50. © 1988 by History Today, Ltd., 20 Old Compton Street, London W1V 5PE.
Reprinted by permission.

pliers of wheat to Lisbon, and England built a six-hundred-year alliance on Portugal's need for northern trade. But in the fourteenth century one new solution to the grain deficit was a colonial venture in the Atlantic.

One thousand miles off the coast of Portugal lay the uninhabited islands of the Azores and Madeira. With the development of better shipping they became more accessible to Lisbon than the much closer interior of mainland Portugal. Colonisation and the setting up of wheat gardens were therefore attempted. Concepts of colonisation were learnt from the Venetians who had established settled colonies around their trading factories in the Near East. The labour supply consisted both of cheap European migrants driven by hunger, and captured slaves raided from the Barbary coast. The necessary capital was raised in the banking houses of Genoa. Patronage was provided by the land owning nobility under the protection of Prince Henry. The beginnings of temperate cereal colonisation in the Atlantic basin were laid. The system was later to spread to the far side of the ocean, and eventually the Canadian and American prairies became a source of wheat not only for Portugal but also for half of Europe. Stage one of the Portuguese expansion, the wheat-based stage, was successful in the initial objective of supplying bread to overcome the Lisbon deficiency. It was also successful in terms of pioneering a colonial system which carried Europe out into the world.

The second stage of Portuguese expansion involved a more subtle development of overseas investment. Wheat was a comparatively low-yielding agricultural enterprise. A much higher return on capital, on labour and on land could be obtained by turning agrarian produce into alcohol. Alcohol could also be better preserved and could be sold when the price was advantageous rather than when the crop was ripe, as in the case of grain. The second stage of Portuguese expansion therefore attempted to establish a wine industry overseas. The necessary skills were available in the wine industry of Portugal. But Portuguese domestic wine, like Portuguese grain, suffered from severe problems of cartage

A detail from Le Testu's 'Cosmographie Universelle' of 1555, showing Portuguese settlements and trading posts in Southern Africa.

to the coast. Even in the eighteenth century, when port wine became a lucrative export, the shooting of the rapids on the Douro river made transport almost suicidal. The prospect of using colonial islands for the growing of vines was therefore attractive. The territory chosen was the Canary Islands, off the Moroccan coast of Africa.

Morocco was known to the Portuguese after a series of raiding wars associated with the militant crusading Order of Christ, of which Prince Henry was the commander. Despite an initial victory in Ceuta in 1415,

these wars had failed to capture the 'bread-basket' of North Africa which had once fed the city of Rome. Instead, the conquerors therefore set their sight on the off-shore islands. Unlike the Azores, the Canaries were already inhabited and conquest was necessary before plantations could be established. Once conquered, however, the surviving islanders could be compelled to slave servitude. Migrants from Portugal's impoverished backlands sailed in to create vineyards using both local and mainland slaves. Even when the colony was transferred in 1479 from

Portuguese suzerainty to control by the Crown of Castile, Portuguese immigrants continued to provide many colonists for Tenerife.

The Canary Islands were a second, wine-based, stage of Portugal's colonial pioneering. The development of colonial wine industries, for instance in California, South Africa and Australia was slower to take off than the development of wheat colonies. Portugal itself imposed restrictions where the interests of metropolitan producers were put at risk, though Canary wine was extensively smuggled into the Portuguese empire. The Canary Islands were important, however, for another reason. They became the base for the conquest and colonisation of Hispanic America. It was from there that Columbus set sail in 1492, and later a significant proportion of the emigrants who went to the Spanish American colonies were Canary islanders, often of Portuguese ancestry. As a stage in the growth of the economic, political and social ideology of imperialism the Canary Islands were of critical significance. The slave vineyards of Tenerife, and the spasmodic raiding of southern Morocco, are a more accurate testimony to the place of Henry the Navigator in history than all the myths about his scientific virtuosity which were put out by the hired praise-singer, the chronicler Azurara.

The third stage of Portuguese experimentation in colonial practices was focused on another set of Atlantic islands, the Cape Verde islands. The Cape Verdes became famous over time for their textile industry. Portugal was almost as severely short of textiles as it was short of wheat. One reason for the development of wine exports was to pay for woolen materials from England. Cotton was also bought in significant quantities from Muslim suppliers in north Africa and, after the rounding of the Cape of Good Hope, from the great texile industries of India. But the Cape Verde islands offered an opportunity to create a colonial textile industry.

Cotton and indigo plantations were established on the islands for spinning and dying. Labour was purchased on the West Africa mainland. Craftsmen were also brought over from the mainland to introduce the necessary weaving skills. The styles of textile adopted were ones which would sell best in Africa. The industry soon became self-perpetuating. Cloth woven in the islands was sold on the mainland in return for more slaves who would further expand the plantations. The only European input was sea transport. The Portuguese shipped cloth up and down the coast in the cabotage trade. The final profits were taken in slaves, the best of which were carried to Portugal to work on the underdeveloped landed estates of the south. By the sixteenth century some 10 per cent of the population of southern Portugal comprised black immigrants. Many were still slaves but others had married into land-owning families, thus increasing the domestic labour force without having to make reciprocal marriage payments. Blacks also became a significant part of the working population of Lisbon.

Slave-grown cotton became, over the colonial centuries, one of the fundamental bases of European relations with the wider world. From its pioneering beginnings the economic system spread to Brazil, which supplied Portugal, to the 'Sea Island' cotton colonies of the Caribbean, and eventually to the great cotton belt of Georgia and Alabama. This particular branch of Portuguese colonial ideology played a more direct part than any other in the development of the industrial revolution in eighteenth-century Britain.

The fourth stage of Portuguese progress towards the discovery of the Cape of Good Hope involved a fourth set of islands and a fourth type of colonial plantation economy. The tropical island of São Tomé, off the Niger delta, proved to have excellent soil and plentiful rainfall. The merchant community of Lisbon, and especially its Jewish economic pioneers, experimented with the introduction of sugar cane. Sugar required a much higher degree of organisation than the temperate or tropical crops hitherto introduced into the new Atlantic colonies. Cane had to be grown on a sufficiently large scale to justify investing in a crushing mill and boiling vats. It also required a labour force which could be compelled to work intensely hard during the harvest season to ensure that mature cane be crushed with a minimum of delay. Sugar seemed to be ideally suited to a slave economy and labour was therefore bought from the nearby kingdoms of Benin and Kongo. The industry so flourished that the island soon became too small, and sugar planting began to spread to other Portugese colonies, notably in north-eastern Brazil.

The success of São Tomé as a pioneering sugar colony was watched with admiration by the European powers which aspired to emulate Portugal's path to colonial prosperity. The Dutch went so far as to conquer the island, and also part of Brazil. The English set up their own black slave sugar colonies in Barbados and the Caribbean in the seventeenth century, and then turned to Indian-worked sugar colonies in the nineteenth century. But the greatest imitator of them all was France whose sugar island, later called Haiti, became the richest colony of all time. It was also the first one to successfully rebel against the racial pattern of servitude that Portugal had evolved and create an independent black state out of a white-ruled colony.

The fifth stage of Portuguese colonial evolution was concerned not with planting but with mining. The mines which the explorers aspired to reach were the gold mines of West Africa. From about 1400 the Akan mines of the coastal forest had begun to supplement gold production in the medieval fields controlled by the inland kingdoms of Ghana and Mali. Information about the trans-Saharan supply of African gold was widely known in the Christo-Islamic financial circles of the Mediterranean and certainly reached the merchants of Lisbon. In 1471 these merchants discovered a back route to the mines by way of the Gold Coast in West Africa. In order to buy gold, however, the Portuguese had to offer prices, and assortments of commodities, which were competitive with those of the experienced Saharan camel caravans. They found, to their surprise, that labour was in scarce supply in the mines and that slaves from their island plantations could fetch a good price. Thus the islands became entrepôts for the selling of slave miners. The business flourished and within a generation Portugal was buying ten thousand and more ounces of gold each year.

The lure of gold became a permanent feature of colonial ambition. The success of Portugal in West Africa became a driving force for all the European powers overseas. All the great gold-bearing regions of the world were explored and often plundered. Africa initially protected its mineral wealth with well-ordered states and effective armies. America was not so strong, and the peoples of the Caribbean died in the Spanish mines while the empires of Mexico and Peru were overthrown and ransacked. Only in the nineteenth century did Africa succumb to the conquering quest for gold by Europeans. Gold lust led to the great Anglo-Boer war of 1899 in which Britain, by now the strongest of the colonising nations, conquered South Africa.

The sixth and last stage of Portuguese expansion before the discovery of the Cape occurred on the western mainland of Central Africa. In Angola the Portuguese made their one and only attempt to create a colony on *terra firma* and among native inhabitants. The trump card which they played to gain access was religion. By offering to introduce more powerful gods and saints to control the supernatural, the Portuguese were able to build up political allies who protected their commercial interests and allowed a limited development of foreign settlement. Africa's first mainland colony was primarily concerned with the buying of slaves, however, and in less than a century it had been stalled by resistance and overrun by rebellion. The Portuguese therefore adopted Spanish military

tactics and sent squads of *conquistadores* to fortify their trading posts. Justification was supplied by accompanying Jesuits who commended armed conversion and established slave-worked plantations to finance their churches and monastries.

Portugal was initially less successful than its latter-day imitators in achieving territorial conquest. But the Jesuits and the soldiers did cross over to Brazil and began the harsh opening up of the eastern half of the South American continent. The colonists included some three million slaves brought over from Africa against their will. All the previous colonial experiments that Portugal had attempted in the fourteenth and fifteenth centuries – cereal farming, wine growing, cotton picking, sugar planting, gold mining – were introduced into Brazil. Sugar in the seventeenth century and gold in the eighteenth proved the most lucrative. Tobacco was added to the cornucopia. By the end of the colonial period in the Americas, the formerly Portuguese United States of Brazil exceeded the size of the formerly British United States of America.

The six stages of Portuguese expansion into the Atlantic were followed in 1488 by the great expedition to the Cape of Good Hope. This was commanded by a common captain called Bartholomew Dias, for whose services the King of Portugal paid an annuity of six thousand reals. Nothing is known of the captain's experience in tropical waters, but in August 1487 he set out with two small exploring caravels, light enough to be beached, and a bulkier store ship of provisions and trade goods. He carried three stone crosses

with which to claim territory on the African mainland. His objective, via Mina and Kongo, was the desert coast of Namibia, beyond the Angolan waters explored by Diego Cão in the three previous seasons. Dias prepared reports on the available anchorages, and conducted a little trade with local Khoi cattle herders. The Portuguese were not welcome intruders, however, and after selling them some sheep and cows the Khoi prudently turned them away. In the skirmish which followed one Khoi was killed by Bartholomew Dias' cross-bow. Relations between Europe and South Africa thus began as badly as they were to continue. At another bay Dias left his store ship with nine men instructed to investigate the commercial opportunities of the region. So unsuccessful were these trade emissaries that six of them had been killed before the main expedition returned to base. The store ship itself had to be fired for want of an adequate crew to sail it back to Lisbon.

After these unhappy encounters, very reminiscent of the hit-and-run exploits of Henry the Navigator's men on the desert coast of North Africa fifty years earlier, Dias sailed on towards the greener coast of the south. After many false promises in the deeply indented bays he gradually realised that the coast he was following had turned eastward. The enthusiasm generated by this discovery

Noble savages? A 1510 woodcut of some of the native peoples the Portuguese encountered: (left to right) West African negroes; Hottentots from Algoa Bay, South Africa; Arab traders from the East African coast.

IN GENNEA   IN ALLAGO   IN ARABIA

was slow to capture the imagination of his homesick crews as bay followed bay along the southernmost shore of Africa. No opening towards the north was encountered. Eventually, at Bushman's River, some five hundred miles east of the Cape of Good Hope, Dias was persuaded to turn for home. He planted his first stone totem on March 12th, 1488, and dedicated it to Saint Gregory. He had discovered no new wealth, no fertile land, and no hospitable islands, not even a source of slaves with which to recompense the entrepreneurial King of Portugal for his outlay of risk capital. Worse still he had not conclusively found the sea lane to Arabia and India, although the direction of the coast had become more promising.

On the homeward journey Bartholomew Dias stopped on Saint Philip's day, June 6th, 1488, and apparently planted his second stone cross on the Cape of Good Hope. This was the most famous landmark of his voyage, though not actually the southernmost point of Africa. It was the rounding of this cape which eventually secured Dias his place in history. Dias did not enter Table Bay, site of the later city of Cape Town, but he did enter the Namibian bay later named Luderitz and mounted his third pillar of territorial assertion of Portuguese rights. He finally arrived back in Lisbon in December 1488 having covered 6,000 leagues in sixteen months.

The international repercussions of the Dias voyage were numerous. In 1491 a major colonising expedition was sent to the kingdom of Kongo, in Angola, which seemed a more promising African political and commercial partner than the sparse communities of coastal South Africa. In 1492 Columbus, no longer in Portuguese service, and armed with absurdly false data on the earth's circumference, sailed on behalf of Castile to find a western route to China, since Dias had failed to find an eastern one round the African coast. Not till 1497, nine years after the Dias voyage and five years after Columbus began to explore the Caribbean, did a new Portuguese king, Manuel I, manage to raise the resources, then men and the ships to attempt another merchant adventure in the far south without guarantee of profit. The expedition of Vasco da Gama, however, did complete the task begun by Bartholomew Dias and opened up the sea route to Asia. Dias himself was called back to royal service and appointed to open a gold trading factory at Sofala in southeastern Africa.

Dias had experience of the gold trade. In 1497 he had accompanied Vasco da Gama on the first leg of his journey down the African coast before turning into the Gulf of Guinea to deliver a cargo of trade cloth and merchant goods to the gold factory of Mina. In 1500 Dias was appointed to accompany the great fleet of Alvares Cabral to the Indian Ocean and set up a similar factory at Sofala. The highland gold of the Zimbabwe mines had recently switched from the old ports of southern Mozambique to reach the international market via the Zambezi route in central Mozambique. Manuel of Portugal hoped that Dias, with his little flotilla of four shallow-draft caravels, would be able to close off the traditional gold route via East Africa to the Muslim precious metal marts of the eastern Mediteranean and divert the Sofala gold round the Cape of Good Hope to Christian bankers and the western Mediteranean. Dias, however, failed to crown his career in such a fashion. After an unscheduled stop on the then unknown coast of Brazil, his boat was lost on the south Atlantic crossing. The trading fortress was indeed built five years later, but Bartholomew Dias was remembered not as a great gold trader but as the first navigator along the coast of South Africa.

The discovery of the Cape of Good Hope was initially of little intrinsic interest. South Africa had few attractions to men seeking trade, minerals, slaves, vacant land and any other kind of entrepreneurial opportunity which would allow an escape from the barrenness of Portuguese provincial society. Few Portuguese visited the Cape, and then only in order to by-pass it and seek the wealthy sea lanes of Asia. Dias' son Antonio and grandson Paulo Dias de Novais invested their capital and energy not in South Africa but in Angola in Central Africa. In 1571 they claimed the rights of Lord-Proprietor in Angola and four years later founded the city of Luanda on a shore that their ancestor had patrolled on his epic voyage.

The Dias family failed, however, to secure their colony and in the 1590s the Hapsburgs repossessed Angola for the united Iberian crown of Spain and Portugal. But despite this check, grandfather Dias had, when reaching the Cape, set eyes on the South Africa that was gradually to become the most powerful of all the foreign colonies of Africa. It was also, five centuries later, to be the one which attracted the largest number of Portuguese migrants.

In 1588, a century after Dias visited South Africa, the country had changed little. Black farming and cattle-herding were as prosperous as ever in the east while sheep-rearing and shell-fishing were important in the dryer areas of the west. Portuguese mariners were regularly shipwrecked on the coast and often hospitably received and given food, shelter, clothing and a safe-conduct along the trade paths to a Portuguese harbour in Mozambique. The first signs of the agricultural revolution which was to bring American maize to South Africa as a staple crop may have been noted, but it was not until the eighteenth century that the new farming, and favourable climatic conditions, led to a large demographic increase in the South African population.

By 1688 the seeds of colonial challenge to South Africa's independence had been sown. The Dutch haven at the Cape had begun to be swelled by Calvinist refugees from European persecution. Wheat and vine colonies, reminiscent of the Azores and Canaries, were set up in the fertile plains of Swellendam and Stellenbosch. Settlers already felt restive at the imperial control imposed on them by the metropolitan government of the Dutch West India company. Slavery was accepted as the normal means to acquire labour both in the artisan shops of the city and on the farms. White women were rare among the settlers and concubines of every race were readily accepted and acknowledged as they had been on the old colonial estates of the Portuguese islands. Indeed, the Cape was seen by the settlers as an 'island' and they tried to hedge themselves off from the mainstream of South Africa.

In 1788, three hundred years after Dias, the Cape had become a frontier society very strongly linked to the rest of South Africa. The indigenous population of the western Cape had been either integrated into colonial society in as subservient caste, or driven out to the northern frontiers and labelled 'the people of the bush'. In the east settlers had adopted the cattle ranching, and cattle rustling, way of life of their black neighbours. Co-operation and conflict between them alternated according to the grazing and watering needs of the herds. Traders cast their eyes on the further horizon and dreamed of fortunes made hunting elephants for ivory. A large creole population of varied racial composition resembled the creole societies which has evolved in all the Portuguese island colonies and in Luanda. Instead of speaking a 'pidgin' Portuguese creole, the people of the Cape spoke a Dutch creole, later known as Afrikaans.

By 1888 South Africa had changed again and was on the brink of a social and economic revolution. Diamonds, gold and coal had been found and the agrarian societies, both black and white, were beginning to be mobilised for the industrial exploitation of their mineral wealth on behalf of investors in Europe. The upheaval was immense and led to the entrenchment of both a racial divide between black and white and a cultural divide between English-speakers and Dutch-speakers. The old Cape population with its mixed heritage, black and white, English and Dutch, was unable to provide a bridge when the demands of industrial profit outweighed the political benefits of reconciliation. The great Boer War and the ideology of racial segregation were the consequences.

Finally by 1988, at the time of the fifth centenary of the first European visit to the Cape, an embattled South Africa had been transformed into Africa's foremost industrial nation. The old black population had become totally overwhelmed by white power. Surplus people not needed for industrial production or capitalist agriculture were carried off to encampments on the remote and dry fringes of the country. The remainder were segregated into urbanised black ghettos with limited economic rights and no political voice. Meanwhile the white population grew in size and prosperity in the fertile heartlands. Its latest recruits were six hundred thousand Portuguese immigrants. Like their predecessors, the Atlantic migrants of the fourteenth and fifteenth centuries, they were seeking an alternative to penury in Europe's poorest yet most innovative colonising nation.

FOR FURTHER READING:
Charles Boxer, *The Portuguese Seaborne Empire, 1415-1825* (Hutchinson, 1969); C. V. Scammell, *The World Encompassed* (Methuen, 1981); V. Malgalhaes Godinho, several works in Portuguese and *L'economie de l'Empire Portugaise* (Paris, 1969); Walter Rodney, *A History of Upper Guinea* (Oxford University Press, 1970); David Birmingham, *Trade & Conflict in Angola* (Oxford University Press, 1966).

A frontier society; the Town Hall of a Dutch-administered Cape of Good Hope, 1764, with Table Mountain in the background and a slave-based economy already in evidence.

That fateful moment when two civilizations came face to face

Cortés and his men were out for gold and glory; Montezuma's Aztec empire was shaky; the cruel result was a tragedy of history

Charles L. Mee Jr.

Even before anyone came, there were amazing events: a comet appeared and split into three; the waters of the lake boiled up in a rage; a sign like a tongue of fire burned up into the sky, up to the heavens.

These and other remarkable things began to happen ten years before the Spaniards landed: omens that foretold their coming, said the old men who drew pictographs of them some 30 years afterward for the Franciscan missionary Fray Bernardino de Sahagún.

According to Sahagún's aged native informants, a messenger brought word of "towers or small mountains floating on the waves of the sea." The ships came in the spring of 1519, off the northern shore of the Yucatán peninsula. There were 11 all told (or, according to other sources, 10 or 12 ships), carrying 10 large bronze cannon, 4 falconets, or light cannon, stores of powder and shot, 16 horses, some large dogs, 550 soldiers (including 32 crossbowmen and 13 musketeers), 100 sailors along with 200 Cuban natives, several black people and a few Indian women.

The Spaniards, with their white skin, their suits of armor, their cannon and their horses, were an arresting sight. "They were very white," the old men told Sahagún. Their faces were like chalk. Indian amazement, in any case, has been the theme of most historians for the past four centuries and more, who have written of the Spanish ships of supernatural size and appearance. The newcomers were observed riding on the backs of extraordinary deerlike beasts, which snorted and bellowed, and whose running made tremors "as if stones were raining on the earth." Perhaps these creatures who rode such beasts were gods, white gods.

Yet the natives of the Yucatán and of Mexico could hardly have been quite as astonished as all that. In truth, just a year before, in 1518, the Indians had seen Spaniards cruise precisely this same coastline, in an expedition led by the adventurer Juan de Grijalva. The Indians had met the Spaniards and traded na-

tive gold ornaments and jewels for green glass beads, some scissors, pins and other trinkets. And the year before Grijalva, Francisco Hernandez de Córdoba had sailed into the Gulf of Mexico looking for gold and silver and slaves.

The new lot of Spaniards was led by Hernán Cortés, a soldier of fortune whose parents had destined him for the law until he had quit school at the age of 16. According to an account written years later by Cortés' private secretary and chaplain, Francisco López de Gómara, this "vexed his parents exceedingly. . . . He was a source of trouble to his parents as well as to himself, for he was restless, haughty, mischievous, and given to quarreling, for which reason he decided to seek his fortune." Cortés arrived in the New World in 1504, and eventually was chosen by Diego Velázquez, governor of Cuba, to command an expedition to Mexico—for exploration and trade but, officially at least, *not* to conquer or colonize.

Even so, many of those who sailed with him were experienced soldiers of fortune, men who had signed up in the hope of getting fame and riches, as well as conquering lands for Spain. Tough as they were, they were also committed, in a way we can hardly understand today, to the mission of converting the Indians to Christianity. Along the route of their journey, searching for members of an earlier journey, they picked up Jerónimo de Aguilar, a Spaniard who had been shipwrecked eight years before, then enslaved by the Maya, learning their language. The Spaniards also picked up a woman sold to the Maya by allies of the Aztecs. They called her Doña Marina. She spoke Nahuatl, the language of the Aztecs, as well as Maya. As the Spaniards moved into Aztec territory, she was helpful, translating from Nahuatl into Maya, while Aguilar translated from Maya into Spanish.

On Holy Thursday, 1519, the fleet found safe harbor on the island of San Juan de Ulúa, as the Spaniards called it, off Mexico's eastern shore. As Bernal Díaz, one of Cortés' foot solders who chronicled these events years later, tells the story, they no sooner had dropped anchor than two large canoes came out filled with Aztec ambassadors. The Indians brought with them some gifts, and they were taken aboard the flagship and given food and wine and some blue beads.

"They said that their lord," relates Bernal Díaz, "a servant of the great Montezuma [as the Spanish spelled it], had sent them to find out what kind of men we were and what we were seeking." According to Gómara, the Indians also asked the Spaniards, with exemplary diplomatic tact, "whether they intended to stop or continue on beyond." Cortés replied that the Spaniards had come to speak to the lord of the Aztecs. (According to Sahagún's native informants the Spaniards were not as polite as all that. They put the Indians in irons and fired off a cannon to scare them.)

By Easter Sunday, a local Aztec governor had arrived. His name was Tentlil, and he was accompanied, says Gómara, by more than 4,000 men, all unarmed, handsomely dressed and loaded with presents. Tentlil had brought along some artists, who made portraits in the style of Aztec picture-writing, of Cortés, his captains and soldiers, his ships and horses and guns—a detailed report to send back to Montezuma. When Cortés asked to see Montezuma himself, saying that the Spaniards came as ambassadors from the greatest king on earth, Tentlil graciously replied that word would be sent to Montezuma. Some sources say that Tentlil at first inquired testily, "How is it that you have been here only two days, and demand to see the emperor?" Cortés asked whether Montezuma had any gold, and Tentlil replied that he did. It was then, apparently, that Cortés said, in a phrase that has rung down through the ages, "Send me some of it, because I and my companions suffer from a disease of the heart which can be cured only with gold."

From his capital city of Tenochtitlán, the present site of Mexico City, the emperor Montezuma II ruled over a vast imperial domain in central Mexico stretching from the Gulf Coast to the Pacific Ocean, and as far south as present-day Guatemala. He was chosen by a group of about a hundred of the richest and most powerful members of the ruling class, and he had to maintain his rule with subtle and skillful maneuvering. Central Mexico at the time probably had a population of perhaps 25 million, with 2 million or so in the region about Tenochtitlán. Of these, perhaps a total of 500,000 could be mustered as soldiers, though the offensive force here comprised, on average, probably about 50,000 men.

Montezuma's reply to Cortés came back to the coast accompanied by more extremely lavish gifts, and word that Montezuma "rejoiced to learn about" Cortés' great king, and that Cortés should determine what he needed for himself and "the cure of his sickness," as

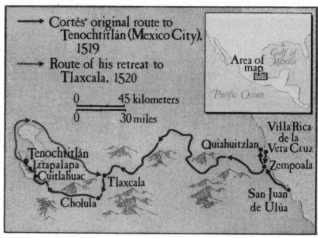

The route of the Spanish conquest of Mexico includes Cortés' retreat to Tlaxcala in the summer of 1520.

well as whatever supplies he needed for his men and his ships. But, as for Montezuma and the Spanish leader meeting, that would be "impossible."

Undismayed, Cortés gathered a sample of Spanish wealth to send to the emperor, inquiring again about a meeting and the possibility of trade. While he waited he had some surprise visitors, five Indians from the city of Zempoala—a city, they said, that had recently been brought under Montezuma's yoke by force of arms.

This piece of news electrified Cortés. As Díaz puts it, he learned "that Montezuma had opponents and enemies, which greatly delighted him." Very quickly, Cortés would come to learn how extraordinarily fragile this great empire of Montezuma's was. Mexico was a loose organization of villages and city-states linked together in an uneasy alliance. Their inhabitants spoke more than 20 different languages and hundreds of different dialects. Their local loyalties made them resentful of central government. The empire, in short, was based upon the conquest and subjugation of many embittered peoples. Cortés instantly saw the possibility of revolt in Mexico, with himself as the leader.

Eager to be rid of Cortés, Montezuma apparently reiterated in his next communication that the Spaniards might have whatever they needed but then must take their fleet and leave. Now surer of his ground, Cortés refused. It was impossible, he insisted, for the Spaniards to leave without seeing the emperor. Montezuma had provided men to wait on the Spaniards, but about this time Cortés saw that these people had disappeared. He called his captains together and told them to prepare for war.

The route the Spaniards eventually took to Montezuma's capital city was circuitous. First they headed north, to Zempoala, finding the people ready to join in an uprising against Montezuma. From there, gathering allies, they moved on to Quiahuitzlan, where they came across some of Montezuma's tax collectors—and had them arrested. (Later Cortés quietly set them free for diplomatic purposes.) As soon as the chiefs of the neighboring towns heard that the Spaniards had arrested Montezuma's tax collectors, they joined forces with Cortés against Montezuma, and even took an oath of allegiance. Almost overnight his tiny force was increased by thousands of fighting men.

Stones came like hail from Indian slings

After establishing a base at Villa Rica de la Vera Cruz, the Spaniards and their new allies ventured into the territory of the Tlaxcalans, where their mettle was tested in battles with several thousand warriors. The Indians fought with clubs, spears, slings, arrows and darts; the Spaniards with lances, artillery, muskets, crossbows and swords. Some days of nearly continuous hand-to-hand fighting occurred. Stones came like hail from the Indians' slings, Díaz says, and "their barbed and fire-hardened darts fell like corn on the threshing-floor."

The Spaniards "wondered what would happen," Díaz adds, "when we had to fight Montezuma if we were reduced to such straits by the Tlaxcalans, whom our Cempoalan allies described as a peaceful people." But in the end they had the victory, the first of many.

How, in fact, was it possible for this little band of Spaniards to march into unknown territory, defeat the vast armies brought against them, and lose only two score or so Spanish lives in such encounters?

First of all, not too much faith should be placed in the numbers used to describe the size of the enemy. Though the various Spanish estimates range from 30,000 to 100,000 warriors, it is clear that if such numbers were accurate, only a miracle could explain a Spanish victory. That miracle would seem less necessary if, say, a decimal point were moved, giving the Tlaxcalans 10,000 warriors at most. Even so, the Spaniards were greatly outnumbered.

Not too much credit can be given to the Spanish crossbows. Although they outclassed Indian bows, they were difficult to use. Nor can too much credit be given to the purely material effects of gunpowder. Spanish powder was often wet, and the rate of fire of cannon and muskets was appallingly slow.

The psychological effect of gunpowder and horses and glistening armor, though, must have been phenomenal. The Spaniards must have impressed the Indians in the way that street demonstrators are impressed—and suddenly made to feel vulnerable—when heavily armed, modern riot police wade into the midst of a crowd. Besides, some Indian tactics helped the Spaniards. They tended not to kill their enemies, hoping to wound and capture them mainly for use as sacrifices to the gods. They also stopped fighting periodically to remove their dead and wounded from the

battlefield. At close range, the Indians used wooden clubs tipped and ridged with razor-sharp obsidian—a vicious weapon against other Indians, but one which probably shattered against Spanish helmets.

The Spaniards brought their swords into this close combat, and they were dreadfully effective. Pointed and double-bladed, they could stab, and slash left and right, quickly killing or maiming. Driving directly at warriors clustered around their leaders, the Spaniards would often capture or kill a local chief. Once their chief was taken, his men usually fell back.

After two weeks the Tlaxcalans surrendered, agreeing to join Cortés against the Aztecs. As the Spaniards penetrated farther and farther into Mexico, they recruited allies until, when they reached Tenochtitlán at last, their force included about 5,000 Indians.

As the Spaniards advanced, they laid waste to the town of Cholula. It was there that Cortés killed 3,000 Indians, because, he said, they had plotted with Montezuma to attack him. Other sources describe it as an unprovoked massacre. In any case, as they approached Tenochtitlán the Spaniards' reputation for savagery and invincibility grew greater and greater.

By the time they had reached the city of Cuitlahuac, just southeast of Tenochtitlán, they had entered the lake country in the Valley of Mexico, where the towns were sometimes built entirely in the water, connected to the land by broad causeways. The towns and stone buildings, says Díaz, "seemed like an enchanted vision. . . . Indeed, some of our soldiers asked whether it was not all a dream."

As they approached the Aztec capital the Spaniards set foot on a causeway—wide enough for ten horsemen to ride abreast. And partway along it, Gómara says, they were met by 4,000 "gentlemen of the court" of Tenochtitlán, "richly dressed after their fashion," who, each in turn, bowed to the Spaniards as a sign of peace. Then, just across a little bridge, the Spaniards saw Montezuma. "He walked," Gómara adds, "under a pallium of gold and green feathers, strung about with silver hangings, and carried by four gentlemen." He was supported on the arms of two royal princes.

Courtiers walked ahead of Montezuma, sweeping the ground and laying down thin mantles so that his feet would never touch the earth. Then came 200 lords, all barefoot, but wearing rich cloaks. Cortés stepped forward to embrace Montezuma; but the two princes put out their hands at once to prevent it. The two leaders exchanged brief greetings. Only then was Cortés permitted to step forward and take a splendid necklace of pearls and cut glass and put it around the neck of Montezuma.

The emperor ordered that Cortés and many of his Indian allies be shown to a beautiful palace. There, Montezuma himself took Cortés by the hand, bidding him, Cortés says, to "sit on a very rich throne . . . and then left saying that I should wait for him." In the heart of Montezuma's empire, the Spaniards and their allies were surrounded. The Aztecs, in turn, were surrounded by more of Cortés' allies outside the city. Frozen in this balance of forces, they commenced a curious diplomatic dance, one whose end was entirely unpredictable.

Montezuma, Díaz reports, was about 40 years old, "of good height, well proportioned, spare and slight." He bathed every afternoon, according to Díaz—twice a day, according to Gómara. The Spaniards, who sometimes slept in their armor without even removing their shoes, were impressed by the frequency of Montezuma's bathing.

For a time the Spaniards were left alone. The city in which they found themselves would have impressed anyone. Tenochtitlán lay at the center of a vast bowl dominated by high mountains. At the bottom was a large plain and many shallow lakes, including Lake Texcoco, a large body of salt water. The Aztec capital had been built up atop mudbanks and islands until, like Venice, it was a wonder of human artifice, laced with canals and bridges. Three long and wide causeways connected it to the mainland. An aqueduct brought fresh water from a hillside spring into the middle of the city.

Cortés describes a marketplace "twice as big as that of Salamanca, with arcades all around, where more than sixty thousand people come each day to buy and sell." The array of goods on sale reflected the far-flung trade that the Aztecs had developed: all manner of birds—chickens, partridge, quail, turtledoves, falcons—used for food, for feathers, for hunting; gold or featherwork in the form of butterflies, trees, flowers; a silver monkey that moved its feet and head; carved turquoise and emeralds; stuff made of conchs and periwinkles; toys for children; ointments, syrups and culinary delicacies, such as little barkless dogs that had been castrated and fattened. There were even cakes made from a sort of scum skimmed from the ooze on the lake's surface and dried, to be eaten like cheese. "Delicious," says Gómara.

All around the city, according to Cortés, were many temples, "beautiful buildings," but among them all, there was one "whose great size and magnificence no human tongue could describe." The main temple occupied a site about 70 by 80 yards at its base, with two staircases leading up nearly 200 feet to a terrace and twin shrines. There the stones were splattered black with the blood of human sacrifices.

Most often, the victim would be led or dragged to the top of the temple steps and stretched out over a block of stone by five priests. A priest would cut him open, reach in and pluck out his still-beating heart. The heart was offered up in a sacred vessel, often to placate the Sun. The body was thrown down the temple steps and then flayed and cut up. Its skull went to a great skull rack (where, according to Gómara, there were 136,000 skulls, arranged in rows, teeth outward),

and the remainder was sometimes ceremoniously eaten, usually by the warriors who had captured the victim.

In the days to come, as Cortés and Montezuma met, Cortés broached his wish to convert Montezuma to Christianity and spoke of the evils of the Aztec gods—a topic of conversation that must have struck Montezuma as outrageously rude, and irrelevant to the business of conducting trade or to negotiations between an emperor and a visiting captain general.

A commander "beset with misgivings"

For their part, the Spaniards evidently became increasingly uneasy about the absurdity and perilousness of their position. Even Cortés himself came to feel "beset with misgivings," sharing a dreadful sense of being caught in a web from which he and his men could never escape. It had begun to dawn on them that there was no reason for Montezuma to let them leave Tenochtitlán alive. Eventually, they devised a most astounding way out of their dilemma. They decided to seize Montezuma and hold him hostage in his own city.

And so, says Gómara, Cortés took some of his soldiers with him to pay a call on the emperor. Cortés greeted Montezuma "as usual, and then began to jest and banter with him, as he had done before." But soon enough Cortés got to the point, and told the emperor that he would need to come and stay with the Spaniards. Montezuma was "profoundly shaken," says Gómara, and replied, "My person is not such as can be taken prisoner, and even if I should consent to it, my people would not suffer it."

According to Díaz, Cortés and Montezuma spent more than half an hour discussing the question. Cortés' soldiers grew jittery. "What is the use of all these words?" one of them burst out. "Either we take him or we knife him. If we do not look after ourselves now we shall be dead men." In the end Montezuma went peacefully with the Spaniards.

How was it that the Aztec emperor could have allowed himself to be placed in such a position? Sahagún's informants gave an explanation of the mystery that has endured ever since: Montezuma and the Aztecs thought that Cortés was none other than the ancient god-king Quetzalcóatl, the Feathered Serpent, who, according to religious myth, had been driven from his kingdom vowing one day to return and reassert his rule. Therefore some historians believe that Montezuma was a prisoner of his own mythology. The myth is a wonderful explanation but, as British archaeologist Nigel Davis points out, it "has been rather overplayed in popular accounts." Besides, purely diplomatic protocol provides a reasonable explanation—Montezuma waited for Cortés to arrive at Tenochtitlán simply because it was the Aztec custom that an ambassador was immune from harm.

Or it may be that, as word came of Spanish military

and diplomatic victories, Montezuma came to comprehend that these strangers needed to be handled with great care. This, in any case, appears to have been Cortés' view. As Gómara explains, Montezuma "did not wish to stir up trouble for himself (and this was the truest reason)" by offering open resistance to Cortés and thus perhaps encouraging more of his discontented subjects to join the Spaniards in an attempt to unseat his power. He would pursue the strategy of the spider and the fly; he would bring Cortés into Tenochtitlán and informally hold him hostage, in the same way that he customarily held numerous rival chiefs as permanent hostages.

While the Spaniards kept Montezuma in captivity—sometimes, indeed, in manacles—the myth of Montezuma's rule had to be maintained. Each day the Spaniards would ask him what his orders and his wants were, and these were carried out. Sometimes Cortés and Montezuma would sit together and play *totoloque*, a game that involved tossing small pellets of gold for higher stakes, usually more gold or jewelry.

Eventually, perhaps trying to quench the Spanish thirst for gold, Montezuma agreed not only to open up his personal treasure but to call in gifts from his whole empire and give them to Cortés. The list of what he gave is breathtaking: gold and silver and pearls, golden nose crescents and necklaces, blowguns inlaid with silver, silver plates and cups, pitchers and saucers. There was so much gold treasure from Montezuma's gifts alone, says Díaz, that it took the Spaniards three days just to examine it all.

Soon afterward it appeared that some of the Aztec leaders, tired of seeing their emperor truckling to the Spaniards, told Montezuma that either the Spaniards should leave or the Aztecs should kill them. Aware of the danger, Cortés ordered that the horses be kept saddled and bridled day and night; Spanish soldiers slept in their armor, their weapons beside them.

But just at the critical point—it was May 1520—Montezuma's messengers brought news that another Spanish fleet, captained by Pánfilo de Narváez, had been spotted back at San Juan de Ulúa, where Cortés had originally landed. A picture painted on cloth was brought to Montezuma. There were 18 ships, 80 horses and 900 soldiers.

Cortés greeted the news with an appearance of relief, even joy. However, out of Montezuma's presence he grew "very thoughtful," Díaz says. He guessed that Diego Velázquez had sent the fleet to put a stop to his enterprise, and he sensed the presence of rivals for the Aztec riches as well as a possible split among the Spaniards that the Aztecs might exploit. Cortés left for the coast, taking about 120 soldiers with him and leaving fewer than 100 at Tenochtitlán, under the command of Pedro de Alvarado, a man with the reputation of being brave but cruel.

At Zempoala, Cortés took Narváez's army by surprise at night. Narváez himself got a pike thrust that cost him an eye and was put into irons. Most of his men joined Cortés, augmenting his force with a large and fresh lot of soldiers, including, as Gómara reports, "a Negro sick with the smallpox"—who would, as we now know, turn out to be a very significant figure in the final tragedy.

Back in Tenochtitlán, however, the whole city had exploded in violence. The Indians had been celebrating the annual festival of Toxcatl in the courtyard of the great temple square with "drums, conch trumpets, bone fifes" and other instruments. They were covered with necklaces and jewels, feathers and pearls, and danced in circles, accompanied by sacred singing. In the midst of the dancing the Spanish soldiers abruptly closed off all the exits and, with swords drawn, waded into the midst of the dancers.

"They attacked the man who was drumming," according to Sahagún's native informants, "and cut off his arms. Then they cut off his head, and it rolled across the floor. They attacked all the celebrants, stabbing them, spearing them. . . . Others they beheaded . . . or split their heads to pieces. . . . Some attempted to run away, but . . . they seemed to tangle their feet in their own entrails."

The next day the Aztecs who had not been trapped in the courtyard counterattacked. Full-scale fighting swept through the city, bringing about all of the horrors that Montezuma apparently had feared and labored for so long to avoid. The emperor watched, powerless, as the city, which had thus far been saved from bloodshed, was threatened with disaster. The Aztecs closed off the causeways, destroyed some of the bridges over which the Spaniards might escape and threw up barricades around the palace, hoping to starve the Spaniards out.

Trapped inside the Aztec city

Hearing the news, Cortés at once rushed back toward Tenochtitlán. As he passed through the countryside, he discovered "all the land was in revolt and almost uninhabited." In late June, when he reentered Montezuma's city, he found the streets almost deserted. There was an ominous quiet, as the Aztecs let the Spaniards back into the trap. By next morning, the roads around Tenochtitlán were filled with angry warriors, all of them enemies of the Spaniards. The thousands of Cortés' native allies now seemed to melt away, except for the few thousand Tlaxcalans trapped with the Spaniards inside the city.

"Such a multitude" of Aztecs now swarmed in to surround the Spaniards' quarters, says Cortés, "that neither the streets nor the roofs of the houses could be seen for them." And soon, so many stones began to be "hurled at us from their slings into the fortress that it seemed they were raining from the sky. . . ."

Wave after wave of Aztecs repeatedly attacked, often running headlong into Spanish guns, cannon and swords. Some tried to scale the walls of the palace. Finally, they shot burning arrows into the fortress, hoping to smoke the enemy out. One whole section of the palace fell, but the attackers never got in.

At last Cortés sent for Montezuma and asked him to go up to the roof of the palace and tell his people to stop the fighting and let the Spaniards leave in peace. According to Díaz, Montezuma mounted to the roof, and a great silence fell over the thousands who swarmed over the streets and nearby rooftops. The emperor begged his people to put down their arms and let the Spaniards go. But, Díaz says, the chiefs replied to Montezuma—"in tears"—that they no longer recognized him as their leader, and they would not stop now until all the Spaniards were dead, "and they begged for his forgiveness."

And then, a shower of darts and stones was thrown at Montezuma. The Spanish soldiers rushed the emperor back inside the palace. But soon thereafter, because he refused to eat or have his wounds tended, Montezuma died.

While most sources agree with this account, some, mostly native sources, say that Montezuma was murdered by the Spaniards back in their palace quarters.

It was now imperative for the Spaniards to get out of the city. In the middle of the night of June 30, 1520, they brought the gold and jewels and silver out into the middle of a hall in the palace. Those who wanted some, took it and stuffed it into their packs and clothes. Shortly before midnight, Cortés and his men made a run for it across one of the causeways.

The horsemen went out first, presumably to charge and scatter any Aztecs who might block the way. They were followed by soldiers carrying a makeshift wooden bridge to be used in place of the bridges the Aztecs had destroyed. The retreating Spanish managed to slam the bridge down across the first break they came to. They had caught the Aztecs by surprise, and so a good many Spaniards slipped past the main mass of Indians. But then an alarm sounded—trumpets, cries and whistles—and their retreat became a headlong dash down the causeway. Crowds of Aztec warriors threw stones and spears at them, and, as Díaz says, they had to leave the bridge behind at the first gap.

Trying to get over the next gap without the bridge was a disaster. As horses slipped and fell into the water, cannon and bundles and boxes followed. The Spaniards rushed on from gap to gap, fleeing ahead of the Aztec warriors, braving the improvised gauntlet of warrior-filled canoes on either side of the causeway. Those who had been most greedy about stuffing gold into their clothes were among the first to sink with the weight of it as they crossed. "So those who died," Gómara notes dryly, "died rich."

According to Díaz, there had been 1,300 Spanish soldiers in Tenochtitlán in those last days (much of Cortés' original army, plus Narváez's reinforcements) as well as 2,000 native warriors, mostly Tlaxcalans. Estimates of those killed in the siege and flight from the city range from 450 to 860 Spaniards and 1,000 to 4,000 Tlaxcalans.

The survivors continued to flee, all the way to the city of Tlaxcala, where their strongest allies took them in. For Cortés and the Tlaxcalans, there was no quitting the struggle with the Aztecs.

Realizing that to take back the Aztec capital he would have to attack and seize the city from both the causeways and the surrounding water, Cortés had boats built so they could be carried piecemeal over land and then assembled to operate in the shallow lake waters. In late December of 1520, Cortés reentered the Valley of Mexico, secured the shores of the lake, and destroyed the aqueduct that brought the main supply of fresh water into the city.

In late April 1521 the siege began, Cortés sending his boats across the water, and his foot soldiers down the causeways. The Aztecs had prepared their defenses by planting sharpened stakes just under the water at the gaps in the causeway. As fighting continued, the Spanish kept filling in the gaps with stones and rubble, but at night the Aztecs reopened them. Once, when the Aztecs took prisoners, they cut off the heads of some and bowled them at the approaching army.

Day and night, the fighting went on. The Spaniards would secure a street, only to find it taken back the next day. At last Cortés instructed his men to advance, slowly and deliberately, removing every Aztec barricade, destroying every Aztec tower and house as they went. The slow, grinding reduction of Tenochtitlán went on for three months, and toward the end the stench of unburied bodies piled high in the streets and rotting in the water was appalling. In the last offensive, so "piteous" was the wailing of women and children, says Gómara, that Cortés urged his men to spare the populace, but they kept on. As the city began at last to collapse, a gush of old men, women and children came flooding out toward the causeways with such force "that they pushed each other into the water, where many drowned."

The end came on August 13, 1521. The few Aztec warriors still alive gathered on the rooftops of the houses that still stood, and "stared at the ruins of their city in a dazed silence." As the Spaniards walked at last down the inner streets of the conquered city, they tied handkerchiefs over their noses to guard against the stench. They went through town, seeing the stagnant and briny water that had served as drinking water in these last days of Tenochtitlán, and the remnants of what the Aztecs had had for food: lizards and salt grasses from the lake, twigs, roots and tree bark.

Among the piles of bodies were people who had died not so much of wounds as of starvation and of various diseases, especially smallpox—the virus that had been brought ashore by the man in Narváez's crew, a virus that had made its way across Mexico with Cortés' army. The populations of the Americas had no resistance to it.

In some regions of Mexico, the mortality rate was so great that the living could not bring themselves to bury the dead. It was said that the Indians, overwhelmed by the task, sometimes pulled down the houses on top of the dead to bury them.

Cortés' story did not end here. Like many other New World adventurers, he went on to great wealth and power. But in the end, accused of murder and mis-management, he died broken-hearted in Spain. The pestilence that his invasion brought did not end with the death of Tenochtitlán, either. Smallpox and other epidemics spread throughout the countryside, subsided and recurred, subsided and recurred, until, eventually, of a total population of perhaps 25 million, as many as 22 million died.

And with the death of so many, a civilization died—not simply a city or a government or an empire, but most of the accumulated knowledge of life and art and skill, so that, in time, practically all that remained of it were its artifacts and its story of the inevitability, in life and in history, of tragedy, and surprise.

Discovering Europe, 1493

A year after Columbus sailed west,
Native Americans sailed east—as envoys and
sightseers as well as captives.

HARALD PRINS AND BUNNY MCBRIDE

HARALD PRINS AND BUNNY MCBRIDE are anthropologists. Prins teaches at Kansas State U. and is co-editor of "American Beginnings: Exploration, Culture and Cartography in the Land of Norumbega," U. of Nebraska Press. McBride ("Modern Medieval Vacation," WM, March '92) is author of "Our Lives in Our Hands," on Micmac basketmakers, Tilbury House, 1991.

"In the yeere 1153...it is written, that there came to Lubec, a citie of Germanie, one canoa with certaine Indians, like unto a long barge: which seemed to have come from the coast of Baccaloaos [Newfoundland]." This intriguing historical snippet comes via geographer Richard Hakluyt (1552-1616), an Oxford lecturer who translated many early accounts of the Americas. Although evidence supporting this very early chronicle of Native Americans in Europe remains elusive, the report hints at things to come. Later, substantiated records show that during the Age of Exploration, launched by Columbus's 1492 voyage across the Atlantic, hundreds of American Indians did travel in the other direction—to Portugal, Spain, France, or England.

In fact, records from 55 transatlantic journeys show that no fewer than 1,600 Indians had landed in Europe by the time Pilgrims sailing on the Mayflower landed on Massachusetts shores in 1620. True, they relied on European ships to get there. True, about two-thirds went as captives, usually sold as slaves. But the balance went for other reasons—as adventurers, envoys, guides, sightseers, or performers.

The first confirmed Native American journey to Europe occurred in 1493, when

Pocahontas as Lady Rebecca: Daughter of intertribal leader Powhatan traveled to England and was celebrated by London society after befriending settlers near Jamestown, Virginia, and marrying colonist John Rolfe. She died in Kent in 1617 as she was about to embark on her voyage home.

Ætatis suæ 21. Aº.1616.

Matoaks als Rebecka daughter to the mighty Prince Powhatan Emperour of Attanoughkomouck als Virginia converted and baptized in the Christian faith, and Wife to the worth Mr. Tho: Rolff.

10 Tainos sailed from Haiti to Spain in the caravels of their Spanish visitors. While there is no clear evidence that they were kidnapped, it is likely that they were lured on board by trade goods, then taken by surprise as the ship lifted anchor and set sail.

Approaching the harbor, the Indians saw a forest of masts belonging to an exotic array of sailing vessels—carracks, caravels, feluccas, galleys, pinnaces, shallops—quite different from their seagoing dugout canoes that carried up to 80 people.

From Seville six of the Indians walked 800 miles with Columbus to Barcelona to visit the royal court. During their five-week stay they were baptized in the city's magnificent cathedral, with King Ferdinand and Queen Isabella acting as godparents. One received the name Don Juan de Castilla (after the king's son), and remained with Ferdinand's household, "where he was well-behaved and circumspect, as if he had been the son of an important caballero," wrote eyewitness Gonzalo de Oviedo, royal chronicler of Spanish possessions in the New World. Seven Tainos, including one who was baptized Diego Colón (after Columbus's brother, no doubt), joined Columbus on his second voyage to the Caribbean. Five of them died en route. Diego, one of the survivors, served Columbus as guide and interpreter during his subsequent explorations in the Caribbean.

The Europe discovered by American Indians during the 16th century was in one of its most dynamic eras—the Renaissance. Stimulated by intellectual revolutions and an aggressive mercantile expansionism born of a quick series of major technological innovations, the Renaissance carried a maelstrom of cultural change that left no city in Europe untouched. Indians arriving on the scene encountered people who no longer believed the earth was the center of the universe. They were introduced to Europe's elite, an enterprising, arrogant, supremely confident lot ready to push back the limits of their traditional worlds to seek wealth and glory in faraway lands still shrouded in mystery. Meanwhile, most of Europe's population remained shrouded in poverty, struggling to survive as rural peasants and laborers.

As far as we know, Native Americans didn't write down their observations of 16th-century Europe. However, the Europeans they had contact with sometimes did. On the basis of ship logs, merchant reports, travel accounts, and other historical records, we know that visiting

Indians viewed European life with a mixture of awe, admiration, and disdain—probably not unlike the way most Europeans viewed them.

No doubt Mexican Indian nobles from the magnificent city of Tenochtitlán (pop. 250,000), with its great temple pyramids and royal palaces, were less moved by a major French riverport such as the merchant city of Rouen (pop. 40,000) than were Algonquian Indians from the Gulf of St. Lawrence, migratory hunters who lived in temporary encampments seldom larger than 300 people.

Overall, however, Indian visitors appear to have been favorably impressed by Europe's technology (especially firearms, windmills, and iron tools) and colorful religious and secular ceremonies, while being appalled at the hordes of beggars, the foul urban odors, and the dirty, flea- and bug-infested homes of so many Europeans at the time.

Some Indian voyagers went to Europe more or less as scouts. One of the first was Essomericq, son of Carijo chief Arosca in southern Brazil. In 1505, Arosca was host to French Capt. Paulmier de Gonneville while they negotiated a trade deal in local brazilwood, prized in Europe as a dye base for scarlet cloth. Before the captain returned to Normandy, Arosca asked him to take his son along to learn "artillery, which they greatly desired to dominate their enemies, and also how to make mirrors, knives, axes, and all that they saw and admired among the Christians." The captain agreed, promising to bring the young man back home on his next run for brazilwood.

Gonneville's guest was "well regarded in Honfleur and in all the places we passed: for there had never been in France a person from so distant a country." Essomericq was baptized and well-educated. He ultimately married the captain's daughter,

Suzanne. His father-in-law bequeathed him property, as well as the family name. Essomericq became Binot de Gonneville, and never returned home.

In 1528, eight years after Hernán Cortés defeated Montezuma, the Aztec emperor's son and several other Mexican *caciques* (lords) from Tenochtitlán and Tlaxcala sailed with Cortés as political envoys to the court of Spanish emperor Charles V, then at Toledo. They traveled in the company of Indian entertainers, including a dozen Aztec jugglers and acrobats. Journeying to Toledo by way of Seville, the cavalcade rivaled the spectacle staged at Columbus's return. Although the Aztec acrobats remained in Europe, having been presented to Pope Clement VII, there is reason to believe that the *caciques* ultimately returned to Mexico.

France entered the global quest for fortune by searching for the imagined Northwest Passage to Cathay (China) and Cipangō (Japan) along North America's Atlantic seaboard. In 1534, the French monarch, Francis I, turned the search over to Jacques Cartier of Saint-Malo. Cartier crossed the Atlantic three times on this mission. Each time he sought native intelligence about the lay of the land.

On his first expedition, Cartier picked up Taignoagny and Domagaya, sons of Iroquois chief Donnacona of Stadacona (present-day Quebec City)—a palisaded farming community of about 1,000 inhabitants. They traveled to France, learned French, and told the navigator that the St. Lawrence was not the strait to China, but a route to a country named Canada which—so they led Cartier to believe—should contain the gold he was seeking. The next year they recrossed the Atlantic and guided Cartier up the St. Lawrence. In 1536, Taignoagny and Domagaya made another voyage with the French navigator. This time Cartier pressed their father, Donnacona, and several other leading Iroquoians to come along.

In France, the Iroquoians mastered French and helped create a French-Iroquois lexicon. A section of the king's commission for establishing a colony in Canada reports that they were "long maintained in our kingdom, [and] instructed...in the Christian doctrine, with the intention of taking them back to said country with a good number of our subjects of good will to help influence the peoples of these lands to believe in the holy faith...." It seems the Iroquois leaders had goals of their own. A Spanish report of the time notes they "were traveling contentedly in the hope of returning quickly to Canada with a good share of wealth." However, all the informants died before they could accompany the French on their first colonizing attempt in North America in 1541.

During the 16th century the city of Rouen became France's center for trade in brazilwood. By the middle of the century, Brazilian Indians arriving in French vessels were a familiar sight here, and it had become fashionable for kings, princes, and powerful barons—each engaged in a brilliant display of social rank—to have American Indians in their entourages.

In the 16th century it was fashionable for European kings to have American Indians in their entourages.

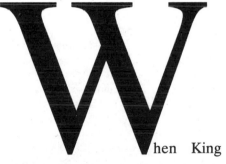

When King Henry II and his wife Catherine de Médici announced intentions to visit Rouen in 1550, city officials and merchants organized a fabulous welcome that included a tableau of Brazilian Indian life. Their aim was to thank the king for giving their city a monopoly on Brazilian imports and to win his support in their struggle against Portuguese and Spanish domination in the Americas. Workers transformed a meadow alongside the Seine River to look like a Tupinambá jungle village in Brazil. They built thatched huts, planted bushes, and enhanced trees with extra branches. Then they festooned the whole green scene with imitation fruit, and released scores of parrots, monkeys, and other South American animals.

An eyewitness report notes that 300 people performed "completely naked, tanned and shaggy, without in any way covering the parts that nature commands, and were decorated and equipped in the manner of those savages of America from whom brazilwood is brought. Among their number were a good 50 natural savages [Tupinambá Indians] freshly brought from that country...."

The pageant opened with a portrayal of everyday life in coastal Brazil—some archery, game chasing, hammock lounging, and loading wood onto a French ship anchored in the river. Then came a mock attack on the Tupinambá village by their hostile Tobajara neighbors, who were allied with the Portuguese. As a climax, the Tupinambás torched the Tobajara hut.

The king and his court were enchanted, which greatly pleased the Rouennais merchants and officials who bankrolled the spectacle.

The France viewed by Indian visitors in the second half of the 16th century was a place of violent turmoil and great inequities. By 1580, some 800,000 people had died in religious wars and famine. French philosopher Michel de Montaigne captured the situation in an essay describing a 1562 discussion between young King Charles IX (son of Henry II) and three Tupinambás visiting Rouen. Asked what they thought of Rouen and its people, the Tupinambás said "they had noticed that there were among us men full and gorged with all sorts of good things, and that [others] were beggars at their doors, emaciated with hunger and poverty; and they thought it strange that these needy halves could endure such injustice...."

These Tupinambá impressions were echoed by a Micmac Indian living in Nova Scotia, who offered this social commentary to a Jesuit priest: "...You [French] are envious and are all the time slandering each other; you are thieves and deceivers; you are covetous, and are neither generous nor kind; as for us, if we have a morsel of bread we share it with our neighbor."

Throughout the 16th century, there was considerable European activity in the bountiful cod fisheries off the coasts of Micmac country in Newfoundland and Nova Scotia. By 1578, thousands of men aboard some 350 vessels were fishing these waters and trading with Indians on the mainland. As in the southern reaches of the Americas, native peoples from the north ventured abroad. Among the most fascinating travelers was Messamoet, chieftain of a Micmac band in Nova Scotia. Probably traveling on a Basque fishing ship, and clad in a beaver or otter robe and moosehide moccasins and leggings, he went to France around 1580 and for two years lived as the guest of the governor of Bayonne, a Basque seaport north of the Pyrenees. No doubt the Micmac and the Basque had mutual vested interests in a friendship: Each offered the other a vital link in the lucrative fur trade.

After Messamoet's trip abroad, he prospered as a fur trader, sailing his own Basque shallop, negotiating deals in pidgin French or Basque. He encountered various explorers in his homeland, including Samuel de Champlain, whose records show that Messamoet guided him on explorations of the Maine coast in 1604, '05, and '06.

Jesuit priest Biard noted that he met a band of Micmacs headed by Chief Cacagous who had also been to France. "...He told me he had been baptized in Bayonne, relating his story to me as one tells about going to a ball out of friendship." This attitude seems typical among the many Indians who allowed themselves to be baptized while visiting Europe. To most, the ritual probably had more to do with business and friendship than religion.

The officials, merchants, or sea captains who played host to the likes of Cacagous surely had a different view on Indian baptisms. Each saved soul enhanced France's campaign to establish its right to evangelize (and by extension to colonize) the Americas.

Sometimes Indian leaders with a "ready capacity" to serve colonial interests were seized and then cajoled into becoming informants. English captain George Waymouth, exploring the Gulf of Maine for the gentleman-entrepreneur Sir Ferdinando Gorges in 1605, locked Chief Nahanada and four other Wabanaki Indians from the Pemaquid area below deck after luring them on board with some friendly trading. They were taken to Plymouth, England, where they lodged with Gorges. In the years that followed these men helped map the New England coast, working with at least eight English explorers, who also participated in fur trade and cod fishing. Among the explorers was Capt. John Smith, who wrote "My main assistance next to God...was my acquaintance among the savages, especially with Dohannida [Nahanada], one of their greatest lords who has lived long in England."

In 1614 English sea captain Thomas Hunt, who had sailed in consort with Capt. John Smith to the Maine coast, ventured on to Cape Cod. There he kidnapped 20 Pawtucket Indians, including a tribesman named Squanto. He sailed on to Spain, hoping to sell the captives, plus 40,000 dried cods. He sold the fish in Málaga, but his slave-trade plans were foiled by Spanish friars who took "them and kept them to be instructed in the Christian faith."

Squanto's life is indicative of how tipped the scales were in the Indian-European encounter during the Age of Exploration. While at least 1,600 Indians ventured to Europe prior to 1620, 400,000 Europeans crossed the Atlantic in the other direction. Though most of the Europeans stayed on as permanent residents in the New World, almost all Native American voyagers chose to return home if they could. In contrast to Europe, which prospered enormously through the encounter, the Americas were devastated. In addition to wars and famines, Indians fell victim to alien diseases, causing the death of perhaps 50 million people—up to 90% of the indigenous population in the Western Hemisphere.

Somehow Squanto "got away for England," found lodging in London, learned English, and linked up with Thomas Dermer, a sea captain. In 1619 Dermer sailed to the Gulf of Maine, taking Squanto along as interpreter-guide. The captain wrote that they traveled to "my savage's native country," where they found "all dead," owing to an epidemic. Following the inland expedition, Dermer sailed on and Squanto joined survivors among the neighboring Wampanoag people.

In 1620 the Pilgrims settled at the site of Squanto's deserted village. The next year Squanto came to their settlement, named New Plymouth. He began serving the Pilgrims as guide and mediator, helping them secure peace with hostile neighboring bands. When Squanto died a year later, Plymouth Colony had a firm foothold in the area.

The Potato Connection

HOW THE NEW WORLD FED THE OLD

Alfred W. Crosby

In the 16th century, Francisco López de Gómara, biographer of Hernán Cortés and historian of Spain's new empire, declared that the European discovery of the New World was one of the two most important events since Creation—the other being the incarnation of God. To Gómara's fellow Europeans, the Americas did indeed provide golden opportunities for conquest and evangelization. But they had no idea that their most influential acquisitions would be the food crops they took home, chiefly maize and the white potato.

For those of us who live in the Western Hemisphere, the importance of Christopher Columbus's landfall in 1492 is self-apparent. But what difference did it make for the peoples on the other side of the Atlantic Ocean?

For some, the impact of contact was undoubtedly negative. The forced migration of millions of Africans to America's plantations, for example, was to Europe's advantage, but certainly not to Africa's. Most Asians, until the mid-19th century, were indifferent to the discovery of the Americas.

But in Europe the fallout from Columbus's find was immense. Europeans extracted enormous sums—in Spanish dollars, French livres and British pounds—from the New World's mines, soils and waters, capital that may have spurred the industrial revolution in Europe. And what would European history, plagued by riot and war, have been like without America to receive 50 million or so people? How would modern science have developed if the unknown plants, animals and peoples of America had not exploded old concepts? The authorities of antiquity had known nothing of America's existence. They had envisioned one-legged men, phoenixes and griffins, which could not be found anywhere; but they had not written of animals with pockets (opossums), birds that fly backwards (hummingbirds) or snakes that rattle, all of which awaited discovery in the New World. Never had they dreamed of the variety of peoples native to America, whose very diversity inspired the invention of anthropology, a scientific outlook many Europeans could not yet embrace, reverting instead to the ancient concept of the subhuman heathen or creating new fictions like Jean Jacques Rousseau's "noble savage." Both concepts still stalk our scholarship and popular culture today.

While such examples of America's shaping influence on Old World *thought* are impressive, they do not reflect direct influence in the way that the transfer of plants and animals does.

Biologically, America was indeed a new world to Europeans, Africans and Asians. It had been separate from the Old World for an immense stretch of time, except for connections in the frigid north, and free from even that frosty link for the past 10,000 years. It had been independent for long enough to have raccoons, skunks, chipmunks, hummingbirds and rattlesnakes, and for Americans to have developed their own distinct civilizations. Politically, America may have become a satellite of the Old World—specifically of Europe—after 1492, but biologically the Old and New Worlds were near equals. The Old World proffered its distinctive flora and fauna—smallpox virus, malaria plasmodia, horses, cattle, sheep, house cats, starlings, wheat, rice, barley, turnips, peas and so on. The New World's most influential contributions were food crops.

A few other life forms—largely valueless exports—made their way over. Turkeys crossed the Atlantic early but never replaced any of the Old World's domesticated fowl; North American gray squirrels have largely displaced the indigenous red squirrels in Great Britain; and American muskrats have spread from central Europe beyond the Urals. But the impact of such transplants has been minimal. The exception may be the spirochete of syphilis, which many scientists and historians claim is as American as the rattlesnake. Europeans first recognized the disease in the mid-1490s, shortly after Columbus's return from America. Voltaire vested his pie-in-the-sky Pangloss with the infection. Pangloss caught it from Paquette, who caught it from a monk and so on back to an early Jesuit, who had caught it from one of Columbus's companions. Did the real Columbus, as many have insisted for the last half millennium, transport the disease across the Atlantic?

THE SCIENTIFIC RECORD IS FRUSTRATINGLY UNCLEAR. Syphilis is one of a close-knit family of diseases, or perhaps one manifestation of an ancient and widely distributed infection. Proving that a given lesion on an ancient bone was caused by syphilis and not by a similar infection is a shaky proposition. In fact, the disease has provoked far more literature than more important illnesses—tuberculosis or malaria, for instance. (Sin is catnip for scientists and scholars alike.) Certainly it has had a decisive influence on the lives of particular individuals—including Gustave Flaubert and Lord Randolph Churchill, Winston's father. But syphilis has not deflected the course of human history. American crops have.

A mention of the important American food crops immediately reveals their significance for Old World agriculture and diet. Who can imagine Italian cooking without the tomato, Indian curries without the chili pepper, or an Irish stew without potatoes to mop up the gravy? Protein-rich American beans (kidney, navy, string, lima, butter, pole, French, haricot, snap, frijol, but not the soybean) have served as "poor man's meat" in Europe, Africa and Asia. These, along with the peanut and fruits like the guava, papaya, squashes, avocado and pineapple, have fed Old World peoples for centuries, but their effects on the course of history are negligible compared with those of America's four abundant sources of carbohydrates: manioc, maize and the two potatoes.

Potatoes, white and sweet, are related not botanically, but only by an accident of comprehension. The Taino Indians of the Greater Antilles and Bahamas used the word "batata" for sweet potato; in the 16th century, the Spanish mistakenly transferred the word to the Andean tuber, and their names have been confused ever since. (The fact that Old World yams are also often called sweet potatoes does not help.)

Manioc, maize, sweet potatoes and white potatoes are extraordinarily hardy and more productive than the staples of Old World agriculture, except for rice. Their cultivation requires human labor, of which the Old World had a surplus, plus a stick, some sort of spade and perhaps a knife. American Indians, who had few beasts of burden and no metal farming equipment, had bred crops that required neither. Their needs adapted these crops for the peasants and poor of the Old World.

Most inhabitants of the temperate zones know manioc only as tapioca, the bulk element of certain desserts. Since its transfer (probably by Portuguese slavers) from Brazil, it has become one of Africa's most basic staples and is often considered a native plant. More than three times as much manioc root is now produced there as in South America. Often known as cassava, it is one of the developing world's great staples. Tropical peoples eat its tender shoots and leaves but value it chiefly for its starchy roots, which can weigh as much as 11 pounds. It is an amazingly hardy plant, resistant to pests and infections, thriving from sea level to 7,000 feet in poor soils, both in flood and drought. In Indonesia, it flourishes where thirsty rice cannot, in the hills and mountains.

The sweet potato probably arrived in the 17th century in New Guinea (brought over by Chinese and Malay traders), where its generous productivity in the highlands may have triggered a population explosion—just as the white potato did in Ireland during the same period. In warm lands the sweet potato (which, like manioc, was first seen by Europeans in the West Indies) also does well on marginal ground. It is important as a staple and particularly as a backup crop or famine food in Africa, China and regions of Indonesia where rice won't grow. Unlike manioc, it thrives in frostless temperate zones; it carried thousands of Japanese through the famines of 1832, 1844, 1872 and 1896 when other crops failed.

BUT MORE IMPORTANT THAN MANIOC AND SWEET POtatoes for feeding the masses of the Old World were maize and the white potato. Their distributions overlap, with more of the grain in warm lands, more of the tuber in cooler. The one spurred population growth in Africa, the other in northern Europe.

The scientific name, *Zea mays,* and the common maize were both derived from the Taino word for the crop, whose fields of it were the first ever seen by Europeans. But somehow English speakers of North America tagged the American cereal "corn," the generic term used in Britain for all cereals (which is incidentally what the word refers to in the King James version of the Bible—Abraham, Joshua, David, Solomon, Jesus and St. Paul never saw an ear of the American grain).

The Maya and a number of other American Indian peoples had maize gods—and no wonder. It provides for more of humanity's needs than any other crop. It is one of the most versatile, thriving in climates as diverse as torrid Nigeria and the cool plains of northern China. In times of need, it can be eaten green. In times of war, it can be left on the stalk after it ripens, protected at least for a while from weather, birds and rodents by its husk. Once harvested and dried, it can be stored for years without spoiling. Its grain makes as good feed for livestock as for humans, and its leaves, unlike those of the other grains, make good fodder. Huts and sheds can be built of its stalks, and smoking pipes fashioned from its cobs.

In 1498, according to Columbus, maize was already growing in Castile, but Europeans hesitated before adopting it. Northern Europe was too cool, and in much of the south the crop required irrigation during dry Mediterranean summers. Iberian Jews and Muslims, fleeing Christian persecution, may have brought it to the eastern Mediterranean, where population pressure was greater than in western Europe in the 16th century, and maize was recorded in the 1570s growing "six, seven or eight cubits high" in fields along the Euphrates and around Jerusalem and Aleppo.

The slave trade, which placed a premium on cheap food that would survive the heat and damp of equatorial passage, was what brought maize to Africa (although linguistic evidence suggests that the grain also came down the coast from the Middle East). West Africans were cultivating maize at least as early as the last half of the 16th century, and shipwrecked Portuguese saw fields of it on the coast of South Africa's Indian Ocean as early as 1630. By the latter half of the 19th century, maize was one of the most widely cultivated of all foods in Africa.

Indonesian chroniclers paid little attention to the arrival of maize (food tends to receive much less attention than kings and battles), but, like manioc, the crop grew in countryside unsuitable for paddy rice, such as the lofty interior of Java. It proved a boon to China, where in the 16th century almost all the level, wet land for rice was already under cultivation, and the Chinese had few crops that would do well in hilly, drier and colder lands. Today China is second only to the United States as a producer of this American grain, and in China, unlike the United States, it is used almost entirely to feed humans.

The potato is to the temperate zone what rice is to the tropics. Given plenty of water, this Andean plant will produce more calories per unit of land in a cool climate than any alternative. Its tuber (a fleshy part of the underground stem) is a rich source of starch and provides some protein and even vitamin C, which was often in chronic shortage in northern winter diets. One can almost live on a diet of potatoes alone, which the Irish proved: A man with no more than a spade, even a wooden one, and an acre and a half of land in potatoes could, with a few supplements such as buttermilk, keep a family of five healthy. Adam Smith, the Scottish economist, recognized the potato's increasing value in this backhanded compliment to it and the Irish:

> The chairmen, porters, and coal-heavers in London, and those unfortunate women who live by prostitution, the strongest men and the most beautiful women perhaps in the British dominions, are said to be, the greater part of them, from the lowest rank of people in Ireland, who are generally fed with this root [sic]. No food can afford a more decisive proof of its nourishing quality, or of its being peculiarly suitable to the health of the human constitution.

The potato's disadvantage is that it does not keep well, and before modern refrigeration those who relied on it were always dependent on the success of the next harvest.

The Old World was slow to take to the potato. European farmers already had the earthy turnip and parsnip, and the fact that the leaves of the potato plant are toxic did not encourage its wholesale cultivation or consumption. But the potato had another appeal: Europeans considered it (like the tomato) an aphrodisiac. That's why when Shakespeare's Falstaff sees the object of his affection approaching in *The Merry Wives of Windsor*, he lustily shouts, "Let the sky rain potatoes!"

The plant arrived in Europe—as an ornamental—in the 16th century. In the 17th century the Irish, pushed off the most fertile land by the English after siding with the Stuart kings against Parliament, adopted the American tuber for its caloric productivity—more than twice that of any alternative in Ireland's climate. In the next century the French and Prussians, driven by war, did likewise. (Not only does the potato fill soldierly bellies cheaply, but when soldiers requisition food, they may leave potatoes in the ground while they trample crops in the field and cart off grain in the barn.)

Eighteenth-century Russians paid little attention to Catherine the Great's suggestion that her subjects plant potatoes, but the failures of the traditional crops in the 19th century convinced them. In the last 40 years of the century, potato production went up 40 percent in the dominions of the czar. Today, the former Soviet Union is the biggest producer of potatoes in the world.

Maize and potatoes were undoubtedly the New World's most precious gifts to the Old World, more valuable than all the silver from Potosí or gold from the Sacramento Valley, but gifts, like swords, can be double edged. The wide spread of maize cultivation in southern Europe, Hungary and the Balkan provinces of the Ottoman Empire made it *the* cash crop for growing cities. But lacking the vitamin-B complex constituents, especially niacin, a diet exclusively of maize causes pellagra, the disease of the three *D's*: dermatitis, dementia and death. In 1755, a medical journal described just such an illness common in Spain's province of Asturias. Soon northern Italian physicians recognized the same symptoms, and by 1856 more than 37,000 cases were reported in Lombardy. Today, with the benefit of vitamin supplements, only in the Third World and in South Africa do maize farmers suffer from the disease.

Too great a dependence on maize eased people into the grave. Too great a dependence on white potatoes killed them swiftly.

Many northern Europeans, notably the Irish, bet their lives on the unvarying productivity of the potato. But as the 19th century progressed and steamship technology reduced the number of days' voyage between America and Europe, American parasites caught up with the plant.

Between 1750 and 1841 the potato-loving population of Ireland had grown from 3 million to more than 8 million, making it one of the most densely populated countries in Europe. In the 1840s ("the hungry '40s") an American parasite, *Phytophthora infestans*, arrived, reducing the tuber to black slime. Between 1841 and the next census, a generation later, Ireland's population dropped by half because of famine, disease and emigration. Ireland became, for its size, the chief exporter of humans on earth; the northeast coast of the United States took on a Celtic cast; and Patrick and Bridget Kennedy, great-grandparents of the first Catholic president of the United States, set sail across the Atlantic (and so did two of my great-grandparents).

THE MOST IMPORTANT CHANGE OF THE LAST FEW centuries, more important than the propagation and shriveling of Marxism, or the industrial revolution, is the population explosion. Between the mid-18th century and the present, the total number of humans on this planet rose from fewer than 800 million to 5.5 billion. Among the various causes of that increase is the nourishment associated with the cultivation of American crops overseas. In some places the connection is undeniable. In China, for example, where the population has grown from 330 million to more than a billion, people depend on a supply of food of which about 37 percent is American in origin.

With little prospect of worldwide population control, we need every productive variety of food plant whose requirements of climate, soil or space differ from our staples. We need strains of maize and potatoes resistant to the insects, worms, rusts and blights that threaten our popular strains. We need plants that will prosper in seasons when we leave the land fallow. We need to squeeze two and three harvests into a single year. We must use the odd corners of land too steep, too dry, too wet, too acidic or too alkaline for our current crops. We need species that will preserve the land's fertility rather than diminish it.

In short, we need another descent of the sort of vegetable manna that Columbus inadvertently introduced to the Old World. Fortunately, we have only begun to exploit the pre-Columbian larder. When Europeans first arrived, the agriculturists of Mesoamerica were cultivating some 67 species of plants (for food and other purposes), those of the Inca region about 70. And this does not include plants first domesticated by the farmers of the Amazon and Orinoco basins. Native American crops account for about one-fifth of the world's crops.

Most of us, except botanists and anthropologists, are ignorant of all but a few of these plants and will remain so, because they do not fit our immediate needs. Other plants will soon be familiar, because they are productive despite saline soils and can survive overabundance or shortage of water, and so on. They make good insurance policies for our uncertain futures. For instance, which of our staple crops is especially tolerant of ozone? None, I suspect; but what about the Andean cereal quinoa, which produces great quantities of starch and protein at 13,000 feet, an altitude at which it is subject to high levels of ozone?

Another neglected crop, amaranth, was cultivated by American

Indians all the way from the desert borderlands of the southwestern United States to the southern Andes. It was one of the most ancient of Mexico's crops: The Aztecs collected half as much of this cereal in tribute as they did of their staff of life, maize. But cultivation fell off sharply soon after the European arrival, probably because the Spaniards saw that it was intricately involved in the old religious practices: Images of the gods were made from its dough, which was even called the "bones of god." (Amaranth is available today in Mexican markets as blocks of candy—seeds bound together with honey or molasses—called *alegría,* joy.)

Yet the crop is a nutritional marvel. Its stems and leaves are as edible as spinach and richer in iron; its prolific seeds are a source of a good grade of starch and are 16 to 18 percent protein of a quality comparable to that of cow's milk. Amaranth flour mixed with wheat or maize flour is about as protein-rich as eggs.

The plant does well at various altitudes in different soils, even tolerating salinity (the curse of irrigated land) better than many cereals. It weathers droughts and cold, though not frosts, and is now being grown in China, Nepal, India and Kenya.

Few Europeans, Africans and Asians know about amaranth—or quinoa, achira, ahipa, oca, maca, kaniwa, lucuma, pepino or tarwi, among scores of other native American crops—but how many Americans knew about China's soybean 75 years ago? Very few indeed. Yet it is now a major crop, nutritionally and economically, in the United States and Brazil, both of which produce far more soybeans than China. And if Europeans, Africans and Asians continue to be as smart about importing crops as American farmers have recently been about soybeans, New World crops will continue to make history in the Old World.

Future Crops

Some traditional Andean crops that have been preserved by native peoples may play an important role in food production around the world:

Achira   Starch from the huge rhizome of this lilylike plant is easily digested, making it an ideal foodstuff for invalids, infants and the elderly. Part of a traditional feast (along with roast guinea pig) in the Andes, achira is already commercially cultivated in Australia and elsewhere.

Kaniwa   Andean farmers regard this grain as a welcome "weed" because it thrives on poor, rocky soil and is resistant to salt, drought, frost and pests. Such resilience along with its richness in protein and amino acids may one day make kaniwa popular in other tropical highlands.

Lucuma   A single tree of this bronze-yellow starchy fruit is said to be able to feed a family year round. Pulped lucuma tastes rather like maple syrup, and is a popular addition to drinks, puddings, pies and cookies. In Switzerland it is used today to flavor ice cream.

Maca   Found at high altitudes—where it endures intense sunlight, violent winds and chilling cold—this relative of the radish has a sweet, tangy root that can be dried and stored for years. It is also said to enhance fertility.

Oca   Brilliant color and pleasant flavor give this potatolike tuber immediate consumer appeal. It is also easy to propagate and can be prepared in so many ways that New Zealanders now serve it with their national dish—roast lamb.

Pepino   A "decadent fruit for the '90s," the versatile but exotic yellow-streaked-with-purple pepino tastes like sweet melon and has now entered international commerce in California, New Zealand and Japan.

Tarwi   This spectacular legume produces protein-packed seeds that contain as much vegetable oil as soybeans. It is being experimentally grown in Europe, South Africa and Australia.

Source: LOST CROPS OF THE INCAS, National Academy Press 1989

Who was responsible?

*Africans were above all victims of the slave trade,
but some of them were partners in it*

Elikia M'Bokolo

To judge from the number of countries taking part in it, the slave trade must have been for Europeans both a profitable business and, considering the number of years it lasted, a familiar fact of life. Even so, in some of the ports involved in the trade, like Nantes, the slave-traders themselves were reluctant to call it by its name and instead spoke of it in more veiled terms as the "matter".

What about the Africans? Were they merely its victims or were they conscious and consenting partners in a business arrangement with whose terms they were perfectly familiar?

A controversial question

There has always been heated debate over the part played by Africans in the slave trade. For a long time, the slave-traders took refuge behind what they saw as the irrefutable argument that the Africans made a regular practice of selling their fellow Africans, and that if the Europeans refused to buy slaves from them, other people—meaning the Arabs, who also used black slaves, among others—would hasten to do so. Nowadays, African intellectuals and statesmen contend that that these exchanges were always unequal (in that human beings were bought with baubles) and that the Europeans always resorted to violence to get the Africans to co-operate against their will.

For historians the story is not quite as simple as that, in the first place because our criteria are not the same as those of 500 or even 150 years ago. We believe that if only one slave had been shipped across the Atlantic, it would have been one too many. But did Africans think like this in the past? Secondly, the slave trade, which went on for almost four centuries, was a very complex process involving a very wide variety of power relationships and participants whose interests and responses were bound to have changed with the course of time. This has prompted the British historian Basil Davidson to say that the "notion that Europe altogether imposed the slave trade on Africa is without any foundation in history. . . . [it] is as baseless as the European notion that institutions of bondage were in some way peculiar to Africa."[*]

From slave-raiding to slave-trading

The first method by which the Europeans acquired African slaves was through straightforward abduction. Striking examples of this can be found in the celebrated *Crónica dos Feitos da Guiné (Chronicle of the Discovery and Conquest of Guinea)*, written by the Portuguese Gomes Eanes de Zurara in the mid-fifteenth century. When the Europeans landed on the coasts of Africa, they stopped at random at places they thought might be suitable for their purpose and set out on man-hunts. This was not without its risks, however, as evidenced by the massacre in 1446 of almost all the members of the expedition led by Nuno Tristao near the Cap Vert peninsula in present-day Senegal. This was not the only such massacre, but it certainly shows that the Africans were determined to fight against enslavement.

The drawbacks of slave-raiding were that its outcome was uncertain and it was incapable of catering for the constantly growing demand, when the plantations and mines of the Americas had to be supplied with slave labour. The Portuguese were the first to switch from merely seizing captives to actually trading in slaves, following a suggestion made by Prince Henry

[*] Basil Davidson, *Black Mother, The Years of the African Slave Trade*, Boston/Toronto, Little, Brown and Company, 1961.

the Navigator in 1444 and subsequently followed by Portuguese sovereigns until the end of the fifteenth century. However, even after this trade had become a routine matter, raiding continued to provide slave-traders with an additional source of supply. The so-called "roving" trade—in which slaving ships sailed along the coast and captured slaves at various places until they had a full consignment—often took the form of armed incursions against villages situated near to the coast. When countries engaged in the slave trade, they often began by organizing raiding expeditions, as did the first vessels hailing from the "twelve colonies" (the future United States of America) in the first half of the seventeenth century.

By that time, however, the leading European nations had imposed a code of ethics of a kind on the slave trade. The English, Portuguese and French agreed to make a joint declaration to the effect that the slave trade was justified only when it involved slaves duly sold by Africans. Forts were built along the coastline in order to organize the trade and at the same time to instill a healthy sense of fear among the Africans. The message they conveyed was perfectly clear: "Sell us slaves—and we shall leave it to you to choose them as you see fit—or else we shall take the slaves we need at random."

The slave trade was therefore a one-sided relationship, founded and maintained on the threat of force. We once again have to agree with Basil Davidson when he says, "Africa and Europe were jointly involved.... Europe dominated the connection, shaped and promoted the slave trade, and continually turned it to European advantage and to African loss."

Affairs of state and lineage societies

At its height, the slave trade was regarded by Africans as a kind of diabolical plot in which they had to be accomplices or perish. Hence almost all the lineage or state societies of the African seaboard were compelled to become involved in it. They did this in ways and under conditions which differed significantly from one region to another and from one period to another.

The social history of pre-colonial Africa shows that slavery was a widespread institution in states where, in some instances, a domestic trade in slaves already existed for military or economic reasons. However, a distinction has to be made between those states which maintained relations with the outside world and those which did not. The former were quicker and more ready to join in the slave-trade cycle. This was true of the states bordering the Sahel, which were already in the prac-

Thinking of the millions of my brothers

Each morning, when I wake up, I have the taste of death in my mouth.... But, after doing a few physical exercises, I open the windows of my bedroom. They overlook the sea and, away in the distance, I can just make out the island of Gorée. And when I think of the millions of my black brothers who were shipped from there to destinations where misfortune and death awaited them, I am compelled not to despair. Their story goads me on....

LÉOPOLD SÉDAR SENGHOR

tice of selling slaves, among other goods, to their Arab and Berber partners, who actually went on to sell some of them to the Europeans. The chronicler Alvise de Ca' da Mósto, who took part in a Portuguese expedition to Senegambia in 1455-1456, reported that the local sovereigns were skilled at taking advantage of the new competition that was growing up between the trans-Saharan trade and the Atlantic trade by selling slaves to the Arabs and Berbers in exchange for horses, and other slaves to the Portuguese in exchange for European goods.

The situation was by no means the same in those states which had no trading links with the outside world. The part these played in the slave trade is a pointer to the ambiguous and contradictory attitudes they displayed and the difficulties they faced when they came to take decisions, often under duress. The kingdom of Kongo, one of the most powerful in Africa at the time of its encounter with the Portuguese at the end of the fifteenth century, is a typical example. In the view of contemporary historians, its economic, political and social standing was on a par with that of Portugal. From the time of the very first contacts, the Kongo nobility became converts to Christianity and the king saw fit to address the Portuguese sovereign as "my brother". Yet the fact was that the slave trade had already started, in violation of the agreements, both tacit and formal, concluded between the two states. A number of letters, in which the king of Kongo protested against the seizure of slaves, including members of noble families, have survived to the present day. There is still some controversy as to what was really the motive behind these protestations. Some historians regard them as being an outburst of nationalist sentiment, but others look upon them more as a sign of the concern of the country's aristocracy not to allow so lucrative a business to slip through their hands. In any event, the kingdom did not survive the impact of the slave trade for very long. The same drama was to be played out to varying degrees elsewhere in Africa.

The kingdom of Dahomey was also exposed to the bitter experience of the slave trade. In the mid-eighteenth century, it took over the port of Ouidah, one of the main centres of the trade in the Gulf of Guinea. The king of Dahomey regarded the port—where there was a growing buildup of firearms—as posing a threat to the security of his possessions, since the slave trade gave it a tactical advantage over its neighbours. Once they took control of Ouidah, the rulers of Dahomey were caught in a vicious circle: in order to maintain a strong state, they needed rifles and gunpowder, but to obtain these they had to sell slaves to the Europeans. The answer was really very straightforward: since the sale of the kingdom's own subjects was strictly forbidden, powerful armies were raised to raid neighbouring peoples and make war on them for the purpose of taking slaves.

Unlike states, lineage societies did not have any means of obtaining slaves by force. In such cases, servitude was based on complex practices in which various categories of social outcasts, such as criminals, misfits, sorcerers and victims of natural or economic disasters, were relegated to being slaves. Even so, this would not have been sufficient to turn the slave trade into the vast and lasting business it became. Other means were therefore found of meeting the Europeans' demands. For example, in the city of Arochukwu ("the voice of Chukwu", the supreme deity), in the Niger delta, a celebrated oracle whose authority was respected by all the population was called on to designate those who, for whatever reason, were condemned to be sold into slavery. This practice continued until the beginning of the nineteenth century.

In other regions, especially in central Africa, trading networks were gradually established, extending from the coast deep into the interior. All the goods exported or imported via these networks—predominantly slaves—transited through the heads of the lineages. In Gabon and Loango in particular, the coastal societies forming the key links in these trading networks had a highly developed ranking social order based on the extent to which their members were involved in the slave trade. Kinship relations, which are fundamental in lineage societies, gradually gave way to relations based on fortunes made in the trade, which came to dictate people's standing in society.

Africans and the abolition of the slave trade

On the African side, however, the basis of the slave trade was very precariously balanced. The part played by Africans in the trade cannot be discussed without reference to the part they played in its abolition. In a one-sided view of history, the role of Europeans—philosophers, thinkers, men of religion and businessmen—is too often stressed, while that played by the Africans is left in the shade. Some people have even gone so far as to tax the Africans with being the main impediment to the phasing-out of the trade in the nineteenth century. Nothing could be further from the truth.

Outside Africa, the resistance of the victims of the slave trade—which took a variety of forms, including the "Back to Africa" movement, the founding of "Maroon" communities and even armed insurrection, like that in San Domingo in 1791—was primarily instrumental in calling the whole institution of slavery into question. Those who had managed to escape its clutches took a very active but often unacknowledged part in the campaign for abolition. They included people like Ottobah Cuguano, who had been born in Fantiland, in present-day Ghana, had been a slave in the West Indies, and published his *Thoughts and Sentiments on the Evil and Wicked Traffic of Slavery* in London in 1787. In 1789, another African, Olaudah Equiano, alias Gustavus Vassa, a native of Iboland, in Nigeria, published, again in London, *The Interesting Narrative of the Life of Olaudah Equiano, or Gustavus Vassa the African, written by himself*. These books played a significant role in the movement of opinion which led to the abolition of the slave trade.

In Africa itself, all through the "years of trial" of the slave trade, along with slaves, blacks continued to sell the produce of their soil and subsoil, such as timber, ivory, spices, gold, vegetable oils, and others besides. Changing European demand was sufficient for the Africans to turn to a more "legal" form of commerce.

ELIKIA M'BOKOLO, Zairean historian, is director of studies at the Ecole des Hautes Etudes en Sciences Sociales in Paris. He is the author of many works on African history, cultures and development problems, including *L'Afrique au 20ᵉ siècle, le continent convoité* (1985) and *Afrique noire, Histoire et civilisations, 19-20ᵉ siècles* (1992).

THE MACARTNEY EMBASSY TO CHINA, 1792–94

Two hundred years ago, a motley collection of Wedgwood china, clocks, a planetarium and a hot-air balloon accompanied an expedition to Peking, designed to open up the Imperial Kingdom to British commerce and diplomacy. How and why it failed, according to **Paul Gillingham,** offers valuable lessons, even today, on the perils of cultural misunderstanding.

Paul Gillingham

Paul Gillingham is a freelance writer and presenter and author of At The Peak: A History of Hong Kong Between the Wars (*Macmillan, 1983*).

Lining the boardroom of Coutts Bank in London's Strand is a striking and unusual wallpaper. Made of mulberry paper, a cross between rice-paper and silk, it depicts scenes of everyday life in Imperial China in the sort of detail that makes it a wallpaper equivalent of a documentary film.

Shopkeepers keep accounts with their abacuses, labourers collect birds' nests for making soup, women adorn a tea house-cum-brothel, bare-footed servants wait on their masters, and horses, dogs and children hang about courtyards. Tea is picked, dried, packed and sold and the stages of silk production are shown, from collecting cocoons off mulberry trees, to spinning and weaving.

Such is the wallpaper's importance to the bank that it has survived being moved twice since it was first hung nearly two hundred years ago. In 1978 it was found to be so firmly glued on that the walls were dismantled and rebuilt as part of the modern bank – just to save the wallpaper.

The wallpaper was a present to the bank's director, Thomas Coutts, from one of his customers, Lord Macartney of Lissamore, who had recently returned to England, in 1794, after a two-year expedition to China. He had seen the paper on the walls of a palace where he and his entourage had stayed in Peking, the home of a Collector of Customs who was in jail awaiting execution for misappropriating the profits of European trade!

It was because of people like the Collector of Customs that the Embassy set off for China in the first place. Trade between Britain and China had been expanding fast throughout the eighteenth century, but not fast enough to satisfy all the merchants involved in it. There was an insatiable desire for things Chinese in Britain, especially China tea, porcelain and silk.

As the directors of the East India Company, which held a monopoly on trade with India and China, grew prosperous on the huge profits to be made, there were nevertheless frustrations at the rigid controls imposed on the one port into China which was open to overseas trade, Canton. Foreigners were allowed to stay there only during a five-month trading season, and then only in 'factories' – which served as warehouse, office and home – in a foreign ghetto outside the main Chinese city. Women, both local and European, were forbidden, as were Chinese servants and sedan-chair bearers, and any Chinese caught teaching the language to a European could face the death penalty.

Moreover, profits were hit by the graft and corruption built into a system dominated by a guild of Chinese merchants known as the Hong or Cohong and the Collector of Customs himself, the all-powerful Hoppo, one of whom owned the palace that provided the Coutts Bank wallpaper.

Thus it was with a view to liberalising the system and opening up trade with China that George III despatched an embassy to the Imperial Court in Peking in 1792 under one of his most experienced ambassadors, Lord George Macartney. The fifty-five year old Irishman had earlier made a name for himself by charming Cather-

ine the Great and performing sterling work as secretary for Ireland, governor-general of British West Indies and governor of Madras.

Lord Macartney's was not the first European embassy to China, but it was certainly the largest. The three ships to set sail from Spithead on September 26th, 1792, carried 700 men including diplomats, scholars, botanists, scientists, painters, musicians, technicians, soldiers, servants and sailors. Also on board were two Chinese interpreters, priests from the Collegium Sinicum in Naples, who spoke no English, but passable Latin.

Because none of the adult members of the embassy spoke Chinese, communication was to prove a major problem during the expedition. English was first translated into Latin and then into Chinese, and vice versa,

a cumbersome process which left much room for misunderstanding.

Only one Briton of the 700 who set sail could read and write Chinese, and that was a boy of twelve, Macartney's page and the son of his second-in-command, Sir George Staunton. Young Thomas Staunton, who was to play a key part in Sino-British relations for the next fifty years, was a precocious child who could recite a page of *The Times* after one reading and spoke Latin, Greek, French and German. He learnt his Chinese from the two priests during the ten-month voyage and was later to prove useful in translating some of the key documents Macartney sent to the emperor, including his views on the *kowtow*.

Aboard the inevitably slow boats to China – the voyage took ten months

The emperor's new toys: Gillray's 1793 cartoon 'Tribute from the Red Barbarians' shows a disdainful emperor receiving the British and plays up the mutually xenophobic under-currents of the meeting.

and went via Rio de Janeiro, Tristan da Cunha, Java and Vietnam – Macartney and his entourage had ample opportunity to reflect on what they might see and experience when they got there. Chinoiserie and 'things Chinese' had been all the rage in Europe for much of the eighteenth century and there was a tendency to idealise China, largely as a result of the writings of European Jesuits who had access to the Peking court. English country estates were landscaped with Chinese gardens, complete with marble pagodas; wall tapestries bore Chinese motifs, and even the Queen of England wore Chinese-style clothes. Philosophers were impressed by the idea of Confucianism, which seemed to hold the key to ideal government and a harmonious social order based on respect for age and authority.

But by the end of the century the love affair with the idea of China was beginning to pall. Louis-Sebastien Mercier wrote: 'What wretched luxuries these Chinese porcelains are! With a touch of its paw, a cat can do more damage than the plunder of twenty acres of land'. Montesquieu was much more devastating in his critique of Chinese government: 'China is a despotic state whose principle is fear', he wrote. 'The stick governs China'.

Apart from the diplomatic and commercial aims of the embassy, there was a powerful need to explore the real China, to separate myth from reality. This was, after all, the age of scientific enquiry when everything under the sun was being weighed, measured and assessed. Sir Joseph Banks who accompanied Captain Cook to the South Seas and was establishing the Royal Botanical Gardens at Kew, gave full instructions to Macartney on what specimens to collect. Both he and Staunton were happy to oblige, being enthusiastic amateur botanists themselves.

On July 20th, 1793, the embassy eventually reached Dengzhou, a city of first rank in the province of Shandung. From there they were to transfer to junks for the journey up-river, stopping briefly at Tientsin, and then marching overland to Peking.

After such a long voyage, first reactions to China were ecstatic. 'O brave new world', Macartney wrote, quoting Shakespeare in his journal. Then, more matter-of-factly, 'great numbers of houses… built of mud and thatched, a good deal resembling the cottages near Christchurch in Hampshire'.

Shortly after arriving, he received a letter from the emperor extending a warm welcome to him and the 'others of England, country of the red hairs' with a promise to replenish their much-depleted stores. Within days, a consignment of 20 bullocks, 120 sheep, 120 hogs, 100 chickens, 100 ducks, 10 chests of tea, 160 bags of flour, 14 boxes of tartar bread and 2,000 melons was lined up on the quayside ready to be loaded on board.

But apart from the significance of having travelled from the other end of the world, the Chinese regarded the embassy as little different from the regular tribute-bearing missions they received from vassal states bordering China, like Burma, Vietnam, Korea and Tibet. As the Chinese script on the yellow pennants fluttering above the junks declared: 'The English Ambassador bringing tribute to the Emperor of China'.

Macartney, however, had no intention of accepting the status of tribute-bearer on the same level as Burma. His aim was to become accredited as an ambassador on equal terms with China, in the European diplomatic tradition of mutual recognition between sovereign states. True, his ships bore gifts for the Chinese emperor and his entourage, but they were intended as presents and not as 'tribute' in the Chinese sense.

Although a basic principle of Chinese good manners is to understate the value of a gift in order not to humiliate the recipient, Macartney did the opposite. It would not, he wrote in the catalogue listing the presents:

...be becoming to offer trifles of momentary curiosity, but little use. His Britannic Majesty has been, therefore, careful to select only such articles as might denote the progress of science, and of the arts in Europe.

Macartney was hoping to impress the emperor with British ingenuity and doubtless win orders for British goods.

The *pièce de résistance* among the presents was a planetarium which, with the aid of complicated gears, showed the movement of the heavens. Also crated up were telescopes, clocks, guns, cannon, Wedgwood china, two carriages, a diving bell used to repair Ramsgate harbour and a newly-invented hot-air balloon.

There were also paintings of people and places, including portraits of George III and Queen Caroline, which later caused a stir among mandarins who thought of portraiture only in terms of 'ancestral portraits' of the dead. A Reynolds portrait of the Duke of Bedford, painted when he was a child was also seen as rather odd. How, the mandarins asked, could a mere boy be a member of the House of Lords when they had to study for years and pass tough exams to achieve a similar rank?

The cultural differences between East and West were especially marked when it came to the *kowtow*. To the Chinese, the act of self-abasement in the form of kneeling three times and 'knocking' the head on the floor nine times was a vital element in court ritual. Its significance went far deeper than merely showing respect, as a deep bow or curtsey might indicate in the West. The kowtow was an acknowledgement of the rights and obligations owed to a higher by a lower power. In Chinese eyes the emperor was the intermediary between heaven and earth, a lynchpin in the preservation of universal order against the forces of chaos, both human and divine. He was, after all, the 'Son of Heaven' and brooked no human equal.

But for Macartney, dropping down on both knees was reserved for begging for mercy, praying to God and proposing marriage. To kowtow to the Emperor of China was an act of abject humiliation which he, as the emissary of an equally proud nation, was simply not prepared to do.

The emperor's mandarins did all they could to persuade the English to change their minds. Zhengrui, Wang and Qiao, who escorted the embassy to Peking, offered to give lessons in kowtowing. They advised the English to replace their tight court breeches, knee buckles and garters in favour of the loose Chinese-style garments that made kowtowing so much easier.

But Macartney remained adamant. How could he make an obeisance before the emperor which he would never perform before his own king? The only terms under which he might agree were if the emperor's emissaries agreed to kowtow before the portrait of King George, which, for the Chinese, was impossible. The furthest he would go was to drop on one knee and kiss the emperor's hand, which was how he greeted his own sovereign. Eventually, the Chinese agreed that Macartney could do as he would at home, though they drew the line at hand-kissing. The concession was granted on the grounds that these were, after all, distant barbarians who could not be expected to understand the real significance of the kowtow anyway.

On August 21st, the embassy eventually reached Peking. Macartney, the Stauntons and the Chinese interpreter entered the city at the Western Gate, carried aloft in palanquins ahead of a procession of 90 wagons, 40 handcarts, 200 horses and nearly 3,000 men. By now, the members of the embassy – unwashed, dishevelled and suffering from lack of sleep and mosquito bites – were hardly a prepossessing sight. According to Macartney's valet, Aeneas Anderson, the Chinese crowds burst into laughter when they saw them. The embassy bore 'greater resemblance to the sight provided by the removal of paupers to their parishes in England than the expected dignity of the representative of a great and powerful monarch', he lamented.

They were given accommodation in the only building in Peking large enough to accommodate the whole embassy, the Palace of Eleven Courtyards with the wallpaper which now graces the boardroom of Coutts Bank. This was to be a short stay, as the imperial audience was to take place not in Peking's Forbidden City, but in the emperor's summer residence 120 miles to the north, at Jehol in Manchuria.

On September 2nd, 1793, the party set out along the Imperial Way. In Peking they had left behind a team to set up the display of the 'presents' and make arrangements for transforming the Palace of Eleven Courtyards into the British embassy. This was an especially bitter blow to the artist William Alexander – and to posterity – because he knew he was losing the opportunity of painting the most dramatic events of the whole expedition.

The Imperial Way was a superbly made road of compacted sand and clay, and travelling along with the young Staunton in his own carriage, 'the first piece of Long Acre machinery that ever rattled up the road to Jehol', Macartney could imagine he was back in England.

But he was soon left in no doubt that this was China, not Surrey, by the Great Wall which loomed ahead of them. 'The most stupendous work of human hands', wrote Macartney, who ordered his men to measure every possible dimension, except of course its 4,000 mile length. As they prepared to leave, some were seen pocketing fragments of the Wall, no doubt to sell to antiquity dealers' back home.

Beyond the Great Wall they were in the land of Tartary – or Manchuria – a barren landscape of mountains and remote valleys. Rising above the plains into cooler air, they approached the emperor's summer retreat at Jehol.

The Emperor Qianlong had been watching the embassy's arrival, unseen, from a hilltop pergola. A remarkably clear-eyed man of benign countenance, he wore his eighty-three years well. Staunton later described him as 'so hale and vigorous that he scarcely appeared to have existed as many years, fifty-seven, as in fact he had governed the empire'. That empire had grown substantially during Qianlong's reign, the population having doubled, along with the area over which it held sway. His energy was prodigious, not least in being able to handle an extensive harem and the whims of the notorious 'perfumed muslim' Xiangfei, his consort. As a young man Qianlong had fallen passionately in love with his father's concubine, Machia, and in his sixties the passion was transferred to a male lover, Heshen, Machia's supposed reincarnation. As a result Heshen enjoyed rapid promotion, becoming the emperor's 'Grand Colao' or chief minister. But he was no friend of the embassy and did much to engineer its failure.

In contemplating the audience he was about to give to the English, Qianlong was highly ambivalent. On the one hand he was flattered by their visit. But, as imperial archives show, he had become increasingly annoyed by what he saw as English bad manners, especially over the kowtow. 'The more magnanimous we are towards them, the more conceited they become,' he wrote. He was especially angered by a letter from the king suggesting China would benefit from English progress and that Qianlong should consider George III his 'friend and brother'. As far as Qianlong was concerned, to imply that China needed anything or that a bar-

barian could be the equal of the Son of Heaven was clearly preposterous.

On Saturday, September 14th, the big day arrived. After setting off at 3am and getting caught up in roaming bands of pigs, cattle and dogs in the darkness, they eventually reached the Garden of Ten Thousand Trees, where Qianlong was to receive them. Approaching a large compound of ceremonial Mongolian tents – or yurts – they could see by the light of paper lanterns that they were in the presence of the entire imperial court. All the Tartar princes were there, plus viceroys, district and city governors and 5-600 mandarins of varying ranks, together with their servants. In addition, there were ambassadors from tributary states, soldiers, balladeers and musicians, all expectantly awaiting the arrival of the Khan of Khans, his arrival perfectly stage-managed to coincide with the rising of the sun.

They waited three hours. Then, at 7am, as the sun flooded the great park, the emperor arrived, carried in an open chair by sixteen men dressed in gold, followed by his ministers and chief mandarins. As he passed the lines of courtiers, everyone present fell to their knees, sweeping their heads to the ground in the kowtow, except for the British, who dropped to one knee, heads bowed.

The emperor entered the largest, most elaborate yurt, followed by the vassals and four members of the British embassy; Macartney, Staunton senior, young Staunton and the Chinese translator. Once inside, they saw that Qianlong was now seated on a raised dais. The nine prostrations were performed again by all present, except the British.

Macartney, followed by Staunton senior, stepped up on to the dais. He handed a pair of enamelled watches to Qianlong, together with a letter from George III in a gilt box. Staunton gave the emperor two airguns. In return, Qianlong presented the two men with a ceremonial jade sceptre each and one in white agate for the king.

Wearying of the long-winded translation provided by Li, the emperor asked if any of the British could speak Chinese. The young Staunton was ushered forward, man and boy conversed briefly and Qianlong presented the twelve-year-old with a yellow silk purse for areca nuts, which had been hanging by his side.

Although the meeting at Jehol had been the high point of the embassy's visit to China, Macartney had no more idea than when he started out whether the British requests would be granted. The answer, in the form of two edicts from Qianlong to George III, came as a shock. There was to be no British ambassador to China and China had no need of British goods. 'As your ambassador can see for himself', Qianlong wrote, 'we possess all things. I set no value on objects strange or ingenious, and have no use for your country's manufactures'.

In the second edict, Qianlong rejected Britain's six proposals for opening up China to British trade. 'Do not say that you were not warned in due time', he concluded. 'Tremblingly obey and show no negligence!' Imperial records show that Qianlong had decided on rejection well before the embassy set foot in China.

Three months later, after a journey across China by land, river and canal, Macartney and his entourage finally rejoined their ships at Canton and set sail for home on January 8th, 1794.

The embassy had been a diplomatic failure, but the long-term effects were profound. Within five years of Macartney's return, six books were published by members of the expedition, all of them best-sellers. Combined with the gossip circulating in England's stately homes and London's salons, they dispelled any romantic notions the West had of China. The celestial empire was now revealed, warts and all.

Macartney chose not to publish his own detailed journal, doubtless for diplomatic reasons. He had concluded that the Chinese were 'barbarians' and the government a 'tyranny of a handful of Tartars over more than three hundred millions of Chinese'. China was like 'an old, crazy, first rate man-of-war' which over-awed its neighbours by its bulk and size but would flounder under the command of a weak leader.

Staunton and John Barrow wrote the semi-official accounts, but it was the populist books by Macartney's valet, Aeneas Anderson, and the soldier, Samuel Holmes, that caught the public imagination. Tales of Chinese peasants eating the fleas they picked off their clothes and defecating in public were far removed from the

earlier, idealised, Jesuit versions of China. 'There is not a water-closet, nor a decent place of retirement in all China', despaired Anderson. His phrase – 'We entered Peking like paupers; we remained in it like prisoners; and we quitted it like vagrants' – stood out as a reminder of the humiliation the embassy had suffered, which, by implication, would one day need to be avenged.

Neither Macartney himself nor any of the books on the embassy advocated using force against China. Yet within fifty years Lord Palmerston had launched the first Opium War against her, extracting by gunboat diplomacy what Macartney had failed to achieve by more peaceful means. Ironically, the leading politician to advocate war against China in the Commons in 1840 was the fifty-nine-year old Sir George Thomas Staunton, that same youth who had conversed with the Emperor Qianlong years before at Jehol.

It is sometimes argued that China missed a golden opportunity and that the history of the country might have been radically different if Qianlong, like Japan's Meiji emperor later, had adopted European techniques of production. But the China of the 1790s was very different from the Japan of the 1860s and China was neither able nor willing to adapt to Western industrialism. Besides, one might ask, what was the relevance of the planetarium – Macartney's great showpiece 'present' – to modern industrialism?

How significant was Macartney's failure to kowtow? Did it cause the failure of the embassy as some, especially the Jesuits in China at the time, believed? The Chinese records of the period significantly make no mention of the kowtow at all. Possibly the embassy might have stayed longer in China and received more courtesies had Macartney agreed to kowtow, but maybe not. Either way, willingness to kowtow did not guarantee success, as a Dutch envoy later discovered. He was treated with disdain after losing face in public when he kowtowed before the emperor so low that his wig fell off!

The Collision of Two Civilisations, by the French historian and former Gaullist diplomat, Alain Peyrefitte, describes the encounter of 1792-94 as 'a collision of two planets … one celestial and lunar; the other with its feet firmly on the ground – mercantile, scientific and industrial.' For him it is a striking instance of the clash

between a dynamic, advanced society and a traditional and unchanging one. Although the book is superbly researched and written, the underlying thesis surely represents a nineteenth century Eurocentric view, which minimises the dynamic, changing aspects of China and the conservatism of much of Britain.

Does the Macartney embassy have a relevance now, 200 years on? On the face of it, yes. China is today an ideological state ruled with an iron hand by an octagenarian. The forces of traditionalism remain strong, Westerners are confined to 'special economic zones' and the capitalist world is knocking hard to enter. Tea, the drink which gave the impetus to eighteenth-century attempts to open up Chinese markets has its modern day equivalent in Coca-Cola. Interestingly, some of the language used recently in connection with Hong Kong Governor Chris Patten's face-off with Beijing over democratic reforms in the colony, echoes 1793. One Hong Kong official praised Britain for standing firm against China over the reforms and refusing to 'tremble and obey', and Britain and Hong Kong are urged by the popular press not to 'kowtow' to Beijing, which must be treated 'like any other country'.

Perhaps it is true that history can repeat itself, but 1793 is not 1993. Qianlong is no more Deng Xiao Ping than George III is John Major or Macartney Chris Patten. What the Macartney embassy offers us is, in the words of Professor Peter Marshall of London University, 'the beam of a searchlight', a fascinating glimpse at the preconceptions two great civilisations had of each other at a particular time in a certain place. No more nor less than that. But it is a thumping good story!

FOR FURTHER READING:
Sir George Leonard Staunton, *An Authentic Account of an Embassy from the King of Great Britain to the Emperor of China* (J. Nicol, 1797); William Alexander, *Picturesque Representations of the Dress and Manners of the Chinese* (John Murray, 1805); Aeneas Anderson, *A Narrative of the British Embassy in China* (J. Debrett, 1795); N. Cameron, 'Kowtow: Imperial China and the West in Confrontation' *Orientations*, Hong Kong, January 1971; J.L. Cranmer-Byng, *An Embassy to China 1793-94* (Longman Green & Co, 1962); Alain Peyrefitte, *The Collision of Two Civilisations: the British Expedition to China in 1792-94*, (Harvill, 1993); Helen Robbins, *Our first Ambassador to China* (John Murray, 1908); Aubrey Singer, *The Lion and the Dragon* (Barrie & Jenkins, 1992).

Coffee, Tea, or Opium?

In 1838, a Chinese drug czar confronted the Age of Addiction

Samuel M. Wilson

Samuel M. Wilson teaches anthropology at the University of Texas at Austin.

In 1839, China's commissioner for foreign trade, Lin Zexu (Lin Tse-hsü), was running out of diplomatic options. Traders from the East India Company and other European enterprises were pressing him ever more forcefully to turn a blind eye to the illegal importation of opium into his country. They were implicitly backed by Britain's heavily armored warships—such as the *Blenheim* and *Wellesley*, carrying seventy-four cannons each—which could crush China's navy and lay waste to her ports. But the opium trade was damaging public health and bleeding China of her wealth. In 1838, the Manchu emperor had given Lin extensive power and ordered him to control the demand of China's people for opium and force the barbarian merchants to cut off the supply.

After his appointment, Lin began to study European culture, looking for clues to barbarian behavior. He obtained a partial translation of Emer de Vattel's 1758 *Le Droit des Gens* ("The Law of Nations"), and he bought and studied the British ship *Cambridge*. Although it was not the largest of the "East Indiamen"—big defended freighters—and although it had been stripped of its guns and its intricate rigging was a mystery to Lin's sailors, the ship was ample evidence that these British were clever at naval warfare.

Lin also visited Macao, the Portuguese trading entrepôt near Canton, and carried out some anthropological fieldwork:

As soon as I entered the wall of Macao, a hundred barbarian soldiers dressed in barbarian military uniform, led by the barbarian headman, greeted me. They marched in front of my sedan playing barbarian music and led me into the city.... On this day, everyone, man and woman, came out on the street or leaned from the window to take a look. Unfortunately the barbarian costume was too absurd. The men, their bodies wrapped tightly in short coats and long "legs," resembled in shape foxes and rabbits as impersonated in the plays.... Their beards, with abundant whiskers, were half shaved off and only a piece was kept. Looking at them all of a sudden was frightening. That the Cantonese referred to them as "devils" was indeed not vicious disparagement. [Chang Hsin-pao, *Commissioner Lin and the Opium War* (Cambridge: Harvard University Press, 1964)]

Although the Chinese forbade opium importation, willing trading partners were easily found among the Chinese merchants. And if trade became too difficult for the foreigners in the principal port of Canton, there were a thousand miles of coastline, and thousands of miles more of inland borders, through which opium could be transported. Lin saw that the opium trade was ruining China. Informed by his reading of de Vattel and by his extensive dealings with the British representatives, in early 1839 he appealed to Queen Victoria, attempting to conceal the sense of superiority that the Chinese rulers felt toward Westerners:

We have heard that in your honorable nation, too, the people are not permitted to smoke [opium], and that offenders in this particular expose themselves to sure punishment.... Though not making use of it one's self, to venture nevertheless to manufacture and sell it, and with it to seduce the simple folk of this land, is to seek one's own livelihood by exposing others to death, to seek one's own advantage by other men's injury. Such acts are bitterly abhorrent to the nature of man and are utterly opposed to the ways of heaven.... We now wish to find, in cooperation with your honorable sovereignty, some means of bringing to a perpetual end this opium, so hurtful to mankind: we in this land forbidding the use of it, and you, in the nations of your dominion, forbidding its manufacture. [Chang Hsin-pao, *Commissioner Lin and the Opium War*]

The British were the biggest traders in China, but merchants from the United States were present too. Lin considered petitioning this other, possibly significant state, but understood that twenty-four chiefs governed the American people, and thought that communicating with them all would be too difficult.

In his letter to Queen Victoria, Lin sought to explain the situation logically. Earlier communications from the Chinese government had not been so diplomatic. The commander of Canton had sent an edict to the Western traders demanding, "Could your various countries stand one day without trading with China?" This threat came in part from the Chinese leaders' delusion that the British would die if deprived of tea, China's largest export (a delusion the British may have shared). The same edict took note that, according to the Western press,

your motives are to deplete the Middle Kingdom's wealth and destroy the lives of the Chinese people. There is no need to dwell on the topic that the wealth of the Celestial Empire, where all five metals are produced and precious deposits abound, could not be exhausted by such a mere trifle, but for what enmity do you want to kill the Chinese people?

China had withstood barbarian traders without difficulty for two thousand years. But now it was feeling the aftershock of the Western encounter with the Americas and with the closely related expansion of European influence across the globe. The importation of opium reached staggering proportions in the early nineteenth century after the British-run East India Company took control of the drug's production in India. During the trading season of 1816–17, about forty-six hundred 150-pound chests of opium entered China. This number rose to 22,000 by 1831–32 and 35,000 by 1837–38. That was more than 5.25 million pounds of opium, the carefully collected and dried sap extruded from 4.8 trillion opium poppies.

The period from the seventeenth century to the present could be termed the Age of Addiction, for the international economy and the fortunes of nations depended on trade in addictive or semiaddictive agricultural products. The young United States exported tobacco, the habit for which spread rapidly across Europe, Africa, and Asia. The Spaniards carried the New World practice of tobacco smoking to Europe and the East Indies, and as its popularity spread, the plant came to be widely cultivated throughout the Old World. In their Indonesian colonies the Dutch tried filling their pipes with a combination of opium and tobacco. The Chinese continued to smoke the opium, but left out the tobacco.

The British became addicted to the carefully processed leaves of *Camellia sinensis,* or Chinese tea (originally, China was the only exporter). Caffeine-rich coffee was another drug for which Europeans and others developed a craving. A native plant of Ethiopia, coffee's range of cultivation expanded hand in hand with European colonialism. Perfect growing conditions were found in both the New World and Southeast Asia, giving rise to the exotic names for coffee familiar today: Jamaica Blue Mountain, Mocha Java, Guatemalan, Sumatran, and Colombian. These and other nonessential but deeply desired plant products—cocaine, chocolate, and marijuana—have captured huge markets.

Addictive substances are wonderful exports for the countries that produce and ship them. They are highly valuable and compact agricultural products that can be exchanged for hard currency, and the demand of addicts is—for physiological reasons—what economists would call highly inelastic. Farmers get much more from their land and effort than they would by growing things for a local market, and middlemen on both sides of the border get rich. The losers in the transaction—apart from the users themselves—are the importing countries, which run up uncontrollable trade deficits.

From the opening of the Silk Road in the Middle Ages, Western countries were eager to obtain Chinese spices, fabrics, and tea, viewing them as superior to European products. The problem for England and other nations was that they had very little that China wanted, so they had to pay in the most respected and accepted international currency, Spanish silver dollars. With good reason, the Chinese thought the British could not live without tea. About all China would take in trade was British woolen and cotton cloth. American merchants, lacking England's textile manufacturing infrastructure, struggled still more to find anything the Chinese would take in trade. They too paid mainly with Spanish silver, but they also brought natural products—sealskins and other furs from the Northwest Coast, aromatic wood, cotton, wild American ginseng—with which to trade (*see* "Yankee Doodle Went to Canton," *Natural History,* February 1984).

By capitalizing upon a massive addiction to smoked opium in China—and in substantial measure helping to create it—England and the other Western nations shifted the balance of trade in their favor. As social historian Fernand Braudel put it, "China was now literally being paid in smoke (and what smoke!)." Most of the rest of what England traded was woven cotton, also grown and spun in India. In return, at the time of Commissioner Lin's appeal to Queen Victoria, the Chinese were trading about 60 percent tea, 12 percent silks, and most of the rest, about 25 percent, silver and gold.

The opium trade was not the only alarming foreign influence in Lin's day. The barbarians seemed to have designs on Chinese territory. The port of Canton lay thirty miles upriver from the great Gulf of Canton, twenty miles wide and fifty miles long. At the western approach to the bay was the Portuguese trading colony of Macao, which the Chinese had allowed to exist since 1557. On the other side of the gulf lay the island of Hong Kong, which the British sought to turn into a secure headquarters for their trading operations. Even if the Europeans had lacked naval superiority, they could have defended both places from invasion by land or sea. China had always insisted that barbarians of any stripe carry out their trade and then leave, but instead of acting as temporary visitors, the Western traders were staying longer and longer, becoming in effect permanent residents.

Another major grievance was that the foreigners would not submit to Chinese laws when in China. Some European sailors murdered Chinese citizens, but their leaders would not turn over the culprits to the Chinese magistrates. Lin's research revealed that foreigners in England were required to obey British law, but when he confronted the British commanders with this double standard, they merely conceded that he had a case and again refused to turn over British subjects to almost certain execution. Other European and American traders acted similarly.

Despite the barbarian offenses, Lin preferred negotiation and reasoned discussion to fighting a battle that he felt would be difficult to win. In a final, carefully worded letter to Queen Victoria, he wrote:

Let us suppose that foreigners came from another country, and brought opium into England, and seduced the people of your country to smoke it. Would not you, the sovereign of the said country, look upon such a procedure with anger, and in your just indignation endeavor to get rid of it? Now we have always heard that Your Highness possesses a most kind and benevolent heart. Surely then you are incapable of doing or causing to be done unto another that which you should not wish another to do unto you. [Chang Hsin-pao, *Commissioner Lin and the Opium War*]

Moral persuasion has not, historically, proved very effective in dealing with drug smuggling or rulers who sanction it. Unofficially, the contents of the letter were probably widely known but, as with his previous attempts, Lin received no official response. Britain was determined that the opium trade would continue, by force if necessary, and because China had been unwilling to open formal diplomatic channels, the British government would not accept a letter to the queen from a commissioner.

Lin's efforts to rein in the barbarians and subdue the Chinese appetite for opium were ultimately unsuccessful, and the emperor harshly accused him of failing:

Externally you wanted to stop the trade, but it has not been stopped. Internally you wanted to wipe out the outlaws, but they are not cleared away.... You are just making excuses with empty words. Nothing has been accomplished but many troubles have been created. Thinking of these things I cannot contain my rage. What do you have to say now?

Lin replied that the Chinese should address the threat and fight the British, falling back to the interior and fighting a guerrilla war if necessary. He warned the emperor not to attempt to placate the British: "The more they get the more they demand, and if we do not overcome them by force of arms there will be no end to our troubles. Moreover there is every probability that if the English are not dealt with, other foreigners will soon begin to copy and even outdo them."

In June of 1839, Lin had 20,000 chests of opium destroyed in Canton, and the foreign merchants fell back to Macao. The British sent a fleet of their most powerful warships on a punitive expedition, and they overwhelmed the Chinese fleet whenever they faced it. Among their warships were the "ships-of-the-line," massively armed vessels that demonstrated the advantage of superior technology over superior numbers in modern warfare. In the summer of 1842, China was forced to sign the humiliating Treaty of Nanking, which required $21 million in reparations, opened five ports to British trade (including Canton and Shanghai), and ceded Hong Kong, surrounding islands, and part of the mainland to Queen Victoria. China also agreed that future Chinese–British relations would be on terms of "complete equality." This condition seems ironic, because the terms of the treaty were certainly in the Western merchants' favor. This wording was insisted upon by the British, however, because previously China had dealt with Westerners as barbarian traders, never recognizing them as official representatives of foreign governments. Nowhere did the treaty mention opium, but everyone knew that the drug had been at the heart of the war.

One hundred fifty years later, China still feels the sting of this defeat. The recently negotiated treaty for the return of Hong Kong in 1997 is viewed as just a fraction of the restitution owed. In 1990, writing in the *Beijing Review*, historian Hu Sheng, president of the Chinese Academy of Social Sciences, lamented the cost of the war in terms of Chinese health, hard currency, and national honor. He also observed that for the next hundred years China was under continuous attack by the West and Japan, but because the emperors were willing to tolerate their presence, the people were unable to rise up and throw out the foreigners. In his view, and in that of many Chinese, "Only the Chinese Communist Party could do this."

For his failure to curb the barbarians, Lin Zexu was demoted and disgraced, and spent the last few years before his death supervising irrigation projects and the repair of dikes. In retrospect, he is regarded as a hero. "The Chinese army, commanded by Lin," writes Hu, "resisted the invaders together with the local people. However, the corrupt Qing court was unable to continue the resistance and succumbed to the invaders."

Commissioner Lin would no doubt feel vindicated, and perhaps even take some pleasure in the way many Western nations are now on the receiving end of the drug policies they helped invent.

After Centuries of Japanese Isolation, a Fateful Meeting of East and West

When Japan's rulers finally let in Yankee trade and technology, they changed the history of their country and of the world

James Fallows

James Fallows, Washington editor of the Atlantic Monthly, *has published* Looking at the Sun, *a Study of Japanese and East Asian economic systems.*

From the deck of the USS *Susquehanna* the sailors watched the sea around them fill with little boats. The *Susquehanna* and its sister ships—the *Mississippi*, the *Saratoga*, the *Powhatan*—had been traveling for more than half a year. From Norfolk, Virginia, they had sailed in the late fall of 1852 across the Atlantic, then down around Capetown, and across the Indian Ocean to the South China Sea. Through the spring of 1853 they labored northward past Macao, Hong Hong, Okinawa and the Bonin island chain—Iwo Jima and Chichi Jima—toward the main islands of Japan.

On the evening of July 8, 1853, they rounded a promontory and came to the entrance of the Uraga Channel, itself the entrance to Edo Wan, now known as Tokyo Bay. At the head of the bay, less than a day's sail away, lay Edo itself, Japan's largest city, insulated from foreign contact for nearly 250 years.

The Japanese guard boats that teemed around the American flotilla in the Uraga Channel were made of wood, with sharply angled prows. Sweating oarsmen propelled the boats through the ocean chop. Above the rowers' heads flapped the geometric- or floral-patterned standards of the Tokugawa shoguns who ruled Japan. The American sailors could not understand the shouts that came to them in Japanese. Yet every crew member knew that in the past, uninvited visitors to Japan had often been jailed, tortured or decapitated.

As the lead guard boat approached the *Susquehanna*, the Americans peering down from the deck found, with relief, that they could make out a few familiar characters from the Roman alphabet, rather than the gracefully swirling *hiragana* of Japanese phonetic writing or the intricate *kanji* ideograms the Japanese had adapted from written Chinese. As the guard boat drew closer still, sharp-eyed crewmen sounded out the first word: *"Départez!"* The entire message was in French, not English. It said, "Depart immediately and dare not anchor!" The two nations that would become the main Pacific powers made their first significant contact in a language neither really understood.

THE LENGTHENED SHADOWS OF TWO MEN

Japan's rulers had not in any way invited the encounter; indeed, the more imminent it had become, the more it filled them with dread. America forced the encounter on Japan for a confused tangle of reasons, many of which the American instigators did not honestly discuss among themselves. Yet the aftereffects of this moment prepared Japan for the most impressive feat in its history, and one of the most surprising in the history of any nation. At the same time American interests were more shrewdly advanced by the man who sat hidden in his cabin on the *Susquehanna* than by other American leaders almost any time in U.S. history. Ninety years afterward, Japan and America would be at war, but that was not the fault of the two men who guided this encounter on a hot summer day in 1853; Masahiro Abe, in the shogun's council at Edo, and Matthew Calbraith Perry, in command of the vessels known today in Japan as *kurofune*, "black ships."

Matthew Perry, bearing the title not of Commodore but of "Commander in Chief, United States Naval Forces Stationed in the East India, China, and Japan Seas," was 59 years old when his fleet reached Uraga. For the era, that was old—especially for a man undertaking a prolonged voyage to an essentially unknown destination. Perry suffered from arthritis and other maladies that confined him to his cabin during much of the long trip. Even at age 25 he had been remarked on for his gravitas; as he grew older he took on the air of a mandarin. This demeanor proved a great asset. Like Douglas MacArthur, another American too regal to fit easily into his home culture, Matthew Perry was well prepared by training and temperament for negotiations in Japan. An aw-shucks, unassuming manner might be an asset on the American frontier, but not surrounded by little boats in Tokyo Bay.

Perry's career, indeed his whole life, was devoted to the expansion of the U.S. Navy. His older brother, Oliver Hazard

From *Smithsonian* magazine, July 1994, pp. 20-24, 26-28, 30, 32. © 1994 by James Fallows. Reprinted by permission of the author.

Library of Congress

北亞墨利加人物
ペルリ像

steamships, American whalers had worked the waters of the North Pacific surrounding Japan. Frequently the ships did not come home. American sailors stranded by typhoon or shipwreck had washed ashore in Japan since the late 1700s. Often they were executed; usually they were jailed; a few were forced to perform ritual disrespect to Christian symbols, for instance by walking on a portrait of the Virgin Mary.

GETTING THE JUMP ON DUTCH, FRENCH AND ENGLISH

These icons of the Blessed Virgin were leftovers from Portuguese Jesuits, who had proselytized in Japan for nearly a century before being driven out in the early 1600s. The shipwrecked Americans, mainly Protestants, found this ordeal less excruciating than the Japanese expected, yet news of such episodes, especially one involving the whaler *Lagoda*, filtered back to America, where at a minimum they stirred a passion for better protection for whalers, and among some people a desire to make the "pagans" atone. "If that double-bolted land, Japan, is ever to become hospitable, it is the whale-ship alone to whom the credit will be due," Herman Melville wrote in *Moby-Dick* in 1851.

The British had won their Opium Wars against China. From the north came Russian vessels. Swarming around were the French and the Dutch. The expansionist U.S. Government watched these plans with care. Finally, to establish America's presence first, the Administration of Millard Fillmore, in by far its most consequential step, commissioned the Japan Expedition and convinced Matthew Perry to command it. For nearly two and a half centuries, since the great warlord Hideyoshi took steps that led to the policies known as *sakoku*, or "closed country," Japan's officials had isolated themselves from the world-and wondered apprehensively when the isolation might end.

In 1549 a Portuguese Jesuit, Francis Xavier, had come ashore on the island of Kyushu. Initially tolerated, even supported by some local noblemen, the Jesuits had in the next 50 years made tens of thousands of Japanese converts. By the end of the century Hideyoshi, weakened by a costly and failed attempt to conquer Korea, and chastened to learn that savage conquistadors had often followed the cross in Latin America, had

Perry, had become a hero at the Battle of Lake Erie before Matthew was out of his teens. Matthew, by contrast, spent his early career in a peacetime navy "where members of a small clique of senior officers scrambled for the limited command opportunities, where feuding, backbiting, and even dueling were a way of life," as Peter Booth Wiley puts it in *Yankees in the Land of the Gods.* "During the navy's first fifty years, thirty-three officers were killed in duels." Perry's first important mission, in 1819, was to transport freed slaves to Africa during the founding of Liberia. He did not see combat until he was in his 50s, at the Battle of Veracruz in the Mexican War, as the nation kept expanding westward toward a second sea frontier on the Pacific.

One great struggle over America's maritime future turned on the relative future roles of clipper ships versus steam-powered vessels. By the 1850s the fast and graceful clippers had given America the lead in the shipping trade. But the British were outbuilding America in steamships, and by the 1840s, Britain's steam-powered Cunard line was winning the battle for passengers and valuable freight on the transatlantic route.

Steam power required coal, and at the time no ship was large enough to carry all the coal it needed to cross the vast Pacific. Clipper ships had to choose routes to China on the basis of favorable winds, but steamers could be more deliberate, following a "great circle" route up toward Alaska and then down the Japanese archipelago. With coaling stations along the way, the great circle route would be possible, and in 1851 Americans learned that Japan had deposits of coal. "The moment is near when the last link in the chain of oceanic steam navigation is to be formed," said Senator Daniel Webster of New Hampshire, not stinting on rhetoric, as he endorsed an American expedition to Japan. The point of this link would not be to buy from the Japanese their own handicrafts and manufactures but to obtain a "gift of Providence, deposited, by the Creator of all things, in the depths of the Japanese islands for the benefit of the human family"—that is, Japan's coal.

The desire to expand a coal-using, steam-powered navy was not the only reason for the expedition to Japan. Beyond lay China, where Americans hoped to find markets to develop and souls to convert. For a century before the age of expelled all missionaries. Soon, the To-kugawa shogunate launched its radical policy of seclusion. As far as possible, Japan and its leaders would function as if there were no world beyond Japan's sea-coast. "So long as the Sun shall warm the earth, let no Christian dare to come to Japan," said the shogun's expulsion order of 1638. If contact with foreigners was unavoidable, it would be handled through an enclave of Dutch traders, concentrated in an island ghetto called Deshima, near Nagasaki in the far south-ern extreme of the country—hundreds of miles from the great, protected centers of Kyoto and Edo.

The sakoku policy worked for a while—indeed, for as many years as the United States has now existed as an independent country. Yet in the early 1800s, as Japan began its third century of near-total isolation, the strains were evi-dent. "In 1642, the year Isaac Newton was born, the last Japanese priest had been crucified and Japan had closed like an oyster," one American historian has written. But the leaders who made the decision "could hardly guess that Japan, which went into seclusion as one of the two or three strongest nations on the globe, would emerge from it, centuries later, as a distinctly second-class power."

The same whalers and fishermen who were inconvenient when washed onto Japanese shores inevitably brought news of the Industrial Revolution and other advancements outside Japan. A young Japanese fisherman named Manjiro Na-kajima was himself shipwrecked and picked up by an American whaler in 1841. Under Japan's seclusion law, it was a capital offense to leave the country—or to come back, if one had escaped. But after spending a decade in New England, under the name John Mung, Manjiro decided to risk returning to Japan.

The *daimyo,* or lord, of the southern province of Satsuma realized, as Samuel Eliot Morison puts it, that decapitating Manjiro would not only sever his head but also "would cut off an important source of information." Instead, the dai-myo sent him to Nagasaki, "where offi-cials pumped Manjiro dry of everything he knew about the United States." Among the facts Manjiro revealed (as Walter McDougall wrote in *Let the Sea Make a Noise . . .*) was that Americans were lewd by nature, and that in their country "toilets are placed over holes in the ground. It is customary to read books in them."

Officially, the Japanese rulers faced news of foreign developments with re-doubled sternness. In 1825, as whaling traffic increased, the shogun issued an edict forbidding any foreign ship to land. When a foreign ship came into view, the order read, it was crucial to shoot at it first and ask questions later. "Have no compunctions about firing on [the Dutch] by mistake," the order went on. "When in doubt, drive the ship away without hesitation. Never be caught off guard."

Behind this bravado was a debate, based on very little information but heated because the Japanese felt the very survival of the nation was at stake. In the town of Mito, a day's walk to the north-east of Edo, the "Mito School" of theor-ists said that an increased threat required increased determination to resist. Japan must shore up its coastal defenses, gird-ing itself for the inevitable battle to the death that would keep the foreigners away. "Today the alien barbarians of the West, the lowly organs of the legs and feet of the world, are . . . trampling other countries underfoot, and daring, with their squinting eyes and limping feet, to override the noble nations," one such scholar wrote in 1825. With such a foe, no compromise could be possible.

COULD JAPAN BEND WITHOUT BREAKING?

In the other camp were the Rangakusha, or "masters of Dutch learning," so called after Holland's role during the closed-country years as the vehicle for all learning from overseas. A realistic assessment of the circumstances, said members of this camp, required Japan to bend so as to avoid being broken. They had evidence of weakness inside the country. Taxes, levied in rice, were be-coming oppressive. In several centuries of peace the samurai class had grown large and dependent; in 1850 Edo alone supported some 17,000 bureaucrats, com-pared with 1,500 in Washington, D.C.

Evidence of the strength of potential invaders was even more dramatic. In 1846, seven years before Matthew Perry's ar-rival, Commodore James Biddle of the U.S. Navy had reached the mouth of the Uraga Channel. He had retreated with humiliating loss of face, after letting Japanese sightseers and officials inspect every inch of his ship and after accepting a letter from the shogun telling him

never to return. Yet the shrewder Japa-nese officials of the era carefully noted the size and power of his ships, and of the American guns. Biddle's vessels repre-sented destructive potential of a sort Japan had barely imagined.

Most of all the Japanese realists no-ticed what had happened to China—no-ticed, and were appalled. China was not just another country but the Middle Kingdom, the Central Country. Its em-peror had historically referred to Japan's emperor as "your little king." A new China had been carved up by West-erners, debauched by opium and left totally unprotected by either the Ch'ing dynasty or armed force. If the British and French could polish off China, what hope was there for little Japan—against Britain, France, Russia and the United States? Japan could try to enforce its seclusion law, said one of its very shrewdest leaders after the Biddle affair, but if "the foreigners retaliated, it would be a hopeless contest, and it would be a worse disgrace for Japan."

This leader was Masahiro Abe, the senior counselor for the shogun's gov-ernment. As the shogun was the power that ruled Japan in the emperor's name, so Abe was the strategist who made plans on behalf of the weakened shogun, Tokugawa Ieyoshi, who was in place when Perry arrived. Abe was a genera-tion younger than Perry, only 34 years old as Perry's flotilla of Black Ships neared Edo. Raised in a scholar's family, he had through force of intellect made himself one of the shogun's most influen-tial advisers while still in his 20s.

In the split between the hard-liners and compromisers in the shogun's court, Abe sided initially with the hard-liners. But after extensive consultation among the daimyos of Japan, he and his allies came up with a brilliant compromise. Japan would open itself to the Western traders—but only for a time—placating them just long enough to learn how to rebuild its own navies and arsenals. Naosuke Ii, the most influential of all the daimyos, re-minded the shogun that, even as Japan had earlier used Dutch traders as its bridge to the outside world, it was time to use the Americans and other for-eigners as another, broader bridge. Across this bridge new discoveries could flow into Japan—providing the country, in the long run, with means to rearm itself, learn from outside technology, and ultimately "gain a complete victory" over the foreigners.

Of gifts given, those from Japanese were more decorative, while Perry's aimed to impress Japan with industrial might. Baby steam engine was biggest hit, but offerings included plow, scythe, grindstone.

Some of the American politicians promoting the Japan Expedition had cast it in missionary terms, a chance to open the Orient to faith and flag. "I am sure that the Japanese policy of seclusion is not according to God's plan of bringing the nations of the earth to a knowledge of the truth," Samuel Wells Williams, a missionary traveling with Perry as cultural expert and interpreter, wrote in his journal as the expedition neared Edo. Perry himself, pious enough, never described his duties in these terms. Instead he concentrated on how to deploy his men, his ships and himself for maximum effect. Before the trip began, Perry foresaw that his fleet's substantial armament "would do more to command their fears, and secure their friendship, than all that the diplomatic missions have accomplished in the last one hundred years." In a set of "Instructions" for the voyage, Perry said that the Commander "will be careful to do nothing that may [compromise] his own dignity or that of the country. He will, on the contrary, do every thing to impress them with a just sense of the power and greatness of this

country, and to satisfy them that its past forbearance has been the result, not of timidity, but of a desire to be on friendly terms with them."

GIFTS TO SHOW A NATION'S STRENGTH

Like Masahiro Abe, Perry had studied the sad history of Commodore Biddle, who had been forced out of Edo Bay in 1846. In Perry's view, Biddle never recovered from setting his first foot wrong with the Japanese: rather than insisting on retaining a mysterious distance, he had let them climb onto his ship and, in effect, imprison it with guard boats. Speaking of himself in the third person, in his memoir of the voyage Perry said, "The Commodore . . . was well aware that the more exclusive he should make himself, and the more unyielding he might be in adhering to his declared intentions, the more respect these people of forms and ceremonies would be disposed to award him." He would meet only with officials of "the highest rank"

in Japan. He would make a threat only when he was absolutely certain he could carry it out.

Power could be demonstrated through generosity as well as reserve. Perry had prepared gifts to demonstrate the range of strengths his nation possessed. Editions of Audubon's *Birds of America* and *Quadrupeds of America* that had cost $1,000 apiece—a decade's earnings for an average American family at the time. Champagne, perfume and mirrors. Whisky, liqueurs, and small weapons from the Colt factory. And, most important, American machines: plows, a telegraph, a crude camera, even a nifty little quarter-scale steam-powered railroad train.

This was the man who appeared in the Uraga Channel in July 1853. He was not one to be driven away by instructions to *"Départez!"* Sweating alone in his cabin, unwilling to present himself prematurely to the crowd of Japanese, he issued his orders. The *Susquehanna* and sister ships were to repel, with all necessary force, any Japanese who attempted to board the boats. They would proceed up the channel, toward Edo, until their wish to meet a truly senior official, one who could speak for the ruler, was fulfilled. After the failure of the French message, a Japanese official had neared the *Susquehanna* and yelled out, in English, "I can speak Dutch!" To him the Americans conveyed their wish to meet someone truly in command.

Throughout Edo, news of the Black Ships' arrival created near-panic. Some citizens fled, carrying their possessions to the countryside, fearing pillage and war. The shogun's council met to consider bleak-seeming alternatives. The usual reflexive responses to outside pressure—asking the foreigners to come back again in a few years, telling them to go on to Nagasaki, the only site where Japan had done business with foreign representatives through the sakoku years—seemed to have lost their potency. The Americans would not retreat—in fact, they kept sending surveying ships farther up the bay, ignoring Japanese assertions that this violated local law and saying that they needed to be sure about anchorages, for "the next time."

As the governing council quarreled, Abe pushed them toward a decision: the Americans must be placated, at least for now. Perry had been asking to meet the emperor; that was out of the question, of course. Indeed, to this point the Americans were not even aware that a real emperor existed, hidden in Kyoto. When they said "emperor," they were referring to the shogun; their official goal was to present him with letters from President Fillmore.

Clearly some meeting was essential, and so on July 14, after elaborate arguments over protocol, Matthew Perry himself came ashore at the town of Kurihama.

In retrospect this result seems inevitable. America was a country on the rise. Japan could not wall itself off eternally. Each party had a stake in negotiating reasonably with the other: Perry, because he was outnumbered on the scene; the Japanese, because other Americans could come back and exact retribution if anything went wrong. But at the time it was very much touch and go. More than once Perry's men came to the brink of violent confrontation. Crewmen on the *Mississippi* had to level a loaded musket at a Japanese official's chest to keep him from climbing aboard. A small American survey boat, commanded by Lieut. Silas Bent, found itself surrounded by three dozen Japanese guard boats. Bent

prepared for hand-to-hand combat, instructing his small crew to fix bayonets—until the mighty *Mississippi* steamed into view and the Japanese retreated.

And so, on the night before Perry's scheduled landing in Kurihama, his crew members watched apprehensively from their decks as more and more Japanese troops filled the shore. Perry considered the possibility that the proposed meeting was really an ambush. After his surveyors reported that Kurihama's harbor was deep enough, Perry ordered his gunboats brought in close to shore, where they could bombard the Japanese if anything went wrong. On the long night before the meeting, 250 American sailors were chosen by lot for the dangerous mission of accompanying their commander ashore. The Japanese worked through the night to prepare a pavilion for the meeting—and to increase the boats guarding the entrance to Edo Bay, in case the Americans were planning a sudden, treacherous assault.

On the morning of July 14, the American boats drew near to shore. Members of the landing party, dressed in their formal uniforms, were issued 20 rounds of ammunition apiece and carefully loaded their muskets and pistols. On the shore they saw three new pavilions, covered with the bright flags and standards of Japanese officialdom. Surrounding the pavilions were files and files of soldiers, armed with swords, bows and arrows, and a few antique firearms.

At 10 o'clock barges full of Americans began arriving on the shore. Miscalculations at this moment might have had historic consequences; long after the event, one of the Japanese commanders revealed that ten swordsmen had been hiding under the floor of a pavilion, with orders to leap out and slaughter the foreigners if they made the slightest aggressive move.

As their numbers grew on the beach, Perry's men formed a double line, through which their commander, arriving at last, marched toward the waiting Japanese. Ahead of Perry was a Marine officer walking with sword in hand. On either side of him were two of the largest men from his ship, both black stewards, loaded with all the weapons they could carry and towering over every other person on the beach. Once Perry was safe ashore, tension eased a bit. He was met by two Japanese governors, to whom the stewards presented large rosewood boxes. Inside were small solid-gold

cases, which in turn contained Millard Fillmore's letters requesting that Japan open itself to the world. The governors, in return, presented Perry with a letter said to be from Japan's ruler. When translated, it turned out to contain warnings that the Americans had broken Japanese law by landing in Kurihama and must not come back. Perry said that, with his mission accomplished, he was leaving Japan—but he would be back the next year to hear the Japanese government's response. With quite as many ships? the interpreter asked. "All of them," Perry replied. "And probably more, as these are only a portion of the squadron."

After the meeting in Kurihama, Perry had compounded Japan's sense of threat by sending surveying parties even deeper into Edo Bay. Then his departing fleet retraced the route it had taken toward Japan, visiting Okinawa and the Bonin Islands before stopping for repairs and refitting in Macao. He studiously ignored suggestions from Washington that he wait and assemble a much larger force before his return trip. Perry knew that French and Russian missions would soon be heading to Japan. He was suffering terribly from arthritis; a winter passage back to Edo would be dangerous and unpleasant. Yet to forestall all other navies and force action from the Japanese, Perry set sail northward from Macao in the middle of January 1854.

Back in Edo everything was till uncertain. What did the Americans really want? What compromise would be enough to make their warships go away? Suppose the shogun's government offered to give the Americans half the trading rights now monopolized by the Dutch? Or dragged out the negotiations themselves over five or ten years; after which time the Americans might lose interest or Japan might come up with a new plan?

FIGHT IT OUT OR FACE UP TO PROGRESS

Masahiro Abe had ordered Japan's coastal defenses fortified as soon as Perry's flotilla headed south after its first visit. He engineered the repeal of a law—enacted at the start of the sakoku era—that prohibited Japanese citizens from building seagoing vessels, and he opened negotiations with the Dutch about buying some steam-powered warships from them. All factions in Japan agreed that negotiations should be strung out as long as possible. Yet when the moment of choice arose, should Japan fight to the death, as influential figures like Tokugawa Nariaki, daimyo of Mito, were advocating? Or should it bow to the reality of superior force and instead plan for long-term survival, and future revenge?

The issue was forced in the middle of February, when American ships arrived once more in the Uraga Channel. This time Perry's flotilla numbered three steam-powered frigates, seven ships under sail, and combined crews totaling more than 1,500 men. Overcoming bitter accusations that he was betraying Japan, Abe at last forced through a decision. Japan would greet the Americans with conciliation. It would accept a code of conduct for shipwrecked whalers and seamen. It would let the Americans obtain coal in Shimoda, near Edo, and trade with them at sites other than the traditional foreigner's ghetto in Nagasaki. It asked only for a transition period of a few years before the full agreement came into effect.

There were still points of detail to be negotiated—how many ports would be open to trade, what tariff the Japanese could impose. But under Abe's guidance Japan had given in. Matthew Perry, confined by disease and dignity to his Black Ship cabin, was ready by early March to deal face-to-face with his Japanese counterparts. On March 8 he came ashore at Yokohama for a detailed, though still touchy, negotiating session.

On March 13 Perry went ashore once again for the first gift-exchanging ceremony. One by one he gave away the marvels of artistry and engineering he had stowed aboard his ships nearly two years before. The Japanese onlookers were entranced by the scale-model locomotive pulling a train. The passenger coach, complete with interior benches and curtains, was too small for human passengers, but samurai and shogun's officials took rides sitting on top of the train. In their turn, the Japanese offered gifts. But because they thought that valuable gifts might be insulting—suggesting the possibility of a bribe or the need to reply in kind—their gifts were modest, though artistic and of fine workmanship. Perry regarded them as trifling. More impressive were their mammoth sumo wrestlers. Perry watched as the *sumotori* strode in, heavy sacks of rice atop their heads. One of the wrestlers approached Perry, who accepted the invitation to punch the immense stomach and feel its strength. Samuel Wells Williams, "Perry's missionary-interpreter, who was generally quite admiring of Japan and who despaired of his crewmates' insensitivity to foreign ways, nonetheless wrote in his diary that the spectacle demonstrated the clash of two cultures: the "success of science and enterprise" on the American side, the "brute animal force" on Japan's.

A final disagreement arose over Perry's desire to walk the streets of the capital city. Here the Japanese held firm: Perry could, if he chose, view Edo from the deck of his ship, but must not come ashore. Perry accepted, sailed to the top of Edo Bay for a look, and then, on April 14, headed south again.

Negotiations between Japan and the United States were just beginning. For most of the next decade an American counsel, Townsend Harris, would accuse Japanese officials of backsliding, dissembling and attempting to evade the treaty's terms. More than a century later in the debate over trading issues, Japanese and American officials have assumed roles very similar to those first played in Uraga and Kurihama, with the Japanese debating the merits of acquiescence or defiance, and the Americans, far less powerful now, attempting to display impressive and intimidating force.

Perry's role in Japan was complete. It was to be a profound role and, though deeply unwished for by the Japanese, in the long run it had quite positive effects. Although Japan had been forced to make concessions and accept "unequal treaties," it had avoided outright defeat—and had prepared for the rapid modernization that began with the Meiji Restoration of 1868. For this progress Japan could, with mixed emotions, thank Perry and the shock he delivered with the Black Ships.

Perry thought he would be lionized by his countrymen on his return, but he was not, in part because his countrymen were preoccupied with tensions over slavery that would lead to the Civil War. Retiring to his town house in New York, the Commodore worked methodically on his *Narrative of the Expedition,* which he submitted to the publisher at the end of 1857. Masahiro Abe, who had skillfully guided Japan through its greatest challenge of the 19th century, died while still in his 30s, a few months before Perry completed the manuscript. On March 4, 1858, shortly before his 64th birthday, Matthew Perry died at home, of rheumatism and heart failure. His cortege was led down Fifth Avenue by the men with whom he had sailed to Japan—the men, that is to say, with whom he had changed history.

The Twentieth Century to 1950

At the beginning of the twentieth century, Great Britain occupied a powerful place in the world. Its fleet with its global reach was the strongest among nations and served as the policeman of the world. It was a factor in the suppression of the slave trade. British financial strength was incomparable and the British pound sterling set the standard for world markets. World War I, however, exhausted its resources and Great Britain changed from being the world's great creditor nation to the world's great debtor nation. The United States emerged at this point as a financial leader, as the article by Clive Lee indicates. Edmund Stillman, looking at World War I, however, says that the goals of the warring nations were very questionable compared to the result of 10 million dead soldiers and a heritage of barbarism. Of course, no one predicted the great losses that occurred, and the losses do not justify the goals of the war.

The Great Depression and World War II brought a further decline in Western control of the world. Again, the great loss of life, the monetary cost, and the internecine fighting among the nations of the West took their toll. Yet, the Allies saw World War II as a just fight, a necessary struggle of good against evil. Adolph Hitler rose from the ashes of World War I and the depression to lead his country into warfare once more. He instigated genocide against the Jews, and proof of his evil policies was found by the Allied soldiers as they overran the Nazi death camps. Other groups also suffered the sentence of genocide, as Jeremy Noakes notes in his article "Social Outcasts in Nazi Germany." Some 25,000 Gypsies were executed and subjected to the infamous medical experiments of the Nazis. The Gypsies were a vagabond people, and no one has paid much attention to their losses. Only 5,000 of them survived the conflict.

The Germans and Italians were defeated by conventional fighting, whereas the Japanese surrendered shortly after the explosion of atomic bombs at Hiroshima and Nagasaki. After Commodore Matthew Perry's fateful visit in 1853, the Japanese quickly industrialized while retaining much of their traditional culture, as Richard Perren explores in his article "On the Turn—Japan, 1900." Reminiscent of other industrial nations, the working class in Japan, especially the women, bore much of the burden. In 1904–1905 the Japanese defeat of Russia announced the success of the transformation. Japan participated in World War I, suffered during the Great Depression, and opened warfare with China in 1937. The Japanese surprise attack against the United States fleet at Pearl Harbor on December 7, 1941, brought the angered American people into World War II.

In earlier wars, even World War I to an extent, it was a part of military ethics to safeguard women, children, and noncombatants. With the advent of submarine warfare in World War I and high altitude bombing in World War II, such ethics were forgotten. Thus began total war—one nationality against another, often with the obliteration of entire cities. This killing of innocents has continued into the conflicts of the postwar world, such as with the "ethnic cleansing" of the Bosnian Serbs against the Bosnian Muslims in the 1990s.

A strategy of island hopping brought U.S. forces ever nearer the Japanese home islands in World War II. The fighting was often bloody and bitter, as demonstrated by the landing at Tarawa (a part of the Gilbert Islands in the West Pacific Ocean). The United States, meanwhile, developed the atomic bomb, and Commander William Parsons was the officer in charge of organization of its construction. He flew on the *Enola Gay* to deliver the bomb at Hiroshima. The decision to use the new weapon was made by President Harry S. Truman, but ever since that moment there has been a continuous debate. Was this bombing necessary to end the war? Does the United States bear special guilt for the only atomic bomb ever used in anger? What concern should there be for the

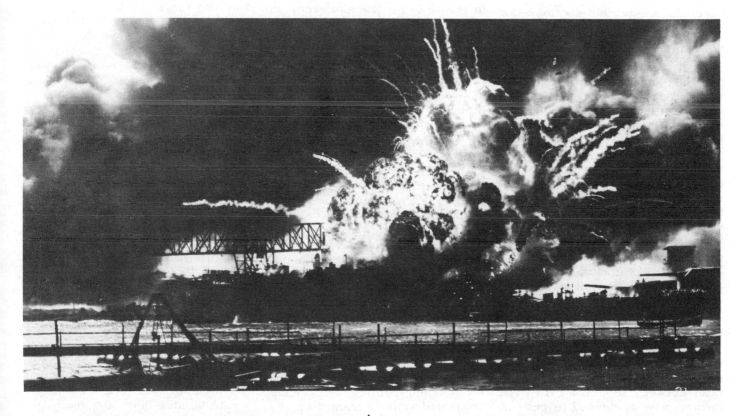

innocent people killed in the blast? William Lanouette summarizes the various positions on this issue. The debate continues even now, as a heated argument over a 1995 display of the *Enola Gay* in the Smithsonian Museum demonstrated. Regardless of the arguments, the United States introduced the world to the atomic age.

Looking Ahead: Challenge Questions

What causes war? Is it rational?

Has anything worthwhile been obtained by fighting wars?

Why did the Nazis carry out genocide against Gypsies?

Compare the lives of Japanese women factory workers with those of the Industrial Revolution.

How did Japan become a "great power"?

Should the United States have used the atom bomb in World War II?

THE INTERNATIONAL ECONOMY

An end to
the older order–
Clive Lee looks
at the pressures and
changes that marked
out the 1890s as a
frontier post in a settled
world economy.

Clive Lee is Professor of Historical Economics at the University of Aberdeen and author of The British Economy since 1700: A Macroeconomic Perspective *(Cambridge University Press, 1986).*

From an economic perspective, especially an international one, history provides few changes dramatic enough to be classified as turning-points. But the 1890s ended a century of relative peace which allowed the international economy to expand and evolve in marked contrast to the twentieth century which combined unprecedented economic advance with immense and frequent dislocation. This decade thus provides a good vantage point from which to evaluate the era of gradual development that preceded it as well as the more intense phase that followed.

By comparison with recent decades, economic growth before the First World War was characterised by modest increases in the principal indicators of income, population and income per head. Between 1860 and 1913 world income grew at about 2.18 per cent each year while population increased at 0.70 per cent. The difference between these measures, 1.48 per cent, is the increase in income per head which is the conventional measure of economic progress. But there were great differences in the progress achieved in different parts of the world. While incomes per head increased greatly in North America and Western Europe, only small improvements were

achieved in Asia and Latin America or, from what little is known, in Africa. While the greater part of world population increase was concentrated in Asia, most of the increase in income was concentrated in North America and Western Europe, increasing the disparity in prosperity between these continents. In 1900, average incomes per head ranged from $890 (in 1953 prices) in the United States, and $450 in the United Kingdom, to $100 in Brazil, $56 in India and $46 in China.

This inequality, which was clearly increasing in the late nineteenth century, was inherent in the structure of the international economy and the nature of economic advance in this period. From the early modern period in embryonic form, and from the eighteenth century in an increasingly distinctive form, the international economy emerged from the trading centres of north-west Europe, centred on London and Amsterdam and extending to northern France, Germany and the Baltic. Access to the sea as the essential medium for any large-scale international trade was crucial, and it was the expansion of the Western European states' trade and colonial empires into the West Indies and North America that provided the foundation for the international economy. By the eighteenth century, supplies of tobacco, sugar and, later, cotton, from the New World in return for hardware and tools represented an exchange which was essential to the prosperity of both continents. The expansion of the nineteenth century, stronger as the century progressed so that it reached a peak in the last two decades, was essentially an amplified and increasingly complex version of the earlier growth. Europe supplied the migrants and the capital which enabled the United States to spread its boundaries west to the Pacific. In the later decades of the nineteenth century almost one million people per year left Europe. Over half of them went to the United States, the rest to British imperial territories like

Australasia and Canada or to South America, notably Brazil and Argentina.

Britain played a central role in the creation and expansion of this international system. By the late eighteenth century London had replaced Amsterdam as the financial centre of Europe, and the City became the heart of the international financial and trading network which developed in the following century. Britain provided two major functions in supplying capital for investment and in co-ordinating the international trade and payments system. The former had its origins in the development of financial institutions in the eighteenth century to provide maritime insurance for commerce and fire, and later life assurance, for both business and households. Loans to the state for military purposes and mortgages on estates for fashionable improvements increased the profits and the resources of the finance houses. In the following century the railway generated unprecedented demands for investment, and the London Stock Exchange became the principal source of funds for railways in Europe, North and South America, India and wherever landlocked territories could be opened to world trade by this new transport. Docks, harbours, warehouses and tramways and public utilities were related infrastructure requirements which were financed from London, as were tea plantations, tobacco and rubber estates in Malaya, cotton estates in India, and Japanese silk manufactures. National and municipal securities and the long-favoured, and exceedingly secure, business of granting mortgages on land absorbed substantial funds. Investments were often extremely diverse. By the late nineteenth century, the London and Lancashire Insurance Company held investments in United States bonds, Brazilian railways, Manchurian railway bonds, Siamese government bonds, the Moscow-Jaroslav Railway, the Honan Railway Gold Loan and City of St Petersburg bonds. In the later decades of the nineteenth century, Bri-

From *History Today*, June 1992, pp. 33-39. © 1992 by History Today, Ltd., 20 Old Compton Street, London W1V 5PE. Reprinted by permission.

tain invested five per cent of its national income abroad, a proportion without historical precedent and unlikely ever to be repeated. From the 1860s to the First World War, securities worth £4,082 million were raised on the London Stock Exchange for overseas investment.

This massive flow of investment reflects the benefits gained by Britain from the expansion of international trade and its dependence on it. Fortunately the success of overseas investment in generating profits allowed Britain to pursue free trade policies which helped the growth of world trade. Throughout much of the eighteenth and nineteenth centuries, Britain had a deficit on trade as imports exceeded exports. But earnings from foreign investment and from services such as insurance and shipping kept the balance of payments in surplus. This extremely unusual balance of payments structure enabled Britain to sustain trade deficits against many countries which, in turn, were encouraged to extend their trade on the basis of such favourable balances.

Even more important was the supremacy of Britain in world trade and finance which meant that the pound sterling was the major currency used in international trade. Such was its strength amongst currencies that it was, literally, as good as gold. Sterling was on the gold standard as early as the 1820s, and was thus exchangeable for gold at a fixed parity. By the end of the century, most of the major trading nations had accepted the gold standard idea and linked their currencies to it. The financial stability that this created was essential for international economic development because it provided the security of monetary values which was necessary to provide the confidence for trade. When that system, and the confidence which it generated, collapsed in the 1930s, the level of international trade and economic activity fell very sharply and the world economy was plunged into a recession which was ended only by the Second World War.

The phase of international economic development which occupied the nineteenth century was characterised by industrialisation in Western Europe, principally Britain and Germany, and the United States. In 1900 these three countries together accounted for 55

per cent of the manufacturing output of the world, a share which had been growing throughout the century and continued to increase until the outbreak of war in 1914. Iron, steel, engineering, all of which were linked to railways and shipbuilding, were major nineteenth-century industries. So too was textile and clothing manufacture, always characteristic activities in early industrialisation. By the beginning of the twentieth century, the three major industrial economies dominated production in all these industries, and the United States was clearly established as the largest, wealthiest and most industrially potent economy. It was in the United States that the beginnings of a more characteristically modern form of manufacturing emerged at the turn of the century. The bicycle boom of the 1890s formed a bridge between the American system of manufacturing, based on machine tooled interchangeable parts as pioneered in the Springfield Armory in the 1830s and 1840s to achieve levels of accuracy and uniformity substantially higher than could be achieved by manual workers, and mass production. During the 1890s bicycle manufacturers in New England began to manufacture many of their components from sheet steel. Punch pressing and stamping were combined with the recently invented electric welding to make parts far more cheaply than had previously been possible. Interchangeable parts and large scale production opened up new opportunities for manufacturers in supplying a mass market with standard goods.

The technology pioneered in bicycle manufacture was very suitable for another relatively new industry, automobile production. Ford adopted both interchangeable parts and the use of pressing and punching techniques to generate an unlimited supply of components. The assembly procedure had to be speeded up to accommodate this flow, and Ford introduced the assembly line in 1911, using the ideas of flow production from the flour milling industry. Fordism which comprised a moving assembly line, high wages (to attract workers to operate under this new pressurised discipline) and low prices made possible by volume production, was firmly established by the First World War. Production soared and price cuts increased the market.

The motor industry, in all its manifestations, was a symbol of the twentieth-century economy, a harbinger of the ending of the old order in the early years of the century.

Despite the growth of industrialisation, often celebrated by historians in terms of soaring output of steel or cotton, the world economy before the First World War was still primarily rural. The most characteristic feature of nineteenth-century development was the extension of the Atlantic economy from its Western European/North American centre into other parts of the world. Other countries, even continents, were drawn into the system through trade because they had some marketable commodity, usually foodstuffs or raw materials, for which a demand existed in the high income economies of the west. The outflow of investment from Britain was, of course, a central part of this development, funding the transport, infrastructure and often the production process itself. Brazil was an economy which was drawn into the international system as a supplier of coffee and rubber, which were the nineteenth-century successors to earlier raw material exports, such as sugar. The Rio and Sao Paulo coffee plantations boomed in the late nineteenth century, and attracted European migrants, especially Italians, who could become major plantation owners within five years. The appearance of the pneumatic tyre in the 1890s stimulated the exploitation of Amazon rubber reserves. American and European companies bought estates, pushing up land values and the price of rubber.

External demand of this kind increased production and exports as the statistical records indicate. By the First World War, Brazil obtained half its export earnings from coffee sold principally to the United States. But there were limitations on this form of development. Plantation agriculture producing coffee, cotton, cocoa and tobacco requires a large input of unskilled labour. It is not, therefore, a suitable medium for increasing skills or generating sufficient incomes either to produce a marked improvement in standards of living or to allow spending beyond the basics of food and shelter.

In the rubber economy, the long gestation period of fifteen years before a tree was ready for tapping restricted the productive capacity. Little advantage was secured by the tappers, and most of the profit was secured by the middlemen who transferred the rubber from the tappers to the exporters. The rubber economy remained pre-capitalist. Production was increased by an extension of the area of exploitation, not by more intensive activity, the many intermediaries fragmented profits between them in a web of debt. At the bottom of the hierarchy, the tapper was dependent on the trader for goods in exchange for the rubber. Little capital or technology was involved.

Other countries were drawn into the international trading system as suppliers of primary products such as cotton, coffee, oilseed, rice and rubber. Often a single commodity comprised a very high proportion of exports, such as cotton in Egyptian trade. In the late nineteenth century the land devoted to cotton cultivation doubled in area, helped by irrigation schemes and railway improvements financed from abroad. But the effect on most of the population was limited as most of the income accrued to the owners of cotton plantations or foreign investors. There was no improvement in traditional agriculture and no widening of the domestic market. By the 1890s population growth was increasing pressure on the land available for food production. Nor did Egypt develop a cotton manufacturing industry. The raw cotton which the country exported returned as manufactured imports from the United Kingdom.

The development of these countries was hampered by their limited economic advantages, but was further inhibited by political and financial dependence on foreign governments and commercial institutions. Egypt had accumulated a massive national debt by the 1880s, partly through funding irrigation schemes and partly as the result of extravagances of the Khedive. The scale of the debt, and the fact that it was owed to British institutions, meant that government policy decisions in the later decades of the century were heavily influenced by advice from Whitehall. More explicit was the control exercised by the British government over its territories in the Indian sub-continent. Industrialisation in India, which had substantial reserves of coal and iron, was restricted by the India Office in London. As a result of

strenuous lobbying by the British cotton manufacturers, import tariffs in India on textiles were abolished in 1882 thus exposing the Indian domestic market to the full force of competition from Lancashire. While the major benefit gained from its imperial status in the Victorian period was the railway, the location of the network was determined not by economic factors such as the need to link iron and coal reserves, but by military concerns such as the need to move troops swiftly to the North West Frontier in case of attack from Russia. Furthermore, the India Office imposed the costs of defence on its imperial territories, and approximately half of total spending was so disposed at the turn of the century.

Apart from cotton production for export to Britain, Indian agriculture did not respond to the great increase in world demand for tropical products in the late nineteenth century. In relation to population, land was in short supply, enjoyed little rainfall, and was exhausted by over-cropping. Most of the land remained devoted to subsistence farming. While acreage per head was greater in India than Egypt, only about a fifth of the land area was irrigated as against most of Egyptian land, so that yields were much poorer. The Egyptians could feed themselves better than the Indians and still export a quarter of their crops.

But not all primary producers were so limited in their opportunities for economic advance. Indeed, Australia, Canada, Argentina and the United States were numbered amongst the highest *per capita* incomes in the world at the end of the nineteenth century. The characteristics of such economies were a rich endowment of natural resources together with labour scarcity. Australia exported wool and later meat when refrigeration made the European market accessible. The migrant flow was limited by demand for labour, the indigenous population was small, and there was no large scale subsistence agriculture. By the 1890s almost all Australian export earnings came from primary products, meat, gold and wheat were prominent amongst these, and contributed towards sustaining the highest *per capita* incomes in the world. Similarly, American and Canadian wheat, Argentinian beef, and New Zealand lamb sustained high incomes based on sales in the

world market. These agricultural activities were relatively capital intensive and required far less unskilled labour than the plantations characteristic of cotton and coffee production.

Limitations to economic advance were not imposed only by a restricted range of natural resources or unfortunate government strategies. In parts of Europe, especially in the east, the shackles of traditional social and economic structures were similarly effective. This was certainly true in the extensive lands of the Russian empire. The Land Census of 1905 revealed that 80 per cent of the land in European Russia, and much in Asia and Transcaucasia, was held under *mir* tenure. The *mir* was a community of peasants within which all members had the right to an allotment of land as well as homestead and kitchen plots of land held in hereditary succession. Land could not be sold or bequeathed without the agreement of the *mir*. Legislation in 1893 decreed that the periodic repartitioning of land by the *mir*, in order to give members a share of both good and bad land, should be no more frequent than every twelve years and that a two thirds majority would be required to sanction change even then. This system was economically extremely inefficient. Small strips of land in scattered locations prevented the introduction of machinery, precious land was lost in demarcating boundaries, farmers were obliged to produce a common crop and improvement was precluded. Furthermore, this tenure system comprised an incentive to early marriage and thence to high fertility rates, since married couples were entitled to an allotment of land. In the second half of the nineteenth century, land per male peasant fell by 50 per cent in European Russia, stimulating migration into Western Siberia and Kazakhstan at the end of the century. But the combination of inefficient farming and rising population undermined the traditional system and forced legislation in the first decade of the twentieth century, which effectively destroyed the old system.

In numerous ways the Russian Empire combined traditional economic and social structures with elements of modernisation as enclaves within it. Even within agriculture economic dualism existed. A survey taken in 1905 showed that 139 million *desiatina* of land was held communally, at an average of 11.6 *desiatina* per household, while a further 79 million belonged to large estates, averaging 592 *desiatina*. These large estates produced most of the grain that reached the market that in turn comprised an extremely important part of Russian exports. They were also far more efficient than the communal farms and were familiar with the use and advantages of mechanised agriculture

Within this massive and mainly backward economy, there existed other pockets of economic modernisation, financed by foreigners and making Russia the world's greatest debtor by 1914. Much of this investment was attracted by the opportunities of exploiting the rich mineral resources of iron and coal in the Ukraine, and oil in the Caucasus which produced half of the total world output in the 1890s. But machinery was poor and productivity low. The best firms were foreign owned and financed, and often provided their own skilled technicians. Shipbuilding, steel, engineering and mining were all foreign dominated. The fact that Russia was the fifth largest industrial power in 1914 reflected more on the limits of world industrialisation than Russian advance. Two thirds of factory workers in St Petersburg retained ownership of village land, and all manufacturing suffered a temporary loss of labour during the harvest. In 1905 and again during the Great War, Russian industry was unable to meet the requirements of warfare between industrial states.

Although the world economy was showing diverse and promising manifestations of growth and change at the end of the nineteenth century, and appeared to have simultaneously achieved a stable economic order through the gold standard to complement the stability of a fairly peaceful century, the reality was less impressive. The advent of unprecedented, extensive warfare in 1914 dispelled the illusion of political security. It also revealed and exacerbated the weaknesses inherent in the international economy. The gold standard system which reached its apogee at the turn of the century depended upon the favourable conjunction between British trade and international finance which made the pound sterling the universally accepted means of exchange. Britain could not have played such a role indefinitely unless these very special conditions could be maintained. The economic advance of other countries, providing their own shipping, insurance and investment services, would eventually have undermined the unique balance of payments surplus achieved by Britain, and with it the undisputed strength of sterling. But that transition would probably have taken several decades to evolve. The First World War achieved it in four years. As a major combatant, and as a country which underwrote much of the costs of war incurred by its imperial territories, the expense of the war turned Britain from the world's greatest creditor nation into its greatest debtor. Conversely, the United States was transformed from a major debtor to a major international creditor. Accordingly, the dollar was greatly strengthened and the pound weakened as a medium of international exchange. The 1920s saw the final attempts to resurrect the old system and the 1929 depression indicated their failure. The search for international financial stability has continued ever since, with varying success but no definitive resolution.

The apparent symmetry in international trade also proved to be temporary. The development of primary exporting countries relied heavily on the buoyancy of the market and the price. But the appearance of competitor producers, as in the growth of Malayan rubber production to rival Brazilian output, cut prices and incomes. Even before the First World War desperate attempts were being made to support prices. The Brazilian government introduced a scheme to store part of the annual coffee crop in order to maintain prices by withholding it from the market. As a short term palliative this was successful, but the coffee mountains continued to grow steadily after the war.

From an economic perspective any short historical period or point in time will reveal both stability and change, the latter usually being the more enduring state. In the 1890s some apparently immutable features of the world economy, like the gold standard and traditional Russian agriculture, were reaching a point beyond which they could no longer be sustained. At the same time, apparently trivial developments as in the evolution of bicycle technology were setting in train changes of universal and fundamental import. The First World War brought to a close this early phase of modern economic development by accelerating certain changes and introducing others. The war stimulated technological and industrial advances in the search for victory, it undermined weak economic structures such as that of the Russian Empire, distorted the patterns of world trade to the advantage of some (United States and Japan) and the detriment of others (Britain, France, Germany), and began the destruction of the gold standard regime. For these reasons the war was a kind of turning point although the fundamental forces of economic life and development remained active and were, in the longer term, more certain in bringing further change and new problems.

FOR FURTHER READING:
James Foreman-Peck, *A History of the World Economy: International Economic Relations since 1850* (Wheatsheaf Books, 1983); David A. Hounshell, *From the American System to Mass Production 1800-1932* (John Hopkins University Press, 1984); A.G. Kenwood and A.L. Lougheed, *The Growth of the International Economy 1820-1960* (George Allen & Unwin, 1971); C.H. Lee, *The British Economy since 1700, A Macroeconomic Perspective* (Cambridge University Press, 1986); Nathaniel H. Leff, *Underdevelopment and Development in Brazil* (George Allen & Unwin, 1982); Roger Owen, *The Middle East in the World Economy 1800-1914* (Methuen, 1981).

ON THE TURN – JAPAN, 1900

From isolation to Great Power status – Richard Perren explains how a mania for Westernisation primed the pump of Japan's transformation at the turn of the century.

Richard Perren

Richard Perren is Senior Lecturer in Economic History at the Department of History, University of Aberdeen and author of Japanese Studies from Earliest Times to 1990: A Bibliographic Guide *(Manchester University Press, 1992).*

Following the Meiji Restoration in 1868, when rule by the emperor replaced the government of Japan by the Tokugawa shogun, the country embarked on a process of modernisation. In the next thirty years Western experts were imported to train the Japanese at home, selected Japanese were sent abroad to learn from the West, and Japan's new leaders embarked on a programme of radical reform. By these means they aimed at transforming a country that was weak and backward into a strong modern industrial nation. This new Japan would be capable of dealing with Western powers on equal terms and of throwing off the humiliating 'unequal treaties' they had imposed between 1858 and 1869.

When the Emperor Meiji died in 1912, control was concentrated in a highly centralised state whose functions were carried out through Western-style political, administrative and judicial institutions operating in the name of the emperor. Western-style armed forces upheld the position of the Japanese state at home and abroad. A modern and efficient education system served the aims of the state. Western-style economic and business institutions were in place, and factory-based industry firmly established. Japan had already been victorious in two major wars, against China in 1894-95 and Russia in 1904-5. She had not only achieved the much desired revision of the unequal treaties, but was a world power with an alliance with Britain, and a possessor of colonies. Yet the country still retained many traditional features, and had only adopted those characteristics of the West that were absolutely necessary to achieve its desired aims.

How far had the transformation process gone by 1900, and can the decade of the 1890s be described as a 'turning point'? To answer this we need to judge when Japan passed beyond that point in time when her modernisation could not have been reversed. Because the whole process of Japanese modernisation involved a complex interaction of social, economic, and political change it is not possible to ascribe a precise date to its completion. Nevertheless, there are a number of factors to suggest that by 1900 it had reached a stage where it was unlikely to be reversed.

It was the authorities that had to provide the necessary pump-priming and make strategic decisions about which areas of Japanese life needed to be transformed. It had become a traditional habit of the Japanese to look to officialdom for example and direction in almost everything, and this habit naturally asserted itself when it became necessary to assimilate a foreign civilisation which for nearly three centuries had been an object of national repugnance. This required the education of the nation as a whole and the task of instruction was divided among foreigners of different nations. The Meiji government imported around 300 experts or *yatoi* – a Japanese term meaning 'live machines' – into the country to help upgrade its industry, infrastructure and institutions. Before the Franco-Prussian War, Frenchmen were employed in teaching strategy and tactics to the army and in revising the criminal code. The building of railways, installing telegraphs and lighthouses, and training the new navy was done by Englishmen. Americans were employed in forming a postal service, agricultural development, and in planning colonisation and an educational system. In an attempt to introduce Occidental ideas of art, Italian painters and sculptors were brought to Japan. German experts were asked to develop a system of local government, train Japanese doctors and, after the Franco-Prussian War, to educate army officers. A number of Western observers believed that such wholesale adoption of an alien civilisation was impossible and feared that it would produce a violent reaction.

Although this did not occur, many early innovations were not really necessary to modernisation but merely imitations of Western customs. At that time the distinction between the fundamental features of modern technology and mere Occidental peculiarities was by no means clear. If it was necessary to use Western weapons there might also be a virtue in wearing Western clothes or shaking hands in the Occidental manner. Moreover, Meiji Japan had good reason to adopt even the more superficial aspects of Western culture. The international world of the nineteenth century was completely dominated by the Occident, and in view of the Western assumption of cultural superiority, the Japanese were probably correct in judging that they could not be regarded as even quasi-equals until they possessed not only modern technology but also many of the superficial aspects of Western culture. The resulting attempts in the 1870s and 1880s to borrow almost anything and everything Western may now seem to us to be amusingly indiscriminate, but it is perfectly understandable.

As the object of modernisation was to obtain equal treatment by the West many of the cultural innovations, besides being more than outward forms to the Japanese themselves, had an important psychological influence on Western diplomats and politicians. Under the shogun, members of the first Japanese delegation to the United States in 1860 wore traditional samurai dress with shaved pate and long side hair tied in a bun and carried swords. Under the emperor, Western-style haircuts were a major symbol of Westernisation. Soldiers and civilian functionaries wore Western-style uniforms, and

politicians often adopted Western clothes and even full beards. In 1872 Western dress was prescribed for all court and official ceremonies. Meat eating, previously frowned on because of Buddhist attitudes, was encouraged, and the beef dish of *sukiyaki* was developed at this time. Western art and architecture were adopted, producing an array of official portraits of leading statesmen as well as an incongruous Victorian veneer in the commercial and government districts of the cities and some rather depressing interiors in the mansions of the wealthy.

Though the pace of change was hectic at first, and the adoption of Western forms seemed indiscriminate, it soon slowed as the Japanese became more selective about which aspects of their society they wanted to transform. Their adaptability meant the contracts of most Western experts and instructors only needed to be short-term, the average length of service being five years, and *yatoi* were less in evidence by the 1890s. The craze for Westernisation reached its height in the 1880s, but thereafter there was a reaction against unnecessary imitations and many of its more superficial features, like ballroom dancing, were dropped. Other social innovations subsequently abandoned were the prohibition of prostitution and mixed bathing, both of which were initially enforced to placate the prejudice of Western missionaries.

In reforming the legal system, Western concepts of individual rather than family ownership of property were adopted. But for purposes of formal registration of the population the law continued to recognise the old extended family or 'house', known in Japanese as the *ie*. This consisted of a patriarch and those of his descendants and collateral relatives who had not yet established a new *ie*. Within this structure the position of women was one of obedient subservience. In the 1870s the theme of liberation of women from their traditional Confucianist bondage was taken up by a number of Japanese intellectuals, influenced by Western writers on the subject. At the same time a number of women activists publicly engaged in politics. As both movements lacked public appeal they waned in the 1880s. In 1887 the Peace Preservation Ordinance, which remained in force to 1922, banned women from political parties and meetings. Women

under the Civil Code of 1898 had no independent legal status and all legal agreements were concluded on a woman's behalf by the male to whom she was subordinate – either father, husband, or son. Women had no free choice of spouse or domicile and while they could in theory protest against this situation, they could do so only in a non-political manner. Such action posed a challenge to the whole social orthodoxy on which the Japanese state was founded, so in practice few women protested.

One Western institution whose adoption would have made a very favourable impression on the West, but which made next to no headway in Japan, was Christianity. Like the women's movement it had some impact among Japanese intellectuals, but prejudices against it ran too deep. In 1889 less than a quarter of one per cent of Japanese were Christians. The only religion that did flourish was Shinto which was one of the traditional faiths of Japan. Revived interest in it had been a key element in the intellectual trends that led to the imperial restoration. But there was little deep interest in religion among Japan's new leaders. Though the government continued to control and support the main Shinto shrines, the many cults that made up the faith lapsed into a traditional passive state forming no more than a ceremonial background to the life of the Japanese people.

There was greater enthusiasm for Westernisation over the matter of constitutional reform, and this dated back to the early 1870s when Meiji rulers realised change here was necessary to gain international respect. In the next decade the major tasks for building a modern political constitution were undertaken. In 1882 the statesman Ito Hirobumi led a study mission to several European capitals to investigate the theories and practices he believed were most appropriate for Japan. Before his departure he decided not to slavishly reproduce any Western system but that whatever example was taken as a model would be adapted to Japan's special needs. Most of his time was spent in Berlin and Vienna, and after his return to Japan work on the new constitution began in the spring of 1884. A new peerage was created, in December 1885 a cabinet type government was introduced, and to support it, a modern civil service with entry by examination was established. The Meiji consitution which took effect from November 1890 was essentially a cautious, conservative document which served to reinforce the influence of the more traditionally-minded elements in Japan's ruling class. While distinctively Japanese, it compared most closely with the German model of the monarchy.

This constitution, though nominally democratic, retained power in the hands of a small ruling élite with minimal interference from or responsiility to, the majority of the population. There was to be a bicameral parliament, called, in English, the Diet. The House of Peers was mostly made up from the ranks of the new nobility and the lower house chosen by an electorate limited to adult males paying taxes of fifteen yen or more. In 1890 this was limited to 450,000 persons or 5 per cent of adult males. Even when the taxation qualification was reduced to ten yen in 1902 it only increased the electorate to 1,700,000 males. The constitution's architects hoped that the provisions for democratic government it contained would be counterbalanced by other safeguarding provisions. Most important of these was the position of the emperor, who was accorded a position of primacy in the state. The imperial family were said to rule over Japan in perpetuity, and under the constitution the emperor was the repository of absolute and inviolable sovereignty. This was underlined by making cabinet and armed forces responsible not to political party, nor to the Diet, or the Japanese people, but to the emperor alone.

The emperor as an individual had little personal influence on events, and was not strong enough to unify the various factions that vied for political power. This was only possible by reference to pre-existing traditions of Japanese culture. These were invoked to stress the duties of loyalty and obedience to the sovereign, and through him to the state. As early as October 1890 the Imperial Rescript on Education, often seen as the basic tool for inculcating the orthodox philosophy of the state, showed the strong influence of the Confucian view that the state was essentially a moral order. This edict made only passing reference to education itself, but showed the revived influence of Confucian ideology in its stress on harmony and loyalty to the

throne. Its central concept of mass indoctrination through formal education was an entirely modern emphasis. Intensive drilling of Japanese children with lessons in patriotism became possible when funds were available for universal compulsory education. In 1885 only 46 per cent of children of statutory school age were in school, though by 1905 this had risen to 95 per cent.

The purpose of educational reform, at its most basic level, was to turn out efficient recruits for the army, factory, and farm. This was because political and military modernisation, as well as industrialisation, depended on new skills, new attitudes and broader knowledge. Japan's leaders realised from the 1870s that social and intellectual modernisation was a prerequisite to success in other fields. But in the social and intellectual areas, as in economics, the responsiveness of thousands of individuals was more important than the exhortations of authority.

While political and social reform and cultural change were limited in extent and selective in their nature by the end of the 1890s, the same picture emerges in economic life. Industrial modernisation took two forms – the reorganisation of traditional industries, and the transplantation of new industries from the West. Some traditional industries, like cotton-spinning, experienced radical change and the introduction of factory production, while others made slower progress. Japan was an important exporter of raw silk but that industry was not dependent upon elaborate or expensive machinery. The production of cocoons was a labour-intensive industry, already carried out as a by-employment in peasant households. Gradually small factories equipped with improved but relatively simple and inexpensive power-driven machines were introduced. The investment in this industry was thus spread thinly over a great number of producers. Where large investments of capital were absolutely necessary, as with Japan's strategic heavy industries like iron and steel, armaments, and shipbuilding, the initial investment was made by the government. But even here success was not immediate and these early concerns were sold off to Japanese businessmen at low prices in the 1880s. In some of the new industries success came sooner than in others. In 1897-1906, 90 per cent of

railway rolling stock was built in Japan but 94 per cent of locomotives were still imported, mainly from England and Germany. It was not until after 1900 that the basis of heavy industry in Japan was firmly established.

Indeed, the whole of Japanese economic and social life in 1900 was still firmly rooted in traditional forms with quite a small modern superstructure. But for Japan the term 'traditional' needs qualification because it does not necessarily mean that pre-modern Japanese economy and society was antagonistic to change. In spite of Japan's decision to isolate itself for almost 300 years, features evolved that could be built upon once the country was forced to accept Western influence. The growing volume of research on the period before 1868, in the form of local and regional studies, has reinforced the view that Japan was a relatively advanced pre-industrial economy. For an underdeveloped country it was already well provided with a basic infrastructure by the time the process of modernisation began in earnest. Agricultural output per head of the population was quite high and premodern Japan possessed a substantial degree of commerce. In the more backward northern regions, on the island of Hokkaido, and also parts of the extreme southern island of Kyushu, medieval forms of social and economic organisation persisted until quite late. But on the more advanced regions of the main island of Honshu, especially the Kanto Plain around Edo – the old name for Tokyo – and Osaka, there was a thriving urban-centred commercial economy. Merchants and traders supplied the wants of the towns of the region and production for exchange, and not just subsistence, was carried on in the countryside.

Much of Japan's growth after 1868 was built upon the foundations of its pre-modern economy. Partly under the protection and encouragement of government most of the capital-intensive investments went into railways, steamships, and mechanised heavy industrial plants. But just as important in promoting development at that time were a vast number of small improvements and minor capital undertakings. Before 1940 the majority of roads were of unsurfaced dirt and bridges were simple wooden structures. Agricultural construction, represented primarily by irrigation works, changed little from

Tokugawa times. Only after the turn of the century did most Japanese make Western products a part of their daily lives, and they were adapted to a traditionally Japanese life-style. In Tokyo in 1910 most of the dwellings were made of wood and only about an eighth used brick, stone, or plaster. Within the houses most furniture was still the traditional kind and most of the food eaten was of a traditional type. This meant that there was still an enormous market to be supplied by peasant farmers, village entrepreneurs, small businesses and traditional craftsmen. In 1890 nearly 70 per cent of Japanese investment was in the traditional sector and it still accounted for 45 per cent, fifteen years later.

But the success of Japan's modernisation efforts needs to be judged not only by what happened within the economy itself, or by the changes within Japanese society. Reform was undertaken as a means to an end and that end was recognition as an equal by the West. This was necessary before there was any chance of removing the unequal treaties of the 1850s and 1860s and contained two major restrictions on Japanese sovereignty. Firstly, there was the provision of 'extra-territorial jurisdiction'. Under this Westerners accused of crimes were not tried by Japanese courts, but by consular courts within the foreign settlements of the seaports of Japan set out in the treaties. The other restriction was the loss of tariff autonomy. Eager for markets, the Western powers placed severe limits on Japanese import and export duties. These measures were the usual way for nineteenth-century Western powers to regulate diplomatic and commercial relations with Oriental countries, the model being the treaties imposed on China after the Opium War of the 1840s. For Japan the actual consequences of the treaties were not particularly damaging. No great market for opium was developed, and the opening of Japanese industry to competition from the West forced the pace of economic change instead of allowing inefficient industries to shelter behind protective tariffs. Foreigners resident in Japan were restricted to the treaty ports and needed official permits to travel outside so were never a great intrusion

into Japanese life. And the justice dispensed in the consular courts was generally fair to both Japanese and Westerners.

Nevertheless, the fact of these treaties' existence was rightly regarded as a great humiliation as they usurped functions which are the proper preserve of a fully independent state. They came up for renewal periodically and from 1871 onwards Japan asked for their revision. In that year refusal was a foregone conclusion, as even the Japanese could see that the conditions originally necessitating extra-territorial jurisdiction had not undergone any change justifying its abolition. In later years Western nations were reluctant to allow their citizens to come under the power of a legal system that was still not fully reformed, despite the abolition of torture as an accepted legal practice in 1876 and the introduction of a Code of Criminal Procedure, framed in accordance with Western ideas, in 1882. But this was the start of what the West wanted and when negotiations were reopened in 1883, Japan included as compensation for the abolition of consular jurisdiction a promise to remove all restrictions on trade, travel, and residence for foreigners within the country. These and subsequent discussions in the 1880s reached no definite conclusion, mainly because the Japanese refused to grant foreigners living in the country the right to own freehold property. It was not until 1894 that a final settlement of the consular question became a real possibility when Britain agreed to abolish consular jurisdiction by 1899.

The five year delay was for two reasons. Before the new treaty came into force Japan had to fully implement a new legal code. The thorough recodification of the law this required was a slow and difficult task as most legal reforms were introduced piecemeal. This area is probably the strongest example of direct Western pressure being applied to change a fundamental feature of Japanese life. Drafts drawn up, largely under French influence, were submitted in 1881 and again in 1888, but a completely revised legal code only went into effect in 1896, removing the final impediment to ending extra-territorial jurisdiction in 1899.

The other cause for delay was to allow Japan to renegotiate the rest of its treaties – of which there were over fifteen – with other Western powers, so that all nations were on an equal footing. This aspect was undoubtedly made possible by the successful outcome with Britain. Tariff autonomy was not finally restored to Japan until twelve years after 1899, but up to 1911 she was allowed to increase import and export duties.

The successful negotiations in 1894 were important as a turning point for the Japanese and for the West. The greatest opponents of the loss of extra-territorial jurisdiction were the few hundred foreign merchants and businessmen who lived and worked in the treaty ports. But for Japan this was a national political question that had provoked fierce debates in the Diet and in the press. The first treaties between Japan and the West were signed when the nation was still in a state of torpor from its long slumber of seclusion, and under circumstances of duress. The redemption of her judicial and fiscal authority had been, for thirty years, the dream of Japanese national aspiration, and both domestic and foreign policies had been shaped with this one end in view. For Japan's rulers, innovation after innovation, often involving sacrifices of traditional sentiments, were introduced for the purpose of assimilating the country and its institutions to the standard of Western civilisation. By 1900 Japan was still not regarded as a full equal by Western nations, but she was now accorded greater respect. In the next decade this was built upon with the Anglo-Japanese Alliance in 1902, the defeat of Russia in 1905, and the annexation of Korea in 1910. By 1912 there was no doubt that Japan had achieved 'Great Power' status.

FOR FURTHER READING:
H.J. Jones, *Live Machines*, (Vancouver, 1980); J.P. Lehnann, *The Roots of Modern Japan*, (Macmillan, 1982); H. Wray and H. Conroy, eds., *Perspectives on Modern Japanese History*, (Honolulu, 1983); J. Hunter, *The Emergence of Modern Japan*, (Longman, 1989); O. Checkland, *Britain's Encounter With Meiji Japan, 1868-1912*, (Macmillan, 1989); E.O. Reischauer and A.M. Craig, *Japan: Tradition and Transformation*, (Allen & Unwin, 1989).

JAPANESE WOMEN AT WORK, 1880-1920

What was it like to be a 'boiled octopus' in the sweatshop silk mills of Japan before the First World War? **Janet Hunter** looks at the life and conditions of the women who bore the brunt of Japan's rapid industrialisation.

Janet Hunter is Saji Research Lecturer and Senior Lecturer in Japanese Economic and Social History at the London School of Economics. She is editor of Japanese Women Working *(Routledge, 1993).*

It is easy to view the growth of Japan's economy over the last century as an unmitigated success story. Notwithstanding the débâcle of 1945, Japan's current position as an economic superpower bears witness to the country's status as the only non-Western nation to acquire both a modern industrial sector and an empire before the Second World War. However, these undoubted achievements too often conceal the problems which Japan, like other late-developing countries, faced, and the burden which rapid industrialisation placed on her people. Among those who paid a high price for national growth were industrial workers.

As Western style factories and the mechanisation of production spread in the late nineteenth century, tens of thousands of individuals, mostly from rural backgrounds, took up factory work. By the late 1920s over 2 million Japanese workers were employed in large, mechanised factories, providing the core of a new, permanent working class.

The silk industry was one of the first branches of industry to be mechanised along factory lines, and throughout the period up to 1929 silk was Japan's most important export. A mechanised cotton spinning industry developed from the 1880s, and by the time of the First World War cotton had become Japan's other major export. These textile exports, by enabling Japan to import capital goods and technology, played a crucial role in the industrialisation process. Moreover, the dynamic success of these industries in both domestic and export markets was the first indicator of the ability of the Japanese economy to compete with the industrialised economies of Western Europe and the United States. At their peak in the 1920s these two industries employed more than half a million workers, over 80 per cent of them female. The growth of a modern industrial sector in pre-war Japan thus depended largely on the labour of women.

Early industrial workers enjoyed relatively favourable conditions. The workers in the first government-owned, model steam-powered silk mill, set up at Tomioka in 1872, were a privileged group. Mostly the daughters of former samurai, they had been persuaded to work in the mill after more conventional recruiting methods had foundered on popular fears of the savage, barbarian habits of for-

From *History Today,* May 1993, pp. 49-55. © 1993 by History Today, Ltd., 20 Old Compton Street, London W1V 5PE. Reprinted by permission.

eigners. Workers in other early silk mills, usually in rural areas, tended to be local girls from a range of social origins. Most had prior experience of handicraft silk production within the home, and were anxious to utilise their labour during the slack agricultural season. Workers in the early cotton mills, which were more likely to be located in urban areas, also drew on local residents, both male and female, some of them recent migrants from agricultural areas.

As the scale of production grew, demand for labour increased. Both silk and cotton mills began to try and recruit workers from further afield. The character of the labour force also started to change. The proportion of women from relatively prosperous backgrounds, and of daily, usually married, workers from the neighbourhood, declined, as did that of male workers. They were increasingly replaced by the young daughters of impoverished rural families. These girls, most of whom were aged between twelve and twenty, were usually housed in dormitories at the mills. Bound by contracts of one to three years, these workers were regarded by employers as short-term, temporary migrants, who were uncommitted to the industrial labour force and would return to their rural homes after a few years to marry. Their motivation for working was assumed to be 'to help the family finances' or to earn pin-money or dowry, justifying employers' payment of low wages.

The growth of the workforce focused attention on working conditions. From the late 1890s graphic accounts of the hardships of mill life shocked many Japanese. A succession of reports, autobiographical accounts and surveys led contemporaries to conclude that many female workers, particularly in the silk industry, were living and working in conditions which were unacceptable. The following extract, written in 1898 by a journalist concerned to enlighten the Japanese public on the conditions of what he termed the 'lower social strata of Japan', is typical:

When I encountered silk workers I was even more shocked than I had been by the situation of weaving workers... At busy times they go straight to work on rising in the morning, and not infrequently work through until 12.00 at night. The food is six parts barley to four parts rice. The sleeping quarters resemble pigsties, so squalid are they. What I found especially shocking is that in some districts, when business is slack, the workers are sent out into service for a fixed period, with the employer taking all their earnings... Many of the girls coming to the silk districts pass through the hands of recruiting agents. In some cases they may be there for two to three years and never even know the name of the neighbouring town. The local residents think of those who have entered the ranks of the factory girls in the same manner as tea house girls, bordering on degradation. If one had to take pity on just one group among all these workers, it must be first and foremost the silk workers.

There is no doubt that many girls took up textile employment in ignorance of the real conditions which they would face in the factory; and mill owners and their agents were hardly anxious to enlighten them, or their families. A labour journal in 1901 castigated the indirect recruiting system through which most workers were hired:

In order to get cheap workers every recruiting master employs the meanest tricks to catch girls from among simple farming families. This slave dealer, pretending to be a gentleman, goes to a country farmer who knows about nothing beyond tilling the land, and tells invitingly of work in silk spinning and the good wages his daughter can earn. These honeyed words are believed by the simple-minded farmer, and without consulting even his wife nor, of course, his daughter, he enters into a contract with the man; the latter pays him 1 yen as contract money, a sum which has to be repaid twenty times over if the contract is not fulfilled.

Hours were immensely long, especially during the peak season, and one report in 1901 found twelve to thirteen-year-olds sleeping as little as four hours in twenty-four, ending up so tired they could not even eat. A 1903 government report commented:

In one silk area, Suwa, the length of working hours are unequalled throughout the country. Average daily working hours do not fall below fifteen, moreover... working hours are repeatedly prolonged to increase production, meaning that daily working hours are often as much as eighteen hours. In factories in some areas working hours are fixed by factory regulations so when they want to extend working hours beyond the specified time they often move back the hands of the clock. Where this happens, if one factory's siren announced the end of work at the correct time, girls working in other mills would also know that they should have reached the end of their shift, so all the factory owners have provisionally agreed not to use their sirens.

In cotton spinning almost all factories operated machinery continuously, with workers taking day or night twelve-hour shifts. If a worker's replacement failed to turn up, a worker could find herself working two shifts of her own and someone else's in between, a total of thirty-six hours. Night work continued until 1929.

The conditions were extremely unhealthy. The air was permeated with dust and fumes and the atmosphere was intensely humid. In the silk reeling mills, reelers' hands were constantly exposed to the boiling water in which the cocoons were placed to soften them. Safety conditions were minimal at least until around 1914, and toilets and other hygiene facilities totally inadequate. Workers were frequently penalised for not paying sufficient attention to their work, for taking time off to go to the toilets or for talking to other workers. In the early days many workers were not permitted meal breaks, having to eat their meals next to their machines, often keeping them running.

Many of the dormitories in which workers lived were equally grim. As late as 1923 one writer commented that:

the dormitories for women workers can be described in a single word - pigsty. With the progress of the times and the growth of the [cotton] industry dormitories do appear outwardly to have undergone a complete change. The external appearance of the dormitories and company housing of companies such as Toyobo and Kanebo [two of the largest spinning companies] suggest that inside as well they must be superior to a middle-class residence. However, this is like saying that someone is a gentleman or lady just because they are wearing beautiful clothes.

Many workers slept together in one room, often sharing bedding. One mill reported a single room for over 700 girls as late as 1926. Light and ventilation were usually inadequate, and residents suffered from extremes of hot and cold in summer and winter. The nutritional standard of the food provided was invariably very low.

Employers, particularly in times of expansion like the late 1890s, sought to restrict worker mobility by confining workers to the factory compound and retaining part of their wages. Government inspectors in 1903 reported that in the silk areas:

girls are not at all free to go out of the mill. In the Suwa region, for example, they are normally banned from doing so. If permission is granted because of some mishap, the worker is supervised by an official who accompanies her. When a mill does have fixed times when workers can go out, it is usually for only one hour after the evening meal, with no more than five girls allowed out on any one evening. In mills lacking a bath girls are sometimes allowed out together at a specified time to go to the bath house, but in all cases exit permits usually have to be handed over.

In retrospect, it is easy to see that employers were not necessarily acting in their own best interests by economising on labour and working conditions. As factory recruiters spread their net ever wider, the reputation of some mills went before them, leading to the supply of labour drying up in particular areas. Competition to recruit labour became ever fiercer and costlier, and the lies told to prospective employees and their families about what they could expect ever more exaggerated. The growing costs of securing adequate labour were a drain on finances which employers could ill afford. Even more serious was the damage inflicted by very high labour turnover. In silk, where many employees were on seasonal contracts, some experienced workers did tend to return annually to the same mill; but even here, and throughout the cotton industry, many workers left after no more than a few months. Turnover in some factories was over 100 per cent per year.

Production at the mills suffered from shortages of experienced workers; many workers did not remain long enough to get properly trained or for the mill to recoup their recruitment expenses. Excessively long hours also took their toll, with productivity on night shifts considerably lower than in the day.

From 1 to around 3 am the bodies of the girl workers are like those of 'boiled octopuses'; some are in a dream, some fall asleep at the machines, some are lying down in corners, but even so the supervisors themselves are overtaken by drowsiness and cannot keep effective watch, and the soulless machines turn endlessly.

Conditions at the mill rendered work in general less productive through worker exhaustion, malnutrition and sickness. Employees worked less efficiently than those enjoying better conditions, and took more time off for illness. Sickness among mill workers was exceptionally prevalent, and the high rates of tuberculosis, especially among cotton mill workers, became a national scandal in the first three decades of the twentieth century. The result of these seemingly shortsighted policies towards labour – not that different from many found in nineteenth-century Europe – was that Japanese labour was unproductive by international standards.

Only gradually did some employers begin to think that such management policies might be against their own best interests. For a long while mill owners and managers continued to hold a poor opinion of their workers, often taking the view that the kind of conditions they complained of were no more than they deserved. A 1898 report by the cotton spinners' federation was typical of the general tenor of management attitudes:

Many of the workers now being taken up by a lot of spinning companies are the daughters of poor people, who are almost totally uneducated and ignorant. When such people are brought together, they have no aim of independence and self-management, therefore no concept of endeavour and frugality, and many have no sense at all of saving on a regular basis. So, if they do not spend what's left of their earnings on food and drink, it immediately goes on clothes. They get money with one hand and let go of it again with the other. While they have money to spend they miss work, and live a life of idleness... in fact, many are absent for several days after payday.

Managers argued that the long working hours did not damage the health of workers. One commented:

The lifestyle of Japanese workers is undisciplined; they draw almost no distinction between work time and leisure time. They cannot even dream of

devoting themselves wholeheartedly to their work during working hours in the manner of European and American workers. For that reason even though working hours may be longer we do not need to worry that this will cause overwork, and any legal attempt to limit working hours must take account of this fact.

The view that employers stood to benefit if they looked after their workforce better was rarely heard prior to the First World War, although the rhetoric of employer paternalism, and the concept of employers acting *in loco parentis* was frequently voiced. Not until the 1920s is there much concrete evidence of employers' drawing the connection between better treatment and wages for workers, better worker skills and productivity, and hence greater employer advantage. There is some evidence that working conditions throughout these industries progressively improved through the inter-war years, producing in a few large cotton companies in particular a structure of management and non-wage benefits more reminiscent of post-war images of Japanese industrial relations. However, employer self-interest was only part of the reason for this change. Equally important was state intervention aimed at factory legislation and recruitment control. Such measures were bitterly resisted by employers on the grounds that such intervention infringed their freedom to deal with their employees and violated the 'traditional harmonious relationship between management and worker', – something which the conditions described above suggest had long been largely illusory.

However, these improvements were only part of the picture. On the other side changes occurred in the labour market, the industrial structure and the international economy, which adversely affected women workers. Extensive rationalisation in the 1920s cut the demand for labour. The Great Depression wrought havoc with the silk industry, which never recovered, and the 1930s witnessed the relative decline of the female-dominated textile industries. In periods of economic difficulty, the failure to view textile workers as long-term, committed members of the workforce (a view which seemed to be supported by the youth and high turnover among workers), and the prevailing conservative view that women's role was essentially domestic, rendered their position particularly vulnerable.

What of the workers' own experience of work? Contemporary report and historical interpretation have combined to convey an image of an exploited workforce whom poverty and sex made easy prey to rapacious industrialists, but whose contribution enabled Japan to compete with the West in early industrialisation. For many historians, the cheap labour of textile workers created profits for greedy capitalists while sustaining a semi-feudal village economy. Above all, they have been widely seen as passive victims of exploitation, suffering worse conditions than almost all other industrial workers, unable to fight back for a variety of reasons, including youth, gender, or capitalist and state oppression.

However, although data giving the workers' perspective is not numerous, we have enough to suggest that workers were far from being the totally passive creatures they have been depicted as, nor were they beguiled by their employers' 'paternalistic' strategies. At the very least they sang protest songs. Some were resigned to their lot, but others protested more vigorously against the extremes of sexual harassment, physical brutality and unhealthy hours and conditions. Workers' willingness to assert their rights against what they considered unjust treatment, especially in the 1920s, have been seriously underestimated. Though unionisation rates remained low, and workers' position as women, as well as state restrictions, discouraged overt forms of protest, there were some incidences of organised strike activity as early as the 1880s. More significantly, relatively few workers completed their full contracts. Despite restrictions and the loss of earnings which departure entailed, the number who managed to leave the mill for another which appeared to offer greater rewards, or to escape to their homes, was quite staggering. This was hardly passive acceptance.

As a group, though, these workers were relatively unsuccessful in pressing for major reforms in the pattern of textile production, and those who absconded were soon replaced by others. One explanation lies in the conditions within the Japanese agricultural sector, from which most

workers came, and which still employed nearly half the gainfully occupied population in 1930. Both male and female members of farming families had a long history of engaging in by-employments at home and had for several centuries left their villages on a temporary or permanent basis to earn in other sectors. The income which came in from such employments helped to sustain the farm family unit, and in bad times or harvest failure the family had one less mouth to feed. The textile workers stood firmly in this by employment tradition. Other factors also contributed to a girl's decision to take up work in textiles. There existed a strong tradition of women's work in textile production. With subsidised board and lodging (however inadequate in quality) thrown in, income in textiles was often higher than the same girl could have earned working as an agricultural labourer or contributing to the family farm. For some, the stimulus was the often illusory attractions of urban life.

There is no doubt that there was in these women's approach to work a life-cycle factor which differentiated them from men. The mills provided a new outlet for employment which could be left on marriage, and a considerable proportion of female textile workers did conform to the stereotype of a few years' work followed by marriage, childbirth and work in an agricultural community. However, it is erroneous to assume, especially for the period after the First World War, that all these women workers were never more than 'supplementary' labour, who remitted all their earnings home and regularly returned to their home villages to marry. Many workers moved from one mill to another to enhance their situations, and many never returned to their villages at all. During the course of the early decades of the twentieth century there emerged from among this group a more permanent female industrial workforce who through work or marriage settled permanently away from their place of birth, became committed to the pursuit of non-agricultural employment, and constituted a significant part of the large flow of people out of agriculture at this time. Like their male counterparts, they were part of the process whereby the occupational structure was gradually changed to one characteristic of an industrialised

country. Features common in early industrialisation, such as seasonal working, temporary industrial employment and short-term migration slowly declined as workers' rural ties were either weakened, or severed completely. Women did not participate in this process just by following their husbands or fathers; many female workers in textiles and other occupations took this step on their own account. Farmers' daughters were gradually transformed into autonomous industrial workers with a collective pride in their status of wage-earners, whose work contributed to the family well-being.

Both at the time and with the hindsight of the late twentieth century, the process of Japanese industrialisation is open to criticism. Contemporaries highlighted the bad conditions, the squalor, the long hours, the lack of safety and the general 'exploitation'; it is difficult for the historian to do other than confirm this picture. From the modern era we can also see more clearly the gendered dimension of Japanese industrialisation. Here, as elsewhere, the fact that these workers were women made control of the workforce easier, and facilitated the payment of low wages. The strongly patriarchal family system formed the background of these workers' employment, of employers' treatment, and of the whole lifecourse of these girls and women. The patriarchal system rested on a bedrock of natural conservatism (of both the individual and society as a whole), and was consciously reinforced by the Japanese state. A fervent rhetoric of domesticity permeated all arguments relating to women workers, who were always seen primarily as wives and mothers, or, if unmarried, as future wives and mothers. Indeed, almost all women did get married. Such ideologies of domesticity, and their reflection in the institutions of society as a whole, played a crucial role in creating the highly segmented labour market based on gender which is apparent not only in Japan, but in most other developing and developed economies as well. This dimension of gender was ignored, because it was taken for granted, by contemporary commentators on the situation of female textile workers in pre-war Japan. While workers slowly forged an identity as workers, and came to make autonomous decisions relating to compliance and protest in the context of the workplace, there is little evidence that the majority of workers seriously questioned the constraints which contemporary perceptions of gender imposed upon their lifecourse and their participation in the labour market.

However, it would be anachronistic to view the early twentieth century purely through late twentieth-century eyes, and to ignore the very real constraints and limited range of choices faced by contemporaries. The transition from an agricultural to an indus-trial society was never going to be easy, especially in the context of a fiercely competitive international economy. Perhaps more striking than the protests at the conditions was the absence of an effective and sustained opposition which could compel employers to alter their policies. This absence reflected a widespread acceptance that industrialisation was the only way forward for the nation and that the social costs associated with it were a price which had to be paid.

FOR FURTHER READING:

G.L. Bernstein 'Women in the Silk Reeling Industry in Nineteenth Century Japan', in G.L. Bernstein & H. Fukui (eds.), *Japan and the World* (St. Martin's Press, 1988); J.E. Hunter, *The Emergence of Modern Japan: an Introductory History Since 1853* (Longman, 1989); J.E. Hunter, 'Women's Labour Force Participation in Interwar Japan', *Japan Forum* 2, 1, April 1990; B. Molony, 'Activism among Women in the Taisho Cotton Textile Industry', in G.L. Bernstein (ed,), *Recreating Japanese Women, 1600-1945* (University of California Press, 1991); E.P. Tsurumi, *Factory Girls: Women in the Thread Mills of Meiji Japan* (Princeton University Press, 1990).

Sarajevo
The End of Innocence

After fifty years of explanations, it is still difficult to see why a political murder in a remote corner of the Balkans should have set off a war that changed the world forever

Edmund Stillman

A few minutes before eleven o'clock in the morning, Sunday, June 28, 1914, on the river embankment in Sarajevo, Gavrilo Princip shot the archduke Franz Ferdinand and brought a world crashing down.

After fifty years and so much pain, Sarajevo is worth a pilgrimage, but to go there is a disappointing and somehow unsettling experience: this dusty Balkan city in its bowl of dark and barren hills, is an unlikely setting for grand tragedy. Blood and suffering are endemic to the Balkans, but Sarajevo is so mean and poor. Why should an age have died *here?* Why did the double murder of an undistinguished archduke and his morganatic wife touch off a world war, when so many graver pretexts had somehow been accommodated—or ignored—in the preceding quarter-century? It was an act that no one clearly remembers today; indeed, its details were forgotten by the time the war it engendered was six months old. Nowadays, even in Sarajevo, few pilgrims search out the place where Princip stood that morning. Nearby, on the river embankment, only a dingy little museum commemorates the lives and passions of the seven tubercular boys (of whom Princip was only one) who plotted one small blow for freedom, but who brought on a universal catastrophe. Within the museum are faded photographs, a few pitiable relics of the conspirators, a fly-specked visitors' book. A single shabby attendant guards the memorials to a political passion that seems, well, naïve to our more cynical age. "Here, in this historic place," the modest inscription runs, "Gavrilo Princip was the initiator of liberty on the day of Saint Vitus, the 28th of June, 1914." That is all, and few visitors to present-day Yugoslavia stop to read it.

There is so much that goes unanswered, even though the facts of the case are so well known: how the failing Hapsburgs, impelled by an unlucky taste for adventure, had seized Bosnia and Herzegovina from the Turks and aggravated the racial imbalance of the Austro-Hungarian Empire; how the southern Slavs within the Empire felt themselves oppressed and increasingly demanded freedom; how the ambitious little hill kingdom of Serbia saw a chance to establish a South-Slavic hegemony over the Balkans; and how Czarist Russia, itself near ruin, plotted with its client Serbia to turn the Austro-Hungarian southern flank. But there is so much more that needs to be taken into account: how Franz Ferdinand, the aged emperor Franz Josef's nephew, became his heir by default (Crown Prince Rudolf had committed suicide at Mayerling; Uncle Maximilian, Napoleon III's pawn, had been executed in Mexico; Franz Ferdinand's father, a pilgrim to the Holy Land, had died—most improbably—from drinking the waters of the Jordan); how the new heir—stiff, autocratic, and unapproachable, but implausibly wed in irenic middle-class marriage to the not-quite-acceptable Sophie Chotek—sensed the danger to the Empire and proposed a policy that would have given his future Slav subjects most of what they demanded; how the Serbian nationalists were driven to panic, and how the secret society of jingoes known as "The Black Hand" plotted Franz Ferdinand's death; how seven boys were recruited to do the deed, and how one of them, Gavrilo Princip, on the morning of June 28, 1914, shot Franz Ferdinand and his Sophie dead.

But why the mindlessness of the war that followed, the blundering diplomacies and reckless plans that made disaster inevitable once hostilities broke out? It is all so grotesque: great and shattering consequences without proportionate causes. When the inferno of 1914–18 ended at last, the broken survivors asked themselves the same question, seeking to comprehend the terrible thing that had happened. To have endured the inferno without a justifying reason—to be forced to admit that a war of such terror and scope had been only a blind, insouciant madness—was intolerable; it was easier to think of it as an unworthy or a wrongful cause than as a ghastly, titanic joke on history. After the event Winston Churchill wrote: "But there was a strange temper in the air. Unsatisfied by material prosperity the nations turned restlessly towards strife internal or external. . . . Almost one might think the world wished to suffer." Yet if this opinion had been widely accepted, it would have been a judgment on human nature too terrible to endure. And so a new mythology of the war grew up—a postwar mythology of materialist cynicism almost as contrived as the wartime propaganda fictions of the "Beast of Berlin" or the wholesale slaughter of Belgian nuns. It embraced the myths of the munitions manufacturers who had plotted a war they were, in fact, helpless

From *Horizon*, Summer 1964. © 1964 by Edmund Stillman. Reprinted by permission of Harold Over Associates, Inc.

to control; of Machiavellian, imperialist diplomacies; of an ever-spiraling arms race, when in fact the naval race between England and Germany had, if anything, somewhat abated by 1914. But no single cause, or combination of such causes, will explain the First World War. Neither the Germans, the Austrians, the Russians, the French, the Italians, nor the British went to war to fulfill a grand ambition—to conquer Europe, or the world, or to promote an ideology. They did not even seek economic dominion through war. The somber truth is that Western civilization, for a hundred years without a major war and absorbed in a social and technological revolution—progress, in short—turned on itself in a paroxysm of slaughter.

On both sides the actual war aims, so far as they were articulated at all, were distressingly small. Merely to humiliate Serbia and to "avenge" a man whose death few particularly regretted, the Austro-Hungarian Empire began a war which cost it seven million casualties and destroyed its fabric: to prevent a senile Austria-Hungary from gaining a precarious (and inevitably short-lived) advantage in the poverty-stricken western Balkans, imperial Russia lost more than nine million men—killed, wounded, or taken prisoner. To support an ally, and to avoid the public humiliation and anxiety of canceling a mobilization order once issued, Germany lost almost two million dead, Alsace-Lorraine, a third of Poland, and its growing sphere of influence in Central Europe and the Middle East. England, to keep its word to Belgium, committed eight million men to the struggle, and lost nearly one million dead. France, to counter its German enemy and to avenge the peace treaty it had accepted in 1870, endured losses of 15 per cent of its population and initiated a process of political decline from which it may not yet have emerged.

This was the price of World War I. Two shots were fired in Sarajevo, and for more than four years thereafter half the world bled. At least ten million soldiers were killed, and twenty million were wounded or made prisoners. But the real legacy of the war was something less tangible—a quality of despair, a chaos, and a drift toward political barbarism that is with us to this day. We have not recovered yet.

In the summer of 1914 the armies marched out to Armageddon in their frogged tunics, red Zouave trousers, and

gilded helmets. Five months later they were crouching in the mud, louse-ridden, half-starved, frozen, and bewildered by the enormity of it all. "Lost in the midst of two million madmen," the Frenchman Céline was to write of the war, "all of them heroes, at large and armed to the teeth! . . . sniping, plotting, flying, kneeling, digging, taking cover, wheeling, detonating, shut in on earth as in an asylum cell; intending to wreck everything in it, Germany, France, the whole world, every breathing thing; destroying, more ferocious than a pack of mad dogs and adoring their own madness (which no dog does), a hundred, a thousand times fiercer than a thousand dogs and so infinitely more vicious! . . . Clearly it seemed to me that I had embarked on a crusade that was nothing short of an apocalypse."

The savagery of the war and the incompetence of the military commanders quickly became a commonplace. The generals proved wholly unprepared for quick-firing artillery, machine guns, field entrenchments, railroad and motor transport; and the existence of a continuous front in place of the isolated battlefield of earlier centuries. They were helpless in the face of a combat too vast, too impersonal, too technical, and too deadly to comprehend. Quite aside from their intellectual shortcomings, one is struck by the poverty of their emotional response. Kill and kill was their motto. No one in command was daunted by the bloodletting, it seems. No more imaginative battle tactic could be devised than to push strength against strength—attacking the enemy's strongest point on the theory that one side's superior élan would ultimately yield up victory. Verdun in 1916 cost the French some 350,000 men and the Germans nearly as many: the German penetration was five miles, gained in a little more than three months. The Somme cost the Allies more than 600,000 casualties, the Germans almost half a million: the offensive gained a sector thirty miles wide and a maximum of seven deep in four and a half months.

That it was an insane waste of lives the combatants realized early, but no one knew what to do. The waste of honor, love, courage, and selfless devotion was the cruelest of all: at the first Battle of Ypres, in the opening days of the war, the young German schoolboy volunteers "came on like men possessed," a British historian records. They were sent in against picked battalions of British regu-

lars who shot them to pieces on the slopes of Ypres with the trained rifle fire for which they were famous. The incident has gone down in German history as the *Kindermord von Ypern*—"The Slaughter of the Innocents at Ypres." No other phrase will do.

It was a strange world that died that summer of 1914. For ninety-nine years there had been peace in Europe: apart from the Crimean War, only eighteen months of all that time—according to Karl Polanyi—had been spent in desultory and petty European wars. Men apparently believed that peace was man's normal condition—and on those occasions when peace was momentarily broken, war was expected to be comprehensible and salutary, an ultimately useful Darwinian selection of the fittest to lead. To us, after the profuse horrors of mustard gas, trench warfare, Buchenwald, the Blitz, Coventry, and Hiroshima, to name only a few, this is incomprehensible naïveté. But that we have been disillusioned and awaked to our condition is due to the events of 1914–18.

In the nineteenth century the belief in progress—automatic progress—went deep. The American anthropologist Lewis Morgan had sounded a note of self-confident hope for the entire age when he said, in 1877, "Democracy in government, brotherhood in society, equality in rights and privileges, and universal education, foreshadow the next higher plane of society to which experience, intelligence and knowledge are steadily tending." The emphasis here was on *steadily*: nothing could stop the onward march of mankind.

And the progress was very real. The age that died in 1914 was a brilliant one—so extravagant in its intellectual and aesthetic endowments that we who have come after can hardly believe in its reality. It was a comfortable age—for a considerable minority, at least—but it was more than a matter of Sunday walks in the Wienerwald, or country-house living, or a good five-cent cigar. It was an imposing age in the sciences, in the arts, even in forms of government. Men had done much and had risen high in the hundred years that came to an end that summer. From Napoleon's downfall in 1815 to the outbreak of war in 1914, the trend had been up.

"As happy as God in France," even the Germans used to say. For France these were the years of the *belle époque*, when all the world's artists came there to learn: Picasso and Juan Gris from Spain,

Chagall and Archipenko from Russia, Piet Mondrian from the Netherlands, Brancusi from Romania, Man Ray and Max Weber from America, Modigliani from Italy. All made up the "School of Paris," a name which meant nothing but that in this Paris of the *avant-guerre* the world of the arts was at home.

"Paris drank the talents of the world," wrote the poet-impresario of those years, Guillaume Apollinaire. Debussy, Ravel, and Stravinsky composed music there. Nijinsky and Diaghilev were raising the modern ballet to new heights of brilliance and creativity. The year 1913 was, as Roger Shattuck puts it in *The Banquet Years,* the *annus mirabilis* of French literature: Proust's *Du Côté de chez Swann,* Alain-Fournier's *Le Grand Meaulnes,* Appolinarre's *Alcools,* Roger Martin du Gard's *Jean Barnis,* Valéry Larbaud's *A. O. Barnabooth,* Péguy's *L'Argent,* Barrès's *La Colline inspirée,* and Colette's *L'Entrave* and *L'Envers du music-hall* appeared that year. "It is almost as if the war *had* to come in order to put an end to an extravaganza that could not have been sustained at this level." That was Paris.

Vienna was another great mongrel city that, like Paris, drank up talent—in this case the talents of a congeries of Austrians, Magyars, Czechs, Slovaks, Poles, Solvenes, Croats, Serbs, Jews, Turks, Transylvanians, and Gypsies. On Sunday mornings gentlemen strolled in the Prater ogling the cocottes; they rode the giant red Ferris wheel and looked out over the palaces and parks of the city; or they spent the morning at the coffeehouse, arguing pointlessly and interminably. It was a pleasure-loving city, but an intellectual one, too. The names of the men who walked Vienna's streets up to the eve of the war are stunning in their brilliance: Gustav Mahler, Sigmund Freud, Sandor Ferenczi, Ernst Mach, Béla Bartók, Rainer Maria Rilke, Franz Kafka, Robert Musil, Arthur Schnitzler, Hugo von Hofmannsthal, Richard Strauss, Stefan Zweig—these hardly begin to exhaust the list. (There were more sinister names, too. Adolf Hitler lived in Vienna between 1909 and 1913, an out-of-work, shabby *Bettgeher*—a daytime renter of other people's beds—absorbing the virulent anti-Semitism that charged the Viennese social atmosphere; so did Leon Trotsky, who spent his evenings listening contemptuously to the wranglings of the Social Democratic politicians at the Café Central.)

England was still gilded by the after-glow of the Edwardian Age: the British Empire straddled the earth, controlling more than a quarter of the surface of the globe. If the realities of trade had begun to shift, and if British industry and British naval supremacy were faced with a growing challenge from the United States and Hohenzollern Germany, the vast British overseas investments tended to hide the fact. England had its intellectual brilliance, too: These were the years of Hardy, Kipling, Shaw, Wells, the young D. H. Lawrence and the young Wyndham Lewis, Arnold Bennett, Gilbert Murray, A. E. Housman, H. H. Munro (Saki)—who would die in the war—and many others, like Rupert Brooke, Robert Graves, Siegfried Sassoon, and Wilfred Owen, who were as yet hardly known.

As for the Kaiser's Germany, it is melancholy to reflect that if Wilhelm II himself, that summer in 1914, had only waited—five years, ten years, or twenty—Germany might have had it all. But Wilhelm was shrewd, treacherous, and hysterical, a chronic bully whose mother had never loved him. His habitual style of discourse was the neurotic bluster of a small man who has had the bad luck to be called upon to stomp about in a giant's boots. Wilhelm II lived all his life in the shadow of "the Great Emperor," his grandfather Wilhelm I, who had created a united Greater Germany with the help of his brilliant chancellor, Prince Otto von Bismarck; he wanted to make the world stand in awe of him, but he did not know, precisely, how to go about it.

If only he could have been patient: Austria-Hungary was really a German satellite; the Balkans and the Middle East looked to Berlin; Germany's industrial hegemony on the continent was secure, and might soon have knocked Britain from her commanding place in the world's trade. By 1914, fourteen Germans had won Nobel Prizes in the sciences (by contrast, their nearest competitors, the French, had won only nine).

But the lesson is something more than a chapbook homily on patience. Wilhelm's personal anxiety merely expressed in microcosm the larger German anxiety about the nation's place in the world. Something strange lay beneath the stolid prosperity of the Hohenzollern Age—a surfeit with peace, a lust for violence, a belief in death, an ominous mystique of war. "Without war the world would quickly sink into materialism," the elder Von Moltke, chief of the German General Staff, had proclaimed in 1880; and he, his nephew the younger Von Moltke, and the caste of Prussian militarists they represented could presumably save the world from that tawdry fate. But this belief in war was not a monopoly of the Right: even Thomas Mann, spokesman of German humanism, could ask, in 1914, "Is not war a purification, a liberation, an enormous hope?" adding complacently. "Is not peace an element in civil corruption?"

There had been peace in the world for too long. From Berlin, in the spring of 1914, Colonel House wrote to Woodrow Wilson: "The whole of Germany is charged with electricity. Everybody's nerves are tense. It only requires a spark to set the whole thing off." People were saying: "Better a horrible ending than a horror without end." In expressing this spirit of violence and disorientation, Germany was merely precocious. It expressed a universal European malaise.

The malaise was evident everywhere—in the new cults of political violence; in the new philosophies of men like Freud, Nietzsche, and Pareto, who stressed the unconscious and the irrational, and who exposed the lying pretentions of middle-class values and conventions; and in the sense of doom that permeated the avant-garde arts of the prewar years. Typical of this spirit of rebellion was the manifesto set forth in 1910 by the Italian Futurist painters: it declared that "all forms of imitation should be held in contempt and that all forms of originality glorified; that we should rebel against the tyranny of the words 'harmony' and 'good taste' . . . ; that a clean sweep be made of all stale and threadbare subject matter in order to express the vortex of modern life—a life of steel, pride, fever, and speed. . . ."

In England and France, as in Germany and Italy, the darker strain was there. When the war came, a glad Rupert Brooke intoned:

Now God be thanked Who has matched us with His hour.

A fever was over Paris as the spring of 1914 slipped into summer. Charles Péguy—Dreyfusard, Socialist, man of good will and reason, to his intellectual generation "the pure man"—had caught this other darker spirit as well. That spring he had written:

Heureux ceux qui sont morts dans les grandes batailles . . .

Happy are those who have died in great battles,
Lying on the ground before the face of God.

By September of that year he himself was dead.

No doubt we shall never understand it completely. What is absolutely clear about the outbreak of the First World War is that it was catastrophic: the hecatombs of dead, the appalling material waste, the destruction, and the pain of those four years tell us that. In our hearts we know that since that bootless, reckless, bloody adventure nothing has really come right again in the world. Democracy in government, brotherhood in society, equality in rights and privileges, universal educa-tion—all those evidences of "the next higher plane of society" to which experi-ence, intelligence, and knowledge seemed to be steadily tending—gave way to mass conscription and the central direction of war, the anonymity of the trenches, the calculated propaganda lie: in short, be-tween 1914 and 1918 Europe evolved many of the brutal features of the mod-ern totalitarian state. And twenty-one years after the last shot was fired in the First World War, a second war came: a war of even greater brutality, moral deg-radation, and purposeful evil, but one where the issues at last matched the scale on which men had, a quarter-century earlier, blindly chosen to fight. Here was a deadly justice. That such a war should be fought at all was the direct outcome of the spiritual wasteland that the first war engendered.

Woodrow Wilson, greeting the Armi-stice, was able to proclaim to his fellow Americans that "everything" for which his countrymen had fought had been accomplished. He could assert that it was America's "fortunate duty to assist by example, by sober, friendly counsel, and by material aid in the establishment of a just democracy throughout the world."

But today we know that the poet Ro-bert Graves more truly expressed the spirit of the nightmare from which the world awakened in 1918 when he wrote, "The news (of the Armistice) sent me out walking alone along the dyke above the marshes of Rhuddlan . . . cursing and sobbing and thinking of the dead."

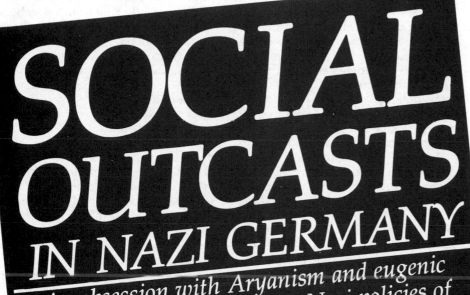

SOCIAL OUTCASTS IN NAZI GERMANY

An obsession with Aryanism and eugenic theory was the catalyst for Nazi policies of repression and extermination against gypsies and other 'asocials' — the forgotten victims of the Third Reich.

Jeremy Noakes

A German gypsy family on the road in the 1920s.

OF ALL NAZI ATROCITIES, THE extermination of the Jews has, rightly, commanded the most attention from historians and the general public. But this understandable preoccupation with the horrors of Nazi anti-Semitism has led people to overlook the fact that the Jews formed only one, albeit the major, target in a broad campaign directed against a variety of groups who were considered to be 'alien to the community' (*Gemeinschaftsfremd*), and who often were defined in biological terms. Only recently have historians begun to focus their attention on this hitherto neglected sphere of Nazi policy and action.

Nazism arose in the aftermath of defeat and revolution. In the view of its leaders, and notably of Hitler, the main cause of Germany's collapse had not been military defeat but the disintegration of the home front weakened by years of incompetent leadership, corroded by pernicious ideas of liberal democracy, Marxism and sentimental humanitarianism, and sapped by biological decline which was the result of ignoring the principles of race and eugenics. Their main domestic goal was to create out of the German people, riven by divisions of class, religion and ideology, a new and unified 'national community' (*Volksgemeinschaft*) based on ties of blood and race and infused with a common 'world view'. They believed this united national community would then possess the requisite morale to enable Germany to make a bid for the position as a world power to which she had long aspired. The members of this national community, the 'national comrades' (*Volksgenossen*), were expected to conform to a norm based on certain criteria. A national comrade was expected to be of Aryan race, genetically healthy (*erbgesund*), socially efficient (*leistungsfähig*), and politically and ideologically reliable, which involved not simply passive obedience but active participation in the various organisations of the regime and repeated gestures of loyalty (the Hitler salute, etc.).

On coming to power the Nazis were determined to discriminate against, or persecute, all those who failed to fulfill these criteria and were therefore regarded as being outside the national community. There were three main types of these outsiders which, although they overlap, can be conveniently considered as separate categories. Firstly, ideological enemies – those who propagated or even simply held beliefs and values regarded as a threat to national morale. Secondly so-called 'asocials' – the socially inefficient and those whose behaviour offended against the social norms of the 'national community'. And thirdly, the biological outsiders – those who were regarded as a threat because of their race or because they were suffering from a hereditary defect. It is with the last two of these categories that this article is concerned.

The third category, that of biological outsiders, consisted of two main groups: those considered undesirable because of their race (the non-Aryans), and those who were unacceptable on eugenic grounds because of hereditary defects which posed a threat to the future of the German race and/or rendered them socially ineffective. Although the racial and eugenic theories which defined these groups were in some respects distinct – not all eugenists were anti-Semitic for example – they shared common origins in biological theories of the late nineteenth century and a common perspective in viewing mankind primarily in biological terms. Individuals were not seen as possessing validity in themselves as human beings and were not judged in terms of their human qualities, but their significance was assessed first and foremost in terms of their physical and mental efficiency as members of a 'race' and they were seen primarily as collections of good or bad genes.

The theory of eugenics – the idea of improving the 'race' through the encouragement of selective breeding – had become increasingly influential in many countries during the 1920s and 1930s and Germany was no exception. It flourished against a background of concern about declining birthrates and particularly about

the destruction of a generation of the healthiest members of the nation in the First World War. There was also growing concern about the impact of modern improvements in welfare, hygiene, and medical care in ensuring the survival of increasing numbers of those with hereditary defects who were thereby allegedly producing a deterioration of the race. Moreover, during this period it was fashionable to attribute many social ills to heredity – habitual criminality, alcoholism, prostitution, and pauperism. Even some on the Left were attracted by eugenics. They tended to make a sharp distinction between the 'genuine' working class and the *Lumpenproletariat*, the 'dregs' of society. Eugenics appeared to offer the prospect of eliminating the *Lumpenproletariat*, traditionally seen since Marx as the tool of reaction.

During the 1920s a number of doctors and psychiatrists in Germany began to propose a policy of sterilisation to prevent those with hereditary defects from procreating. Such a policy of 'negative selection' had already been carried out on a limited scale in the United States where the technique of vasectomy had been developed and was first applied by a prison doctor in 1899. With the economic crisis which began in 1929 such proposals gained increasing support among those involved in the welfare services, since they appeared to offer the prospect not only of substantial savings in the future but also of facilitating the release of some of those in institutional care without fear of their producing defective offspring. Towards the end of 1932 the Prussian authorities prepared a draft law permitting the voluntary sterilisation of those with hereditary defects. Those who drafted the law had felt obliged to make sterilisation voluntary since they believed that public opinion was not yet ready for compulsion. The logic of the eugenist case, however, required compulsion and, significantly, the Nazi medical experts who took part in the preceding discussions had demanded compulsion. The sterilisation issue was given priority by Hitler himself who overruled objections from his Catholic Vice-Chancellor, von Papen. On July 14th, 1933, within six months of its coming to power, the new regime had issued

a Sterilisation Law ordering the sterilisation – by compulsion if necessary – of all those suffering from a number of specified illnesses which were alleged to be hereditary.

Apart from the moral issues raised by the question of compulsory sterilisation as such, the criteria used to define hereditary illness were in many respects exceedingly dubious. Thus, while there could be no doubt about the hereditary nature of some of the diseases specified, such as Huntingdon's Chorea, others such as 'hereditary simple-mindedness', schizophrenia, manic depressive illness, and 'chronic alcoholism' were not only more difficult to diagnose but their hereditary basis was much more questionable. Moreover, even if it were granted, the elimination of these diseases through the sterilisation of those affected was an impossible task in view of the role played by recessive genes in their transmission. Finally, although an impressive apparatus of hereditary courts was established to pass judgment on the individual cases, the evidence used to justify proposals for sterilisation sometimes reflected more the social and political prejudices of the medical and welfare authorities involved than objective scientific criteria. Thus a reputation for being 'work-shy' or even former membership of the Communist Party could be used as crucial supporting evidence in favour of sterilisation. From 1934 to 1945 between 320,000 and 350,000 men and women were sterilised under this law and almost one hundred people died following the operation. After the war few of those sterilised received any compensation for what they had suffered since they could not claim to have been persecuted on political or racial grounds. The new measure appears to have had at least tacit support from public opinion. It was only when people found members of their own families, friends and colleagues affected by it that they became concerned.

The Nazis claimed that sterilistion was an unfortunate necessity for those with hereditary defects and that once it was carried out the sterilised were thereby in effect restored to full status as 'national comrades'. In practice, however, in a society in which health, and in particular fertility, were key virtues the sterilised were bound to feel discriminated against, and the fact that they were forbidden to marry fertile partners underlined this point. However, for those who were not merely suffering from hereditary defects but were socially ineffective as well the future was far bleaker. Already in 1920 a distinguished jurist, Karl Binding, and a psychiatrist, Alfred Hoche, had together published a book with the title: *The Granting of Permission for the Destruction of Worthless Life. Its Extent and Form.* In this book, written under the impression of the casualties of the First World War, the two authors proposed that in certain cases it should be legally possible to kill those suffering from incurable and severely crippling handicaps and injuries — so-called 'burdens on the community' (*Ballastexistenzen*). This proposal assumed, first, that it was acceptable for an outside agency to define what individual life was 'worthless' and, secondly, that in effect an individual had to justify his existence according to criteria imposed from outside (i.e. he had to prove that his life was worthwhile). These assumptions were indeed implicit in the biological and collectivist approach to human life which had become increasingly influential after 1900.

With the take-over of power by the Nazis it was not long before this biological and collectivist approach began to be transferred from theory into reality. In addition to the sterilisation programme, this took the form, firstly, of a propaganda campaign designed to devalue the handicapped as burdens on the community in the eyes of the population and, secondly, of a programme of systematic extermination of the mentally sick and handicapped – the so-called Euthanasia Programme, a misleading title since the term 'euthanasia' was in fact a Nazi euphemism for mass murder.

The euthanasia programme began in the spring or early summer of 1939 when the parents of a severely handicapped baby petitioned Hitler for the baby to be killed. He agreed to the request and ordered the head of his personal Chancellery, Phillip Bouhler, to proceed likewise in all similar cases. Bouhler set up a secret organisation to carry out the programme which initially covered children up to three years old, later

extended to twelve-sixteen years. By the end of the war approximately 5,000 children had been murdered either by injection or through deliberate malnutrition. In August 1939 Hitler ordered that the extermination programme be extended to adults, for which the *Führer*'s Chancellery set up another secret organisation. So large were the numbers involved – there were approximately 200,000 mentally sick and handicapped in 1939 – that a new method of killing had to be devised. Experts in the Criminal Police Department came up with the idea of using carbon monoxide gas. After a successful trial on a few patients, gas chambers were constructed in six mental hospitals in various parts of Germany to which patients were transferred from mental institutions all over the *Reich*. By the time the programme was officially stopped by Hitler in August 1941 under pressure from public protests some 72,000 people had been murdered.

During the next two years under a separate programme also run by the *Führer*'s Chancellery under the code number 14F13, the reference number of the Inspector of Concentration Camps, another 30-50,000 people were selected from concentration camps and gassed on the grounds of mental illness, physical incapacity, or simply racial origin, in which case the 'diagnosis' on the official form read 'Jew' or 'gypsy'. In the meantime, however, the majority of the personnel who had developed expertise in operating the gas chambers had been transferred to Poland and placed at the disposal of the SS for the death camps which opened in the winter of 1941-42. These notorious death camps – Belsen, Treblinka, Sobibor, Majdanek, and Auschwitz-Birkenau – were intended to destroy the other biological outcasts of Nazi Germany, the non-Aryans, of whom the Jews formed by far the largest group. However, the understandable preoccupation with the Holocaust has tended to divert attention from another group which came into this category – the gypsies. For they also suffered genocide at the hands of the Nazis.

Long before the Nazis came to power the gypsies had been treated as social outcasts. Their foreign appearance, their strange customs and language, their nomadic way of life and

lack of regular employment had increasingly come to be regarded as an affront to the norms of a modern state and society. They were seen as asocial, a source of crime, culturally inferior, a foreign body within the nation. During the 1920s, the police, first in Bavaria and then in Prussia established special offices to keep the gypsies under constant surveillance. They were photographed and fingerprinted as if they were criminals. With the Nazi take-over, however, a new motive was added to the grounds for persecution – their distinct and allegedly inferior racial character.

Nazi policy towards the gypsies, like the policy towards the Jews, was uncertain and confused. Initially they were not a major target. With their small numbers – 30,000 – and generally low social status they were not seen as such a serious racial threat as the Jews. They were, however, included in the regulations implementing the Nuremberg Law for the Protection of German Blood and Honour of September 15th, 1935, which banned marriage and sexual relations between Aryans and non-Aryans. From then onwards they were the subject of intensive research by racial 'experts' of the 'Research Centre for Racial Hygiene and Biological Population Studies'. The aim was to identify and distinguish between pure gypsies and the part-gypsies (*Mischlinge*) who had been lumped together in the records of the Weimar police. Whereas in the case of the Jews the *Mischlinge* were treated as less of a threat than the 'full' Jews, among the gypsies the *Mischlinge*, some of whom had integrated themselves into German society, were treated as the greater threat. The leading expert on the gypsies, Dr Robert Ritter, insisted that:

> The gypsy question can only be regarded as solved when the majority of a-social and useless gypsy *Mischlinge* have been brought together in large camps and made to work and when the continual procreation of this half-breed population has been finally prevented. Only then will future generations be freed from this burden.

In December 1938 Himmler issued a 'Decree for the Struggle against the Gypsy Plague', which introduced a more systematic registration of gypsies based on the research of the racial experts. Pure gypsies received brown papers, gypsy *Mischlinge* light blue ones and nomadic non-gypsies grey ones. The aim was 'once and for all to ensure the racial separation of gypsies from our own people to prevent the mixing of the two races, and finally to regulate the living conditions of the gypsies and gypsy *Mischlinge*'. After the victory over Poland the deportation of gypsies from Germany to Poland was ordered and in the meantime they were forbidden to leave the camps to which they were assigned and which were now in effect turned into labour camps. In May 1940 2,800 gypsies joined the Jewish transports to Poland. However, this deportation programme was then stopped because of logistical problems in the reception areas.

During 1941-42 gypsies and gypsy-*Mischlinge* were included in the discriminatory measures introduced against Jews within the Reich and they were also removed from the Armed Forces. However, while there was unanimous contempt for the gypsy *Mischlinge*, Nazi racial experts had a certain admiration for the way in which the pure gypsies had sustained their separate identity and way of life over the centuries, an achievement attributed to their strong sense of race. Dr Robert Ritter suggested that the 'pure bred' gypsies in Germany (*Sinti*) and in the German-speaking areas of Bohemia and Moravia (*Lalleri*) should be assigned to an area where they would be permitted to live according to their traditional ways more or less as museum specimens, while the remainder should be sterilised, interned, and subjected to forced labour. Himmler sympathised with this view and in October 1942 issued orders for appropriate arrangements to be made. However, he ran into opposition from Bormann and probably Hitler and so, on December 16th, 1942, he issued an order for the German gypsies to be transferred to Auschwitz. Between February 26th and March 25th, 1943, 11,400 gypsies from Germany and elsewhere were transported to a special gypsy camp within Auschwitz. Here, unlike other prisoners, they were able to live together with their families, probably to facilitate the medical experiments which were carried out in a medical centre established in their camp by the notorious Dr Mengele. Of the 20,000

gypsies in all transported to Auschwitz, 11,000 were murdered there, while the others were transferred elsewhere. At the same time, thousands of gypsies were being murdered throughout occupied Europe, notably by the *Einsatzgruppen* in Russia. It has been estimated that half a million European gypsies died at the hands of the Nazis. Of 30,000 gypsies living in Germany in 1939 only 5,000 survived the war.

The gypsies offended against the norms of the 'national community' not only on the grounds of their non-Aryan character (although ironically since they had originated in India they could legitimately claim to be more 'Aryan' than the Germans!), but also on the grounds of their 'a-social' behaviour. The 'a-socials' formed another major category of social outcasts. The term 'a-social' was a very flexible one which could be used to include all those who failed to abide by the social norms of the national community: habitual criminals, the so-called 'work-shy', tramps and beggars, alcoholics, prostitutes, homosexuals, and juvenile delinquents. The Nazis introduced much tougher policies towards such groups, in some cases – as with the Sterilisation Law – implementing measures which had been demanded or planned before their take-over of power. Above all, there was a growing tendency for the police to acquire more and more control over these groups at the expense of the welfare agencies and the courts. It was the ultimate ambition of the police to take over responsibility for all those whom it defined as 'community aliens' (*Gemeinschaftsfremde*). To achieve this goal, in 1940 it introduced a draft 'Community Alien Law' which, after being held up by opposition from other government departments, was finally intended to go into effect in 1945. According to Paragraph 1.i of the final draft:

A person is alien to the community if he/she proves to be incapable of satisfying the minimum requirements of the national community through his/her own efforts, in particular through an unusual degree of deficiency of mind or character.

The official explanation of the law maintained that:

The National Socialist view of welfare is

that it can only be granted to national comrades who both need it and are worthy of it. In the case of community aliens who are only a burden on the national community welfare is not necessary, rather police compulsion with the aim of either making them once more useful members of the national community through appropriate measures or of preventing them from being a further burden. In all these matters protection of the community is the primary object.

In September 1933, the Reich Ministries of the Interior and Propaganda initiated a major roundup of 'tramps and beggars' of whom there were between 300,000 and 500,000, many of them homeless young unemployed. Such a large number of people without fixed abode was regarded as a threat to public order. However, the regime lacked the means to provide shelter and work for such vast numbers. Moreover, there were advantages in having a mobile labour force which could if necessary be directed to particular projects. The Nazis, therefore, initially made a distinction between 'orderly' and 'disorderly' people of no fixed abode. Those who were healthy, willing to work, and with no previous convictions were given a permit (*Wanderkarte*) and were obliged to follow particular routes and perform compulsory work in return for their board and lodging. 'Disorderly' persons of no fixed abode on the other hand could be dealt with under the Law against Dangerous Habitual Criminals and concerning Measures for Security and Correction of November 24th, 1933, and the Preventive Detention Decree of the Ministry of the Interior of December 14th, 1937, which introduced the practice of preventive detention. Many tramps were also sterilised.

After 1936, as a result of the economic recovery, Germany faced a growing labour shortage and the regime was no longer willing to tolerate either numbers of people of no fixed abode or the 'work-shy'. Apart from their significance for the labour force, such people contradicted basic principles of the national community – the principle of performance and the principle of being 'integrated' (*erfasst-eingeordnet*). As one Nazi expert put it:

In the case of a long period without work on the open road where he is entirely free to follow his own desires and instincts, he (the tramp) is in danger of becoming a freedom fanatic who rejects all integration as hated compulsion.

As a result, persons of no fixed abode increasingly came to be regarded as a police rather than a welfare matter. Even before 1936 some people designated as 'work-shy' had been sent to concentration camps forming the category of 'a-socials' who wore a black triangle. A big round-up had taken place before the Olympic games and in 1936 two of the ten companies in Dachau were composed of this category. In the summer of 1938 an even bigger round-up took place under the code word 'Work-shy Reich' in the course of which approximately 11,000 'beggars, tramps, pimps and gypsies' were arrested and transferred largely to Buchenwald where they formed the largest category of prisoner until the influx of Jews following the 'Night of Broken Glass' on November 8th. It has been estimated that some 10,000 tramps were incarcerated in concentration camps during the Third Reich of whom few survived the ordeal. This harsh policy towards the 'a-socials' appears to have been popular with many Germans and was welcomed by local authorities who were thereby able to get rid of their 'awkward customers'.

Having set up a utopian model of an ideologically and racially homogeneous 'national community', the Nazis increasingly sought an explanation for deviance from its norms not in terms of flaws within the system itself and its incompatibility with human variety but rather in terms of flaws which were innate within the individual. As an anti-type to the racially pure, genetically healthy, loyal and efficient 'national comrade', they evolved the concept of the 'degenerate a-social' whose deviance was *biologically* determined. As the Reich Law Leader, Hans Frank, put it in a speech in October 1938:

National Socialism regards degeneracy as an immensely important source of criminal activity. It is our belief that every superior nation is furnished with such an abundance of endowments for its journey through life that the word 'degeneracy' most clearly defines the state of affairs that concerns us here. In a decent nation the 'genus' must be regarded as valuable *per se*: consequently, in an individual degeneracy signifies exclusion from the normal *genus* of the decent nation. This state of being degenerate, this different or alien quality tends to be rooted in miscegenation between a decent representative of his race and an individual of inferior stock. To us National Socialists criminal biology, or the theory of congenital criminality, connotes a link between racial decadence and criminal manifestations. The complete degenerate lacks all racial sensitivity and sees it as his positive duty to harm the community or member thereof. He is the absolute opposite of the man who recognises that the fulfillment of his duty as a national comrade is his mission in life.

These ideas represent a variation on concepts which had emerged from research into so-called 'criminal biology' which had been going on in the Weimar Republic. Nor was this simply a matter of theory. For the Nazis had actually begun to apply the principles of criminal biology in the sphere of juvenile delinquency. This was another area in which the police usurped the responsibility of the welfare agencies and the courts. In 1939 they exploited the Preventive Detention Decree of 1937 to set up their own Reich Central Agency for the Struggle against Juvenile Delinquency and the following year established a Youth Concentration Camp in Moringen near Hanover. Perhaps the most significant feature of the camp was the fact that the youths were subjected to 'biological and racial examination' under the supervision of Dr Ritter, now the Director of the Criminal-Biological Institute of the Reich Security Main Office. Then, on the basis of highly dubious pseudo-scientific criteria, they were divided into groups

according to their alleged socio-biological character and reformability. This process of socio-biological selection pioneered in Moringen was an integral part of the concept of the Community Aliens Law. Thus, according to the official justification of the Law:

The governments of the period of the System (Weimar) failed in their measures to deal with community aliens. They did not utilise the findings of genetics and criminal biology as a basis for a sound welfare and penal policy. As a result of their liberal attitude they constantly perceived only the "rights of the individual" and were more concerned with his protection from state intervention than with the general good. In National Socialism the individual counts for nothing when the community is at stake.

Defeat preserved Germans from being subjected to the Community Aliens Law and a future in which any deviation from the norms of the 'national community' would be not merely criminalised but also liable to be defined as evidence of 'degeneracy', i.e. biological inadequacy, for which the penalties were sterilisation and probably eventual 'eradication' (*Ausmerzen*) through hard labour in concentration camp conditions. The Third Reich's policy towards social outcasts stands as a frightful warning both against the application of pseudo-science to social problems and against the rationalisation of social prejudices in terms of pseudo-science.

FOR FURTHER READING:
Gitta Sereny, *Into that Darkness* (Picador Books, 1977); D. Kenrick and G. Puxon, *The Destiny of Europe's Gypsies* (Chatto, 1972); J. Noakes, 'Nazism and Eugenics: The Background to the Nazi Sterilization Law of 14 July 1933' in R.J. Bullen et.al., eds., *Ideas into Politics. Aspects of European History 1880-1950* (Croom Helm, 1984); E. Klee, 'Euthanasie' im NS-Staat. Die 'Vernichtung lebensunwerten Lebens' (Frankfurt, 1983); D. Peukert, 'Arbeitslager und Jugend-KZ: die Behandlung Gemeinschaftsfremder im Dritten Reich', in D. Peukert & J. Reulecke, *Die Reihen fast geschlossen. Beiträge zur Geschichte des Alltags unterm national sozialismus* (Wuppertal, 1981).

'...heavy fire... unable to land... issue in doubt'

For the Second Marine Division, the taking of tiny Tarawa on the way to Japan in 1943 exacted a cruel toll in blood and courage

Michael Kernan

Michael Kernan writes often for Smithsonian. *His first novel,* The Lost Diaries of Frans Hals, *was published by St. Martin's Press.*

August 1943: Marine Maj. Gen. Julian C. Smith stands before a mahogany conference table in K Room, on the third floor of the Windsor Hotel in Wellington, New Zealand. General Smith blinks behind his glasses as a neat, small man in an admiral's uniform spreads a large chart across the table. Vice Adm. Raymond Spruance has come all the way from Hawaii to tell Smith that, in November, his 18,088-man Second Marine Division will be attacking Tarawa.

The map shows an atoll, more or less triangular, 18 miles long, a coral spine studded with tiny huts and trading stations. To the southwest is Bititu Island, more commonly known as Betio (see map), where the Japanese have dug in. Spruance pronounces it "BAY-SHOW." The atoll itself he calls "TAR-A-WA." Hardly anyone has heard of it.

Smith and his staff study the chart of Betio. They see a curious little island shaped like a cockatoo lying on its back. The legs are represented by a pier that juts straight out from its belly. The whole thing covers less than 300 acres; it is less than half a mile wide at its widest point and only a shade over two miles long. The 700-yard-long pier and the new airfield, on which the Japanese are still working, are the only noticeable features. Those and the wiggly lines that mark the reef surrounding it.

The Battle of Tarawa is not as famous as the earlier attack on Guadalcanal or later assaults on Iwo Jima and Okinawa, although more than 1,000 Americans were killed in the 76 hours required to take the island. But it was at Tarawa that the Marines made the first American seaborne assault against a heavily defended coral atoll.

After Tarawa we would send in frogmen to clear the beach approaches, measure water depths, study local tides. The percentage of casualties for the number of men involved was appalling. In the public mind, both during the war and to this day, it produced an indelible image of men, up to their waists in water, helplessly slogging across hundreds of yards of Pacific shallows into the teeth of Japanese fire.

It is the fall of 1943. In Western Europe the war is approaching a sort of climax with the invasion of Italy. But in the Pacific, four months after the U.S. victory at Midway, things are going slowly. Like Midway, Guadalcanal had been a turning point. After landing August 7, 1942, the Marines had to fight for six months, finally winning the island and its crucial airfield. Now another stage in the long, island-hopping road to Japan is about to begin.

The new major American objective in the Central Pacific is Kwajalein, 65 miles long, the largest atoll in the world and a superb base for planes and ships. But to take it, you need forward airbases in Tarawa and elsewhere in the Gilberts.

At the historic meeting in Wellington, Julian Smith diffidently remarks that the reef is going to be the main problem. His operations officer, Lieut. Col. David M. Shoup, glances around the table. Shoup, 38, had met the Japanese in jungle combat on Guadalcanal. "Amtracs," he mutters. Spruance shakes his head at this mention of amphibians. The landing will have to be made in ship's boats, he says. He does not give a reason.

October 1943: Julian Smith flies into Honolulu for a talk with Maj. Gen. Holland M. Smith, known to history as "Howlin' Mad" Smith, an expert on amphibious warfare who commands the Fifth Amphibious Corps under Admiral Spruance.

The two Smiths huddle over yet another map. This one shows the Tarawa atoll, Betio and its lagoon, with the depths marked at various points: seven, nine, five feet. There is one little problem. The soundings were

From *Smithsonian* magazine, November 1993, pp. 118-122, 124, 126-128, 130, 132. © 1993 by Michael Kernan. Reprinted by permission of the author.

taken by the Wilkes Expedition, a remarkable naval exploration of the Pacific and the Northwest coast of America (SMITHSONIAN, November 1985). The map, drawn in 1841, carried a notation: "This chart should be used with circumspection; the surveys are incomplete."

Any attack will have to be blunt, head-on and quick, Julian Smith explains. The ocean side, to the south, is out of the question; aerial photographs show the enemy has mounted his most powerful defenses on that shore. Besides, there is a heavy surf.

This leaves the lagoon side. But here, say the New Zealanders who know these waters, the tides are tricky. They have a nasty way of "dodging," rising and falling at uneven rates in the shallow lagoon. Because of tactical considerations the attack will have to be made during a period of neap tides. Such tides occur near the first- and third-quarter phases of the moon and do not crest as high as the spring tides of the full and new moons. They sometimes remain at nearly the same depth for hours and on Tarawa they could be as low as three feet. Rear Adm. Harry Hill, put in command of the amphibious force, consults with local mariners and reaches a cautious consensus that neap high tide in the lagoon on November 20 will surely be close to five feet deep. A loaded Higgins boat, the conventional landing craft of 1943, draws between three and a half and four feet, leaving a narrow margin for error.

Nevertheless, Julian Smith quietly spells out his fears that the water may be too low for the Higgins boats. His people could be stranded far out on the reef and forced to wade for hundreds of yards under deadly fire. He has 75 amtracs (amphibious tractors) at Wellington, enough to get the first assault waves ashore, but will need at least 100 more. Holland Smith nods agreement. But when he is consulted, Rear Adm. Richmond Kelly Turner, who oversaw the Marine landings on Guadalcanal, insists that more of the 25-foot-long amtracs won't be needed. They're slow, he adds. All but impossible to steer in any kind of a sea and no armor to speak of. Once they stall, they ship water over their low freeboard and swamp.

To the end of his life, Holland Smith would insist Tarawa should have been bypassed in the island-hopping campaign to reach Japan. Now he is outraged by the Navy's reluctance to give the Marines the equipment they need. Face darkening, he bursts out: "No amtracs, no operation!" Finally Turner agrees to give the Second Marine Division more amtracs. If the tide does come in low, he notes, they can ferry men from the larger Higgins boats to shore.

Since taking Tarawa from the British shortly after Pearl Harbor, the Japanese have been making it impregnable. Reconnaissance reveals a network of dugouts, coral-block machine-gun nests and interlocking communication trenches. Lines of fire have been sighted in so that every spot on the island can be crisscrossed with withering fire from many different angles.

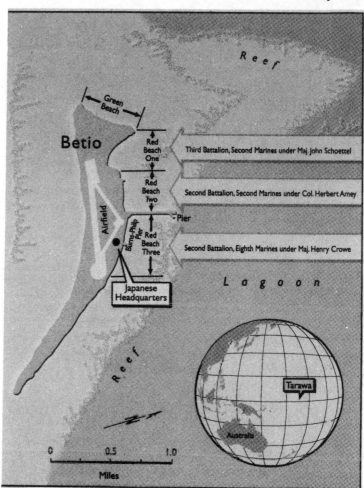

Map shows Tarawa atoll in the Pacific (inset). To reach cockatoo-shaped Betio Island, Schoettel's men face a 900-yard wade from reef to beachhead; Amey's men slosh 700 yards; Crowe's men trek some 500 yards.

The defenses include four eight-inch guns that threaten virtually every inch of the seaward approach to the shore; ten 75-millimeter mountain guns, six 70-millimeter cannon, nine 37-millimeter field pieces, four pairs of five-inch coastal guns, 14 light tanks and many antiaircraft guns and mortars. Tank traps have been sunk in the beach. There are concrete blockhouses up to 40 feet in diameter and 17 feet high, and an incredible 500 pillboxes, sunken miniforts with shallow-curved cupolas and walls of reinforced concrete five feet thick. Rear Adm. Keiji Shibasaki, who has lately taken over the defenses, boasts that if they had a hundred years, "a million men could not take Betio." Along with 2,217 Korean laborers, Shibasaki has 4,836 men, of whom about 3,000 are fighting effectives, including 2,600 first-rate *rikusentai*, or special landing forces.

Most are concentrated on the south side, facing the open sea, where it is thought the Americans will land and be stopped at the beach by the mines and tank obstacles, wire tangles and guns. The American attack is expected at high tide in the morning, but the Japanese expect to counterattack at night and sweep every living enemy off the beach. The assumption is that Americans cannot see in the dark.

Latrines have been set on pilings out over the water. Based partly on the count of latrines visible from the air, American intelligence has underestimated the number of defenders at 2,800. The six Marine battalions scheduled to attack number twice that, though doctrine has it that success requires three times as many attackers as defenders. Torrents of steel and high explosives are to be hurled at the island from three battleships, four cruisers and nine destroyers. Waves of planes are scheduled to bomb and strafe the tiny patch of sand.

Lieut. Col. Shoup draws up the final attack plan. Three battalions will hit the lagoon-side beach at once: the Second Battalion, Second Marines and the Second Battalion, Eighth Marines side by side athwart the pier (Red Beach Two and Three, respectively) and the Third Battalion, Second Marines slightly to the west, at the cove that forms the cockatoo's throat (Red Beach One). As the landing drills wind up, the assault commander falls sick. Suddenly Shoup finds himself promoted to full colonel, commanding the Second Marines, the reinforced combat regiment that will lead the assault that he has planned.

Years later, when the taciturn, poetry-writing Shoup becomes commandant of the U.S. Marine Corps, it is partly because of what he did at Tarawa. His experience there will also influence advice that he gives President John F. Kennedy in 1963 when the feasibility of invading Cuba comes up. Showing Kennedy a map of tiny Tarawa—as compared with the 800-mile-long Cuba—Shoup reminds the President of the "trouble we had" taking the little triangle of sand and coral.

The landing is now firmly set for neap tide on November 20, at 8:30 A.M. The date is a compromise. In November the only tides coming just after daybreak are neaps, with their lesser highs. During most of the month the spring tides, with their higher highs—the ideal time to run boats over the reef—are expected either before dawn or late in the afternoon. Predawn attack would rule out effective bombardment beforehand. An afternoon attack would mean that reinforcements would have to land at night.

Navy experts are still promising five feet of water at the end of the pier on the morning of November 20. One New Zealand Army Reserve officer who knows the island warns that there will be less than four feet over the reef, with a dodging tide making it even shallower. Everyone agrees that by the 22d the dodging tendencies will be over, but Admiral Turner decides not to put off the attack. Each day that passes, he has been told, increases the danger of a west wind, which would push waves up perhaps too steep for a landing. The landing of heavy matériel will certainly be delayed. Turner figures he has a two-to-one chance that the tides won't be a crucial problem. He is wrong.

Saturday, November 20, 2:20 A.M.: Transports heave to northwest of the island, which looms black in the path of the moon. By 2:55 A.M. 13 transports are reported in position 10,000 yards offshore. Boats are lowered and men begin clambering down the rope nets, but it turns out they are within range of Japanese guns—and in the wrong position, exactly in the line of fire between the battleships and the Japanese.

The whole timetable is thrown off. Transports are laboriously moved out of the way, as landing craft loaded with men bob along behind. The time of attack has to be postponed, first 15 minutes, then another 15. The revised H-Hour is 9 A.M.

5:42 A.M.: Everyone listens for the planes which at that moment are supposed to dump 1,500 tons of bombs on the island. Bolloxed communications hold them up. It is 6:20 A.M. before carrier-based Dauntless, Avenger and Hellcat aircraft roar overhead. They drop 500 tons of bombs, only a third of what Shoup had counted on to kill enemy troops and level buildings near the beaches.

6:22 A.M.: The naval bombardment opens, lasting nearly 90 minutes, littering every foot of the atoll with fragments from 3,000 tons of shells. It is 8:25 before the first waves of amtracs peel off from the line of departure and head for shore, some 6,000 yards away. Of the amtracs available, 87 are in the first three waves—42, then 24 and 21. The rest will come later. Each wave is 300 yards from the last. Some, at Shoup's suggestion, have been equipped with light armored shields specially welded in New Zealand. Each vehicle holds 20 to 25 men. They make less than four knots at sea.

At 8:55 A.M. all guns stop firing. Smoke has obscured the beach where the marines are landing, and for 20 crucial minutes the big guns have to remain silent. The Japanese use this moment to rush men massed on the south beach to cover the lagoon.

At 4,000 yards shells from the Japanese 75s start splashing around the amtracs. Then the 37s kick in, and at 2,000 yards long-range machine guns begin to spray bullets all over the sea. Soon rifle fire joins in. At 800 yards, amtracs reach the reef, crawl up over it and down into the water on the shore side. "Little boats on wheels," the Japanese call them.

A few hundred yards ahead of the first wave, two landing boats, miraculously unscathed, touch the end of the pier and men pour out, firing at the Japanese machine guns hidden in the pier. This is the scout-sniper platoon led by First Lieut. William Deane Hawkins, 30, a rangy Texan. Everybody calls him "Hawk." He has worked his way up through the ranks and does not believe he will survive the war.

Hawkins and his men race down the pier, hurling grenades at machine-gun nests, squirting fire from flamethrowers. Soon the pilings are ablaze.

The first wave of amtracs scrapes the sand in uneven increment: 9:10 on Red One; 9:17 on Red Three; 9:22 on Red Two. The beachhead is only ten yards wide. Amtrac drivers discover their machines can't climb over the four-foot seawall. Engines scream, throwing up showers of sand and splinters. The vehicles get hung up on the wall, sink back peppered with holes. In the chaos, some Second Battalion, Second Marines amtracs slant west to land on Red One with the Third Battalion, which the ferocity of the defense has already forced many yards west of its intended landing point. This is Maj. John F. Schoettel's battalion, but he is still trying to get to shore.

"Casualties 70 percent. Can't hold"

To men in the next wave of boats plugging toward the island, the noise is unbelievable: vast shuddering explosions that squeeze the body; the howl of steel fragments tearing the air apart just overhead; the spang of lead smashing into steel; gigantic splashes, underwater explosions that heave tons of green sea with enormous white-water crowns up into the air; guns chattering in long bursts, ripping the water into froth. And above the din a roar of human shouts, screams and cries.

Many of the amtracs are blasted to bits. Bodies sprawl on their decks. Men pile out, to sink under their packs or to float face down. Unhit amtracs start back for another load, running in reverse to keep their armored fronts to the enemy, but many lie dead in the water or skewed crazily on the torn sand. A message from an unidentified sender flashes to Gen. Julian Smith aboard the flagship *Maryland*: "Have landed. Unusually heavy opposition. Casualties 70 percent. Can't hold." In the three-day assault, 90 out of 125 amtracs will be lost.

Now it is the turn of the Higgins boats.

Pounded for hours by wind and ocean chop as they wallowed and circled on the line of departure, the men are relieved to be moving in at last. But some can see the reef just under the surface ahead. Here and there, the coral is actually out of the water, drying in the sun.

With an ominous squeal of metal the front boat, halfway across the lagoon, scrapes its bottom, lurches, stops dead on the coral. Others join it. The second wave piles into the lead wave, and the third follows. Some boats back off. Men leap over the side, holding their rifles high. They are in shallow water 800 yards from shore.

All around them the surface is whipped by curtains of bullets. Shells explode among the men with towering splashes. Marines watch as first one, then another Higgins boat takes a direct hit, splitting them wide open, spilling men and gear into the sea. The rusty, barnacled wreck of a local freighter that foundered on the reef during an earlier air strike plagues marines with crossfire from Japanese snipers hidden inside.

A wave of larger craft carrying Sherman tanks stops at the reef and disgorges the tanks into the sea. Time-Life correspondent Robert Sherrod, who came in with the fifth wave, reports: "One marine picked a half-dozen pieces of shrapnel from his lap, stared at them. Another said, 'Oh God, I'm scared. I've never been so scared in my life'.... Said the wild-eyed small-boat boss: 'It's hell

in here. They've already knocked out a lot of boats and there are a lot of wounded men lying on the beach from the first wave....'"

All along the front, men slosh in, waist-deep in bloody water, rifles over their heads, dodging and ducking as the bullets sing past. Their trousers are torn by the sharp coral, their knees and hands are bleeding.

On the concave beach at Red One, exposed to fire on three sides, of the 880 men of the Third Battalion, Second Marines only about 100 are still in action. One company reports only 40 survivors. Major Schoettel, the battalion commander, still in a boat half a mile from shore, radios Shoup at 9:59: "Receiving heavy fire all along beach. Unable to land. Issue in doubt." Minutes later, another message: "Boats held up on reef of right flank Red One. Troops receiving heavy fire in water."

Shoup replies: "Land Red Beach Two and work west."

Schoettel: "We have nothing left to land."

This news so shocks Shoup that he calls in his regimental reserve battalion to land on Red Two and work over toward Red One.

Despite his report, Schoettel's headquarters and weapons detachments are, in fact, still waiting in their Higgins boats; he has already lost 17 officers and believes his assault waves have been shattered to pieces. Only late in the day does a peremptory message from Julian Smith stir him to action: "Direct you land at any cost." Later Schoettel reports to Shoup on Red Two, saying he got separated from his men–who land without him. Despite being demoralized, the major takes command of what is left of his battalion along with the First Battalion, Eighth Marines and battles for 18 hours to wipe out the "Pocket," the toughest enemy complex on the island. Later, Schoettel is cited for bravery; he will die in action on Guam.

A pilot observer swooping back and forth over the battle notes, "The water seemed never clear of tiny men, their rifles held over their heads, slowly wading beachward. I wanted to cry."

Red Two is the worst. Some 200 yards out, Lieut. Col. Herbert Amey's amtrac runs into a submerged wire fence. He jumps out, waves his pistol in the air, shouts, "Come on! These bastards can't stop us!" and sprints hard for shore. A cone of fire hits him in the throat and kills him instantly.

The terrible test of the seawall

Some of Amey's men hide behind a wrecked amtrac until Lieut. Col. Walter Jordan, who had come as an observer, leads them to the beach. He can't contact other landing teams because most radios are waterlogged, so he sends out runners. Marines are scattered on the spiky coral sand in small groups. Some are as far as 100 yards inland, but most lie at the foot of the seawall, heads down, out of the storm of lead that rakes the beach.

Men huddled at the seawall watch their reinforcements die in the water. Sergeants and lieutenants shout to them, taunting and bullying them. Now and then an officer rises by himself to storm over the wall into the spray of lead. Very few follow. Those who do, scuttling madly across the sand, flop prone after five or six yards to shoot blindly at whatever is ahead. Some lie where they fall. Some inch their way back to roll exhausted over the seawall and lie there wide-eyed, panting.

Sgt. William Bordelon, a combat engineer attached to the Second Battalion, Second Marines, is one of five survivors of his 22-man platoon. His amtrac was blown up offshore. He crouches behind the coconut logs, large hands clenched on some satchel charges, a silent man with deepset gray eyes and a long, unsmiling face.

"Cover me!" he suddenly shouts and springs up over the wall and runs, zigzagging through the rain of bullets, to a Japanese pillbox squatting in the sand a few yards away. He swerves to the side and jams a satchel into the firing slit. A moment later the whole structure explodes in a mushroom of sand and log fragments. Bordelon races to the next pillbox, which covers the first. He throws a satchel inside that one too, and then blows up a third. Finally he runs back and slides down over the wall to get more satchels.

The front of his shirt is blossoming red.

Bordelon ducks back to the beach to pull in a fellow engineer, foundering at the water's edge. Then the sergeant lopes up to the wall, picks up more satchels and starts forward again. Instantly he is stitched by gunfire from three directions and killed. He will get the Medal of Honor.

In one makeshift hospital in a captured pillbox, more than 100 wounded have been collected. In the gloom, doctors have to operate by flashlight. Suddenly a wounded man lifts his rifle and fires at a figure huddled in a corner. Shocked, ears ringing, the marines look at the sprawled body. It is a Japanese soldier who has crept inside. Marines find another and crush his head with a rifle butt. With the rage of battle on them, they keep fighting despite their wounds. Some don't bother to stop for bandages but press on, faces, hands, shirts smeared with blood.

It is about noon. Down the length of the beach, pockets of marines wait by the seawall. Behind them lies the carnage of blasted boats and bodies, spread-eagled on the rocks, hanging head down from wrecked craft, lying half submerged in the water, face down, rocking gently with the waves. Out in the lagoon, landing craft circle, dodging the constant fire.

As troops keep straggling onto the beach, the confusion mounts. Hardly any radios are intact. Officers are separated from their men. Entire units have come ashore at the wrong place. Aboard the cruiser *Indianapolis*, naval officers mill about in Admiral Spruance's cabin, some suggesting that the Fleet Commander take direct control of the operation. Spruance raps the table once. His cold eyes rake the room. The noise

stops. "Gentlemen," he says crisply, "there are a number of senior officers in this landing in whom I have the utmost confidence. The operation will proceed."

The chaos on the beach at last sorts itself out. Colonel Shoup wades ashore after two boats fail under him. He finds 20 men cowering under the pier and rousts them out. A mortar shell knocks him off his feet, peppering his legs with shrapnel. He gets up, pulls himself together and sets up HQ 50 yards past the seawall, next to a ruined air raid shelter.

The sun sinks. Yard by yard, the marines push beyond the seawall. One by one the pillboxes and shelters and dugouts get the treatment: satchel charges or bangalore torpedoes thrust by hand inside the portholes. Flamethrowers are used if they can be taken close enough.

Dawn will break on a hellish scene

By nightfall 5,000 marines have crossed the line of departure. Fifteen hundred are dead or wounded, the others are crowded onto the tiny island's fringes. Medical supplies are so short that corpsmen wade out into the surf to take first-aid kits from dead bodies. Morphine Syrettes are at a premium. There is hardly any water.

November 21: The sun rises, so hot and bright that it makes the eyes ache even before its orange-balloon image has fully lifted above the horizon. On the beach lie bodies exposed by the receding tide, dangling from smashed amtracs, tanks and wire traps. At 6 A.M. a reserve battalion that has been circling offshore for 20 hours swarms in over the reef at low tide. The men start wading in. Marines on the beach watch warily, knowing that the Japanese have plenty of ammunition still on hand in their bunkers.

This second day landing is worse than the first. The Japanese, whose concrete bunkers reinforced with palm trunks had enabled them to survive the bombings and strafings, are still alive, it seems. Machine guns smuggled at night aboard the grounded freighter cut down marines in rows. The men on the shore scream as they helplessly watch their reinforcements cut to pieces. Of 199 men in the first wave this day, only 90 reach shore. It takes five hours to land all the reserves. Almost half of the 800 are killed or wounded. The battalion loses all its flamethrowers in the water.

Nevertheless, this is a pivotal point. Shoup orders a head-on attack over the seawall. In a fury inspired by the slaughter they have just watched, the men charge inland.

Lieut. Deane Hawkins and his scouts take the point as usual, 150 yards into the trees. They reach the airstrip, but Hawkins is wounded again and again. He attacks a machine-gun nest with grenades, presses on with his men to knock out three more nests. He dies at an aid station during the night. He too wins the Medal of Honor.

Backed by the fresh reserve troops, the invasion gains momentum. Leapfrogging ahead, teams of engineers carrying flamethrowers and satchel charges alternate with covering groups of riflemen. They reach the airstrip in force and push beyond. By midafternoon, Colonel Jordan learns that some 150 men, all that are left of his battalion, have reached the south shore and are holed up there with little ammo and no water. They have cut the island in two.

The First Battalion, Sixth Marines lands on Green Beach, bringing the first complete unit ashore with all weapons, including light tanks. Now pillboxes don't have to be removed by hand. Shoup, who had come in commanding a regimental combat team and wound up running eight battalions, gets a little relief. He will win the third Medal of Honor here.

Day Three: Marines begin the final drive. Jeeps are coming ashore, always a good sign because they mean the front has moved on ahead. The First Battalion, Sixth Marines, bypassing the four-acre Pocket at the cove, advance down the long south shore, tanks in the lead, relieving the beleaguered platoons by the airstrip. On Red Three, 400 yards east of the pier, Maj. Henry Crowe, the only one of three assault team commanders to reach shore with his men on D-day morning, is blocked by a huge, sand-covered, concrete bombproof impervious to the heaviest fire.

Enter Lieut. Alexander Bonnyman. Slim, diffident, Princeton, he is an engineer who owns several copper mines near Santa Fe, New Mexico. His men have killed dozens of Japanese as they sortied out from the bomb proof. Now Bonnyman and five others scramble up the sandy mound in the face of desperate firing.

For a moment Bonnyman is king of the mountain, 17 feet high. Then the Japanese rush him, racing up their side of the hill with shrill yells. Bonnyman stands alone, firing his carbine. He is hit, falls to his knees, rips out a magazine, jams in a fresh one, fires until the enemy turns and runs back down the hill. He follows, rubber-legged, tumbles and rolls to the bottom, dead. Behind him other engineers shove grenades into the ventilators of the bombproof and pour cans of gasoline down the vents. With a tremendous roar it blows up. The marines count 150 corpses inside. Bonnyman becomes the battle's fourth and final Medal of Honor winner.

By nightfall on the third day the marines hold a line across the western half of the island and most of the north side. There are 7,000 ashore now, with perhaps 1,000 Japanese still hidden in dugouts. And now, in the dark, the Japanese counterattack at last. Three times they rush forward, at the end reduced to brandishing swords and bayonets. Many commit suicide. Three times they are repelled. Next morning, aided by strafing planes and naval guns, the marines break down the last bombproofs. It is over. Second Marine Division casualties: 1,027 killed, 2,292 wounded, 88 missing. Japanese and Korean casualties: 4,690 dead, 146 captured.

The American public will be outraged at what some call a modern Charge of the Light Brigade. Shortly after the battle, according to a 1962 issue of the *Nava[Institute Proceedings*, a naval board of inquiry took up the question of the tides, although no other report surfaced. Admiral Spruance and all of the principals in the battle denied repeatedly that any such meeting took place. Other top-level conferences after the battle discussed many aspects of Tarawa, among them the need for more amtracs, better early bombardment, improved communications and the creation of underwater demolition teams. But the tides were not listed as a topic.

"Invaluable" information—inaccurate details

Admiral Turner—whose position has always been that he took a calculated risk and lost—will report on the local experts and their "dodging tides": "The information obtained from them was invaluable, in spite of some of it being inaccurate in matters affecting many of the details. . . ." Adm. Chester Nimitz in his report says: "Hydrographic information was known to be incomplete. Tidal conditions were about as expected." Admiral Turner's biographer concludes: "All those in command at Pearl [Harbor] realized that the shallow coral reef, aptly called a barrier reef . . . was a major hazard for the assault forces. . . . All were acquainted with the possibility of a 'dodging tide,' but the chances of it occurring on 20 November 1943 were judged slim. The risk was accepted along with dozens of other risks."

In a 1987 issue of *Sky & Telescope*, physicist Donald W. Olson, a professor at Southwestern Texas State University, analyzed the Tarawa tides and calculated that "from 9 A.M. until 10 P.M. on November 20, 1943, the water hovered within 6 inches of its mean level, 3.3 feet. It was a neap tide of reduced range, technically neither a dodging nor a vanishing tide. . . ." But, Olson says, Navy experts at the time could not have predicted the atoll tides accurately because they did not then possess the detailed tidal "harmonic constants" for Tarawa.

As for "Howlin' Mad" Smith's postwar opinion that the battle should never have been fought at all, it is not widely shared. That early in the war no one could predict the effect of bypassing Tarawa and Makin. "Smith advocated going straight on into the Marshalls," former correspondent Sherrod points out. "But we know now that the Japanese were prepared to resist an invasion there. Tarawa had to be fought."

Sherrod, 84, who saw the action all through World War II, including Iwo Jima and Okinawa, says no experience matched wading in for 700 yards under shattering fire with the fifth wave at Tarawa. His book *Tarawa: The Story of a Battle* makes you feel you were there.

After the battle, in the quiet, naked Marines splash happily about in the cove, ignoring the signs warning of mines. As they look to the blue horizon, they get a nagging sense that something is missing. The dazzling white line of surf that brought death to so many has disappeared. At last the tide is up. The reef is gone!

MAKING IT HAPPEN

DEAK PARSONS MADE SURE that the Manhattan Project's scientific theories got converted into a weapon of awesome destructive force. He oversaw the ordnance design; he made scientists, engineers, and military men work together; he set up and equipped assembly facilities and machine shops thousands of miles from home. And when the *Enola Gay* took off for Hiroshima, Parsons was on board to complete assembly of the bomb.

AL CHRISTMAN

Al Christman is a journalist and historian in San Marcos, California.

In May 1943 Cmdr. William S. ("Deak") Parsons returned from a secret mission to the South Pacific, where he had successfully introduced a new weapon in the war against Japan. He expected his next assignment to be the command of a ship. Instead he found himself on a train heading toward a most unlikely posting for a Navy officer: Los Alamos, New Mexico. His traveling companion was a nuclear physicist, J. Robert Oppenheimer.

The name Oppenheimer meant little then outside a limited circle of scientists. Still less known was the Los Alamos laboratory, where Oppenheimer had recently been appointed director. Even those privy to the laboratory's secrets referred to it obliquely as Project Y of the Manhattan Engineer District. What Parsons learned on his return from the South Pacific was that Los Alamos was working on a new type of bomb with power virtually beyond comprehension—and that he would be intimately involved in building it.

As the train rattled its way west, Oppenheimer and Parsons discussed the officer's future role among the scientists who were being brought together at Los Alamos. They agreed that the scientists would be entrusted to produce the nuclear guts of the "gadget" (as the bomb was referred to), while Parsons, as head of ordnance, would take charge of transforming their scientific results into a reliable service weapon.

During the next twenty-seven months Parsons would accomplish this and more. Vannevar Bush, the wartime leader of American science, summarized Parsons's importance: "The fact that [the atomic bomb] came to fruition and into actual use, the fact that the first uses were fully successful . . . all this was due in no small measure to [Parsons's] devotion to his task and his high skill in carrying it out." In wartime instructions Brig. Gen. Leslie Groves, executive head of the Manhattan Project, expressed the same sentiment more tersely: "Don't let Parsons get killed! We need him."

The story of the naval officer who transformed the theory of atomic fission into a weapon that ended a war begins with a shy boy of exceptional brilliance. William Parsons was seven years old in 1909 when his father, a lawyer, moved the family from Chicago to rustic Fort Sumner, New Mexico. Fort Sumner was deep in Billy the Kid country and about 150 miles southeast of Los Alamos, then the isolated mountain site of a boys' school. Young Parsons outperformed his classmates and skipped grades to graduate from high school and pass the Naval Academy examination by age sixteen.

In a rather labored pun on his last name, classmates at Annapolis turned "Parsons" into "Deacon," which was soon shortened to "Deak." Parsons proved to be an outstanding student in mathematics and physics and graduated from the academy in 1922. Hyman Rickover, who would lead the postwar development of nuclear submarines, was a classmate.

On his first tour of duty, as a gunnery officer aboard the USS *Idaho*, Ensign Parsons set the tone for his naval career by questioning long-standing assumptions about the dispersal pattern of the fourteen-inch batteries. His analysis was so convincing that it led the ship's captain to recommend new procedures for the fleet at large.

In May 1927 Parsons's analytical skills took him to the Naval Postgraduate School, which was then at Annapolis, for advanced studies in ordnance. By this point the social shyness of his earlier days at the Naval Academy had given way to a comfortable modesty. When he spied the beautiful Martha Cluverius on a tennis

From *American Heritage of Invention & Technology*, Summer 1995, pp. 22-25, 28-31, 34-35. © 1995 by Forbes, Inc. Reprinted by permission of *American Heritage* magazine, a division of Forbes, Inc.

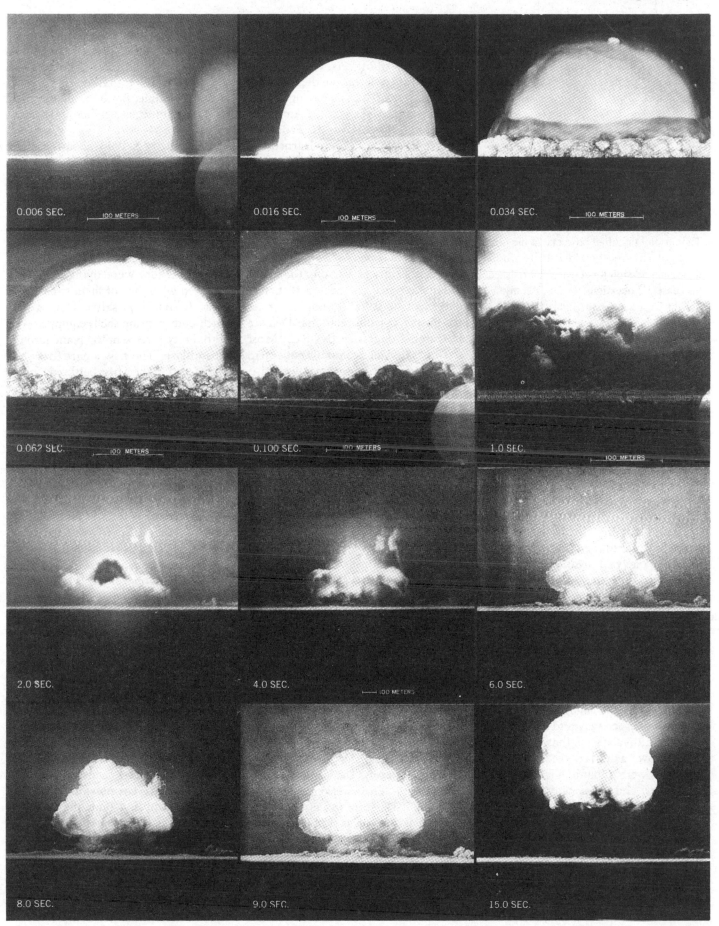

0.006 SEC.   100 METERS

0.016 SEC.   100 METERS

0.034 SEC.   100 METERS

0.062 SEC.   100 METERS

0.100 SEC.   100 METERS

1.0 SEC.   100 METERS

2.0 SEC.

4.0 SEC.   100 METERS

6.0 SEC.

8.0 SEC.

9.0 SEC.

15.0 SEC.

court, he did not hesitate to challenge her to a set. The tall, slightly balding junior officer appealed to Martha, who was delighted to find him undaunted by the knowledge that her father was an admiral, Wat Tyler Cluverius.

DEAK AND MARTHA MARRIED in November 1929, during his reassignment to the Naval Proving Grounds at Dahlgren, Virginia, where he had come to complete a research project. L. T. E. Thompson, a civilian physicist at the proving grounds, recognized Parsons's brilliance and passion for science and relished his ceaseless questions. In Dr. Tommy, as the physicist was known, Parsons found a mentor who agreed with him that the Navy should look beyond the mere incremental improvement of guns and other conventional weaponry. The next war, they agreed, could be won or lost with weapons yet unknown, and creating these weapons would require ending the indifference with which scientists and officers viewed each other. As long as only a few scientists understood the military environment and only a few officers could speak the scientists' language, advances would be limited.

Parsons's ability to speak with scientists was put to the test in July 1933, when the Navy's Bureau of Ordnance made him its liaison officer to the Naval Research Laboratory (NRL). The NRL was then a little-known facility in Washington, D.C., and Parsons was astounded to learn that Navy brass did not understand the revolutionary possibilities of its investigations into high-frequency radio waves. NRL scientists and engineers had found a way to use such waves to detect ships and aircraft—a system that would later be known as radar—yet only three engineers were pursuing high-frequency studies, and those only part-time. Through the commanding officer, Parsons requested $5,000 to pursue the research full-time. The funds were not approved. None of the Navy's bureaus saw the detection of airplanes as their business; radio was for communication.

But Parsons's appeal for support of radar was not in vain. By June 1936,

when he went back to sea as executive officer and navigator on the destroyer USS *Aylwin*, he had passed his zeal to other technical officers. One of these, Rear Adm. F. I. Entwistle, credited Parsons for the Navy's having operational radar by the time of America's entry into World War II. From his NRL experience Parsons learned the vulnerability of new ideas to the inflexibility of large bureaucracies.

In September 1939 Parsons reported back to the Naval Proving Grounds. His arrival coincided with Hitler's invasion of Poland, which started World War II in Europe. As Dahlgren's experimental officer Parsons took special interest in a secret device that civilian scientists were developing under the auspices of the National Defense Research Committee (NDRC). Most scientists in American universities had been indifferent, if not openly hostile, to military research, but with Dunkirk and the fall of France in 1940, that changed abruptly. Scientists who did not know a howitzer from a mortar descended on Washington with weapon ideas and gadgets to test.

The NDRC device that intrigued Parsons was the proximity fuze, the ancestor of today's "smart" weapons. This fuze consisted of a radio transmitter and receiver, the size of a pint of milk, inside an antiaircraft gun shell. The mechanism, glass vacuum tubes and all, had to withstand acceleration of up to 20,000 g's when fired from a gun. While speeding through the sky, the fuze had to detect the presence of an enemy aircraft and, at optimum distance, trigger the shell's explosive charge.

Bush asked the Navy to attach "one damn good officer" to the secret project. The Navy assigned Parsons to the management team of the newly formed Applied Physics Laboratory (APL) of Johns Hopkins University. The team's chief scientist, Merle Tuve, welcomed Parsons. He wrote, "The mere fact that we had a qualified officer with us right in the actual work, knowing every detail, gave everybody confidence that this wasn't just a silly exercise invented by some civilian."

After three years of painstaking development, in November 1942 Parsons took 5,000 of the fuzes to the

South Pacific for battle trials. An officer in the Solomons campaign recalled: "Parsons came to see if he could get these things battle tested. . . . We weren't anxious to go looking for trouble. But he came out there saying, 'Come, let's go; let's go get into a fight.'"

On January 5, 1943, aboard the light cruiser USS *Helena*, Parsons watched as four Japanese Aichi dive bombers broke formation and attacked the American task force. Defying hundreds of antiaircraft rounds with conventional fuzes, the enemy bombers struck a cruiser and scored two near misses. The attackers were flying away unscathed when one of them streaked by the *Helena*. Two salvos from a five-inch battery firing shells equipped with proximity fuzes sent the plane into the sea ablaze. The new smart fuzes had succeeded in their first battle encounter.

The proximity fuze came along soon enough to counter Japanese kamikaze attacks and German V-1 buzz bombs. When adapted to artillery shells, it would help blunt Hitler's counteroffensive in the Battle of the Bulge. The military man most responsible for winning these battles against time was Deak Parsons.

Upon returning from the Pacific in May 1943, Parsons had every reason to expect command of a ship. He had had more than his share of shore duty, and by tradition a line officer in time of war belongs at sea. But tradition cut no ice with President Roosevelt's Military Policy Committee (MPC), a board of scientists and officers, chaired by the ubiquitous Vannevar Bush, that governed the Manhattan Engineer District.

At the May meeting of the MPC, General Groves reported on Project Y. Research under way at Los Alamos was aimed at answering the critical question, How much fissionable material would be needed to make an atomic bomb? The previous December Enrico Fermi had built the first self-sustaining chain-reacting pile using an enormous heap of uranium oxide. Now fairly pure uranium 235 metal was slowly becoming available, as was fissionable plutonium. To make bombs from these materials, though, one first had to determine their critical mass—

the minimum amount needed to ensure that neutrons from fission would continue the chain instead of simply passing into the outside world. Experimenters and theorists were investigating this question intensely, and there was much scientific discussion and speculation in the air. Until that question was answered, many of the physicists believed it would be a waste of time to try to design the bomb itself.

This worried Groves, who was focused on the project's ultimate objective: building a bomb. He told the committee, "I need an ordnance officer, particularly in the development of the bomb itself, so that we will have service equipment instead of some dream child." Groves added that he knew of no one available in the Army who could fill the bill.

"Would you have any objection to a naval officer?" Bush asked.

"Not at all, if he's good," Groves replied.

Bush recommended Deak Parsons. Rear Adm. William Purnell added, "You can't get a better man."

On May 5 Parsons was summoned to the office of Adm. Ernest J. King, commander in chief of the U.S. fleet. King was brief and pithy. As Parsons later put it, he was "plunged into the Manhattan District with a set of verbal orders and a discussion with Admiral King lasting less than ten minutes." A few days later Parsons was on the train with Oppenheimer.

The physicist and the officer delineated responsibilities, engaged in what Parsons called "a highly satisfactory exchange of philosophies," and laid out the laboratories, machine shops, and firing ranges of Parsons's ordnance division—all this before Parsons had seen the site. That train ride opened a highly effective military-civilian partnership. Scientist and officer alike were driven by a desire to end the war and a belief that the bomb could do it.

Parsons's two-week visit to Los Alamos came at a critical time. Recommendations had just arrived from a review committee set up by Groves under Warren Lewis, the dean of American chemical engineering. After inspecting the work

under way at Los Alamos in respect to the final objective—a bomb to end the war—the committee had called for major expansion, thereby breaking the last strand in Oppenheimer's earlier dream of a small think-type laboratory.

Working together, the new military-scientific team of Oppenheimer and Parsons authored a joint memorandum to Groves on May 21 with a detailed plan for expanding Project Y. Most of the additions were for Parsons's division: 175 specialists in ordnance and engineering, an ordnance laboratory, engineering shops, and test ranges. The other major addition was a chemistry and metallurgy laboratory for the final purification of uranium.

All of Parsons's involvement in the planned expansion occurred before he was officially transferred to the Manhattan Project. The same was true of his early design work on the bomb that occurred upon his return to Washington. There on June 4 he brought together five ordnance leaders, including his old Dahlgren friend L. T. E. Thompson, who by now was the dean of Navy ballistics experts, and George Chadwick, a seasoned ordnance engineer. Parsons asked them to design a most unusual gun—one that would fit inside a bomb.

Parsons's request was prompted by a basic consideration in atomic-bomb design. To create an effective explosion, you have to assemble a critical mass—that is, at least the minimum amount needed for a sustained reaction—of fissionable material as quickly as possible. The ensuing reaction releases enormous amounts of energy, which destroys whatever the bomb is dropped on; in the process, of course, it also blows the mass apart. The separate parts of the mass have to be brought together very quickly, to make sure the chain reaction proceeds to the maximum possible extent before the explosion disperses them. If they are not assembled quickly enough, the bomb will fizzle.

When the material in an atomic bomb approaches criticality, it starts releasing energy; as soon as it crosses the threshold and becomes critical, it begins to blow apart. The trick is to keep it supercritical (that is, with a propagation factor, k,

greater than 1) for as long as possible before it breaks up, so that the bomb can deliver its full force. That means that it's important to rush through the subcritical range, where k is close to 1, as fast as you can; otherwise you will merely blow a chunk of metal apart instead of destroying a city.

A simple way to assemble such a mass in a hurry had already occurred to project scientists: Shoot one subcritical piece of fissionable material into another with a gun. Thompson and Chadwick set to work designing one to the preliminary specifications coming from Los Alamos. They eventually came up with a five-inch smoothbore capable of firing a sixty-pound projectile at 3,000 feet per second.

In mid-June, with the gun-design team already at work, Deak and Martha Parsons arrived at Los Alamos with their daughters, Margaret and Clara. Martha, a daughter and granddaughter of Navy admirals, was used to military bases. But nothing in her experience matched the remoteness of this pine-covered mesa, and never had she seen so much frenzied construction—block after block of newly framed offices, laboratories, and rapid-rise apartments. When the Parsons family arrived, the base employed about 150 civilian and military personnel, not counting hordes of construction workers on contract. The number grew daily. By the end of the war there would be about 5,000 residents, including 1,000 spouses and children.

When Parsons got to the nuclear boomtown, his Ordnance Division joined three previously established scientific divisions: Chemistry and Metallurgy, Experimental Physics, and Theoretical. Edwin McMillan and, later, Lt. Cmdr. A. Francis Birch concentrated on developing the 3,000-feet-per-second gun, which was slated for a design called Thin Man. Calculations revealed that it would have to be seventeen feet long, which made it rather unwieldy. The difficulties ahead were revealed in an early drop test of a scale model: A report from the Naval Proving Grounds described it as "an ominous and spectacular failure."

Meanwhile a completely different type of device was being tested. Seth

Neddermeyer, head of Parsons's implosion group, had begun blowing up explosives tamped around pipes and metal of various shapes, in an attempt to provide an alternative to the gun. His plan was to surround a core of fissionable material with explosives that would compress it inward. (When a sphere of metal is compressed, its surface area decreases, giving neutrons less of a chance to escape. Using this principle, it is possible to squeeze a subcritical sphere into a supercritical one.) Although later implosion studies focused on spheres, Neddermeyer tried a variety of shapes in his early work.

Neddermeyer did not originate the idea of using implosion, but he was its most persistent advocate. Parsons did not actively oppose the idea, but he had serious doubts about Neddermeyer's methods. Others did too. L. T. E. Thompson wrote, "It seems to me there is fundamental difficulty with the system which makes it quite certain to be unsatisfactory." Richard Feynman, then a young member of the theory group, was more succinct: "It stinks."

Parsons took a fresh look at implosion in late September 1943, when John Von Neumann, the wizard of many scientific disciplines (see "How Von Neumann Showed the Way," *Invention & Technology,* Fall 1990), visited Los Alamos. Von Neumann had recently been working on shaped charges—the use of explosives as precision weapons—at the Navy's Bureau of Ordnance in Washington, D.C. His visit was timely, because by this point the implosion alternative had acquired new importance. Efforts at several sites to separate fissionable uranium 235 from nonfissionable uranium 238 were not going well, and it was far from certain that enough U-235 could be accumulated to build a bomb. Unless a breakthrough occurred, plutonium, which was produced by irradiating the far more plentiful U-238, might be the only material available in significant amounts.

Unfortunately there was also a problem with plutonium. When it was first isolated and named, in March 1941, its chemistry was a mystery; no one was even sure if it emitted neutrons when it underwent fission. Within a year it became clear that plutonium emits

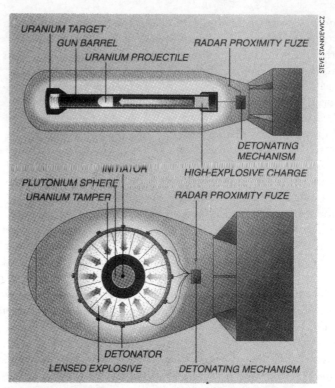

URANIUM TARGET
GUN BARREL
URANIUM PROJECTILE
RADAR PROXIMITY FUZE
DETONATING MECHANISM

INITIATOR
PLUTONIUM SPHERE
URANIUM TAMPER
HIGH-EXPLOSIVE CHARGE
RADAR PROXIMITY FUZE

DETONATOR
LENSED EXPLOSIVE
DETONATING MECHANISM

STEVE STANKIEWICZ

Little Boy, the gun bomb, and Fat Man, the implosion bomb.

plenty of neutrons—too many, in fact. When you get a critical mass together, it blows apart at the drop of a hat, usually before the energy release has had a proper chance to build up.

Calculations showed that there was no way to avoid this pre-detonation problem with the gun design; doing so would require an unfeasibly large muzzle velocity. If implosion could be made to work, however, it could collapse a core of plutonium into supercriticality much faster than any gun. To make a successful bomb, then, project workers had to either scrape together enough U-235 to use the simple and sturdy gun method or else rely on relatively plentiful plutonium, which would require mastering the problematic implosion method. In the end they managed to do both, but in the fall of 1943, with war proceeding in Europe and the Pacific at a horrifying pace, it was hard to tell if either one could be worked out in time to make a difference.

The difficulty with implosion lay in making the explosive behave properly. Getting a plutonium ball the size of an orange to implode symmetrically is a very tricky proposition, since as any ballistics engineer knows, a charge of explosive

does not ignite all at once. As the explosion progresses within the tight confines of the plutonium-bomb shell, it sets off shock waves that interfere with one another. If some parts of the plutonium ball are brought together too early, they will explode before the other parts can come fully into play. The result will be a very expensive dud.

Von Neumann and Parsons closeted themselves in an office with a blackboard, agreeing not to come out until they found a solution to the implosion problem. Once they had hashed things out, Parsons joined Von Neumann in advocating a new method known as "fast" implosion. This made use of "lenses"—carefully shaped pieces of high explosive in which the detonation waves would behave differently. By placing the lenses properly, it would be possible to "focus" the pressure from different sections of the explosive and make the implosion proceed symmetrically. That way the chain reaction would occur to the maximum extent possible in the brief time that the ball of plutonium held together. With Von Neumann's help, implosion got a new lease on life. Thus was born a new bomb, Fat Man, measuring approximately nine feet in length and five feet in diameter.

To try out full-scale models and components of both designs, Parsons formed a field-test group of Los Alamos scientists, military officers, and enlisted technicians. Using a modified B-29 bomber, they began drop tests in March 1944 at Muroc Army Air Base (now Edwards Air Force Base) in California. These tests revealed numerous problems: Models of Fat Man yawed and rolled violently; fuzes failed; three Thin Man models got caught and hung in the plane up to ten seconds after release; and one fell ahead of release onto the bomb-bay doors—a nightmare if it had been a fully armed nuclear bomb. The engineering went little better than the testing. George Chadwick, Parsons's pick for chief engineer, refused to move to the isolated laboratory site from his home in the Detroit area.

THROUGH ALL THE DIFFIculties, Oppenheimer and Parsons retained confidence in each other. Parsons wrote later, "We had two ingredients essential to success: (1) the compulsion of war, (2) the inspired leadership of Oppenheimer." Oppenheimer gave his view of Parsons in a January 1945 letter to Groves: "It is impossible to overestimate the value which Captain Parsons has been to the project. . . . He has been almost alone in this project to appreciate the actual military and engineering problems which we should encounter. He has been almost alone in insisting on facing these problems at a date early enough so that we might arrive at their solution."

In the summer and fall of 1944 Oppenheimer reorganized the laboratory for the aggressive development of fast implosion. Part of Parsons's ordnance organization, including engineering for Fat Man, went into a new explosives division under George Kistiakowsky. Parsons was made an associate director, the only high-ranking official of the Los Alamos laboratory in uniform and the only one who was

not an eminent scientist. The project depended on the Army Air Forces for bombers, crew, and air support, so Parsons sought an air officer who could work closely with him and the Los Alamos scientists. The Air Forces sent Col. Paul W. Tibbets, Jr., a veteran bomber pilot, to meet with Parsons for project approval and briefing.

Tibbets took charge of a bombardment squadron at Wendover Field in Utah, the new center of flight activities for the Manhattan Project. Flight testing out of Wendover began in October with the arrival of fifteen B-29s modified for the new bombs. By the end of the year, Tibbets's original squadron became the nucleus of the 509th Composite Group, a unique military entity that had to respond to the often mysterious needs of a secret scientific laboratory. The first items drop-tested by the 509th included inert models of the new Little Boy, a six-foot gun-type bomb with a muzzle velocity of 1,000 feet per second designed to use U-235.

By March 1945 the scientific and engineering ends of the project were nearing completion, but the uncertainties of implosion had added the need for a full-scale live nuclear test of Fat Man. (The simpler ballistics of Little Boy were considered foolproof enough that no test was needed; besides, there wasn't enough U-235 available to make a second bomb.) To prepare the way, Oppenheimer again shuffled the organization, forming Project Trinity under Kenneth T. Bainbridge to handle the test and Project Alberta under Parsons to prepare for overseas delivery and use of the bombs. At the same time, Oppenheimer made Parsons a member of the forceful Cowpuncher Committee, which "rode herd" on implosion.

From March to June of 1945 Parsons juggled two critical functions. As head of ordnance he spurred the completion of all nonnuclear components, including, among others, fail-safe electronics in the bomb to prevent explosion before the delivery plane had time to escape the blast, reinforcement of Little Boy's tail assembly, proximity fuzes to detonate the bombs at the op-

timum altitude above ground for maximum damage, and special armor to protect the bombs against enemy gun fire. Also, to give Tibbets's crews realistic training, Parsons designed and put into production high-explosive bombs, called Pumpkins, which had the aerodynamic characteristics of Fat Man. As head of Project Alberta he organized one of the most complex technical operations ever undertaken at a distant location in a theater of war. He selected personnel and arranged for their training, and through Norman Ramsey's delivery group he made sure that everything that would be needed overseas—from screwdrivers to hydraulic lifts to gun-assembly buildings—would be in place when the time came.

In June 1945 Parsons turned his full attention to overseas preparations. The mission for which he was now preparing would symbolize his role in bringing together talent and knowledge from many sources: As weaponeer on the Hiroshima flight he would be a Navy officer on an Army Air Forces plane in charge of a weapon developed by civilian scientists under an Army general.

In February Parsons had sent Cmdr. Frederick L. Ashworth to the Pacific to choose a suitable site for the overseas operation. Ashworth selected Tinian, a recently captured island of the Marianas on which six parallel runways had been rushed to completion for launching massive bombing raids on mainland Japan. (While it was in operation, Tinian was the world's largest airport.) In April Navy Seabees had begun construction of Project Alberta facilities, including fourteen buildings for bomb assembly, shops, and storage, as well as explosives magazines and loading pits.

Parsons spent much of June in whirlwind travel between the Air Forces installation at Wendover; the secret rocket station at Inyokern, California, and the California Institute of Technology in Pasadena, where explosive lenses were being developed; and naval commands at San Diego, for logistical support from the Pacific fleet. From July 2 to 13 he visited Tinian; then he headed back to New Mexico to watch the test of the implosion bomb.

ON THE EVENING OF JULY 15, Parsons arrived in the rain at Kirtland Army Air Base. One hundred miles south, at Trinity Site, the first nuclear bomb hung from a hundred-foot tower awaiting countdown. Plans had called for Parsons to fly over the tower moments before the explosion with Luis Alvarez's instrument team as it dropped pressure gauges by parachute, but poor weather made the mission too risky. The flight could occur, Oppenheimer decided, but no closer to the bomb tower than twenty-five miles.

Alvarez, a future Nobel laureate, was upset; he would be a mere observer in the most spectacular scientific experiment of the century. Parsons's primary concern, however, was not science. For military purposes, his own eyes were as important as the scientists' instruments. And in any case, failure of the Trinity bomb would not cancel his mission in the Pacific. Regardless of any problems with the implosion bomb, the gun-type Little Boy was going to be dropped.

Before dawn on July 16 Parsons stood behind the pilot of a plane circling the Alamogordo test site. Alvarez knelt between the pilot and the copilot. As the countdown came over the radio, the pilot banked and headed in the direction of the tower. From twenty-five miles away at an altitude of 24,000 feet, they would have a grandstand view of the first display of the awesome power of the atom.

The count droned toward zero. Officers and scientists pulled special Polaroid goggles over their eyes. At 5:29 A.M., the bomb was detonated. Clouds concealed the initial ball of fire, but neither they nor the darkened lenses could contain the burst of illumination that filled the sky. The sensation, according to Alvarez, was one of intense light covering the whole field of vision. A deep orange-red glow pierced the clouds. Shortly after, they saw a new ball of fire developing. Colors danced across the sky, and a mushroom cloud began to form. After eight minutes the cloud towered

an estimated 40,000 feet above the ground.

The goals of Trinity had been achieved. Scientific theories had been proven, calculations had been calibrated, weapon feasibility had been established. President Truman was told that atomic bombs would be available for use against Japan within three weeks.

One week after Trinity, Parsons headed back to Tinian aboard a C-54 with photographs and films of the Trinity test. He immediately took charge of final preparations by the technical group from Los Alamos. In the days that followed, elements of Parsons's planning came together with the same precision as the bombs themselves:

• July 23. The first of three dummy Little Boys is dropped near Tinian to rehearse the plane's breakaway maneuver to escape the bomb's blast.
• July 26. USS *Indianapolis* delivers Little Boy's gun assembly and U-235 projectile. At Potsdam, Truman, Prime Minister Clement Attlee of Great Britain, and President Chiang Kai-shek of China issue a declaration urging Japan to surrender or suffer "prompt and utter destruction."
• July 29. The last of the U-235 target inserts for Little Boy arrive, conveyed as three separate parts in three otherwise empty C-54 cargo planes. Japan declines to accept the terms of the Potsdam Declaration. Parsons requests permission to drop the first bomb as early as August 1.
• July 29–30. A Japanese torpedo sinks the *Indianapolis,* resulting in the death of 880 men out of a crew of 1,196.
• July 31. The 509th completes rehearsals for the first mission. Little Boy is assembled and readied for loading. Brig. Gen. Thomas F. Farrell, deputy of General Groves, arrives at Tinian.
• August 1. The first of three Fat Man dummies is dropped near Tinian to test electronic fuzing and detonators and to rehearse for the live delivery.
• August 2–3. All hands—and Little Boy—stand ready, waiting for the weather over Japan to clear.
• August 4, 2:00 P.M. Storms continue over Japan. Crewmen of seven B-29s en-

ter a Quonset hut surrounded by armed military police and are finally told what they have been preparing for. Tibbets discloses that a new weapon equivalent to perhaps 20,000 tons of TNT has recently been tested. "We have received orders to drop it on the enemy," he says.

Parsons tells the airmen: "The bomb you're going to drop is something new in the history of warfare. It is the most destructive weapon ever produced. We think it will knock out almost everything within a three-mile area." Crewmen find it reassuring that Parsons, one of the makers of the new superweapon, will be with them on the mission.
• August 5. Forecast calls for clear weather over Japan the next day. Preparations proceed accordingly.

Parsons and Farrell face an unexpected last-minute problem. Four B-29s have crashed the night before while taking off from Tinian as part of a mass bombing raid on Japan. The plane with the atomic bomb will have a seven-and-a-half-ton overload. If it crashes on takeoff, Parsons warns, "We could get a nuclear explosion and blow up half the island." He recommends completing the final assembly of the bomb after takeoff. Farrell, fully aware of Groves's opposition to in-flight tinkering because of cramped conditions in the bomb bay, asks Parsons whether he has ever done this before. "No," Parsons responds, "but I've got all day to try it." Farrell agrees to the plan.
• 2:00 P.M. Little Boy is trailered to the loading pit, and technicians scribble pungent messages to the enemy on the bomb. The *Enola Gay* named after Tibbets's mother) is backed over the pit.
• 3:00 P.M. The bomb is loaded. Parsons squeezes in behind Little Boy. For two hours he balances himself on an improvised catwalk straddling the bomb-bay doors. Working by flashlight, he methodically practices the assembly, following an eleven-step list.
• August 5–6, midnight. Tibbets begins the day with a final briefing. Breakfast follows. To Parsons's consternation, klieg lights and popping flashbulbs from military photographers documenting the event illuminate the *Enola Gay* and crew.

Shortly before takeoff, Parsons borrows a .45-caliber automatic from a security agent. In the event of capture the pistol will be the only certain safeguard for the secrets in his head.

• 2:45 A.M. Takeoff. As the *Enola Gay* approaches the last hundred feet of runway, Tibbets pulls the overloaded bomber off the ground. Fifteen hundred miles ahead, via Iwo Jima, lies the target, Hiroshima.

Minutes into the flight Parsons nods to the electronics officer, Lt. Morris R. Jeppson. They make their way to the bomb bay. Parsons squeezes in behind the bomb. Jeppson hands him tools and holds the flashlight. As Parsons completes each step, he reports by intercom to the cockpit. His progress is relayed by low-frequency radio to Farrell on Tinian.

• Around 3:15 A.M. Parsons withdraws his nicked and graphite-blackened hands. The assembly is complete. He and Jeppson return to the bomb's electronic monitoring panels in the crew compartment.

• 6:00 A.M. The *Enola Gay* makes rendezvous at Iwo Jima with two observation and instrument planes, which will accompany it to Hiroshima.

• 7:30 A.M. Parsons returns to the bomb bay and replaces the green safety plugs with red plugs, arming the bomb. Tibbets begins the climb to bombing altitude.

• 8:38 A.M. The *Enola Gay* levels off at 32,700 feet. Jeppson continues to monitor Little Boy's circuitry.

• 9:09 A.M. Parsons is standing behind Tibbets as Hiroshima comes into sight. Tibbets asks Parsons to verify the target. He does so, thereby authorizing release.

• 9:15:17 A.M. A mere seventeen seconds after the scheduled drop time, the *Enola Gay* bolts upward from the release of its five-ton cargo. "Now it is in the lap of the gods," Parsons says to himself.

Parsons pulls down his protective goggles and listens intently for the bomb-bay doors to close. If they fail, it could mean disaster; open doors would impede the breakaway turn, which will allow them to escape from the blast. Upon hearing the doors snap shut, he feels intense relief.

Forty-three seconds after the bomb is dropped, a bright purple flash penetrates his goggles. A heavy shock rocks the plane. Someone yells, "Flak!"

"No, no, that's not flak," Parsons responds. "That's it—the shock wave. We're in the clear now."

A second shock wave follows, caused by reflection of the first one from the ground. Parsons pushes back the goggles and looks toward Hiroshima. He is, as he will say later, "completely awestruck by the tremendous mushroom and dust cloud covering the blasted parts of the city." He watches as the boiling dust and debris rise to 20,000 feet. He sees a white plume climb upward from the center to some 40,000 feet. He watches "an angry dust cloud" spread over the city.

• 9:40 A.M. As the trio of planes heads back to Tinian, Parsons sends a coded radio message: "Deak to Farrell: Results in all respects clear-cut and successful. Immediate action to carry out further plans [for a second atomic bomb] is recommended. Greater visible effects than at Alamogordo. Target was Hiroshima. Proceeding to Tinian with normal conditions in airplane." The results are relayed to President Truman aboard the USS *Augusta*, returning from Potsdam. Truman approves release of the news to the world, again calling on the Japanese to surrender.

• 2:58 P.M. After twelve hours and thirteen minutes in the air, the *Enola Gay* lands on Tinian, ending the world's first atomic mission.

Cheers rose from two hundred or more officers, enlisted men, and scientists when the *Enola Gay* landed. As Tibbets led the crew down the hatch, Gen. Carl Spaatz, commander of the Strategic Air Forces, strode forward and pinned the Distinguished Service Cross on the breast of Tibbet's coveralls. The subsequent award of a Silver Star, a lesser honor, to Parsons stirred this comment from Groves: "There was never any question on the part of anybody [familiar with the mission] but that Parsons was running the show. The only person who did not get that right was apparently General Spaatz." The Navy also responded, at

first, with a half-measure. It promoted Parsons to commodore, a rank one star less than the normal progression from captain direct to rear admiral.

THE DAY AFTER THE HIROshima mission, in the quiet tent, Parsons wrote a letter to his father: "Depending on how the Japs felt before there is a definite possibility that this kind of attack may crack them and end the war without an invasion. If so it will save hundreds of thousands of American (and even Japanese) lives."

Parsons, like Groves, believed it would take the shock of a second bomb to persuade the Japanese to surrender. He sped up the Fat Man assembly line so that the second bomb could be dropped before storms forecast for the scheduled date, August 11. In the meantime American bombers showered Japan with leaflets calling for surrender and warning of more bombs with "the most destructive explosive ever devised by man." On August 9, with Japan still holding out, the Fat Man implosion bomb destroyed almost half the city of Nagasaki. This time Parsons stayed on Tinian.

The following day the Japanese initiated surrender negotiations. With their formal surrender on September 2 aboard the USS *Missouri*, the wartime mission of the Manhattan Project—and the personal objective of its ordnance chief, Deak Parsons—was fulfilled.

Two days after the surrender the Navy Department awarded Commodore Parsons the Distinguished Service Medal for exceptionally meritorious service in the development of the atomic bomb. On January 8, 1946, it finally promoted him to rear admiral, a rank not usually given to a line officer without a sea command.

Parsons's immediate positions in postwar Washington included stints as the Navy Department's director of atomic defense, Navy representative to the military liaison committee of the Atomic Energy Commission, and deputy chief of the Armed Forces Special Weapons Project. In all these roles he spearheaded the development of the Navy's postwar nuclear policy. As the master link between science and the military, he profoundly influenced the structure and operating philosophy of today's Navy laboratories.

Between January 11 and August 18, 1946, Parsons, as deputy to the commander of Operation Crossroads, provided technical direction for the testing of two atomic bombs, one an air burst and the other underwater, in Bikini atoll. He held a similar position two years later in Operation Sandstone, a series of three atomic tests at Eniwetok, making him the only person to witness seven of the first eight atomic explosions.

Parsons never fulfilled his desire to have a ship of his own, but in 1951 he commanded Cruiser Division Six in the Atlantic and Mediterranean. In 1952, as deputy chief in the Bureau of Ordnance, he promoted innovative development programs, including the Bumblebee beam-riding guided missiles and the heat-homing Sidewinder. He influenced the establishment of the Navy's postwar laboratories on a foundation of military-scientific cooperation.

On December 4, 1953, Parsons learned that Robert Oppenheimer's security clearance was to be suspended. Parsons, so long known for his calm demeanor, became, according to his wife, "extremely upset." He exclaimed, "This is the biggest mistake that the United States could make!"

The next morning, only minutes after arriving at the Bethesda Naval Hospital, Deak Parsons died of a heart attack at age fifty-two.

Why We Dropped The BOMB

**The U.S. wanted to
end the war against
Japan and save
American lives. But
diplomatic and political
factors also played a
role in the decision**

William Lanouette

At 8:16 on the morning of August 6, 1945, the world got a glimpse of its own mortality. At that moment, the city of Hiroshima was obliterated by a fireball that sent waves of searing heat, then a deafening concussion, across the landscape. Three days later, a second bomb hit Nagasaki. In another five days, Japan surrendered, ending World War II.

Fifty years later, the destructive potential of nuclear weapons is terrifyingly familiar. What continues to cause controversy is why the United States used atomic weapons against Japan in the first place. The explanation given at the time, which has since been widely accepted, is that the U.S. dropped the bomb to end the war quickly and to save the thousands of lives that would have been lost in an invasion of Japan.

After half a century of historical investigation, this answer no longer seems so clear-cut. Respected scholars have found archival evidence suggesting that other considerations—not just military but diplomatic and political as well—influenced the decision. The mere mention of other factors angers many Americans, who

have long believed that the decision to use this horrific weapon had an unambiguous *moral* foundation.

After the bomb was dropped, President Harry S. Truman said flatly that its purpose was to save lives, and his secretary of war, Henry L. Stimson, elaborated that view in a 1947 *Harper's Magazine* article. Not surprisingly, the official explanation is embraced most strongly by the veterans who were preparing for Operation Olympic, an attack scheduled for November 1945 on Japan's southern island of Kyushu, and for Operation Coronet, a planned March 1946 assault on the main island of Honshu.

Since early last year, many of these veterans—and their lobbies in Washington—have mounted a vigorous defense of Truman's decision. Their chief target has been an exhibit about the bomb that is scheduled to open in May at the Smithsonian Institution's National Air and Space Museum. "The Last Act: The Atomic Bomb and the End of World War II" features the restored forward section of the *Enola Gay*, the B-29 that dropped the Hiroshima bomb. After seeing early drafts of the exhibit's text, erans' groups denounced it as biased against the American war effort and too sympathetic to Japan—"historical revisionism at its worst." The *Enola Gay's* pilot, retired Gen. Paul W. Tibbets, called the exhibit "a package of insults."

The controversy spread through Op-Ed pages, letters to the editor, opinion columns, editorials and radio talk shows. Two dozen U.S. Representatives sent a letter protesting many examples of the exhibit's "anti-American prejudice and imbalance," and the Senate joined the cause with a nonbinding resolution that called the exhibit "revisionist, unbalanced and offensive." In the end, the text went through five drafts, with the result that the exhibit has been altered significantly to reflect the veterans' views.

The debate is bound to intensify this year as the world reflects on the 50th anniversary of Hiroshima. Army Air Force veterans have threatened to picket the Air and Space Museum; peace activists, who feel that their views have been drowned out by the veterans, plan to do the same when the Smithsonian exhibit opens. Here and there, historians are arranging campus teach-ins—a forum popular during the bitter days of the Vietnam War—to educate their students, the press and the public about the fateful decisions that ushered in the nuclear age.

CHALLENGING THE OFFICIAL VIEW

WAS ENDING THE PACIFIC WAR PROMPTLY THE ONLY REASON for leveling two cities, instantly killing 70,000 at Hiroshima and 40,000 at Nagasaki, and within the next five years, an estimated 230,000 more people from the aftereffects of the two bombs? The official view first came under serious challenge in 1965, with the publication of *Atomic Diplomacy* by historian Gar Alperovitz. Drawing on Secretary of War Stimson's unpublished diaries, Alperovitz argued that postwar relations with the Soviet Union were an important consideration in the decision to drop the bomb. During the three decades since, other evidence that raises questions about Truman's explanation has surfaced in the Manhattan Project records at the National Archives, the papers of physicist J. Robert Oppenheimer and others at the Library of Congress, and the official and personal documents of America's wartime presidents, diplomats, military leaders and scientists. Taking this information into account, it still seems fair to conclude that the predominant reason for dropping the bomb was the belief that it would end the war quickly and spare American soldiers. But other factors clearly influenced the decision. These include:

• Postwar diplomacy. Truman's new secretary of state, James F. Byrnes, and a number of military leaders saw the awesome weapon as a way to make the Soviets "more manageable"—first, by ending the Pacific war before they could join it in earnest; second, by countering political gains the Soviets had made in Europe.

• Bureaucratic momentum. Fearing that Germany was working on an atomic bomb, President Franklin D. Roosevelt began America's A-bomb research in 1939 and agreed to make it a high-priority project days before Japan's surprise attack on Pearl Harbor in 1941. Building the bomb required billions of dollars and the efforts of many of the nation's leading scientists—an undertaking that became known as the Manhattan Project. In the end, the commitment to build the bomb produced a powerful impulse to *use* it.

• Political justification. Some American military and civilian leaders pushed the White House to use the bomb before Japan could surrender in order to justify those billions that had been spent on the project—without congressional knowledge or approval. As an aide to Under Secretary of War Robert Patterson said, "If this thing works, they won't investigate anything and if it doesn't work … they won't investigate anything else."

• Psychological factors. After four costly years of war, Americans in high office were eager to crush the enemy and bring the boys home. Public feeling was running so high against the Japanese and their wartime behavior—the slaughter of civilians at Nanking, the surprise attack on Pearl Harbor, the Bataan death march, the barbaric treatment of Allied POWs (one study after the war found that 27 percent died in custody, compared with 4 percent of those held by Germany and Italy)—that many American leaders were in no mood to take additional casualties. They were appalled at the thought of more American boys, who found glory in life, being killed by Japanese kamikaze pilots and suicide fighters, who found glory in death. In the eyes of war-weary Americans, the enemy had become merely "Japs," creatures who needed to be blasted and burned out of island caves.

Historians sometimes use a "rational actor" model to analyze decisions. The model works like this: Truman wanted to end the war and save American lives; the only way to do that was to use atomic weapons; therefore Truman ordered the bombing of Hiroshima. But with so many factors influencing American leaders, the rational-actor model cannot fully explain the decision to drop the bomb. Even Stimson admitted as much. "No single individual can hope to know exactly what took place in the minds of all of those who had a share in these events," he wrote in 1947. Because all the principal figures have since died, it is chiefly with archival evidence that the various arguments are now being made.

Set against this inconclusive scholarly debate is the emphatic verdict of the men who believed they were preparing to invade the Japanese home islands. Paul Fussell, professor emeritus at the University of Pennsylvania and author of *The Great War and Modern Memory* and *Wartime: Understanding and Behavior in the Second World War*, articulated the veterans' view in a 1981 essay in *The New Republic*. Fussell was a grunt himself, a second lieutenant in the 45th Infantry Division, which had finished a bloody march through Europe and in the summer of 1945 was preparing to ship off to be trained for the final assault against Japan.

Under the defiant headline "Thank God for the Atom Bomb," Fussell dismissed revisionist interpretations as "tidy hindsight." He saw the dispute between historians and veterans as a collision between theory and experience. "What's at stake in an infantry assault is so entirely unthinkable to those without experience of one, even if they possess very wide-ranging imaginations and sympathies, that experience is crucial in this case," he wrote.

Fussell accepted as a given that the Japanese would have sacrificed their lives to defend their homeland, taking untold thousands of Americans with them. "Why delay and allow one more American high school kid to see his own intestines blown out… when with the new bomb we can end the whole thing just like that?" Fussell asked.

The soldiers' rallying cry in 1945 was "Golden Gate in '48," meaning that they didn't expect to be back stateside in San Francisco for another three years. No wonder, then, that Fussell and others in the 45th "cried with relief and joy" when the bomb was dropped. "We were going to live."

But the perceptions of soldiers in the field "are of little value in understanding why U.S. policymakers made the choices they did," contends J. Samuel Walker, a diplomatic historian and expert on nuclear issues who is not associated with either side in the debate. Walker notes in the journal *Diplomatic History* that "although scholars generally agree that Truman used the bomb primarily to shorten the war, the number of American lives saved, even in the worst case, would have been in the range of tens of thousands rather than hundreds of thousands." Scholarly consensus, he writes, also holds that "the war would have ended within a relatively short time without the atomic attacks and that an invasion of the Japanese islands was an unlikely possibility. It further maintains that several alternatives to ending the war without an invasion were available and that Truman and his close advisors were well aware of the options."

This scholarly view is sharply at odds with Truman's assessment several months after the bombings: "It occurred to me that a quarter of a million of the flower of our young manhood were worth a couple of Japanese cities, and I still think they were and are."

As questions were raised after the war about whether it was really necessary to use the atomic bomb, administration officials cited higher and higher casualty figures to justify their decision. "When Truman wrote his memoirs in 1955, he said 500,000 American lives were saved as a result of the bombing," says Dartmouth College historian Martin J. Sherwin, whose 1975 book on the bomb and the origins of the Cold War, *A World Destroyed*, examined in detail how U.S. leaders decided to use nuclear weapons. Winston Churchill, who later called the bomb "a miracle of deliverance," wrote that more than 1 million lives were saved. These upward revisions, according to Sherwin, suggest that the two wartime leaders felt a serious need to justify its use.

The debate over whether the United States was justified in dropping the bomb starts with two words: "unconditional surrender." With their defeat on Okinawa in June 1945, the Japanese were clearly going to lose the war. Should the U.S. have modified the terms of surrender, approved by the Allies at their Casablanca conference in 1943, and allowed one condition: a guarantee that the emperor and the imperial throne would survive? And if the U.S. had offered this guarantee, would the powerful war faction in Japan have allowed the nation to lay down its arms?

THE AMBIGUOUS SURRENDER TERMS

HISTORICAL RESEARCH SINCE THE WAR SHOWS THAT IN THE spring and summer of 1945 there were profound disputes in Washington about unconditional surrender. Churchill had suggested "mitigation" of the "unconditional surrender" terms when he met with Stalin and Roosevelt at Yalta in February 1945. The U.S. Army chief of staff, Gen. George C. Marshall, and the White House chief of staff, Adm. William D. Leahy, both favored retaining the emperor. So did Assistant Secretary of War John J. McCloy and Joseph C. Grew, the former U.S. ambassador to Japan who was then acting secretary of state. But other influential advisors held to the original terms, among them FDR's personal advisor, Harry Hopkins, and two assistant secretaries at State: Archibald MacLeish and Dean Acheson.

An ad hoc committee of Stimson, Grew and Navy Secretary James Forrestal was charged with drafting surrender terms. On July 2, the group recommended to Truman that the U.S. promise Japan it could retain a "constitutional monarchy under the present dynasty" as long as the regime remained peaceful. But a Gallup Poll that month showed one-third of Americans favored

executing Hirohito as a war criminal and another 20 percent wanted him jailed or exiled. Only 7 percent wanted him to stay.

Byrnes, Truman's new secretary of state, took office on July 3. A novice at diplomacy but a skilled politician, he worried that public opinion would turn against the president unless Japan was brought to its knees, and he was convinced that negotiating a surrender with an all but vanquished foe would make the president appear weak. Byrnes had special stature within the government. He had been a Supreme Court justice. He had headed the federal economic stabilization and war mobilization programs. He had been an influential colleague of Truman's in the Senate, and until FDR had dissuaded him, Truman intended to nominate Byrnes for vice president at the 1944 Democratic convention.

When Truman went to the Big Three conference in Potsdam in mid-July 1945, he took along the draft of the surrender terms prepared by Stimson, Grew and Forrestal. Truman also took along Byrnes. During the meeting, the Americans received word that the first test of the A-bomb on July 16 in New Mexico had been a stunning success. Byrnes persuaded the president to delete from the draft declaration the section that would have guaranteed the continuation of the imperial system.

The July 26 Potsdam Declaration demanded "the unconditional surrender of all Japanese armed forces," while warning that the alternative would be "prompt and utter destruction." The surrender terms had been softened only to the extent that they promised that "a peacefully inclined and responsible government" could be formed "in accordance with the freely expressed will of the Japanese people. ..."

The wording was vague enough to support almost any interpretation. In an editorial published in the first week of July, *Life* magazine, arguably the most influential American publication during the war, had warned the U.S. against being "unnecessarily inscrutable" in its diplomacy. "If we fail to define 'unconditional surrender' as precisely as possible before the invasion, we are failing to use that mixture of reason and force known as statesmanship." *Life* predicted that Japan would go through an internal upheaval after the war. "Out of its tragic turmoil there may come no emperor at all, or an emperor of purely religious and no political significance, or even a 'constitutional monarchy.' In any case, the intelligent thing for us to do is to let the Japs figure it out for themselves."

In Tokyo, pressures for a settlement had been rising all spring in various government circles. The Japanese had been fighting a losing defensive war for more than two years, and they seemed ready to break in April when Allied forces invaded Okinawa and the government of retired Gen. Kuniaki Koiso resigned.

Japan's leaders had considered Okinawa a "decisive" battle that would show the Allies that continued fighting would be dreadfully costly. And it was. During the three-month island campaign, 7,000 American soldiers and Marines died, along with 5,000 sailors. It was the highest death toll for any single battle in the Central Pacific campaign, surpassing the total of 6,800 in the yard-by-yard battle for Iwo Jima that had ended in late March. But the number of Japanese killed on Okinawa was far higher, with some estimates approaching 100,000. (At least 80,000 Okinawan civilians died in the fighting.) When it was over, the war faction in Japan set about preparing for one more "decisive" battle—a suicidal defense of the home islands.

4. THE TWENTIETH CENTURY TO 1950

1939	1940	1941	1942	1943	1944
● August 2: Einstein warns Roosevelt about German nuclear-weapons research and urges an all-out U.S. effort	● June 12: FDR establishes the National Defense Research Committee under Vannevar Bush to oversee the nuclear effort	● November 27: Bush tells Roosevelt the nuclear bomb is feasible ● December 7: Japan attacks Pearl Harbor	● December 2: Manhattan Project scientists create the first self-sustaining nuclear chain reaction	● January 24: At Casablanca, Roosevelt calls for the "unconditional surrender" of Germany, Italy and Japan	● September 19: Roosevelt and Churchill agree that the atomic bomb might be used against Japan

Emperor Hirohito and such older advisors as retired Adm. Mitsumasa Yonai and Gen. Koiso hoped to end a war they knew was lost. Also favoring peace was the emperor's political confidante, Marquis Koichi Kido, the Lord Privy Seal. After two weeks of private conversations with many of his country's senior officials, Hirohito called in the chief cabinet members and urged them to seek peace by any diplomatic means. Throughout the summer, Adm. Kantaro Suzuki's government continued to approach the Soviet Union, which was still officially neutral in the Pacific war, about brokering a favorable peace with the Allies.

The Soviets, however, dragged their feet on the Japanese overtures. Months earlier at Yalta, before Japan's crushing defeats in the Central Pacific, the Americans and the British had thought it was crucial to get the Soviets into the Asian conflict. They promised the Soviets the use of Dairen and Port Arthur on the Manchurian coast, recovery of the southern half of Sakhalin Island, and control of the Kurile Islands. In return, the Soviets pledged to enter the hostilities by mid-August. Now, with Japan enfeebled, it was clearly in the Soviets' interest to prolong the war until they could get into it—and collect the concessions they had won at Yalta.

The Americans had cracked the Japanese diplomatic code as early as 1939, and through radio intercepts they knew about Tokyo's urgent approaches to Moscow. "Unconditional surrender is the only obstacle to peace," the foreign minister, Shigenori Togo, instructed his representative in Moscow on July 13. But the intercepts also showed dissension within Suzuki's cabinet. While Hirohito and his civilian advisors wanted to accept the surrender terms in the Potsdam Declaration, despite its ambiguity about the fate of the emperor, intercepts led U.S. intelligence analysts to conclude that the Japanese government would ultimately balk at "unconditional surrender" and was "still determined to exploit fully the possible advantage of making peace first with Russia," according to an intelligence analysis quoted by military historian Ronald H. Spector in *Eagle Against the Sun*. On July 28, after pondering the Allied ultimatum for two days, Suzuki told the Japanese press that his cabinet was *mokusatsu*. Translated in a journalistic context, *mokusatsu* could mean the cabinet was "without comment"; translated in a diplomatic context, it could mean the cabinet was responding "with silent contempt." Faced with this ambiguity, the Allied leaders waiting in Potsdam interpreted the statement as a rejection of their declaration.

After the war, two top U.S. military men expressed deep misgivings about dropping the bomb. Adm. Leahy said he told President Truman in June that peace could be achieved if the surrender terms were modified. "The use of this barbarous weapon at Hiroshima and Nagasaki was of no material assistance in our war against Japan," he later wrote. When Stimson told Gen. Dwight D. Eisenhower in mid-July 1945 that the bomb would be used, Ike was disheartened by the news, he later recalled. "Japan was at that very moment seeking some way to surrender with a minimum loss of 'face,'" Eisenhower said in 1963. "It wasn't necessary to hit them with that awful thing."

On July 25, the day before the Potsdam Declaration was issued, Stimson approved a directive instructing the 509th Composite Group on Tinian Island in the Pacific to "deliver its first special bomb as soon as weather will permit visual bombing after about 3 August 1945 on one of the targets: Hiroshima, Kokura, Niigata and Nagasaki." The directive ordered that "additional bombs will be delivered on the above targets as soon as made ready by the project staff." Missing from the list was the city of Kyoto, which Stimson ruled out because of its religious and cultural importance. The four urban targets had been spared conventional bombing so U.S. military observers could see the A-bomb's full effect on large cities. Some atomic scientists—along with Vannevar Bush, who directed the Office of Scientific Research and Development, which was created to oversee scientific work for the war, and James B. Conant, chief science administrator for the Manhattan Project—believed that it was necessary to demonstrate the weapon on a city in order to alert the public to the horrors of nuclear weapons and the perils of a postwar arms race.

THE EMPEROR INTERVENES

THE EMPEROR HAD ENORMOUS SWAY OVER HIS SUBJECTS, WHO believed he was descended from the sun god. But when Hirohito's survival was at stake, military and civilian leaders became protective rather than deferential. Even after Hiroshima was destroyed on August 6 and the Soviet army invaded Japanese-occupied Manchuria on August 8, the cabinet debated whether to hold out for a promise from Washington that the emperor and the imperial system would remain in place. Only hours before the bombing of Nagasaki, Japan's Supreme Council for the Direction of the War was still arguing whether to accept the two-week-old Potsdam Declaration. Again the emperor intervened, urging that the terms be approved with the condition that his throne survive. On August 10, the day after the Nagasaki bombing, the Japanese government announced that it would accept the Potsdam formula provided that "it does not compromise any demand which prejudices the prerogatives of His Majesty as a Sovereign Ruler."

On August 14, worried that hard-liners would try to scuttle the surrender, Hirohito decided to take the unprecedented step of explaining his decision in a recorded message to be broadcast the next day. That night, a group of fanatical army officers broke into the palace grounds, murdering the commander of the Imperial Guards, in hopes of finding and destroying the recorded message. They were unable to find it, and loyal troops put down the uprising.

Studying Tokyo's surrender message at the White House with his top advisors, Truman noted that telegrams from the public were running 8-to-1 for *unconditional* surrender, a course favored by Byrnes. But Stimson argued that only the emperor

1945

JANUARY	FEBRUARY	MARCH	APRIL	MAY	JUNE	JULY	AUGUST
	● February 4: Allied leaders meet at Yalta ● February 19: Battle of Iwo Jima	● March 9-10: U.S. planes fire-bomb Tokyo, killing 83,000	● April 1: Battle of Okinawa begins; 12,000 Americans and up to 180,000 Japanese and Okinawans are killed ● April 12: Roosevelt dies; Truman is sworn in ● April 25: Stimson briefs Truman on the atomic bomb	● May 7: Germany surrenders ● May 28: Szilard and other scientists urge Byrnes not to use the bomb, but to place it under international control to prevent a U.S.-Soviet arms race. Byrnes believes the bomb will make the Soviets "more manageable"	● June 8: Japan's cabinet resolves to continue the war to the "bitter end" ● June 22: Emperor Hirohito pushes the Japanese government for a diplomatic end to the war	● July 12-13: Intercepted messages reveal that "unconditional surrender" is blocking Hirohito's peace efforts ● July 17: The Potsdam conference begins; Stalin tells Truman that the Soviets will invade Manchuria in August ● July 25: Stimson issues the order to use the bomb "after about August 3" ● July 26: The Potsdam Declaration warns Japan to surrender unconditionally or suffer "prompt and utter destruction" ● July 28: Japan's cabinet responds ambiguously to the Potsdam Declaration	● August 6: Hiroshima bombed ● August 8: The Soviets invade Manchuria ● August 9: Nagasaki bombed as Japan's cabinet debates surrender terms ● August 10: Japan accepts the Potsdam terms provided that the emperor stays ● August 14: Japan surrenders with assurances of retaining the emperor

could command Japan's army to surrender and prevent "a score of bloody Iwo Jimas and Okinawas." Byrnes finally agreed to a compromise: With surrender could come the guarantee that "the ultimate form of the Government of Japan shall be established by the freely expressed will of the Japanese people," as the Potsdam Declaration had stated. As the options were being considered, Truman permitted sea and air attacks to continue, including a 1,000-plane firebombing of Tokyo that ended on August 14 as he was announcing Japan's surrender. (The surrender produced an outcome similar to the one favored by Grew, Stimson and Forrestal. Under its postwar constitution, which was drawn up by U.S. occupation authorities, Japan became a constitutional monarchy. Sovereignty was given to the people, not to the emperor, whose powers were greatly diminished.)

If Japan's leaders were preparing to surrender, then what was the rush by the United States to use not one but two bombs "as soon as made ready"? Here diplomatic considerations come more strongly into play.

Historians Alperovitz, Sherwin and Robert Messer of the University of Illinois argue that Byrnes's main motive in wanting to use the bomb was not ending the Pacific war but preparing for what would become the Cold War with Russia. Byrnes had two objectives in mind: First, to halt Russian advances into Japanese-occupied Manchuria, thus limiting Moscow's territorial claims and influence in the Far East. Second, as Manhattan Project physicist Leo Szilard recalled from a May 1945 meeting with Byrnes, the future secretary of state did not argue that the bomb was necessary to win the war but that "the possession of the bomb by America would render the Russians more manageable in Europe."

A few scientists like Szilard felt caught between their ominous invention and the political and military leaders who would determine its use. Szilard had drafted for his friend Albert Einstein the 1939 letter to FDR that helped launch the Manhattan Project, and in the spring of 1945 he enlisted Einstein to write the president again, this time about the scientists' fears of a postwar nuclear arms race with Russia. But FDR had died in April before receiving the message, and when Szilard approached the Truman White House, he was sent to talk to Byrnes, who was about to be named secretary of state. When Byrnes proved unresponsive, scientists at the University of Chicago, led by Nobel laureate James Franck, drafted a report to the Interim Committee, which had been formed to advise President Truman on the new weapon.

The Franck report urged that the use of nuclear bombs in this war be considered as a problem of long-range national policy rather than of military expediency and recommended *demonstrating* the bomb to force Japan's surrender, rather than using it against cities. (In July, a poll of 150 Manhattan Project scientists revealed that 124 favored some sort of demonstration. But their leaders, including J. Robert Oppenheimer, director of the secret Los Alamos, New Mexico, laboratory where the bomb was designed and built, and several other Interim Committee members, argued for using the bomb on an actual target.) Byrnes was Truman's personal representative on the committee, and he threw the president's weight against demonstrating the new weapon without causing casualties.

Byrnes was very sensitive to domestic concerns about the Soviets' role after the war. He had been with Roosevelt at Yalta when the Allies worked out plans for dividing the territory conquered by Hitler, and he was responsible for selling that settlement to important voter blocs skeptical about Soviet intentions. Historian James Hershberg, of the Smithsonian's Woodrow Wilson Center and the author of a recent biography of Conant, notes that Stimson acknowledged in his memoirs, *On Active Service in War and Peace*, published in 1948, that the bomb was seen as a way to keep the Soviets from joining the war against Japan. The bomb also gave Britain and the U.S. what Stimson called "a badly needed 'equalizer'" to contain Soviet expansionism in the Far East and Europe. "You open up Stimson's diaries from April 1945 on," says Sherwin, "and you see, week after week, discussions that the bomb is central in dealing with the Russians."

Recalling the decision during a *U.S. News & World Report* interview in 1960, Byrnes said, "In the days immediately preceding the dropping of that bomb [Truman's] views were the same as mine—we wanted to get through with the Japanese phase of the war before the Russians came in." In this light, using the bomb so soon after the Potsdam Declaration, with the first planned invasion still almost three months off, seems driven not so much by a desire to save lives as to enhance American influence after the war. "It's important to recognize how much of American memory is myth," argues historian John W. Dower of M.I.T., author of *War Without Mercy*, a book about racial hatreds in the Pacific war. "For example, that we used the bomb simply to win the war and save American lives is the dominant myth." Dower believes the bomb was dropped "to make a political point to the Russians."

If the bombs were intended to impress the Soviets, they were an immediate success, as Stanford University historian David Holloway makes clear in his 1994 book, *Stalin and the Bomb*. Stalin had approved a modest atom bomb research program in early 1943, but he let months pass before he allowed his chief scientist, Igor Kurchatov, to see intelligence data gleaned by Soviet agents from British and American atomic research. At Potsdam on July 24, Truman mentioned casually to Stalin that the U.S. had "a new weapon of unusual destructive force." Stalin feigned lack of interest, although he already had reports from Soviet agent Klaus Fuchs at Los Alamos that a test had been scheduled for a week earlier. Stalin simply urged Truman to make "good use of it against the Japanese." But when Truman did use the bomb, Stalin was suddenly furious. He saw that Russia's place as a world power, gained with its victory against Hitler at the cost of 26 million lives, had just been erased. "Hiroshima has shaken the whole world," Stalin told Kurchatov. "The balance has been destroyed."

"AFTER MATURE CONSIDERATION"

ALSO DRIVING THE DECISION TO BOMB JAPAN WAS THE bureaucratic momentum that had been building since 1939 and the assumption that the new weapon would be used if it was ready in time. Although the original race to build the bomb was with Germany, Roosevelt and Churchill agreed at Hyde Park, New York, in September 1944 that when the bomb became available, "it might perhaps, after mature consideration, be used against the Japanese, who should be warned that this bombardment will be repeated until they surrender."

For his part, Gen. Leslie R. Groves, military director of the Manhattan Project, had no doubt about his mission. "Whenever anyone asked him," says Groves biographer Stanley Goldberg, "he said his work was 'To build the atomic bomb in the shortest time possible and thereby end the war.'" It was Groves who drafted the July 25 directive to bomb Japan as soon as weather permitted.

Several historians emphasized this point during a CIVILIZATION roundtable discussion at the Library of Congress. "The Interim Committee never received a military briefing to consider the alternatives relevant to the bomb in the context of the military situation," said Hershberg. "Use of the weapon was just as-

sumed." Noted Dower: "There were so many forces saying, 'Do it.' Only scientists like Szilard and Franck asked, 'What are we doing?'" As Janne Nolan, a historian of nuclear strategy, pointed out, "One of the enduring lessons of the A-bomb decision is the disconnection between the science and the politics of nuclear strategy. The Hiroshima decision was the birth of it."

Besides the Manhattan Project's internal momentum was an external motive. Its leaders had to justify the $2 billion ($26 billion in today's dollars) expense to Congress and the public, which had no idea of the scope of the A-bomb work, for the more than 160,000 workers at 37 top secret factories and labs around the country. These sites included the "Metallurgical Lab" at the University of Chicago, where the first nuclear chain reaction had been attained in 1942; huge plants for purifying uranium at Oak Ridge in Tennessee and for creating plutonium at Hanford in Washington state; and Los Alamos.

One of the reasons some in the Truman administration feared postwar investigations of the bomb effort was old-fashioned politics. If members of Congress were in the dark about the bomb, they nevertheless picked up the sweet scent of political pork. Truman was no exception. When he was still a senator, Truman became suspicious of huge public-works projects in Washington state and tried to investigate—hoping to lure jobs to Missouri. He pressed for hearings and wasn't dissuaded until Stimson himself said the work was secret and was FDR's highest priority.

By March 1945, after Byrnes had learned about the bomb, he warned Roosevelt that political scandal would follow if it was not used. And in May, Byrnes told Szilard: "How would you get Congress to appropriate money for atomic energy research [after the war] if you do not show results for the money which has been spent already?"

"There were people with responsibility for building the bomb who were scared to death that the war would end before they could use it," says historian Goldberg. Groves was stuck on the fact that the U.S. had produced two types of bombs—one using uranium, the other plutonium. Whenever anyone suggested that the moment the bomb was dropped the war would be over, Groves countered, "Not until we drop two bombs on Japan." As Goldberg explains Groves's actions, "One bomb justified Oak Ridge, the second justified Hanford." Hiroshima was hit with the uranium bomb, nicknamed "Little Boy"; the plutonium bomb, "Fat Man," was used against Nagasaki.

Even the strongest defenders of the Hiroshima bombing had difficulty justifying the attack on Nagasaki. For one thing, it was carried out before the Japanese could respond to Hiroshima; Japanese leaders were urgently reassessing their position on peace terms in the hours *before* the Nagasaki bombing. For another, the moral justification of Nagasaki was shaky at best. The attack was set in motion by the July 25 order, then propelled by bureaucratic momentum and weather conditions. The attack was supposed to take place on August 11, but was moved up to August 9 at Groves's urging. The primary target was Kokura, but overcast skies prompted U.S. fliers to hit Nagasaki instead. The clouds opened up just long enough for them to see the stadium that showed their location over the city.

Reasonable people will continue to disagree on whether the U.S. *needed* to bomb Hiroshima and Nagasaki to end the war. But it is beyond dispute that the decision to do so was messy and more haphazard than we might expect. President Truman, the "rational actor," was buffeted at every turn by strong constituencies: the ad hoc science panels headed by Bush and Conant, for example, and the secret Manhattan Project itself, which developed outside normal cabinet and congressional scrutiny. Other committees offered recommendations on surrender terms and on bomb policy. Groves's Target Committee, which selected the four Japanese cities, heightened the sense that using the bomb was inevitable.

Moreover, the new president was pushed and pulled by strong personalities who were determined to have a hand in shaping policy. Acting Secretary of State Grew believed that diplomacy would win the war—by modifying the unconditional-surrender terms, or by responding to the peace feelers that Japan was sending to neutral governments. When Byrnes succeeded Grew in July, however, his preoccupation with both domestic politics and U.S.-Soviet relations changed the department's focus. At Potsdam, Byrnes may have foreordained the use of the bomb when he deleted from the Allied declaration the section that would have clearly guaranteed the imperial institution in Japan.

The president should be exposed to the widest possible range of views—military, political, moral and practical. And this advice should be articulated by strong-minded and serious advisors. The problem with the bomb decision was that these points of view were not isolated, weighed and examined for ulterior motives. Taken together, they simply added to the bureaucratic momentum in favor of using the bomb.

In any event, Truman was in a weak position to reverse course on the bomb. While he is viewed today as a strong and successful president, in 1945 he was considered a lightweight by both the political establishment and ordinary Americans. FDR's death badly shook the nation's confidence. "To many it was not just that the greatest of men had fallen, but that the least of men—or at any rate the least likely of men—had assumed his place," wrote recent Truman biographer David McCullough. A measure of Truman's low standing is the fact that he had been president for two weeks before Stimson deigned to brief him on the bomb. Perhaps Roosevelt alone had the political stature *not* to use the weapon he had helped create.

Sometimes it seems that the only constant in history is the law of unintended consequences. Sherwin and other historians argue that archival evidence shows that the bomb, instead of shortening the war and saving many lives, may actually have prolonged the fighting. They conclude that the Japanese were ready to surrender as early as the spring of 1945—if Truman had only assured them that they could retain the emperor. But by anticipating that the bomb would soon be available, Stimson and others held out for the Allies' "unconditional" terms. Stimson conceded much in his memoirs, observing that "history might find that the United States, by its delay in stating its position [on the surrender terms], had prolonged the war."

Most historians believe that the Cold War, growing out of Western efforts to contain Soviet expansionism, would have occurred even if the bomb had not been used against Japan. The Soviets would have developed their own bomb anyway, which would have touched off a nuclear arms race. But the specter of Hiroshima and Nagasaki always hung over the world. For nearly half a century, the United States and the Soviet Union held each other at bay by following a policy with the fitting acronym MAD: mutually assured destruction. Even today, with the Cold War over, the civilized world lives in fear that a renegade state might resort to nuclear weapons and set off a global cataclysm.

As rational people, we like to think that momentous decisions are based on reason and conviction or, in the words used in 1944 at Hyde Park, "mature consideration." Hiroshima reminds us that fear and doubt are every bit as important as reason and conviction. Whatever the verdict on the bombing of Japan, one thing is certain: It was not done after "mature consideration." At a time when humanity has developed weapons powerful enough to destroy the planet, that failure may be the most important legacy of the Pacific war.

BOOKS ABOUT THE BOMB

ATOMIC DIPLOMACY: Hiroshima and Potsdam, *Gar Alperovitz.* Pluto Press, 1994.

THE ATOMIC BOMB AND THE END OF WORLD WAR II, *Herbert Feis.* Princeton University Press, 1966.

THE ATOMIC BOMB: The Critical Issues, *Barton J. Bernstein* (ed.). Little, Brown, 1976.

JAMES B. CONANT: Harvard to Hiroshima and the Making of the Nuclear Age, *James G. Hershberg.* Alfred A. Knopf, 1993.

DANGER AND SURVIVAL: Choices about the Bomb in the First 50 Years, *McGeorge Bundy.* Vintage Books, 1990.

EAGLE AGAINST THE SUN: The American War with Japan, *Ronald H. Spector.* Vintage Books, 1985.

STALIN AND THE BOMB: The Soviet Union and Atomic Energy, 1939-1956, *David Holloway.* Yale University Press, 1994.

THE DECISION TO DROP THE BOMB, *Len Giovannitti and Fred Freed.* Coward-McCann, 1965.

THE MAKING OF THE ATOMIC BOMB, *Richard Rhodes.* Simon & Schuster, 1986.

MANHATTAN, THE ARMY AND THE ATOMIC BOMB, *Vincent C. Jones.* Center of Military History, U.S. Army, 1985.

TENNOZAN: The Battle of Okinawa and the Atomic Bomb, *George Feifer.* Ticknor & Fields, 1992.

WAR WITHOUT MERCY: Race and Power in the Pacific War, *John W. Dower.* Pantheon, 1986.

A WORLD DESTROYED: The Atomic Bomb and the Grand Alliance, *Martin J. Sherwin.* Vintage Books, 1977.

THE END OF AN ALLIANCE: James F. Byrnes, Roosevelt, Truman, and the Origins of the Cold War, *Robert L. Messer.* University of North Carolina Press, 1982.

The Era of the Cold War, 1950–1990

With the threat of atomic warfare ever present, the "cold war" began between the United States and the Soviet Union at the end of World War II. It was a war of competition for political and military supremacy, but no direct shooting. Nuclear-tipped missiles, atomic submarines, H-bombs, elaborate defensive lines of bases, and huge armies were a part of this war. In "Heating Up the Cold War," T. A. Heppenheimer describes this military technology. In part, because of its cost, the United States, like Great Britain in an earlier period, changed from the largest creditor nation in the world into the world's greatest debtor. Perhaps there was little choice.

In cold war history there are various major events, such as the Cuban missile crisis, Korean War, Vietnam War, and Afghanistan War. With the breakup of the Soviet Union, information has become increasingly available that indicates how close the superpowers came to attacking one another. One occasion was during the Berlin crisis in 1961, when tanks aimed their guns at each other across Checkpoint Charlie. Raymond Garthoff explains what happened and how it was stopped by negotiation through informal channels. The cold war came to a surprise end with the breakdown of the Soviet Union and the breakup of this former superpower into constituent pieces. Shlomo Avineri, in "The Return to History: The Breakup of the Soviet Union," points out that the pieces reflect earlier historical patterns, even with the return of old street names.

The reasons for the breakdown are still unclear, but American politicians have been quick to claim that it was a victory of foreign policy and pressure. Soviets tend to blame the event upon internal economic problems. The article "Who Broke Down This Wall?" summarizes these various views. The shock waves of the breakup of the USSR are still in motion around the world. In Central America there has been a necessary adjustment by leftist revolutionary forces. They no longer receive aid and inspiration from the Soviet Union. What will happen in Cuba remains to be worked out. In China, where the

1989 student rebellion of Tiananmen Square was crushed, there also seems to be a sort of waiting. The world and the Chinese are waiting to see what will happen to the last great communist nation with its aging leaders.

During this period of the cold war, the colonial empires ended and new nations, inspired by Western ideals about nationalism, liberalism, socialism, and capitalism, stepped onto the world stage. The West, exhausted by warfare, stepped aside. There was little choice. Between 1944 and 1990, 90 countries became independent. The United Nations started with 51 members after World War II, and in 1990 it listed 159 members.

Africa changed almost totally from being white-controlled to black-controlled in 30 year's time. The African states, however, often lacked economic balance and democratic traditions. Westerners generally have thought that nationalism has failed in Africa. In June 1987, for example, the Central African Republic sentenced its former dictator, Jean-Bedel Bokassa, to be shot to death. He was responsible for over 20 murders and for spending $100 million for his coronation as emperor in 1977. His poor, landlocked nation had a population of only 3 million people. In "A Decade of Decline," George Ayittey reports a negative growth rate for Africa during the 1980s that has left the continent on the edge of economic and political chaos. Perhaps we tend to judge Africa too much in Western terms, but the presence of AIDS, as reported in unit 6, will likely strike the hardest in Africa. It is an additional storm cloud for the continent.

The West not only retreated from Africa, but also from India and the Middle East. In India, Mohandas Gandhi led a long struggle for independence that played upon British weaknesses and their sense of law and ethics. In 1947 the British left behind a nation of enormous population that spoke 16 different languages. The British also gave up in the Middle East, but worked to leave behind the independent state of Israel. Unfortunately, there were Arab claims to the same land. In the time

since World War II, the Middle East has remained a land simmering with complaints, bitterness, and war. There are many great misunderstandings, as Akbar Ahmed explains in his essay, and the cultural power of the West is a basic problem for people of Islamic faith.

Looking Ahead: Challenge Questions

What was the role of technology in the cold war?

Who won the cold war? How was this accomplished?

Why did the cold war remain "cold" between the superpowers?

Why did the colonial empires end?

What were the results of colonialism in Africa? How can national progress be measured?

Of what use is history for prediction about the future of the Middle East, Africa, and the former USSR?

Heating Up The Cold War

Missiles and nuclear submarines and hydrogen warheads came forth in a single decade, transfiguring both war and peace forever

T. A. Heppenheimer

T. A. Heppenheimer is an associate fellow of the American Institute of Aeronautics and Astronautics. He writes often for *Invention & Technology*.

It was mid-June of 1952, and President Harry Truman was at the Electric Boat Company shipyard in Groton, Connecticut. Off to his side lay a huge, bright yellow steel plate that was to become part of the keel of a new submarine. Truman gave a speech, and then a crane lifted the plate and laid it before him. He walked down a few steps and chalked his initials on its surface, whereupon a welder stepped forward and burned them into the steel. The USS *Nautilus*, the world's first nuclear submarine, was under construction.

At that moment the Korean War was under way. For the United States the struggle was proving to resemble the Pacific war of nearly a decade earlier. Jet planes ruled the skies, but otherwise the weaponry was essentially the same. The B-29, with its four piston-driven engines, was still the standard Air Force bomber, and the massive air raids against Pyongyang recalled the destruction of Tokyo. At sea the Navy was operating the battleships, cruisers, and submarines of the last war.

Yet less than a decade later, the basic principles of American defense would be undergoing the most sweeping of transformations. The nuclear sub would be on its way to becoming the Navy's most important craft, supplanting even the aircraft carrier, and—equipped with long-range Polaris missiles—would pro-

vide a means to destroy the Soviet Union that could not be countered or even detected. On land the Air Force's ballistic missiles—Atlas, Titan, and Thor—would offer a similar prospect of sudden and devastating strikes. Meanwhile, at Cape Canaveral, Florida, the first of an even more advanced type of missile, the quick-firing, solid-fueled Minuteman, would be undergoing flight tests.

The shift would be under way from delivering ordnance near the point of attack from planes, ships, and artillery to delivering it from subs and silos hundreds or thousands of miles away. Although America's armaments of the early 1950s, and the strategies behind them, were those of World War II, within ten years they looked very much as they do today.

This shift took place during the Presidency of Dwight Eisenhower. Yet there would prove to be great symbolism in the fact that it was Truman laying that keel plate. His administration had prepared much of the technical groundwork for the weapons revolution, sowing the seeds that Ike would reap. And the *Nautilus*, the work of the Navy's Capt. Hyman Rickover, would be more than just an essential component of these changes. It would stand as a demonstration of how a few brilliant people could creatively seize vast opportunities.

RICKOVER

Nothing as specific as a nuclear submarine was in the minds of the Navy's

senior commanders immediately after World War II, when they began to consider the possibilities of atomic fission. They envisioned only a succession of experimental projects, at least for some time into the future. But an advance at flank speed, leading to real fighting ships powered by the atom, quickly became Hyman Rickover's personal agenda.

Rickover knew that a nuclear-powered submarine would have enormous advantages over conventional ones. The submarines of World War II ran on a combination of diesel and electric power. The diesel engines were fired up upon surfacing, and they both propelled the craft and charged its batteries. Below the sea a submarine had to rely on battery power. This limited underwater speeds to a maximum of eight or nine knots; more important, it meant that a submarine could stay submerged only until its batteries ran out. At peak speeds this could be as little as one hour.

A nuclear submarine, its reactors driving steam-turbine engines, not only would go faster—cruising at speeds of twenty knots—but would be able to stay submerged for weeks at a time, with purification equipment providing oxygen for the crew to breathe. Few had the vision to see that far ahead, but Hyman Rickover did, and he had the tenacity to make his vision a reality. His start came in 1946 with an assignment to the Oak Ridge nuclear laboratory, where he was to take part in designing an experimental reactor.

From *American Heritage of Invention & Technology*, Fall 1992, pp. 21-30. © 1992 by Forbes, Inc. Reprinted by permission of *American Heritage* magazine, a division of Forbes, Inc.

(Many scientists from Oak Ridge would later follow Rickover to his submarine-reactor group.)

Rickover was an Annapolis graduate, but definitely not one to play the social games of the officers' club. He was already known as a plainspoken man who would set his own standards of excellence and insist that they be met. He had made his name during the war as head of the electrical section in the Bureau of Ships (BuShips), a post that in other hands might have involved no more than administering contracts and keeping track of schedules. He had built up a staff of the best engineers he could find, both naval and civilian. He inspected every war-damaged ship he could visit, to learn how electrical equipment was standing up to combat, and he uncovered scores of deficiencies: circuit breakers that popped open at the firing of a ship's guns, cables that leaked and carried water to switchboards, junction boxes that emitted poisonous gases in a fire.

His staffers not only designed new types of equipment but even developed basic engineering data on such topics as shock resistance. Rickover picked the contractors who would build the equipment, worked with them closely, and made sure that their products would be ready on time and meet his demanding specifications. He would use the same methods as head of the Navy's nuclear program.

Of course no such program existed right after the war, and no one anywhere had even built the kind of reactor a Navy nuclear program would need. The wartime Manhattan Project had used low-power atomic piles to produce plutonium. A high-power reactor, capable of driving a ship, would be a completely different matter, requiring new engineering knowledge. Rickover thus had a threefold task: to set up a department with the necessary authority; to gain the technical understanding that would make his reactors feasible; and to overcome bureaucratic inertia, pushing ahead far more rapidly than many of his superiors thought possible. And he would have to do these things while

holding no higher rank than captain.

It helped that he had strong support from the chief of BuShips from 1946 to 1949, Vice Adm. Earle Mills. In August 1948, after a year of military-civilian bickering and turf wars, Mills set up within his bureau a new Nuclear Power Branch, which would develop into the core of Rickover's organizational empire. But this naval office could do little on its own; the Atomic Energy Act of 1946 had specified that the new Atomic Energy Commission (AEC), a civilian agency, would have the prime responsibility for developing nuclear power. The AEC originally tried to concentrate on peaceful uses of nuclear power, but the needs of the military were pressing; it soon established an office to develop reactors for submarine propulsion, while the Navy designed the submarines themselves. By early 1949 the AEC's Naval Reactors Branch was in business, and Rickover was running it. He thus was wearing two hats, naval and civilian.

Such an arrangement might have diluted his authority amid endless committees, but characteristically he made it into a source of strength. If he ran into an obstacle within the Navy, he could always don his AEC hat and try anew within that agency. He found that the AEC would give him considerable leeway as a Navy man, and vice versa. He would even draft letters for his boss at the commission to sign, requesting naval help, and then draft the approving letter for Mills's signature at BuShips.

Within this dual office Rickover sought to sweep away distinctions based on hierarchy, whether military or civilian. He knew only too well how naval officers could pull rank to get their way, and he wanted to ensure that all decisions were based on technical merit. He thus sponsored a major educational program for his staff, arranging for courses in nuclear science. He also encouraged vigorous debate over technical issues at free-for-all staff meetings and made sure that everyone had the license to declare that the emperor had no clothes. If you worked for Rickover, you had no time for protocol or organization

charts; what mattered was what you knew and how much responsibility you could take.

From the outset Rickover had to watch out for two pitfalls. The first he knew from his wartime days: not to assume that industrial contractors were fully capable. His people would have to do far more than merely sign off on routine paperwork. The second pitfall was peculiar to the nuclear community. It was top-heavy with physicists more interested in research than in practical engineering. Thus, when the principal AEC contracts went to such monoliths as General Electric and Westinghouse, Rickover took care to direct some of their effort into accumulating data for engineering handbooks that would form a foundation for the technology. His reactors would rely on exotic materials—zirconium, hafnium, beryllium, liquid sodium—and he made sure that the necessary know-how would be as solidly established as the production facilities.

Under traditional procedures Rickover would have had the AEC build a succession of test reactors, eventually using one in an experimental vessel. The Navy, in its own good time, might then have gotten around to setting forth requirements for an actual nuclear-powered fighting ship. But Rickover insisted that there must be only a single test reactor, Mark I. (In fact, Rickover's group pursued two independent prototypes, Mark I and Mark A. The former was water-cooled; the latter got its power from more energetic neutrons and used liquid sodium as a coolant. Mark A ultimately formed the basis for the Seawolf class of submarines, but it took longer to develop.) As far as possible Mark I would be the same as the succeeding operational version, Mark II; in Rickover's words, "Mark I equals Mark II." This focus on Mark I would cut years off the program and would enable Rickover, with his two-hat management, to put the Navy on the spot. There would have to be a hull ready to receive Mark II when it was built.

That vessel was to be the *Nautilus*, and Rickover insisted that it be a real fighting ship, complete with torpedoes. Moreover, to meet his schedule, he wanted the necessary high-level approvals ready by the spring of 1950. Events lent him a hand, for in August of 1949 the Soviets detonated their first atomic bomb. Truman, told of the news, shook his head and asked, "Are you sure? Are you sure?" Finally he said heavily, "This means we have no time left." Early in 1950 he approved a top priority effort to develop the hydrogen bomb, a project that had Air Force written all over it. Rickover's submarine offered the Navy a chance to hitch its own wagon to the nuclear star, and in April the Navy's general board, which had responsibility for shipbuilding plans, decided that the *Nautilus* would proceed as Rickover wished.

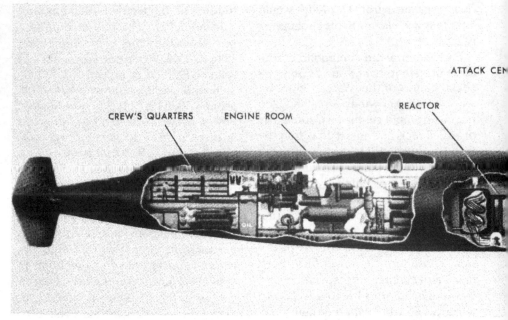

CREW'S QUARTERS   ENGINE ROOM   REACTOR   ATTACK CEN

MISSILES

While the Navy was working on submarines, the Air Force and Army were nurturing the concepts that would lead to the long-range missile. The point of departure was the wartime German V-2 rocket, which had struck London by the hundreds during 1944 and 1945. Its designers, led by Wernher von Braun, were guests of the Army at the White Sands Proving Ground in New Mexico, where in 1946 they began firing captured V-2s while dreaming of better things. They constituted one of three principal groups working in this area.

The second group was at North American Aviation, in the Los Angeles area. It pursued a concept called Navaho, which in its earliest versions was to resemble a V-2 fitted with wings and ramjet engines. The wings would allow it to glide, increasing its range; the ramjets would extend its range further still. The Navaho project was eventually canceled by the Air Force, but it formed the basis for several other types of military and scientific rockets.

The third group was at Convair, in San Diego. Its leader, the Belgian-born Karel Bossart, had a particularly far-reaching plan involving three interrelated projects. First there would be an unmanned jet aircraft to test a guidance system. This would be Teetotaler, the only one of the three projects that would not burn alcohol as its fuel. Next

Rickover would draft a letter for his boss at the AEC to sign, then draft a reply for his Navy boss.

would come Old Fashioned, a missile incorporating many new features but still in many ways resembling the V-2. The third project, Manhattan, would be an intercontinental rocket and carry the atomic bomb.

Teetotaler never got anywhere, and Old Fashioned quickly emerged as the centerpiece of the effort. Whereas the V-2 had been built in aircraft fashion, with a framework covered with sheet metal enclosing propellant tanks, Old Fashioned would eliminate the framework and have internal bulkheads walling off sections to serve as the tanks. Nitrogen gas, pressurizing the interior, would give it rigidity and strength, like an inflated automobile tire.

The V-2 had flown in one piece, hur-

tling through the atmosphere like an arrow. Old Fashioned, by contrast, would carry its payload in a nose cone that would detach from the rest of the missile once fuel ran out, avoiding the drag of the empty rocket. Its engines would steer the missile by swiveling on gimbals, to give steady thrust. That would improve on the V-2, which had steered by dipping graphite vanes into its exhaust, a procedure that reduced thrust by up to 17 percent. Old Fashioned was to combine light weight and high performance, using technical features that could later be employed in Manhattan.

There was enough money in the budget for Convair to build three Old Fashioneds, and all of them flew at White Sands during 1948. Hopes were high that the rockets would reach an altitude of a hundred miles, but premature engine cutoffs kept them from topping thirty. Still, the flights sufficed to show that Bossart's design was basically sound.

Nevertheless, the Air Force, which had been funding the work, declined to follow it up. The reason was that the guidance systems of the day were too inaccurate. Vannevar Bush, the wartime head of the U.S. Office of Scientific Research and Development, had summed up the matter as early as December 1945: "People have been talking about a 3,000-mile, high-angle rocket, shot from one continent to

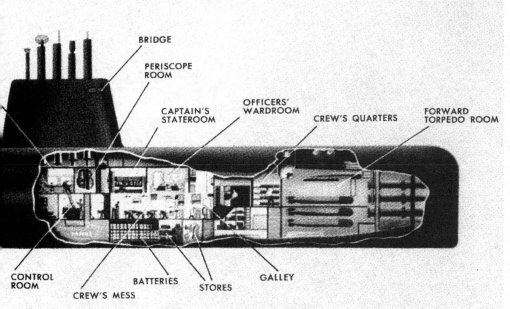

BRIDGE

PERISCOPE ROOM

CAPTAIN'S STATEROOM

OFFICERS' WARDROOM

CREW'S QUARTERS

FORWARD TORPEDO ROOM

CONTROL ROOM

CREW'S MESS

BATTERIES

STORES

GALLEY

COURTESY OF ELECTRIC BOAT COMPANY, GENERAL DYNAMICS CORPORATION

another, carrying an atomic bomb . . . which would land exactly on a certain target, such as a city. I say, technically I don't think anybody in the world knows how to do such a thing, and I feel confident it will not be done for a very long period of time to come. I wish the American public would leave that out of their thinking."

The first challenge to this conviction emerged in December 1950, when an Air Force study concluded that such significant advances were under way in both rocket engines and guidance systems that a long-range missile might indeed be practical. The report brought new life to Convair's Manhattan concept, and the following August Manhattan was rechristened Atlas. Atlas, according to Bossart's new studies, would have the capability of being the first intercontinental ballistic missile (ICBM)—one that could cross oceans on an accurate path. It was eventually to carry an 8,000-pound bomb 5,000 nautical miles and strike within 1,500 feet of its target. Under various proposed designs, the rocket would stand as much as 180 feet tall, lifting off with a million pounds of thrust provided by seven engines.

Such a behemoth was far too large for a practical weapon, but there was hope that emerging technology would enable it to be scaled down. Under the Navaho program, North American

Aviation was pursuing an alcohol-fueled engine of 120,000 pounds' thrust, which was likely to become an industry standard. And advances in weapon design were promising to shrink the atom bomb to as little as 3,000 pounds. The size and thrust of Atlas could then decrease concomitantly. Between 1952 and 1954, as Eisenhower entered the White House, these hopes were realized to the fullest.

THE H-BOMB

Ike's election coincided with the first test of a true hydrogen bomb, in November 1952. The experiment was called Mike. Its fireball reached a diameter of several miles, spreading so far and fast that it terrified observers who had seen many previous tests, even though the nearest of them were forty miles away. In the words of the weapons physicist Theodore Taylor, it "was so huge, so brutal—as if things had gone too far. When the heat reached the observers, it stayed and stayed, not for seconds but for minutes." It blew an island completely out of existence as it delivered its yield of 10.4 megatons, nearly a thousand times that of the Hiroshima bomb.

For advocates of Atlas, Mike meant that bombs of arbitrarily great destructive power were at hand. That could vastly ease the problem of missile guidance, because such a warhead might

miss by several miles and still wipe out its target. But Mike was not a practical weapon; it was more like a railroad tank car, 22 feet long, 5.5 feet wide, and weighing more than 40,000 pounds. It also required refrigeration apparatus weighing 65 tons to keep its liquid tritium and deuterium cold. Could such megaton yields could be had from a design small enough to fly atop an Atlas of reasonable size?

It fell to John Von Neumann, one of the world's leading mathematicians and physicists, to answer this question. He was an old nuclear hand, having been among the principal designers of the plutonium bomb dropped on Nagasaki. He gathered a review panel that reported in June 1953 that a half-megaton H-bomb could be made to weigh just 3,000 pounds and could fit in a missile. In September the Air Force Special Weapons Center revised this estimate, stating that bombs with that yield could weigh only 1,500 pounds. That meant Atlas could be reduced to a three-engine rocket of little more than one-third the weight of the 1951 design.

Events quickly accelerated, driven by a new urgency: the Soviets had exploded their own hydrogen bomb, and intelligence estimates pointed to a Soviet lead in missile development. Trevor Gardner, a special assistant to Air Force Secretary Harold E. Talbott, responded by having Von Neumann head another panel to review the entire strategic-missile program. The group, code-named the Teapot Committee, declared that the required accuracy "should be relaxed from the present 1,500 feet to at least two, and probably three, nautical miles."

The committee's report came in February 1954. Its message was strongly underscored on March 1 with a test of Bravo, a new lightweight, high-yield H-bomb using lithium deuteride, which needed no refrigeration. Bravo yielded fifteen megatons, more than even Mike, and could be delivered by air. It was abundantly clear now that small bombs could become destructive enough to make pinpoint accuracy unnecessary. Armed with this knowledge, less than three weeks later Talbott directed an immediate and major step-up in Atlas development. Gardner described this as "the maximum effort possible with no limitation as to funding." In mid-May the Secretary of Defense, Charles Wilson, granted Atlas the Air Force's highest priority for funding. The break from World War II weapons had been made.

There was more. Wilson decided that the need for an ICBM was so great that the nation could not risk putting all its eggs into the Atlas basket; there would have to be a second ICBM program. This emerged as Titan. The Titan missile would be built with aircraft-type structures rather than Atlas's pressurized steel shell and by a completely separate set of principal contractors, led by the Glenn L. Martin Company.

Defending against an unknown but potentially terrifying Soviet threat was so urgent that even in a crash program Atlas and Titan would take unacceptably long to build. So the government instituted two more programs to build stopgap missiles of 1,500-mile range more quickly. These missiles, to be based in Europe, were the Air Force's Thor, built by Douglas Aircraft, and the Army's Jupiter, designed by von Braun's group, which had moved from White Sands to Redstone Arsenal in Huntsville, Alabama.

Thus by 1954 the United States was going full throttle with four nuclear-missile programs: intercontinental Atlas and Titan (both Air Force) and intermediate-range Thor (Air Force) and Jupiter (Army). In both categories the government was banking on diversity and competition, hoping that having separate programs would create interservice and intercompany rivalries and spur project workers to greater achievement.

PROBLEMS AND SOLUTIONS

The development of these projects called for far more than just money; there were wrenching technical dif-

U.S. NAVY

The USS *Sam Rayburn* at Newport News, Virginia, in 1964. The sixteen tubes were used to launch Polaris missiles.

ficulties. At the top of the list was the re-entry problem. Near the end of its flight a warhead would re-enter the atmosphere at up to 16,000 miles an hour, carrying enough energy to vaporize five times its weight in iron. Its front end would face temperatures hotter than the sun's surface. How could it survive?

An initial answer came in 1951 in a classified document from two scientists, H. Julian Allen and Alfred Eggers, of the National Advisory Committee for Aeronautics. They calculated that if a nose cone was blunt enough, the adjacent airflow would carry away virtually all the heat, leaving only one part in two hundred to sink into the warhead. Soon Arthur Kantrowitz, a Cornell University physicist who would be dubbed "Mr. Nose Cone" by *Time* mag-

azine, gave experimental data leading to the "heat sink" concept, in which a missile's front end would be made of solid copper—heavy but able to absorb the heat. Kantrowitz later developed a lightweight "ablative" nose cone that carried away the heat by actually letting its outer layers slowly vaporize. But heat-sink designs were good enough for the early missile flights.

Atlas, Titan, Thor, and Jupiter were all liquid-fueled. They ran on kerosene (or similar hydrocarbons) and liquid oxygen, which offered high energy and accurate control. But rocket engines were a plumber's nightmare, and the propellants took time to load, time that would be in very short supply during a Soviet attack. (Liquid oxygen could not be stored in the rockets because it would evaporate.) A solid-propellant rocket, on the other hand, would come with its fuel in place, ready to be fired at a moment's notice, and would theoretically be far simpler to design and operate.

Such weapons had been in use for centuries; fueled with black powder, they had produced Francis Scott Key's "rockets' red glare" during the War of 1812. The propellants of World War II often used a potent solid mix of nitroglycerin and nitrocellulose, but the resulting charges of fuel tended to develop cracks and then explode. This could be prevented only by fabricating the charges in modest sizes, and so the largest such rocket of the war, Germany's Rheinbote, had no more than 539 pounds of fuel in a single chunk.

The path toward solid-fueled rockets of large size proved to lie in a liquid polysulfide polymer called Thiokol, produced by a struggling firm known as Thiokol Chemical Corporation. It could easily be cured into a solvent-resistant synthetic rubber, and during World War II it had found use sealing aircraft fuel tanks. After 1945 this market disappeared, and business was so slow that almost any small order would draw the attention of Thiokol's president, Joseph Crosby. When he learned in 1946 that the California Institute of Technology's Jet Propulsion Laboratory was buying five- and ten-gallon lots in a steady stream, he became interested enough to fly out and see what its people were up to. He found that a rocket-research group was mixing the polymer with an oxidizer and adding powdered aluminum for extra energy, then using the result as a propellant. What was more, the group was on its way toward using this propellant in ways that would make possible long-range solid-fuel rockets.

Crosby soon decided that with help from the Army, he would go into the rocket business himself. The Army could spare only $250,000 to help Thiokol get started, but to him this was big money. Then in 1950, at the start of the Korean War, Army Ordnance awarded Thiokol a contract to build a rocket called Hermes with 5,000 pounds of propellant. Hermes was a demonstration project, meant to show that solid fuel could work in a large-scale rocket. It was successfully fired the following year, and with this the prospect was at hand for solid fuels that could challenge the liquids.

MISSILES AT SEA

The Army and Air Force were still fully committed to liquid fuels, but within the Navy a few people were open to the new possibilities presented by solids. The Navy's Bureau of Aeronautics (BuAer) was developing submarine-launched cruise missiles—small, unmanned aircraft that would fly over short ranges under the control of advanced autopilots. In 1954 two BuAer scientists, Robert Freitag and Abraham Hyatt, decided to lobby for a ballistic-missile program with long-range rockets. Such a program could give the Navy a striking power comparable to the Air Force's. And with the missiles carried in nuclear submarines, such a force could stay at sea for long periods—mobile, difficult to detect, and nearly invulnerable.

Freitag and Hyatt soon won support from James R. Killian, president of MIT and an influential adviser to Eisenhower. They also gained strong backing from their superior, the chief of BuAer, Rear Adm. James Russell. Then, in August 1955, these two were joined by the heaviest of naval guns, Adm. Arleigh Burke, a wartime destroyer-man who took over as chief of naval operations and endorsed the new concept within a week.

The next move lay with Defense Secretary Wilson, who promptly put the Navy in bed with the Army. Amid furious interservice rivalries, he wanted to keep budgets under control, and he and Ike agreed that no new rocket programs must be started beyond the four already being funded. In November Wilson approved the Navy's ballistic-missile proposal but directed Burke to use someone else's rocket. The only choices were the two 1,500-mile missiles, Thor and Jupiter. The lesser of these evils was the Army's liquid-fueled Jupiter, not for technical reasons but because Army officials feared that Wilson would cancel their program. This encouraged them to hold their noses and work with the admirals.

Navy officials were frank in stating that they would switch to solid fuel as soon as such a move was technically feasible. The first step, completed early in 1956, was to commission a study of a solid-fueled missile with the performance of Jupiter. It proved to be a monster, 44 feet long and 10 feet in diameter, weighing 160,000 pounds. A follow-up study examined the feasibility of shrinking major components, including the nose cone and guidance system. This produced a far more encouraging conclusion: Such a missile could weigh 30,000 pounds. The question then was the same that had faced Atlas: Could the missile's nuclear warheads be similarly shrunk while preserving a useful yield?

The physicist Edward Teller, a co-inventor of the hydrogen bomb, believed that while such shrinking was not yet possible in 1956, the trend of nuclear development would permit it

U.S. MISSILE PROGRAMS OF THE 1950s					
Name	Begun	Deployed	Range	Sponsoring Service	Fuel
Atlas	1954	1960	Intercontinental	Air Force	Liquid
Jupiter	1955	1959	Intermediate	Army	Liquid
Thor	1955	1959	Intermediate	Air Force	Liquid
Titan	1955	1962	Intercontinental	Air Force	Liquid
Polaris (Sea-based)	1956	1960	Intermediate	Navy	Solid
Minuteman	1958	1962	Intercontinental	Air Force	Solid

in due time. Early in September the AEC confirmed Teller's prediction, stating that a suitable warhead could weigh as little as 600 pounds. With this estimate the Navy could make a new pitch to Secretary Wilson. This time, though, it had a sweetener: a projection that the new missile program would save half a billion dollars over the continued use of Jupiters. In December the Secretary gave his approval, ensuring that the nation would now have a fifth long-range missile to go along with Atlas, Titan, Thor, and Jupiter. Its name would be Polaris.

Polaris drew on the technologies supporting the other programs, but it faced a problem peculiar to its alliance with the submarine. Nuclear subs, navigating beneath the sea for long periods, would have to rely on inertial guidance, a system of determining motion and position by using sensitive accelerometers and exquisitely precise gyroscopes. Developing such guidance systems for the missiles themselves was a high priority, and work was under way in that area at MIT's Instrumentation Laboratory. But missile guidance systems would need to work for only a few minutes; a Ships Inertial Navigation System (SINS) would have to maintain its accuracy for weeks.

Fortunately, the necessary precision could be had by making SINS larger than its missile-borne cousins, because a submarine would offer plenty of room. The first version of such a system made its debut late in 1953. It was tested by being carried in a truck from Boston to Washington, and it gave an error of sixteen miles during the nineteen-hour run, which wasn't much to brag about. Tests in ships followed, demonstrating some improvement, but it still wasn't good enough, and it never got past the testing phase. However, there was another major source for inertial guidance, the Autonetics Division of North American Aviation, which had been developing such a system for the Navaho missile program. Navaho would be canceled in 1957, as Secretary Wilson decided that it could not compete in performance with the ICBMs. But by early 1958, with help from Autonetics, SINS was navigating

with an accuracy of an eighth of a mile during a sixty-day cruise.

GETTING THE JOB DONE

In both the Navy and the Air Force, the emphasis was very much on accomplishing things in a hurry with a minimum of fuss. (The Army placed less emphasis on missiles, so its lone program had lower bureaucratic priority.) The drama and challenge of these projects attracted the talented and capable, and as Gen. Bernard A. Schriever, who headed the Air Force effort, later recalled, "we did not always have lawyers at our elbows, and every time we decided to do something, we did not have a long legal brief to contend with. I could tell any contractor, do this or do that, and the paperwork would follow."

Rear Adm. William F. Raborn, the head of the Polaris project, ran his program virtually as a navy within the Navy. His authority came from Admiral Burke, who had written him in a letter: "If Rear Admiral Raborn runs into any difficulty with which I can help, I will want to know about it at once, along with his recommended course of ac-

During little more than two years, Atlas, Polaris, and Minuteman all came through with flights at full range.

tion. . . . If more money is needed, we will get it. If he needs more people, those people will be ordered in. If there is anything that slows this project up beyond the capacity of the Navy and the department, we will immediately take it to the highest level and not work our way up through several

days." With this authority Raborn was able to seize the crown jewels from Rickover himself, who remained in charge of naval reactors. Raborn needed a submarine, and he learned that a successor to the *Nautilus* was approaching completion at Electric Boat's yard in Groton, Connecticut. Raborn took charge of it, cut it in two, inserted a 130-foot bay in its midsection that would hold the Polaris missiles, and had it in commission by the end of 1959 as the USS *George Washington*.

"We used a philosophy of utter communication," Raborn said later. "There was no such thing as hiding anything from anybody who had an interest in it. And there was nothing that got a person into trouble, whether he was a civilian contractor or in uniform or in civil service, quicker than to delay reporting potential trouble. And, boy, if he waited until he had trouble, then he really had trouble."

To run their programs, though, Raborn and particularly Schriever needed more than lavish funds and overriding authority; they needed raw courage. Their developmental policy was literally to shoot first and ask questions later: to fire off unarmed test missiles knowing full well that they would explode, then pick through telemetered data and recovered wreckage to seek the source of the failures. Since figures used for stresses and forces within the engines were often no more than estimates, engineers had to see what parts would fail before they could fix them. As one veteran of those days put it, "It wasn't that the first vehicle that flies must be a demonstrated success and capable of being advertised to the world at large."

But the project directors were living in a political goldfish bowl, and what people could see were the test-missile explosions. Fortunately, the spirit of total communication extended to Congress as well as to the contractors, and Raborn and Schriever, along with Rickover, found they were being relied on as national resources.

It also helped that Congress and the President offered all the money that was needed. In an odd twist this policy kept costs down, for overruns occur when large numbers of people draw salaries for long periods of time while producing little of value. Professional challenges drew in a generation of the best managers and technical people, and their only mandate was to get the job done quickly.

A KICK IN THE PANTS

Then came October 1957, and the biggest shock yet: the launch of *Sputnik*, the first Soviet satellite. Its effect within Washington was cataclysmic, for it pointed all too sharply toward a substantial Soviet lead in the development of the strategic missile, which was the means for launching such spacecraft. A month later Moscow struck again with *Sputnik II*, which carried a live dog and weighed a shocking 1,120 pounds, compared with 21 pounds for the corresponding American satellite, which was still very much on the ground. "How long, how long, O God, how long will it take us to catch up with Russia's two satellites?" wailed Lyndon B. Johnson, chairman of the Senate Preparedness Subcommittee. Styles Bridges, a Senate Republican leader, was equally apocalyptic: "The time has clearly come to be less concerned with the depth of pile on the new broadloom rug or the height of the tail fin on the new car and to be more prepared to shed blood, sweat and tears."

Eisenhower had raised the long-range missile to the highest national priority in mid-1955; now even further attention and emotion would be the order of the day. Projects and plans were re-evaluated. The Army's poky Jupiter program, limping along amid the likelihood of cancellation because it duplicated the Thor, now went forward like a Sherman tank. Polaris had been scheduled for deployment in 1963, using an energetic solid fuel to achieve a range of 1,500 nautical miles. But it needed heat-resistant materials to cope with the hot exhaust, and these were not yet ready. By substituting a less energetic fuel, Polaris could be

built with available metals. Its range would be limited to 1,200 miles, but it would be ready by 1960.

The time was also right to start yet another missile program, the Air Force's Minuteman. That would be the nation's sixth missile overall, the Air Force's fourth, and its third ICBM, along with Atlas and Titan. Like Polaris, the Minuteman would use solid fuel. Its advocates said it would be the ultimate land-based weapon, able to hide for years in a hardened underground silo while remaining ready to fly at a moment's notice. Minuteman was the concept of Col. Edward Hall, a propulsion expert, program manager on the Thor, and a member of Schriever's staff. Hall was all too familiar with liquid-fueled rockets and was convinced that solids were the answer. In 1955 Schriever had directed a committee to determine whether anything like the Minuteman was feasible, and in February 1958 this program, too, received its go-ahead.

Finally, after years of furious design, testing, and preparation, the various long-range missile projects began to bear fruit. During little more than two years, between November 1958 and February 1961, the Atlas, Polaris, and Minuteman programs all came through with successful tests at full range. Atlas was first, flying 6,300 miles from Cape Canaveral to a spot in the South Atlantic near the island of St. Helena. In July of 1960 it was Polaris's turn. The submarine *George Washington* lay submerged off the cape with Raborn aboard. At a signal it ejected a missile that breached the surface like a dolphin, ignited, and soared downrange to its full distance. Then the skipper launched another one, just to show that it was all routine.

Minuteman's turn came the following February, twelve days after President John F. Kennedy's inauguration. Its guidance system had never flown before, nor had any of its three stages. It didn't matter; they all worked, and the nose cone hurtled 4,600 miles to the South Atlantic. Schriever himself had ordered this all-up test; its success cut a year off the schedule for deployment.

THE CONTINUING REVOLUTION

By the time JFK entered the White House, Atlas, Thor, and Jupiter were all in the field and ready for war. Titan and Minuteman became operational in 1962, around the time of the Cuban missile crisis. With Minuteman's numbers scheduled to grow to a thousand, it was clear that big liquid-fueled missiles were already on the way out. The short-range Thors and Jupiters, which were based overseas, came home during the months that followed the Cuban crisis. The Atlas and Titan ICBMs were also soon deactivated, for in the rapid pace of postwar technology both proved to be no more than interim weapons. Liquid-fueled rockets found a niche only by imitating the characteristics of Minuteman. And so the Titan II, a follow-up to the original version, was built to use storable propellants that could be held in the missiles' own tanks without evaporating like volatile liquid oxygen. Titan II then could be held down-hole like Minuteman, ready for quick action. Fifty-four Titan IIs served in this fashion until 1987.

The intervening quarter-century saw just one more major advance in missilery: multiple warheads, each aimed at a separate target. These emerged in the late 1960s and reflected further work in cutting down the sizes of both bombs and guidance systems while improving their accuracy. The original Atlas, in late 1954, had been designed to carry a single one-megaton bomb with a miss distance of three miles; the latest submarine-launched missile, Trident II, can carry up to fourteen 150-kiloton warheads, each with more than ten times the destructive power of the Hiroshima bomb, and place them on target to within 400 feet. The range is 6,000 nautical miles, five times that of the early Polaris. A Trident sub could launch a strike against a target as distant as Moscow while moored in South Carolina.

The nuclear sub has indeed become the Navy's mainstay, and it has since been supplemented by the nuclear carrier. The *Nautilus* joined the fleet in

1955, and following its successful first missions, naval officials decided to build no more diesel-powered subs. Instead, they would pursue only nuclear-powered designs. During the Reagan Presidency more than a hundred were in commission, counting both attack and missile-carrying versions, and they had advanced considerably in both size and quietness. The Skipjack class of the late 1950s, which incorporated the lessons of *Nautilus*, had a submerged displacement of 3,500 tons. The Ohio class, which carries the Trident missile, weighs in at 18,700 tons, which puts it on a par with some World War II aircraft carriers. As for its silence, two Ohios could reportedly pass within a thousand yards of each other, each listening with sensitive sonar, without detection.

The nuclear sub also gave rise to the civilian nuclear-power industry, as the *Nautilus* brought the power reactor into existence for the first time. The influence of the early naval designs remained pervasive, even as the reactors' power grew a hundredfold, from 11,000 kilowatts in the Skipjacks to nearly 1.1 million kilowatts at such major installations as Browns Ferry, Alabama. And that influence was more than technical; it involved people as well. Following the accident at Three Mile Island in 1979, a number of Rickover's men went in to set things right by doing them the Navy way. This permitted a second reactor at TMI, undamaged in the accident, to resume service in 1985. Industrywide, the nation's utilities were turning to a new Institute of Nuclear Power Operations

to keep their nuclear plants up to the mark. Its founder, Vice Adm. Eugene Wilkinson, had been the first skipper of the *Nautilus*.

Moreover, despite their early obsolescence as weapons, the Atlas, Titan, and Thor missiles found new life as space launchers. They acquired upper stages to carry payloads into orbit and solid-fuel boosters to help them lift the heavy weights.

After Three Mile Island, Rickover's men came in to set things right by doing them the Navy way.

In 1961 Air Force spy satellites launched by Thor showed that the Soviets were lagging in their missile programs. This ended the decade-long fear that the Russians were ahead of us. More recent payloads have included communications satellites that provide worldwide television and telephone service. Reconnaissance satellites keep a wary eye on potential

trouble spots. Planetary missions have landed on Mars and turned Jupiter and Saturn into subjects for stamps and posters. Beyond those services, these rockets and their successors have carried astronauts as far as the moon, nurturing dreams of a new age of exploration and discovery.

These have been the legacies of the postwar military revolution: weapons that helped win the Cold War, nuclear power as an energy source, rockets for space flight. Their influence has not been as pervasive in our lives as that of the jet airliner or electronics, but they certainly are among the more noticeable of the postwar technologies. All grew up in the shadow of Hiroshima as responses to the dangers and opportunities that had loomed beneath the mushroom cloud.

"I am become Death, the destroyer of worlds," a quote from the *Bhagavad Gita*, was the thought of J. Robert Oppenheimer on seeing the first detonation of his atom bomb. The commentator Edward R. Murrow put it differently: "Had we walked through midnight, toward the dawn, without knowing it?" Such thoughts today have not lost their pertinence. Yet from the perspective of nearly a half-century, we can say that the true consequences of Hiroshima, manifested in rocketry and nuclear power, have been far more modest. They have not ushered in new worlds, but neither have they brought death on even a small scale, let alone a large one. The shadow of the atomic bomb, which in our time has loomed so fearsomely, has thus far yielded consequences that deserve

to be viewed not with sweeping emotion but with irony.

There is irony in noting that nuclear power has found no more than a modest role within an electric-power industry that remains dominated by the burning of coal. Irony also lies in that other cynosure of attention, the space program, which has found few markets and whose uses have been even more specialized. And the weapons of the Cold War, built with such passionate ingenuity, today appear likely to succumb to arms-control agreements. Such are the results that have flowed

A 1960s Titan II missile is launched from its underground silo at Vandenberg Air Force Base, near Lompoc, California.

from those postwar years when feelings ran so high and when, for good or ill, all things seemed possible.

BERLIN 1961: THE RECORD CORRECTED

Raymond L. Garthoff

RAYMOND L. GARTHOFF, *a senior fellow at the Brookings Institution, was serving in the State Department at the time of the 1961 Berlin crisis. He is now working on a sequel to* Détente and Confrontation: American-Soviet Relations from Nixon to Reagan *(1985) and studying other aspects of the Cold War.*

Anniversaries of critical events in the late and unlamented Cold War still provide useful occasions to review presumably well-known events and to reconsider the lessons we believe we have learned. One of the most dangerous confrontations of the Cold War occurred in late October 1961 when, for the first and only time, U.S. and Soviet tanks squared off against each other. The setting was Checkpoint Charlie, the famed crossing point in the recently constructed Berlin Wall. The tanks were armed and had contingent instructions to fire. The world came closer than ever to a nuclear-age equivalent of the Wild West showdown at the OK Corral.

Recalling this event for a new generation that did not experience it, or for an older one that has forgotten it, would be reason enough for an article. Now, however, startling information on the *Soviet* view of that crisis has become available for the first time—information that changes the whole picture as understood until today. The new sources reveal why the confrontation was even more dangerous than believed at the time and tell the undisclosed story of how it was peacefully resolved. Even as the Cold War fades, with the Wall and what it symbolized now gone, a proper understanding of this crisis will help us cope less perilously with new crises in the future.

The West saw the 1961 incident as a bold Soviet test of Western resolve to defend West Berlin, a challenge U.S. forces overcame by facing down the Soviet tanks. Soviet leaders, on the other hand, viewed the episode as a *Western* provocation challenging their position in East Berlin, a test they withstood by facing down the U.S. tanks. Political leaders have enough difficulty resolving real conflicts of interest; they should not approach the brink of war through an unnecessary confrontation involving serious misperceptions on both sides. Western observers have not understood the Soviet perspective at all, much less that there was foundation for the Soviet view, even though it was in error. There were real conflicts of interest and ambition in the Cold War, and in the recurrent Berlin crises of that era; but the dangerous tank confrontation would not have occurred had each side not believed the other was posing a challenge to its vital interest. New information shows that *both* sides were mistaken.

The logical starting point is to recall the Western perception in 1961 that has held ever since. Soviet leader Nikita Khrushchev touched off the Berlin crisis in November 1958 with an arbitrary demand that the Western Powers withdraw from West Berlin, an enclave in communist East Germany and, for the Soviets, a disruptive anomaly complicating the consolidation of Soviet hegemony in Eastern Europe. West Berlin was, in Khrushchev's words, a "bone stuck in our throat" that needed to be removed. Apart from not wanting to facilitate communist control in Eastern Europe, the West feared Soviet attempts to undercut the Western Alliance. While the Western view understated the "defensive" Soviet aim in the East, concern over the "offensive" aim of weakening the West was valid. By the summer of

1961, after a series of actions and counteractions, tensions were high. But after the building of the Berlin Wall in August 1961 checked the massive outflow of East Germans, the crisis seemed to abate. On October 17 of that year, in a speech to the 22d Congress of the Soviet Communist party in Moscow, Khrushchev withdrew his unilateral year-end deadline for signing a German peace treaty. The crisis appeared to be ending, but the West remained watchful for renewed probes and demands.

On Sunday evening, October 22, the senior American diplomat in Berlin, Deputy Commandant Allan Lightner, and his wife were about to enter East Berlin at the Friedrichstrasse crossing point, nicknamed Checkpoint Charlie. The couple was taking a routine trip to attend the theater. The East German police (*Volkspolizei*) asked to see their diplomatic passports. While the request may seem reasonable (the Lightners were in their private automobile), compliance would have implied recognition of East German (rather than Soviet) authority in East Berlin—a concession the United States was determined not to offer. (British officials in Berlin, regarding the matter as less important, had acceded to similar requests.) In accordance with precedent, Lightner refused and demanded to see a Soviet officer. He then tried, initially without success, to drive through without permission. When he returned with his car escorted by a squad of eight American soldiers on foot with fixed bayonets, backed up by four M-48 tanks and additional troops at the checkpoint, the East German border guards stepped aside. When news of the incident reached Washington, the State Department instructed the U.S. mission in Berlin to cool it. But General Lucius Clay, recalled to Berlin as President John Kennedy's special representative a few months earlier in a demonstrative move at a time of high tension, personally called the president and obtained approval to maintain a tough stance. What followed was a series of assertive American probes, East German attempts to check the documents of American civilian officials, and, after refusal, entries into East Berlin by these Americans accompanied by U.S. military escorts. On October 25, Clay decided to drive the point home a little harder by moving 10 M-48 tanks near Checkpoint Charlie, assembling a force of unprecedented strength near the Wall.

The next morning, October 26, a battalion of 33 Soviet tanks entered East Berlin, matching the American tank force in West Berlin. (Soviet tanks were not normally deployed in the city

The world came closer than ever to a nuclear-age equivalent of the Wild West showdown at the OK Corral.

itself.) The Soviet tanks did not then approach the crossing points. The next day, however, 10 of the Soviet tanks moved up to the East German side of Checkpoint Charlie, facing the 10 American tanks still there in a symmetrical standoff.

Many officials in Washington, including the president, were alarmed. The British, too, expressed their concern over what they regarded as an unnecessary confrontation. An irritated Kennedy reportedly had said with reference to Lightner's initial foray that "We didn't send him over there [to West Berlin] to go to the opera in East Berlin." But he had not wanted to override Clay on an issue concerning the possible erosion of Allied rights in East—and, by extension, West—Berlin.

Only 17 years later did it become known, although virtually without public notice, that Kennedy had resorted to an unofficial line of communication with Khrushchev to defuse the crisis. In 1978, Arthur Schlesinger reported that then Attorney General Robert Kennedy had revealed that the president asked him to convey to Khrushchev through Georgi Bolshakov, press attaché at the Soviet Embassy in Washington (and, as then suspected, a KGB officer), that "the President would like them to take their tanks out of there in twenty-four hours."

On the morning of October 28, within 24 hours, the Soviets withdrew their tanks from the checkpoint. Half an hour later, the United States did the same. The tank confrontation had ended. To borrow a phrase coined by Secretary of State Dean Rusk during the Cuban missile crisis just a year later: "We are eyeball to eyeball, and the other fellow just blinked." The American show of force had succeeded. From Clay's standpoint, he had forced *Soviet* intervention, thus reemphasizing Four Power, not East German, authority in East Berlin. As Peter Wyden put it in his book *Wall* (1989): "Clay had been correct again: the Soviets were bluffing," and Khrushchev had backed away.

Except for the important later footnote about Kennedy's back-channel message to Khrushchev, this has been the story of the confrontation at Checkpoint Charlie from October 1961 to this day. When the Soviets tested Allied will, the United States stood up firmly, forcing the Soviets to back down. The only risk was not to have met the challenge. As Clay is reported to have commented to an associate at the height of the confrontation, "If the Soviets don't want war over West Berlin, we can't start it. If they do, there's nothing we can do to stop them."

The Soviet Perspective

Published Soviet accounts of the confrontation have been sparse. But their image of the outcome is the mirror image of the American view: From their perspective the *Soviet* dispatch of tanks to Checkpoint Charlie effectively deterred an assertive *American* challenge.

Khrushchev himself, in his taped memoirs and in conversations with foreigners (including West German Ambassador Hans Kroll and Kennedy's press secretary Pierre Salinger) and close associates (his son Sergei, and his son-in-law Alexei Adzhubei), has given slightly varying accounts. All focus on his decision to match the American force with Soviet tanks, despite the concern of his military, and on his move to defuse the crisis by ordering the Soviet tanks to withdraw, confident that the Americans would follow suit.

Soviets have thus viewed the crisis as an American provocation and Soviet response. Khrushchev relied successfully on matching force with force, and then initiated a deescalation. The West has interpreted this view as an attempt to put the best face possible on a Soviet backdown—an explanation that fits the U.S. account and has undergirded the judgment of Western historians.

New disclosures and a reexamination of the record now yield an entirely new Soviet perspective on the crisis. Khrushchev and the Soviet leadership did not intend to put pressure on the West; instead, they discerned an aggressive Western challenge. Similarly, they believed that with a firm reaction and prudent crisis management *they* had succeeded in facing down the Western threat.

Over the years, Soviet accounts have proclaimed this outcome, but in very terse reference, with no explanation of how the Soviets perceived a Western provocation. Accordingly, Westerners have simply rejected such statements as attempts to camouflage a Soviet defeat. Until very recently, Khrushchev's unofficial memoir was the only source to specify a Western threat. Khrushchev claimed the Americans intended to knock down the Wall and burst into East Berlin—until they encountered Soviet tanks. And, he said, he ordered the Soviet tanks to move back once he was sure the U.S. commanders would then promptly with-

draw their tanks, ending the confrontation. Again, because no Western sources believed that the United States intended to dismantle the Wall, his account was dismissed as self-serving.

Today historians can reconstruct the situation, and a new picture emerges. General Clay was skeptical of the U.S. decision to accept the Berlin Wall. Clay's principal objectives were first to prevent any further Soviet or East German encroachments on West Berlin or on Allied access to East Berlin, and second to boost the morale of West Berlin and its confidence in the Allies. But he also hoped to roll back the communist position if the opportunity arose. Clay had been in command in Berlin during the Berlin airlift in 1948; to the German population, he embodied Western resolve. Clay understood that his appointment on August 30 as the president's personal representative in West Berlin was designed as a signal of U.S. fortitude, but he went further in taking his position as a mandate for vigorous action.

Soon after Clay returned to Berlin on September 19, he secretly ordered the U.S. military commandant in West Berlin, Major General Albert Watson, to have combat engineers replicate a section of the Berlin Wall in a secluded, forested area of greater West Berlin. Clay wanted to determine the best way to breach the Wall. After construction of the model barrier, tanks with bulldozer attachments experimented with assault techniques to break it down. When, presumably through Watson or his staff, the commander-in-chief of U.S. forces in Europe, General Bruce Clarke, learned of this action—taken without his knowledge or approval—he angrily countermanded Clay's order. In an unpublished personal communication, Clarke later wrote: "As soon as I learned of it, I stopped it and got rid of what had been done." Clarke bawled Clay out, but did not report the incident to Washington.

In fact, *no one* in Washington was fully aware of the project, much less knew that Clay had actually built a section of wall and tested specially configured bulldozer tanks against it. But Soviet military intelligence, probably through the East Germans, quickly learned of the construction and its purpose. Again, until today, only Khrushchev had claimed, in his heavily discounted memoir, that Marshal Ivan Konev, Clay's counterpart (also recalled from retirement to Berlin in a reciprocal move), reported that "he had learned through intelligence channels on what day and at what hour the Western powers were going to begin their actions against us. They were preparing bulldozers to break down our border installations [i.e., the Wall]. The bulldozers would be followed by tanks and wave after wave of jeeps with infantrymen."

In fact, two knowledgeable retired Soviet military intelligence officers said in recent interviews that the GRU (Soviet military intelligence) not only learned of the mock wall and the exercises to breach it, but photographed them. This visual evidence powerfully supported reports of an American plan to break down the Wall. A third source, a senior Communist party adviser directly involved in the crisis, Valentin Falin, has confirmed this account and reported that the intelligence reached the leadership in Moscow, by his recollection, on October 20–21.

Soviet military intelligence closely monitored Western moves to gradually increase the number of tanks intermittently stationed near the Wall. With these maneuvers, the Allies apparently sought to establish a pattern of accepted deployments. On August 30, for example, three U.S. tanks and five armored personnel carriers (APCs) approached the Wall during a routine dispute over border access. Four U.S. tanks and two APCs came within 500 yards of Checkpoint Charlie on October 22, just hours after Lightner's first incident. On October 25, when the United States first brought as many as 10 tanks to Checkpoint Charlie, three APCs and several jeeps of soldiers accompanied them. Later that day, the force withdrew from the immediate border area. At the same time, three British tanks and a company of infantry appeared at the Brandenburg Gate crossing point, even though there had been no incident there. Soviet intelligence closely monitored these movements. At that juncture, Konev, then in Moscow for the Communist Party Congress, reported personally to Khrushchev.

The next day, October 26, three U.S. tanks returned to the checkpoint during another incident. Later that day, as earlier noted, the Soviets moved 33 tanks (one tank battalion, roughly equal to the number of U.S. tanks then in West Berlin) into East Berlin. Soviet tanks had not entered the city since the suppression of rioting in June 1953. The tanks stayed about one mile from the checkpoint.

The critical confrontation began on October 27. Another dispute over credentials occurred at Checkpoint Charlie that afternoon. Yet even *before* that incident, the U.S. command brought up 10 M-48 tanks, accompanied by two APCs and five jeeps carrying infantry. The lead tanks were equipped with bulldozers.

These were hardly the "waves" that Khrushchev colorfully described, but the force was far stronger than had been required to obtain access earlier. Bulldozer tanks could clear away parked vehicles or other obstructions at the checkpoint—or could batter through the Wall. After obtaining access again, the American contingent, with the tanks, began to withdraw. Ten Soviet tanks, however, arrived just after the U.S. tanks had departed. The Soviets, in turn, soon departed—but by then the U.S. tanks, advised of the arrival of the Soviet tanks, had returned. So, then, did the Soviet tanks as well. At the conclusion of this bizarre dance, 10 U.S. tanks and supporting units faced 10 Soviet tanks. All remained through the night, in all for 16 hours. The lead tanks kept their engines running, even "gunning" them at times. On both sides, the tank guns were uncovered and (as recently confirmed) ready to fire.

A massive Berlin crisis management system had been functioning in the Kennedy administration for five months. The State Department and Pentagon watched the developments of October 22–28 closely. Kennedy did not, however, "unleash" the Berlin Task Force. On October 23, he talked by phone with Clay, confirming his determination to prevent Soviet encroachments. But it seems clear that the president did not regard Clay as the one to resolve the confrontation. Since the incident began, the State Department had tried to cool the ardor of the U.S. mission in Berlin, suggesting the suspension of all "probes." During their conversation on October 23, however, Clay felt the president had endorsed the stiff stance he subsequently assumed.

The State Department, with White House approval, instructed the U.S. ambassador in Moscow, Llewellyn (Tommy) Thompson, to see Foreign Minister Andrei Gromyko and protest the East German attempts to change the procedures for U.S. access to East Berlin. Thompson conveyed the message on October 27. But his State Department instructions preceded and did not mention the tank confrontation. Gromyko, in turn, rejected this démarche and protested the repeated entry of armed American soldiers into East Berlin.

On October 27, President Kennedy turned to a confidential back channel of communication with Khrushchev, bypassing the Soviet and U.S. embassies and foreign ministries. As noted, Robert Kennedy passed a message from the president to Khrushchev through his contact, Soviet embassy information attaché (and KGB

The dangerous tank confrontation would not have occurred had each side not believed the other was posing a challenge to its vital interest. New information shows that *both* sides were mistaken.

colonel) Georgi Bolshakov. Robert Kennedy's account, posthumously disclosed, was this: "I got in touch with Bolshakov and said the President would like them to take their tanks out of there in twenty-four hours. He said he'd speak to Khrushchev and they took their tanks out in twenty-four hours. So he [Bolshakov] delivered effectively when it was a matter of importance." This contact has only been known to a few historians of the Berlin confrontation, in particular Peter Wyden and Michael Beschloss.

The incident that triggered the crisis, from the U.S. perspective, was the East German attempt on October 22 to obtain a display of identification from Lightner. The Soviets in East Berlin, however, did not even know of this action until later, much less instigate it. Upon learning of the dispute, they did permit the East Germans to repeat the demands. Soviet leaders in Moscow, however, had not intended to test Western resolve, nor were they aware that the West saw the tank confrontation as such a test.

On the contrary, when U.S. activity escalated on October 25 with the arrival of 10 tanks, Soviet leaders saw confirmation of the military intelligence report that had arrived some four days earlier with allegations of an American plan to assault the Wall. Moreover, the timing seemed deliberate and sinister. First, the Soviet Communist Party Congress was in session, and the leadership had problems in other areas—in an internal dispute over de-Stalinization, and in the international communist movement, with both Albania and, more important, China. The time might have seemed opportune for the United States to open a "second front" while the Soviets were occupied elsewhere. Second, the Soviet Union had just made a major concession on Berlin itself, defusing the intensifying crisis of the preceding four months. As noted, on October 17, the opening day of the Congress, Khrushchev had removed the ultimatum demanding the resolution of the German problem by the end of the year. The United States, instead of reciprocating Soviet moderation, seemed to press its advantage.

Finally, underlying these considerations was the strategic context, marked by new U.S. assertiveness. On October 21, just one day before the Lightner episode, Deputy Defense Secretary Roswell Gilpatric, in a major Kennedy administration statement, exploded the "missile gap" and coolly affirmed vast U.S. strategic superiority, claiming that "we have a second strike capability which is at least as extensive as what the Soviets can deliver by striking first." Gilpatric not only deflated exaggerated Soviet claims of military superiority, but also Moscow's political expectations based on a changing "correlation of forces." And he specifically warned the Soviets over Berlin.

No one in Washington had the offensive strategy the Soviets discerned. Nor did any Americans realize that such was the perception in Moscow. But even if incorrect, the Soviet view was reasonable, based on the information available to the leadership.

Khrushchev, in contrast to Kennedy, created an ad hoc brain trust on the crisis, almost prefiguring Kennedy's creation of an "ExComm" (Executive Committee of the National Security Council) a year later during the Cuban missile crisis. His advisers were Gromyko; senior Central Committee official Leonid Ilychev; party foreign affairs adviser Valentin Falin; Defense Minister Marshal Rodion Malinovsky; the chief of the Main Operations Directorate of the General Staff, Colonel General Semyon Ivanov; and the commander in East Germany, Marshal Konev. The Soviet plan was to meet and match U.S. moves—the United States was the apparent initiator and pace-setter in the crisis. The U.S. threat looked real: The appearance of tanks with bulldozer attachments seemed, along with the evidence of the mock "target" wall, to validate intelligence reports of U.S. and West German designs to knock down the Wall. Firm countermeasures seemed necessary—thus the stationing of armed Soviet tanks at the checkpoint on October 27.

Robert Kennedy, it is now clear, described the president's back-channel message to Khrushchev incompletely. Falin, a member of Khrushchev's brain trust in October 1961 and now chief of the International Department of the Communist party Central Committee, recently disclosed to this author more about this exchange. In the message, received late on October 27, President Kennedy did ask Khrushchev to remove the Soviet tanks—but only to do so first in the context of a mutual disengagement. Kennedy promised that if Khrushchev did so, the American tanks would withdraw in turn. Thus, instead of the some-what improbable unilateral demand described by Robert Kennedy, the message was a plea from the president for mutual restraint and deescalation, asking Khrushchev to take the initial step. From Khrushchev's standpoint, the request delineated a reciprocal course of action compatible with Soviet objectives. Indeed, the withdrawal of the U.S. tanks would constitute a Soviet victory, removing the threat to the Wall.

On the morning of October 28, at about 10:30 a.m., some 16 hours after the confrontation at Checkpoint Charlie began, the 10 Soviet tanks withdrew. Khrushchev later described his decision in his memoir, though without revealing the secret exchange with President Kennedy. He said he ordered Konev to pull the tanks back, telling him:

> I'm sure that within twenty minutes or however long it takes them to get their instructions, the American tanks will pull back, too. They can't turn their tanks around and pull them back as long as our guns are pointing at them. They've gotten themselves into a difficult situation, and they don't know how to get out of it. They're looking for a way out, I'm sure. So let's give them one. We'll remove our tanks, and they'll follow our example.

Khrushchev explained his decision to initiate mutual deescalation to several foreigners, as well as in his taped memoir. His son Sergei said in an interview that his father had described the situation (a year before Rusk's similar remark) as one in which the two sides stood eyeball to eyeball, and he decided to take the first step back. Even then he did not disclose the clandestine deal with President Kennedy.

About half an hour after the Soviet tanks withdrew, only a little later than the 20 minutes Khrushchev claimed to have predicted, the American tanks departed. On October 27, the day before, President Kennedy had telephoned General Clay; it is now clear that Kennedy advised Clay that the Soviet side might withdraw its tanks and instructed him to follow suit promptly in that event.

No more tanks returned to the checkpoint, and no standoff resumed. Khrushchev's contention that he removed the tanks confident of a reciprocal U.S. response has heretofore been considered a belated invention or a lucky gamble. Now it is clear that Khrushchev had Kennedy's prior assurance, and the parallel withdrawals were the result of a tacit agreement to defuse the confrontation.

With this new information, the Soviet proclamation of triumph is comprehensible. In retrospect, it is also clear why some Soviets, including Falin, regarded this as perhaps the most dangerous confrontation of the Cold War. Such claims now make sense—a U.S. breach of the Berlin Wall would have violated a vital Soviet interest.

The Confrontation in Retrospect

The tank standoff at Checkpoint Charlie marked the last serious challenge of the Berlin crisis. Although minor incidents continued for some months, by April 1962 both Clay and (nine days later) Konev had been recalled. The outcome of the Cuban missile crisis the following October rendered unlikely the renewal of the Berlin crisis that a difficult outcome in Cuba would probably have presaged.

The revelation that Kennedy and Khrushchev used a back-channel exchange to defuse the confrontation at Checkpoint Charlie places their communication during the Cuban missile crisis in a new light. One year after the Berlin conflict, Khrushchev resorted to the same channel, asking Bolshakov to convey misleading assurances that the Soviet Union would not send missiles to Cuba. While this deceit damaged Khrushchev's credibility, the secret resolution of the Berlin crisis undoubtedly encouraged mutual confidence and facilitated communication during the Cuban conflict.

Three decades after the confrontation of Soviet and U.S. tanks at Checkpoint Charlie, new disclosures challenge the Western understanding of the crisis. There is therefore an opportunity for reflection not only on the conduct of yesterday's Cold War, but also on the lessons of that experience for future instances of crisis management. The absence of key information, largely—though not entirely—regarding the Soviet side of events, contributed most to previous misconceptions. At the same time, Kennedy administration officials were surprisingly reticent about the affair in their historical papers. The memoirs and accounts of Arthur Schlesinger, Walt Rostow, Roger Hilsman, Charles Bohlen, Dean Rusk, and Paul Nitze make no reference to the incident. Those of Theodore Sorensen, Pierre Salinger, McGeorge Bundy, Foy Kohler, and Martin Hillenbrand refer to it only fleetingly, as does Schlesinger's book on Robert Kennedy. Incidentally, Rusk, Bundy, and Sorensen were all unaware of Kennedy's use of the Bolshakov channel. Schlesinger discovered it only belatedly from unpublished notes of an interview with Robert Kennedy in 1964 by historian Robert Bartlow Martin.

Why have veterans of the Kennedy administration ignored an incident some historians consider perilous? Since the Soviets appeared to cower before a display of U.S. force, why have American officials not gladly recalled the episode, in pride if nothing else? The answer seems to be that President Kennedy and his chief advisers, few of whom he closely consulted, regarded the crisis largely as the result of Clay's overreaction to minor harassments at the Berlin border. Clay, of course, was able to trigger the dispute only because Kennedy had called him to Berlin. Rusk's assessment may be typical: When I recently asked him about the incident, he referred to it as "the silly tank confrontation at Checkpoint Charlie brought on by the macho inclinations of General Clay."

Historians, on the other hand, have devoted considerable attention to the crisis, though most, as indicated, had to rely on incomplete Western sources. Those scholars of the Cold War include Peter Wyden, Norman Gelb, Robert Slusser, Jean Edward Smith, Curtis Cate, Howard Trivers, James McSherry, and John Newhouse; Wyden and Newhouse, who have written recently, have parts of the fuller story. But the most recent account, by far the best on this episode, is Michael Beschloss's *The Crisis Years: Kennedy and Khrushchev 1960–1963* (1991).

Clearly, it is Soviet *glasnost* that has allowed a far more accurate reconstruction of this Cold War confrontation. Without access to the Soviet perspective, scholars could never recount the complete story of the standoff at Checkpoint Charlie. This experience underscores the importance of encouraging full Soviet participation in the historiography of the Cold War.

Now that the narrative is complete, both political leaders and historians have a unique opportunity to learn from this episode. Politicians, for their part, ought to strive to understand the perspective of adversaries. In this instance, had either side understood the extent to which the other felt threatened, the mutual provocations might have stopped. The Berlin crisis also highlights the potential value of confidential communication between leaders—the Bolshakov channel was crucial to the resolution of this confrontation. In addition, politicians should recognize the importance of tight managerial control. The unauthorized construction of the mock wall generated anxieties that the Kennedy administration could have avoided altogether.

Historians and analysts also have much to learn. Those who seek to reconstruct a situation must relentlessly pursue the perspective and interest of all parties, as well as the information available to all sides. To the detriment of their work, Western scholars of the Berlin crisis woefully lacked an appreciation of the Soviet viewpoint. Today's fuller account of this incident underscores the importance of detail—historians must work to supplement the documentary record, seeking, for example, intelligence information that is often sparse in declassified papers. Scholars hoping to penetrate the actual motivations of key figures must rise above prevailing assumptions and consider unorthodox approaches.

These ideas are hardly novel; nonetheless, historians and policymakers often fail to apply them. At Checkpoint Charlie, similar failures gave rise to a potentially explosive situation. The world, in retrospect, was fortunate to escape armed conflict. Recalling this episode may help drive its lessons home.

Who broke down this wall?

Bush says tough U.S. policies did, but the Russians disagree

The cold war is over, but the combatants have just begun to fight over who deserves credit for the West's victory.

George Bush insists that he and Ronald Reagan prevailed with a combination of ideological fortitude and military might. "We didn't listen to the . . . nuclear-freeze group . . . " Bush argued during the second presidential debate. "President Reagan said no, peace through strength. It worked."

Democrats counter that the West's victory was the product of a bipartisan effort that began with the Truman administration's strategy of containment. Moreover, argues former National Security Adviser Zbigniew Brzezinski, writing in *Foreign Affairs*, it was Carter who began rebuilding the U.S. military, responded to the Soviet deployment of SS-20 nuclear missiles with a plan to put American missiles in Europe, began supporting the mujeheddin who drove the Soviets out of Afghanistan, improved America's relations with China and started pressing Moscow to respect the human rights of its people.

Other Western experts insist that the West prevailed not because tough-minded American policies and military strength brought communism to its knees but because the Soviet system collapsed from within. In this view, argued by Daniel Deudney of the University of Pennsylvania and G. John Ikenberry of Princeton University in *Foreign Policy* magazine, Mikhail Gorbachev, who abandoned superpower confrontation for a "new thinking" Soviet foreign policy of cooperation, deserves much of the credit for ending the cold war.

Changing stories. The group that may be in the best position to know what effect American policies really had on the Soviet Union's collapse has been largely silent, however. Until now,

the policy makers who were in the Kremlin as the Soviet ship went down have been content to let Americans duel over how the cold war ended. Now, in a series of interviews with *U.S. News*, two dozen former top Soviet officials offered their versions of how the cold war ended, why the West prevailed and whether Bush and Reagan are the architects of victory or just its beneficiaries.

The Russian versions of history are no less self-serving than the American ones: Once taciturn officials claim the superpower confrontation dragged on a decade longer than it need have because the Reagan-Bush hard line undercut a Soviet desire to mend fences. By 1980, the Russians now say, they knew the Soviet Union was in deep economic trouble, and they were seeking détente with the West.

Many former Soviet officials still harbor lifelong grudges against the United States and are nursing wounded pride over history's verdict. Others, mindful of the new Russian leadership's antipathy toward the old Soviet system, are eager to recast themselves as closet reformers who chafed under the tyrannical communist regime. Some of their accounts flatly contradict the historical record.

Misunderstandings. It may take historians longer to resolve all the competing versions of events, if they ever do, than it did to fight the cold war. But even now, comparing the Russian views with the American ones underscores how little each side understood about the other and how poorly each calculated the effect its policies would have on its adversary. It also suggests that misunderstandings, miscues and missed opportunities probably did more to determine how the cold war ended than the best-laid plans of either side.

In fact, former Soviet officials now say, Kremlin blunders

1982 Yuri Andropov, the former KGB chief who became Soviet leader after Leonid Brezhnev died, was a hard-liner who backed the 1979 invasion of Afghanistan. But he knew the Soviet system needed reform and wanted a new détente with the United States. He died in 1984, just before relations began to improve.

1983 Superpower relations hit rock bottom. Ronald Reagan denounced the Soviet Union as an "evil empire," proposed the Star Wars program and began deploying new nuclear missiles in Western Europe. The Russians shot down KAL Flight 007 and walked out of arms negotiations. By year's end, Moscow was rife with rumors of impending war with the United States.

---

helped bring Reagan to power in the first place. "Reagan should thank us," says Georgi Arbatov, head of the U.S.A.-Canada Institute in Moscow and a Kremlin foreign-policy adviser since the 1960s. "He came to power in part because of some of our stupid policies of the late 1970s."

Two of the dumbest, some former Kremlin policy makers now concede, were the invasion of Afghanistan in December 1979 and the deployment, beginning in 1977, of the SS-20, a three-warhead mobile missile that sharply upped the nuclear ante in Europe. But the Russians now insist that both decisions were the products of lackluster leadership in the Kremlin and mistakes by the Soviet military, not the drive for global domination that American conservatives saw.

Bad moves. Viktor Karpov, a top Soviet arms negotiator, says the Soviet Foreign Ministry was never consulted about the decision to deploy the SS-20, a move that prompted the United States and its allies of the North Atlantic Treaty Organization to begin deploying new American medium-range nuclear missiles in Western Europe in 1983. Karpov says he and other Soviet diplomats could have predicted in West's tough response, but insists that the decision to build the SS-20 was made solely by the Soviet defense establishment.

The decision to invade Afghanistan, former Soviet officials say, was made by three top officials—then KGB chief Yuri Andropov, Foreign Minister Andrei Gromyko and Defense Minister Dimitri Ustinov—and handed to the feeble Soviet leader Leonid Brezhnev for rubber-stamp approval.

Having inadvertently helped Reagan to power, former Soviet officials recall, Moscow proceeded to misread its new adversary. The Kremlin expected the conservative Reagan to evolve into a pragmatic partner in the mold of Richard Nixon, who despite his visceral hatred of communism had pursued détente and arms control. "There was dancing in Moscow when Reagan was elected in 1980," says former Soviet Foreign Minister Alexander Bessmertnykh.

But in his first presidential press conference, Reagan charged that the Soviets "reserve unto themselves the right to commit any crime, to lie, to cheat," in the cause of global revolution. Ignoring this slap, Brezhnev called a month later for a summit with Reagan and "active dialogue" to ease U.S.-Soviet strains. Reagan rejected the offer, leaving the Kremlin's America watchers to eat their predictions of Détente II.

Reagan stayed on the offensive, boosting military spending and sending aid to Moscow's adversaries in the Third World. All that, the Soviets say, frustrated any attempt to improve relations. "It was precisely his talent for saying things simply and succinctly that made for trouble," says Arbatov. "Even our dullest leaders could pick up a Reagan speech and understand that it was aimed at them. It didn't do any good to try to explain to them it was a speech made partly for domestic purposes, as was the case with his famous 'evil empire' speech in 1983. Our hard-liners understood just one thing: Reagan was a threat."

"The evil-empire speech showed us clearly what America's real intentions were," says Marshal Viktor Kulikov, a former Warsaw Pact commander. "Reagan was a logical extension of what had started with Truman, a concentrated effort to weaken and intimidate the Soviet Union."

But former Soviet officials concede that any attempts at détente also were frustrated by a lack of leadership in the Kremlin. Brezhnev, they say, was a sick, befuddled figurehead. He died in 1982, to be replaced by KGB chief Andropov, who died after 15 months in power. Then came Konstantin Chernenko, who lasted only 13 months. Reagan complained: "I can't get down to business with Soviet leaders; they keep dying on me."

Miscues. The Soviets also failed to understand how their own policies were playing in Washington. The Soviet military buildup continued long after 1979, when the Soviets calculated that they had reached parity with the United States. Between 1977 and 1986 the Soviet military built 24,400 new tanks, 81 surface warships, 90 submarines and 3,000 strategic missiles. The Soviets also continued to support Marxist movements and regimes in the Third World and terrorists in the Mideast.

"The mindset in Moscow was that the Soviet Union was a superpower and had achieved parity," recalls Georgi Shakhnazarov, a senior Communist Party official. "The U.S. intervened around the world, so why couldn't we? In the end, the only way we could get the generals to change their thinking on Angola, Nicaragua and other places was through strict Communist Party discipline, by ordering them as communists to obey the political leadership. But they went kicking and screaming, partly because the Americans were so active in hurting our allies."

Rewriting history. Western experts dismiss much of this as historical revisionism. "You can't explain away Soviet actions of the late 1970s as mistakes," argues Soviet expert William Hyland. "It is absurd to say a small group of old crocks launched a major military campaign in Afghanistan that everyone else first heard about on the radio. There was no indication at the time that anyone in the Soviet government opposed the invasion. At the same time, the Soviets were trying to change the military balance in their favor, giving the green light to Vietnam to invade Cambodia, getting ready to crack down on Poland—a whole range of actions that doesn't square with professed desires for détente."

Relations hit bottom in 1983. In March, just two weeks after the evil-empire speech, Reagan proposed his Strategic Defense Initiative, a space-based missile shield that was dubbed "Star Wars." Credited by Western conservatives with pushing the Soviets to the wall with its high technology, SDI is recalled differently in Moscow.

Pyotr Korotkevich, a scientist and adviser to Boris Yeltsin, says Soviet researchers quickly devised a series of relatively low-cost methods to foil SDI. One plan the Soviets studied—

1984 The Reagan Doctrine kept pressure on the Soviets in global regional conflicts, to the consternation of the Kremlin. Washington supplied arms and other support to the Nicaraguan Contras and other anti-Marxist movements.

1985 Superpower relations began to improve under Konstantin Chernenko, but his successor, Mikhail Gorbachev, quickly found common ground with Reagan. The two met in Geneva just eight months after Gorbachev came to power.

1986 Stormy friendship: Afghan fighters got deadly Stinger missiles from the United States; Reagan and Gorbachev met at Reykjavik, where they nearly agreed to sweeping arms cuts but went home empty-handed and angry.

which American experts acknowledge would have complicated SDI's task—consisted of making minor modifications to their ballistic missiles so they would rotate as they rose, making it difficult for a laser or other beam weapon to focus on one spot on the rocket long enough to destroy it.

The event Boris Yeltsin calls "the most horrible catastrophe of the cold war"—the 1983 downing of Korean Air Lines Flight 007—was another Soviet blunder. Georgi Kornienko, a former first deputy foreign minister, says the incident "could not have been handled more stupidly" by the Soviet side.

"[Defense Minister] Ustinov told the leadership that the best thing to do was lie, that it never could be proven we had shot down the plane," says Kornienko, who with Gromyko's blessing called Andropov to recommend—unsuccessfully— that the Soviet Union admit it had shot down the plane and its 269 passengers and crew. The United States quickly produced intercepted radio conversations in which a Soviet fighter pilot reported that "the target is destroyed."

In Europe, the Soviets blundered again by mounting a vitriolic propaganda campaign to prevent the deployment of U.S. medium-range nuclear missiles. Soviet commentator Valentin Falin, a former ambassador to West Germany, warned that if the missiles were deployed, "West Germans will live in constant expectation of the worst, only minutes away from catastrophe," because they had "invited nuclear death into their home." When the threats failed, the Soviets walked out of negotiations on intermediate-range nuclear forces and suspended strategic-weapons talks.

With the Soviet economy groaning and Reagan facing reelection, however, neither side could sustain a confrontation, and early in 1984 peace feelers were sent out from Washington and Moscow. Reagan administration officials say their firmness finally forced the Soviets to negotiate seriously.

The Reagan-Bush hard line "played no role" in ending the cold war, replies Alexander Yakovlev, one of Gorbachev's closest confidants. "By the mid-1980s we were ready for changes in policy toward the West, whether there was Reagan, Kennedy or someone even more liberal."

Reagan 1 and 2. "The end of the cold war came less because of Reagan's hard line than as a result of his soft line starting in 1984," argues Andrei Kortunov, a top analyst of U.S.-Soviet relations at the U.S.A.-Canada Institute in Moscow. "The communist system was shaped by Stalin and could not survive without a hostile environment. We needed an enemy, which 'Reagan 1,' the hard-liner, provided. Once we had 'Reagan 2,' the peacemaker, the enemy disappeared and our system had no reason to exist."

"If there had not been a Gorbachev, Reagan would not have made any difference," insists Anatoly Dobrynin, who served as Moscow's ambassador to Washington from 1962 until 1986. "The older generation, the one that had fought the war, felt you could prevent war only by being strong,"

says Kornienko. "The younger generation, people like Gorbachev and [Foreign Minister Eduard] Shevardnadze, were more flexible and open to solutions based on something other than military might."

Soviet trap? U.S. officials, however, were slow to accept the idea that Gorbachev was anything other than an old communist in a new suit. Some Western analysts, for example, argued that the Reagan-Gorbachev summit meeting in Reykjavik, Iceland, in October 1986 was a trap laid by Gorbachev to sucker Reagan into trading away his SDI program. "When we were planning the summit, we never discussed anything of the scale that emerged in Reykjavik," says Bessmertnykh.

Even as the Iron Curtain collapsed and Reagan warmed to Gorbachev, the two old adversaries continued to see things very differently. The Russians, for example, dispute Bush's campaign claim that he and Reagan brought down the Berlin Wall.

"We didn't look at events in Eastern Europe purely from a military point of view," says Yegor Ligachev, the former No. 2 man in the Soviet Communist Party and a harsh critic of Gorbachev. "By the mid-1980s, when I joined the Politburo, there was a clear understanding that given the realities of modern warfare, simple physical possession of territory was no guarantee of security. We needed good, neighborly relations with Eastern European states, so we took a principled decision in 1985 not to interfere under any circumstances in events in Eastern Europe.

"... Also, the region was a terrible economic drain on the U.S.S.R., and we had to take urgent action to fix our own house. This meant that Eastern Europe had to take more control over its own fate. Of course," adds Ligachev, "we didn't expect events to work out the way they did, and Gorbachev and Shevardnadze are largely to blame for the ultimate disaster there."

Other Russian conservatives question whether the struggle has ended. "You didn't win the cold war, our leadership caved in," says Ivan Polozkov, former head of the Russian Communist Party. "Gorbachev, Yakovlev, Shevardnadze— they betrayed their motherland, their people and their system. And it's still not a final victory for you. Genghis Khan and the Mongols thought they would rule forever, Napoleon burned Moscow, Hitler was at the city's gates. The Russian people are proud. They won't long stand for outsiders telling them what to do."

Although that may seem far-fetched, there is a danger that George Bush and other Americans who are now celebrating the defeat of communism and the triumph of democracy in Moscow may understand today's Russia as poorly as they understood the old Soviet Union.

JEFF TRIMBLE IN MOSCOW

1987 Mathias Rust, a West German pilot, landed his Cessna near Red Square and did Gorbachev a favor: The Soviet leader promptly fired many old-school generals and promoted men more attuned to his "new thinking" foreign policy.

1988 Reagan's summit visit to Moscow was the heady high point of his relationship with the Soviet leader. Gorbachev's critics now accuse him of being seduced by the West into making overly generous concessions.

1989 Withdrawal of forces from Afghanistan ended Moscow's 10-year foreign-policy disaster. Revolution swept through Eastern Europe; Bush met Gorbachev in Malta for the first post-cold-war summit.

THE RETURN TO HISTORY

THE BREAKUP OF THE SOVIET UNION

Shlomo Avineri

Shlomo Avineri, professor of political science at the Hebrew University of Jerusalem, was guest scholar in the Brookings Governmental Studies program last year. He is the author, among other books, of The Social and Political Thought of Karl Marx.

SINCE 1989

events in Central and Eastern Europe have given rise to a number of questions—and false hopes—about the alternatives to communism in countries that have been ruled by Marxist-Leninist governments for many decades. The dissolution of communist regimes in the former Warsaw Pact countries and the disintegration of the former Soviet Union make the question of the alternatives into a central issue of current international politics. They also pose some tough challenges for political analysts about the limits of their own professional expertise.

It is obvious that the defeat of communism is primarily seen in the West through an ideological prism. It is equally obvious that such a prism may sometimes impose triumphalist distortions on the interpretive faculties of the observer. Thus in the rush of the initial enthusiasm over the demise of communism, some Western analysts went so far as to announce the End of History. Finally—so they argued—liberal democracy, with the free market as its mainstay, had won its ultimate victory. After defeating fascism and Nazism in World War II, Western liberalism had triumphed over the other alternative ideology confronting it, communism. No other system or ideology could ever successfully challenge it. The Sons of Light had finally vanquished the Sons of Darkness. Gloria in excelsis.

Actual developments in Eastern Europe and the currently unfolding drama in the former Soviet Union itself, however, advise caution. Although there is no doubt that the communist system as such—a one-party dictatorship coupled with a planned command economy—is dead and buried in Central and Eastern Europe (China, Vietnam, and North Korea may be a different story), it becomes less and less clear whether the emerging alternative is a democratic and free-market society. Even in the brief period since the autumn of 1989, clear differences in developments in several postcommunist societies suggest that not all these societies are traveling on the same tracks or even necessarily moving in the same direction. Czechoslovakia and Romania, for example, show completely different patterns of development.

If one begins to look more carefully at these differences, as well as at the vastly different course taken by the various former Soviet republics, it becomes clear that the most pronounced determinants in these different developments are historical factors. Far from seeing an end of history, Eastern Europe now goes through a massive return of history and to history. Past structures and ideologies become a more reliable guide to the general contour of things to come than any other indicator, just as pre-1914 atlases give a better picture of the tangled conflicts emerging in postcommunist societies (for example, Yugoslavia) than recent atlases. Paradoxically, they are more up to date

From *The Brookings Review*, Spring 1992, pp. 30-33. © 1992 by the Brookings Institution. Reprinted by permission.

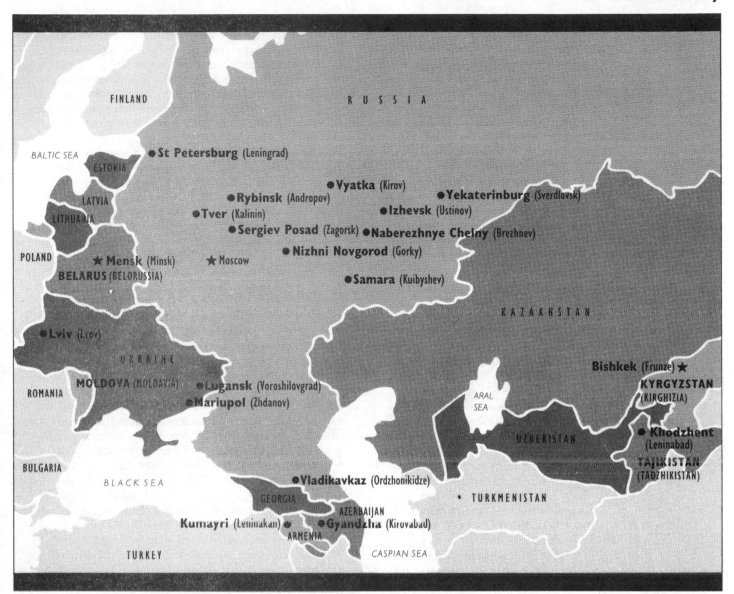

Changing Place Names in the Commonwealth of Independent States, 1992

Map by Margaret Bauer

precisely because they are older. And anyone who has studied the Balkan wars of the 1910s is better equipped to understand the current developments in Yugoslavia than anyone conversant only with recent GNP or other indicators of these societies.

Taking the Long View

In assessing the meaning of this return to history, it is helpful to try to fit the developments of the past few years into a broader historical perspective. Otherwise, the picture is fragmented, and the fragments do not make much sense, nor are they helpful in trying to formulate policies for the future. What we are witnessing is, in historical terms, much more encompassing and complex than the mere disintegration of communism.

In the wake of World War I, three centuries-old continental empires collapsed: the Ottoman, the Austro-Hungarian, and the Russian.

While the collapse of the first two empires was final, the reverberations of the collapse are still very much with us in the form of lingering regional conflicts. In the Middle East, the Israeli-Palestinian conflict, the civil war in Lebanon, the Greek-Turkish conflict in and over Cyprus, and even some aspects of the Iraqi-Kuwaiti dispute are, in essence, disputes between successor states of the Ottoman Empire over the heritage left by it. Similarly, in Central and Eastern Europe, tension between Hungary and Romania over questions connected with Transylvania, the current war in former Yugoslavia, even the possibility of the breakup of the Czechoslovak federation all stem from the unfinished business of carving up the defunct Austro-Hungarian Empire.

That the breakup of these two continental empires has continued to haunt the successor states for more than 70 years now (with no end yet in sight) should be a cautionary note for anyone expecting a quick fix to the collapse of the Soviet Union and the Warsaw Pact.

For the collapse of the old Russian Empire in 1917 was more complex than that of the Ottoman or Austro-Hungarian systems. On coming to power in November 1917, Lenin and the Bolsheviks recognized and announced the right of the non-Russian nations within the old czarist empire to secede and form their own states. As a consequence, Finland and the Baltic states attained their independence with Soviet blessing. The Russian part of Poland aligned itself with the Polish areas under German and Austrian rule to establish the independent Polish republic. The Ukraine declared its independence, as did the Transcaucasian nations of Georgia and Armenia and other regions in the Central Asian parts of the old czarist empire.

The policy of self-determination, however, was reversed during the ensuing civil war and Western anti-communist interventions, when some of the seceding republics became involved in the war against communist rule in Russia. Eventually, central authority was reestablished by force in most of the seceding areas, mainly in the Ukraine and the Transcaucasus. Up to a point, the old Russian Empire was reestablished, this time with a revolutionary, internationalist ideology. During and after World War II this old-new Russian-Soviet empire was able to re-annex the Baltic republics and some other areas in Eastern Poland and Northern Romania. And with the Soviet victory over Nazi Germany in World War II, the Soviet army was instrumental in imposing communist rule over Poland, Czechoslovakia, Hungary, Romania, Bulgaria, and East Germany (Yugoslavia was a different story)—thus adding an unprecedented outer rim to Russian-Soviet domination.

Not by Arms Alone

It would, however, be a mistake to attribute the existence of this extended empire to force alone. It was held together by a powerful combination of force and ideology—a messianic vision of communism as the harbinger of a New World Order of equality, social justice, and solidarity. Flawed as communist society was, one can never understand its staying power only in terms of its coercive instruments of repression. There was always the vision—the vision that made it possible for people in Moscow and Kiev, Riga and Tashkent, Yerevan and Tbilisi to believe that despite their differences in language and customs, religious background and national origin, culture and race, they were still united in an unprecedented effort to create a new world and a new man.

Indeed, for many, *homo sovieticus* was seen to arise out of the debris of the old world. Some of the best and the brightest of the Eastern European intelligentsia believed that given the history of the region's economic backwardness, social conservatism, ethnic strife, and fascist or near-fascist governments, only the promise of communism could deliver these societies and lead them to a new, bright, and peaceful future. The dream might have been naive, but it was born out of the noblest sentiments, and the nobility of the vision makes the abyss of Stalinist horrors even more tragic, as so poignantly shown in Arthur Koestler's *Darkness at Noon*. Only those who understand the attraction of communism for Eastern European intellectuals can understand the depth of the catastrophe brought upon that dream by Stalinism and its aftermath.

Today, the two pillars of communism—force and ideology—have both crumbled. The repressive system has disintegrated, and so has the dream. Nobody believes any more in the redemptive potential of communism. The void is almost fathomless, and frightening.

What will replace this dream and the political structures erected by it? Those who, in their early enthusiasm, naively saw communism as being inevitably replaced by democracy and a market economy are beginning to realize that the countries of Central and Eastern Europe lack the social building blocks—the network of voluntary associations, modes of thinking, traditions, and institutions—cultural, economic, and religious—that make democracy, and the market, possible. The fact of the matter is that before the advent of communism only one country in Eastern Europe—Czechoslovakia—had a viable democratic system coupled with a thriving market economy, and even that was encumbered by grave problems of ethnic minorities (Sudeten Germans, Slovaks, Ruthenians, and Hungarians). Poland did try, between the two World Wars, to achieve a democratic structure, but the nobility of its intention was not matched by the reality of its politics and economics. Parliamentary fragmentation and the fact that almost a third of its population consisted of non-Polish ethnic minorities (Ukrainians, Germans, Jews) undercut its fledgling democratic structures. Hungary, Romania, Bulgaria, Yugoslavia, and the Baltic States developed, between 1918 and 1939, a variety of authoritarian regimes, with various degrees of xenophobic repression and semi-fascist tendencies. And last and not least, Russia itself, despite the historical yearnings of many of its poets and scholars, never had a viable democratic tradition of self-government, pluralism, civil society, tolerance, and individualism. For all the best intentions in the world, post-communist societies find themselves, in most cases, lacking the building stones of democracy that made the West European and North American experience of freedom possible.

The Past as Prologue

Events since 1989 suggest that the best predictive indicator of a country's postcommunist future is—its past. Not that the past is about to be repeated. Heraclitus knew long ago that you cannot step twice into the same river. But the past does, to a large degree, circumscribe the contours of the future political discourse—and its potentialities.

Thus Czechoslovakia, with its liberal, secular, Western-oriented traditions, has made the most successful attempt to develop along democratic lines. Even so, the success has been greater in the Czech lands than in Slovakia, whose historical tradition is much more lacking in these ingredients and which went through an autochthonous fascist phase (the Slovak fascist independent state between 1938 and 1945). Poland and Hungary are able to draw with some success on historical resources and traditions to which representative government was not wholly foreign. But countries like Romania and Bulgaria, let alone Albania, with hardly any democratic or civil society tradition, show how difficult the transition is. And in Yugoslavia, two parallel throw-backs to history are discernible: the historical enmities, mainly between Serbs and Croats, are coming back in all their ferocity, and in the vortex of this ethnic conflict, both independent Croatia and the Serb-dominated rump Yugoslavia show clear signs of developing along the historical authoritarian lines of their past traditions. Only Slovenia, with a history of relative tolerance and decency (mainly under benevolent Habsburg rule) may yet escape the slide into ethnocentric authoritarianism of various stripes now engulfing the former communist attempt to bridge those centuries-old conflicts.

The return to historical patterns is also exemplified by the unification of Germany. Few thought the two Germanies would come together so quickly when the Berlin Wall came down on November 9, 1989. But once the wall was down, and the communist system in East Germany was being transformed, there was no *raison d'etre* for a separate existence of the German Democratic Republic, and the forces of national unity and historical memory very quickly turned the battle cry of East German dissenters *Wir sind das Volk* (We are the people) to *Wir sind ein Volk* (We are one people).

What once seemed Soviet permafrost blanketing Central and Eastern Europe is now melting. And all the grass and all the dirt are coming back. Fifty or seventy-five years of communism appear to be a hiatus in time, and postcommunist societies go back to the political discourse of pre-1917 or pre-1945, respectively.

In the former Soviet Union, with the disappearance of communism as an ideology and a system of power, the disintegration of the world's second-strongest superpower into its national components appears complete. Even Russia itself is being challenged by some of the smaller nations incorporated into it by the czars and commissars alike (Tartars, Chenens—and the list will grow). Erstwhile communist leaders become overnight champions of nationalism—so Leonid Kravthuk in the Ukraine, Nursultan Nazarbayev in Kazakhstan. Georgia and Armenia emerge as separate nation states, with at least the former showing some rather repressive features. Russia itself, while possessing a leadership hailing democracy and the market, lamentably lacks the infrastructure for both, and the dangers for an authoritarian, populist regime are evident. That 25 million ethnic Russians live outside the borders of the Russian Republic (11 million of them in the Ukraine) suggests enormous potentialities for Yugoslav-like problems.

The breakup of the old Russian empire—postponed for 75 years by Soviet power—appears to be now final.

The return to history is nowhere more evident than in the return to the old names of streets, squares—and cities: so Leningrad becomes Saint Petersburg again; Kalinin, Tver; Sverdlovsk, Yekaterinburg; Ordzhonikidze, Vladikavkaz (the last one, a nice czarist triumphalist name: 'the conqueror of the Caucasus').

A Return to Religion

And with the return to history and historical memory comes a return to religion, which in Eastern Europe is closely intertwined with ethnicity and national consciousness. The void left by the demise of communism in the belief system of Eastern European societies is being replaced by a revival (sometimes uncritical) of religiosity and religious symbolism. During the days of Solidarity's fight against communism in Poland, the Church was both a system of beliefs and a helpful alternative organizational structure. But the phenomenon is much wider. Not only Czestechowa, but also Zagorsk and many other shrines in Eastern Europe now enjoy a place in the public realm that few comparable religious sites can claim in the West.

Out of the communist experience many societies may emerge as being more religiously devout than most contemporary Western societies—but also more devout than these societies were themselves before the advent of communism. In Soviet Central Asia, fundamentalist Islam may become a strong political force in the processes of replacing communist structures. Similarly, many Jews in Russia who saw communism (with all its repressive anti-Jewish policies) as a passport into general society are now discovering that with the demise of Soviet Man and the reassertion of Russian, Ukrainian (or Uzbek) nationalism, often coupled with religious connotations, they have to redefine the problems of their own identity. No longer can they claim to be Soviet citizens "of Jewish origin." It is this, as much as economic hardships and the ravings of some marginal anti-Semites, that drives so many (former) Soviet Jews to seek a new homeland in Israel.

History at the Heart of Social Science

This return to history, with all its accompanying dangers, also poses a question to social scientists. After all, social science was not very successful in grasping, let alone predicting, the dramatic processes that brought about the disintegration of communism.

The lesson in this for social scientists, and it can be touched on only briefly here, is a need for more humility with regard to the usefulness of quantitative data, for more reverence for historical contexts—that is, for the role of human consciousness in human affairs. History is not an ontological entity, existing outside human consciousness. Ultimately, it is the totality of choices human beings make about what they remember and transmit to their next generations. As Hegel once remarked, all revolutions are preceded by a quiet and lengthy revolution in human consciousness, "a revolution not visible to every eye, especially imperceptible to contemporaries, and as hard to discern as to describe in words." And "it is the lack of acquaintance with this spiritual revolution which makes the resulting changes astonishing."

Changes in the core of human thinking cannot be captured through diagrams or observed from a distance through digests of official statements and press cuttings (usually in translation). They can be glimpsed in the way human beings express themselves and behave—in their language, their literature, their concrete human discourse. Two examples suffice. In 1974, on Assumption Day in Zagorsk, thousands of young female pilgrims, none of whom was even born when the communist revolution broke out, gathered at the shrine. And in 1986 Moscow intellectuals were preoccupied with whether local street names should be changed to their prerevolutionary names to preserve the meaning of 19th-century Russian literature. It is fair to guess that these two foreshadowings of the dramatic events of the past several years were never documented in the voluminous files kept by professional Western observers of the Soviet Union.

Some humility, then, is in order. If we are to understand in the future the momentous events connected with the decline and fall of communism and the Soviet empire, we must be guided by humility before the obdurate nature of human consciousness.

A Decade of Decline

The 1980s were years of staggering economic decline for Africa.

George B.N. Ayittey

George B.N. Ayittey, a native of Ghana, is currently an associate professor of economics at Bloomsburg University in Bloomsburg, Pennsylvania. He is the author of Africa Betrayed, *1992.*

nce a region with bountiful stores of optimism and hope, the African continent now teeters perilously on the brink of economic disintegration, political chaos, and institutional and social decay. The decline in per capita income has been calamitous for many African countries. Agricultural growth has been dismal, with output growing at less than 1.5 percent since 1970. Industrial output across Africa has also been declining, with some regions experiencing deindustrialization. Export volumes for many African countries faltered, leading to a fall by almost half in Africa's share of world markets.

To maintain income and investment, African governments borrowed heavily in the 1970s. Total African foreign debt has risen 19-fold since 1970 to a staggering $130 billion, equal to its Gross National Product (GNP), making the region the most heavily indebted of all (Latin America's debt amounts to around 60 percent of GNP). Debt service obligations absorbed 47 percent of export revenue in 1988, but only half were actually paid; the arrear payments are constantly being rescheduled.

With scarce foreign exchange increasingly being devoted to service debt obligations, less money was available to import spare parts, drugs, textbooks, and other essential supplies. Infrastructure began to crumble for lack of maintenance, roads started to deteriorate, and telephones refused to work. Hospitals in many African countries had no running water. At the Akomfo Anokye Hospital in Ghana, patients were asked to bring their own bandages, blankets, and food.

Educational facilities soon began to disintegrate. Makerere University in Uganda, once called "the Harvard of Africa," is now in total ruins. The University of Ghana at Legon, once a world-class institution, has not seen a single coat of fresh paint since the colonialists left in the fifties.

In sub-Saharan (or black) Africa, the economic deterioration has been so severe that this region

GNP Per Capita: Average Annual Rates of Growth

	1965-73	1973-80	1980-87
Black Africa	2.9	0.1	-2.8
Excluding Nigeria	1.2	-0.7	-1.2
Exceptions			
Botswana	9.3	7.3	8.0
Mauritius	0.8	3.9	4.4
Cameroon	-0.4	5.7	4.5
Senegal	-0.8	0.5	0.1

Source: World Bank Report, *Sub-Saharan Africa: From Crisis to Sustainable Growth,* Nov. 1989.

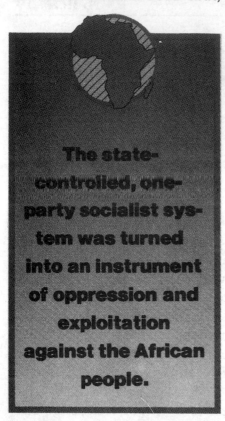

The state-controlled, one-party socialist system was turned into an instrument of oppression and exploitation against the African people.

now has the dubious distinction of being home to twenty-four of the world's thirty-six poorest nations. Economic performance of this region, measured crudely by the rate of growth of per capita income, has been pathetic, as the table indicates.

The overall picture is even more depressing when compared to the performance of other Third World regions. Social and economic indicators of development, such as output growth, health, and literacy, have shown persistently weak performance in black Africa. For example, black Africa's per capita GNP for the two periods 1965–1987 and 1980–1988 were 0.6 and -2.5, respectively. For Asia, these were 4.0 and 5.5 while those for Latin America and the Caribbean were 2.1 and -0.6, respectively. While all other regions of the Third World advanced, black Africa retrogressed.

The exceptions to the general economic atrophy in black Africa have been few. Botswana continues to serve as a shining black success story, followed by Mauritius and Cameroon, while Senegal struggles to keep its head above water. In the early 1980s, Ivory Coast and Kenya used to be members of this select club but now suffer from serious economic crises.

The worst performers have been Ethiopia, Ghana, Liberia, Mozambique, Niger, Nigeria, Sao Tome and Principe, Sudan, Uganda, Zaire, and Zambia—all of which are presided over by civilian/military dictatorships.

What went wrong?

Back in the 1960s, euphoria punctuated much of Africa. Freedom had been won; the colonial "infidels" had been driven out of Africa. There was a fervid desire to prove to the "racists" that Africa, too, was capable of charting its own course—in its own image. But today, most Africans are worse off than they were at independence. What happened?

The new leaders faced the daunting task of developing Africa and delivering the goods to their people. There was widespread belief among African leaders, intellectuals, and even American development experts that the state had to assume a predominant role in economic development. It was argued that markets were underdeveloped, infrastructural facilities were inadequate, capital or funds were insufficient, the middle class was nonexistent, the colonial economic structure had to be

transformed, and so forth. Africa could not rely on free markets and private enterprise, so the state had to spearhead economic development. The U.S. Agency for International Development, the U.S. State Department, and even development experts from Harvard University supported those arguments and channeled aid resources to African governments.

To initiate development, it was widely held that the state needed wide-ranging powers to marshal resources. Extensive powers were conferred upon some African heads of state; others simply arrogated unto themselves additional powers. If a piece of land was needed for highway construction, the state simply appropriated it. In this way, *all* African governments, regardless of their professed ideology, came to assume immense powers.

It can be argued justifiably that the governments needed these powers to spur development. But almost everywhere, the mistake or pernicious oversight was the failure to attach countervailing checks or safeguards to prevent the abuse of these powers. That failure led to the rise of tyranny in Africa. There are tyrannical regimes on *both* the left and the right, but the leftist ones are more numerous since most African countries took the "socialist" route after independence with only a few countries such as Ivory Coast, Kenya, Malawi, and Senegal going the "capitalist" way.

In many places in Africa capitalism was identified with colonialism; since the latter was evil and exploitative, so, too, was the former. Socialism, the antithesis of capitalism, was advocated as the only road to Africa's prosperity. The state-controlled, one-party socialist system, copied from the East, was widely adopted, and, in its wake, followed economic atrophy, exploitation, repression, and dictatorship. The gap between government and people widened. Worse, the "socialism" instituted in most African countries was of the peculiar type that allowed the heads of state and a phalanx of kleptocrats to rape and plunder African treasuries for deposit in overseas banks.

In April 1989, the Christian Association of Nigeria revealed that more than 3,000 Nigerians maintained Swiss bank accounts, putting Nigerians near the top of the list of Third World patrons of Swiss banks. Wealthy Kenyans have hoarded over $5 billion abroad, an amount that exceeds their own country's foreign debt of $4 billion. While Africa's peasants were being exhorted to tighten their belts, vampire elites were loosening theirs with fat bank balances abroad.

By 1980, almost every African economy was dominated by one large sector—the state sector —created by a maze of laws, controls, and regulations. Public sector expenditures in 1986 were more than 27 percent of GNP, compared with only 19 percent in low-income countries outside Africa. The state sector had become an albatross, characterized by a huge civil service, overlapping bureaucracies, stifling red tape, hideous waste and corruption, and hopelessly inefficient state enterprises (SEs). Many of these enterprises were acquired haphazardly with little planning and foresight and

overstaffed with party functionaries.

In the early 1980s, there were more than 3,200 SEs in Africa whose collective performance was nothing short of scandalous. A state-run shoe factory in Tanzania continues to operate at no more than 25 percent of capacity. Here are some other examples:

● For 14 months, from November 1978 to January 1980, the State Jute Bag Factory in Ghana was closed due to a shortage of raw materials. Yet the 1,000 workers received full pay for the entire period of closure.

● In Niger, the cumulative deficit of 23 loss-making SEs exceeded four percent of Niger's Gross Domestic Product (GDP) in 1982.

● In Tanzania, between 1976 and 1979, one-third of all SEs were losing money.

● In Togo, the losses of just eight SEs reached 4 percent of GDP in 1980 while in Ghana 75 percent of SEs posted losses.

Many of the SEs were set up with foreign loans and aid. But in many cases, the investment decision was poorly appraised and riddled with graft and corruption. For instance, a cement plant serving Ivory Coast, Ghana, and Togo was closed in 1984 after only four years of operation. (A 1987 evaluation of rural development projects in Africa financed by the World Bank revealed that half had failed.) After Somalia built a plant to box bananas in 1976, it was discovered that the production level needed for the plant to break even exceeded the total national banana production. In 1975, Tanzania built a $2.5 million bakery in Dar es Salaam with Canadian aid, but there was no flour to make bread. When

Ghana's state-owned sugar factory at Asutsuare was built, it stood idle for more than a year because somebody forgot to include a water supply system. Ghana's state-owned shipping company, Black Star Line, had so many redundant employees that 254 workers were paid for three years (1981–84) simply to stay at home.

The state-owned railways, once the backbone of Africa's transportation system, are now in shambles. Between 1985–87, only 2 black African railways out of 22 derived any modest financial surplus. In 1985, out of 9 railways for which reliable data are available, 1 had operating costs of 90 percent, another, 50 percent of revenue.

Ghana Railways used to carry 2.6 million tons of freight in the early 1970s, but only 0.4 million tons by the middle of the 1980s. Nigeria Railways lost 33 percent of traffic from 1979 to 1986. In Sudan, 40 percent of exports were carried by rail in 1980, but by 1986, the railway's share had fallen to 5 percent. Staff costs of railways absorb up to 75 percent of revenue in some cases. Nigerian Railways, for example, had six times the staff per traffic unit of European railways in 1987.

The civil service is the one segment of the state sector that has experienced phenomenal growth. In Ghana, the civil service increased at a rate five times the growth of the labor market—14 percent each year between 1975 and 1982. In The Gambia, the civil service doubled between 1974 and 1984. By 1986, Guinea's 75,000 civil servants' wages accounted for 50 percent of current expenditures. In the Central African Republic, civil service salaries absorbed 63 percent of current revenues. More than 20 percent of Ghana's civil servants were declared superfluous. In February 1987, some 30 percent of the staff in all government ministries in Sierra Leone were considered useless.

Reform of the hideously inofficient African state sector began in the latter part of the 1960s, when the military seized power and threw out kleptocrats. The soldiers embarked on a "housecleaning" drive to inject discipline and efficiency into the public sector. Many Africans applauded enthusiastically.

The military claimed greater political powers for "housecleaning," national "redemption," and "reconstruction." Constitutions were suspended, curfews imposed, political parties and associations proscribed, and so forth. The military did not ask for these powers; it simply usurped them. But since there were no checks or safeguards, the military, too, abused its power.

The military itself succumbed to the sweet taste of power and overstayed its welcome. In most countries, they turned out to be far worse than the governments they had replaced. They looted national treasuries with "discipline" (Liberia, Nigeria, and Zaire) and ruined one African economy after another with brutal "efficiency" (Benin, Burkina Faso, Ethiopia, Ghana, Somalia, and Uganda).

A new breed of "dedicated" military officers, such as Jerry Rawlings of Ghana and Thomas Sankara of Burkina Faso, emerged and overthrew the corrupt stratocrats. But this new breed was not significantly better.

They resorted to draconian measures, as if more of the wrong medicine would cure the patient. By 1984, the situation had become hopeless.

To add to Africa's woes, civil wars and political strife now rage in at least 15 African countries, as supposed liberators scatter refugees in all directions, leaving carnage and human debris in their wake across the continent. Some of these wars have been waged for 10 years or more, with no end in sight. Meanwhile, Africa's refugee problem mounts; the count now exceeds 10 million, which excludes those trapped within their own countries. In Mozambique, for example, the 12-year-old civil war has cost at least $8 billion and an estimated 900,000 civilian lives; over a third of Mozambique's people have been displaced. The UN High Command for Refugees observed recently that Africa has more than half of the world's refugees.

Studies undertaken by the ECA (UN Economic Commission for Africa) and UNICEF indicate that wars and armed conflicts in southern Africa cost somewhere between 25 to 40 percent of GDP annually, even more in Mozambique and Angola. Military spending has diverted resources from southern Africa's development and accounts for nearly 50 percent of government expenditures. Exports have suffered throughout the region, and import costs have risen due to disruptions in transport routes.

Going back to African roots

To survive in the 1990s, Afri-

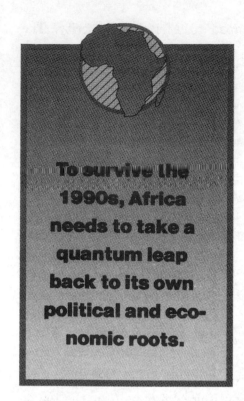

To survive the 1990s, Africa needs to take a quantum leap back to its own political and economic roots.

ca needs to take a quantum leap back to its own indigenous political and economic roots. It is true that in the native system of government, the African chief rules for life. But he is appointed with the advice and consent of the Queen Mother and the council of elders—he does not appoint himself. There is a fundamental difference. No one just gets up and declares himself "chief-for-life" and his village to be "a one-party state" in Africa.

The chief rules as long as his people allow it. Sanctions can be brought against any chief who flouts the will of his people. He is first admonished privately by his advisers and then publicly. If he persists, his people can resort to several remedies. The Igbo people go on a village strike, bringing life to a halt; that usually forces the authorities to mend their ways. In other societies, the people simply abandon their chief and move elsewhere. The history of Africa is full of migrations of people to escape oppression. Nobody loves freedom and independence more than African natives. That explains why there are more than 2,000 different tribes in Africa today—rather than submit to despotic rule, the natives moved somewhere else to preserve their culture and independence. This course of action is still evidenced today by Africa's growing number of refugees.

In other tribes, an erring chief or king is simply *destooled* (removed). According to the Ghanaian historian Dr. Kwame Arhin, "The people of Asante destooled three kings in 1799, 1874, and 1883. They destooled Osei Kwame in 1799 for absenting himself from Kumasi and failing to perform his religious duties during the Adae festival. They destooled Karikari in 1874 for extravagance. They destooled Mensa Bonsu in 1883 for excessively taxing his people."

Furthermore, Africa's indigenous economic system was never fundamentally socialist, as was mistakenly assumed by such African leaders as Ghana's Kwame Nkrumah and Tanzania's Julius Nyerere. Socialism entails government ownership of the means of production, the operation of state enterprises to the exclusion of privately owned businesses, price fixing by the state, and a plethora of state regulations and controls. In other words, there is an absence of private ownership or property, free enterprise, and free markets. Africa's indigenous economic system may be "backward" and "primitive," but it is not characterized by these absences and is therefore not socialism.

The means of production in traditional Africa are not owned by the chief or the tribal government. Certainly, all the cattle in Zululand do not belong to the Zulu Chief—nor do the huts, hunting gear, machetes, and other agricultural implements or farm produce. Even land, erroneously characterized as communally owned, is not owned by the chief; he holds land only in trust. Any African will affirm that chiefs do not fix prices in village markets—one bargains over prices. Nor do African chiefs operate tribal government enterprises to the total exclusion of their subjects. Businesses and commercial enterprises (goldsmiths, bakeries, sculpturing, trade houses) are privately owned; Africans do not need permits to operate them. In fact, one notable feature of the indigenous African system is the absence of pervasive economic controls and regulations. So why impose on black Africans an economic system alien to their culture?

True, African peasants are communalistic and socialistic in the sense that they pool their resources to care for their neighbors and family members. But so, too, do people elsewhere, who work together to rebuild after a natural calamity. That hardly makes them socialists. Communalism does not necessarily imply communism or socialism. Failure to make this important distinction has led many African leaders and experts astray.

Moreover, profit is not an alien concept to Africa. The Asante call it *mfaso*. But the traditional practice was to share it. Under the *abusa* system of the cocoa farmers of West Africa, profit was divided into three: a third to the workers, another third to the owner of the

Africa's future prosperity requires peace and economic freedom.

farm, and the remaining third was set aside for farm maintenance and expansion. In the West, profit was appropriated by capitalists; in the East, by the state. In Africa, the natives shared it in a system that exploited no one. This is this same profit-sharing scheme that the Japanese successfully used to engineer their economic miracle. The "backward" peasants of Africa had been using this scheme for centuries.

But because profit was shared in Africa, some Western writers dismissed African natives as primitive communists. And looking at the same scheme, many African leaders concluded that Africans were ready for socialism. Both groups were wrong.

Instead of copying foreign systems to impose upon their people, African leaders should build upon their indigenous political and economic heritage. Black Africans are not lazy or unresponsive to

Gabon: Lost Opportunities

For many African nations, the 1980s became the time to pay the piper for years of neglect, waste, mismanagement, and plain corruption. African leaders like the Central African Republic's self-appointed emperor Jean Bedel Bokassa misspent millions to live in grandiose splendor while their people scratched a bare existence out of the earth. Marxist Ethiopia's President Mengistu Haile Mariam spent millions to celebrate the 10th anniversary of his "people's revolution" in 1984 while his real people starved —proving that communists were susceptible to the lures of self-aggrandizement. Other countries, like impoverished Mauritania or Burkina Faso (formally Upper Volta), arguably had little to invest and less to lose in socialist experimentation. But some, like Gabon, were blessed with a golden chance to propel themselves into lasting prosperity, only to squander the opportunity away.

Gabon's goose that laid the golden egg was oil. First discovered in the late 1950s, its peak production coincided with soaring world oil prices in 1974. At its height, Gabon's modest though respectable output made it Africa's third largest oil producer—with Nigeria being the region's leading oil exporter. It also made Gabon the wealthiest black African nation, with a per capita income of $3,670 in 1985. During the 1970s and early 1980s, the oil bonanza accounted for 83 percent of the country's export earnings and 63 percent of government revenues.

With its coffers bulging, Gabon sought ways to spend its booty. But its leaders fell prey to the siren call of centrally managed economic planning and the ambitious infrastructure projects that so often accompany it. Large state companies with bloated bureaucracies became breeding grounds for corruption and waste. During the period from 1980 to 1985, capital expenditures rose twice as fast as revenue. More than a third of this money went to the government-owned Trans-Gabon Railway, a stretch of 433 miles through some of the world's densest jungle is meant to connect the mineral-rich interior with the Atlantic coast. Huge cost overruns brought the final amount for completing the line to almost $3 billion—making it the most expensive railway per mile in the world. International lending agencies say that it is unlikely that the money spent to build the line will ever be recovered.

In the spirit of the times, Gabon, which was to be host to the 1977 Organization of African Unity conference, went to great expense to build a cavernous, ultramodern convention center surrounded by sumptuous villas intended for Africa's visiting heads of state. President Omar Bongo doled out the villas to his political cronies after the conference. The convention center itself remains largely unused.

Bongo shipped imported Italian marble—despite the fact that Gabon has a generous supply of its own—to build a sprawling, heavily fortified presidential palace that includes its own movie theater, nightclub, tennis courts, swimming pools, and private apartments for top government officials. Living in a virtually self-contained world cut off from his own citizens, Bongo himself rarely leaves the palace grounds. Security reasons are often cited.

But more than just profligate government spending, the oil boom created a gold-rush atmosphere as Gabon's newly moneyed elite embarked on conspicuous consumption. Luxury imports soared. Shops selling everything from French wines, pâtés, and cheeses to fresh-killed grouse flown in from Europe did a booming business, appealing both to the newly acquired tastes of wealthy Gabonese as well as to the largely French expatriate community (numbering some 20,000), looking for a taste of home in the tropics. Gabon earned the somewhat dubious reputation of being the leading per capita importer of French champagne in the world. Even the country's former first lady couldn't resist the urge to make a killing. She opened up 14 luxury shops, using Gabonese military planes to ferry in everything from Cartier diamond necklaces to Dior evening gowns and charging eager customers exorbitant prices. The ultimate Third World status symbol, the Mercedes Benz, jammed the capital's streets, whisking Gabon's beautiful people to trendy foreign restaurants and glittering nightclubs.

In the midst of this spending spree, little was done to make Gabon more self-sufficient in feeding itself. Even though more than half of the country's working population is engaged in agriculture, it is mostly subsistence farming, contributing only 6 percent to the country's GNP. Today Gabon spends precious foreign earnings to import an incredible 85 percent of its food.

Some good did emerge from all this. Gabon's small population of barely one million was given one of black Africa's best social security and health care systems, all government subsidized. Money was invested in education and the construction of new primary and secondary schools. Education is compulsory until age 16, and adult illiteracy stands at 38 percent, an impressive figure for the region. A university—named after President Bongo, of course—was built. A deep-water port just south of the capital was dredged out and the tourist infrastructure was developed.

But the world oil glut in 1986 brought the good times to an abrupt and wrenching end. In just one year, Gabon's export earnings dropped 44 percent, real economic growth declined 10 percent, and the country's foreign debt soared to $1.7 billion.

Faced with impending disaster, once-proud Gabon went hat in hand to the international lending agencies. In 1986 it received $99 million in standby credit from the International Monetary Fund, rescheduled public debt, and instituted austerity measures. In December 1989, Gabon signed a structural adjustment program with the World Bank and the African Development Bank for loans amounting to $112 million. The government also agreed to restructure, privatize, or liquidate 22 government-owned enterprises.

But austerity measures have this year caused the worst antigovernment riots in 20 years, with widespread strikes of public workers who fear that their long-cherished benefits and job security are in danger. Economic discontent has led to political unrest as many Gabonese now charge that the country's fiscal mess stems from President Bongo's autocratic one-party rule. Bongo has now had to grudgingly accept democratic reforms and multiparty rule. Like it or not, the winds of perestroika and glasnost have reached Gabon.

—*Raymond J. Mas*

Raymond J. Mas is a current issues editor for THE WORLD & I. *He lived in Gabon for three years.*

market incentives. Their indigenous institutions may be backward and primitive, but they used these same institutions to prosper in the late 19th century. The period from 1880 to 1950 stands out in Africa's history as one of unparalleled peasant economic advancement. During this time, Africans proved themselves to be remarkably industrious and enterprising, in spite of their backwardness and primitive implements. This is not primitive romanticism but a statement of fact. African natives prospered in the late 19th century because they had economic freedom and a peaceful environment. Africa's future prosperity requires this economic freedom that was wrenched from its people after independence by deluded leaders with misguided social, political, and economic policies alien to Africa.

Africa also needs freedom from the civil wars and political strife that plague it today. While colonialism may have been invidious, one of its least-acknowledged benefits was the peace it brought to Africa. Tribal wars and rivalries came to a virtual halt, giving Africa a much-needed atmosphere of peace for productive economic activity. Basic forms of infrastructure (roads, railways, bridges, schools, post offices, etc.) were laid down during this period, which greatly facilitated the movement of goods and people. Infrastructural development gave production and economic expansion an enormous boost.

The secrets of prosperity in Africa are thus not hard to find. A mere two words unveil them: peace and economic freedom.

The pipes of peace?
Sir Sidney Smith and
officers with the
Pasha of Acre, 1799 – a
time when the
Napoleonic
intervention in Egypt,
and the accelerating
decay of the Ottoman
Empire brought Islam
and the West again
into sharp contact.

ISLAM
THE ROOTS OF MISPERCEPTION

Akbar Ahmed offers the most timely review of how history
and stereotype have often combined to make Western
Orientalism a hindrance rather than a help in mutual
understanding between two cultures.

*Akbar S. Ahmed is Iqbal Visiting Fellow and
Fellow of Selwyn College, Cambridge.*

In an earlier article for *History
Today* (November 1989) I had
pointed out the ongoing and complex confrontation between Islam and
the West which was explained by the
three historical encounters between
them. The encounter first began with
the rise of Islam, the conquest of Spain
and the appearance of Islamic armies in
France and Sicily. It reached its drama-

tic climax with the Crusades, which in
a sense symbolise it for the popular
imagination. It ended in the seventeenth century when the Ottomans
were halted at Vienna.

The second encounter was brief but
ferocious. During it the entire Muslim
world would be included in the grip of
European colonial imperialism. When
this encounter concluded, after the
Second World War, it was assumed that
a period of harmony and friendship
based on equality between Islamic and

western nations would follow. However, this was not to be. The hoped for
symmetry was destroyed as Western
civilisation, driven by the USA and UK,
began to dominate the world, a process
sharpened by the collapse of Communism in Eastern Europe in the late 1980s.

The present encounter is perhaps
the most complex and bitter of all. The
weapons are culture and media propaganda. Television and the video-recor-
der penetrate the most inaccessible
Muslim homes. Muslims appear more
threatened than ever before and unable
to cope with the cultural onslaught of
the West. Their responses to *The Satanic Verses* sum up this encounter; Muslim fury met Western incomprehension
reflecting the complete lack of communication, the great cultural gaps.

I want to further the discussion by
arguing broadly the study of Islam and
perception of Muslim society are
embedded in the socio-political context of these encounters. Scholars are
thus not innocent bystanders in this
confrontation. Indeed, in an important
sense they are active participants. For
many, the confrontation with Islam
would be a kind of *Glaubenskrieg*, the
doctrinal war to be fought to the finish.
In turn, their work would help form

From *History Today*, April 1991, pp. 29-37. © 1991 by History Today, Ltd., 20 Old Compton Street, London W1V 5PE.
Reprinted by permission.

the popular contemporary perception of Muslims.

In the first historical encounter in the Middle Ages, Islam, to Europe, appeared as a minatory, all-conquering and all too-real threat knocking on its very doors. Church and state were united in condemning it. Writers and scholars enthusiastically lent their talents to the effort. In this phase religion is the main understanding of the 'other'; the conflict was reduced to Christianity versus Islam. Islamic civilisation was on the ascendant and Europe a backward area, of peripheral interest to it. Paradoxically for Muslims, the enemy hammer-head that would strike at the heart of their greatest empire, the Abbasids, would come not from Europe but from the opposite direction. Just when the Crusades were fizzling out, the Mongols in 1258 captured and destroyed Baghdad.

Recognising the central role of the Prophet, critics of Islam concentrated their attacks on his character. In particular they criticised his marriages and certain incidents, namely the deaths of the vituperative poet and the Jewish group, Quraiza. From Voltaire to Gibbon, there is a long list of the writers and scholars of Europe who participated in this attack. In Dante's *Divine Comedy* the Prophet is constantly split in two as eternal punishment for the sin of religious schism. 'Muhammad remained in his moral corruption and debauchery a camel thief, a cardinal who failed to reach the throne of the Papacy and win it for himself,' declared the French *Encyclopedie Larousse*. Pope Innocent III identified him as the Anti-Christ. The Royal Chaplain and Father Confessor of Spain, Jaime Bleda, introduced the Prophet, in what became a standard history, as the 'deceiver of the world, false prophet, Satan's messenger, the worst precursor of the Anti-Christ'.

The Quran, because it is so directly linked to the Prophet, also remained a target. This would continue into modern times. For Carlyle it was a 'wearisome, confused jumble, crude, incondite'. Contemporary scholars, such as Montgomery Watt, would continue to reflect this strain. By imputing authorship of the Quran to the Prophet, who was unlettered, Watt complained of the lack of logic and method in its arguments. In spite of these arguments, for Muslims the power and sublimity of the Quran remained unchanged. For

them it is the 'inimitable symphony, the very sound of which moves men to tears and ecstasy' (Pickthall in his introduction to his translation of the Quran, still a standard version even though it was first published in 1930).

There are many examples of synthesis, and sympathetic understanding between East and West. Spain under the Arabs is an example of the former, Saladin of the latter. With its libraries, colleges and baths, its dynamic interaction between Christian, Jew and Muslim, Arab Spain produced a gloriously rich and tolerant culture. From here western Europe learned of many things, including the Greeks. The Oxford and Cambridge colleges are believed to be modelled on those of Cordoba and Granada.

Saladin (1138-93) – a European corruption of Salah-al-din, rectitude of the faith – perhaps more than any Muslim has captured the Western imagination. He features in popular films and novels like those of Walter Scott and Rider Haggard; Saladin's dealings with Richard Coeur de Lion – battling against him one day and exchanging gifts the next – added to the lustre of his name.

The high point of Saladin's career was the re-taking of Jerusalem in 1187. His legendary generosity was displayed when he allowed the Christian priests to stay on and keep their churches – this in spite of the fact that some had encouraged Crusaders to acts of barbarity like eating Muslim corpses. When the French general in 1920, preparing to partition Arab lands, knocked on his tomb in Damascus and said, 'Awake Saladin, we have returned,' he expressed the continuity of the first encounter.

The second encounter was for Muslims an unmitigated disaster which arguments about railways and the telegraph, or maintaining law and order, cannot assuage. Europe – England, France, Germany, Spain, Portugal, Italy – absorbed Muslim lands; Russia took the Central Asian states. One by one, kingdoms and states, large and small, fell. The Europeans were able to subjugate what had been established and complex civilisations. Colonial rule paralysed Muslim societies, congealed thought and froze their history. Muslims were finding it difficult to reconcile themselves with what was rapidly becoming the European phase of world history, and in their failure and anger

they rejected the symbols of modernity.

It was easy to fall back to old, pre- or non-Islamic, superstition and beliefs. Muslim leaders would successfully convince their followers to face European bullets with sticks and lances. They had blessed Muslim weapons, bestowed on them magical powers which would prevent injury to the true believers. Beliefs such as these assisted the Europeans in consolidating their hold.

However, what is notable in the turbulence of the nineteenth century and in the face of advancing Europe, across Africa and Asia, is Muslim leadership which vigorously clung to the Quran and *Shariah*, Islamic tradition. The Sanusi and Mahdi orders fighting Europeans in Africa; Imam Shamyl in the Caucasus struggling against Russians; Ummar Tal Al Haji whose theocratic state the French eventually absorbed; Muhammad Abdul Hassan in Somalia, Abdul Qadir in Algeria, the Akhund of Swat and Sayyed Ahmad Barelvi in north India, and Haji Shariatullah in Bengal fought to preserve the Islamic order. By the time the century turned the Muslim world was still smouldering, but it was subdued.

A distinct transformation is evident in the European perceptions of Muslims during the second encounter. For Lord Clive, the conqueror of India, the 'typical' Indians 'are servile, mean, submissive and humble. In superior stations, they are luxurious, effeminate, tyrannical, treacherous, venal, cruel'. 'A Persian is a coward at the best of times,' concluded Lord Curzon, Viceroy of India, and imperial expert on Persia. Lord Cromer of Egypt describes the Egyptian mind, making comparisons with Europeans: 'Sir Alfred Lyall once said to me "Accuracy is abhorrent to the Oriental mind. Every Anglo-Indian should always remember that maxim." Want of accuracy, which easily dengenerates into untruthfulness, is in fact the main characteristic of the Oriental mind'.

Lord Macaulay, the President of the Indian Law Commission whose Minute on Education in 1835 would devastate Muslim society, dismissed the entire body of Arabic and Sanskritic learning as worthless. Kipling, though he is capable of illuminating shafts of understanding, nonetheless created in his poems racist stereotypes. The native is the 'big black boundin' beggar' ('Fuzzy-Wuzzy'); the women, 'Funny an' yel-

East meets West; (left) a sketch of Kipling with the Orient 'on the brain'; (right) a sketch of an Imam by Sir Edwin Landseer – two facets of the 'Orientalism' generated among Victorian and Edwardian writers and artists.

low' ('The Ladies'); the 'natives' are a 'blackfaced crew' ('Gunga Din'), 'Half devil and half child' ('The White Man's Burden').

Scholarship, again, adds to, lends credence to and further caricatures this endeavour. 'Orientalism', the study of the Orient, emerges during this encounter. It is often traced to that first body of scholars who accompanied Napoleon to Egypt. Along with interest in the ethnography and geography of the Orient these scholars were fascinated by what they saw as primitive social and sexual customs.

Though he did not coin the term 'Orientalism' Edward Said's book of that title gave it currency in the late 1970s. In a nutshell, he argued that the West cannot know the Orient (for him mainly the Muslim Orient) except as irrational, depraved and infantile. This perception is rooted in the power relationship between a dominating West and subjugated Orient. It is in the interest of the West, therefore, to depict the Orient in negative stereotypes.

If for Muslims the second encounter, European colonialism, was a siege, the present encounter is a *blitzkrieg*. Unlike the earlier encounters it is neither primarily religious, nor colonial nor racist – but at certain points reflects all three. It is marked by a bewildering fusion of media images, scholarly opinions and atavistic cultural responses. In an age where plurality of cultures and belief in the practice of democracy are widely accepted the abrasiveness of

the debate is notable. Matters are exacerbated by what is seen as Islamic resurgence or revivalism.

The present phase of intense Islamic activity began in the 1970s: the Ramadan war in 1973, the Arab Oil embargo in the same year led by the vigorously dedicated King Faisal, General Zia's assuming power in 1977 and his Islamisation programme and finally the culmination of the decade with the coming to power of Ayatollah Khomeini at the head of the Islamic revolution in 1979. The Russian invasion of Afghanistan in 1979 triggered an Afghan *jihad* (holy war), to liberate it.

Muslim activity was not confined to guns and battlefields. A period of vigorous and confident intellectual activity was noted. An international attempt towards an 'Islamisation of Knowledge' was made by scholars like Ismail Faruqi which challenged many existing modernist ideas associated with the West. Muslim economists like Khurshid Ahmad laboured to create an 'Islamic economics', anthropologists an 'Islamic anthropology'. The publication of books like *Orientalism*, further provided ideas fuelling the challenge to Western scholarship.

A key feature in these endeavours is the perception of the West; it is seen as determined to humiliate and ridicule Islam. In this campaign the Western media are identified as the chief villains, as simply anti-Islamic. In turn the Western attacks on Muslim extremists the fundamentalists of the popular press – easily convert and carry over to an attack on the entire body of Muslims. For some non-Muslims beneath every Muslim there appears to be a mullah struggling to emerge; the sooner, the more effectively, he is put down the better.

How is contemporary scholarship of Islam, both among Muslims and non-Muslims, affected by these perceptions? For the traditionalist Muslim scholar, the larger message of Islam, rather than the narrower sectarian or personal squabbles, is of importance. They believe in the universal message of God and in inter-faith dialogue. Established names like Ismail Faruqi, Hossein Nasr and Ali 'Ashraf are to be

found here. Some, like Aziz Ahmad, 'connect' with Western Orientalists.

If the traditionalists suggest harmony and balance, even a *modus vivendi* with the non-Muslim world, the radicals, like Shabbir Akhtar, Ziauddin Sardar and M. W. Davies,—reflect the general Muslim sense of anger at its injustice. Kalim Siddiqui is the best known radical in the UK demanding an Islamic order and the death of Salman Rushdie. Most Western scholarship, including that of a different and more sympathetic younger generation, is rejected by the radicals as tainted.

The radicals are contemptuous of the modernists, and in turn, branded fundamentalists by them. For modernists, Islam as nostrum, or relevant system, is no longer valid. Salman Rushdie and Tariq Ali are held as the modernists par excellence. Their knowledge of Islam is limited and usually derived from a cursory reading of the Orientalists. They also serve the negative stereotypes of Islam; Rushdie's *The Satanic Verses* and the play Ali wrote with Howard Brenton, *Iranian Nights,* are examples (these positions may shift as Rushdie's declaration of faith in Islam indicates; see Ahmed 1991).

Recently religious pride and nationalist anger have combined to create a reaction against Orientalism which is seen as tainted by colonialism. One inevitable consequence is the outright rejection of Western scholarship by Muslims. Muslim scholars in the West whether Arab, like Rana Kabbani, or

Pakistani, like Asaf Hussain, are deeply suspicious of Western Orientalism in their work.

Another consequence is the growth of a kind of Occidentalism among Muslim writers. Unfortunately, there are many in whose work paranoia and hysteria pass for thought and analysis. Fulminating against Princeton and Harvard is no answer; it is intellectual bankruptcy. The distortions, the travesty, are not only incorrect but also a sad reminder of what Muslim scholarship once was.

After all, Muslims are exhorted in the holy Quran to know and marvel at the variety of people created. The holy Prophet urged his followers to go as far as China to acquire knowledge. To an Arab in the seventh century, China would have been at the outermost limits of the known universe. The bankruptcy today is made poignant by the achievements and observations in foreign lands of the great Muslim travellers, like Al-Beruni and Ibn Battuta, centuries ago.

This Occidentalism merits study. An examination of what contemporary Orientals think of the Occident would reveal images as distorted and dishonest as those in Orientalism. It derives almost entirely from the Western mass media. Muslims have still to produce scholarly studies of the West. This includes Muslims, over ten million in number, who live permanently in the USA and Europe, and in whose interest it is to study the countries they have made their home. Knowledge of their host population is critical, not only for academic reasons but also practical ones. Employment, immigration controls, housing, cultural integration are all affected. As a result immigrants, especially in Europe, live in intellectual and cultural ghettoes often facing serious discrimination.

In concluding our arguments we turn to the non-Muslim commentators. Said is dismissive of even the most renowned universities 'like Princeton, Harvard, and Chicago' where Islam is taught. However the work of the older Orientalists was marked, *pace* Said, by many positive features. These included a life-time's scholarship, a command of languages, a wide vision and breadth of learning, and an association with the established universities. In this category are the well-known names – H. Gibb, B. Lewis, A. Arberry, M. Watt, L. Massignon. We must not allow their

links of various kinds with the colonial powers and a consciousness of the larger encounter between Islam and the West to detract from their contribution. While decrying some of their political assumptions I, for one, am grateful to the translators of the work of Al-Beruni, Ibn Battuta, Ibn Khaldun and, nearer home to me, Babur, the founder of the Mughal dynasty in India.

However, one of the major contemporary failures of the Orientalists was not to be able to predict, and later to make much sense of, the political changes occurring in Muslim countries. For them Muslim society, as in Iran, was progressing along a linear, modernising, secular path, the outward signs of which were discos, cinemas and jeans. Scholars who had spent a life-time on Persian studies were projecting a secure and long future for the Shah up to the revolution. After the

revolution their previous commitment to, or association with, the Shah barred them from the country. Their knowledge was of little avail in dealing with the new leaders.

Moreover, in the very premise of Orientalism something central and indispensable is absent: it is the notion of a common, universal humanity embracing human society irrespective of colour and creed. By denying a common humanity Orientalism corrodes the spirit and damages the soul, thus preventing a complete appreciation or knowledge of other people. In this light Orientalism is either cultural schizophrenia or a complex form of racism.

Though most of the renowned Orientalist names are no longer with us, their influence is pervasive and the ideas of younger writers continue to be shaped by them. However, there is

'Science versus Pluck or Too Much for the Mahdi' – a cartoon comment on war in the Sudan, 1884.

emerging a new breed of Western scholars, born from the Orientalist tradition yet different in sympathy and style. John Esposito, Michael Fischer and William Chittick in the USA, and Francis Robinson in the UK, represent this trend. Their work is scholarly and fair; their aim is sympathetic scholarship, a need to know and understand. Unfortunately in their numbers and viewpoint these are still in the minority.

William Chittick's most recent study of the Sufi figure, Ibn Arabi, is a good example of this scholarship. It is nothing short of a magnificent labour of love. His defence of Arabi's themes of humility and compassion are deep-felt; his identification with his subject moving. It is impossible to see this kind of Orientalist work through Saidian eyes.

The final group commenting on Islam is the ragbag body of instant media expert, journalist and novelist. For people in this group Islam is the media villain, a monstrosity to be reviled and beaten. It is the volume and power of these voices in the media that have drowned the more sober tones of the scholar. Indeed they raid the Orientalist cupboard for alimentation picking up stereotypes and scatological bits of information. In turn they use these in the most tendentious and egregious manner.

Into 1990, when the Gulf crisis was building up, the tabloids were distorting anything on Islam, even a straight, academic lecture. After my talk at the Royal Anthropological Institute in London on September 13th, 1990, arranged for Her Royal Highness the Princess of Wales, the tabloids illustrated this point. 'Princess Di was swept up in the Gulf crisis yesterday as Muslims gave her a lecture on "holy war"', declared the opening lines of *The Sun* (September 14th, 1990). It then chided me: 'newspapers were accused of "distorting" the religion that holds thousands of Britons hostage.' Once again Islam was equated as the religion of hostage-takers.

Numerous academics, including many Islamic experts abandoned their role as observers and became active participants in the efforts to portray Islam in an unsympathetic light. During crises involving Muslims – Iran, the Rushdie affair, the Gulf war – they advise governments, prepare reports and appear in the popular media. The voices of scholars explaining the gentle aspects of Islam – Persian paintings, Arabic calligraphy, Sufi mysticism – can be drowned by those arguing about geo-political strategy and imperatives. Indeed some experts, like J.B. Kelly in *Arabia, the Gulf and the West*, demanded outright invasion of Muslim countries, like those in the Gulf, in order to capture their wealth, their oil wells and ports, to make them safe for the West.

Kelly's words were prophetic. In 1990 the large army of Western troops that gathered on the Arabian peninsula and the war against Iraq in early 1991 were a logical outcome of this thought. Again, the perception of events revealed how differently the conflict was seen by the two sides. For most Americans it was an attempt to establish the New World Order, one that was post-colonial and post-Cold War. It was to be based on justice, promising hope for humanity. For most Arabs it was a continuation of the old order; a desire by the West to order their politics and control their destiny. It was also rooted in the encounters we have identified; Saddam was being called a modern Saladin by his supporters in the Middle East and there was talk of *jihad*.

The position is complicated by inter-penetrating networks in our age. Not all Arabs are enemies for the Americans: Saudi, Egyptian and Kuwaiti troops were fighting alongside them. For many of these Arabs Saddam was a murderous tyrant.

It is time, however, to move beyond Edward Said's arguments. In an important sense he has led us into an intellectual cul-de-sac. In attempting to transcend the idea of the Orientalist system he ends up by replacing one system with another. There remains the real danger of simplifying the complex problem of studying the 'other' or the 'foreign'. Said has left us at the end of the trail with what he set out to denounce: stereotypes, like the Orientalists; and the application of terms like Orient, Orientalist, Oriental, to such wide blocs as to make them meaningless. Said's Arab passion may have ultimately damaged his own case. The *rite de passage,* the ritual slaying of the elders (Grunebaum, Gibb and Lewis) was too noisy and too bloody.

One way forward is through ordinary human contact. By reducing Said's serious arguments to caricature, that the West can know the Orient only in a negative, exploitative way, friendship across borders is removed from human relationships. Yet we know of the many long-lasting and fruitful friendships between people from the West and Muslims: Thomas Arnold and Muhammad Iqbal, Olaf Caroe and Iskander Mirza, E.M. Forster and Ross Masood; or nearer our times, Salim Ali and Dillon Ripley, Ralph Russell and Khurshid ul Islam.

These were equal friendships, symmetrical in their balance, not represented by 'border, nor breed, nor birth'. Renowned books were dedicated, *A Passage to India,* to Ross Masood, *The Pathans,* to Iskander Mirza, and odes written for the fraternity, Iqbal's for Arnold, Ripley's for Ali.

Perhaps the post-modernist phase of history, with its emphasis on fragmentation and plurality, equality and tolerance, will encourage such friendship; that is one ray of light in an otherwise bleak picture. The great divides, the polarisation, in the study of and dealing with Islam may thus be lessened. The need to understand the other is more imperative than ever before in our world because it is so interlocked through technology and communications.

FOR FURTHER READING:
The themes behind the three historical encounters between Islam and the West are reflected further in A.S. Ahmed, *Discovering Islam: Making Sense of Muslim History and Society,* (Routledge, 1988); Interview with Salman Rushdie, *The Guardian* (Review), January 17th, 1991; A.S. Ahmed and E. Gellner (forthcoming), *Post-Modernism and Islam,* Routledge, London (under publication); W. Chittick, *The Sufi Path of Knowledge,* State University of New York Press, 1989; J.B. Kelly, *Arabia, the Gulf and the West,* Weidenfeld and Nicolson, London, 1980; E. Said, *Orientalism,* New York, 1978 and *Covering Islam,* New York, 1981.

Global Problems, Global Interdependence

The cold war and its aftermath left problems for the contemporary world, a world in which every nation is linked to the welfare of others. The Soviet landscape has been left in an environmental shambles with poisoned air, food, and water. Particularly worrisome are the pockets of atomic waste and nuclear technology left in the wake of military competition with the United States. The new nations of the former USSR are too poor to repair the environmental damage, and, as the essay "Toxic Wasteland" reports, the recovery will likely take decades. At the moment (mid-1995), former Soviet countries that are in desperate need for electricity are beginning to activate

unsafe nuclear reactors, and disasters similar to the blowup at the Chernobyl nuclear plant in Ukraine can be predicted.

Another problem left over from the cold war is the proliferation of nuclear technology. Almost any determined nation now can build an atom bomb, and recent scares from North Korea and Iraq confirm the possibility. American policies of secrecy, inspection, and trade restrictions will probably not work for the future, as noted in the article "The Nuclear Epidemic." There is a question about what the world should do about this problem. It may be that the era of the cold war, when two superpowers controlled most of the atomic weaponry, will seem a simple world indeed. Possibly, humankind is too oriented towards violence for its survival. Even in the Punjab, a success story of the green revolution, the profits have gone in part to buy weapons. Richard Critchfield tells about this development in his report "Sowing Success, Reaping Guns."

The green revolution has provided the means to greater crop yields and brought famine to a temporary end in India. The technology has given a respite, but world population continues to grow. World population, now over 5 billion, will double by 2050. Then what? Can such a number be fed? John Bongaarts provides arguments on both sides of the question. Where will they live? Can our cities grow into megacities of 50 million people without problems of governance? What will be done with megalomaniacs like Hitler who wanted "living room" for his people, and who was willing to kill others to get it?

In contrast, there is the threat of the pandemic of AIDS, a disease that is almost always fatal. No one knows for certain the origin of the disease, but the best guess at the moment is that it jumped from monkeys in central Africa to humans. The spread of the disease coincided with the growth of African cities and has since spread worldwide. The World Health Organization estimates that 40 million people will have AIDS by the year 2000. About 2 percent of the adult population in Bombay already have the disease, yet India with its 900 million people lags behind the devastation of the disease in central Africa. Can these nations deal with the cost of treatment and the loss of productive citizens? In addition, there are other diseases, such as the Ebola virus, which recently broke out in Africa, that can decimate the human population. Would it not be ironic if our overpopulation problem is solved by a disease that our science and technology cannot cure?

Still, the world is a beautiful place and human beings have learned some things during their brief sojourn on the planet. Thus far, industrialization and the earlier agricultural revolution have provided for an increasing population. We have made progress concerning human rights, and there is historical evidence that a mixing of cultures can lead to greatness. Cultural diversity can be good, as Thomas Sowell argues in his report. It can also go the other way and result in "dead-end tribalism." This seems to confirm that our world is filled with wonders, opportunities, perils, and disasters. A global wisdom and perspective will be necessary in order to preserve "spaceship Earth" for the future.

Looking Ahead: Challenge Questions

Compare the position of the United States at the end of the cold war with that of Great Britain at the end of World War I.

What problems have been left over from the cold war?

What progress has been made in respect to human rights since 1500?

Does an overpopulation problem exist, or is it a myth?

Why is AIDS so difficult to cure? Is this considered a new disease?

What is the value or detriment in cultural diversity?

TOXIC WASTELAND

*In the former Soviet Union, economic growth was worth any price.
The price is enormous.*

In satellite photos of the Eurasian landmass at night, the brightest pools of light do not emanate from London, Paris or Rome. The largest glow, covering hundreds of thousands of acres and dwarfing every other light source from the Atlantic to the Pacific, can be found in the northern wilderness of Siberia, near the Arctic Circle. It comes from thousands of gas flares that burn day and night in the Tyumen oil fields, sending clouds of black smoke rolling across the Siberian forest. During the past two decades, the steady plume of noxious sulfur dioxide has helped to ruin more than 1,500 square miles of timber, an area that is half again as large as Rhode Island.

Siberia's acid rains are just one more environmental catastrophe in a land where man has run roughshod over nature and is now facing the deadly consequences. The former U.S.S.R. had no monopoly on pollution and environmental neglect, as residents of Minamata, Mexico City and Love Canal can testify. But Soviet communism's unchecked power and its obsessions with heavy industry, economic growth, national security and secrecy all combined to produce an environmental catastrophe of unrivaled proportions.

Thirty Percent of All Foods Contain Hazardous Pesticides

"When historians finally conduct an autopsy on Soviet communism, they may reach the verdict of death by ecocide," write Murray Feshbach, a Soviet expert at Georgetown University and Alfred Friendly Jr. in the new book, "Ecocide in the U.S.S.R." (Basic Books, $24). "No other great industrial civilization so systematically and so long poisoned its air, land, water and people. None so loudly proclaiming its efforts to improve public health and protect nature so degraded both. And no advanced society faced such a bleak political and economic reckoning with so few resources to invest toward recovery."

In the name of progress. Communism has left the 290 million people of the former Soviet Union to breathe poisoned air, eat poisoned food, drink poisoned water and, all too often, to bury their frail, poisoned children without knowing what killed them. Even now, as the Russians and the other peoples of the former U.S.S.R. discover what was done to them in the name of socialist progress, there is little they can do to reverse the calamity: Communism also has left Russia and the other republics too poor to rebuild their economies and repair the ecological damage at the same time, too disorganized to mount a collective war on pollution and sometimes too cynical even to try. Even when the energy and the resources needed to attack this ecological disaster do materialize, the damage is so widespread that cleaning it up will take decades. Among the horrors:

■ Some 70 million out of 190 million Russians and others living in 103 cities breathe air that is polluted with at least five times the allowed limit of dangerous chemicals.

■ A radiation map, which has never been released to the public but which was made available to *U.S. News*, pinpoints more than 130 nuclear explosions, mostly in European Russia. They were conducted for geophysical investigations, to create underground pressure in oil and gas fields or simply to move earth for building dams. No one knows how much they have contaminated the land, water, people and wildlife, but the damage is almost certainly enormous. Red triangles on the map mark spots off the two large islands of Novaya Zemlya where nuclear reactors and other radioactive waste were dumped into the sea. Tapping one location, Alexei Yablokov, science adviser to Russian President Boris Yeltsin, says a nuclear submarine sank there 10 years ago, its reactor now all but forgotten. "Out of sight, out of mind," he says with disgust.

■ Some 920,000 barrels of oil—roughly 1 out of every 10 barrels produced—are spilled every day in Russia, claims Yablokov. That is nearly the equivalent of one Exxon Valdez spill every six hours. To speed up construction of oil pipelines, builders were permitted to install cutoff valves every 30 miles instead of every 3, so a break dumps up to 30 miles worth of oil onto the ground. One pool of spilled oil in Siberia is 6 feet deep, 4 miles wide and 7 miles long.

■ According to Yablokov, the Siberian forests that absorb much of the world's carbon dioxide are disappearing at a rate of 5 million acres a year, posing a bigger threat to the world environment than the destruction of the Brazilian rain forests. Most of the damage is caused by pollution and by indiscriminate clear-cutting, mostly by foreign companies, in soil that can't tolerate such practices.

■ Because the rivers that feed it were diverted, the Aral Sea is evaporating, altering rainfall patterns, raising local temperatures as much as 3 degrees and releasing so much salt and dust that the level of particulate matter in Earth's atmosphere has risen more than 5 percent.

■ Officials in Ukraine have buried 400 tons of beef contaminated by radiation from the Chernobyl nuclear accident. An additional 920 tons will be buried in June.

A confidential report prepared by the Russian (formerly Soviet) Environment Ministry for presentation at the Earth Summit in Rio de Janeiro this summer blames the country's unparalleled ecological disaster primarily on a policy of forced industrialization dating back to the 1920s. The report, a copy of which was obtained by *U.S. News*, notes the "frenetic pace" that accompanied the relocation of plants and equipment to the Urals and Siberia during World War II and their rapid return to European Russia after the war. This, the report says, created a "growth-at-any-cost mentality."

The communist state's unchallenged power also was reflected in its obsession with gigantism and in its ability to twist science into a tool of politics. The late Soviet President Leonid Brezhnev planned to reverse the flow of the Irtysh River, which flows north, in order to irrigate parts of arid Central Asia for rice and corn growing. But to redirect 6.6 trillion gallons of water each year would have required building a 1,500-mile canal. Critics warned that the project would alter world weather patterns, but Soviet officials gave up only after spending billions of rubles on the plan. "Soviet science became a kind of sorcerer's apprentice," write Feshbach and Friendly.

Unexplained anthrax. Not surprisingly in a nation obsessed with national security and secrecy, another culprit was the military-industrial complex, which the Environment Ministry's report says, "has operated outside any environmental controls." In 1979, some 60 people died in a mysterious outbreak of anthrax near a defense institute in Sverdlovsk (now renamed Ekaterinburg). After years of Soviet denials of any link with defense matters, the Presidium of the Supreme Soviet voted in late March to compensate the victims of the incident and conceded that it was linked to "military activity."

At the same time, the report says, communism's reliance on central planning and all-powerful monopolies produced an "administrative mind-set" that created huge industrial complexes that overtaxed local environments. The report says the emphasis on production over effi-

ciency has led to some 20 percent of all metal production being dumped—unused—into landfills. Nor did Soviet industries, shielded from competition, feel any need to improve efficiency or switch to cleaner, more modern technology.

Worse, it became virtually impossible to shut down even the worst offenders, because doing so could wipe out virtually an entire industry. In Estonia, for example, the Kohtla-Jarve chemical plant, a major polluter, squeezes 2.2 million barrels of oil a year from shale and provides 90 percent of the energy for the newly independent country. Environment Minister Tanis Kaasik says flatly that it is "impossible" to shut down production.

Terrible secrets. A pervasive secret police force, meanwhile, ensured that the people seldom found out about the horrors visited on them in the name of progress and that, if they did, they were powerless to stop them. It took Soviet officials more than 30 years to admit that an explosion had occurred at a nuclear storage site near Chelyabinsk in 1957. The blast sent some 80 tons of radioactive waste into the air and forced the evacuation of more than 10,000 people. Even with *glasnost*, a cult of silence within the bureaucracy continues to suppress information on radiation leaks and other hazards. Indeed, the No. 1 environmental problem remains "lack of information," says former Environment Minister Nikolai Vorontsov.

Even now, with the fall of the Communist Party and the rise of more-democratic leaders, there is no assurance that communism's mess will get cleaned up. Its dual legacy of poverty and environmental degradation has left the new political leaders to face rising demands for jobs and consumer goods, growing consternation about the costs of pollution and too few resources to attack either problem, let alone both at once.

Although 270 malfunctions were recorded at nuclear facilities last year, economic pressure will make it difficult to shut down aging Soviet nuclear power plants. In March, radioactive iodine escaped from a Chernobyl-style plant near St. Petersburg, prompting calls from German officials for a shutdown of the most vulnerable reactors. Yeltsin adviser Yablokov warns that "every nuclear power station is in no-good condition, a lot of leaks." In the short term, Russia has little choice but to stick with nuclear power, which provides 60 percent of the electricity in some regions.

Environmental consciousness has permeated only a small fraction of society, and rousing the rest will require breaking the vicious circle of social fatalism. "We haven't got any ecological culture," says Dalia Zukiene, a Lithuanian official. Russian aerosols still contain chlorofluorocarbons, though Russia has now banned them, but if a Russian is lucky enough to find a deodorant or mosquito repellent, he will grab it—regardless of the consequences to the ozone layer. "We still bear the stamp of *Homo sovieticus*—we're not interested in the world around us, only in our own business," says Zukiene. Adds Alla Pozhidayeva, an environmental writer in Tyumen, in the oil fields of western Siberia: "Sausage is in the first place in people's minds."

Despite the mounting toll, the environmental activists who rushed to the barricades in the early days of *glasnost* have largely disappeared. When the Social Ecological Union recently tried to update its list of environmental groups, it found that more than half of them had disbanded in the past year. "If people go to a meeting at all, it isn't for the sake of ecology," says Vladimir Loginov, an editor of *Tyumen Vedomosti*, a newspaper in the Tyumen oil region. "They have to eat."

In fact, the crisis of leadership afflicting much of the former Soviet Union poses a whole new set of threats to the environment. The loosening of political control from Moscow already has turned the provinces—especially Siberia—into the Wild West. Local authorities, particularly in the Far East, have extended vast timber-cutting rights to foreign companies, especially Japanese and South Korean, without either imposing strict controls on their methods or requiring reforestation. "The economic chaos here presents enormous opportunities for local administration, without any government control, to cut forest, to sell it abroad and to receive some clothes, cars, video equipment," says Yeltsin adviser Yablokov. "If you visit the Far East forest enterprises, you will be surprised how many Japanese cars you will find."

The breakup of the Soviet Union is adding to the tensions. Despite Chernobyl, Ukraine, facing an energy crisis as the price of the oil it imports from other regions rises to world levels, is quietly contemplating building new nuclear power plants. But a stepped-up Ukrainian nuclear power program would create its own problems: Krasnoyarsk, the traditional dumping ground in Russia for nuclear waste, is refusing to accept Ukraine's spent reactor fuel because Ukraine is demanding hard currency for its sugar and vegetable oil.

In the mountainous Altai region of Russia, which recently declared itself autonomous and elected its own parliament, newly elected officials are trying to revive a controversial hydroelectric project on the Katun River. Victor Danilov-Danilyan, the Russian minister of ecology and natural resources, says local officials in Altai, many of whom are former Communist Party leaders, are now trying to cast the battle over the project as a nationalist issue. He says local authorities have deliberately ignored the danger of increased toxic wastes in the water and intentionally underestimated both how much the project will cost and how long it will take to build. "They're just deceiving people," Danilov-Danilyan charges. "They just want to grab as much as they can while they're in power, to build *dachas* for themselves."

Still, there are some glimmers of progress, including the recent creation of three new national parks in Russia. In February, President Yeltsin signed a new environmental law that empowers local officials or even individuals to sue an offending enterprise and demand its immediate closure. It also holds polluters, not some distant ministry, responsible for their actions. The new law further permits aggrieved parties to sue for damages, not just fines. The environmental ministry's report notes that over the years, "few ministries, if any, chose to clean up their act and didn't go beyond paying lip service to the need to protect the environment." In most cases, polluters got off with small fines or escaped punishment altogether by passing the buck to government ministries.

But Vladislav Petrov, a law professor at Moscow State University and the main author of the new legislation, says that if it is strictly enforced, the law would shut down 80 percent of the country's factories overnight. In the sooty steel town of Magnitogorsk, in the Urals, an independent radio journalist says he will try to force the Lenin Steel Mill, which employs 64,000 people, to close. He doubts he will succeed.

Growth industry. Moreover, while the new, 10,000-word statute has teeth, only a handful of lawyers, and ever fewer judges, are familiar with environmental law. Petrov says the courts are ill-equipped to handle claims from individuals and would be overwhelmed if people tried to collect damages from polluters. "In order for this article of the law to be effective, the whole court system should be changed," he says.

Still, environmentalism is a growth industry in the former Soviet Union. Many scientists in fields such as nuclear physics hope to recast themselves as ecologists. Mindful that the Russian government does not have the funds for large projects, they are looking for foreign partners to join them in cleanup projects. So far, most Western groups have offered advice but not much money.

Some Western input may be necessary, however, to prevent the environmental effort from succumbing to its own form of gigantism. One Central Asian academic's plan for saving the Aral Sea, for example, calls for building a 270-mile canal from the Caspian Sea to divert water into the depleted Aral. But because the Caspian Sea is lower than the Aral, the water could have to be pumped into the canal, and that would require considerable electricity. The proposed solution: Build a network of solar power stations.

The spreading ecological disaster may yet force change on an impoverished and cynical people. "We have a Russian saying: 'The worse, the better,' " says Yablokov. "This situation has now become so obvious for all people that I feel that a lot of decision makers began to turn their minds in this direction." The Stalinist idea, he says, was to build socialism at any cost because afterward there would be no more problems. "It was an unhealthy ideology," he says. "Now I feel that my people are coming to understand the depths of this tragedy."

By Douglas Stanglin with Victoria Pope in Moscow, Robin Knight in Tyumen, Peter Green in Tallinn, Chrystia Freeland in Kiev and Julie Corwin

THE NUCLEAR EPIDEMIC

The West's attempt to prevent the spread of nuclear weapons has failed, and a dangerous new era of nuclear proliferation has begun

Don't blame it on penurious Russian physicists selling their souls for 5,000 rubles and a Big Mac, or on accommodating German trading companies that are only too happy to ship sensitive electronic triggers under the label "automobile parts."

The North Koreans, who CIA Director Robert Gates recently warned may be only a few months away from building an atomic bomb, did it all by themselves. Saddam Hussein's Iraq got much closer to the bomb than anyone realized. And if the North Koreans and the Iraqis can do it, anyone can do it. "Things that were very difficult for the smartest people in 1943 are easy for ordinary people now," says Richard Garwin, a physicist at IBM's Thomas J. Watson Research Center and a former nuclear-weapons designer.

At the same time, the collapse of the Russian economy is unleashing a flood of uranium ore and other nuclear materials onto world markets; it may be only a matter of time before more dangerous products, including tons of plutonium from spent Soviet reactor fuel and perhaps even uranium-processing technology from the Central Asian republics, reach the black market. The West's attempt to prevent the spread of nuclear weapons, based on the premise that a combination of secrecy, export controls and inspections of civilian nuclear reactors could thwart the world's nuclear wannabes, has failed, and a new and much more dangerous era of nuclear proliferation has begun.

Lost opportunity. U.S. officials privately concede that the system has failed — and that America blew an important opportunity to strengthen it after the gulf war. "We should have pointed to Iraq as proof positive that the system doesn't work and that something much more aggressive must be put in place — an assertive nonproliferation policy instead of the passive one we have now," admits a senior U.S. official.

Now America and its allies may be facing a painful choice: Either use military force to prevent North Korea and others from going nuclear, or learn to live in a world in which nearly every nation that wants nuclear weapons has them. U.S. officials fear that a North Korean bomb could destabilize all of Northeast Asia, triggering a nuclear arms race that could bring South Korea, Japan and Taiwan into the nuclear club as well. A white paper issued by the South Korean Defense Ministry last autumn ominously warned that North Korea's bomb program "must be stopped at any cost."

But it would be much harder to muster allies for an attack on North Korea than it was to round up support for driving Saddam Hussein out of Kuwait. A commando raid, a cruise missile attack or a Stealth bomber raid on the North's nuclear installations could trigger another Korean war. In addition to its million-man Army, North Korea has thousands of artillery pieces and hundreds of Scud missile launchers lined up just across the demilitarized zone — well within range of Seoul, just 35 miles away. Japan would be likely to oppose the use of bases on its soil for such a mission; using them anyway could jeopardize the U.S.-Japan Security Treaty and magnify the growing tensions between Washington and Tokyo. "We'd like to see a political solution to this," says U.S. Under Secretary of Defense Paul Wolfowitz. "It's not the time to start discussing military options. But we haven't ruled anything out."

The wrong door. North Korea's approach to building the bomb is a case study of how a determined country can evade international controls—and without much outside help, either. The primary aim of the nuclear safeguards regime, first developed in the 1950s, was to let developing countries have commercial nuclear-power plants without allowing their by-products to be funneled into bombs.

As a result, almost all of the International Atomic Energy Agency's inspection and monitoring efforts are devoted to keeping tabs on the uranium fuel that's fed into nuclear-power plants and on the plutonium-containing waste that comes out of them. Inspectors attach seals to the reactor vessel of a power plant after fuel is loaded or install cameras to monitor the cooling pools where spent fuel rods are kept after being removed from a reactor. The safeguards regime did not anticipate that instead of trying to divert nuclear raw materials from power plants bought from abroad, even technologically primitive countries such as North Korea might simply build their own, complete nuclear infrastructures—in effect, reproducing the Manhattan Project.

In fact, every country that has built a bomb or even come close has done it the same way—not by hijacking the operations of a civilian reactor but by building a dedicated bomb-making complex. That means the IAEA safeguards are largely focused in the wrong direction.

The hardest part of building a bomb is obtaining plutonium or highly enriched uranium to fuel the explosive chain reaction. Neither substance exists in nature. Plutonium is formed when uranium fuel is bombarded by neutrons inside a nuclear reactor; it must be extracted from the spent fuel, a step called reprocessing. Highly enriched uranium is made in an industrial process that selectively concentrates the isotope uranium-235 from 1 percent or less—its abundance in natural uranium ore—to the 20 percent, or ideally 90 percent, that is required for a nuclear explosive.

North Korea picked the plutonium route, which meant it needed a nuclear reactor. IAEA rules control the sale of reactors, as well as the hard-to-come-by materials needed to fuel and operate most power-producing reactors: low-enriched uranium fuel, which is needed for the water-cooled reactors typical in the United States and Europe, and heavy water (a combination of deuterium—a heavy isotope of hydrogen—and oxygen), which is needed for reactors fueled by more easily obtainable natural, unenriched uranium.

The North Koreans sidestepped these obstacles entirely. The design they chose went back to the dawn of the nuclear age. It uses natural uranium fuel and, in place of heavy water, graphite—which North Korea has in abundance. "The first reactor, which we built at the University of Chicago football field, was a graphite reactor," notes Michael Golay, a professor of nuclear engineering at MIT. "It was built by stacking blocks [of graphite]" on a wooden scaffold. North Korea, like just about every country in the world, also has its own source of uranium ore.

The North Korean reactor, completed in 1987, is tiny by commercial standards, with a power output of 30 megawatts compared with 1,000 megawatts for a typical electric power plant. Yet it can produce at least 20 pounds of plutonium a year—more than enough to build one nuclear weapon.

"If you're in a weapons program, you don't want to tie in to your electric power system; you want a reactor that's especially for that purpose," says A. David Rossin, a nuclear engineer and a former U.S. assistant secretary of energy. Trying to divert plutonium from a power reactor presents a host of technical hurdles. Fuel in a power reactor is left in the core for a long time to maximize energy production; that makes it highly radioactive and hard to handle. Then it has to be reprocessed by remote control behind heavy shielding.

Moreover, long irradiation leads to undesirable nuclear reactions that complicate the bomb maker's task. When the neutrons produced in a nuclear reactor strike uranium-238—the abundant and otherwise uninteresting isotope of natural uranium—it is converted to plutonium-239, the stuff that bombs are made of. But in subsequent reactions the Pu-239 can in turn capture more neutrons itself, forming Pu-240 and -241. These isotopes not only are highly radioactive, but because they tend to undergo nuclear fission spontaneously, they can cause the nuclear chain reaction of a bomb to begin a fraction of a second too soon—making a whimper instead of a bang. To overcome this problem, a bomb has to be designed so the conventional explosives that squeeze the plutonium together to create a critical mass do their job much more quickly, an extremely difficult technical challenge. "But if your whole thing is oriented to production of the bomb, you avoid some of the headaches," says Leonard Spector, an expert on nuclear proliferation at the Carnegie Endowment for International Peace.

The obstacles that secrecy and techni-

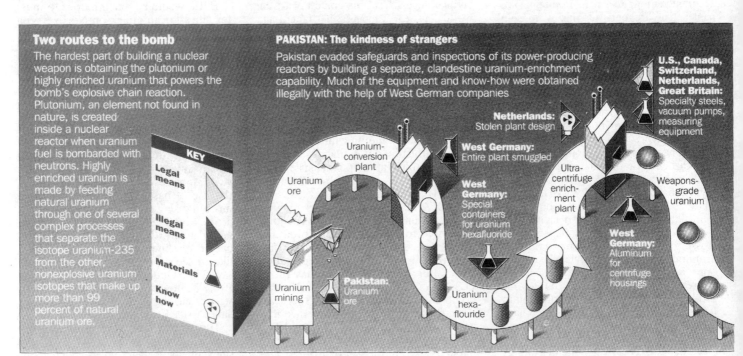

Two routes to the bomb
The hardest part of building a nuclear weapon is obtaining the plutonium or highly enriched uranium that powers the bomb's explosive chain reaction. Plutonium, an element not found in nature, is created inside a nuclear reactor when uranium fuel is bombarded with neutrons. Highly enriched uranium is made by feeding natural uranium through one of several complex processes that separate the isotope uranium-235 from the other, nonexplosive uranium isotopes that make up more than 99 percent of natural uranium ore.

KEY
Legal means
Illegal means
Materials
Know how

PAKISTAN: The kindness of strangers
Pakistan evaded safeguards and inspections of its power-producing reactors by building a separate, clandestine uranium-enrichment capability. Much of the equipment and know-how were obtained illegally with the help of West German companies

Uranium ore
Uranium mining
Pakistan: Uranium ore
Uranium-conversion plant
Netherlands: Stolen plant design
West Germany: Entire plant smuggled
West Germany: Special containers for uranium hexafluoride
Uranium hexaflouride
Ultra-centrifuge enrichment plant
Weapons-grade uranium
West Germany: Aluminum for centrifuge housings
U.S., Canada, Switzerland, Netherlands, Great Britain: Specialty steels, vacuum pumps, measuring equipment

cal backwardness once presented to the world's would-be bomb makers have largely vanished, too. Perfectly legal assistance has provided countries such as North Korea with a cadre of skilled technicians. Technicians from the former Soviet Union are working in Libya and Algeria. North Korea even received technical aid from the IAEA in uranium mining and assaying, and had reactor operators trained by the Soviet Union as part of an IAEA-sanctioned deal during the 1960s in which the Soviets provided a small, safeguarded research reactor at Yongbyon, the site of North Korea's burgeoning nuclear complex.

Even designing a nuclear weapon, once the most closely guarded of secrets, is now not a terribly difficult task for a physicist anywhere. "What's classified today is how to build a *good* weapon," says Golay, "not how to build a weapon." Mathematical problems that challenged some of the best minds in the world during the Manhattan Project can now be solved on a personal computer. What's more, not all the best minds in the world are in the West anymore. Citizens of Taiwan, South Korea and India, for example, account for more than 2,600 of the science and engineering Ph.D.'s awarded annually by American universities.

The United States has been pressing its allies and the IAEA to tighten up export controls and inspection procedures to eliminate the kind of loopholes that North Korea exploited. All the major nuclear nations—with the notable exception of China—have now agreed that they will not sell *any* nuclear technology to a nation that refuses to open all its facilities to IAEA inspection—so-called

full-scope safeguards. Under the non-proliferation treaty, the only obligation of a supplier nation is that the particular plant or material it sells be placed under safeguards. That loophole allowed Pakistan, India, Algeria and Israel, none of which have signed the treaty, to receive nuclear help from abroad while pursuing nuclear-weapons programs at uninspected sites.

Germany, embarrassed by the prominent role played by German companies in the legal, quasi-legal and blatantly illegal sales of nuclear technology to Pakistan, Iraq and other proliferators, has recently tightened its export controls. And a new IAEA policy announced late last month has affirmed the agency's right to conduct inspections at undeclared facilities in countries that have signed the treaty or otherwise accepted full safeguards. Such inspections might have detected Iraq's clandestine nuclear program, for example, and may be invoked soon in an IAEA demand to see North Korea's undeclared production reactor and reprocessing plant.

But with the equivalent of only 40 full-time inspectors to cover close to 1,000 *declared* nuclear installations, the IAEA has its hands full already. And what especially concerns many nuclear experts is the increasing ease with which a determined nation can gain direct access to the critical technologies needed to enrich uranium or reprocess plutonium, as well as to weapons-grade materials themselves. Once a nation has the ability to manufacture its own highly enriched uranium or plutonium, no inspection regime is worth very much. It takes only a few weeks to make plutonium from a sealed

and monitored storage depot into a nuclear bomb. Argentina, Brazil, Pakistan, India, Israel and South Africa all have declared or undeclared reprocessing or enrichment plants in operation. "Good intentions in peaceful times last for years; plutonium lasts forever once it's separated into weapons-usable form," says Paul Leventhal of the private Nuclear Control Institute.

China continues to provide legal nuclear assistance to Iran, Algeria and Pakistan, insisting that the technology will be used only for "peaceful" purposes; it rejected as "totally groundless" charges that a 15-megawatt research reactor it provided Algeria could be used to make nuclear fuel for weapons. But the reactor, which Algeria agreed only last week to place under IAEA safeguards, is in theory capable of producing 12 pounds of plutonium a year, almost enough for one bomb. "At the center of the hub, again and again we see China," says one top U.S. official. "This is the kind of network which we really have no control of." U.S. officials fear that Algeria and Iran, following North Korea's lead, could use such legal help to build up indigenous nuclear weapons programs.

In the case of North Korea, U.S. officials are especially worried that Pyongyang may continue its foot dragging on allowing IAEA inspections just long enough to reprocess a couple of bombs' worth of plutonium, which it could then hide—or sell to the highest bidder.

But if the North Koreans try to peddle plutonium, they could face stiff competition. Russia has recovered at least 20 tons of plutonium from power reactors, in addition to military stockpiles of 115 tons of

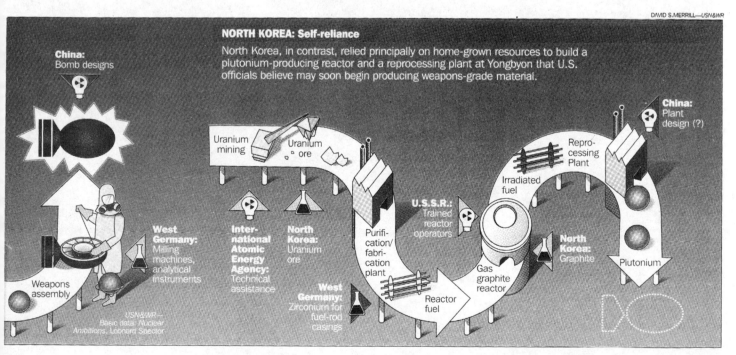

NORTH KOREA: Self-reliance
North Korea, in contrast, relied principally on home-grown resources to build a plutonium-producing reactor and a reprocessing plant at Yongbyon that U.S. officials believe may soon begin producing weapons-grade material.

plutonium and 500 tons of highly enriched uranium, all of which the government is eager to sell as reactor fuel.

Peaceful uses? "It could conceivably be sold to companies and consumers, as can any other valuable commodity. Hopefully it will be used in a beneficial method," says Boris Nikipelov, first deputy minister of Russia's Ministry of Atomic Power and Industry. "We see no technical or political restrictions against utilizing the materials." The fact that they have a market value of close to $1 billion is no doubt a factor, too. The Soviet Union sold 12 million pounds of uranium in the United States last year, worth $110 million, nearly 30 percent of the entire U.S. consumption; Russian shipments reached as much as 5 million pounds in the first month of 1992 alone. American uranium producers have filed an antidumping suit against the Russian sales.

The plutonium trade, meanwhile, is getting a boost from Japan, which is reprocessing reactor fuel in France and Britain, and plans this year to ship a *ton* of plutonium aboard a freighter escorted by a single Japanese patrol boat armed with a light cannon and machine guns. Japan plans to reprocess a total of 100 tons of plutonium over the next 20 years.

"You have an impossible task of accounting for it all," says Leventhal, "and ensuring that the 15 pounds you need to blow up a city doesn't fall into the wrong hands" through theft, terrorism, or black-market sales.

Leventhal argues that a global ban on the production of weapons-grade material would shut this door. "We haven't produced any plutonium for two or three years because our production reactors are all unsafe or broken," adds physicist Richard Garwin, "and we haven't produced any highly enriched uranium since 1964." The only remaining use the United States has for HEU is as fuel for reactors in ships and submarines, a demand Garwin says could easily be met from the U.S. stockpile of 500 tons. Russia says it no longer makes HEU and will stop plutonium production by 2000.

But it is unclear whether France and Britain, eyeing lucrative Japanese reprocessing contracts, would go along. And even some U.S. officials, while acknowledging that the nation no longer needs to produce weapons-grade material, are apathetic about a ban on the production of weapons-grade nuclear fuel. "I don't believe that I see any downside to it," says Everet Beckner, an official at the U.S. Department of Energy who works on defense programs, "but there are more important problems to consider."

In any event, nuclear experts are virtually unanimous in believing that no "technical fix" alone can do the job. "It's effectively impossible to keep the lid on," says MIT's Golay. "The only way you're going to control these things is to make them uninteresting." Unfortunately, some of the most unsavory regimes in the world are just now discovering that their motives and their opportunities for going nuclear are converging.

STEPHEN BUDIANSKY WITH TIM ZIMMERMANN, BRUCE B. AUSTER, DOUGLAS PASTERNAK, JIM IMPOCO IN TOKYO, SUSAN V. LAWRENCE IN BEIJING, LOUISE LIEF, JULIE CORWIN AND EMILY MACFARQUHAR

Sowing Success, Reaping Guns

It's the Green Revolution's greatest success story. Punjab went from dune-blown desert to California-like food surplus in one generation. And, oh yes, the fate of India also happens to hang on Punjab's forgotten little war.

Richard Critchfield

Richard Critchfield ("Is It Still Out There?" WM, January) has lived in villages in India over a period of three decades. An American Midwesterner, he received one of the first MacArthur "genius awards" and is the author of noted cultural studies of the third world ("Villages"), America ("Those Days"), and Britain ("An American Looks at Britain")—all lively studies of how societies change.

A little after midnight there is gunfire out in the darkness of the village fields. Five shots. The Punjabi farmer hastens to turn out his yard lights. His family holds its breath until the *khadkus*, as young Sikh militants are called, go away.

"They may come back and kill somebody," he warns his children. "Don't speak of this. Everybody has heard the firing. But nobody must talk of it."

Helplessly caught in crossfire and pillaging between trigger-happy rebels and corrupt police, the ordinary Punjabi villager just tries to wish it all away. More than 15,000, most of them ordinary people, have been killed in the past eight years as Sikh fundamentalists fight for an independent homeland they call Khalistan, or Land of the Pure.

Is this just another distant ethnic/political/religious conflict? Just part of the global balkanization that looks and sounds so eerily similar whether your TV screen is filled with Croats and Serbs, Armenians and Azeris, rival Kenyan tribesmen, or Peruvian troops and Shining Path guerrillas?

No. Those gunbursts in the Punjab night mean more than just a struggle over ownership of the rich valleys of Indus River tributaries in northern India. The lesson emerging from this apparently haphazard warfare is one that applies to many other parts of the third world.

To understand Punjab's story is to understand how parts of the poorer world can be rescued from hunger and poverty and brought to the brink of an almost California-valley agricultural prosperity. But it is also to understand how cultural rootlessness and strife arrived along with the prosperity. And, finally, to understand what is needed if the justly famous agricultural successes of the

Green Revolution are to translate into a stable society.

The Punjab struggle—nobody calls it an insurgency—has been going on ever since June 1984, when Indira Gandhi sent the Army into the Golden Temple of Amritsar, the Sikhs' most holy place, to kill militants holed up there. That October Mrs. Gandhi herself was murdered in retaliation by her own Sikh bodyguards and nearly 10,000 Sikhs were massacred across northern India in riots that followed.

An election in February, after five years of direct rule from Delhi, was won by India's ruling Congress Party, after a boycott by Akali Dal, the most popular moderate Sikh political force in Punjab. All told, only 22% of Punjab's 13 million registered voters cast their ballots, a mere 15% out in the villages. The turnout in previous elections had been around 55%.

So the violence is expected to worsen, with the Akalis turning to agitation and strikes, the militants shooting, bombing, and kidnapping anybody connected with the government, and a big force from the Indian Army staying on in Punjab.

That is the political side of the story.

The reason Punjab matters so much to the rest of us, aside from its crucial role in feeding India's 883 million people, is that it has become the 20th century's greatest Green Revolution success (see box). If the Punjabi government were to post signs at the border similar to those in California's central valley that tell visitors 43% of America's fruits and vegetables are grown there, the Punjabi signs might well brag that more than two-thirds of the wheat for the Indian government's nationwide food distribution program comes from Punjab. All this with just 20 million people, half of them farming, on not much more than 19,000 square miles of farmland. No one has made the shift in modernizing a subsistence peasant society—nor gotten richer—faster than the Punjabi Sikh farmers.

Nor is this coincidental. Experts agree that, Delhi's political bumbling and machinations aside, the rise of Sikh fundamentalist gunmen in Punjab is a direct result of the Green Revolution.

How can this be?

When we say "Green Revolution" we often are talking of two things. In the narrowest sense, it is a purely scientific phenomenon: a breakthrough in plant genetics which allows the breeding and growing of artificially dwarfed, stiff-stemmed grains—most importantly, wheat and rice—which can take up to 120 pounds of nitrogen per acre to support heavy grainheads without falling over.

In Punjab this increased tolerance for fertilizer, combined with a quicker maturation period, makes seeds widely introduced since 1967 *six or seven* times more productive, providing they get plenty of water. By double cropping wheat and rice to produce 12.2 million tons of wheat and 8 million tons of rice per year (compared to 1.7 million tons of wheat and almost no rice 30 years ago), Punjab has become the cornucopia of India. Punjabis eat only

about a third of the grain their state produces and it now supplies about 60% of India's *food reserve* in wheat and 45% in rice. Boosted by the Punjabi Sikh farmers, India has been able to increase its overall annual wheat *production* fivefold since 1967, from 11 million tons to 55 million tons. So the fate of India pretty much hangs on what happens in Punjab, even if Sikhs are only 2% of the country's population.

The second meaning of Green Revolution embraces the whole continuing process of transferring the West's biological, chemical, and mechanical science to a peasant society—one whose technology had hardly changed for thousands of years. In the late 1960s dwarf wheat was introduced to Punjab. It had been bred in Mexico by American scientists led by Iowa plant geneticist Norman Borlaug, later to win the Nobel Peace Prize as father of the Green Revolution. Along with the dwarf wheat came tractors, threshers, combines, chemical fertilizers, pesticides, and tubewells (steel pipes drilled to reach underground water) pumped by diesel or electricity produced by Punjab's Bhakra-Nangal hydro-run turbines.

The area around Punjab Agricultural University, Ludhiana district, is sometimes called the Green Revolution's launching pad. As late as 1947 the terrain was practically desert, with sand dunes drifting over the Grand Trunk Road, famed from Kipling's "Kim." Just about the only crop there was a little groundnut.

When I first saw it, in 1959, the desert had been reclaimed, irrigated, and cultivated by Sikh Jat refugees from Pakistan, but Ludhiana's villages still had a timeless feeling. Fodder and grain were cut by squatting turbaned-and-bearded men with sickles. Camels and bullocks turned age-old waterwheels. The commonest tree was the sparse and thorny acacia. And just about the only sounds were the creak of wooden bullock-cart wheels on rutted dirt roads, the caws of crows, and the monotonous *poop-poop* of village flour mills.

Today all but the crows are gone. The fields are dotted with electrified tubewells, lit up at night like suburban Chicago. There is the roar of tractors and combines, gushing water from underground piped irrigation; village houses have biogas plants, solar panels, maybe even a satellite TV dish. Express buses, cars, trucks, and motorcycles clog the now-paved roads, doctors hold daily village hours, letters arrive from sons and daughters postmarked Dubai, Beirut, Frankfurt, Phoenix, and Yuba City, and one ex-village chief writes he has opened a pizza parlor in Toronto.

The fields are dotted with electrified tubewells, lit up at night like suburban Chicago. There is the roar of tractors and combines.

With so much irrigation, the landscape of Punjab has become stunningly beautiful, especially in winter and early spring. Tall, stately eucalyptus trees, planted by the millions in the 1980s, line country roads, as poplars do in Europe. Fields of vivid green wheat and clover are broken by bright yellow patches of mustard, which also grows along the edges of fields; and marigolds and sunflowers have become popular. Indeed, since the introduction of rice in the 1970s, there is so much overpumping that some experts warn that Punjab's groundwater level could fall so drastically as to turn the land once more into desert in the mid-21st century.

After India's partition in 1947 vast numbers of Sikh Jats had fled south from reclaimed-desert colonies in West Punjab (which had been irrigated and settled at the turn of the century). The newly independent government in Delhi gave them land previously owned by Muslims, who had either been killed in the partition holocaust or had escaped to Pakistan.

There were Sikhs already living in Punjab's villages, but these were mainly Mazhbi or Chamar landless laborers, untouchables whom Mahatma Gandhi called Harijans, or "children of God." As hired field workers they had been tillers of the soil under the Muslims as they now became under the Jats.

The Punjabi Jats, who tend to be tall and fair, are the most European-looking of Indians. (Their looks have made many of them film stars.) They are relative latecomers to the country. One theory is that they are descended from Scythians, nomadic people who displaced less warlike rivals on the Eurasian steppes, seizing their lands and establishing themselves as overlords of settled agricultural populations. Certainly the Jats retain a warrior spirit, glorying unabashedly in the strength of arms and the destruction of foes. Until recent years they formed the main ranks of the Indian Army. These Jats—now divided into Sikhs, Hindus, and Pakistani Muslims—did not enter India until the time of Caesar and did not fully occupy the greater Punjab Plain down as far as Delhi until the collapse of the Mogul Empire in the late 19th century.

Much of the social impact of the Green Revolution has been on the interrelationship of the Harijans and Jats. Their Sikh religion was founded in the 17th-century to combine the concepts of Islam and Hinduism based on human equality. The Sikhs' sacred scripture, the "Guru Granth Sahib," an anthology of religious teaching, is specific about this: "The Hindus say there are four castes/ But they are all of one seed . . ./ How can one amongst them be high/ and another low?"

Jats and Harijans pray together at Sikh temples, both become holy men, and the devout wear beards and turbans. Harijans tend to be shorter and darker, especially Mazhbis, but some can be so fair and tall it is hard for an outsider to tell their caste. Social distinctions are still rigid in Sikh Punjabi villages. Intermarriage is unthinkable and until very recently Jats never ate or drank in Harijan homes (and if Harijan workers ate in Jat homes they sat subserviently on the ground; many still do).

India's Hindu caste system, while it offends Western ideals of equality, provides a sense of belonging to a community of one's own and has always held India's 576,000 villages together.

Since caste is occupation-based, it has been hard put to survive the coming of modern farming. In Punjab, tractors, combines, and electronically powered irrigation very rapidly displaced human labor. Yet strip away the age-old economic basis for caste—the exchange of labor for grain and fodder—and the old Jat-Harijan system of mutual rights and obligations shatters like overripe wheat.

In the village I know best this happened in 1970, the third harvest of the new dwarf wheat. Until then a Harijan harvester got every 20th bale of wheat he cut and gathered. That year the Jats, to offset their new costs in fertilizer and fuel, demanded this be reduced to every 30th bale. No compromise was reached and there was a mutual boycott. The Harijans went off to cut wheat in other villages. Half of them never returned to field labor but got manual jobs in the booming nearby towns, commuting by bicycle, bus, or motor scooter. To compensate for this loss of manpower, migrants from the much poorer Ganges plain states of Uttar Pradesh and Bihar came in to work as harvesters. Today the number of these migrants, who do not bring their families and often live in the fields, has risen to more than 450,000.

The Jats also turned to machines. In 1991, 65–70% of the wheat harvest in Punjab was gathered by just under 4,000 leased combines. Tractors now number 236,000, seed-fertilizer drills 180,000, and threshing machines close to 300,000.

Field wages have risen from 5 to 25 rupees per day. Annual per capita cash purchasing power has gone from 559 rupees in 1965 to 5,477 rupees, or about $220. Both Jats and Harijans produce some of their own food (especially milk for the Harijans). There is no question most Punjabis, Jat and Harijan alike, are today much better off than when the Green Revolution began 25 years ago.

An exception are a small number of Jat landowners with less than 10 acres, who increasingly have gone into debt and been forced to sell their land.

The most alarming trend is the subdivision of farmland. Example: a grandfather who came as a refugee from Pakistan in 1948 and was allotted 14 acres, a common amount. He may plan to leave his two middle-aged sons seven acres apiece. But what about their sons, now in their 20s? Or their sons' sons, now being born?

Rural overcrowding is a world-wide problem, but thanks to the way Punjab was resettled in 1947, land fragmentation did not frustrate the Green Revolution in the 1960s and '70s. It is only coming now.

Punjabi Jat farmers, to whom land is everything and farming the only truly respectable profession, have tried to solve this problem by educating all but one son for nonfarm jobs in the towns. Punjab's high school enrollment has doubled to 3 million since 1970. In 1947 Punjab had one university and a few colleges. There are four universities now and more than 150 colleges, turning out more than 20,000 graduates a year. Half of these get BA degrees, which means they study subjects like history, geography, home economics, political science, and sociology. White collar jobs are hard to find; you reportedly have to pay a $1,000 bribe to land a bank teller's job. One Punjabi professor says, "You have so many arts colleges. They create a useless person. He doesn't want to go back to the farm and dirty his hands, and he's not fit for any technical job. So he's badly frustrated."

Only belatedly has it been realized that manpower training in micro-electronics, computers, telecommunications, and other high-tech skills should have accompanied the Green Revolution to absorb the surplus young people.

Punjab is currently developing food processing industries as fast as it can. From very few in 1970, it now has 21 roller flour mills, 4,400 rice huller mills, 442 sheller mills, 1,965 modern rice mills, and 21 large sugar mills. Sixteen modern milk plants now process more than 500,000 gallons a day.

But, aside from Punjab's two fertilizer plants, agriculture-related industries such as irrigation and tubewell equipment, fungicides, herbicides, and most farm machinery are mostly located in other Indian states. From Delhi's standpoint, this was a way to spread prosperity around.

It should not be forgotten that India could barely feed its 360 million people at the time of independence in 1947; 1.5 million Bengalis had died in the famine of 1943. India's annual steel production was just over 1 million tons, less than a month's output at a single American mill. Literacy was below 25% among males and 8% among females. Smallpox (now eradicated) and cholera were endemic. Today India not only feeds its 883 million people but makes jets, rockets, and nuclear devices, and its computer software engineers are in demand all over the world. It exports cars and trucks and has a large merchant navy.

A growing middle class has emerged, some of it in Punjab, which frantically pursues Western-style consumerism.

A growing middle class of 100 million-plus has emerged, some of it in Punjab, which frantically pursues Western-style consumerism. With this

goes a very rapid spread of commercial television culture. The glorification of instant material gratification as the way to happiness and success is promoted in Punjab, as all over India, by pop music, TV commercials, Bombay films, and videos. Punjab has seen a big rise in alcohol consumption. Many young Sikhs have "modernized" by trimming their once-long hair, shaving off their beards, or smoking, all in contravention of Sikh religious taboos.

Historian Arnold Toynbee called this "Herodianism," adopting foreign ways to live as comfortably as possible. It created a backlash Toynbee called "Zealotism," the impulse to frantically retreat into one's own traditional culture. We see it constantly in Islamic fundamentalism and its aversion to the West.

In Punjab the prime Zealot was Sant Bhindranwale, a young preacher of village origin who has been called the "messiah of Sikh fundamentalism." Originally promoted by Indira Gandhi and her son Sanjay as a way of dividing the Sikhs, Bhindranwale got out of control, turned to violence, and fortified the Golden Temple. He was killed there when Mrs. Gandhi ordered the Army to attack the temple in June 1984.

Educated Sikhs today say Bhindranwale is irrelevant and belongs to history. Among Sikh peasants, though, he is a martyr. Some claim he is still alive—and his ideas form the credo of the young Sikh *khadkus*, armed militants.

Just about everybody heard him preach. His message was simple: Go back to the 17th- and 18th-century ways of the Sikh gurus and renounce the evils of modernism. As in Sikh scripture, he made no distinction between Jats and Harijans and welcomed Harijans among his followers. The bodyguards who assassinated Mrs. Gandhi were low-caste Sikhs. The second one was low-caste but not a Mazhbi or Harijan. The bodyguard who shot Mrs. Gandhi first was a Mazhbi Harijan, the other killer was another low-caste Sikh though not a Mazhbi.

In practice most of Bhindranwale's men were, like himself, Jats. Sikh militancy has essentially been Jat militancy. It may be that Harijans feel their rights are better protected constitutionally than by Jat overlords.

So who are the *khadkus*? Most Punjabis say they are college-educated, unemployed, frustrated Jat youth. The Green Revolution goes on— wheat yields have continued to go up every year since 1975 as ever-more-dwarfed varieties come in—but the margin of profit is down, the size of holdings is down, and the aspirations of these young Sikhs have gone way up. A few get to England, Canada, or the US by hook or crook. But when all else fails, a gun offers a way out.

Both *khadkus* and the Punjab police may have an interest in keeping their shooting war going, something you sense when jeeps full of stern-faced turbaned-and-bearded men in uniforms manning machine guns roar by in a cloud of dust, scattering everyone else to the roadsides. The *khadkus* can extort protection money and the police can go into a village and grab villagers and then charge them money to get released. Both sides profit.

As Mark Tully, BBC's veteran correspondent in India, says, "You go to Kashmir and it's collapsed completely. Whereas Punjab is all go, go, go." It is a phenomenon of terrorism among a people who don't easily terrorize.

K. P. S. Gill, a Jat Sikh who came back in 1991 as Punjab's police chief and is said to be top of the *khadkus'* hit list, says the young rebels have "love of a good gun, a good faith, and abhorrence of surrender." This reflects a swaggering Jat mythology that goes back centuries.

It is hard to imagine what will happen next in Punjab. The Sikhs are a small community, only about 11 million strong, though their distinctive appearance and entrepreneurial success make them seem more numerous. Some 80% of Sikhs

How India's Green Machine Has Grown

Punjab's statistics are awesome: Wheat production since 1950 has gone from 1 million tons to 12 million, rice from virtually none to 8 million tons. No land was irrigated in 1950; today 91% of it is. Fertilizer consumption has gone from 5,000 in 1950 to 1.1 million tons, tubewells from just under 2,000 to over 750,000, tractors from 1,392 to over 260,000, paved roads from 2,800 kilometers to 46,000, and the villages they reach

from 1,300 to more than 12,000. Traffic has grown even faster. In 1975-88, the number of "two-wheelers" (motor scooters and motorcycles) rose from 80,000 to 614,000, cars from 19,000 to 50,000, and the total of all motorized vehicles from 173,000 to 975,000. Punjab now has four-lane superhighways. The accident rate is grim.

Farm machinery also takes its toll. Punjab, Haryana and eastern Uttar Pradesh states, the main Green Revolution setting, now count more than 5,000 farm machinery deaths a year, along with many more thousands of injuries. India passed a Dangerous Machines Act in 1983, requiring safety devices on threshers and fodder-cutters, but it is practically unenforced.

In the boom, land values in Punjab have shot up to $6,000 an acre, five times what they are in neighboring states (compared to $1,000-$1,200 per acre in Iowa in 1990). Storage capacity has gone from next to nothing to 14 million tons. More than 4,000 village co-ops now provide farm credit to just under 2 million members. Railway freight cars to haul all the grain and dairy products out have gone from 72,000 to 608,689.

The Green Revolution succeeded so spectacularly, it is said, because Punjab had all the right preconditions: a homogenous, well-educated farming population culturally prepared for change, plus some degree of capital, water control, and farm policies that included land reform. In Ludhiana district, for instance, in 1967 42% of villagers were literate. Population was dense (773 persons per square mile) but two-thirds of it worked in non-farming jobs in Ludhiana or small towns—making bicycles, spare parts, small farm machinery, or knitting and weaving textiles.

Most crucial, there was little pressure on the land: 37% of farmer-owners had more than 20 acres each, another 43% between 10 and 20 acres. Virtually all were Sikhs of the Jat farmer-warrior caste. —R.C.

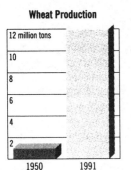

Wheat Production

12 million tons / 10 / 8 / 6 / 4 / 2

1950 — 1991

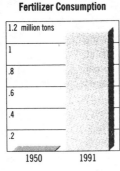

Fertilizer Consumption

1.2 million tons / 1 / .8 / .6 / .4 / .2

1950 — 1991

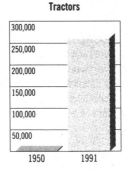

Tractors

300,000 / 250,000 / 200,000 / 150,000 / 100,000 / 50,000

1950 — 1991

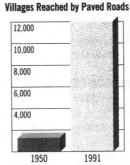

Villages Reached by Paved Roads

12,000 / 10,000 / 8,000 / 6,000 / 4,000

1950 — 1991

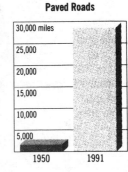

Paved Roads

30,000 miles / 25,000 / 20,000 / 15,000 / 10,000 / 5,000

1950 — 1991

live in Punjab, but even with the Harijans they make up just 56% of its people.

Most Punjabis, including, one suspects, a good many Sikh Jats, do not actually want a separate Sikh state—or are at least ambiguous about it, as if Khalistan really is some kind of dreamlike golden age. Many complain, justifiably, that Delhi's Hindu Brahmin rulers have repeatedly neglected Punjab. They would like more understanding and justice. It is

a scandal that three Congress leaders who everyone knows instigated mobs during the 1984 massacre of Sikhs in Delhi have never been brought to trial.

Then, aside from settling long-standing and vital water and boundary disputes, the Punjabis want more investment in high-tech training and industry.

In the end, I think, these good Sikh farmers would happily settle for something like the rewarding life

described in their "Guru Granth Sahib":

As a team of oxen are we driven
By the ploughman, our teacher;
By the furrows made are thus writ
Our actions—on the earth, our
paper.
The sweat of labor is as beads
Falling by the ploughman as seeds
sown.
We reap according to our measure—
Some for ourselves to keep, some to
others give.
O, Nanak, this is the way to truly
live.

Can the Growing Human Population Feed Itself?

*As human numbers surge toward
10 billion, some experts are alarmed,
others optimistic. Who is right?*

John Bongaarts

JOHN BONGAARTS has been vice president and director of the Research Division of the Population Council in New York City since 1989. He is currently a member of the Johns Hopkins Society of Scholars and the Royal Dutch Academy of Sciences. He won the Mindel Sheps Award in 1986 from the Population Association of America and the Research Career Development Award in 1980-85 from the National Institutes of Health.

Demographers now project that the world's population will double during the next half century, from 5.3 billion people in 1990 to more than 10 billion by 2050. How will the environment and humanity respond to this unprecedented growth? Expert opinion divides into two camps. Environmentalists and ecologists, whose views have widely been disseminated by the electronic and print media, regard the situation as a catastrophe in the making. They argue that in order to feed the growing population farmers must intensify agricultural practices that already cause grave ecological damage. Our natural resources and the environment, now burdened by past population growth, will simply collapse under the weight of this future demand.

The optimists, on the other hand, comprising many economists as well as some agricultural scientists, assert that the earth can readily produce more than enough food for the expected population in 2050. They contend that technological innovation and the continued investment of human capital will deliver high standards of living to much of the globe, even if the population grows much larger than the projected 10 billion. Which point of view will hold sway? What shape might the

future of our species and the environment actually take?

Many environmentalists fear that world food supply has reached a precarious state: "Human numbers are on a collision course with massive famines.... If humanity fails to act, nature will end the population explosion for us—in very unpleasant ways—well before 10 billion is reached," write Paul R. Ehrlich and Anne H. Ehrlich of Stanford University in their 1990 book *The Population Explosion.* In the long run, the Ehrlichs and like-minded experts consider substantial growth in food production to be absolutely impossible. "We are feeding ourselves at the expense of our children. By definition farmers can overplow and overpump only in the short run. For many farmers the short run is drawing to a close," states Lester R. Brown, president of the Worldwatch Institute, in a 1988 paper.

Over the past three decades, these authors point out, enormous efforts and resources have been pooled to amplify agricultural output. Indeed, the total quantity of harvested crops increased dramatically during this time. In the developing world, food production rose by an average of 117 percent in the quarter of a century between 1965 and 1990. Asia performed far better than other regions, which saw increases below average.

Because population has expanded rapidly as well, per capita food production has generally shown only modest change; in Africa it actually declined. As a consequence, the number of undernourished people is still rising in most parts of the developing world, although that number did fall from 844 million to 786 million during the 1980s. But this decline reflects improved nutritional conditions in Asia alone. During the

same period, the number of people having energy-deficient diets in Latin America, the Near East and Africa climbed.

Many social factors can bring about conditions of hunger, but the pessimists emphasize that population pressure on fragile ecosystems plays a significant role. One specific concern is that we seem to be running short on land suitable for cultivation. If so, current efforts to bolster per capita food production by clearing more fertile land will find fewer options. Between 1850 and 1950 the amount of arable land grew quickly to accommodate both larger populations and greater demand for better diets. This expansion then slowed and by the late 1980s ceased altogether. In the developed world, as well as in some developing countries (especially China), the amount of land under cultivation started to decline during the 1980s. This drop is largely because spreading urban centers have engulfed fertile land or, once the land is depleted, farmers have abandoned it. Farmers have also fled from irrigated land that has become unproductive because of salt accumulation.

Moreover, environmentalists insist that soil erosion is destroying much of the land that is left. The extent of the damage is the subject of controversy. A recent global assessment, sponsored by the United Nations Environment Program and reported by the World Resources Institute and others, offers some perspective. The study concludes that 17 percent of the land supporting plant life worldwide has lost value over the past 45 years. The estimate includes erosion caused by water and wind, as well as chemical and physical deterioration, and ranks the degree of soil degradation from light to severe. This degradation is least prevalent in North

Chronically Undernourished Individuals

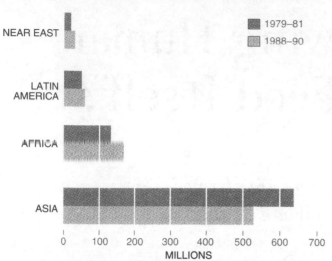

Legend: ■ 1979–81 ■ 1988–90

(Bar chart, horizontal axis MILLIONS: 0, 100, 200, 300, 400, 500, 600, 700)

Regions: NEAR EAST, LATIN AMERICA, AFRICA, ASIA

INCIDENCE OF CHRONIC UNDERNUTRITION fell in the developing world from an estimated 844 million sufferers in 1979 to 786 million in 1990, showing evidence of dramatic nutritional improvements in Asia (*left*). Agricultural productivity

Crop Yields Needed in 2050

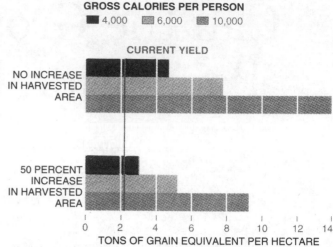

GROSS CALORIES PER PERSON
■ 4,000 ■ 6,000 ■ 10,000

CURRENT YIELD

NO INCREASE IN HARVESTED AREA

50 PERCENT INCREASE IN HARVESTED AREA

(Bar chart, horizontal axis TONS OF GRAIN EQUIVALENT PER HECTARE: 0, 2, 4, 6, 8, 10, 12, 14)

must improve to continue this trend (*right*). Even if more land is harvested in 2050, the average yield must rise sharply as well to offer the projected Third World population of 8.7 billion the current diet of 4,000 gross calories per day.

America (5.3 percent) and most widespread in Central America (25 percent), Europe (23 percent), Africa (22 percent) and Asia (20 percent). In most of these regions, the average farmer could not gather the resources necessary to restore moderate and severely affected soil regions to full productivity. Therefore, prospects for reversing the effects of soil erosion are not good, and it is likely that this problem will worsen.

Despite the loss and degradation of fertile land, the "green revolution" has promoted per capita food production by increasing the yield per hectare. The new, high-yielding strains of grains such as wheat and rice have proliferated since their introduction in the 1960s, especially in Asia. To reap full advantage from these new crop varieties, however, farmers must apply abundant quantities of fertilizer and water.

Environmentalists question whether further conversion to such crops can be achieved at reasonable cost, especially in the developing world, where the gain in production is most needed. At the moment, farmers in Asia, Latin America and Africa use fertilizer sparingly, if at all, because it is too expensive or unavailable. Fertilizer use in the developed world has recently waned. The reasons for the decline are complex and may be temporary, but clearly farmers in North America and Europe have decided that increasing their already heavy application of fertilizer will not further enhance crop yields.

Unfortunately, irrigation systems, which would enable many developing countries to join in the green revolu-

tion, are often too expensive to build. In most areas, irrigation is essential for generating higher yields. It also can make arid land cultivable and protect farmers from the vulnerability inherent in natural variations in the weather. Land brought into cultivation this way could be used for growing multiple crop varieties, thereby helping food production to increase.

Such advantages have been realized since the beginning of agriculture: the earliest irrigation systems are thousands of years old. Yet only a fraction of productive land in the developing world is now irrigated, and its expansion has been slower than population growth. Consequently, the amount of irrigated land per capita has been dwindling during recent decades. The trend, pessimists argue, will be hard to stop. Irrigation systems have been built in the most affordable sites, and the hope for extending them is curtailed by rising costs. Moreover, the accretion of silt in dams and reservoirs and of salt in already irrigated soil is increasingly costly to avoid or reverse.

Environmentalists Ehrlich and Ehrlich note that modern agriculture is by nature at risk wherever it is practiced. The genetic uniformity of single, high-yielding crop strains planted over large areas makes them highly productive but also renders them particularly vulnerable to insects and disease. Current preventive tactics, such as spraying pesticides and rotating crops, are only partial solutions. Rapidly evolving pathogens pose a continuous challenge. Plant breeders must maintain a broad

genetic arsenal of crops by collecting and storing natural varieties and by breeding new ones in the laboratory.

The optimists do not deny that many problems exist within the food supply system. But many of these authorities, including D. Gale Johnson, the late Herman Kahn, Walter R. Brown, L. Martel, the late Roger Revelle, Vaclav Smil and Julian L. Simon, believe the world's food supply can dramatically be expanded. Ironically, they draw their enthusiasm from extrapolation of the very trends that so alarm those experts who expect doom. In fact, statistics show that the average daily caloric intake per capita climbed by 21 percent (from 2,063 calories to 2,495 calories) between 1965 and 1990 in the developing countries. These higher calories have generally delivered greater amounts of protein. On average, the per capita consumption of protein rose from 52 grams per day to 61 grams per day between 1965 and 1990.

According to the optimists, not only has the world food situation improved significantly in recent decades, but further growth can be brought about in various ways. A detailed assessment of climate and soil conditions in 93 developing countries (excluding China) shows that nearly three times as much land as is currently farmed, or an additional 2.1 billion hectares, could be cultivated. Regional soil estimates indicate that sub-Saharan Africa and Latin America can exploit many more stretches of unused land than can Asia, the Near East and North Africa.

Even in regions where the amount of potentially arable land is limited, crops could be grown more times every year than is currently the case. This scenario is particularly true in the tropics and subtropics where conditions are such—relatively even temperature throughout the year and a consistent distribution of daylight hours—that more than one crop would thrive. Nearly twice as many crops are harvested every year in Asia than in Africa at present, but further increases are possible in all regions.

In addition to multicropping, higher yields per crop are attainable, especially in Africa and the Near East. Many more crops are currently harvested per hectare in the First World than elsewhere: cereal yields in North America and Europe averaged 4.2 tons per hectare, compared with 2.9 in the Far East (4.2 in China), 2.1 in Latin America, 1.7 in the Near East and only 1.0 in Africa.

Such yield improvements, the enthusiasts note, can be achieved by expanding the still limited use of high-yield crop varieties, fertilizer and irrigation.

The Potential Impact of Global Warming on Agriculture

The scientific evidence on the greenhouse effect indicates that slow but significant global warming is likely to occur if the emission of greenhouse gases, such as carbon dioxide, methane, nitrogen oxide and chlorofluorocarbons, continues to grow. Agriculture is directly or, at least in some cases, indirectly responsible for releasing a substantial proportion of these gases. Policy responses to the potentially adverse consequences of global climatic change now focus primarily on hindering emissions rather than on halting them. But considering the present need to improve living standards and produce more food for vast numbers of people, experts doubt that even a reduction in global emissions could occur in the near future.

In a 1990 study the Intergovernmental Panel on Climate Change estimated that over the next century the average global temperature will rise by three degrees Celsius. The study assumes that agriculture will expand considerably. This forecast of temperature change is uncertain, but there is now broad agreement that some global warming will take place. All the same, the effect that temperature rise will have on human society remains an open question.

Global warming could either enhance or impede agriculture, suggest Cynthia Rosenzweig of Columbia University and Martin L. Parry of the University of Oxford. Given sufficient water and light, increased ambient carbon dioxide concentrations absorbed during photosynthesis could act as a fertilizer and facilitate growth in certain plants. In addition, by extending the time between the last frost in the spring and the first frost in the fall, global warming will benefit agriculture in cold regions where the growing season is short, such as in Canada and northern areas of Europe and the former Soviet Union. Moreover, warmer air holds more water vapor, and so global warming will bring about more evaporation and precipitation. Areas where crop production is limited by arid conditions would benefit from a wetter climate.

If increased evaporation from soil and plants does not coincide with more rainfall in a region, however, more frequent dry spells and droughts would occur. And a further rise in temperature will reduce crop yields in tropical and subtropical areas, where certain crops are already grown near their limit of heat tolerance. Furthermore, some cereal crops need low winter temperatures to initiate flowering. Warmer winters in temperate regions could therefore stall growing periods and lead to reduced harvests. Finally, global warming will precipitate a thermal swelling of the oceans and melt polar ice. Higher sea levels may claim low-lying farmland and cause higher salt concentrations in the coastal groundwater.

Techniques used to model the climate are not sufficiently advanced to predict the balance of these effects in specific areas. The most recent analysis on the impact of climatic change on the world food supply, by Rosenzweig and Parry in 1992, concludes that average global food production will decline 5 percent by 2060. And they anticipate a somewhat larger drop in the developing world, thus exacerbating the problems expected to arise in attempts to feed growing populations. In contrast, their report predicts a slight rise in agricultural output in developed countries situated at middle and high latitudes.

POSSIBLE BENEFITS OF GLOBAL WARMING ON AGRICULTURE

POSSIBLE DRAWBACKS OF GLOBAL WARMING ON AGRICULTURE

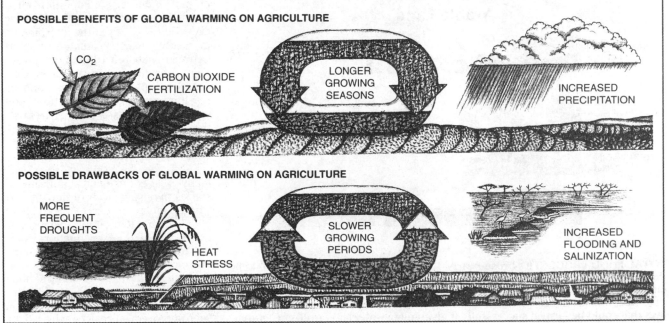

Change in Food Production between 1965 and 1990

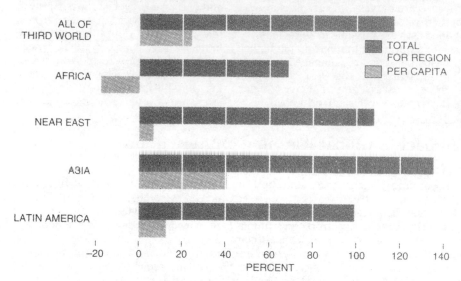

ALL OF THIRD WORLD

AFRICA

NEAR EAST

ASIA

LATIN AMERICA

TOTAL FOR REGION
PER CAPITA

PERCENT

Soil Erosion of Vegetated Land

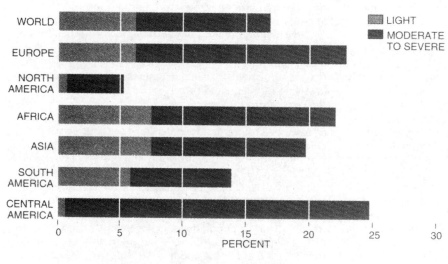

WORLD

EUROPE

NORTH AMERICA

AFRICA

ASIA

SOUTH AMERICA

CENTRAL AMERICA

LIGHT
MODERATE TO SEVERE

PERCENT

Arable Land

SUB-SAHARAN AFRICA

NEAR EAST AND NORTH AFRICA

ASIA (EXCLUDING CHINA)

LATIN AMERICA

IN USE
POTENTIAL

MILLIONS OF HECTARES

TOTAL FOOD PRODUCTION rose nearly 120 percent between 1965 and 1990 in the developing world. Per capita food production showed little change in regions outside Asia (*top*). Soil erosion has debased much of the land worldwide on which that food was produced (*middle*). But many Third World nations have vast holdings that could be farmed successfully if given more water and fertilizer (*bottom*).

In *World Agriculture: Toward 2000*, Nikos Alexandratos of the Food and Agriculture Organization (FAO) of the United Nations reports that only 34 percent of all seeds planted during the mid-1980s were high-yielding varieties. Statistics from the FAO show that at present only about one in five hectares of arable land is irrigated, and very little fertilizer is used. Pesticides are sparsely applied. Food output could drastically be increased simply by more widespread implementation of such technologies.

Aside from producing more food, many economists and agriculturalists point out, consumption levels in the developing world could be boosted by wasting fewer crops, as well as by cutting storage and distribution losses. How much of an increase would these measures yield? Robert W. Kates, director of the Alan Shawn Feinstein World Hunger Program at Brown University, writes in *The Hunger Report: 1988* that humans consume only 60 percent of all harvested crops, and some 25 to 30 percent is lost before reaching individual homes. The FAO, on the other hand, estimates lower distribution losses: 6 percent for cereals, 11 percent for roots and 5 percent for pulses. All the same, there is no doubt that improved storage and distribution systems would leave more food available for human nutrition, independent of future food production capabilities.

For optimists, the long-range trend in food prices constitutes the most convincing evidence for the correctness of their view. In 1992–93 the World Resources Institute reported that food prices dropped further than the price of most nonfuel commodities, all of which have declined in the past decade. Cereal prices in the international market fell by approximately one third between 1980 and 1989. Huge government subsidies for agriculture in North America and western Europe, and the resulting surpluses of agricultural products, have depressed prices. Obviously, the optimists assert, the supply already exceeds the demand of a global population that has doubled since 1950.

Taken together, this evidence leads many experts to see no significant obstacles to raising levels of nutrition for world populations exceeding 10 billion people. The potential for an enormous expansion of food production exists, but its realization depends of course on sensible governmental policies, increased domestic and international trade and large investments in infrastructure and agricultural extension. Such improvements can be achieved, the optimists believe, without incurring irreparable damage to global ecosystems.

Proponents of either of these conflicting perspectives have difficulty accepting the existence of other plausible points of view. Moreover, the polarity between the two sides of expert opinion shows that neither group can be completely correct. Finding some common ground between these seemingly irreconcilable positions is not as difficult as it at first appears if empirical issues are emphasized and important differences in value systems and political beliefs are ignored.

Both sides agree that the demand for food will swell rapidly over the next several decades. In 1990 a person living in the developing world ate on average 2,500 calories each day, taken from 4,000 gross calories of food crops made available within a household. The remaining 1,500 calories from this gross total not used to meet nutritional requirements were either lost, inedible or used as animal feed and plant seed. Most of this food was harvested from 0.7 billion hectares of land in the developing world. The remaining 5 percent of the total food supply came from imports. To sustain this 4,000-gross-calorie diet for more than twice as many residents, or 8.7 billion people, living in the developing world by 2050, agriculture must offer 112 percent more crops. To raise the average Third World diet to 6,000 gross calories per day, slightly above the 1990 world average, food production would need to increase by 218 percent. And to bring the average Third World diet to a level comparable with that currently found in the developed world, or 10,000 gross calories per day, food production would have to surge by 430 percent.

A more generous food supply will be achieved in the future through boosting crop yields, as it has been accomplished in the past. If the harvested area in the developing world remains at 0.7 billion hectares, then each hectare must more than double its yield to maintain an already inadequate diet for the future population of the developing world. Providing a diet equivalent to a First World diet in 1990 would require that each hectare increase its yield more than six times. Such an event in the developing world must be considered virtually impossible, barring a major breakthrough in the biotechnology of food production.

Instead farmers will no doubt plant more acres and grow more crops per year on the same land to help augment crop harvests. Extrapolation of past trends suggests that the total harvested area will increase by about 50 percent by the year 2050. Each hectare will then have to provide nearly 50 percent more tons of grain or its equivalent to keep up with current dietary levels. Improved diets could result only from much larger yields.

The technological optimists are correct in stating that overall world food production can substantially be increased over the next few decades. Current crop yields are well below their theoretical maxima, and only about 11 percent of the world's farmable land is now under cultivation. Moreover, the experience gained recently in a number of developing countries, such as China, holds important lessons on how to tap this potential elsewhere. Agricultural productivity responds to well-designed policies that assist farmers by supplying needed fertilizer and other inputs, building sound infrastructure and providing market access. Further investments in agricultural research will spawn new technologies that will fortify agriculture in the future. The vital question then is not how to grow more food but rather how to implement agricultural methods that may make possible a boost in food production.

A more troublesome problem is how to achieve this technological enhancement at acceptable environmental costs. It is here that the arguments of those experts who forecast a catastrophe carry considerable weight. There can be no doubt that the land now used for growing food crops is generally of better quality than unused, potentially cultivable land. Similarly, existing irrigation systems have been built on the most favorable sites. Consequently, each new measure applied to increase yields is becoming more expensive to implement, especially in the developed world and parts of the developing world such as China, where productivity is already high. In short, such constraints are raising the marginal cost of each additional ton of grain or its equivalent. This tax is even higher if one takes into account negative externalities—primarily environmental costs not reflected in the price of agricultural products.

The environmental price of what in the Ehrlichs' view amounts to "turning the earth into a giant human feedlot" could be severe. A large inflation of agriculture to provide growing populations with improved diets is likely to lead to widespread deforestation, loss of species, soil erosion and pollution from pesticides, and runoff of fertilizer as farming intensifies and new land is brought into production. Reducing or minimizing this environmental impact is possible but costly.

Given so many uncertainties, the course of future food prices is difficult to chart. At the very least, the rising marginal cost of food production will engender steeper prices on the international market than would be the case if there were no environmental constraints. Whether these higher costs can offset the historical decline in food prices remains to be seen. An upward trend in the price of food sometime in the near future is a distinct possibility. Such a hike will be mitigated by the continued development and application of new technology and by the likely recovery of agricultural production and exports in the former Soviet Union, eastern Europe and Latin America. Also, any future price increases could be lessened by taking advantage of the underutilized agricultural resources in North America, notes Per Pinstrup-Andersen of Cornell University in his 1992 paper "Global Perspectives for Food Production and Consumption." Rising prices will have little effect on high-income countries or on households possessing reasonable purchasing power, but the poor will suffer.

In reality, the future of global food production is neither as grim as the pessimists believe nor as rosy as the optimists claim. The most plausible outcome is that dietary intake will creep higher in most regions. Significant annual fluctuations in food availability and prices are, of course, likely; a variety of factors, including the weather, trade interruptions and the vulnerability of monocropping to pests, can alter food supply anywhere. The expansion of agriculture will be achieved by boosting crop yields and by using existing farmland more intensively, as well as by bringing arable land into cultivation where such action proves economical. Such events will transpire more slowly than in the past, however, because of environmental constraints. In addition, the demand for food in the developed world is approaching saturation levels. In the U.S., mounting concerns about health have caused the per capita consumption of calories from animal products to drop.

Still, progress will be far from uniform. Numerous countries will struggle to overcome unsatisfactory nutrition levels. These countries fall into three main categories. Some low-income countries have little or no reserves of fertile land or water. The absence of agricultural resources is in itself not an insurmountable problem, as is demonstrated by regions, such as Hong Kong and Kuwait, that can purchase their food on the international market. But many poor countries, such as Bangladesh, cannot afford to buy food from abroad and thereby compensate for insufficient natural resources. These countries will probably rely more on food aid in the future.

Low nutrition levels are also found in many countries, such as Zaire, that do possess large reserves of potentially cultivable land and water. Government neglect of agriculture and policy failures have typically caused poor diets in such countries. A recent World Bank report describes the damaging effects of direct and indirect taxation of agriculture, controls placed on prices and market access, and overvalued currencies, which discourage exports and encourage imports. Where agricultural production has suffered from misguided government intervention (as is particularly the case in Africa), the solution—policy reform—is clear.

Food aid will be needed as well in areas rife with political instability and civil strife. The most devastating famines of the past decade, known to television viewers around the world, have occurred in regions fighting prolonged civil wars, such as Ethiopia, Somalia and the Sudan. In many of these cases, drought was instrumental in stirring social and political disruption. The addition of violent conflict prevented the recuperation of agriculture and the distribution of food, thus turning bad but remediable situations into disasters. International military intervention, as in Somalia, provides only a short-term remedy. In the absence of sweeping political compromise, hunger and malnutrition will remain endemic in these war-torn regions.

Feeding a growing world population a diet that improves over time in quality and quantity is technologically feasible. But the economic and environmental costs incurred through bolstering food production may well prove too great for many poor countries. The course of events will depend crucially on their governments' ability to design and enforce effective policies that address the challenges posed by mounting human numbers, rising poverty and environmental degradation. Whatever the outcome, the task ahead will be made more difficult if population growth rates cannot be reduced.

FURTHER READING

POVERTY AND HUNGER: ISSUES AND OPTIONS FOR FOOD SECURITY IN DEVELOPING COUNTRIES. World Bank, 1986.

ENERGY, FOOD, ENVIRONMENT: REALITIES, MYTHS, OPTIONS. Vaclav Smil. Clarendon Press, 1987.

WORLD AGRICULTURE: TOWARD 2000. Nikos Alexandratos. New York University Press, 1988.

WORLD RESOURCES 1992-93. World Resources Institute. Oxford University Press, 1992.

The Future of AIDS

New research suggests HIV is not a new virus but an old one that grew deadly.
Can we turn the process around?

Geoffrey Cowley

Ten years ago, Benjamin B. got what might have been a death sentence. Hospitalized for colon surgery, the Australian retiree received a blood transfusion tainted with the AIDS virus. That he's alive at all is remarkable, but that's only half of the story. Unlike most long-term HIV survivors, he has suffered no symptoms and no loss of immune function. He's as healthy today as he was in 1983—and celebrating his 81st birthday. Benjamin B. is just one of five patients who came to the attention of Dr. Brett Tindall, an AIDS researcher at the University of New South Wales, as he was preparing a routine update on transfusion-related HIV infections last year. All five were infected by the same donor. And seven to 10 years later, none has suffered any effects.

The donor turned out to be a gay man who had contracted the virus during the late 1970s or early '80s, then given blood at least 26 times before learning he was infected. After tracking him down, Tindall learned, to his amazement, that the man was just as healthy as the people who got his blood. "We know that HIV causes AIDS," Tindall says. "We also know that a few patients remain well for long periods, but we've never known why. Is it the vitamins they take? Is it some gene they have in common? This work suggests it has more to do with the virus. I think we've found a harmless strain."

He may also have found the viral equivalent of a fossil, a clue to the origin, evolution and future of the AIDS epidemic. HIV may not be a new and inherently deadly virus, as is commonly assumed, but an old one that has recently acquired deadly tendencies. In a forthcoming book, Paul Ewald, an evolutionary biologist at Amherst College, argues that HIV may have infected people benignly for decades, even centuries, before it started causing AIDS. He traces its virulence to the social upheavals of the 1960s and '70s, which not only sped its movement through populations but rewarded it for reproducing more aggressively within the body.

The idea may sound radical, but it's not just flashy speculation. It reflects a growing awareness that parasites, like everything else in nature, evolve by natural selection, changing their character to adapt to their environments. Besides transforming our understanding of AIDS, the new view could yield bold strategies for fighting it. Viruses can evolve tens of thousands of times faster than plants or animals, and few evolve as fast as HIV. Confronted by a drug or an immune reaction, the virus readily mutates out of its range. A few researchers are now trying to exploit that very talent, using drugs to force HIV to mutate until it can no longer function. A Boston team, led by medical student Yung-Kang Chow, made headlines last month by showing that the technique works perfectly in a test tube. Human trials are now in the works, but better drug treatment isn't the only hope rising from an evolutionary outlook. If rapid spread is what turned HIV into a killer, then condoms and clean needles may ultimately do more than prevent new infections. Used widely enough, they might drive the AIDS virus toward the benign form sighted in Australia.

I. WHERE DID HIV COME FROM?

Viruses are the ultimate parasites. Unlike bacteria, which absorb nutrients, excrete waste and reproduce by dividing, they have no life of their own. They're mere shreds of genetic information, encoded in DNA or RNA, that can integrate themselves into a living cell and use its machinery to run off copies of themselves. Where the first one came from is anyone's guess, but today's viruses are, like any plant or animal, simply descendants of earlier forms.

Most scientists agree that the human immunodeficiency viruses—HIV-1 and HIV-2—are basically ape or monkey viruses. Both HIVs are genetically similar to viruses found in African primates, the so called SIVs. In fact, as the accompanying tree illustrates, the HIVs have more in common with simian viruses than they do with each other. HIV-2, found mainly in West Africa, is so similar to the SIV that infects the sooty mangabey—an ash-colored monkey from the same region—that it doesn't really qualify as a separate viral species. "When you see HIV-2," says Gerald Myers, head of the HIV database project at the Los

Alamos National Laboratory, "you may not be looking at a human virus but at a mangabey virus in a human." HIV-1, the virus responsible for the vast majority of the world's AIDS cases, bears no great resemblance to HIV-2 or the monkey SIVs, but it's very similar to SIV cpz, a virus recovered in 1990 from a wild chimpanzee in the West African nation of Gabon.

The prevailing theory holds that humans were first infected through direct contact with primates, and that the SIVs they contracted have since diverged by varying degrees from their ancestors. It's possible, of course, that the HIVs and SIVs evolved separately, or even that humans were the original carriers. But the primates-to-people scenario has a couple of points in its favor. First, the SIVs are more varied than the HIVs, which suggests they've been evolving longer. Second, it's easier to imagine people being infected by chimps or monkeys than vice versa. Humans have hunted and handled other primates for thousands of years. Anyone who was bitten or scratched, or who cut himself butchering an animal, could have gotten infected.

Until recently, it was unclear whether people could contract SIV directly from primates, but a couple of recent accidents have settled that issue. In one case, reported last summer by the Centers for Disease Control, a lab technician at a primate-research center jabbed herself with a needle containing blood from an infected macaque. The infection didn't take—she produced antibodies to SIV only for a few months—but she was just lucky. Another lab worker, who handled monkey tissues while suffering from skin lesions, has remained SIV-positive for two years. In a recent survey of 472 blood samples drawn from primate handlers, health officials found that three of those tested positive as well. No one knows whether the people with SIV eventually develop AIDS, but the potential for cross-species transmission is now clear.

Far less clear is when the first such transmission took place. The most common view holds that since AIDS is a new epidemic, the responsible vi-

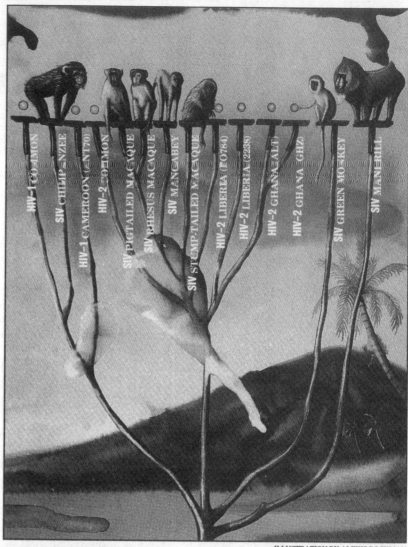

ILLUSTRATION BY ALEXIS ROCKMAN

HIV'S EXTENDED FAMILY: Today's viruses are descendants of earlier forms. This family tree shows that the human AIDS viruses, HIV-1 and HIV-2, are more closely related to viruses found in primates (the SIVs) than to each other.

ruses must have entered humans within the past few decades. That's a reasonable suspicion, but it raises a sticky question. Why, if people have been handling primates in Africa for thousands of years, did SIV take until now to jump species?

One possibility is that humans recently opened some avenue that hasn't existed in the past. Some theorists argue, for example, that AIDS was spawned by a polio-vaccination program carried out in Africa during the late 1950s. During that four-year effort, 325,000 Africans received an oral polio vaccine produced in kidney cells from African green monkeys. Even if the vaccine was contaminated with SIV—which hasn't been estab-

lished—blaming it for AIDS would be hasty. For the SIVs found in African green monkeys bear too little resemblance to HIV-1, the primary human AIDS virus, to be its likely progenitor. In order to link HIV-1 to those early lots of polio vaccine, someone would have to show that they contained a monkey virus never yet found in actual monkeys.

The alternative view—that the HIVs are old viruses—is just as hard to prove, but it requires fewer tortured assumptions. Dr. Jay Levy, an AIDS researcher at the University of California, San Francisco, puts it this way: "We know that all these other primates harbor lentiviruses [the class that includes the SIVs and HIVs]. Why should humans be any exception?" If the HIVs were on hand before the AIDS epidemic began, the key question is not where they came from but whether they always caused the disease.

II. WAS HIV ONCE LESS DEADLY?

If HIV had always caused AIDS, one would expect virus and illness to emerge together in the historical record. Antibodies to HIV have been detected in rare blood samples dating back to 1959, yet the first African AIDS cases were described in the early 1980s, when the disease started decimating the cities of Rwanda, Zaire, Zambia and Uganda. When Dr. Robert Biggar, an epidemiologist at the National Cancer Institute, pored over African hospital records looking for earlier descriptions of AIDS-like illness he didn't find any. It's possible, of course, that the disease was there all along, just too rare to be recognized as a distinct condition. But the alternative view is worth considering. There are intriguing hints that HIV hasn't always been so deadly.

Any population of living things, from fungi to rhinoceri, includes genetically varied individuals, which pass essential traits along to their progeny. As Charles Darwin discerned more than a century ago, the individuals best designed to exploit a particular environment tend to produce the greatest number of viable offspring. As generations pass, beneficial traits become more and more pervasive in the population. There's no universal recipe for reproductive success; different environments favor different traits. But by preserving some and discarding others, every environment molds the species it supports.

Viruses aren't exempt from the process. Their purpose, from a Darwinian perspective, is simply to make as many copies of themselves as they can. Other things being equal, those that replicate fastest will become the most plentiful within the host, and so stand the best chance of infecting other hosts on contact. But there's a catch. If a microbe

reproduces too aggressively inside its host, or invades too many different tissues, it may kill the host—and itself—without getting passed along at all. The most successful virus, then, is not necessarily the most or the least virulent. It's one that exploits its host most effectively.

As Ewald and others have shown, that mandate can drive different microbes to very different levels of nastiness. Because they travel via social contact between people, cold and flu viruses can't normally afford to immobilize us. To stay in business, they need hosts who are out coughing, sneezing, shaking hands and sharing pencils. But the incentives change when a parasite has other ways of getting around. Consider tuberculosis or diphtheria. Both deadly diseases are caused by bacteria that can survive for weeks or months outside the body. They can reproduce aggressively in the host, ride a cough into the external environment, then wait patiently for another host to come along. By the same token, a parasite that can travel from person to person via mosquito or some other vector has little reason to be gentle. As long as malaria sufferers can still feed hungry mosquitoes, their misery is of little consequence to the microbe. Indeed, a

host who can't wield a fly swatter may be preferable to one who can.

These patterns aren't set in stone. A shift in circumstances may push a normally mild-mannered parasite toward virulence, or vice versa. One of the most devastating plagues in human history was caused by a mere influenza virus, which swept the globe in 1918, leaving 20 million corpses in its wake. Many experts still regard the disaster as an accident, triggered by the random reshuffling of viral genes. But from an evolutionary perspective, it's no coincidence that the flu grew so deadly when it did. World War I was raging in 1918. Great numbers of soldiers were huddled in the European trenches, where even the most ravaged host stood an excellent chance of infecting many others. For a flu virus, the incentives favoring restraint would have vanished in those circumstances. Rather than rendering the host useless, extreme virulence would simply make him more infectious.

Ewald suspects that HIV has recently undergone a similar transformation. Unlike influenza viruses, which infect cells in the respiratory tract and

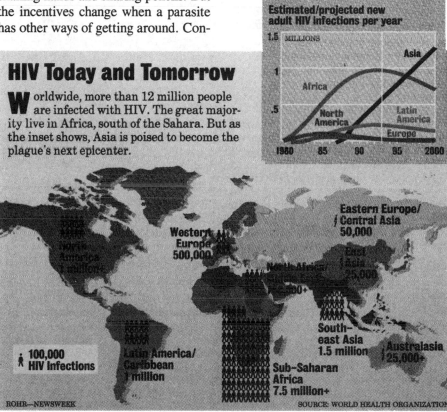

HIV Today and Tomorrow

Worldwide, more than 12 million people are infected with HIV. The great majority live in Africa, south of the Sahara. But as the inset shows, Asia is poised to become the plague's next epicenter.

Estimated/projected new adult HIV infections per year

1.5 MILLIONS

Asia

Africa

North America

Latin America

Europe

1980 85 90 95 2000

Eastern Europe/ Central Asia 50,000

Western Europe 500,000

North Africa

East Asia 25,000

Southeast Asia 1.5 million

Australasia 25,000+

Sub-Saharan Africa 7.5 million+

Latin America/ Caribbean 1 million

North America 1 million

100,000 HIV Infections

ROHR—NEWSWEEK

SOURCE: WORLD HEALTH ORGANIZATION

spread through coughs and sneezes, the HIVs insinuate themselves into white blood cells. Infected cells (or the new viruses they produce) can pass between people, but only during sex or other exchanges of body fluid. Confined to an isolated population where no carrier had numerous sex partners, a virus like HIV would gain nothing from replicating aggressively within the body; it would do best to lie low, leaving the host alive and mildly infectious for many years. But if people's sexual networks suddenly expanded, fresh hosts would become more plentiful, and infected hosts more dispensable. An HIV strain that replicated wildly might kill people in three years instead of 30, but by making them more infectious while they lasted, it would still come out ahead.

Is that what actually happened? There's no question that social changes have hastened the spread of HIV. Starting in the 1960s, war, tourism and commercial trucking forced the outside world on Africa's once isolated villages. At the same time, drought and industrialization prompted mass migrations from the countryside into newly teeming cities. Western monogamy had never been common in Africa, but as the French medical historian Mirko Grmek notes in his book "History of AIDS," urbanization shattered social structures that had long constrained sexual behavior. Prostitution exploded, and venereal disease flourished. Hypodermic needles came into wide use during the same period, creating yet another mode of infection. Did these trends actually turn a chronic but relatively benign infection into a killer? The evidence is circumstantial, but it's hard to discount.

If Ewald is right, and HIV's deadliness is a consequence of its rapid spread, then the nastiest strains should show up in the populations where it's moving the fastest. To a surprising degree, they do. It's well known, for example, that HIV-2 is far less virulent than HIV-1. "Going on what we've seen so far, we'd have to say that HIV-1 causes AIDS in 90 percent of those infected, while HIV-2 causes AIDS in 10 percent or less," says Harvard AIDS specialist Max Essex. "Maybe everyone infected with HIV-2 will progress to AIDS after 40 or 50 years, but that's still in the realm of reduced virulence." From Ewald's perspective, it's no surprise that HIV-2, the strain found in West Africa, is the gentle one. West Africa has escaped much of the war, drought and urbanization that fueled the spread of HIV-1 in the central and eastern parts of the continent. "HIV-2 appears to be adapted for slow transmission in areas with lower sexual contact," he concludes, "and HIV-1 for more rapid transmission in areas with higher sexual contact."

The same pattern shows up in the way each virus affects different populations. HIV-2 appears particularly mild in the stable and isolated West African nation of Senegal. After following a group of Senegalese prostitutes for six years, Harvard researchers found that those testing positive for HIV-2 showed virtually no sign of illness. In laboratory tests, researchers at the University of Alabama found that Senegalese HIV-2 didn't even kill white blood cells when allowed to infect them in a test tube. Yet HIV-2 is a killer in the more urban and less tradition-bound Ivory Coast. In a survey of hospital patients in the city of Abidjan, researchers from the U.S. Centers for Disease Control found that HIV-2 was associated with AIDS nearly as often as HIV-1.

The variations within HIV-1 are less clear-cut, but they, too, lend support to Ewald's idea. Though the evidence is mixed, there are hints that IV drug users (whose transmission rates have remained high for the past decade) may be contracting deadlier strains of HIV-1 than gay men (whose transmission rates have plummeted). In a 1990 study of infected gay men, fewer than 8 percent of those not receiving early treatment developed AIDS each year. In a more recent study of IV drug users, the proportion of untreated carriers developing AIDS each year was more than 17 percent.

Together, these disparities suggest that HIV assumes different personalities in different settings, becoming more aggressive when it's traveling rapidly through a population. But because so many factors affect the health of infected people, the strength of the connection is unclear. "This is exactly the right way to think about virulence," says virologist Stephen Morse of New York's Rockefeller University. "Virulence should be dynamic, not static. The question is, how dynamic?

A Hypothetical History of AIDS

Why did HIV suddenly emerge as a global killer? According to one theory, the virus has infected people for centuries, but recent social changes have altered its character.

BEFORE 1960
Rural Africans contracted benign ancestral forms of HIV from primates. Because the viruses spread so slowly among people, they couldn't afford to become virulent.

1960 TO 1975
War, drought, commerce and urbanization shattered African social institutions. HIV spread rapidly, becoming more virulent as transmission accelerated.

1975 TO PRESENT
Global travel placed HIV in broader circulation. Shifting sexual mores and modern medical practices, such as blood transfusion, made many populations susceptible.

THE FUTURE
If social changes can turn a benign virus deadly, the process should be reversible. Simply slowing transmission may help drive fast-killing strains out of circulation.

We know that a pathogen like HIV has a wide range of potentials, but we can't yet say just what pressures are needed to generate a particular outcome."

The best answers to Morse's question may come from laboratory studies. A handful of biologists are now devising test-tube experiments to see more precisely how transmission rates shape a parasite's character. Zoologist James Bull of the University of Texas at Austin has shown, for example, that a bacteriophage (a virus that infects bacteria) kills bacterial cells with great abandon when placed in a test tube and given plenty of new cells to infect. Like HIV in a large, active sexual network, it can afford to kill individual hosts without wiping itself out in the process. Yet the same virus becomes benign when confined to individual cells and their offspring (a situation perhaps akin to pre-epidemic HIV's). With a good animal model, researchers might someday manage to test Ewald's hypotheses about HIV with the same kind of precision.

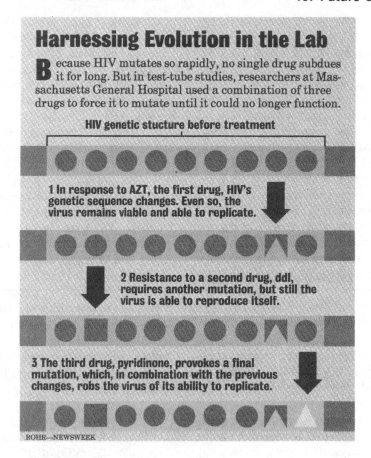

Harnessing Evolution in the Lab

Because HIV mutates so rapidly, no single drug subdues it for long. But in test-tube studies, researchers at Massachusetts General Hospital used a combination of three drugs to force it to mutate until it could no longer function.

HIV genetic stucture before treatment

1 In response to AZT, the first drug, HIV's genetic sequence changes. Even so, the virus remains viable and able to replicate.

2 Resistance to a second drug, ddI, requires another mutation, but still the virus is able to reproduce itself.

3 The third drug, pyridinone, provokes a final mutation, which, in combination with the previous changes, robs the virus of its ability to replicate.

ROHR—NEWSWEEK

III. CAN HIV BE TAMED?

Until recently, medical science seemed well on its way to controlling the microbial world. Yet after 10 years and billions of dollars in research, HIV still has scientists over a barrel. The secret of its success can be summed up in one word: mutability. Because HIV's method of replication is so error prone (its genes mutate at a million times the rate of our own), it produces extremely varied offspring, even within an individual host. Whenever a drug or immune response successfully attacks one variant, another arises to flourish in its place. Even when an AIDS drug works broadly enough to check HIV's growth, it rarely works for long. AZT, for example, can help prevent symptoms for a couple of years. But people on AZT still get AIDS, as the viral populations in their bodies evolve toward resistant forms.

There may not be a drug or vaccine on earth that could subdue such a protean parasite. But from a Darwinian perspective, killing HIV is not the only

way to combat AIDS. We know the virus changes rapidly in response to outside pressures. Logic suggests that if we simply applied the right pressures—within a community, or even within a patient's body—we might begin to tame it.

It's well known that condoms and clean needles can save lives by preventing HIV infection. From an evolutionary perspective, there is every reason to think they could do more. Used widely enough, those same humble implements might push the virus toward more benevolent forms, simply by depriving virulent strains of the high transmission rates they need to survive. Gay men are already engaged in that exercise. Studies suggest that, thanks to safer sex, the rate of new infections among gays declined five to tenfold during the 1980s. There are tantalizing hints that HIV has grown less noxious in the same population over the same period. In a 1991 study, researchers at the National Institutes of Health (NIH) calculated the rates at which infected people from different

risk groups were developing AIDS each year. They found that as of 1987, the rate declined sharply among gay men, suggesting the virus was taking longer to cause illness. Part of the change was due to AZT, which can delay the onset of symptoms. But when the NIH researchers corrected for AZT use, there was still a mysterious shortage of AIDS cases. From Ewald's viewpoint, the shortfall was not only unsurprising but predictable.

How far could such a trend be pushed? Would broader, better prevention efforts eventually turn today's deadliest HIV-1 into something as benign as Senegal's HIV-2? No one knows. But the prospect of domesticating the AIDS virus, even partially, should excite public-health officials. Condoms and clean needles are exceedingly cheap medicine. They can save lives even if they fail to change the course of evolution—and judging from the available evidence, they might well succeed.

In the meantime, more than 12 million people are carrying today's HIV, and those who get AIDS are still dying. Fortunately, as Yung-Kang Chow and his colleagues at Massachusetts General Hospital showed last month, there's more than one way to manipulate viral evolution. The researchers managed, in a test-tube experiment, to outsmart HIV at its own game. Their trick was to combine three drugs—AZT, ddI and pyridinone—that disarm the same part of the virus (an enzyme called reverse transcriptase).

Any of those drugs can foil HIV's efforts to colonize host cells. When HIV encounters them individually, or even in pairs, it gradually mutates into resistant forms and goes on about its business. But each mutation makes the virus slightly less efficient—and as Chow's group demonstrated, there comes a point where mutation itself hobbles the virus (see chart on previous page). By engineering an HIV mutant that contained three different mutations (one in response to each of the three drugs), the researchers ended up with a virus that was too deformed to function at all. If virgin HIV can't function in the presence of the three drugs—and if triply mutated HIV can't function at all—then the three-drug regimen should, theoretically, do wonders for patients.

It's a long way from the test tube to the clinic; many treatments have shown great promise in lab experiments, only to prove ineffective or highly toxic in people. Upcoming clinical trials will determine whether patients actually benefit from Chow's combination of drugs. The beauty of the new approach, however, is that it's not limited to any particular combination. While the Boston team experiments with drugs directed against reverse transcriptase, researchers at New York's Aaron Diamond AIDS Research Center are trying the same tack against another viral target (an enzyme called protease). "This virus has impressed us again and again with its ability to change," says Dr. David Ho, director of the Aaron Diamond Center. "It always has a new strategy to counter our efforts. Now we're asking it to make a tradeoff. We're saying, 'Go ahead and mutate, because we think that if you mutate in the right place, you'll do less damage to the patient'."

IV. CAN THE NEXT AIDS BE AVOIDED?

The forces that brought us this plague can surely bring us others. By encroaching on rain forests and wilderness areas, humanity is placing itself in ever-closer contact with other animal species and their obscure, deadly parasites. Other activities, from irrigation to the construction of dams and cities, can create new diseases by expanding the range of the rodents or insects that carry them. Stephen Morse, the Rockefeller virologist, studies the movement of microbes among populations and species, and he worries that human activities are speeding the flow of viral traffic. More than a dozen new diseases have shown up in humans since the 1960s, nearly all of them the result of once exotic parasites exploiting new opportunities. "The primary problem," Morse concludes, "is no longer virological but social."

The Ebola virus is often cited as an example of the spooky pathogens in our future. The virus first struck in August 1976, when a trader arrived at a mission hospital in northern Zaire, fever raging and blood oozing from every orifice. Within days the man died, and nearly half of the nurses at the hospital were stricken. Thirty-nine died, and as hospital patients contracted the virus, it spread to 58 neighboring villages. Ebola fever ended up striking 1,000 people in Zaire and nearby Sudan, killing 500. Epidemiologists feared it would spread more widely, but the outbreaks subsided as quickly as they had begun. From a

As Human Habits Change, New Viruses Emerge

VIRUS, DISEASE	SYMPTOMS	ORIGIN	STATUS
JUNIN Argentine Hemorrhagic Fever	Fever, muscle pain, rash, internal bleeding and, sometimes, tremors or convulsions. Mortality rate: 10 to 20 percent.	First recognized in 1953, Junin has emerged as a result of an increase in corn cultivation in northern Argentina. Carried by mice.	A rodent-control program brought the virus's Bolivian cousin, Machupo, under control, but Junin has expanded its reach in recent decades. It strikes 400 to 600 people annually.
EBOLA African Hemorrhagic Fever	Fever, vomiting, rash, muscle pain, gastrointestinal bleeding, shock. A deadly virus, Ebola kills at least half its victims.	Virtually identical to Marburg, a virus found in Germany in 1967, Ebola was first reported in 1976. Its origin is unknown.	An outbreak in Africa killed 500 in 1976. Philippine monkeys sent to a Reston, Va., research lab brought a related—but not lethal—virus here in 1989, leading to curbs on monkey imports.
DENGUE Dengue Fever	Headache, fever, muscle pain, chills. More severe dengue hemorrhagic fever can cause internal bleeding and death.	Dengue has long plagued tropical Asia, South America and the Caribbean, favoring densely populated, mosquito-infested areas.	Infects more than 30 million people annually. Rare in U.S. but could spread more widely since a shipment of used tires brought virus-transmitting Asian tiger mosquitoes ashore in 1985.
HTLVs Leukemia, TSP	Leukemia is a cancer of white blood cells which can spread to other organs. TSP is a degenerative neurological disorder.	HTLV-1 was first reported in 1980, but studies suggest that it and the related virus HTLV-2 have attacked humans for millenniums.	HTLVs are transmitted in the same manner as HIV but, so far, appear less deadly. One recent study found that up to 20 percent of IV drug users in Los Angeles are infected.

SOURCE: STEPHEN S. MORSE—THE ROCKEFELLER UNIVERSITY, PAUL EWALD—AMHERST COLLEGE

Darwinian perspective, that's no great surprise. A parasite that kills that rapidly has little chance of sustaining a chain of infection unless it can survive independently of its host.

More worrisome is a virus like HTLV, a relative of HIV that infects the same class of blood cells and is riding the same waves through new populations. Though recognized only since the 1970s, the HTLVs (HTLV-1 and HTLV-2) appear to be ancient. About one in 20 HTLV-1 infections leads eventually to leukemia, lymphoma or a paralyzing neurologic disorder called TSP. The virus is less aggressive than HIV-1—it typically takes several decades to cause any illness—but its virulence seems to vary markedly from one setting to the next. In Japan, the HTLV-related cancers typically show up in 60-year-olds who were infected by their mothers in the womb. In the Caribbean, where the virus is more often transmitted through sex, the average latency is much shorter. It's not unusual for people to develop symptoms in their 40s.

HTLV may not mutate as readily as HIV, but it is subject to the same natural forces. If human activities can turn one virus into a global killer, it's only prudent to suspect they could do the same to another. "HTLV is a threat," says Ewald, "not because it has escaped from some secluded source, but because it may evolve increased virulence." HTLV-1 is only one tenth as prevalent as HIV in the United States, but it has gained a strong foothold among IV drug users, whose shared needles are a perfect breeding ground for virulent strains.

No one knows whether HTLV could cause an epidemic like AIDS. Fortunately, we don't have to wait passively to find out. We're beginning to see how our actions mold the character of our parasites. No one saw the last epidemic coming. This time, that's not an excuse.

CULTURAL DIVERSITY
A WORLD VIEW

STEPPING BACK FROM
TODAY'S DIVISIVE
DEBATES ON
MULTICULTURALISM,
PLURALISM, AND EXCELLENCE
TO LOOK AT HOW
CIVILIZATIONS ADVANCE

THOMAS SOWELL

Thomas Sowell is a senior fellow at the Hoover Institution, Stanford University. This article is Mr. Sowell's Francis Boyer Lecture delivered at the American Enterprise Institute's annual dinner in Washington, D.C., on December 5, 1990.

"Diversity" has become one of the most often used words of our time—and a word almost never defined. Diversity is invoked in discussions of everything from employment policy to curriculum reform and from entertainment to politics. Nor is the word merely a description of the long-known fact that the American population is made up of people from many countries, many races, and many cultural backgrounds. All that was well known long before the word "diversity" became an insistent part of our vocabulary, an invocation, an imperative, or a bludgeon in ideological conflicts.

The very motto of the country—*E Pluribus Unum*—recognizes the diversity of the American people. For generations, this diversity has been celebrated, whether in comedies like *Abie's Irish Rose* (the famous play featuring a Jewish boy and an Irish girl) or in patriotic speeches on the Fourth of July. Yet one senses something very different in today's crusades for "diversity"—certainly not a patriotic celebration of America and often a sweeping criticism of the United States, or even a condemnation of Western civilization as a whole.

At the very least, we need to separate the issue of the general importance of cultural diversity—not only in the United States but in the world at large—from the more specific, more parochial, and more ideological agendas which have become associated with that word in recent years. I would like to talk about the *worldwide* importance of cultural diversity over centuries of human history before returning to the narrower issues of our time.

The entire history of the human race, the rise of man from the caves, has been marked by transfers of cultural advances from one group to another and from one civilization to another. Paper and printing, for example, are today vital parts of Western civilization—but they originated in China centuries before they made their way to Europe. So did the magnetic compass, which made possible the great ages of exploration that put the Western Hemisphere in touch with the rest of mankind. Mathematical concepts likewise migrated from one culture to another: trigonometry from ancient Egypt, and the whole numbering system now used throughout the world originated among the Hindus of India, though Europeans called this system Arabic numerals because it was the Arabs who were the intermediaries through which these numbers reached medieval Europe. Indeed, much of the philosophy of ancient Greece first reached Western Europe in Arabic translations, which were then retranslated into Latin or into the vernacular languages of the West Europeans.

Much that became part of the culture of Western civilization originated *outside* that civilization, often in the Middle East or Asia. The game of chess came from India, gunpowder from China, and various mathematical concepts from the Islamic world, for example. The conquest of Spain by Moslems in the eighth century A.D. made Spain a center for the diffusion into Western Europe of the more advanced knowledge of the Mediterranean world and of the Orient in astronomy, medicine, optics, and geometry. The later rise of Western Europe to world preeminence in science and technology built upon these foundations, and then the science and technology of European civilization began to spread around the world, not only to European offshoot societies such as the United States or Australia but also to non-European cultures, of which Japan is perhaps the most striking example.

The historic sharing of cultural advances, until they became the common inheritance of the human race, implied much more than cultural diversity. It implied that some cultural features were not only different from others but *better* than others. The very fact that people—all people, whether Europeans, Africans, Asians, or others—have repeatedly chosen to abandon some feature of their own culture in order to replace it with something from another culture implies that the replacement served their purposes more effectively: Arabic numerals are not simply different from Roman numerals, they are *better* than Roman numerals. This is shown by their replacing Roman numerals in many countries whose own cultures derived from Rome, as well as in other countries whose respective numbering systems were likewise superseded by so-called Arabic numerals.

It is virtually inconceivable today that the distances in astronomy or the complexities of higher mathematics should be expressed in Roman numerals. Merely to express the year of American independence—MDCCLXXVI—requires more than twice as many Roman numerals as Arabic numerals. Moreover, Roman numerals offer more opportunities for errors, as the same digit may be either added or subtracted, depending on its place in the sequence. Roman numerals are good for numbering kings or Super Bowls, but they cannot match the efficiency of Arabic numerals in

most mathematical operations—and that is, after all, why we have numbers at all. Cultural features do not exist merely as badges of "identity" to which we have some emotional attachment. They exist to meet the necessities and forward the purposes of human life. When they are surpassed by features of other cultures, they tend to fall by the wayside or to survive only as marginal curiosities, like Roman numerals today.

Not only concepts, information, products, and technologies transfer from one culture to another. The natural produce of the Earth does the same. Malaysia is the world's leading grower of rubber trees—but those trees are indigenous to Brazil. Most of the rice grown in Africa today originated in Asia, and its tobacco originated in the Western Hemisphere. Even a great wheat-exporting nation like Argentina once imported wheat, which was not an indigenous crop to that country. Cultural diversity, viewed internationally and historically, is not a static picture of differentness but a dynamic picture of competition in which what serves human purposes more effectively survives while what does not tends to decline or disappear.

Manuscript scrolls once preserved the precious records, knowledge, and thought of European or Middle Eastern cultures. But once paper and printing from China became known in these cultures, books were clearly far faster and cheaper to produce and drove scrolls virtually into extinction. Books were not simply different from scrolls; they were *better* than scrolls. The point that some cultural features are better than others must be insisted on today because so many among the intelligentsia either evade or deny this plain reality. The intelligentsia often use words like "perceptions" and "values" as they argue in effect that it is all a matter of how you choose to look at it.

They may have a point in such things as music, art, and literature from different cultures, but there are many human purposes common to peoples of all cultures. They want to live rather than die, for example. When Europeans first ventured into the arid interior of Australia, they often died of thirst or hunger in a land where the Australian aborigines had no trouble finding food or water. Within that particular setting, at least, the aboriginal culture enabled people to do what both aborigines and Europeans wanted to do—survive. A given culture may not be superior for all things in all settings, much less remain superior over time, but particular cultural features may nevertheless be clearly better for some purposes—not just different.

Why is there any such argument in the first place? Perhaps it is because we are still living in the long, grim shadow of the Nazi Holocaust and are understandably reluctant to label anything or anyone "superior" or "inferior." But we don't need to. We need only recognize that particular products, skills, technologies, agricultural crops, or intellectual concepts accomplish particular purposes better than their alternatives. It is not necessary to rank one whole culture over another in all things, much less to claim that they remain in that same ranking throughout history. They do not.

Clearly, cultural leadership in various fields has changed hands many times. China was far in advance of any country in Europe in a large number of fields for at least a thousand years and, as late as the sixteenth century, had the highest standard of living in the world. Equally clearly, China today is one of the poorer nations of the world and is having great difficulty trying to catch up to the technological level of Japan and the West, with no real hope of regaining its former world preeminence in the foreseeable future.

Similar rises and falls of nations and empires have been common over long stretches of human history—for example, the rise and fall of the Roman Empire, the "golden age" of medieval Spain and its decline to the level of one of the poorest nations in Europe today, the centuries-long triumphs of the Ottoman Empire—intellectually as well as on the battlefields of Europe and the Middle East—and then its long decline to become known as "the sick man of Europe." Yet, while cultural leadership has changed hands many times, that leadership has been real at given times, and much of what was achieved in the process has contributed enormously to our well-being and opportunities today. Cultural competition is not a zero-sum game. It is what advances the human race.

If nations and civilizations differ in their effectiveness in different fields of endeavor, so do social groups. Here there is especially strong resistance to accepting the reality of different levels and kinds of skills, interests, habits, and orientations among different groups of people. One academic writer, for example, said that nineteenth-century Jewish immigrants to the United States were fortunate to arrive just as the garment industry in New York began to develop. I could not help thinking that Hank Aaron was similarly fortunate—that he often came to bat just as a home run was due to be hit. It might be possible to believe that these Jewish immigrants just happened to be in the right place at the right time if you restricted yourself to their history in the United States. But, again taking a world view, we find Jews prominent, often predominant, and usually prospering, in the apparel industry in medieval Spain, in the Ottoman Empire, in the Russian Empire, in Argentina, in Australia, and in Brazil. How surprised should we be to find them predominant in the same industry in America?

Other groups have also excelled in their own special occupations and industries. Indeed, virtually every group excels at something. Germans, for example, have been prominent as pioneers in the piano industry. American piano brands like Steinway and Schnabel, not to mention the Wurlitzer organ, are signs of the long prominence of Germans in this industry, where they produced the first pianos in colonial America. Germans also pioneered in piano-building in Czarist Russia, Australia, France, and England. Chinese immigrants have, at one period of history or another, run more than half the grocery stores in Kingston, Jamaica, and Panama City and conducted more than half of all retail trade in Malaysia, the Philippines, Vietnam, and Cambodia. Other groups have dominated retail trade in other parts of the world—the Gujaratis from India in East Africa and in Fiji or the Lebanese in parts of West Africa, for example.

Nothing has been more common than for particular groups—often a minority—to dominate particular occupations or industries. Seldom do they have any ability to keep out others—and certainly not to keep out the majority population. They are simply *better* at the particular skills required in that occupation or industry. Sometimes we can see why. When Italians have made wine in Italy for centuries, it is hardly surprising that they should become prominent among wine-makers in Argentina or in California's Napa Valley. Similarly, when Germans in Germany have been for centuries renowned for their beer-making, how surprised should we be that in Argentina they became as prominent among beer-makers as the Italians were among wine-makers? How surprised should we be that beer-making in the United States arose where there were concentrations of German immigrants—in Milwaukee and St. Louis, for example? Or that the leading beer producers to this day have German names like Anheuser-Busch or Coors, among many other German names?

Just as cultural leadership in a particular field is not permanent for nations or civilizations, neither is it permanent for given racial, ethnic, or religious groups. By the time the Jews were expelled from Spain in 1492, Europe had overtaken the Islamic world in medical science, so that Jewish physicians who sought refuge in the Ottoman Empire found themselves in great demand in that Moslem country. By the early sixteenth century, the sultan of the Ottoman Empire had on his palace medical staff 42 Jewish physicians and 21 Moslem physicians. With the passage of time, however, the source of the Jews' advantage—their knowledge of Western medicine—eroded as successive generations of Ottoman Jews lost contact with the West and its further progress. Christian minorities within the Ottoman Empire began to replace the Jews, not only in medicine but also in international trade and even in the theater, once dominated by Jews. The difference was that these Christian minorities—notably Greeks and Armenians—maintained their ties in Christian Europe and often sent their sons there to be educated. It was not race or ethnicity as such that was crucial but maintaining contacts with the ongoing progress of Western civilization. By contrast, the Ottoman Jews became a declining people in a declining empire. Many, if not most, were Sephardic Jews from Spain—once the elite of world Jewry. But by the time the state of Israel was formed in the twentieth century, those Sephardic Jews who had settled for centuries in the Islamic world now lagged painfully behind the Ashkenazic Jews of the Western world—notably in income and education. To get some idea what a historic reversal that has been in the relative positions of Sephardic Jews and Ashkenazic Jews, one need only note that Sephardic Jews in colonial America sometimes disinherited their own children for marrying Ashkenazic Jews.

Why do some groups, subgroups, nations, or whole civilizations excel in some particular fields rather than others? All too often, the answer to that question must be: Nobody really knows. It is an unanswered question largely because it is an *unasked* question. There is an uphill struggle merely to get acceptance of the fact that large differences exist among peoples, not just in specific skills in the narrow sense (computer science, basketball, or brewing beer) but more fundamentally in different interests, orientations, and values that determine which particular skills they seek to develop and with what degree of success. Merely to suggest that these internal cultural factors play a significant role in various economic, educational, or social outcomes is to invite charges of "blaming the victim." It is much more widely acceptable to blame surrounding social conditions or institutional policies.

But if we look at cultural diversity internationally and historically, there is a more basic question whether blame is the real issue. Surely, no human being should be blamed for the way his culture evolved for centuries before he was born. Blame has nothing to do with it. Another explanation that has had varying amounts of acceptance at different times and places is the biological or genetic theory of differences among peoples. I have argued *against* this theory in many places but will not take the time to go into these lengthy arguments here. A world view of cultural differences over the centuries undermines the genetic theory as well. Europeans and Chinese, for example, are clearly genetically different. Equally clearly, China was a more advanced civilization than Europe in many scientific, technological, and organizational ways for at least a thousand years. Yet over the past few centuries, Europe has moved ahead of China in many of these same ways. If those cultural differences were due to genes, how could these two races have changed positions so radically from one epoch in history to another?

All explanations of differences between groups can be broken down into heredity and environment. Yet a world view of the history of cultural diversity seems, on the surface at least, to deny both. One reason for this is that we have thought of environment too narrowly—as the immediate surrounding circumstances or differing institutional policies toward different groups. Environment in that narrow sense may explain some group differences, but the histories of many groups completely contradict that particular version of environment as an explanation. Let us take just two examples out of many which are available.

Jewish immigrants from Eastern Europe and Italian immigrants from southern Italy began arriving in the United States in large numbers at about the same time in the late nineteenth century, and their large-scale immigration also ended at the same time, when restrictive immigration laws were passed in the 1920s. The two groups arrived here in virtually the same economic condition—namely, destitute. They often lived in the same neighborhoods, and their children attended the same schools, sitting side by side in the same classrooms. Their environments—in the narrow sense in which the term is commonly used—were virtually identical. Yet their social histories in the United States have been very different.

Over the generations, both groups rose, but they rose at different rates, through different means, and in a very different mixture of occupations and industries. Even wealthy Jews and wealthy Italians tended to become rich in different sectors of the economy. The California wine industry, for example, is full of Italian names like Mondavi, Gallo, and Rossi, but the only prominent Jewish wine-maker—Manischewitz—makes an entirely different kind of wine, and no one would compare Jewish wine-makers with Italian wine-makers in the United States. When we look at Jews and Italians in the very different environmental setting of Argentina, we see the same general pattern of differences between them. The same is true if we look at the differences between Jews and

Italians in Australia, or Canada, or Western Europe.

Jews are not Italians and Italians are not Jews. Anyone familiar with their very different histories over many centuries should not be surprised. Their fate in America was not determined solely by their surrounding social conditions in America or by how they were treated by American society. They were different before they got on the boats to cross the ocean, and those differences crossed the ocean with them.

We can take it a step further. Even among Ashkenazic Jews, those originating in Eastern Europe have had significantly different economic and social histories from those originating in Germanic Central Europe, including Austria as well as Germany itself. These differences have persisted among their descendants not only in New York and Chicago but as far away as Melbourne and Sydney. In Australia, Jews from Eastern Europe have tended to cluster in and around Melbourne, while Germanic Jews have settled in and around Sydney. They even have a saying among themselves that Melbourne is a cold city with warm Jews while Sydney is a warm city with cold Jews.

A second and very different example of persistent cultural differences involves immigrants from Japan. As everyone knows, many Japanese-Americans were interned during World War II. What is less well known is that there is and has been an even larger Japanese population in Brazil than in the United States. These Japanese, incidentally, own approximately three-quarters as much land in Brazil as there is in Japan. (The Japanese almost certainly own more agricultural land in Brazil than in Japan.) In any event, very few Japanese in Brazil were interned during World War II. Moreover, the Japanese in Brazil were never subjected to the discrimination suffered by Japanese Americans in the decades before World War II.

Yet, during the war, Japanese-Americans, overwhelmingly, remained loyal to the United States, and Japanese-American soldiers won more than their share of medals in combat. But in Brazil, the Japanese were overwhelmingly and even fanatically loyal *to Japan*. You cannot explain the difference by anything in the environment of the United States or the environment of Brazil. But if you know something about the history of those Japanese who settled in these two countries, you know that they were culturally different *in Japan, before* they ever got on the boats to take them across the Pacific Ocean—and they were still different decades later.

These two groups of immigrants left Japan during very different periods in the cultural evolution of Japan itself. A modern Japanese scholar has said: "If you want to see Japan of the Meiji era, go to the United States. If you want to see Japan of the Taisho era, go to Brazil." The Meiji era was a more cosmopolitan, pro-American era; the Taisho era was one of fanatical Japanese nationalism.

If the narrow concept of environment fails to explain many profound differences between groups and subgroups, it likewise fails to explain many very large differences in the economic and social performances of nations and civilizations. An eighteenth-century writer in Chile described that country's many natural advantages in climate, soil, and natural resources—and then asked in complete bewilderment why it was such a poverty-stricken country. That same question could be asked of many countries today. Conversely, we could ask why Japan and Switzerland are so prosperous when they are both almost totally lacking in natural resources. Both are rich in what economists call "human capital"—the skills of their people. No doubt there is a long and complicated history behind the different skill levels of different peoples and nations. The point here is that the immediate environment—whether social or geographic—is only part of the story.

Geography may well have a significant role in the history of peoples, but perhaps not simply by presenting them with more or less natural resources. Geography shapes or limits peoples' opportunities for cultural interactions and the mutual development that comes out of that. Small, isolated islands in the sea have seldom been sources of new scientific advances or technological breakthroughs—regardless of where such islands were located and regardless of the race of the people on these islands. There are islands on land as well. Where soil fertile enough to support human life exists only in isolated patches, widely separated, there tend to be isolated cultures (often with different languages or dialects) in a culturally fragmented region. Isolated highlands often produce insular cultures, lagging in many ways behind the cultures of the lowlanders of the same race—whether we are talking about medieval Scotland, colonial Ceylon, or the contemporary Montagnards of Vietnam.

With geographical environments as with social environments, we are talking about long-run effects not simply the effects of immediate surroundings. When Scottish highlanders, for example, immigrated to North Carolina in colonial times, they had a very different history from that of Scottish lowlanders who settled in North Carolina. For one thing, the lowlanders spoke English while the highlanders spoke Gaelic—on into the nineteenth century. Obviously, speaking only Gaelic—in an English-speaking country—affects a group's whole economic and social progress.

Geographical conditions vary as radically in terms of how well they facilitate or impede large-scale cultural interactions as they do in their distribution of natural resources. We are not even close to being able to explain how all these geographical influences have operated throughout history. That too is an unanswered question largely because it is an unasked question—and it is an unasked question because many are seeking answers in terms of immediate social environment or are vehemently insistent that they have already found the answer in those terms.

How radically do geographic environments differ—not just in terms of tropical versus arctic climates but also in the very configuration of the land and how that helps or hinders large-scale interactions among peoples? Consider one statistic: Africa is more than twice the size of Europe, and yet Africa has a shorter coastline than Europe. That seems almost impossible. But the reason is that Europe's coastline is far more convoluted, with many harbors and inlets being formed all around the continent. Much of the coastline of Africa is smooth—which is to say, lacking in the harbors which make large-scale maritime trade possible by sheltering the ships at anchor from the rough waters of the open sea. Waterways of all sorts have played a major role in the evolution of cultures and nations around the world. Harbors on the sea are not the only waterways. Rivers are also very important. Virtually every major city on Earth is located either on a river or a harbor. Whether it is such great harbors as those in Sydney, Singapore, or San Francisco; or London on the Thames, Paris on the Seine, or numerous other European cities on the Danube, waterways have been the lifeblood of urban centers for centuries. Only very recently has manmade, self-powered transportation like automobiles and airplanes made it possible to produce an exception to the rule like Los Angeles. (There is a Los Angeles River, but you don't have to be Moses to walk across it in the summertime.) New York has both a long and deep river and a huge sheltered harbor.

None of these geographical features in themselves create a great city or develop an urban culture. Human beings do that. But geography sets the limits within which people can operate—and in some places it sets those limits much wider than others. Returning to our comparison of the continents of Europe and Africa, we find that they differ as radically in rivers as they do in harbors. There are entire nations in Africa without a single navigable river—Libya and South Africa, for example. "Navigable" is the crucial word. Some African rivers are navigable only during the rainy season. Some are navigable only between numerous cataracts and waterfalls. Even the Zaire River, which is longer than any river in North America and carries a larger volume of water, has too many waterfalls, too close to the ocean for it to become a major artery of international commerce. Such commerce is facilitated in Europe not only by numerous navigable rivers but also by the fact that no spot on the continent, outside of Russia, is more than 500 miles from the sea. Many places in Africa are more than 500 miles from the sea, including the entire nation of Uganda.

Against this background, how surprised should we be to find that Europe is the most urbanized of all inhabited continents and Africa the least urbanized? Urbanization is not the be-all and end-all of life, but certainly an urban culture is bound to differ substantially from nonurban cultures, and the skills peculiar to an urban culture are far more likely to be found among groups from an urban civilization. (Conversely, an interesting history could be written about the failures of urbanized groups in agricultural settlements.)

Looking within Africa, the influence of geography seems equally clear. The most famous ancient civilization on the continent arose within a few miles on either side of Africa's longest navigable river, the Nile, and even today the two largest cities on the continent, Cairo and Alexandria, are on that river. The great West African kingdoms in the region served by the Niger River and the long-flourishing East African economy based around the great natural harbor on the island of Zanzibar are further evidences of the role of geography. Again, geography is not all-determining—the economy of Zanzibar has been ruined by government policy in recent decades—but nevertheless, geography is an important long-run influence on the shaping of cultures as well as in narrowly economic terms.

What are the implications of a world view of cultural diversity on the narrower issues being debated under that label in the United States today? Although "diversity" is used in so many different ways in so many different contexts that it seems to mean all things to all people, there are a few themes which appear again and again. One of these broad themes is that diversity implies organized efforts at the preservation of cultural differences, perhaps governmental efforts, perhaps government subsidies to various programs run by the advocates of "diversity."

This approach raises questions as to what the purpose of culture is. If what is important about cultures is that they are emotionally symbolic, and if differentness is cherished for the sake of differentness, then this particular version of cultural "diversity" might make some sense. But cultures exist even in isolated societies where there are no other cultures around—where there is no one else and nothing else from which to be different. Cultures exist to serve the vital, practical requirements of human life—to structure a society so as to perpetuate the species, to pass on the hard-earned knowledge and experience of generations past and centuries past to the young and inexperienced in order to spare the next generation the costly and dangerous process of learning everything all over again from scratch through trial and error—including fatal errors. Cultures exist so that people can know how to get food and put a roof over their head, how to cure the sick, how to cope with the death of loved ones, and how to get along with the living. Cultures are not bumper stickers. They are living, changing ways of doing all the things that have to be done in life.

Every culture discards over time the things which no longer do the job or which don't do the job as well as things borrowed from other cultures. Each individual does this, consciously or not, on a day-to-day basis. Languages take words from other languages, so that Spanish as spoken in Spain includes words taken from Arabic, and Spanish as spoken in Argentina has Italian words taken from the large Italian immigrant population there. People eat Kentucky Fried Chicken in Singapore and stay in Hilton Hotels in Cairo.

This is *not* what some of the advocates of "diversity" have in mind. They seem to want to preserve cultures in their purity, almost like butterflies preserved in amber. Decisions about change, if any, seem to be regarded as collective decisions, political decisions. But that is not how any cultures have arrived where they are. Individuals have decided for themselves how much of the old they wished to retain, how much of the new they found useful in their own lives. In this way, cultures have enriched each other in all the great civilizations of the world. In this way, great port cities and other crossroads of cultures have become centers of progress all across the planet. No culture has grown great in isolation—but a number of cultures have made historic and even astonishing advances when their isolation was ended, usually by events beyond their control.

Japan was a classic example in the nineteenth century, but a similar story could be told of Scotland in an earlier era, when a country where once even the nobility were illiterate became—within a short time, as history is measured—a country which produced world pioneers in field after field: David Hume in philosophy, Adam Smith in economics, Joseph Black in chemistry, Robert Adam in architecture, and James Watt, whose steam engine revolutionized modern industry and transport. In the process, the Scots lost their language but gained world preeminence in many fields. Then a whole society moved to higher standards of living than anyone ever dreamed of in their poverty-stricken past.

There were higher standards in other ways as well. As late as the eighteenth century, it was considered noteworthy that pedestrians in Edinburgh no longer had to be on the alert for sewage being thrown out the windows of people's homes or apartments. The more considerate Scots yelled a warning, but they threw out the sewage anyway. Perhaps it was worth losing a little of the indigenous culture to be rid of that problem.

Those who use the term "cultural diversity" to promote a multiplicity of segregated ethnic enclaves are doing an enormous harm to the people in those enclaves. However they live socially, the people in those enclaves are going to have to compete economically for a livelihood. Even if they were not disadvantaged before, they will be very disadvantaged if their competitors from the general population are free to tap the knowledge, skills, and analytical techniques which Western civilization has drawn from all the other civilizations of the world, while those in the enclaves are restricted to what exists in the subculture immediately around them.

We need also to recognize that many great thinkers of the past—whether in medicine or philosophy, science or economics—labored not simply to advance whatever particular group they happened to have come from but to advance the human race. Their legacies, whether cures for deadly diseases or dramatic increases in crop yields to fight the scourge of hunger, belong to all people—and all people need to claim that legacy, not seal themselves off in a dead-end of tribalism or in an emotional orgy of cultural vanity.

Credits/ Acknowledgments

Cover design by Charles Vitelli

1. The Ferment of the West, 1500–1800
Facing overview—Reproduced from the collections of the Library of Congress.

2. The Industrial and Scientific Revolutions
Facing overview—Source unknown. 36—From *The Textile Manufactures of Great Britain* by George Dodd, London, 1844. 38—(top) From the *Book of English Trades,* London, 1804; (bottom) From *Cotton Manufacture in Great Britain* by Edward Baines, London, 1835. 39—(left top and bottom) From *The Book of English Trades*; (right top) From *Days at the Factories* by G. Dobb, London, 1843; (right bottom) From *Penny Magazine,* November 1944. 40-42—Mansell Collection. 53-60—Department of Rare Books and Special Collections, Princeton University Libraries. 74-75, 78—Drawings by Tomo Narashima.

3. The West and the World, 1500–1900
Facing overview—Reproduced from the collections of the Library of Congress. 82-83—Weidenfeld Archives. 85—*History Today* Archives. 87—Mansell Collection. 89—Bowring Cartographic. 107—*History Today* Archives.

4. The Twentieth Century to 1950
Facing overview—Official U.S. Navy photo. 139—From *Die Zigeuner* by Hermann Arnold, Freiburg, 1965. 145—Bowring Cartographic. 151—Los Alamos National Laboratory, Los Alamos, New Mexico.

5. The Era of the Cold War, 1950–1990
Facing overview—AP/Wide World photo by Alexander Zemlianichenko. 201—Weidenfeld Archives. 203—(top left) Mansell Collection; (top right) Weidenfeld Archives. 204—*History Today* Archives.

6. Global Problems, Global Interdependence
Facing overview—United Nations photo by Milton Grant. 222, 224—*Scientific American* graphics by Johnny Johnson. 223—*Scientific American* illustrations by Patricia J. Wynne.

ANNUAL EDITIONS ARTICLE REVIEW FORM

■ NAME: _____ DATE: _____

■ TITLE AND NUMBER OF ARTICLE: _____

■ BRIEFLY STATE THE MAIN IDEA OF THIS ARTICLE: _____

_____

■ LIST THREE IMPORTANT FACTS THAT THE AUTHOR USES TO SUPPORT THE MAIN IDEA:

_____

_____

_____

_____

_____

_____

■ WHAT INFORMATION OR IDEAS DISCUSSED IN THIS ARTICLE ARE ALSO DISCUSSED IN YOUR TEXTBOOK OR OTHER READING YOU HAVE DONE? LIST THE TEXTBOOK CHAPTERS AND PAGE NUMBERS:

_____

_____

_____

_____

_____

_____

■ LIST ANY EXAMPLES OF BIAS OR FAULTY REASONING THAT YOU FOUND IN THE ARTICLE:

_____

_____

_____

_____

_____

■ LIST ANY NEW TERMS/CONCEPTS THAT WERE DISCUSSED IN THE ARTICLE AND WRITE A SHORT DEFINITION:

_____

_____

_____

_____

_____

*Your instructor may require you to use this Annual Editions Article Review Form in any number of ways: for articles that are assigned, for extra credit, as a tool to assist in developing assigned papers, or simply for your own reference. Even if it is not required, we encourage you to photocopy and use this page; you'll find that reflecting on the articles will greatly enhance the information from your text.

ANNUAL EDITIONS: WORLD HISTORY, VOLUME II, Fourth Edition
Article Rating Form

We Want Your Advice

Here is an opportunity for you to have direct input into the next revision of this volume. We would like you to rate each of the 41 articles listed below, using the following scale:

1. **Excellent: should definitely be retained**
2. **Above average: should probably be retained**
3. **Below average: should probably be deleted**
4. **Poor: should definitely be deleted**

Your ratings will play a vital part in the next revision. So please mail this prepaid form to us just as soon as you complete it.
Thanks for your help!

Annual Editions revisions depend on two major opinion sources: one is our Advisory Board, listed in the front of this volume, which works with us in scanning the thousands of articles published in the public press each year; the other is you—the person actually using the book. Please help us and the users of the next edition by completing the prepaid article rating form on this page and returning it to us. Thank you.

Rating	Article	Rating	Article
	1. Luther: Giant of His Time and Ours		21. After Centuries of Japanese Isolation, a Fateful Meeting of East and West
	2. Scotland's Greatest Son		22. The International Economy
	3. The First Feminist		23. On the Turn—Japan, 1900
	4. A World Transformed		24. Japanese Women at Work, 1880–1920
	5. China: Rethinking the Revolution		25. Sarajevo: The End of Innocence
	6. The French Revolution, North Africa, and the Middle East		26. Social Outcasts in Nazi Germany
	7. Cottage Industry and the Factory System		27. '. . . Heavy Fire . . . Unable to Land . . . Issue in Doubt'
	8. For a While, the Luddites Had a Smashing Success		28. Making It Happen
	9. Looking beyond Aristotle and Alchemy		29. Why We Dropped the Bomb
	10. The Scientific Importance of Napoleon's Egyptian Campaign		30. Heating Up the Cold War
	11. James Watson and the Search for Biology's 'Holy Grail'		31. Berlin 1961: The Record Corrected
	12. How Von Neumann Showed the Way		32. Who Broke Down This Wall?
	13. The Scientific Legacy of Apollo		33. The Return to History: The Breakup of the Soviet Union
	14. Portugal's Impact on Africa		34. A Decade of Decline
	15. That Fateful Moment When Two Civilizations Came Face to Face		35. Islam: The Roots of Misperception
	16. Discovering Europe, 1493		36. Toxic Wasteland
	17. The Potato Connection		37. The Nuclear Epidemic
	18. Who Was Responsible?		38. Sowing Success, Reaping Guns
	19. The Macartney Embassy to China, 1792–94		39. Can the Growing Human Population Feed Itself?
	20. Coffee, Tea, or Opium?		40. The Future of AIDS
			41. Cultural Diversity: A World View

(Continued on next page)

ABOUT YOU

Name _____ Date _____

Are you a teacher? ❑ Or student? ❑

Your School Name _____

Department _____

Address _____

City _____ State _____ Zip _____

School Telephone # _____

YOUR COMMENTS ARE IMPORTANT TO US!

Please fill in the following information:

For which course did you use this book? _____

Did you use a text with this Annual Edition? ❑ yes ❑ no

The title of the text? _____

What are your general reactions to the Annual Editions concept?

Have you read any particular articles recently that you think should be included in the next edition?

Are there any articles you feel should be replaced in the next edition? Why?

Are there other areas that you feel would utilize an Annual Edition?

May we contact you for editorial input?

May we quote you from above?

ANNUAL EDITIONS: WORLD HISTORY, VOLUME II, Fourth Edition

BUSINESS REPLY MAIL

First Class   Permit No. 84   Guilford, CT

Postage will be paid by addressee

**Dushkin Publishing Group/
Brown & Benchmark Publishers**
Sluice Dock
Guilford, Connecticut 06437

No Postage
Necessary
if Mailed
in the
United States